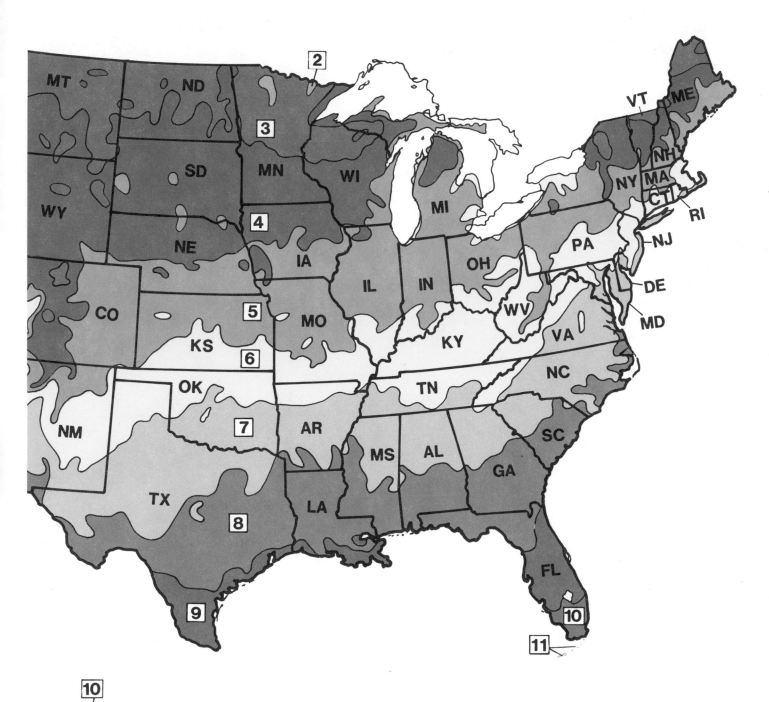

**THE USDA PLANT HARDINESS MAP
OF THE UNITED STATES**

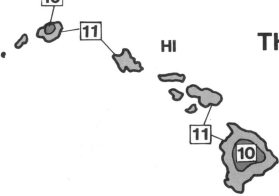

THE NATIONAL ARBORETUM BOOK OF OUTSTANDING GARDEN PLANTS

The Authoritative Guide to Selecting and Growing the Most Beautiful, Durable, and Care-free Garden Plants in North America

By Jacqueline Hériteau

with Dr. H. Marc Cathey, Director, and the staff and consultants of
The U.S. National Arboretum

Introduction by Dr. H. Marc Cathey

A Stonesong Press Book

Simon and Schuster

New York London Toronto Sydney Tokyo

A Stonesong Press Book

Simon and Schuster
Simon & Schuster Building
Rockefeller Center
1230 Avenue of the Americas
New York, New York 10020

Designed by Michaelis/Carpelis Design Associates, Inc.

Manufactured in the United States of America

10   9   8   7   6   5   4   3   2   1

Library of Congress Cataloging in Publication Data

Hériteau, Jacqueline.
    The National Arboretum Book of outstanding garden plants : the
authoritative guide to selecting and growing the most beautiful,
durable, and care-free garden plants in North America / by
Jacqueline Hériteau with H. Marc Cathey and the staff and
consultants of the U.S. National Arboretum.
        p.   cm.
    "A Stonesong Press book."
    ISBN 0-671-66957-5
    1. Plants, Ornamental.   2. Plants, Ornamental—North America.
3. Plants, Ornamental—Pictorial works.   4. Plants, Ornamental—
North America—Pictorial works.   5. Landscape gardening—North
America.   I. Cathey, Henry Marcellus, 1928–   .   II. National
Arboretum (U.S.)   III. Title.
SB407.H493   1990
635.9'517—dc20   89-19704
                            6   89-19704
                                            CIP

Title page photo: Yellow daylilies and irises naturalized at the U.S.
National Arboretum in Washington, D.C. (Cathey)

Genesis 1:28
And God blessed them, and God said unto them,
Be fruitful, and multiply, and replenish the earth,
and subdue it: and have dominion . . .

Entrance to the National Herb Garden. (Cathey)

ACKNOWLEDGMENTS

The author warmly thanks Dr. Waldemar Klassen, Director of the U.S.D.A. Agricultural Research Service (ARS), for his support at the inception of the project, and for ARS permission to publish the work, which has been completed under the guidance of Dr. Edward Knipling. The author thanks Dr. H. Marc Cathey, Director of the U.S. National Arboretum, and Friends of the National Arboretum (FONA) for making the book possible. The book is a FONA project. As public agencies, ARS and the National Arboretum cannot endorse any product; nothing in this work is to be construed as an endorsement of any product.

The stature of the outside contributors to this project is a measure of the affection and respect won by the U.S. National Arboretum. Early support came from the late Robert F. Lederer, and Gordon Dunlap and Duane Jelinek of the American Association of Nurserymen. The late Col. Charles A. H. Thomson, horticultural consultant, made an enormous contribution in editorial help and photo research. Elvin McDonald, Special Projects Director for the Brooklyn Botanic Garden, provided hundreds of photos of flowers from his private collection. Longwood Gardens, W. Atlee Burpee & Co., and Geo. W. Park Seed Co. filled photo gaps.

The substance of the book was contributed by the National Arboretum staff members and consultants named below. The work owes much to the extracurricular efforts of Erik Neumann, Head, Education and Public Services, who acted as liaison between the author and the National Arboretum staff. Fay's good cheer, T. C.'s smile, and Christine's bouquets were very helpful.

My deep appreciation goes to my husband, Earl Hubbard, for bearing with my working weekends and midnight oil.

Special thanks, too, go to Caroline Herter at Simon & Schuster, who quickly saw the need for this book, and to Anne Halpin, a meticulous editor and expert who gave me many good suggestions. Bouquets of roses are due to: Felice Levy and Alexandra Koppen for their copyediting skills; Tom Robertson, my computer consultant; Woodrow F. Dick, Jr., for the American Association of Nurserymen (AAN) Nursery Crops Coding System; and Sylvain Michaelis, who was able to fit a two-foot-high collection of script and photos into a pleasant and practical design.

TABLE OF

CONTENTS

END PAPERS
The New U.S.D.A. Plant Hardiness Map
of North America

ACKNOWLEDGMENTS   vii

**U.S. NATIONAL ARBORETUM
STAFF AND CONSULTANTS**   xiii

FOREWORD   xvii
Dr. H. Marc Cathey,
Director U.S. National Arboretum

ABOUT THE NATIONAL ARBORETUM   xviii

HOW TO USE THIS BOOK   xxiv

SECTION ONE

FLOWERS

Introduction To Flowers 4

BULBS, CORMS, RHIZOMES
(Flowers–1) Small Spring Bulbs,
Corms, and Rhizomes 6

(Flowers–2) Summer Bulbs, Corms,
and Rhizomes for Sun 8

(Flowers–3) Summer Bulbs, Corms,
and Rhizomes for Shade 9

(Flowers–4) Fall and Winter Bulbs,
Corms, and Rhizomes 10

(Flowers–5) Crocuses 11

(Flowers–6) Daffodils 12

(Flowers–7) Irises 15

(Flowers–8) Lilies 17

(Flowers–9) Tulips 19

PERENNIALS
(Flowers–10) Spring Perennials
for Sun 22

(Flowers–11) Spring Perennials
for Shade 24

(Flowers–12) Summer Perennials
for Sun 26

(Flowers–13) Summer Perennials
for Shade 29

(Flowers–14) Fall Perennials for Sun ... 31

Fall Perennials for Shade . 33

(Flowers–15) Daylilies 34

(Flowers–16) Peonies 35

(Flowers–17) Annuals, Biennials,
and Tender Perennials 36

SPECIAL USES
(Flowers–18) Bulbs for Containers
and Forcing 41

Flowers for Baskets and
Window Boxes 42

(Flowers–19) Flowers to Attract Bees,
Birds, and Butterflies 43

(Flowers–20) Fragrant Flowers 47

AQUATIC PLANTS

Introduction To Aquatic Plants 52

WATER LILIES
(Aquatics–1) Frost-Hardy Perennial
Water Lilies 54

(Aquatics–2) Frost-Tender Perennial
Water Lilies 55

LOTUS
(Aquatics–3) Lotuses 57

BOG PLANTS
(Aquatics–4) Frost-Hardy Perennial
Bog Plants 57

(Aquatics–5) Tropical Bog Plants 59

HERBS

Introduction To Herbs 62

HERBS
(Herbs–1) Trees and Shrubs
for Herb Gardens 64

GARDENS
(Herbs–2) Flowering Herbs 66

(Herbs–3) Popular Culinary Herbs 68

(Herbs–4) Unusual Culinary Herbs ... 70

(Herbs–5) Fragrant Herbs for Drying .. 71

(Herbs–6) Fragrant Herbs
for the Garden 74

(Herbs–7) Old Garden Roses 75

(Herbs–8) Historic Herbs 78

SPECIAL USES
(Herbs–9) Herbs for Baskets
and Pots 80

(Herbs–10) Herbs for Nooks
and Crannies 81

ORNAMENTAL GRASSES

Introduction To Ornamental Grasses . 86

GARDENS OF GRASSES

(Ornamental Grasses–1) Grasses for
Color and Texture 88

SPECIAL USES

(Ornamental Grasses–2) Grasses for
Naturalizing and Slopes 90

(Ornamental Grasses–3) Grasses for
Rapid Growth and Summer Screening . 91

(Ornamental Grasses–4) Grasses for
Seashore Gardens 93

(Ornamental Grasses–5) Grasses for
Shade 94

(Ornamental Grasses–6) Grasses for
Sunny, Dry Urban Areas 97

(Ornamental Grasses–7) Grasses for
Wet Conditions 98

GROUND COVERS

Introduction To Ground Covers 102

COLOR

(Ground Covers–1) Flowering
Ground Covers 104

FOLIAGE

(Ground Covers–2) Ground Covers
with Deciduous Foliage 106

(Ground Covers–3) Ground Covers
with Evergreen Foliage 107

(Ground Covers–4) Ferns for Ground
Cover 109

SPECIAL USES

(Ground Covers–5) Lawn Alternatives . 111

(Ground Covers–6) Ground Covers
for Nooks and Crannies 113

(Ground Covers–7) Ground Covers
for Seashore Gardens 114

(Ground Covers–8) Ground Covers
for Shade 116

(Ground Covers–9) Fast-Growing Ground
Covers for Slopes and Erosion Control . . 118

(Ground Covers–10) Ground Covers
for Wet Conditions 120

VINES

Introduction To Vines 124

COLOR

(Vines–1) Flowering Vines 126

(Vines–2) Flowering Vines: Roses . . . 129

FOLIAGE

(Vines–3) Vines for Foliage:
Deciduous 131

(Vines–4) Vines for Foliage:
Evergreen 132

SPECIAL USES

(Vines–5) Vines with Fragrant
Flowers 134

(Vines–6) Vines Attractive to Birds . . . 135

(Vines–7) Vines for Rapid Growth
or Screening 136

(Vines–8) Vines That Grow
in Shade 138

(Vines–9) Vines for Urban
Conditions 140

SHRUBS

Introduction To Shrubs 144

COLOR

(Shrubs–1) Flowering Shrubs for Early
and Mid-Spring 146

(Shrubs–2) Azaleas
(Rhododendron) 149

(Shrubs–3) Rhododendrons 153

(Shrubs–4) Flowering Shrubs
for Late Spring 156

(Shrubs–5) Flowering Shrubs
for Summer and Fall 157

(Shrubs–6) Shrub Roses 159

FOLIAGE

(Shrubs–7) Broadleaved and Needled
Evergreen Shrubs 161

(Shrubs–8) Shrubs with Red Foliage
All Season 166

(Shrubs–9) Shrubs with Yellow Foliage
All Season 167

(Shrubs–10) Shrubs with Blue, Gray,
and Silver Foliage 168

(Shrubs–11) Shrubs with Variegated
Foliage 170

(Shrubs–12) Shrubs with Red, Orange,
and Yellow Foliage in Fall 172

FORM

(Shrubs–13) Dwarf and Slow-Growing
Shrubs 174

(Shrubs–14) Shrubs for Topiary
and Espalier 176

SPECIAL USES

(Shrubs–15) Shrubs with
Fragrant Flowers 178

(Shrubs–16) Shrubs Attractive
to Birds 180

(Shrubs–17) Deciduous Shrubs
for Hedges, Edging, and Screening . . . 182

(Shrubs–18) Evergreen Shrubs
for Hedges, Edging, and Screening . . . 184

(Shrubs–19) Roses for Hedges
and Edging 186

(Shrubs–20) Shrubs for City Streets
and Dry Places 188

(Shrubs–21) Shrubs for Container
Planting 189

(Shrubs–22) Shrubs for
Seashore Gardens 192

(Shrubs–23) Shrubs for Shade 194

(Shrubs–24) Shrubs for Slopes
and Erosion Control 196

(Shrubs–25) Shrubs for Wet
Conditions 198

TREES

Introduction To Trees 202

COLOR

(Trees–1) Trees with Colorful,
Exfoliating, or Distinctive Bark 204

(Trees–2) Trees with Flowers in Early
and Mid-Spring 205

(Trees–3) Trees with Flowers in Late
Spring and Summer 210

FOLIAGE

(Trees–4) Trees with Evergreen
Foliage 212

(Trees–5) Trees with Red or Yellow
Foliage All Season 217

(Trees–6) Trees with Silver
or Variegated Foliage 219

(Trees–7) Trees with Red Foliage
in Fall 220

(Trees–8) Trees with Yellow Foliage
in Fall 221

FORM

(Trees–9) Trees with Columnar
Form 223

(Trees–10) Trees with Weeping
Form 224

SPECIAL USES

(Trees–11) Trees with Fragrant
Flowers 226

(Trees–12) Trees Attractive
to Birds 227

(Trees–13) Large Shade Trees 229

(Trees–14) Small or Dwarf
Shade Trees 232

(Trees–15) Trees for City Conditions
and Dry Places 233

(Trees–16) Trees for Container
Planting 236

(Trees–17) Trees for Screening 238

(Trees–18) Trees for Seashore
Gardens 241

(Trees–19) Shade-Tolerant Trees 243

(Trees–20) Trees for Wet
Conditions 246

SECTION TWO

**GARDENING VIEWS AT THE
U.S. NATIONAL ARBORETUM**   251

**U.S.D.A. AGRICULTURAL
EXTENSION SERVICES**   255

A READY REFERENCE GUIDE   257

**INDEX AND AAN NURSERY CROP
CODE NUMBERS**   258

**HARDINESS ZONES FOR
CANADA AND MEXICO**   292

The New American Garden entrance to the National Arboretum gift shop. (Cathey)

Henry Marc Cathey, who acted as director and senior editor for this project, became the fourth director of the U.S. National Arboretum in 1981. He is known for original research in the interrelations of light, temperature, and chemicals in plant growth, conducted during nearly three decades at the Beltsville Agricultural Research Center. Among prestigious awards he received are the Norman J. Coleman Award from the American Association of Nurserymen, and the Silver Seal and Gold Seal awards from the National Council of State Garden Clubs in recognition of contributions of national and world significance. Dr. Cathey is a Fulbright Scholar, has M.S. and Ph.D. degrees from Cornell University, was the first scientist appointed to the D. C. Kiplinger Chair in Floriculture at Ohio State University, and has served as president of the American Horticulture Society (1974–1978), which presented him its highest award, the Liberty Hyde Bailey Medal, in 1981. A popular lecturer, he hosts a Saturday morning Washington, D. C., radio talk show on WRC AM 980 and is a frequent network television guest.

Erik A. Neumann, liaison and coordinator, as well as consultant and co-editor for the Ground Covers lists, has been Head of Education and Public Service since 1972. He holds a B.A. in botany from Indiana University, an M.S. from Purdue University, has done graduate work in horticulture at Cornell and Michigan State universities, and was Curator for Native Plant Gardens at the New York Botanical Garden. Mr. Neumann has photographed botanic gardens and arboreta all over the world and is a major contributor of photography for this book. He is author of *The United States National Arboretum—America's Living Museum* (John D. Lucas Printing Company). He established the Arboretum series of education programs, garden tours, nature walks, lectures, and flowers shows. He also established the National Arboretum Horticulture Series of the U.S.D.A. Graduate School and serves on the Board of Directors of the George Washington University Landscape Design Program.

The late Charles A. H. Thomson, researcher and editor for the Trees, Shrubs, and Flowers lists, was a consultant to the U.S. National Arboretum with special reference to perennials, annuals, and flowering bulbs and gardening in southern California. A talented horticulturist with four decades of experience in the mid-Atlantic and southern California regions, he served with many plant societies, including those interested in lilies, daylilies, daffodils, roses, azaleas, rhododendrons, magnolias, and maples. Col. Thomson was a founding member of FONA and a long-term member of the American Horticultural Society, the Los Angeles State and County Arboretum, the Southern California Horticultural Institute, and the Royal Horticultural Society. He taught short courses in horticultural subjects at the Smithsonian Institution and the U.S. Department of Agriculture, lectured to gardening organizations, and served as co-host for WTTG's show "Plant Talk." He was an early member of the Men's Garden Club of Montgomery Country and general editor of their *Successful Gardening in the Greater Washington Area,* 1975 and 1989. He received a doctorate in political economy from Harvard University and served as a colonel in the United States Army.

Frederick G. Meyer, consultant taxonomist for the project and a contributor for the Trees lists, is Supervisory Botanist in charge of the Herbarium at the U.S. National Arboretum. He conducts research on the taxonomy and nomenclature of cultivated plants, in particular woody landscape plants of southeastern United States. Dr. Meyer holds a Ph.D. degree from Washington University in St. Louis. He has contributed extensively to the scientific literature on ornamental plants.

Susan (Sue) Frost Martin, editor for conifers and a contributor, is the National Arboretum Curator of Conifer Collections, responsible for the Gotelli Collection of Dwarf and Slow-growing Conifers, the Watnong Collection of Dwarf and Slow-growing Pines, and the Japanese Maple Collection.

FOR FLOWERS:

Charles A. H. Thomson was consultant, coauthor, and editor for the Flowers lists. He provided photo research and photos from his personal collection for this section.

Elvin McDonald, valued friend and longtime associate of the author, provided most of the photos for the Flowers section. A noted journalist and author on gardening subjects, he teaches, lectures, and serves as the Brooklyn Botanic Garden's Director of Special Projects. Among current activities, he serves on the Horticulture Advisory Council of the Board of Education of the City of New York, and on the boards of the New York City Flower Show and *Garden Design* magazine. The Elvin McDonald Research Fund of the American Gloxinia and Gesneriad Society supports related research projects.

Additional information was provided by researchers at the U.S.D.A. Florist and Nursery Crop Laboratory, in Beltsville, Maryland, notably Dr. R. H. Lawson, director, Dr. Mark Roh, and Dr. R. J. Greisbach.

FOR AQUATICS:

Charles B. Thomas, president of Lilypons Water Gardens, Lilypons, Maryland, and grandson of its founder, was coauthor and editor for the Aquatics lists and provided the Aquatics photos. Mr. Thomas, who has an M.S. degree from George Washington University in business and a B.S. from the University of Maryland, holds several water lily patents. He has been a guest lecturer at Cornell, the University of Maryland, Ohio State University, George Washington University, Virginia Tech, and the American Horticulture Society, and is a consultant for *Horticulture* magazine, *American Horticulturist*, Time/Life Publications, *Southern Living, The New York Times*, and Ortho Books. He received the American Horticultural Society's Commercial Individual Citation for outstanding work in the field of horticulture and is the author of *Water Gardens for Plants and Fish* (T. F. H. Publications, Inc.). Mr. Thomas is founder and secretary of the International Water Lily Society. He was awarded the Nurseryman of the Year Award by the Mailorder Association of Nurseries.

Robert DeFeo, former plant propagator and curator of the Aquatic Plant Collection at the National Arboretum, acted as first consultant on this subject. He is presently with the National Botanic Garden.

Lynn Batdorf, a consultant for the Aquatics lists, has been curator for the past twelve years for the National Aquatic Garden. He is also Curator for the Boxwood and Crab Apple evaluation collections. Mr. Batdorf teaches classes and provides technical information on these plant groups.

FOR HERBS:

Holly Shimizu, who provided the lists, basic information, and photos for the Herbs section, was first curator of the National Herb Garden in 1980 and remained with the project until 1988, when she joined the U.S. Botanic Garden as head of public programs. In 1986 the Herb Society of America gave her the Nancy Putnam Howard Award for outstanding achievements in horticulture. A horticulturist, she has worked at Longwood Gardens, the Hillier Arboretum in Hampshire, and at Wisley, the garden of the Royal Horticultural Society in England, the Hatt Nursery in Munster, West Germany, and Arboretum Kalmthout in Belgium. Mrs. Shimizu holds a B.A. from Temple University's Ambler School of Horticulture, a B.S. in horticulture from Pennsylvania State University, and an M.S. from the University of Maryland. She is an active lecturer and writes on a variety of horticultural subjects, particularly heritage roses, herbs, and perennials.

Ruth Smith, who edited the lists with Holly Shimizu, is a member of the Potomac Unit of the Herb Society of America and chairman of the group that researched the more than 1,000 herbs featured in the National Herb Garden. Mrs. Smith, whose special interest is native American uses of plants, teaches a course on the subject at the U.S.D.A. Graduate School.

FOR ORNAMENTAL GRASSES:

Wolfgang Oehme, ASLA, consultant, coauthor and coeditor of the Ornamental Grasses section, is cofounder and president of Oehme, van Sweden & Associates, Inc. OVS is a landscape architectural firm with special interest in horticulture, known nationally and internationally for the development of dramatic low-maintenance multi-seasonal gardens. Mr. Oehme's achievements earned him the Perennial Plant Association's Distinguished Service Award in 1987. Oehme, van Sweden & Associates, Inc., donated the design of the New American Garden to the National Arboretum. Mr. Oehme, whose degree in landscape architecture is from the University of Berlin, is known for the Maryland parks and playgrounds he developed in his early years in America. Photos in the Ornamental Grasses lists were contributed by Oehme, van Sweden & Associates, Inc.; some were taken by Mr. Oehme for this book.

James A. van Sweden received the Thomas Roland Gold Medal from the Massachusetts Horticultural Society for exceptional skill in horticulture. He holds a Bachelor of Architecture from the University of Michigan, did his graduate study of landscape architecture at the University at Delft, the Netherlands, and was former assistant town planner for Amsterdam. He is cofounder and vice-president of Oehme, van Sweden & Associates, Inc.

Kurt Bluemel, Czech-born founder and president of Kurt Bluemel, Inc., Landscape Design-Construction and Nurseries, Baldwin, Maryland, was coeditor of the Ornamental Grasses lists. Mr. Bluemel introduced the use of ornamental grasses to this country in the 1960s. He grows over 500 varieties, follows extensive testing programs for new varieties and cultivars, and searches out wild grasses in America, Europe, and Africa. He is sought after as a consultant to the nursery trade and is a frequent speaker at colleges, universities, garden clubs, and seminars.

FOR GROUND COVERS:

Sylvester G. March, consultant and coeditor for the Ground Covers lists, is horticulturist for the National Arboretum. He heads the Gardens Unit and coordinates the activities of the gardens curators. He participates with the director in planning new gardens. Mr. March has traveled extensively in Japan, Korea, and the United Kingdom, collecting wild and elite plants. He is the U.S. member of Council for the International Dendrology Society, past director of the American Association of Botanic Gardens and Arboreta, and a member of the Royal Horticultural Society. He holds an Associate degree in applied science from New York State University at Farmingdale.

Erik Neumann (see above) is consultant and coeditor of the Ground Covers lists.

Peter Mazzeo, botanist and consultant for ferns (Ground Covers 4), is a curator in the Herbarium at the National Arboretum. He has conducted taxonomic and floristic research on various native and cultivated plants. He is the author of a guidebook on trees, and another on the ferns and fern allies of the Shenandoah National Park. He is also a faculty member of the U.S.D.A. Graduate School. He was the 1976 corecipient of the J. Shelton Horsley Research Award, the highest research honor bestowed by the Virginia Academy of Science. Mr. Mazzeo has been featured in various national media, including *The New Yorker*, *The Explorer*, and *American Forests*. He conducts botanical tours for Smithsonian Associates and lectures extensively.

Joan W. Feely, coauthor and editor for Ferns, is curator for Native Plant Collections and for Daffodils and Ivies at the National Arboretum. She develops and maintains native plant collections including woodland, swamp, and meadow habitats. She teaches classes and provides technical information on these plant groups.

FOR VINES:

Theodore R. Dudley, consultant and coauthor for the Vines lists, is a research botanist and internationally recognized plant scientist specializing in the biosystematics, nomenclature, and phytogeography of woody plants. He is Coordinator of National Arboretum Documented Germplasm Explorations and serves on the organizing committee of the IV International Congress of Systematics and Evolutionary Biology. He is a veteran of plant exploration expeditions all over the world to collect potentially significant woody landscape plants and scientific materials, and is experienced in germ plasm introduction and the floristics, phytogeography, and ecology of rare, threatened, and endangered species, as well as their conservation, and the preservation of natural habitats in areas where he has traveled. He has published over 250 papers and one book and is a frequent speaker at national and international conferences, symposia, and congresses. Dr. Dudley is also a botanical consultant for numerous organizations, and general editor for Dioscorides Press, publisher of plant science books. Dr. Dudley holds a doctorate from the University of Edinburgh, Scotland, and has served at Harvard as horticultural taxonomist at the Arnold Arboretum. Most of the photos for the Vines lists are from his personal collection.

FOR SHRUBS:

Gene Eisenbeiss, consultant and editor for Trees and Shrubs, is a horticulturist and support scientist for the National Arboretum in shrub-breeding research, specializing in *Ilex*.

Charles A. H. Thomson (see above) coordinated the Shrubs section with several members of the National Arboretum staff, and designated consultants.

Charles Bell, Jr., coauthor of the four lists for roses (Shrubs 6, Shrubs 19, Vines 2, and Herbs 7) was with the U.S.D.A. for many years and is a consulting rosarian. He has grown roses of all types since 1946. Author, lecturer, hybridizer, and exhibitor of roses, past president of two local rose societies, former vice-director and editor of *The Colonial District*, American Rose Society, he was instrumental in the planning and development of the Heritage Rose Garden at the National Arboretum. Col. Bell is a member of the American Rose Society's Old Garden Rose Committee. Most of the photos of historic roses are from Col. Bell's collection.

William C. Miller III was coauthor of the list on Azaleas (Shrubs 2), and most photos on that list are his. He is a lecturer on and hybridizer of azaleas, and in his home garden grows some 600 azaleas, many of which are his own crosses. Mr. Miller is co-chairman, Glenn Dale Preservation Project, Azalea Society of America; past governor, Board of Governors, Azalea Society of America; past president, Brookside Gardens Chapter, Azalea Society of America; chairman of horticulture, Brookside Gardens Chapter Flower Show, Azalea Society of America; and Director of Science and Education, *The Azalean* (the journal of the Azalea Society of America). Mr. Miller is also a member of FONA, the American Rhododendron Society, the American Horticultural Society, Brookgreen Gardens, and the Brooklyn Botanic Garden.

Normal Beaudry coauthored and provided photos for the list on Rhododendrons (Shrubs 3). A native of Washington state, he has been active in amateur Rhododendron hybridizing for ten years, pursuing yellow flowers adaptable to the more severe climates found on the East Coast. Mr. Beaudry has served in numerous American Rhododendron

Society offices, including president of the Potomac Valley chapter, and grows over 500 varieties of azaleas and rhododendrons at his Bethesda, Maryland, home. He is a biochemist and director of immunochemistry research and development for the Hazleton Laboratories Division of Corning Glass.

Lisa S. Kratz, Curator of Azalea and Rhododendron Collections at the National Arboretum, also assisted with these subjects.

Dr. Francis Gouin, Extension Specialist Ornamental Horticulture at the University of Maryland, was consultant for the culture of container plants.

FOR TREES:

Frank S. Santamour, Jr., contributor for the Trees lists, has a national and international reputation in genetics, cytology, and the biochemistry of trees and woody plants. He is project leader at the National Arboretum in landscape tree genetics and improvement, with specialties in cytological and biochemical verification of hybrids, insect and disease resistance, wound compartmentalization, graft incompatibilities, and cultivar nomenclature. He has authored more than 210 publications in these fields. Dr. Santamour holds a B.S. degree from the University of Massachusetts, an M.F. from Yale University, an A.M. from Harvard University, and a Ph.D. in forestry and plant genetics from the University of Minnesota.

Alden M. Townsend, contributor and cooperator for the Trees lists, is a research leader and geneticist, investigating genetic improvement of elms, red maples, blue spruce, and European alder. Dr. Townsend holds a Master's degree in forest genetics from Yale University and a Ph.D. from Michigan State University.

J. Frank Schmidt, Jr., consultant for Trees, is founder and president of the Boring, Oregon, wholesale nursery that bears his name, and is a former member of the National Arboretum Advisory Council. Mr. Schmidt holds eleven plant patents, including the well-known maple cultivar 'Red Sunset'.

Bill Flemer III, consultant for many Trees and Shrubs lists, is a distinguished horticulturist and the president of Princeton Nurseries, Princeton, New Jersey, a major East Coast wholesale nursery. Mr. Flemer is at this writing chairman of the National Arboretum Advisory Council, past president of the American Association of Nurserymen and the International Plant Propagators' Society, and the author of four books on trees and shrubs. His speciality has been the breeding and introduction of trees and shrubs. He holds B.S. and M.S. degrees in botany from Yale University.

Richard J. Henkel, sales manager for Princeton Nurseries, was a consultant for Trees and Shrubs. He is a member of the Board of Directors of the American Association of Nurserymen, and is a frequent speaker to arboretum groups and municipal bodies on the use of shade trees and landscaping.

Don Shadow, consultant on Shrubs and flowering trees, is owner and president of Shadow Nursery, Inc., Winchester, Tennessee, a wholesale nursery specializing in woody ornamentals and rare and unusual plants. Mr. Shadow is also a member of the National Arboretum Advisory Council.

Roland M. Jefferson, consultant on flowering trees, was until recently a member of the National Arboretum research staff. Mr. Jefferson has contributed significantly to research on and detailed literature about the nomenclature of flowering cherries.

Frederick G. Meyer (see above) was consultant, contributor, and editor for several Trees lists, and coeditor with Erik Neumann (see above) for trees with ornamental bark, (Trees).

FOR REGIONS:

Audrey C. Teasdale, botanist for the Monrovia Nursery Company of California and Oregon, was a consultant and coeditor for warm-region plants, California and southern California, and the West Coast. She is a world-traveled botanist who has practiced horticulture in Belgium, southern France, West Germany, and with the Hillier Arboretum in England. She holds a Bachelor of Science degree from the University of California, Davis, has contributed articles to *American Horticulturist* and several other publications, and has taught at the college level.

Alan W. Meerow, taxonomist and assistant professor at the Fort Lauderdale Research and Education Center of the University of Florida, was a consultant for Florida plantings and supplied photos from his collection. He holds M.S. and Ph.D. degrees from the University of Florida, and is an authority on the Amaryllis family, currently acting as specialist for tropical ornamentals.

Henry Donselman, formerly with the University of Florida Fort Lauderdale Research and Education Center, acted as early consultant for Florida. He is presently vice-president, director of research at Rancho Soledad Nurseries in Rancho Santa Fe, California.

Additional assistance for Florida research was contributed by members of the Gainesville Extension Service, namely Dr. R. J. B. Black, Dwayne Ingram, and Ray Oglespeak.

PHOTOGRAPHY

The photographers whose works are included are:
Robert Armstrong, Longwood Gardens
Norman Beaudry, amateur rhododendron hybridizer
Col. Charles Bell, Jr., consulting rosarian
W. Atlee Burpee & Co., Stephen D. Cobden
Dr. H. M. Cathey, Director, U.S. National Arboretum
Elizabeth Corning
Dr. Theodore R. Dudley, plant scientist, National Arboretum
Lilypons Water Gardens
Longwood Gardens, Director Fred Roberts
Elvin McDonald, journalist, author, photographer
Alan W. Meerow, Fort Lauderdale Research and Education Center of the University of Florida
William C. Miller III, Azalea Society of America
Monrovia Nursery Co.
Erik Neumann, Head, Education and Public Services, National Arboretum
Wolfgang Oehme, President, Oehme, van Sweden & Associates, Inc.
Oehme, van Sweden & Associates, Inc.
Caroline Sequi, Oehme, van Sweden
Holly Shimizu, first curator, National Herb Garden
Bill Thomas, Longwood Gardens
Charles B. Thomas, President, Lilypons Water Gardens
George Leicester Thomas III, Lilypons Water Gardens
Col. Charles A. H. Thomson, horticultural consultant
Wayside Gardens and Geo. W. Park Seed Co., John Elsley, Leonard Park, and Louise Raborn
Louis Williams, National Arboretum

Flowering cherry and daffodils frame a view of the Capitol Columns at the U.S. National Arboretum. (Cathey)

DR. H. MARC CATHEY

The summer of 1988 brought us to painful awareness of vital environmental issues. It was an extremely trying year in gardens, private and public. It was not an isolated year, but rather part of a larger picture of change. Rainfall is diminishing from many sections of the United States. Rainfall supplied at the rate of three to four inches per month spaced properly should sustain the growth of most of our landscape plants over the spring, summer, and fall growing months. This seldom happens anymore, anywhere. The high heats, colder winters, and drying winds of the last decades are expected to continue.

In ages past, plants growing in the wild maintained ecological balances by adapting to climatic change. Some plant species "migrated" with the winds and the birds to regions suited to their needs. Some seeds of plants that survived change grew into species adapted to the new conditions. And some species vanished, making way for the new.

By replacing jungle, wetlands, and prairie with ranch and farm, city and road, we have limited plants' opportunities to adapt to environmental changes. The price for this interruption of the natural cycle is that we must now take over the development and select plants adapted to projected climate changes.

We once said, "My garden, my land." Now we must think and act, "Our gardens, our land."

I am calling for a new ethic for all gardeners, a determination to conform to professional standards and conduct. When water is in short supply, it is unethical to plant water-guzzling species. When air, water, or particulate pollution is a threat to the environment, we must choose plants without chemical dependencies. The meadow garden whose prototype at the National Arboretum is called "The New American Garden" is a style, a combination of plants and space use, conforming to the new ethic. There will be others. We need to grow tough plants for tough times and sites.

I invite you to join me as we learn together how to grow tough plants in our private gardens, public spaces, and along our interstate highway systems. It will require the cooperative dreams of millions of North American gardeners to introduce durable beauty into all of our living spaces. We have tough plants right at hand—we need to encourage their development, availability, and use. We need to learn how to grow them in tough sites and tough times. I do not know of a more worthy, fulfilling, or necessary endeavor. Green is the color of hope. In our garden plants is our hope for survival.

I commend the staff of our U.S. National Arboretum and our consultants for the excellence of the plant information here. I thank Jacqueline Hériteau for her determination to gather and publish the information and congratulate her on the book's brilliant organization and presentation.

It is most timely.

Dr. H. Marc Cathey
Director, U.S. National Arboretum
Washington, D.C.
Agricultural Research Service
U.S. Department of Agriculture

NATIONAL ARBORETUM

The purpose of our National Arboretum is threefold: to collect and evaluate trees, shrubs, and flowers that can be cultivated over relatively wide areas of the country; to breed them for increased hardiness, disease and insect resistance, enhanced fragrance, broader ranges of color and seasonal change, better flowers and fruit; and to educate the public regarding these plants through collections, native plants, and designed gardens. We are invited to choose the best of their discoveries for our own gardens.

A century ago a handful of enthusiasts dreamed of an arboretum in the nation's capital that would take its place among the world's noted botanic gardens. The first attempt to turn the dream into reality was in 1901. In 1927 Congress approved a bill that directed the secretary of agriculture to establish the National Arboretum.

(The United States Botanic Garden, established·in 1842, is a separate entity. It is located just below the Capitol on the Mall.)

The early planning and acquisition of land were directed by F. V. Coville and B. Y. Morrison of the Division of Plant Exploration and Introduction. Dr. Coville was principal botanist of the Department of Agriculture. Mr. Morrison was principal horticulturist and head of the division before he became the first director of the Arboretum in 1951.

Today the National Arboretum is one of the largest arboreta in the country. It is directed by the Agricultural Research Service and the U.S. Department of Agriculture, and aided by an advisory council of citizens appointed by the secretary of agriculture in accordance with the provisions of the act of establishment. In 1975, legislation was enacted allowing the secretary of agriculture to accept gifts in support of the National Arboretum and its development through Friends of the National Arboretum (FONA).

The National Arboretum's operational and research facilities include 9.5 miles of paved roads, an administration building, a brick service court, cut stone entrances, and a range of six 100-foot greenhouses. Caretaker residences were constructed at two of the gateways; one has since been converted to an information center, headquarters, and gift shop for the National Capitol Area Federation of Garden Clubs, Inc. The second is used for curators' offices.

A headhouse-greenhouse complex is equipped with laboratory and refrigeration facilities for plant research and production purposes, for plant breeding programs, and for laboratory work in cytology (the study of cells) and plant hardiness.

THE ARBORETUM GROUNDS

The U.S. National Arboretum is one of the largest gardens in the world. It occupies 444 acres in the Mount Hamilton section of Washington, north and east of the Capitol. The higher hills look southward to the

Glenn Dale azaleas on Mount Hamilton. (Neumann)

Asian Valley. (Cathey)

The Gotelli Collection.

The National Arboretum's first camellia plantings were started in Cryptomeria Valley with a gift in 1949 of a collection of the fall-blooming *Camellia sasanquas*, which were planted along trails leading to the nearby dogwood collection. 'Frost Queen' and 'Cinnamon Cindy' are among the introductions that came from research conducted on this group.

Flowering dogwoods, *Cornus florida*, donated by the Woman's National Farm and Garden Association, are set among hemlocks and formal plantings of other dogwoods. In the collection are over 70 kinds of dogwood including the weeping, upright, and pink forms of *Cornus florida*, our native dogwood.

The holly trail abounds in native and exotic species that are parents to brilliant new hybrids introduced by the National Arboretum. It leads to a unique six-sided teakwood bench from which can be viewed plantings of the towering hybrid magnolias (*Magnolia virginiana* × *M. grandiflora*), deciduous hollies (*Ilex serrata*, *I. decidua*, and *I.* 'Sparkleberry'), and the adjacent crab apple planting.

There are 300 or more species and cultivars of crab apples, and important collections of magnolia, fire thorn, viburnum, crape myrtle, flowering cherries, lilacs, daffodils, and wildflowers. Collections of boxwood, peonies, daylilies, and irises are planted in formal garden settings.

Fern Valley is a naturalistic planting of ferns, wildflowers, trees, and shrubs native to eastern North America; adjacent to it is a collection of thousands of daffodils. Lime-loving ferns in the valley cling to a wall made from limestone rocks once used in a parapet constructed by General Braddock's army during the French and Indian War.

The Asian Valley is a hilly area planted with materials from Korea, Japan, and China. It includes a watercourse and overlooks the dam toward the Anacostia River.

The Gotelli Collection of conifers is one of the most significant at the Arboretum. It is planted on a 5-acre hillside site in the northeast part of the grounds. Donated by William T. Gotelli, the collection includes numerous cultivars of *Abies, Cedrus, Chamaecyparis, Cryptomeria, Juniperus, Picea, Pinus, Taxus, Thuja, Tsuga,* and miscellaneous additional genera. Most of the conifers originated in the United States and Europe, but there are also specimens from Japan, Australia, New Zealand, and Canada.

There are other minor plant collections, and every year brings fresh opportunities to add to these invaluable banks of plant germ plasm. All told, almost 100 gardens and collections are placed on the grounds. The

Kalmia in the bonsai collection.

Capitol and the Washington Monument, and in the east, break in dramatic drops to the Anacostia River.

Although not a park in the usual sense, miles of roads (with frequent parking spaces) and walking trails wind through elegant plant displays and stream-edged woodlands. There is a steady flow of visiting scientists, landscape architects, nurserymen, schoolchildren, and tourists at all seasons.

Though the first purpose of the plant collections is scientific, they are meant to be beautiful as well. In late April and early May, the slopes of Mount Hamilton glow with the spring color of 70,000 azaleas. On weekends, they are visited by as many as 20,000 people daily. A mass planting of Glenn Dale azaleas on Mount Hamilton was the National Arboretum's first major project—in 1947. Glenn Dale, now a research facility of the Arboretum, was a plant introduction station. Here B. Y. Morrison developed his Glenn Dale azaleas. He later became the Arboretum's first director.

Of particular interest to horticulturists and home gardeners are the azalea study collections. Evergreen types—the Glenn Dale hybrids, Satsuki azaleas, and Kurumes—are centered in and around the Morrison and Lee azalea gardens. In the woodlands below is an extensive collection of azaleas native to the eastern United States.

Historic roses in the National Herb Garden. (Cathey)

dominant landscape is almost 300 acres of climax Eastern deciduous forest—all a 10-minute drive from the U.S. capital.

GARDEN AND MUSEUM

The U.S. National Arboretum also is the repository for valuable plant gifts from other countries, in particular collections of bonsai and penjing, which add to our knowledge of plants and their meaning to other peoples.

In commemoration of America's bicentennial, a rare and priceless gift of 53 bonsai was presented to the American people by the Nippon Bonsai Association of Japan. Many of the plants were donations from private sources—including some from the Japanese royal family. Bonsai, dwarfed ancient trees in pots without landscape, has great significance for the Japanese people. It represents one of their nation's oldest, highest, and most revered art forms. The bonsai at the National Arboretum comprise some of Japan's most treasured specimens, some dating back more than 350 years.

Several bonsai have been added to the collection, among them a white pine and a persimmon presented in 1983 to President and Mrs. Ronald Reagan by His Majesty Hassan II, King of Morocco, from his personal collection and transferred to the National Arboretum for display.

The same love for natural form expressed in bonsai is also found in suiseki, or stone viewing, long associated with bonsai. Part of the bicentennial gift from Japan was a collection of priceless, unique viewing stones which is displayed in the administration building.

Penjing is the Chinese art of shaping trees and shrubs in miniature with a landscape. It began in China before A.D. 700 and was introduced to Japan some 500 years later. In 1986, Dr. Yee-sun Wu of Hong Kong presented to the American people a collection of 31 penjing ranging in age from 15 to 200 years. Some grow in irreplaceable antique containers. Additional plants in the collection were the gift of Shu-Ying Lui of Hong Kong.

Eventually the National Bonsai and Penjing Museum will be a complex of Oriental gardens and pavilions with teaching and support facilities funded through private donations to the National Bonsai Foundation. Currently, the complex occupies 2.5 acres on the east side of the Arboretum's administration building, and includes the Japanese gardens, the bonsai pavilion, and winter storage pavilion.

The National Herb Garden, a gift of the Herb Society of America with matching funds from Congress, was donated in 1980. Actual herb plantings occupy about an acre, with walkways, terraces, and background shrubs. The garden includes a formal "knot" garden. The collection of historic roses is one of the most complete in the country. Among several special herb gardens is a Dioscorides Garden of medicinal plants and others used in the first century and described by him in A.D. 60. There are gardens of herbs for cooking, fragrance, dyes, bees, and teas, as well as herbs used by Indians and early colonial settlers, and an Oriental Garden.

The National Aquatic Garden. (Williams)

From the first herb curator's experience in combining pungent herbs and roses comes the view that beneficial insects outweigh nuisances—even Japanese beetles—in the chemical-free garden.

The design of the New American Garden fronting the Activities Center and Arbor House Gift Shop was a gift of landscape architects Wolfgang Oehme and James van Sweden, of Washington, D.C. It replaces a traditional lawn and foundation plants with wild grasses and naturalized perennials and bulbs, and is an ongoing investigation in this increasingly accepted new type of garden.

The coast-to-coast interest in this style of garden suggests that it is a real direction rather than just a trend. It is endorsed by all the scientists at the Arboretum as well. The mowed, clipped, pruned landscape we inherited from Europe is changing into a flowering meadow, unabashedly American, democratic and free. It displays masses of almost-wild flowers, catches the light in tall grasses, flows and murmurs with each breeze, irresistibly transporting consciousness to a moment in a sunny field when the United States was brand new. For an increasing number of Americans, the home landscape also includes water gardens and reflecting pools. Birds nest here as some of the original ecological balance is restored, and insects join rather than combat the gardener in making all things beautiful.

The Carl W. Buchheister National Bird Garden, centered by an enormous butterfly pattern, is designed to display plants that provide food, cover, and nesting materials for birds. It is named for a past president of the National Audubon Society, a member of the National Arboretum Advisory Council.

A transformed Brickyard Garden fronting New York Avenue Northeast will eventually include a demonstration center for silver plants, vegetables, shade plants, container plantings, watering systems and recycling, and red flowers for hummingbirds.

The Aquatic Garden surrounds part of the administration building, a colonnaded auditorium that seats 175 people. In summer and into autumn, water lilies, lotuses, and flowering bog plants bloom. A black dye added to the water reduces algae and furnishes a velvety black surface that reflects plants and clouds. Nearly 600 Koi live in its 115,000 gallons of water. Twenty-six fountain nozzles provide aeration for the fish.

THE ARBORETUM'S SCIENTIFIC WORK

A small staff of dedicated professionals and scientists have made the National Arboretum internationally known for research and taxonomy of woody plants, and for the development of new and superior trees and shrubs. They have produced many of the best new woody plants in America and distribute them freely to other research centers and to the wholesale nursery industry, much as NASA distributes its scientific knowledge without charge to American industry.

The starting point of a new plant variety is plant germ plasm. The National Arboretum is the leader in ornamental plant germ plasm collection. To visitors, the Arboretum is a big, beautiful green space planted with common and unusual species in numerous gardens and collections, among them azaleas, daylilies, dwarf conifers, hollies, magnolias, native wildflowers and ferns, Asian plants, and magnificent heirloom bonsai and penjing. To local families, it is as friendly as a zoo—a place where children help to feed the fish, fall in love with miniature bonsai forests, and Friends of the National Arboretum (FONA) hold their educational events and fund-raising fall plant fair. But to scientists, the collections are vast living stores of plant germ plasm.

The Gotelli Conifer Collection alone numbers about 2,000 dwarf and slow-growing conifers and is one of the most extensive of its kind, providing a treasury of genetic resources for the future. In contrast, a nearby grove of *Metasequoia*—the rare, ancient dawn redwood that once extended over the Northern Hemisphere—seems to scrape the sky. This tree dates back 25 to 40 million years and was known only in fossil form until discovered in the 1940s growing along the Yangtze River in China.

The plants and collections are acquired through exploration, gifts, and exchanges with other arboreta and botanic gardens. Plant exploration expeditions are regularly undertaken to places as diverse as an uninhabited island in northern Korea, the mountains of China, and the highlands of Peru and Ecuador. Horticulturist Sylvester G. March recently brought back from Great Britain's historic gardens over 500 accessions of "elite" plants to be added to the National Arboretum's collections; the most useful will eventually be distributed to the trade and other arboreta and botanic gardens throughout the world.

Arboretum plants are labeled, documented, and arranged in generic botanical groupings, in gardenlike or naturalistic settings, or in demonstration plantings. A curator is responsible for each major collection. The knowledge gained is evaluated and shared with the Agricultural Research Service (ARS), U.S. Department of Agriculture (U.S.D.A.), cooperating institutions, and through publication, with scientists, industries, nurserymen, botanic gardens, and arboreta.

Not all introductions are hybridized from plants collected abroad. For instance, a new clematis with the amazing ability to bloom when clematis never bloomed before was sired in an American backyard. This story began when Dr. Theodore R. Dudley, National Arboretum research botanist and plant explorer, noticed an unusual clematis in an abandoned garden in Albany, New York. Unlike other clematis, it bloomed past summer and into early fall. Dr. Dudley collected the plant and began the long, slow process of breeding, evaluation, and propagation at the Arboretum. (To introduce a new woody plant often requires as long as fifteen years, and in some instances we may not know too much about how it performs for another twenty.) Finally, a new clematis with beautiful flowers and the extended blooming period of the Albany maverick was ready for testing by growers outside the Arboretum. Today, Dr. Dudley's late-spring-through-fall-flowering 'Betty Corning' clematis is available in commercial quantities from nurseries. It is an all-time winner.

Then there's the willow that happened to fall where a National Arboretum scientist was bound to notice. It blew down outside a window next to the desk of Dr. Frank S. Santamour, a Ph.D. in forestry and plant genetics with a national and international reputation in genetics, cytology, and the biochemistry of trees and woody plants. Dr. Santamour observed that one side of the willow's root system was strangely stunted and began a series of tests that related the damage to a nematode (parasitic worm). He discovered that nematode damage is responsible for the inadequate root system that often causes willows to go over in storms. The next decade will likely see long-lived, strong weeping willows added to the National Arboretum's distinguished list of plant introductions.

THE INTRODUCTIONS

The National Arboretum has introduced over 150 improved plants, most of them woody, in some twenty-five genera—a magnificent contribution for an institution barely sixty years old. Others are in the pipeline and will be released to the nursery trade in future years.

Many ARS and National Arboretum plant introductions already are acclaimed. A few of them are: the Glenn Dale azaleas; the Bradford pear cultivars, which are magical when seen in bloom by spring moonlight and handsome when the foliage turns burgundy-red in fall; a selection of the Chinese elm; a perky red magnolia, 'Galaxy' (developed by Dr. Frank S. Santamour); 'Columbia' and 'Liberty', the new anthracnose-resistant plane trees for city streets (Dr. Santamour); *Ilex* 'Sparkleberry', a deciduous holly that covers itself with shiny lipstick-red berries in winter and literally glows in the snow (William Kosar and Gene Eisenbeiss); a palate of mildew-free crape myrtles in melting pink and white, lavender and melon tones; and many viburnums, pyracantha (fire thorn), and hibiscus (Dr. Donald Egolf).

Current National Arboretum plant research emphasizes the breeding of better selections of woody and herbaceous ornamental plants. Research has been conducted in the past, and continues in many instances, on camellias, hibiscus, irises, lycoris and other amaryllises, deciduous azaleas, crape myrtles, hollies, flowering pears, and other plants.

Based on present research, we may expect to see long-lived mimosas and stronger and more insect- and disease-resistant flowering and shade trees, the result of basic research by Dr. Santamour. On the horizon are hybrid crab apples with disease resistance built in, and scale-free euonymus. Roselike flowers with fifty petals are anticipated for flowering cherries. New introductions will be developed from 200,000 seeds and cuttings of exotic flowering cherries collected in the Far East by Arboretum botanist Roland M. Jefferson. New types also will thrive for the first time in cold northern states and in southern parts of Florida and Texas.

Ilex 'Sparkleberry'. (Eisenbeiss)

Lagerstroemia indica 'Seminole', one of the many mildew-free crape myrtles introduced by the National Arboretum.

Promising selections are first tested on the Arboretum grounds, then locally and by cooperating institutions. Finally they are released gratis to wholesale nurseries, but with an agreement that the nurseries will develop commercial quantities and make these available to the retail nursery trade. The National Arboretum annually distributes many thousands of plants and plant propagations to botanic gardens and other cooperators. These efforts are supported and encouraged by the American Association of Nurserymen.

More limited attention is given to problems of plant propagation and to assisting other agencies and institutions through the dissemination of needed plants stocks, materials, and information.

THE NEW TECHNOLOGY

Plant introductions are the glamorous aspect and end product of the breeding work at the National Arboretum. But contributions to the world's pool of basic research have the greatest impact on the future. When scientists talk about genetic engineering, predictions hinge on how much "basic research" and "applied research" has been com-

Magnolia 'Galaxy'. (Neumann)

pleted. Basic research is the time-consuming work that uncovers principles governing appearance, form, everything we call growth and life. Applied research leads to applications to specific goals.

In the 21st century we can expect the research efforts of the National Arboretum and other research centers around the world to transform our gardens and farms. Genetic engineering and hybridizing have the potential to give us roses in forget-me-not-blue, corn as high as an elephant's eye, and a whole sequence of fall and winter color. Even more important will be resistance to pests and stresses, and immunity to otherwise toxic agents.

Their ultimate goal is gardens satisfying in all seasons, without need of laborious or ecology-shattering chemical interventions. Such marvels require "high risk research" which will take time and the kind of money only publicly funded institutions provide. Key pieces of the basic research are already in place.

A revolution in worldwide grafting techniques now under way is the result of basic research conducted by Dr. Santamour, who studied enzymes of more than 2,000 trees and found that each tree has only three or four major lignin-forming enzymes—the peroxidase enzyme in the cambial tissue. He discovered that trees form a solid graft when the stems and rootstocks have matching enzymes. Weak grafts result if the enzymes are different, even if from the same species. Some 4,000 years of grafting fruit trees had evolved a data base governing fruit tree grafting, but no comparable information was developed for the trees important to municipal plantings and those that supply the forestry industries. One incalculably valuable result of Dr. Santamour's work may be the return of forests of chestnut trees to America.

THE HERBARIUM

Crucial to all plant research and development is accurate botanical identification. The Herbarium, a plant reference collection similar to a library, is located in the administration building of the National Arboretum. A collection of over 600,000 dried, pressed, cultivated, and wild specimens, it is the principal facility that makes accurate identification possible.

Research here emphasizes taxonomy (the orderly classification according to presumed natural relationships of plants and animals). The value of the Herbarium increases as its overall collection grows through active exchange with other institutions, both foreign and domestic. It includes sizable reference collections of native plants of the United States, China, Tierra del Fuego, and Peru. The collection of commercial nut varieties is extensive and a collection of willows (*Salix*), assembled by

the late Carleton R. Ball, is one of the largest in the country. The I. C. Martindale Herbarium, acquired in 1964, includes valuable historic specimens dating from the late 18th century.

The Herbarium inventory includes the den Boer collection of crab apple materials and a special collection of plants indigenous to the western United States. The latter forms the basis of the National Arboretum's "Medicinal Uses of Plants by Indian Tribes of Nevada," which has provided leads of considerable medical and industrial significance. A by-product of taxonomic work of the Herbarium was the development by Dr. Frederick G. Meyer of the use of plastics to attach herbarium specimens—a technique that has been adopted by many of the world's leading herbaria.

The Herbarium's staff answers technical inquiries and loans its collections to visiting scientists and others both here and abroad.

EDUCATIONAL SERVICES

On an intermittent basis the National Arboretum publishes a series of technical papers, "National Arboretum Contributions," and provides technical advice to the Agricultural Research Service in the preparation of publications for a gardening audience. Its education programs reach the general public through year-round lectures, horticultural demonstrations, exhibits, and films given in the auditorium and classroom in the administration building. A monthly event is the program of Living Legends—educational lectures given by National Arboretum researchers, staff, and consultants.

In cooperation with the U.S. Department of Agriculture Graduate School, horticultural short courses are given for beginners interested in practical gardening, botany, landscape design, and related subjects. The classes are taught by members of the Arboretum staff, nurserymen, and specialists from local chapters of plant societies.

In cooperation with local chapters of various plant societies, the National Arboretum hosts a series of free flower shows. It also provides land for the "Washington Youth Gardens," where children learn and practice the fundamentals of gardening under the direction of the District of Columbia Department of Recreation.

The National Arboretum exchanges seed and plant material with other scientific institutions throughout the world in order to provide researchers with needed genetic resources and to enrich the educational display collections at the National Arboretum.

—with Erik Neumann,
Head, Education and
Public Services

USE THIS BOOK

This book was developed in order to provide an easy-to-use guide for gardeners to consult when deciding which plants to grow in their gardens and yards. It is not an encyclopedia or dictionary of plants. Instead, it is a plant finder; the plants are organized first, by major plant groups (flowers, aquatics, herbs, ornamental grasses, ground covers, vines, shrubs, and trees), and within each group, by qualities possessed by the plants or the purposes the plants serve in the landscape. A complete listing can be found in the Table of Contents. Most gardeners will approach this book—and their search for the perfect plant—in terms of landscaping need. This includes aesthetic qualities (color, height, blooming season, etc.) and cultural requirements (light, soil, moisture). The beauty—and ease—of the plant finder concept is that you will be able to look up plants according to your landscaping needs.

The **Plant Finder** lists in the Table of Contents include plants whose excellence has been established over wide areas of the country, those on which the future will be built. They also contain beautiful southern plants that gardeners in cooler regions are encouraged to use as indoor/outdoor container material.

All the plants on the lists are judged by the staff of the U.S. National Arboretum and their consultants as having enduring beauty and resistance to pests and diseases, and as being likely to flourish in the home garden with little maintenance or chemical/physical intervention. Many of the plants are brilliant new problem-solving introductions of the National Arboretum.

The lists of plants included in the book, and the descriptions of species and cultivars, are based on information from Arboretum curators and research scientists and their consultants. This project began with an exhaustive compilation of plants for special purposes prepared by the author from data bases at the universities of Florida and North Carolina, and elsewhere, various West Coast sources, and major nurseries in varied climates. Each entry was reviewed by at least two specialists. Nevertheless, there will be areas of disagreement; in gardening, the variables are almost infinite. Trees in the North may grow at a different rate and reach a different mature height than the same species in the South. Where this book doesn't appear to fit local facts, consult with regional plantsmen, arboreta and botanic gardens, and Agriculture Extension Services offices at state universities (see the Appendix).

Study the titles of the plant lists in the Table of Contents. Your first step is to select a plant group—such as Flowers, for example. Look under Flowers in the Table of Contents and you will find a listing of all the flower categories included in the book, along with the page number of each. General planting and landscaping advice, supplied by renowned specialists, can be found in the introduction to each plant group. The introduction to Flowers gives tips on designing flower gardens, planting different types of flowers, and dividing perennials and bulbs. We highly recommend that you take a minute to review the introduction to the plant group in which you are interested, to find helpful advice and additional information.

Following the introduction you will find the plant lists themselves—106 lists in all, covering a total of 1,786 outstanding plants. Each list is identified by a number, and refers to the particular qualities that make the plants most desirable. By reviewing all of the lists in the Table of Contents, you will find the one that best suits your needs. (If you do not find the exact criteria you are looking for, refer to the list that comes closest.)

Suppose you want some summer flowers for a shady spot. You will find that Flowers 13 covers Summer Perennials for Shade. Turn to that page and you will find descriptions of five genera of perennials that bloom in

---

FLOWERS 13
SUMMER PERENNIALS FOR SHADE

In hot regions shade may be almost as bright as direct sun in the North. These plants thrive in light shade in the moderate regions of the country; they will tolerate more sun farther north, and succeed with even less farther south.

summer and thrive in shady locations. In some cases, such as *Hosta*, several species and cultivars are described. These plants are considered

H. 'Honeybells'   Zones 3–9.
Grass-green leaves, and in July and August, 3-foot lavender-lilac, fragrant flower spikes.

H. lancifolia var. *albomarginata*
Narrow-leaved Hosta   Zones 3–9.
Narrow leaves brushed with white, to 2 feet, and lavender blooms in August and September.

H. montana 'Aureo-marginata' Zones 3–9.
Large green leaves irregularly margined in yellow which turns to cream as the season progresses. The clumps reach 40 inches wide and stand more sun than other hostas.

H. plantaginea 'Grandiflora'
Fragrant Hosta   Zones 3–9.
White-flowering, 20 inches high, this is a fragrant hosta that blooms in late summer. The light green leaves are large, 10 inches long and 6 inches wide. One of the most beautiful and useful for the flower border.

by the National Arboretum staff and consultants to be the best plants for this particular use in American gardens. With each entry you will find several important pieces of information:

TIME OF BLOOM for any given plant differs from region to region. It is expressed here as early spring, mid-spring, late spring, and so on. Plants whose performance spans seasonal boundaries may appear on several lists.

MATURE HEIGHT given for woody plants is usually height attained in cultivation, which is 30 to 50 percent less than the mature height of a plant growing in the wild. Cultivated trees are long-lived, and our judgment of how they perform in North America is sometimes based on relatively incomplete information.

LIGHT requirements are given in terms of three different categories. Full sun means a minimum 6 hours full sun daily; semi-sunny, 2 to 6 hours sun daily; shade, 2 hours full sun, or dappled sun all day; and versatile, a range of light. Where two different light requirements are given for a plant (such as both full sun and semi-sunny), it means the plant tolerates both conditions.

MOISTURE needs are given as follows: surface moist means a moist atmosphere is best; roots moist means the plant needs sustained moisture at the root level, but the surface can be dry; versatile means the plant adapts to drought and some wetness.

> Outstanding spring and summer gold or golden orange buttercuplike flowers for damp, shady places. Lovely massed by a small stream in light woodlands. 'Golden Queen' is deep orange. Plant container-grown plants in early spring. Easy to grow in fairly heavy garden soil. Seeds are slow to germinate.
>
> MATURE HEIGHT: 2'
> GROWTH RATE: slow
> LIGHT: semi-sunny, shade
> MOISTURE: soil surface damp

For each plant category you will find several pieces of information in addition to the descriptive list of featured plants. At the beginning of the section are suggested **Companion Plants**—that is, other kinds of

> COMPANION PLANTINGS
> Shrubs: Azalea (*Rhododendron*) cvs; *Aucuba japonica* 'Variegata', Gold-dust Tree.
> Background plant: Ferns.
> Ground cover: *Vinca minor*, Periwinkle.
> Flower: *Impatiens wallerana*, Zanzibar Balsam, Busy Lizzy.

plants to grow along with the featured plants. The Companion Plants for Summer Perennials for Shade include shrubs, background plants, ground covers, and other flowers. At the end of each section, following the list of featured plants, you will find two additional lists of plants. One is headed **See also**, and refers you to plants covered elsewhere in this

> SEE ALSO:
> *Astilbe* × *arendsii* 'Feuer', 'Professor van der Wielen', Spiraea, Flowers 11
> *Chrysanthemum* × *superbum* 'Polaris', Shasta Daisy, Flowers 14
> *Dianthus* × *allwoodii*, Allwood Pink, Flowers 20
> *Sedum maximum* 'Atropurpureum', Great Stonecrop, Flowers 14
> *Veronica spicata*, 'Blue Fox', 'Snow White', 'Sunny Borders', Speedwell, Flowers 10
> *Yucca glauca*, Soapweed, Flowers 12

book. The most important quality of the See also plants is the one under which they are listed, but these plants also fit into this category as well. For example, under See also for Summer Perennials for Shade, *Dianthus*

× *allwoodii* is noted. This plant can be found under Flowers 20, Fragrant Flowers, because it is loved for its spicy scent. But it also blooms in summer and grows in partial shade.

Following the list of See also plants you will find another list of plants headed **Alternates**. These plants can also serve the same purpose as the featured plants, and are included to give you some third choices. Some of the Alternate plants are covered elsewhere in the book and others are

> ALTERNATES:
> *Alchemilla mollis*, Lady's Mantle
> *Astilbe simplicifolia*, Spiraea
> *Chrysogonum virginianum*, Golden Star
> *Cimicifuga racemosa*, Black Cohosh, Black Snake-root
> *Filipendula ulmaria*, Queen-of-the-meadow
> *Lythrum salicaria*, 'Dropmore Purple', 'Morden's Pink', Purple Loosestrife

not. To find out if Alternate plants are covered elsewhere in the book, consult the Index.

The **zone map** included in this book, The U.S.D.A. Plant Hardiness Map of North America, outlines a new view of climate in the 50 United States. The boundaries of the 10 climate zones outlined in the old U.S.D.A. Hardiness Zone Map have been redrawn to reflect changing climatic conditions. This map has several differences and replaces the map published in 1960 and revised in 1965.

The U.S.D.A. Plant Hardiness Map of North America is offered by the Government Printing Office in a four-foot-wide color version, showing A and B regions for zones 1 through 11. The A zones are 5 degrees cooler than the B zones. A smaller map is offered by the U.S.D.A. in black-and-white without A or B zones. The map here repeats the U.S. portions of the 4-foot color map without the A and B zones.

Gardeners will find this new map better reflects with their experience of local climates and pocket-climates. Be aware that the climates in most regions is averaging up to 5 degrees more cold than the previous map indicated. The warmer zone around the Great Lakes is much smaller than in the previous map. Maine, New Hampshire, Washington, Oklahoma, are a little warmer. The 4-foot map shows many large urban areas are warmer than the surrounding countryside, while small pockets of higher elevation are colder. States such as California, where mini-climates are created by abrupt changes in elevation, will find the new map closer to their experience.

A and B plant hardiness information is not in the text because current, reliable U.S.D.A. information on the hardiness of all plants is not available. The ongoing National Arboretum Plant Performance Guide research project is developing new data, including the extremes of cold and heat in which the 1800 gardens plants here will flourish. More than 60,000 North American gardeners are involved in the National Arboretum PPG project.

The new map shows in detail the average annual minimum temperatures (lows) recorded from 1974 to 1986 for the United States and Canada and from 1971 to 1984 for Mexico. The map shows 10 different zones, each of which represents an area of winter hardiness for the plants of agriculture and our natural landscape. It also introduces Zone 11, to represent areas that have average annual minimum temperatures above 40° F (4.4° C) and that are therefore essentially frost free.

The zone ratings are intended to indicate where *satisfactory to excellent adaptability* of the plants can be expected. Many plants may survive in warmer or colder climates than those given. Usually, however, mere survival does not represent satisfactory performance.

INDEX: To find a particular plant, look up either the botanical (Latin) or common name in the Index. Learn botanical names for plants—they are universal as well as accurate in a way few common names can be.

AAN NURSERY CROP CODES are listed with botanical names in the Index. These codes were developed by the American Association of Nurserymen in order to standardize the identification of specific plants, so that confusion caused by different names is eliminated. Eventually it is hoped that all plant suppliers in the United States will use these codes, and many already do. When you use these codes you will be sure of getting exactly the plant you want.

Choose plants that will thrive where you are, they'll be the most rewarding. A palm has a hard time of it in Alaska, and so does its owner. Consult with regional U.S.D.A. Agricultural Experimental Stations, page 255, and area nurseries and plant societies when the local success of a species or cultivar is in question. There are truly outstanding mail order suppliers who are excellent sources for newly introduced or hard-to-find plants.

Reference works consulted for generally held information were Cornell University's *Hortus Third*, Michael A. Dirr's *Manual of Woody Landscape Plants* and similar works, and several books by Donald Wyman, Horticulturist Emeritus of Harvard University's Arnold Arboretum.

Botanical and common plant names conform to *Hortus Third*, though many of the common names seem more common to the British past than to North America's present. The author has usually chosen a single common name, the first listed by *Hortus*. Occasionally she has added a second or third name universally associated with the plant. Perhaps this can help to standardize common names. The director of the National Arboretum recommends that gardeners learn the botanical (Latin) names of plants they grow. The National Arboretum Herbarium expects soon to complete the compilation of reliable botanical records for woody landscape plants for the nation.

Pronunciations are given for genus names, and usually follow authoritative gardening literature. They are scripted in the clear and simple style initiated in Ralph Bailey's sixteen-volume *The Good Housekeeping Illustrated Encyclopedia of Gardening*, unfortunately now out of print.

Jacqueline Hériteau
Washington, D.C.

THE NATIONAL ARBORETUM
BOOK OF OUTSTANDING
GARDEN PLANTS

Tulipa 'Sorbet', a single late-blooming tulip, sparkles in a mass planting. (Thomson)

FLOWERS

FLOWERS

In the next century, genetic engineering will push beyond its modification of simple annual flowers, such as petunias and impatiens, to develop flowers that bloom in what is today's off-season, and in new colors, forms, sizes, and fragrances. For the time being, most available research funds go to improving other more economically viable crop plants. Our need for resistant plants is rising dramatically as chemicals are discouraged to avoid pollution and the destruction of life-giving ecosystems. Flowers, along with other plants, will need to be part of research efforts.

The term perennial is used in this book to mean a flowering herbaceous plant lasting more than two seasons, and bulbs are included. In the new gardening ethic, they provide the drama on a stage set by evergreen shrubs, ornamental grasses, and ground covers that flourish without wasteful watering and weekly mowing. Where possible, perennials are naturalized—planted once and left for several years to renew themselves.

In designing with perennials, the sequence of bloom established by the Plant Finder lists will be helpful. Bulbs are the core of early spring color, tucked under high-branched shrubs and tall trees. Lists Flowers 1 through Flowers 6 suggest a progression of bulb color from late winter through fall. All bulbs require well-drained soil and moderate levels of nutrients. The perennial show is for mid-spring through early summer, but the new interest is in those that bloom in late summer and autumn, a rich complement to the fall color of trees and shrubs.

Use the annuals and tender perennials listed in Flowers 17 for quick cover of bare spots and for container and basket planting—color movable according to need. In November you can plant cold-hardy annuals, like pansies, that bloom amazingly through winter in mild regions.

To experience your flower garden in a new way, let the flower season end more as it does in nature, where seedheads ripen amid stems rooted in autumn-gilded leaves. In the warmth of Indian summer, bees drone lazily over a few asters and mums, and insects hum as they shred summer's organic structures. There are some exceptions to the ideal, alas—peony vegetation, for instance, had best be cut to the ground and burned to avoid carrying over disease problems to the next season.

Perennials blooming in early summer. (Orndorf)

PLANTING PERENNIALS AND ANNUALS

With the exceptions noted on the Plant Finder lists, flowers bloom best when given 6 hours of direct sun. Often there is more light available than there appears to be--light reflected from a white wall or mirrorlike surface increases the footcandles in the vicinity.

Planting in slightly raised beds or borders ensures good drainage. Before planting, test the soil to determine its fertility and pH. Add fertilizer, lime, and gypsum as recommended by a soil test to bring the soil pH to 6.0–7.0, the range for most perennials and annuals. Use a low-nitrogen fertilizer such as 5–10–5, 50 percent organic, at a rate of 3 to 5 pounds for each 100 square feet. Dig or till a 2-inch-thick layer of organic material, such as compost, rotted sawdust, shredded composted leaves, or peat moss to a depth of 8 to 12 inches. Fertilize the garden every three to five weeks for the continued growth of the annuals over the summer and fall months.

Do not plant seedlings or seeds before the soil has drained and the air warmed. They sulk, and may rot in spring's cold, wet weeks. Annuals in particular need to grow unchecked.

Keep seedlings out of direct sun; plant them in late afternoon, after the sun has gone by. Container-grown plants are sold in 1- to 3-inch pots or pocket strips, or in flats of 6 to 12. Water them with diluted fertilizer. Make the holes deep enough to set plants a little above the level at which they are growing in the container. Always pull apart the roots winding around or binding the root balls of container-grown plants before planting. Divide plants in flats with a sharp, clean knife, giving each a good root system. Half fill each hole with diluted fertilizer, plant the seedling, push earth up around the stem, and with the fingers of both hands firm the soil around the stem gently but firmly so the plant will not come out of the ground if tugged. Broadcast 1 to 3 inches of mulch around the plants, but do not let it touch the stems.

Pinching out the leader (tall, central shoot) encourages branching in plants that bloom in spires, and each branch produces new spires with flowers.

DIVIDING PERENNIALS

Every three to five years, you will need to divide perennials to rejuvenate them. Divide spring-flowering perennials one month before the ground freezes in autumn or before growth begins in early spring; divide autumn-flowering perennials in spring.

With a spading fork, lift the clump of roots and shake off loose dirt. The crown makes it obvious where to divide. Firm pressure will break apart a plant with a multiple crown, or you can force it apart using two spading forks back to back. Discard the old central portion of the root clump and replant the younger outer roots. Cut rhizomes and plants with a large single crown into sections, allotting to each a bud, or "eye," and sufficient roots for survival. To divide a plant that multiplies by rooting runners or stolons, cut the offshoot seedlings from the parent plant, then dig and replant them.

"Volunteers" are plants that seed themselves and pop up the next season. Usually they are late in maturing, and their color can make a welcome show after the parent plants have finished blooming. They may be off color or form and should be rogued (plants of unwanted colors removed) to maintain the desired horticultural form.

PLANTING BULBS

Early to late fall is the season to plant spring-flowering bulbs. Plant fall-flowering bulbs in late summer for fall bloom, in late fall for bloom the following fall. In late August or September, plant the small early bulbs in Flowers 1 and spring-flowering crocus. Plant daffodils a little later, after the soil has begun to cool down. Otherwise, they may start to grow and even bloom before the snow flies. Plant tulips in late fall, before the soil freezes. Forgotten bulbs, if held in a cool, dry place, may succeed when planted as late as early February in northern sites if the ground is workable.

Bulbs naturalize well in beds prepared as for perennials. When planting individual bulbs in established borders, at the bottom of each hole place a small handful of a slow-release fertilizer especially marketed for bulbs. Pelleted slow-release fertilizers are also recommended. Bulbs benefit from an annual liquid early spring fertilization just as the foliage emerges from the ground. The rule of thumb for planting bulbs, as with seeds, is to plant at a depth three or four times the largest measurement of the bulb or seed.

Recommended mulches for bulbs are up to 3 inches of pine needles, oak leaves, wood chips, or shredded bark. Avoid mulches that pack and shed water, such as peat moss and uncomposted leaves.

Naturalized bulbs at the National Arboretum are fertilized and watered during their maturing season, but they are not deadheaded. (Deadheading is a term describing the removal of spent blossoms.) Foliage is not cut, but as the season advances it is covered over with the emerging foliage of other plants. However, tulip foliage may be removed when it is yellow halfway down. Leave daffodils undisturbed until the foliage begins to yellow (6–8 weeks); then it may be cut back close to the soil.

DIVIDING BULBS

To reset bulbs, dig them up in late spring after the foliage has partially yellowed, allow them to dry down in a cool, shaded spot, and store in a cool place until fall planting time. Or set rootballs in a holding bed when the foliage becomes yellow.

FLOWERS 1
SMALL SPRING BULBS, CORMS, AND RHIZOMES

Planted in early fall, these small bulbs are heralds of a new growing season, providing a succession of bright little blooms from late winter into spring. Most require a chilling period, which makes them poor subjects for frost-free areas.

COMPANION PLANTINGS
Shrubs: *Acer palmatum*, Japanese Maple; Azalea (*Rhododendron*); *Buxus*, Boxwood.
Bulbs: *Chionodoxa luciliae*, Glory-of-the-snow; *Crocus*; *Eranthis hyemalis*, Winter Aconite; *Tulipa*, Species Tulips.
Flowers: *Aquilegia flabellata* 'Nana', Dwarf Fan Columbine; *A.* 'Spring Song Strain', Columbine; *Viola* × *wittrockiana*, Pansy.

ANEMONE *an-nem-on-ee* Windflower

Rhizomatous or tuberous-rooted perennials with ferny foliage and showy red, pink, white, or purple flowers, blooming in spring. The species here grow from corms or tubers: plant them in well-drained soil, in fall in warm regions, spring in cold areas. Set out 8 to 12 inches apart, and mulch over winter. Maintain moisture in somewhat neutral, well-drained soil.

GROWTH RATE: fast
LIGHT: semi-sunny
MOISTURE: roots moist

A. blanda 'White Splendor'
Greek Windflower Zones 6–8.
Spreads rapidly and produces a cloud of yellow-centered, white daisylike flowers on stems to 8 inches high. Great for rock gardens and the front of

Endymion hispanicus, Spanish Bluebell. (McDonald)

Galanthus nivalis, Snowdrop. (McDonald)

the border. Soak tubers overnight and plant 3 inches deep in rich, well-drained soil, in partial shade.

A. coronaria Poppy Anemone Zones 8–10.
Also called florist's anemone, perennial outdoors only in southern California and Florida. Ruffled blooms in a range of brilliant colors—reds, purples, and blues, as well as creamy white. In cooler regions, handle as a tender perennial to be lifted in fall and stored over winter in a dry, cool place. Choose reds from the 'DeCaen' series.

A. pulsatilla 'Rubra'
Cloak Pasque-flower Zones 5–8.
Lovely feathery foliage and bright color. Interesting fruiting heads. Blooms with *Viola* in spring. 'Red Cloak' is a handsome cultivar.

ENDYMION *en-dim-ee-on*
hispanicus Spanish Bluebell Zones 3–9.

In late spring, nodding bells appear on graceful stems 8 to 12 inches high, in white, pink, or lavender. Lovely in mixed-color batches with ferns, or late narcissus and tulips. It spreads. Formerly classified as Scilla hispanica. Plant bulbs in fall, 2 to 3 inches deep, in rich, sandy, well-drained soil, in partial shade.

MATURE HEIGHT: 15"
GROWTH RATE: medium
LIGHT: semi-sunny, shade, versatile
MOISTURE: roots moist, versatile

GALANTHUS *gal-anth-us*
elwesii Giant Snowdrop Zones 2–9.

Earlier-blooming than the crocus, a hardy little bulb with 2 to 3 straplike leaves, and 12-inch-high delicate, pendulous, bell-shaped white flowers with emerald green markings. It spreads. Plant bulbs 3 to 4 inches deep in early autumn in moist, fairly heavy but well-drained soil, in full sun or partial shade. Good choice to follow *Eranthis hyemalis*, Winter Aconite, another early bloomer. Plant in well-drained soil.

MATURE HEIGHT: 10"
GROWTH RATE: medium
LIGHT: full sun, semi-sunny
MOISTURE: roots moist

HYACINTHUS *hye-uh-sinth-us*
orientalis Hyacinth, Dutch Hyacinth
Zones 4–9.

Exquisitely sweet fragrance in early spring is a sign that hyacinth is blooming. The scent can be enjoyed outdoors or indoors, for hyacinth is an excellent forcing bulb. Single, sturdy, formal spikes 8 to 12 inches high cover themselves with outfacing bells in white, shades of purple-blue, pink, rose, or yellow. 'Carnegie', one of the best for forcing, is white; 'Blue Magic' is a rich blue with a white eye. The variety *albulus*, Roman Hyacinth, is smaller and earlier, and has white or blue flowers. Plant bulbs in fall, 6 inches deep in well-worked loam with excellent drainage. Spreads in the garden.

MATURE HEIGHT: 18"
GROWTH RATE: fast
LIGHT: full sun, semi-sunny
MOISTURE: roots moist

Hyacinthus orientalis, Hyacinth. (McDonald)

Dutch Iris cultivar. (McDonald)

IRIS *eye-riss*
Dutch Hybrids   Dutch Iris   Zones 6–8.

A bulbous plant about 20 inches high, with a very large, elegant, airy, beardless bloom, choice for the border and cutting garden. Available in white and yellow, blues, bicolors. 'Wedgewood' is the earliest and best. Most effective massed in the border or naturalized. Plant in early fall, 6 inches apart, 4 to 5 inches deep, in well-drained soil in a sunny place. Protect with winter mulch in the North. See also Flowers 7.

MATURE HEIGHT: 20"
GROWTH RATE: medium
LIGHT: full sun, semi-sunny
MOISTURE: roots moist, versatile

LEUCOJUM *lew-koh-jum*
aestivum   Giant Snowflake,
Summer Snowflake   Zones 3–8.
Long-lasting, 14-inch-high, dainty, bell-shaped flowers, white with green markings. In early to mid-spring, charming with the small, early daffodils. Plant bulbs in early fall, 3 to 4 inches deep, 4 inches apart, in rich, well-drained soil, full sun or partial shade,

Muscari azurem, Grape Hyacinth. (McDonald)

and leave undisturbed to multiply. 'Gravetye Giant' is an improved cultivar.

MATURE HEIGHT: 14"
GROWTH RATE: medium
LIGHT: full sun, semi-sunny
MOISTURE: roots moist, versatile

MUSCARI *muss-kar-eye*
azureum   Grape Hyacinth   Zones 5–7/8.

Like a miniature hyacinth, this early spring bloomer bears tiny, pale to deep blue flowers thickly clustered on a stem to 8 inches high, and grows its grassy leaves in fall. The cultivar 'Album' has white flowers.

Leucojum aestivum 'Hidcote', Giant Snowflake. (McDonald)

Scilla siberica, Siberian Squill. (McDonald)

Plant in late summer or very early autumn, 2 inches deep, 3 inches apart, in well-drained, rich soil. Best in clumps or drifts under trees or in full sun, at the edge of the lawn or in the border with taller bulbs, such as bright red tulips. 'Heavenly Blue' is a superior cultivar. Lovely forced in bulb baskets or shallow pots with other bulbs.

MATURE HEIGHT: 8"
GROWTH RATE: medium
LIGHT: full sun, semi-sunny
MOISTURE: roots moist, versatile

SCILLA *sill-uh*
siberica   Siberian Squill   Zones 2–9.

Tiny bulb that produces one or more slender 4- to 6-inch stems bearing the bluest bell-shaped flowers in early spring. Multiplies rapidly. Plant in early fall, 3 inches apart, 2 to 3 inches deep, in well-worked, slightly moist but well-drained, enriched soil, in semi-shade. Nice in lawns, where it will ripen before mowing begins, in borders, or naturalized. 'Spring Beauty' is a superb blue with large flowers.

MATURE HEIGHT: 6"
GROWTH RATE: fast
LIGHT: semi-sunny
MOISTURE: roots moist, versatile

ALTERNATES:
Agapanthus orientalis 'Peter Pan', Lily-of-the-Nile
Allium moly, Lily Leek
Galanthus nivalis, Snowdrop
Gladiolus 'The Bride', Corn Flag, Sword Lily
Iris danfordiae, Danford Iris
Iris reticulata 'Cantab', Netted Iris
Iris reticulata 'Joyce', Netted Iris
Iris reticulata 'Springtime', Netted Iris
Iris reticulata 'Jeannine', Netted Iris
Iris xiphioides, English Iris
Ornothogalum nutans, Nodding Star-of-Bethlehem
Puschkinia scilloides var. *libanotica*, Striped Squill

FLOWERS 2
SUMMER BULBS, CORMS, AND RHIZOMES FOR SUN

These flowers are perennial in frost-free climates. Where there is frost in winter, they are planted in spring, dug after the foliage dies down, dried, and stored in vermiculite for winter in a cool, dry place. They are among the plants treated as annuals in cold regions, and set out where gaps will be created by the dying away of the early spring-flowering bulbs.

COMPANION PLANTINGS
Foliage plants: *Sedum ewersii* 'Album', Ewers Stonecrop; *Sempervivum arachnoideum* 'Silver Carpet', Cobweb Houseleek; *Yucca filamentosa* 'Bright Edge', Adam's-needle.

ACIDANTHERA *ass-id-anth-er-uh*
bicolor var. *murieliae*   Peacock Orchid
Zones 9–10.

Tender, summer-blooming corm similar to *Gladiolus*, with fragrant, creamy white flowers blotched with crimson-maroon in the center. Excellent cut flower and pot plant. A perennial bedding plant in central Florida. Plant when weather warms, 4 to 6 inches deep, 6 inches apart. Thrives in clay soils. In the North, dig after foliage yellows, lift, dry, and store over winter. Also called Abyssinian or fragrant gladiolus.

MATURE HEIGHT: 2'
GROWTH RATE: fast
LIGHT: full sun, semi-sunny
MOISTURE: roots moist

Allium sphaerocephalum 'Drumsticks', Round-headed Garlic. (Thomson)

Gladiolus. (McDonald)

ALLIUM *al-lee-um*
sphaerocephalum   Round-headed Garlic,
Drumsticks   Zones 3–8.

Grows to 30 inches tall; blooms in midsummer; small round heads of densely packed reddish purple, bell-shaped florets. Foliage is like wild onion. Excellent in flower arrangements, and with Aurelian lilies. Plant bulbs in full sun to light shade, in sandy, well-drained soil. Unusual and striking allium. See also Flowers 20.

MATURE HEIGHT: 30"
GROWTH RATE: fast
LIGHT: full sun, semi-sunny
MOISTURE: soil surface damp

CRINUM *krye-num*
× *powelli*   Crinum Lily, Spider Lily
Zones 6–10.

This big bulb sends up a tall stem that by late summer is 3 to 4 feet high, and topped with a cluster of 5 to 10 sweetly fragrant trumpets that bloom in succession. 'Cecil Houdyshel' is rosy pink. Winters over with protection in Zone 6 and is used as a bedding plant in Florida. High salt tolerance. Plant in fall, in porous soil, with one-third of the bulb above ground. Provide ample moisture during growth; let soil dry down after blooming and through winter. Full sun or partial shade.

MATURE HEIGHT: 3'–4'
GROWTH RATE: fast
LIGHT: full sun, semi-sunny
MOISTURE: roots moist

GLADIOLUS *glad-ee-oh-lus*
Corn Flag, Sword Lily   Zones 7–10.

Tall—18 inches to 3 feet—showy flower spikes in every color but blue, long-lasting when cut. Cut when the first bud shows color. Bedding plant in north and central Florida. Plant corms every 10 days from spring to midsummer for a succession of bloom. Plant in early spring, 5 to 6 inches deep, 6 inches apart in well-drained, moderately rich soil with lots of peat moss. In the North, plant in mid-spring; after the foliage dies down, dig and store corms for winter.

MATURE HEIGHT: 1½'–3'
GROWTH RATE: fast
LIGHT: full sun
MOISTURE: roots moist

HYMENOCALLIS *hye-men-oh-kal-iss*
narcissiflora   Basket Flower,
Peruvian Daffodil   Zones 7–10.

Fragrant white flowers bloom on a fleshy stalk with the 3-foot-high straplike leaves. Plant in clumps in

Hymenocallis, Peruvian Daffodil. (McDonald)

Sprekelia formosissima, Jacobean Lily. (McDonald)

rich, moist, well-drained soil, in full or partial sun. Blooms 10 days to several weeks after planting. In Florida it requires protection from full sun and is a bedding plant with a short blooming season; it is allowed to dry down in winter. In the North, plant out in late spring, and dig in early fall for winter storage in vermiculite. 'Sulphur Queen' is an interesting yellow. Good drainage is important.

MATURE HEIGHT:	3'
GROWTH RATE:	fast
LIGHT:	full sun, semi-sunny
MOISTURE:	roots moist

SPREKELIA *sprek-keel-ee-uh*
formosissima   Jacobean Lily, Aztec Lily

Zones 7–10.

Like a big *fleur-de-lis*, red to crimson, on a stalk 1 to 1½ feet high, and blooming spring to summer. Plant in clumps in rich, moist, well-drained soil, in full or semi-sun. A bedding plant in Florida that handles much like *Hymenocallis* (above), requires good drainage, and must be kept dry in winter. In the North, plant out in late spring, and dig in early fall for winter storage in vermiculite. May repeat bloom if conditions are alternately wet and dry in summer. Good pot plant.

MATURE HEIGHT:	1'–1½'
GROWTH RATE:	fast
LIGHT:	full sun, semi-sunny
MOISTURE:	roots moist

SEE ALSO:
Clivia × *cyrtanthiflora*, Kaffir Lily, Flowers 18

FLOWERS 3
SUMMER BULBS, CORMS, AND RHIZOMES FOR SHADE

These are some of the loveliest plants for summer bloom in semi-shady places. The begonias are among the most important shade-blooming flowers for container planting.

COMPANION PLANTINGS
Annuals: Blue *Ageratum houstonianum*, Flossflower; *Impatiens*.
Foliage plants: *Artemisia schmidtiana* 'Nana', Silvermound Artemisia; Ferns; dwarf *Hosta*.

BEGONIA *beg-goh-nee-uh*

Indispensable bedding plants, from the sprightly wax begonias to the big, gorgeous tuberous begonias, whose blooms rival those of the tea rose. Both begonias bloom from summer into fall. Plant in late spring in rich, well-drained, humusy soil in the acid range and fertilize often during the blooming season.

GROWTH RATE:	fast
LIGHT:	semi-sunny
MOISTURE:	roots moist

B. grandis   Hardy Begonia   Zones 6–8.
Valuable, hardy, tuberous-rooted little begonia, with small pink blooms beginning in late July and lasting until frost. Interesting seed heads, and colorful leaves in late summer. In fall, remove the spent plants without disturbing the tubercles (bulbs).

B. × *semperflorens-cultorum*
Bedding Begonia, Wax Begonia   Zones 9–10.
Shiny, bright green or reddish green leaves, and blooms that can be cool white, soft pink, coral, or red. Sizes range from 8 to 12 inches high. Bloom

Begonia × *tuberhybrida*, Hybrid Tuberous Begonia. (McDonald)

Caladium × *hortulanum*, Fancy-leaved Caladium. (McDonald)

from late May until, with a little protection, real frost. If cut back by one-third and potted up in fall, they'll bloom indoors all winter.

B. × *tuberhybrida*
Hybrid Tuberous Begonia   Zones 9–10.
Beautiful large-leaved begonias about 1 foot high, with erect or procumbent branches and many rose-like flowers, single or double, in red, yellow, orange, pink, white, and combinations. The flowers may be crested, frilled, daffodil-form, picotee, and several other types. In Florida these are cool-season bedding plants. Farther north, when the first sprouts appear on the tubers in spring, pot in an acid-range, humusy mixture and set in a semi-sunny window. Move outdoors when weather warms to grow in partial sun. The *B.* × *tuberhybrida* Pendula, or Hanging Basket Group, has trailing branches suitable for hanging baskets with good overhead light.

CALADIUM *kal-lay-dee-um*
× *hortulanum*   Fancy-leaved Caladium

Zones 9–10.

Exquisite airy foliage plant with shield-shaped leaves in red, pink, green, and white designs. Beautiful color for moist, shady places, in pots or beds. In Florida beds, it becomes dormant in winter. In the North, plant the tubers indoors, right side up, about 2 inches deep, in rich, well-drained loam 2 or 3 weeks before danger of frost is past. Requires well-drained soil. Before frost in fall, dry down, dig, and store indoors for winter. Most effective in groups of 4 to 6.

MATURE HEIGHT:	1'–2'
GROWTH RATE:	fast
LIGHT:	semi-sunny, shade
MOISTURE:	roots moist

LYCORIS *lye-kor-iss*
squamigera   Magic Lily, Resurrection Lily

Zones 5–8.

The magic of this plant is that the straplike leaves appear in spring, die down, then in late summer tall

Lycoris squamigera, Magic Lily. (McDonald)

stems rise—resurrect—bearing fragrant, exotic, airy, rose-pink, trumpet-shaped flowers tinged with pale amethyst-blue. Wonderful companion planting for azaleas, hostas, and silvery foliage plants. In August, plant bulbs 5 inches deep in partial shade in rich, humusy, well-drained soil where they can remain undisturbed. Naturalizes and multiplies, but needs winter chilling to flower. Divide after foliage dies down in spring. Avoid transplanting. Grows well in pots. Requires good drainage.

MATURE HEIGHT: 1½′–2′
GROWTH RATE: medium
LIGHT: semi-sunny, shade
MOISTURE: roots moist

ALTERNATE:
Canna, dwarf cultivars

FLOWERS 4
FALL AND WINTER BULBS, CORMS, AND RHIZOMES

Here are crocuslike flowers for seasons when the spring crocuses do not bloom. The fall bulbs carpet barren shrub borders as the rest of the garden dies down, and the little *Zephyranthes* celebrate the rain. Autumn crocuses are covered under Crocuses (Flowers 5). Where not winter-hardy, the bulbs may

Colchicum autumnale 'Waterlily', Autumn Crocus. (McDonald)

be lifted and stored indoors for winter. See Flowers 14 for perennials that make good companion plantings.

COMPANION PLANTINGS
Shrubs: Azalea (*Rhododendron*) cvs.; *Rhododendron* cvs.

COLCHICUM *kol-chik-um*
autumnale Autumn Crocus,
Meadow Saffron   Zones 5–9.

Showy, crocuslike flowers that bloom in the fall. 'The Giant', big lavender-pink flowers white at the base, is early; 'Album' is later and pure white; 'Waterlily' has lilac-pink, large, double flowers that are long lasting and good for cutting. Plant in late summer for fall bloom, in late fall for bloom the following fall.

MATURE HEIGHT: 6″–8″
GROWTH RATE: medium
LIGHT: full sun, semi-sunny
MOISTURE: roots moist, versatile

STERNBERGIA *stern-berj-ee-uh*
lutea Winter Daffodil, Lily-of-the-field
                                    Zones 6–8.

Beautiful fall-blooming bulb with narrow, strap-shaped leaves about 1 foot long, which die down and are followed by bright yellow, crocuslike blooms in fall, even after frost. Plant in early fall, in well-drained

Sternbergia lutea, Winter Daffodil. (McDonald)

soil, with top of bulb an inch below the soil surface, in full sun to half shade, in dry, rather heavy, soil. Naturalizes. Nice with *Colchicum autumnale*, Autumn Crocus (above).

MATURE HEIGHT: 1'
GROWTH RATE: medium
LIGHT: full sun, semi-sunny
MOISTURE: roots moist

ZEPHYRANTHES *zeff-er-ranth-eez*
Zephyr Lily, Rain Lily, Fairy Lily

Charming grassy plants that grow from bulbs and produce crocuslike blooms after rain, 2 to 3 inches

Zephyranthes candida, Rain Lily. (McDonald)

across, 6 inches high, in pink, purple, white, orange, or red. There's also a yellow type sold as *Z. sulphurea*. In Florida and other frost-free areas, the species sold locally are good as lawn substitutes, perennial edging for borders, or seashore ground cover. Where winter temperatures go below 25° F grow as tender perennials. Constant moisture is essential.

MATURE HEIGHT: 6"–12"
GROWTH RATE: slow
LIGHT: full sun, semi-sunny
MOISTURE: soil surface damp

Z. candida   Autumn Zephyr Lily   Zones 6–9.
Leaves are narrow, stiff, and up to 12 inches high, appearing in late summer and lasting until the following spring in frost-free areas. The flowers are white, about the same height as the leaves, sometimes pink outside. They bloom in late summer and autumn.

Z. rosea   Cuban Zephyr Lily   Zone 10.
This species grows to 12 inches with spreading, flat leaves and rose red flowers, about an inch long, that bloom in fall.

SEE ALSO:
Crocus, Flowers 5
ALTERNATE:
Callistephus chinensis, China Aster

FLOWERS 5
CROCUSES

These delightful small bulbs produce a chalice-shaped flower before the leaves rise. Some of the small spring-flowering crocus species bloom so early they preside over the last snowfall, and do it without faltering. The fall-flowering species may be small or large. Among them is the crocus whose dried stigmas are sold as saffron.

COMPANION PLANTINGS
Flowering tree: Flowering Cherry, especially weeping.
Early bulbs: *Eranthis hyemalis*, Winter Aconite; *Galanthus elwesii*, Giant Snowdrop.
Flowering shrubs: Azalea (*Rhododendron*) and *Rhododendron*, white and pink cultivars.

CROCUS *kroh-kus*

The sight of a purple or golden crocus blooming above late spring snow, or shining out from behind a fallen autumn leaf, is memorable. Some crocuses are so early they flower in late winter, but most bloom in early to mid-spring, and a few in fall. In warm areas, they may bloom from September through May. The leaves are attractive—grassy, with the midrib streaked white or silver. The flowers are white, pink, lavender, purple, yellow, or orange, and may be streaked or mottled. Crocuses are delightful by rock outcroppings, in rock gardens, by rock walls and steps, at the wood's edge, or in the border. In lawns they thrive and multiply; the early bloomers are ready for mowing just when the lawn needs its first trim. Crocuses naturalize quickly, and also make

good pot plants. They can be forced for winter flowers indoors. Most withstand temperatures to −10° F.

Plant fall-flowering types in August. They may bloom that same fall, though later than usual. Set out winter or spring bloomers in September. Plant the bulbs with pointed end up, 3 to 4 inches deep, in light, well-drained soil, in partial shade. They are tolerant of variations in moisture.

EARLY SPECIES
These species are among the first crocuses to bloom in late winter and early spring. Most of them are about 3 inches high.

C. chrysanthus   Zones 4–7.
Many stemless yellow, blue, white, or bicolored flowers rise from each tiny bulb before the grassy leaves appear. 'Blue Pearl' is a superb blue-purple. 'E. A. Bowles', a long-time favorite, is a solid yellow-bronze.

C. sieberi   Sieber Crocus   Zone 7.
The flowers are lilac and bloom in early spring or winter. 'Firefly' has showy stamens and is effective massed.

C. tomasinianus   Zones 5–7.
The flowers are purple to mauve. 'Whitewell Purple', the best cultivar, is very early, and squirrels don't dig it up. Good purple color, silver-gray when in bud. Opens in full sun to show a cobalt-violet interior. Multiplies evenly and quickly. Excellent edger, perfect with *Eranthis hyemalis*, Winter Aconite.

C. vernus   Zones 4–7.
These have larger flowers, with thicker foliage. The colors are white, yellow, or purple, the height 4 to 6 inches. 'Remembrance' is violet with a silver gloss and a dark base, blooms with *Galanthus nivalis*, Snowdrop.

Crocus tomasinianus. (Thomson)

Crocus 'Remembrance'. (Thomson)

Crocus 'Yellow Mammoth'. (Thomson)

EARLY HYBRIDS
Later to bloom, these are the very popular, large-flowered crocuses. They multiply amazingly and produce up to 6 blooms per bulb. Good for pots and forcing indoors.

C. 'Lady Killer', white tinged with purple, many blooms per bud.

C. 'Peter Pan', pure ivory-white with orange stigma.

C. 'Purpureus Grandiflorus', uniform deep violet-purple, base purple, fine oval flower. Large flower and showy.

C. 'Pickwick', silver-lilac with darker lilac stripes.

C. 'Yellow Mammoth', also 'Mammoth Yellow', huge rich yellow flower; may not force well.

C. 'Vernus Vanguard', pale lavender, often blooms

with *Narcissus asturiensis,* the tiny, earliest daffodil (see Flowers 6).

FALL SPECIES
A large group of crocuses that produce refined, elegant flowers in early and mid-fall. They are tender to cold and most successful if they have a chance to dry out in summer, after the spring foliage has died down. Best in sun, in sandy soil. Plant 4 inches deep in late summer—they may bloom the same season, but late.

C. sativus Saffron Crocus   Zones 6–9.
The large flowers are 3 to 6 inches tall, purple with deep purple veins, and large bloodred pistils that hang beyond the petals. The yellow stigmas, dried,

become saffron, a very costly herb that flavors Mediterranean and Eastern foods.

C. speciosus   Zones 6–9.
Best of the fall-flowering species; can last for weeks until a hard frost. The flowers are light lavender with bright orange stigmas, about 4 inches high. A superb bulb for naturalizing, tolerates a wide range of soil conditions and more moisture than *sativus.*

FLOWERS 6
DAFFODILS

Daffodils are rewarding and easy to grow, have few diseases, and generally are not bothered by squirrels. They are suitable for naturalizing: they tend to become smaller but more numerous, and eventually make lovely drifts of color. Particularly attractive with rocky outcroppings or evergreens in the background. See also Herbs 6. The fading of daffodils planted in flower beds leaves empty spaces which can be quickly filled by planting annuals (see Flowers 17).

COMPANION PLANTINGS
Blue and white *Crocus* with *Narcissus asturiensis*; *Muscari* 'Heavenly Blue', Grape Hyacinth, with small early daffodils; *Dicentra spectabilis*, Bleeding-heart; Double Tulip 'Peach Blossom' with late white daffodils; *Aquilegia*, Columbine, and *Endymion hispanicus*, Spanish Bluebell, behind the late and mid-season Triandrus Hybrid Daffodils.

NARCISSUS *nar-siss-us*
Daffodil, Narcissus, Jonquil   Zones 3–9.

Golden or creamy trumpets on slender green stems bloom in spring from southern Canada to northern Florida. Not all daffodils are hardy everywhere, but there are varieties for a wide range of climates, cold to warm.

Narcissus 'Unsurpassable', Trumpet. (Thomson)

Narcissus 'Salome', Large Cup. (McDonald)

Most gardeners use the term daffodil to refer to yellow, large-flowered trumpets, while the names narcissus and jonquil often are taken to mean white flowers with short trumpets. But hybridizing has produced variations of the original flower forms. Now all *Narcissus* species and hybrids are classified in numbered divisions published by the American Daffodil Society and the Royal Horticultural Society and described below. There are hundreds of impressive hybrids, old and new. Some outstanding cultivars are named here.

Plant the bulbs in early or mid-autumn, in ordinary, well-drained soil, 6 to 8 inches deep and 6 inches apart. Good drainage is critical. Add a scoopful of slow-release fertilizer to the bottom of each hole. Daffodils and narcissus are especially effective if placed in irregular patterns or drifts of at least 12 bulbs. They thrive in full sun or partial shade. After the flowers have faded, allow them to remain undisturbed until the foliage begins to yellow, then both stems and leaves may be cut back close to the soil. This is a new view—until recently, it was believed that letting the foliage die to the ground before removing it enhanced the next season's flowers.

DIVISION 1. TRUMPETS
Plants have one flower to a stem, and the central trumpet is as long as, or longer than, the petals. This is the familiar, well-loved daffodil form. A few fine cultivars are:
'Foresight', to 16 inches, early midseason; very large with white petals and golden yellow trumpets. Unusual.
'Mount Hood', to 15 inches, midseason; outstanding, bold, vigorous white, flushed with yellow when it opens. Magnificent naturalized.
'Spellbinder', to 18 inches, midseason; reverse-bicolor, with yellow petals surrounding a greenish, sulfur yellow trumpet.
'Unsurpassable', to 24 inches, midseason; immense, magnificent, deep golden yellow. Very vigorous grower.

DIVISION 2. LARGE CUPS
One flower to a stem, and the cup is more than a third, but less than equal to, the length of the petals.

The most popular division.
'Ceylon', to 14 inches, early midseason; yellow and orange.
'Ice Follies', to 18 inches, early midseason; white petals around a cup that opens lemon yellow, then fades to white. Extremely vigorous naturalizer.
'Binkie', to 16 inches, midseason; reverse-bicolor, the flower opens sulfur yellow and fades to pure white.
'Salome', to 15 inches, late midseason; white petals perfectly frame an almost trumpet-length coral-pink cup rimmed with gold. A frequent prize winner in flower shows and the best all-purpose pink.

DIVISION 3. SMALL CUPS
One flower to a stem. The cup, not more than a third the length of the petals, may be so shallow it is called an "eye." These flowers are also called "flatcup" narcissus.
'Sunapee', 14 to 16 inches, midseason; yellow petals and yellow and red cup.
'Amor', to 20 inches, late midseason; enormous flower with pure white petals that weather well. Yellow frilled cup with a red margin.
'Silver Salver', to 14 inches, so late it can be spoiled by an early heat spell, but it is a beautiful white-on-white.

DIVISION 4. DOUBLES
Tall, blooming midseason to late, with one large double flower on each stem.
'Sir Winston Churchill', to 15 inches, late midseason; white with white and orange in the doubled cup.
'White Lion', to 18 inches, midseason; creamy double white with a yellow center.
'Tahiti', to 16 inches, late midseason; full double flowers have yellow petals interspersed with tufts of red.

DIVISION 5. TRIANDRUS HYBRIDS
Several small, graceful, pendant flowers on each stem, with petals turned back (reflexed) and sometimes twisted. Often fragrant.

Narcissus 'April Tears', Triandrus. (Thomson)

Narcissus 'Silver Salver', Small Cup. (Thomson)

Narcissus 'February Gold', Cyclamineus Hybrid. (Thomson)

Narcissus 'Orangery', Split Corona. (Thomson)

Narcissus poeticus var. recurvus, Pheasant's-eye. (Thomson)

'Thalia', to 12 inches, late midseason; called "the orchid daffodil," and one of the loveliest. Two or more flowers to each stem, with reflexed petals. Fragrant.

'Hawera', 6 to 8 inches, late; miniature, with dainty, pendant, lemon yellow flowers. Excellent in the rock garden and for forcing.

'April Tears', 5 to 6 inches, late midseason; 3 drooping flowers on each stem, with reflexed petals. Trumpet and petals are clear yellow. Fragrant. Good edger in part shade.

DIVISION 6. CYCLAMINEUS HYBRIDS

Low, with small, drooping single flowers, recurved petals, long narrow cup. Among the first narcissus to bloom in spring.

'February Gold', to 12 inches, very early; large yellow-on-yellow, long-lasting flowers.

'Peeping Tom', to 12 inches, yellow-on-yellow, early.

'Tete-a-tete', to 6 inches, early; 1 to 3 small golden yellow and orange flowers on each stem. Good forcing bulb for small pots.

'Jack Snipe', to 8 inches, midseason; miniature white blooms with clear lemon yellow cups. Spreads quickly.

DIVISION 7. JONQUILLA HYBRIDS

Clusters of 2 to 6 yellow flowers on each stem, most with a short cup, some fragrant. Dwarfs and full-size.

'Baby Moon', to 12 inches, late midseason; pale yellow, free-flowering, highly fragrant miniature.

'Trevithian', to 16 inches, early midseason; broadly overlapping petals and a wide shallow crown. Pale lemon yellow.

'Kinglet', to 12 inches, late midseason. Naturalizes easily.

DIVISION 8. TAZETTAS

Four to 8 small flowers per stem, usually fragrant, with short cups. Also known as Poetaz and Polyanthus Daffodils, this is the oldest type in cultivation. Some of the best forcing bulbs are in this division.

'Cragford', to 15 inches, early midseason; fragrant, a good forcer with creamy white overlapping petals and a bright orange-red cup.

'Geranium', to 15 inches, late midseason; 4 to 7 fragrant flowers on each stem, with crisp white petals around frilled orange cups.

DIVISION 9. POETICUS HYBRIDS

Single, fragrant flowers on each stem, each having a short, yellow cup with a wavy, red-edged border, white petals. Old-time favorites.

'Actaea', to 16 inches, midseason; the whitest of all narcissus petals frame a small yellow cup edged with red and sporting a green eye. Naturalizes beautifully under trees and in the lawn. Long

Narcissus 'Cantabile', Poeticus Hybrid. (Thomson)

established as one of the best varieties. Sweetly fragrant. Prefers cooler climates, Zones 3 to 7.
'Cantabile', to 16 inches, late; white with a greenish cup edged in red. Good in clumps and massed.

DIVISION 10. SPECIES
This division includes all botanical species and their varieties. Two of the best are described here.
N. asturiensis, Zone 4, to 4 inches, the earliest of all daffodils; nodding flowers in 2 shades of yellow. Good naturalizer.
N. poeticus var. *recurvus* (Pheasant's-eye), Zone 4, to 15 inches, very late; white with yellow and red, and very fragrant.

DIVISION 11. SPLIT CORONAS
The cup is split for at least one-third of its length into 6 separate parts, which form a flat collar. These flowers are also known as Butterfly Daffodils.
'Orangery', to 14 inches, early midseason; an orange, broadly flared crown, speckled with pink and yellow against white petals.
'Baccarat', to 20 inches, midseason; hardy. Yellow petals with a yellow crown.

FLOWERS 7
IRISES

IRIS eye-riss

Irises have luminous beauty, variety of size and form, useful foliage, and are valuable cut flowers. The color range includes pink, blue, lilac and purple, white, yellow-brown, orange, and near black, in solid colors and color combinations. Many are fragrant. Some bloom in wet places.

Irises bloom for three to five weeks in spring and early summer in most areas, but a selection can be made that will bloom from spring to mid-fall. A few

rebloom in summer and may flower again in fall (rebloomers). Some, like 'Immortality', may be in bloom from spring all the way until frost, depending on weather and growing conditions.

Since most irises do not rebloom, companion flowering plants are needed to continue color in the border. Good choices are plants that contrast well in leaf and form with the narrow, spiky, gray green foliage of the iris. Among annuals, zinnias, marigolds, and bedding dahlias are all suitable. So are daylilies and chrysanthemums.

Thousands of hybrids and cultivars have been developed. In this work the irises are divided into two main groups: the bearded irises and the beardless. The flowers of both have the iris form, but there are significant differences, including cultural requirements.

The flower of the bearded iris has a "beard"—a pattern of hairs on the lower half of the falls. "Falls" are the three horizontal or drooping sepals located under the three upper, usually erect, petals, which are called "standards." The plant has sword-shaped, durable foliage that is an excellent anchor for the middle border through the season.

The flower of the beardless iris is more horizontal in structure and the falls have no hairs. This type is easier to grow, and less subject to pests and diseases. The foliage varies according to species.

Irises are hardy in a range of climates, usually to − 15° F. They require full sun and well-drained, moderately fertile soil. In rich, moist soil they are susceptible to root rot. Moisture requirements are individual to the species.

Following are a few excellent cultivars, most of which grow well at the National Arboretum.

COMPANION PLANTINGS
See individual classes, below.

BEARDED   Zones 3–9.

It is probable that somewhere in the background of many bearded iris cultivars is *I. × germanica,* Flag.

Iris 'Beverly Sills', a tall bearded iris. (Thomson)

The foliage is sword-shaped, a valuable architectural accent in the border from spring through fall. The bearded flowers, some of them huge, bloom on tall, sturdy stems that fork to show several buds.

Handsome grouped in clumps proportionate to the size of the bed. Beautiful when naturalized. Early spring bulbs, peonies, and daylilies are all good companion plants.

The bearded irises are tolerant of pH. Fertilize the soil with slow-release fertilizer three weeks before planting. Planting depth is critical; rhizomes are planted with their tops right at soil level. These irises require full sun. The rhizomes of the bearded irises do not need moisture during the summer when they are resting after blooming, and are healthier when maintained on the dry side at that time. Keep the rhizomes free of vegetation. Protect with winter mulch in the North. Fall planting is recommended, but early spring is acceptable.

There are three major bearded iris divisions: dwarf, intermediate, and tall. The irises covered here are all rhizomatous; bulbous irises are covered under bulbs (see Flowers 1).

DWARF
Grow to 15 inches tall.
'Baby Blessed', to 12 inches. This is a yellow rebloomer for the front of the border.
'Canary Prince' is a good yellow.

INTERMEDIATE
Grow 15 to 28 inches tall.
'Butter Pecan', to 28 inches, with yellow falls, brownish plicata stitching. "Plicata" in iris language means a flower having a white base and a colored margin.

TALL
Grow from 28 inches to 4 feet and over.
'Beverly Sills', an early, fragrant iris, laced coral pink.

Siberian and Spuria irises bloom near a pond. (McDonald)

Iris 'Blue Burgee', Siberian Iris. (Thomson)

'Corn Harvest', yellow rebloomer that flowers mid-season to fall.

'Denver Mint', yellow, midseason.

'Immortality' is a striking white and one of the few that can bloom from spring until frost.

'Orange Parade', a lovely orange that blooms at midseason.

'Pink Sleigh', a delicate shade of blue-pink with a red beard, midseason to late.

BEARDLESS

This class includes cultivars of the magnificent Siberian iris, the Japanese irises, and several other species. The flowers are more horizontal than those of bearded irises.

SIBERIAN

I. sibirica Siberian Iris Zones 3–8.
To 24 inches. The foliage is slender, grasslike, and waving. The colors are clear blue-purple, lavender, and white, and there are two or three flowers in a cluster. To thrive the plant needs sun, rich soil, and good drainage. Mass for best effect. Excellent cut flowers.

Good companion plants are early spring bulbs, peonies, daylilies, and annuals; see Flowers 17.

'Blue Burgee', to 24 inches, with 4½-inch flowers, ruffled, flaring, compact, on low stalks. Violet-blue. Tetraploid. Early midseason.

'Blue Pennant', to 24 inches, a light violet. Early midseason.

'Early Bluebird', to 36 inches, with 4½-inch flowers, medium violet-blue. Diploid. Early to late.

'Harpswell Haze', to 35 inches, 5½-inch flowers, soft medium blue with flaring 2½-inch falls. Tetraploid. Mid- to late season.

'Outset', to 28 inches, 5½-inch flowers, dark violet-blue semi-flaring falls with white spots. Very early to late.

'White Swirl', to 30 inches, 4- to 5-inch flowers and a long season of bloom.

JAPANESE

I. kaempferi Japanese Iris Zones 4–8.
Heights are to 24 inches and the bloom period is mid- to late spring. The huge, gorgeous flowers are flat, to 8 inches across. They are beardless, marbled and mottled in exotic combinations of blue, pink, reddish purple, mauve, and white. Valuable cut flowers, border specimens, and container plants. These thrive in soil consistently moist and may be planted in water up to 4 inches deep. Acid soil is essential—pH 5.5. Avoid lime, wood ashes, or bone meal. Peat moss, oak-leaf mold, or sulfur will acidify alkaline soils. Plant in either spring or fall in full sun or light shade. Divide only in spring.

Good companion plants are hardy ferns, azaleas, and rhododendrons.

'Grape Fizz', to 40 inches, a vigorous, long-blooming Ackerman Hybrid.

'Marhigo', to 36 inches, comes in a range of white, blue, and lavender.

SPECIES

I. cristata Crested Iris Zones 3–8.
Creeping species, 3 to 4 inches high, that makes vigorous growth soon after flowering in spring, spreading in all directions. It can be used as a ground cover in wild places. Lavender-blue, wide-spreading 4-inch flowers have narrow petals with white or yellow crests. Needs dividing every several years and is best moved just before growth begins. Deteriorates when crowded. Combines well with *Stachys byzantina*, Woolly Betony, Lamb's-ears (see Ground Covers 2).

Iris cristata, Crested Iris. (Thomson)

Iris kaempferi 'Grape Fizz', Japanese Iris. (Thomson)

Iris pseudacorus, Yellow Iris.

I. pseudacorus **Yellow Iris** **Zones 5–8.**
Another common name for this plant is Water Iris. It is tall—4 to 7 feet— with bright yellow flowers with brown veins in spring or early summer. It grows in full sun in wet places and up to 10 inches underwater, developing stately clumps of 1-inch-wide leaves. It will also bloom in consistently moist garden soil, but will be smaller. Flowers in late spring and early summer. There is a variegated form whose foliage is highly ornamental. Plant root divisions in early spring or fall. Soil should be heavy, slightly acid, and contain some humus. Naturalized in the northeastern U.S. Easy to grow.

I. tectorum **Roof Iris** **Zones 4–8.**
To 12 inches tall with wide-open, lavender-blue 3-inch flowers that bloom from late spring to midseason. The flowers stand almost as tall as the foliage, and the stem forks to bear several flowers, as with the bearded types. Spreads well. It is grown on the thatched rooftops of Japanese homes, and from this comes the common name. There is a white form, *I. t.* 'Alba', that is lovely in the spring border. Plant in moist, humusy, acid-range soil in spring just before growth begins.

ALTERNATES:

TALL BEARDED
'Beaux Arts', phlox-pink and purple
'Gingersnap', ginger-brown
'Indiglow', dark blue

'Rainbow Gold', large yellow, ruffled
'Snow Cloud', soft blue and white
'Ultrapoise', yellow and white

SIBERIAN
'Snow Bounty', white

FLOWERS 8
LILIES

There is enough variation in the bloom time of these regal flowers to carry the garden from June until the first frosts in fall. They are most effective grouped in twos and threes, or massed at the back of the border. The bulbs here are listed in order of flowering time.

COMPANION PLANTING
Chrysanthemum; *Cleome hassleriana*, Spider Flower; and *Dahlia* take over from spent lilies and bloom into fall.

LILIUM *lil-ee-um* Lily

Tall, stately, dressed in narrow leaves, and bearing up to 25 or more recurved bells, bowls, or trumpets on a stem. Thousands of hybrids have been named. The four divisions described here cover the bloom season

from summer through early fall and include wild species that prosper where other lilies fail.

Early-blooming lilies flower in June and early July; midseason lilies bloom in mid-July and early August; late bloomers flower in mid-August and early September.

Lilies are fast-growing in well-drained, humusy, slightly acid soil, with sustained moisture but no soaking, and no competition from vigorous woody plants. Ground cover is the best mulch. The tallest plants need staking and shelter from gusts of wind. Plant lilies in fall, the later the better. Do not plant in soil that has been limed recently or heavily. Loosen the soil to a depth of 2 feet to ensure good drainage, especially in clay. Add a handful of bone meal to each hole and plant the bulb 4 to 6 inches deep, depending on size.

Lilies do best in full sun where temperatures remain under 90° F, but need shade in hotter regions. Four to 6 hours of full sun, plus partial sun the rest of the day, is the rule of thumb. Lilies in pastel shades do better in partial shade. Remove dead blooms as they wither. When the last one is gone, cut the stalk just below the lowest blossom, but above the leaves. When all the leaves have yellowed, cut the stalk back to the ground. The Royal Horticultural Society and the North American Lily Society group lilies in divisions; those here thrive readily in the home garden.

DIVISION 1. ASIATIC HYBRIDS **Zones 4–8.**
Early blooming. Beautiful 4- to 6-inch flowers with exotically recurved petals on plants 2 to 6 feet tall.

17

Lilium 'Gold Lode', Asiatic Hybrid. (Thomson)

These are the most disease-resistant and cold hardiest lilies, hardy to −40° or −50° F. The blooms face up, out, or down, according to the type. Examples of each follow:

'Gold Lode', 4 to 5 feet, is bright gold, and has upward-facing flowers.

'Showtime', to 4 feet, has big, spotless gold flowers that face out.

'Burgundy Strain', 3 to 4 feet, is vibrant cherry-red to deep burgundy, with up to 20 3-inch buds on each stem; flowers face out or down.

'Tiger Babies', to 3 feet, is salmon with chocolate spots and faces down.

DIVISION 6. AURELIAN OR TRUMPET HYBRIDS   Zones 4–8.

These midseason hybrids stage a major show in July, and a few continue on into August. Sturdy, vigorous plants often 6 feet tall, with up to 12 blooms on a stem, large trumpet-shaped flowers that may be intensely fragrant. Very disease-resistant, and cold hardy to −10° or −15° F.

'Black Dragon', 5 to 7 feet, pure white trumpet inside and shades of purple-brown or maroon on outside. Intensely fragrant. Up to 20 blooms on each stem. Easily grown in containers.

'Gold Eagle', 5 to 6 feet, golden yellow, very fragrant. Blooms in July.

'White Henryi', to 6 feet, beautiful white flowers with yellow-spotted centers. Virus-resistant. Blooms in July.

DIVISION 7. ORIENTAL HYBRIDS

Spectacular late-blooming lilies which may have either bowl-shaped or flat-faced flowers, or blossoms with sharply recurved petals, up to 10 inches in diameter, 8 to 10 on a stem, on stems up to 6 feet tall.

Lilium auratum var. *platyphyllum*, Gold-band Lily. (National Arboretum)

Prefer acid soil. Hardy to −10° or −15° F, but they tend to come up early and require protection from late spring frosts.

'Stargazer', 18 inches, with carmine flowers edged in white, is a small Oriental, good for the middle border and pots. Blooms in June, earlier than other Oriental hybrids.

'Imperial Silver' strain, to 6 feet, huge white, fragrant flowers with maroon spots.

'Jamboree' strain, to 6 feet, rose to red flowers, some white. Fragrant and a persistent bloomer.

'Black Beauty', 6 to 7 feet, 4- to 5-inch recurved red flowers with a green starlike center. It is a healthy triploid, the last to bloom and the hardiest.

DIVISION 8. SPECIES LILIES

L. auratum var. *platyphyllum*   Gold-band Lily   Zones 4–8.

To 6 feet tall. Colors range from ivory tinged yellow with red speckles to almost solid carmine. Very beautiful and often quite fragrant. Blooms August to September. Look for improved cultivars. Likes slightly rich soil.

L. canadense   Canada Lily, Wild Yellow Lily   Zones 3–8.

Height of 3 to 5 feet, grows wild in the Northeast, and has clusters of 2- to 3-inch, bell-shaped flowers of canary yellow with an orange interior spotted dark purple. It is one of the few lilies that tolerates swampy conditions. 'Coccineum' has orange-red blossoms.

L. candidum   Madonna Lily   Zones 4–8.

Height of 3 to 5 feet. The hauntingly perfumed, pure white, upturned flower clusters are trumpet-shaped with showy golden stamens. They bloom in late spring and early summer. This species requires alkaline soil, unlike most lilies. Plant no more than 1 inch deep. Look for improved, disease-resistant strains, like 'Cascade'.

Lilium 'Black Dragon', Aurelian Hybrid. (Thomson)

Lilium 'Jamboree' strain, Oriental Hybrid. (Thomson)

L. hansonii   Hanson Lily   Zones 3–8.
Height of 3 to 4 feet, with clusters of 2-inch, spicily fragrant, star-shaped flowers in yellow or orange. The petals are slightly recurved, pendant, waxy, and spotted brown. Tolerant of semi-shade or sun, and limed soils. Increases readily in humusy, moist locations.

L. lancifolium   Tiger Lily   Zones 3–8.
Tall—to 7 feet—beautiful, invulnerable species that grows wild in the eastern U.S. and has 7-inch-long orange to orange-red flowers with recurved petals and purple-black spots. Blooms in July and August. Its progeny now range in color from white to dark red. Most share the parents' hardiness.

L. regale   Regal Lily   Zones 3–8.
Height to 6 feet, a beautiful, fragrant, July-blooming lily with 7-inch flowers, as many as 25 to a stalk, white with yellow base, rose-purple outside. Widely available.

FLOWERS 9
TULIPS

Tulipa 'Mickey Mouse', Single Early. (Thomson)

A major spring event is the blooming of tulips early and late, in brilliant hues, fantastic color combinations and forms, frilled, splotched, striped, tall, small, fat, thin, elegant, informal, lily-flowered, peony-flowered, and more. Tulips require a frosty period in order to bloom. Only a few succeed without special treatment in frost-free areas. Most described here force well and are long-lasting cut flowers. Plant early- and late-blooming cultivars together for a long season of color.

COMPANION PLANTINGS
Background plants: *Aucuba japonica* 'Variegata', Variegated Gold-dust Tree; *Dicentra spectabilis*, Bleeding-heart; *Kalmia latifolia*, Mountain Laurel; *Viburnum odoratissimum*, Sweet Viburnum; *V. plicatum* var. *tomentosum* 'Shasta', Double File Viburnum.
Annuals: *Ageratum houstonianum*, Flossflower; *Antirrhinum majus*, Snapdragon; *Pelargonium* × *hortorum*, House Geranium.
Perennials: *Chrysanthemum*, range of colors.

TULIPA *tew-lip-uh*   Tulip

Tulips are solid-fleshed bulbs from the Middle East. In 17th-century Holland, "tulipomania" drove the price of a single bulb to the equivalent of $50,000. Most of the tulip bulbs on the market are still produced in the Netherlands.

Species tulips can bloom in February in a sunny, sheltered place. They are charming under small trees, next to steps, in front of walls and entrances. The big tulip show begins with the later daffodils and goes on until early summer. Tulips are striking planted in twos and threes as specimens in a small border. More often they are massed in single or mixed colors in big beds.

Maintain bulbs at temperatures below 70° F until ready to plant. The refrigerator crisper is a suitable cold storage place. Plant tulips late in fall but before the ground freezes.

Set large tulips 6 inches apart, 8 inches deep; small wild species 3 to 4 inches apart, 4 to 5 inches deep. They prefer full sun. Ideal soil is deeply dug, well-drained, sandy, and enriched with compost and humus. Work a scoopful of balanced slow-release fertilizer into each hole before planting. Soon after blooming, treat established tulip plantings with a cup of slow-release fertilizer for every square yard and keep the area moist until the leaves start to die down.

At the National Arboretum tulip foliage is removed when it is yellow halfway down.

The most popular classes of tulips are listed below.

SINGLE EARLY   Zones 3–8.
Large single flowers, 12 to 18 inches high, that bloom two weeks before the Single Late tulips (which were formerly classified as Cottage Tulips and Darwins). Superb cut flowers, long lasting and fragrant. Good forcing bulbs.
'Bellona', to 15 inches, large flowers of rich, golden yellow.
'Mickey Mouse', 16 inches, early, with a long bloom season. Yellow and scarlet.

Tulipa 'Jewel of Spring', Darwin Hybrid. (Thomson)

DOUBLE EARLY   Zones 3–7.
About 8 to 12 inches high. Superb, softly colored double blooms.
'Peach Blossom', to 8 inches tall, deep, soft rose, early to midseason. Lovely with white daffodils (Flowers 6) and *Dicentra spectabilis*, Bleeding-heart (see Flowers 10).

TRIUMPH   Zones 3–7.
Midseason tulips blooming between Single Early types and the late varieties. Handsome in front of the taller midseason Darwin Hybrids. Substantial flowers on medium-tall stems.
'Garden Party', to 16 inches; white, edged with glowing carmine.

DARWIN HYBRIDS   Zones 3–7.
Tall—to 30 inches—classic tulip form, brilliantly colored. Long lasting, they bloom with the Fosteranas and a little later than Single Early tulips. Darwins and Fosteranas are nice together.
'Golden Parade', to 24 inches, early to midseason, almost perennial in a cool climate.
'Jewel of Spring', to 24 inches, early to midseason, cream-white with delicate red picotee. Almost as persistent as 'Golden Parade'.
'Parade', to 24 inches, splendid fire-engine red, early to midseason.

BUNCH-FLOWERING   Zones 4–7.
Tall tulips with 4 to 5 large, cup-shaped flowers on each stem. Brilliant colors.
'Georgette', to 25 inches tall; rich, buttery yellow with edges just brushed with red, and 3 to 5 flowers per stem.

LILY-FLOWERED   Zones 4–7.
Striking designer favorite, elegant, vase-shaped, with pointed, reflexed petals on slender stems. Long-lasting cut flowers. Wonderful in contemporary settings and with ornamental grasses. Midseason.

Lily-flowered Tulip. (McDonald)

Fringed or Lace Tulip. (McDonald)

'Mariette', to 18 inches, deep satin rose with a white
   base.
'Queen of Sheba', to 22 inches, a glowing brownish
   red edged with orange. Long lasting.

FRINGED OR LACE   Zones 4–7.
Also called Orchid-flowering, and Crispa. The top
edges of the petals are fringed, and some are frosted.
Resembles Parrot Tulips. Blooms late, along with the

Single Lates. Long-lasting flowers. To 20 to 30 inches.
'Burgundy Lace', to 28 inches, deep burgundy with
   fringed petal edges, often shows color breaking to
   red and white. Midseason; good for cutting.

SINGLE LATE   Zones 3–8.
Includes tulips formerly classified as Darwins and
Cottage Tulips. Excellent in the border.
'Ace of Spades', to 14 inches; best "black" tulip
   (actually deep, deep purple), repeats well.
'Sorbet', to 18 inches, late; cream-flamed carmine
   with yellow anthers, sturdy. Great when massed.

Tulipa 'Ace of Spades', Single Late. (Thomson)

Parrot Tulip. (McDonald)

PARROT   Zones 4–7.
Informal tulip that opens wide and has frilled and
curled edges and many striking and brilliant color
combinations. To 20 inches.
'Estella Rynveld', to 20 inches; extraordinarily beautiful frilled petals, streaked red and white. Mid-
   season.

DOUBLE LATE   Zones 3–7.
Similar to Double Early but tall, to 18 and 24 inches,
and looks like a peony. Blooms toward the end of

Double Late, or peony-flowered, Tulip. (McDonald)

spring, before the peonies. Wonderful planted in groups of 4 or 5 with tall blue irises in a long border. 'Mount Tacoma', to 14 inches; a beautiful white, unusual in this class.

KAUFMANNIANA HYBRIDS
Waterlily Tulips   Zones 3–8.
Early-flowering tulips with short stems and long, pointed petals. Very colorful. Many have mottled or striped leaves.
'Shakespeare', 6 inches high, bright salmon to vermilion-red outside, yellow-tinged red inside. Good edger for beds of later-blooming perennials and shrubs.

FOSTERANA HYBRIDS   Zones 3–7.
Early, medium-tall, with some of the largest flowers in the genus; truly immense petals.
'Red Emperor', 18 inches high, with flame-red flowers. Very early. The Emperor tulips are the largest and most striking of all varieties.
'Purissima', 18 inches high, a pure white Emperor tulip.

Tulipa 'Heart's Delight', Kaufmanniana Hybrid. (McDonald)

GREIGII HYBRIDS   Zones 3–7.
Low-growing, open tulips, with broad foliage streaked or mottled with purple. For the front of the border.
'Red Riding Hood', to 6 inches, bright scarlet-red with black base; dependable, beautiful. Purple-striped green foliage.

SPECIES TULIPS
Also called Botanical Tulips. Forms range from flamboyant to extremely delicate. Heights vary. Some are quite small. Plant all 4 to 5 inches deep, and provide good drainage. They persist for years; some are hardy in frost-free regions.

T. clusiana   Zones 3–10.
About 12 to 14 inches high. Also called Lady Tulip, Lipstick Tulip, and Radish Tulip. White inner petals,

Tulipa pulchella 'Violacea'. (Thomson)

Greigii Hybrid Tulip. (McDonald)

Tulipa 'Red Emperor', Fosterana Hybrid. (McDonald)

outer petals white with a broad cherry-red band from top to bottom, deep purple center, and purple anthers. Blooms early and prospers even in Zone 9.

T. marjolettii   Zones 3–8.
About 20 inches. A slim-leaved tulip with ivory-white petals brushed with red on the edges. Late.

T. pulchella 'Violacea'   Zones 5–8.
About 3½ inches tall, early. Purple-red petals, the lower outer segment tinged green, and a green-black basal blotch. Many cultivars.

FLOWERS 10
SPRING PERENNIALS FOR SUN

The perennials described here bloom in spring; some keep flowering all summer, and some bloom again in fall. They have been chosen for foliage as well as for flowers, and will enhance the border all season long. They are intended to complement the lilies, peonies, irises, and other classic border flowers that bloom in spring and early summer.

COMPANION PLANTINGS
Bulbs: *Anemone pulsatilla rubra* 'Red Cloak', Pasque-flower.
Edging plants: *Ageratum houstonianum*, Floss-flower; *Iberis sempervirens* 'Autumn Snow', Evergreen Candytuft.

CAMPANULA *kam-pan-yew-luh*
carpatica   Tussock Bellflower,
Carpathian Bellflower   Zones 3–9.

Vigorous, low-growing plants, with bell-shaped blue, or lavender- or violet-blue, flowers from spring (depending on region) to summer's end, especially if sheared back at midsummer. There are white varieties also. Lovely in front of daylilies and as edgers. Plant root divisions in summer for bloom the following spring. Plant in well-drained soil and mulch to protect roots from summer heat.

Dicentra spectabilis, Bleeding-heart. (McDonald)

MATURE HEIGHT: 6″–10″
GROWTH RATE: fast
LIGHT: full sun, semi-sunny
MOISTURE: soil surface damp

DICENTRA *dye-sent-ruh*
spectabilis   'Adrian Bloom'
Bleeding-heart   Zones 2–3.

Blooms from spring to early fall. Feathery foliage and charming little heart-shaped flowers, rosy with a white tongue. Thrives in semi-sun or light shade. Plant root divisions in early spring in well-drained, light, humusy soil. Can follow spring crocus (Flowers 5) and makes a nice contrast for coreopsis (see Flowers 12).

MATURE HEIGHT: 18″
GROWTH RATE: slow
LIGHT: semi-sunny, shade
MOISTURE: roots moist

DICTAMNUS *dik-tam-nus*
albus   Dittany, Gas Plant   Zones 4–8.

Shrublike, with lemon-scented, long-lasting white or pink flowers in terminal clusters about 1 inch long, during spring and summer. Sow seeds where plant is to bloom; does not transplant well. Sun or partial shade. Plant in spring, in deeply dug, well-drained, rich soil. Seedpods and other parts of the plant are poisonous.

MATURE HEIGHT: 30″
GROWTH RATE: fast
LIGHT: full sun, semi-sunny
MOISTURE: roots moist

Campanula carpatica, Carpathian Bellflower. (McDonald)

Dictamnus albus, Gas Plant. (McDonald)

EUPHORBIA *yew-**forb**-ee-uh*
epithymoides var. *griffithii* Spurge
Zones 5–9.

Stems packed with narrow leaves and topped with long-lasting, colorful bracts. The species is yellow, but 'Fire Glow' is a fiery red, from spring to summer. Contains a milky juice which can cause allergies. Plant root divisions in spring, in well-drained soil, in full sun. Stands some shade.

MATURE HEIGHT: 2'
GROWTH RATE: medium
LIGHT: full sun
MOISTURE: versatile

GERANIUM *jer-**ray**-nee-um*
sanguineum var. *prostratum*
Bloodred Cranesbill   Zones 3–8.

Geranium is a common name for some species of the genus *Pelargonium* (see Flowers 17; Herbs 6), but *Geranium* also is a genus name of a group whose common names are Cranesbill or Hardy Geranium. This dwarf pink with deeper pink veining has lovely spreading foliage, and is attractive with evergreen azaleas and smaller rhododendrons. Plant root divisions in spring, in sun or light shade.

MATURE HEIGHT: 6"
GROWTH RATE: fast
LIGHT: full sun, semi-sunny
MOISTURE: versatile

HEUCHERA *hew-ker-uh*
sanguinea Coralbells   Zones 3–9.

Semievergreen basal clusters of round, scalloped, veined, dark green leaves. In late spring and summer, tiny bell-shaped flowers top wiry stalks high above the foliage. Long lasting. Bressingham Hybrids are

Heuchera sanguinea 'Bressingham Hybrids', Coralbells. (McDonald)

Oenothera species. (McDonald)

superior, in colors of white, pink, coral-red, and deep red. Excellent and persistent edger and ground cover for borders and pockets in partial shade or full sun. Plant root divisions in spring in well-drained, humusy soil with plenty of moisture. Good with later bloomers with contrasting foliage, such as *Echinops ritro*, Small Globe Thistle.

MATURE HEIGHT: 2'
GROWTH RATE: medium
LIGHT: full sun
MOISTURE: roots moist

OENOTHERA *ee-noh-**theer**-uh*
tetragona Evening Primrose   Zones 3–9.

Charming yellow flowers that open after the sun sets. 'Fireworks' and 'Illuminations' are superior cultivars, blooming in spring and repeating in fall. Hardy and resistant to drought. Plant root divisions in spring. Lovely with blue or white hybrids of *Tradescantia virginiana*, Spiderwort.

MATURE HEIGHT: 1½'
GROWTH RATE: fast
LIGHT: full sun
MOISTURE: versatile

PHLOX *flox*
subulata Moss Pink, Moss Phlox
Zones 2–3.

Ground-hugging evergreen mats of mossy foliage that cover themselves in early spring with tiny pink flowers. There also are cultivars in white, deep rose, lavender, and lovely blues. 'Millstream Coraleye' is blue with a coral eye. Charming in the border, under bare-legged spring-flowering shrubs, in rock gardens, and on banks. Plant root divisions in early spring in full sun and divide every few years. Easy to grow.

Phlox subulata, Moss Pink. (McDonald)

MATURE HEIGHT: 6"
GROWTH RATE: medium
LIGHT: full sun
MOISTURE: versatile

VERONICA *ver-**ron**-ik-uh* Speedwell

Very valuable filler plants and among the most invulnerable perennials. The foliage is attractive, and there are abundant flowers in densely packed spikes starting in mid-spring. Plant root divisions in early spring in well-drained soil. Remove spent flower heads to prolong blooming.

GROWTH RATE: fast
LIGHT: full sun
MOISTURE: versatile

V. latifolia   Zones 3–8.
Blue to reddish flowers in mid- to late spring. 'Crater Lake Blue' bears gentian blue starlike blooms with

Veronica 'Crater Lake Blue'. (McDonald)

tiny white eyes. Good for the middle of the border. It can precede smaller daylilies and accompany later ones.

V. spicata   Zones 3–8.
Later-blooming species. Cultivars like 'Blue Peter', almost navy-blue, 18 to 24 inches high, extend the blooming period through summer. 'Snow White' is a beautiful white. 'Sunny Borders' has a very long flowering season and interesting tridentlike flower spikes. 'Blue Fox' is one of many small veronicas, 8 to 12 inches tall. Prefers soil in the acid range, pH 5.0–6.0.

SEE ALSO:
Iberis sempervirens 'Autumn Snow', Evergreen Candytuft, Ground Covers 6

ALTERNATES:
Aethionema cordifilium, Lebanon Cress
Armeria maritima, Thrift
Cerastium tomentosum, Snow-in-summer
Nepeta mussinii, Catmint

FLOWERS 11
SPRING PERENNIALS FOR SHADE

These plants bloom around and under shrubs, taller herbaceous perennials, and flowering spring trees, and will naturalize in the dappled light of woodsy places. Most thrive with 2 to 6 hours of sun daily, some with a little less; others can handle a little more.

COMPANION PLANTINGS
Background plants: Azalea (*Rhododendron*) cvs.; *Buxus* Boxwood; *Dicentra spectabilis*, Bleeding-heart; *Euonymus japonica* 'Aurea-variegata', Golden Variegated Spindle Tree, Golden Variegated Japanese

Aquilegia, Columbine. (Thomson)

Spindle Tree; *Ilex × crenata* 'Golden Heller', Japanese Holly; *Kalmia latifolia*, Mountain Laurel. Ground covers: *Hosta* 'Antioch'; Ferns. Annuals: *Impatiens; Viola × wittrockiana*, Pansy.

AQUILEGIA *ak-wil-leej-ee-uh*
Columbine

Spring and early-summer bloomer to 2 or 2½ feet tall, with graceful, usually spurred blooms, nodding above dainty leaves. The flowers come in a wide range of colors. The many species and varieties are lovely, and the foliage is attractive for many weeks after the flowers are gone. The most striking are hybrid strains with giant spurs, such as 'Spring Song'. There are also double-flowered strains, and dwarfs good for the rock garden. Nice cut flower, and attractive to bees. Seed sown in spring produces flowers the following year. Or plant root divisions 12 to 15 inches apart in well-drained, humusy, moist soil, preferably in partial shade. Most species tolerate sun if moisture is maintained. Self-sows vigorously.

GROWTH RATE:	medium
LIGHT:	full sun, semi-sunny
MOISTURE:	roots moist

flabellata 'Nana' Dwarf Fan Columbine
Zones 3–9.
Short, gracefully hooked spurs on blue or lilac flowers in late spring and summer, and pretty, soft blue-green foliage. 'Alba' has white flowers and blooms a little earlier. The plants are 12 to 18 inches tall, and tolerate full sun except in hot regions.

ARISAEMA *ar-riss-seem-uh*
triphyllum Jack-in-the-pulpit   Zones 4–9.

Wildflower, very early bloomer in a shady, moist garden or a wild garden. Naturalizes. Nice with ferns. The flower is a spathe sheltering "Jack." It is green on the outside and purplish bronze inside. It is

Astilbe × arendsii cultivar. (McDonald)

followed by a fruit cluster, bright red in autumn. Plant in early spring, in loose, well-drained, humusy soil that is somewhat acid.

MATURE HEIGHT:	1'–2'
GROWTH RATE:	fast
LIGHT:	semi-sunny, shade
MOISTURE:	soil surface damp

ASTILBE *ass-till-bee* Spiraea

Feathery flower heads standing well above deeply cut green foliage, in shades from palest pink to coral to bright red and creamy white, June through August. Belongs in every shaded border. Remove spent flower heads to keep blooms coming. Plant root divisions in spring in neutral-range, deeply worked, rich soil with lots of organic matter, and maintain moisture. In hot climates, especially if the plants receive a lot of sun, mulch well.

GROWTH RATE:	fast
LIGHT:	semi-sunny, shade
MOISTURE:	roots moist

A. × arendsii   Zones 4–8.
There are many beautiful cultivars: 'Fanal' has garnet-red 12-inch flower panicles on plants to 24 inches high with handsome bronzy foliage. Long lasting. 'Feuer' is a real red; 'Professor van der Wielen' is a beautiful, tall white.

A. chinensis 'Pumila'   Zones 4–8.
Dwarf, to 12 inches, with raspberry-red flower panicles July to September. Most drought-resistant of the astilbes. Shade or partial shade. Good successor for 'Fanal'.

HELLEBORUS *hel-leb-bor-rus*
orientalis Lenten Rose   Zones 3–8.

Blooms for a long period in late winter in mild areas, early spring in cool areas—large, nodding, white to purple flowers and nearly evergreen foliage. Naturalizes easily. Rated by some as one of the ten best perennials. Plant root divisions in early spring in moist, humusy soil. Good contrast for *Skimmia* (see Shrubs 7).

MATURE HEIGHT: 12″–15″
GROWTH RATE: fast
LIGHT: semi-sunny, shade
MOISTURE: versatile

MERTENSIA *mer-ten-see-uh*
virginica Bluebells, Virginia Bluebells
Zones 3–9.

Early spring bloomer, nodding sprays of pink buds that open violet-blue on tall stems with fresh, pale green foliage. Foliage disappears early, making way

for other perennials. Plant root divisions in early spring, in rich, humusy, well-drained soil, in partial shade. Nice contrast with *Aquilegia*, Columbine (above).

MATURE HEIGHT: 2′
GROWTH RATE: fast
LIGHT: semi-sunny
MOISTURE: roots moist

PRIMULA *prim-yew-luh* Primrose

Low-growing, spring-blooming, dense clusters of small flowers in bright colors above basal tufts of gray green crinkled leaves. Thrives in the partial shade of a border, under shrubs, and in moist, woodsy situations. Especially lovely sheltered by rock outcrop-

Pulmonaria saccharata, Bethlehem Sage. (McDonald)

pings, stone walls, and steps. Combines beautifully with spring-flowering bulbs, especially daffodils and tulips. An especially attractive species, *P. malacoides*, Fairy Primrose, has rounded leaves and small, dainty pink or lavender-blue flowers that stand well above the foliage. It is not recommended here because it rarely is grown outdoors. A dwarf, to 4 inches, known as *P. × hybrida*, is sold as a houseplant and thrives in a sunny window indoors, as long as it is not allowed to dry out.

Set out container plants in fall in mild regions, or early spring in cooler areas, in rich, humusy soil, and provide plenty of water all summer.

MATURE HEIGHT: 6″–12″
GROWTH RATE: fast
LIGHT: semi-sunny
MOISTURE: soil surface damp

P. × polyantha
Polyanthus, Polyantha Primrose Zones 3–8.
'Pacific Giants' offer a great range of vibrant primary colors. About 12 inches high.

P. vulgaris English Primrose Zones 3–8.
Yellow, blue, and purple varieties bloom in spring. To 6 inches. Provide light mulch for winter. Barnhaven Strains are superior.

PULMONARIA *pull-mon-nay-ree-uh*
saccharata 'Mrs. Moon' Bethlehem Sage
Zones 3–8.

Beautiful white-spotted, dark green leaves persist after the flowers, which are blue as they open and turn toward pink as they mature. *P. officinalis*, Jerusalem Sage, is grown in the National Arboretum's American Herb Garden for its attractive blue flowers. Early bloomer for the spring border or wild garden, combines well with *Helleborus* (above). Set out container plants in well-drained, moist, humusy soil, and divide every 3 or 4 years.

Mertensia virginica, Virginia Bluebells. (McDonald)

Trillium grandiflorum, White Wake-robin. (McDonald)

MATURE HEIGHT: 1'
GROWTH RATE: fast
LIGHT: semi-sunny
MOISTURE: soil surface damp

SANGUINARIA *san-gwi-nay-ree-uh*
canadensis   Bloodroot, Red Puccoon
                                    Zones 5–8.

Small, starry white flowers bloom very early above rich, dark green leaves which continue to grow through spring. Double-flowered forms are also available. Plant root divisions in early spring in light, well-drained, humusy soil and provide plenty of moisture.

MATURE HEIGHT: 1'
GROWTH RATE: fast
LIGHT: semi-sunny, shade
MOISTURE: soil surface damp

TRILLIUM *trill-ee-um*
grandiflorum   White Wake-robin Zones 3–8.

Lovely wildflower now domesticated. It blooms all spring, an orchidlike pure white flower above a whorl of 3 leaves—changes to pink as it matures. Especially good with azaleas and ferns in a woodsy place. Set out container plants in early spring in rich, well-drained, humusy soil that is somewhat acid.

MATURE HEIGHT: 18"
GROWTH RATE: fast
LIGHT: semi-sunny, shade
MOISTURE: soil surface damp

SEE ALSO:
Asarum europaeum, European Wild Ginger, Herbs 8
Epimedium grandiflorum 'Rose Queen', Red Alpine
    Epimedium, Ground Covers 6
Viola odorata, Sweet Violet, Flowers 17

ALTERNATES:
Galium odoratum, Woodruff, Sweet Woodruff

FLOWERS 12
SUMMER PERENNIALS FOR SUN

Here are some of the most enduring and rewarding of the summer border flowers. They begin to be a presence in the border as the spring bulbs are fading away and come into bloom in early summer. Many last well into fall.

COMPANION PLANTINGS
Edging plants: *Ageratum houstonianum*, Floss-flower; *Dianthus* × *allwoodii*, Allwood Pink; *Lobularia maritima*, Sweet Alyssum; *Zinnia* dwarfs 'Peter Pan', 'Liliput', 'Tom Thumb', 'Small World Pink', or 'Fantastic Light Pink'. See also Flowers 17.
For massing: *Allium moly*, Lily Leek; *Veronica latifolia* 'Crater Lake Blue', Blue Speedwell.
To tie it all together: *Gypsophila paniculata* 'Bristol Fairy', Baby's-breath.

ACHILLEA *ak-il-lee-uh*   Yarrow

Bears masses of flowers throughout the summer. An ancient herb (see *A. tomentosa*, Herbs 10), it is semievergreen, mat-forming, and long-lived, with ferny, woolly, aromatic foliage. Long-lasting spring and summer single or double flowers in shades of white, pink, or yellow. Good cut flowers, fresh or dried. Survives heat and drought. Planted at the base of rocks and stone walls, it makes a transition to the lawn. Tolerates light foot traffic. Set out container plants 12 to 18 inches apart in well-drained soil in early spring. Good seashore plant.

MATURE HEIGHT: 18"–3'
GROWTH RATE: medium
LIGHT: full sun
MOISTURE: roots moist

A. filipendulina   Fern-leaved Yarrow
                                    Zones 3–9.
Showy all-summer bloomer, to 3 feet, with large heads of golden yellow flowers. 'Coronation Gold' has large, flat heads of deep gold and is beautiful when dried.

Baptisia australis, False Indigo. (McDonald)

A. millefolium Yarrow, Milfoil   Zones 3–9.
Good ground cover, to 2 feet, can be mowed, and survives droughts and neglect. 'Fire King' is a striking pink with ferny foliage.

A. taygetea   Zones 3–7.
Gray green foliage. The cultivar 'Moonshine', 18 to 24 inches, has flat, sulfur-yellow flower heads from early summer into fall. Good for cutting.

BAPTISIA *bap-tiz-ee-uh*
australis   False Indigo   Zones 3–8.

Lovely back-of-the-border plant, to 3 or 4 feet, with gray green leaves, and spikes of indigo-blue flowers in early summer, followed by prominent dark seedpods. The plant was the source of indigo-blue dye. Good

Achillea filipendula 'Coronation Gold', Fern-leaved Yarrow. (McDonald)

Coreopsis verticillata 'Moonbeam', Threadleaf Tickseed. (Burpee Co.)

cut flower. Naturalizes, and thrives in sun or the bright shade of light woodlands. Plant root divisions in well-drained, moist, humusy soil in early spring.

MATURE HEIGHT: 3'–4'
GROWTH RATE: fast
LIGHT: full sun, semi-sunny
MOISTURE: soil surface damp

COREOPSIS *ko-ree-op-sis* Tickseed

Sunny, profuse summer bloomer with a daisylike face, that goes on for months, is a wonderful cut flower. Airy, attractive foliage and small but long-lasting, showy yellow flowers. It is one of the easiest perennials to grow, and a staple of any low-mainte-nance garden. Plant seeds or root divisions 15 to 18 inches apart in spring in somewhat acid soil.

GROWTH RATE: fast
LIGHT: full sun
MOISTURE: roots moist

C. grandiflora 'Sunray' Bigflower Tickseed
Zones 4–10.
Fluffy, double-flowered, sturdy, compact plants to 20 inches tall. Very tolerant of heat and drought.

C. lanceolata 'Goldfink' Zones 4–10.
Handsome dwarf, 9 inches tall, with the broad flower head typical of *C. grandiflora*, and perfect for the front of the border. Blooms from early summer to frost.

C. verticillata Threadleaf Tickseed
Zones 3–9.
Taller (to 30 inches) lemon yellow flowers in late spring and summer, with beautiful fernlike foliage. The cultivar 'Moonbeam' grows to about 18 inches and is light yellow. 'Golden Showers', to 18 inches, is a strong yellow.

ERYNGIUM *ee-rinj-ee-um*
giganteum Eryngo Zones 6–9.

Belongs to a group of thistlelike plants that are impos-ing in the large border. This species has striking 2- to

3-inch flowers and sea green foliage variegated with silvery white, about 2 feet high. Excellent for drying. Prefers sandy, well-drained soils. Sow seeds in early spring. The species *E. maritimum*, Sea Holly, with bright blue flower heads and whitish foliage, is a good seashore plant, but hard to find.

MATURE HEIGHT: 2'
GROWTH RATE: medium
LIGHT: full sun
MOISTURE: rather dry

HIBISCUS *hye-bisk-us*
moscheutos Rose Mallow Zones 5–9.

Huge hollyhocklike pink or white flowers with a dark eye bloom from late summer into mid-fall on very big plants. Handsome in the back of the border or massed in the larger landscape. Self-sows freely. Native to salt marshes, it needs ample moisture. Lord Baltimore series flowers are 10 inches across, brilliant red, ruffled, on 4-foot plants, from July to frost; sterile, so there are no volunteers. Plant seedlings in late summer or spring, in deeply dug, well-drained, well-fertilized soil.

MATURE HEIGHT: 3'–5'
GROWTH RATE: fast
LIGHT: full sun, semi-sunny
MOISTURE: roots moist

PAPAVER *pap-pay-ver* Poppy

Spring-to-summer perennials and annuals with shim-mering, silky petals, usually crinkled, in beautiful colors from pastels to brights. The leaves are hairy and die down soon after the plants finish blooming. Soil must be well-drained, light, somewhat sandy. Transplants with difficulty. Do not transplant until foliage has died down completely after flowering, in late summer or early fall (late July through September at the National Arboretum). Or plant pot-

Eryngium giganteum, Eryngo. (McDonald)

Hibiscus moscheutos, Rose Mallow. (McDonald)

grown specimens in early spring. Plant in deep, rich loam and maintain moisture. Deadhead after bloom-ing.

GROWTH RATE: fast
LIGHT: full sun
MOISTURE: roots moist

P. nudicaule Iceland Poppy Zones 1–8.
Smaller poppy with wonderful colors from white-green and sunny yellow to coral, pink, and red; somewhat fragrant. Tender perennial that can flower the first year from seed sown the fall before, and is

Papaver nudicaule, Iceland Poppy. (McDonald)

Phlox paniculata. (McDonald)

usually grown as a biennial. There are double-flowered types.

P. orientale   Oriental Poppy   Zones 3–8.
Dramatic, exotic, 5- to 8-inch flowers in vibrant reds, oranges, and combinations, usually with a sooty black center. Interesting foliage. Oriental Poppies are stars of the late spring–early summer show. Last when cut if the stem is seared by flame and placed in warm water. Seedheads may be removed—or left—but the foliage must be allowed to ripen on the plant before it is removed. 'Minicap' and other Mohn hybrids have small seed capsules and adapt well to warm-winter climates. 'Tara' (pink) and 'Maya' (salmon) may reach 6 feet.

PHLOX *flox*
paniculata   Perennial Phlox, Garden Phlox
Zones 3–9.

Mid- to late-summer pastels, oval-to-round flower heads, each floret usually with a contrasting eye. The color combinations are almost limitless. Clumps multiply and should be divided every 3 or 4 years. Their seedlings revert to magenta. 'Mount Fujiyama', lovely white with a golden eye, exceptionally weatherproof, often reblooms and is mildew-resistant—many varieties are not. Water the ground, not the plants, and set plants 18 inches apart. Good cutting flower. Plant root divisions in spring, in well-drained, well-fertilized soil rich in compost and humus. A spring-blooming, creeping phlox is *P. subulata,* Moss Pink (Flowers 10).

MATURE HEIGHT: 2'–4'
GROWTH RATE: fast
LIGHT: full sun, semi-sunny
MOISTURE: roots moist

PLATYCODON *plat-ik-koh-don*
grandiflorus var. *mariesii*
Dwarf Balloon Flower   Zones 3–9.

Pretty, starry, blue, white, or lilac-pink flower that opens to 3 inches across from a balloon-shaped bud on a plant 18 inches high. Freely flowering with glossy foliage from early summer to early fall, reliable, durable, and easy.
There are some exquisite doubles. 'Apoyama' is a dwarf about 6 inches high, a good follow-up flower for *Veronica* 'Crater Lake Blue' (see Flowers 10). 'Autumnalis' is a late-flowering variety that extends the bloom season. Sow seeds in spring in well-drained sandy or loamy soil and be patient. Transplant badly, and are slow to grow in spring, so mark the place. Last as cut flower if stems are seared.

MATURE HEIGHT: 18"
GROWTH RATE: slow
LIGHT: full sun
MOISTURE: soil surface damp

RUDBECKIA *rud-bek-ee-uh*
fulgida var. *sullivanti*
'Goldsturm'   Coneflower   Zones 3–9.

Hybrid of the durable wild Black-eyed Susan, this easy perennial blooms all summer and into fall, depending on the weather. Leave the cone-shaped ripening flower heads on the plant to reseed. Tolerates heat and drought and is a good cut flower. Often included in gardens of ornamental grasses for its summer color and ease of maintenance. Plant root divisions 12 to 15 inches apart in early spring. *R. hirta*, Black-eyed Susan, is the annual (actually a binennial grown as an annual). It self-sows aggressively and is a good naturalizer for wild places.

MATURE HEIGHT: 18"–24"
GROWTH RATE: fast
LIGHT: full sun
MOISTURE: versatile

YUCCA *yuk-uh*

Bold rosette of big, sword-shaped leaves, and once established, a long-lasting, astonishing, 4- to 6-foot woody spike of big white or purple bell-shaped flowers 2 inches or more across in early summer. Evergreen, good companion to cacti. In fall or spring, plant root divisions in well-drained, preferably neutral-range, sandy soil, not too rich.

GROWTH RATE: fast
LIGHT: full sun
MOISTURE: versatile

Y. filamentosa 'Bright Edge'   Adam's-needle
Zones 5–10.
Specimen plant also useful in hedges. The floral spike rises to 5 feet with creamy white flowers. The leaves

Yucca glauca, Soapweed. (McDonald)

Rudbeckia species, Coneflower.

are 15 inches long, 1 inch across, with shaggy threads along the edges.

Y. glauca Soapweed Zones 4–10.
Smaller, better for the Midwest, more tolerant of shade, and one of the hardiest of the genus. Narrow, white-edged, gray green leaves, 3 feet long and ½ inch wide. The flowers are greenish white on a 3-foot spike.

SEE ALSO:
Aster × frikartii 'Wonder of Staffa', Flowers 14
Chrysanthemum × superbum 'Polaris', Shasta Daisy, Flowers 14
Liatris spicata 'Kobold', Spike Gay-feather, Flowers 14
Liriope platyphylla 'Christmas Tree', Lilyturf, Ground Covers 5
Sedum spectabile 'Autumn Joy', Stonecrop, Flowers 14
Veronica spicata 'Blue Peter', Speedwell, Flowers 10

ALTERNATES:
Delphinium elatum Blackmore and Langdon and Pacific Giant Hybrid strains
Echinacea purpurea 'Bright Star', Purple Cone-flower
Echinops ritro 'Taplow Blue', Small Globe Thistle
Gazania spp., Treasure Flower
Ligularia 'The Rocket'
Lythrum salicaria 'Morden's Pink', Purple Loosestrife
Lythrum salicaria, 'Rose Queen', Purple Loosestrife
Monarda didyma 'Croftway Pink', Bee Balm
Perovskia atriplicifolia, Russian Sage
Potentilla × tonguei, Cinquefoil

FLOWERS 13
SUMMER PERENNIALS FOR SHADE

In hot regions shade may be almost as bright as direct sun in the North. These plants thrive in light shade in the moderate regions of the country; they will tolerate more sun farther north, and succeed with even less farther south.

COMPANION PLANTINGS
Shrubs: Azalea (*Rhododendron*) cvs; *Aucuba japonica* 'Variegata', Gold-dust Tree.
Background plant: Ferns.
Ground cover: *Vinca minor*, Periwinkle.
Flower: *Impatiens wallerana*, Zanzibar Balsam, Busy Lizzy.

ARUNCUS *ar-runk-us*
dioicus Goatsbeard Zones 4–9.

Tall background or specimen plant with big, feathery panicles of off-white flowers in summer and fall, and handsome foliage. It thrives in light shade and moist places. Self-sows once established. The cultivar 'Kneiffii' is shorter—to 3 feet—has finely cut foliage, and is worth the effort to get it started. Plant container-grown plants or seeds in early spring, in well-drained soil.

Aruncus dioicus, Goatsbeard. (McDonald)

MATURE HEIGHT: 4'–7'
GROWTH RATE: fast
LIGHT: semi-sunny
MOISTURE: soil surface damp

CAMPANULA *kam-pan-yew-luh*
poscharskyana Serbian Bellflower
Zones 3–9.

Resembles the beautiful *C. carpatica*, Carpathian Bellflower (Flowers 10), but the 2-foot stems have a sprawling habit useful for planters and border edges. The bell-shaped flowers are lavender-blue, and bloom through summer into fall, especially if plants

are sheared back at midsummer. It prefers light shade, withstands drought. Plant container-grown plants in spring, in well-drained soil in the neutral range. Mulch against summer heat.

MATURE HEIGHT: 4"
GROWTH RATE: fast
LIGHT: full sun, semi-sunny
MOISTURE: soil surface damp

HOSTA *hoss-tuh* Plantain Lily

Magnificent clump-forming ground cover, foliage plant, and flower for shade. Tall lavender or white flower spikes rise above the foliage in summer and early fall. The foliage is bold, sometimes wavy-edged, in rich shades of green, blue-green, gold, and variegated combinations. Sizes from dwarf to giant clumps 5 feet across. They need 3 years to develop into handsome specimens. Culture is easy. Set out container-grown plants in spring, late summer, or early fall, in soil well supplied with humus and well drained.

GROWTH RATE: slow
LIGHT: semi-sunny, shade
MOISTURE: soil surface damp

H. 'Honeybells' Zones 3–9.
Grass-green leaves, and in July and August, 3-foot lavender-lilac, fragrant flower spikes.

H. lancifolia var. *albomarginata*
Narrow-leaved Hosta Zones 3–9.
Narrow leaves brushed with white, to 2 feet, and lavender blooms in August and September.

H. montana 'Aureo-marginata' Zones 3–9.
Large green leaves irregularly margined in yellow which turns to cream as the season progresses. The clumps reach 40 inches wide and stand more sun than other hostas.

H. plantaginea 'Grandiflora'
Fragrant Hosta Zones 3–9.
White-flowering, 20 inches high, this is a fragrant hosta that blooms in late summer. The light green

Hosta sieboldiana 'Frances Williams'. (McDonald)

leaves are large, 10 inches long and 6 inches wide. One of the most beautiful and useful for the flower border.

H. sieboldiana 'Frances Williams'
Zones 3–9.
Also known as 'Gold Edge' or 'Gold Circle', 4-foot clumps with very large puckered leaves—like seersucker—blue-green with broad golden margins that deepen as the season progresses. Foliage-height, soft lilac flowers in late spring and early summer—the bold foliage remains to envelop bare-legged late bloomers like *Lycoris,* the beautiful Resurrection Lily (see Flowers 3).

H. tardiflora
Zones 3–9.
Narrow, dark green leaves form a clump 12 inches high, and the pale purple flowers bloom late, at about foliage height, and hold their flowers until well into fall. Needs moist, organic soil in partial shade.

H. undulata
Zones 3–9.
Wavy green leaves with white centers, and lavender flowers in late spring and early summer. Foliage enhances the early summer blooms of *Allium giganteum* and *A. rosenbachianum* (see Flowers 20). Best color develops in plants growing in shade. There are variegated types.

LOBELIA *loh-beel-ee-uh*

Perennials and half-tender perennials, as well as an annual species, that bear red or blue flowers from

Lobelia cardinalis, Cardinal Flower. (McDonald)

summer into fall, and love moisture and partial shade. Beautiful when massed to naturalize, and beside streams. Plant container-grown plants in fall or spring, in soil enriched with compost.

GROWTH RATE:	medium
LIGHT:	semi-sunny, shade
MOISTURE:	soil surface damp

L. cardinalis Cardinal Flower   Zones 2–8.
Wildflower found by streams. With its feet in water, it can stand some sun but is most valuable in the shade. Slender spikes of dazzlingly red flowers, 24 to 30 inches high, and dark red-bronze foliage. Superb color for late summer and fall. Hummingbirds come to it. Not too vigorous, but self-sows in hospitable environment. Lovely with ferns (Ground Covers 4).

L. erinus Edging Lobelia   Annual.
Annual, intense blue, and a superb edger. There are whites, purples, and rose reds, on plants that can be compact, dwarf, or pendulous, the latter excellent in baskets and pots. Sow seeds indoors, plant out after the ground warms, and cut back plants after each flush of bloom to continue flowering through the season. Tolerates sun or light shade.

L. siphilitica Blue Cardinal Flower, Great Blue Lobelia   Zones 4–9.
Superb, long-lasting late summer show of blue and deep blue flower spikes to 30 inches tall. Quickly reseeds and multiplies in moist, shady situations. More adaptable and tolerant of heat and sun than the red species.

Trollius ledebourii, Globeflower. (McDonald)

TROLLIUS *troh-lee-us*
ledebourii Globeflower   Zones 3–8.

Outstanding spring and summer gold or golden orange buttercuplike flowers for damp, shady places. Lovely massed by a small stream in light woodlands. 'Golden Queen' is deep orange. Plant container-grown plants in early spring. Easy to grow in fairly heavy garden soil. Seeds are slow to germinate.

MATURE HEIGHT: 2'
GROWTH RATE: slow
LIGHT: semi-sunny, shade
MOISTURE: soil surface damp

SEE ALSO:
Astilbe × *arendsii* 'Feuer', 'Professor van der Wielen', Spiraea, Flowers 11
Chrysanthemum × *superbum* 'Polaris', Shasta Daisy, Flowers 14
Dianthus × *allwoodii*, Allwood Pink, Flowers 20
Sedum maximum 'Atropurpureum', Great Stonecrop, Flowers 14
Veronica spicata, 'Blue Fox', 'Snow White', 'Sunny Borders', Speedwell, Flowers 10
Yucca glauca, Soapweed, Flowers 12

ALTERNATES:
Alchemilla mollis, Lady's Mantle
Astilbe simplicifolia, Spiraea
Chrysogonum virginianum, Golden Star
Cimicifuga racemosa, Black Cohosh, Black Snakeroot
Filipendula ulmaria, Queen-of-the-meadow
Lythrum salicaria, 'Dropmore Purple', 'Morden's Pink', Purple Loosestrife
Lythrum salicaria, Purple Loosestrife

FLOWERS 14
FALL PERENNIALS FOR SUN

Many fall-flowering plants are container-grown by nurseries and can be purchased ready to bloom in early autumn.

COMPANION PLANTINGS
Shrubs: *Cotoneaster; Euonymus alata* 'Compacta', Dwarf Winged Spindle Tree.
Ground cover: *Ceratostigma plumbaginoides,* Blue Ceratostigma, Plumbago.
Edging plants: *Ageratum houstonianum,* Flossflower; *Aster,* dwarf cultivars.
Fall bulbs: *Colchicum autumnale,* Autumn Crocus; *Crocus speciosus.*

ANEMONE *an-nem-on-ee*   Windflower

These are very beautiful, readily available, and not very well known. Ferny foliage and showy red, pink, white, or purple flowers. In warm regions plant in fall or spring; in cold areas plant in spring. Set out 8 to 12 inches apart in neutral-range, well-drained soil, and mulch over winter. Maintain moisture. See Flowers 1 for spring bloomers.

Aster, Michaelmas Daisy. (McDonald)

GROWTH RATE: fast
LIGHT: semi-sunny
MOISTURE: roots moist

A. hupehensis var. *japonica*
Japanese Anemone   Zones 5–8.
Often listed as *A.* × *hybrida.* Tall fall-flowering anemone with pink or white blooms on stems to 5 feet tall that dance in autumn winds. Many cultivars are available. Prettiest when several colors are massed against evergreens or a stone wall.

A. vitifolia   'Robustissima'
Grape-leaved Anemone   Zones 4–8.
Hardy, fall-flowering, with silvery pink blooms on 2- to 3-foot stems. Lovely, long-lasting display, easy to grow.

ASTER *ass-ter*   Michaelmas Daisy

Late summer and fall daisylike fluffy flowers in purples, blue, pink, red, and white that stand up to early frost. Among cultivars are dwarfs for edging and tall back-of-border plants. Good cut flowers, easy to grow. Plant root divisions in neutral-range, well-drained soil in spring. Pinch plants back in spring and again a month later. Divide the plants every 3 to 4 years.

GROWTH RATE: slow
LIGHT: full sun, semi-sunny
MOISTURE: roots moist, versatile

A. × *frikartii*   Zones 4–8.
Compact hybrids 1½ to 2 feet tall with large, fragrant violet-blue flowers. This is the earliest blooming aster, and it lasts until frost. Lovely in the mid border with yellow, pink, or white perennials. 'Wonder of Staffa', a beautiful blue, blooms earlier and lasts long. Check hardiness for your area.

A. novae-angliae   New England Aster
     Zones 3–8.
Late-flowering 3- to 4-foot plants with pink flowers. 'Harrington's Pink' bears a profusion of salmon-pink

flowers, prefers sun and a moist location. Stake, don't pinch back.

A. novi-belgii   Zones 2–8.
Also called New York Aster, the flowers are blue-violet. Very hardy. Cultivars in many shades of red, white, and blue. 'Professor Kippenburg' is a compact blue, 14 inches high; a good edger for fall color.

BOLTONIA *bolt-toh-nee-uh*
asteroides 'Snowbank'   Zones 3–8.

Like the Michaelmas daisy, a tall, branching, self-supporting perennial that bears showers of white 1-inch daisies in late summer and fall. Sparse grayish foliage remains attractive. Tolerates extremes of heat and humidity. Spreads rapidly in moist, well-drained, sandy soil but is not a nuisance.

MATURE HEIGHT: 4'
GROWTH RATE: fast/medium
LIGHT: full sun
MOISTURE: roots moist

CHRYSANTHEMUM *kriss-anth-em-um*

Late-blooming daisy-flowered perennials that last until hard frost and succeed in every growing condition. Plant in spring, and pinch back monthly until midsummer. "Cushion" types need no pinching. Apply fertilizer liberally through the growing season until buds show color. Divide every spring and discard old, woody growth. Good successor for spring bulbs. Or plant blooming root divisions in early fall; they will rebloom the next spring.

GROWTH RATE: slow
LIGHT: full sun
MOISTURE: versatile

C. × *morifolium*   Florist's Chrysanthemum, Mum   Zones 5–8.
Colors range from pure white to red, bright yellow, shades of orange, rust, and bronze, many pinks and

Chrysanthemum hybrid. (McDonald)

lavenders (which look great with yellow). Classes range from the button mums, less than an inch across, to large-flowered hybrids like 'Cloud 9'—a beautiful, hardy, yellow-centered white flower 4 to 5 inches across even if not disbudded. Good container plants.

C. × superbum Shasta Daisy   Zones 5–9.
Early-summer-flowering mum—the classic yellow-centered white daisy—2 to 4 feet tall. 'Polaris' grows to 28 inches, and has large, single flowers to 7 inches across. Plant 1 foot apart in deep, rich soil. Remove spent blooms, and divide every other year. Single types need full sun; doubles do better in light shade.

HELENIUM *hel-leen-ee-um*
autumnale Sneezeweed   Zones 3–8.

Bright yellow daisylike flowers from late summer to mid-fall on tall plants. There are also dwarfs and reds, but they aren't easily found. 'Butterpat' is a strongly colored beauty about 40 inches high. Plant root divisions in spring.

MATURE HEIGHT:	4'–5'
GROWTH RATE:	fast
LIGHT:	full sun
MOISTURE:	soil surface damp

LIATRIS *lye-ay-triss* Gay-feather

Handsome purple or white sprays in late summer and early fall, on tall plants with dense foliage. Good at the back of the border and very hardy. Tolerates heat and drought, but thrives in light, fairly moist soil. Plant root divisions in spring.

MATURE HEIGHT:	3'–6'
GROWTH RATE:	fast
LIGHT:	full sun
MOISTURE:	soil surface damp

L. scariosa Tall Gay-feather   Zones 2–8.
For fall. Close-set fuzzy blossoms on 3- to 5-foot, wandlike spikes, with very dense linear foliage. Toler-

Liatris, Gay-feather. (McDonald)

ates semi-sun, but doesn't grow straight. 'September Glory' is a late hybrid with deep purple flowers, to 60 inches tall.

L. spicata Spike Gay-feather   Zones 3–9.
For mid- and late summer, ragged-edged florets on spikes 2 to 5 feet tall, opening from the top down. 'Kobold' is an established hybrid to 18 inches high, compact, and dark purple, lovely with pale yellows and greens, good for the border and island beds.

SALVIA *sal-vee-uh* Sage

Hardy and tender perennial summer bloomers with tall, graceful violet, blue, or white flower spikes. The sage used in cooking—see Herbs 9—is less orna-

mental. In the North where lavender isn't hardy, the blue *S. farinacea* 'Blue Bedder', and *S. X superba* 'East Friesland' are used to set off roses and pink plants in the border. Good cut flowers. Salvias attract bees and butterflies. Plant seedlings of tender perennials, or root divisions of perennials, in spring, in well-drained soil.

GROWTH RATE:	fast
LIGHT:	full sun
MOISTURE:	versatile

S. azurea var. grandiflora Blue Salvia
Zones 4–9.
Perennial with beautiful deep blue flowers and narrow leaves prominently veined with lighter green, on plants 1 to 5 feet high. Flowers from midsummer to mid-fall.

S. elegans Pineapple Sage   Zone 9.
Shrubby, with leaves scented of pineapple, and red flowers about an inch long. Grows as an annual except in frost-free climates.

S. farinacea Mealycup Sage   Zones 8–9.
Tender perennial grown as an annual in the North, it has showy violet-blue blossoms on stems 2–3 feet tall from summer to frost. Plant seeds indoors and set out in spring when the weather has warmed. 'Blue Bedder' is a bright Wedgwood blue, 2 feet high. There are also whites.

S. splendens Scarlet Sage   Zones 9–10.
Includes compact, very vibrant reds. Welwyn Hybrids in pink and salmon tones are cultivars that continue blooming until frost. Grown as an annual except in warm climates.

S. × superba   Zones 5–8.
Violet-purple blooms with red bracts from early to late summer.

SEDUM *seed-um* Stonecrop

Nearly indestructible, but not invasive, this group of succulent, evergreen plants includes ground covers

Salvia × superba 'East Friesland'. (McDonald)

(see Ground Covers 6) and some species valued for late summer and early fall flowers. Dense clusters of small, star-shaped pink or salmon to lavender blooms. There are some yellows, too. Ideal for nooks and crannies, rock gardens, pockets in rocks and walls, by steps, and in the flower border. Self-sows, and grows readily from root divisions set out in well-drained soil in early spring or late summer.

GROWTH RATE: medium
LIGHT: full sun, semi-sunny
MOISTURE: versatile

S. ewersii 'Album' Ewers White Stonecrop
Zones 4–9.
Blooms in late summer and into fall. The flowers are purplish pink, on plants 6 to 12 inches tall.

S. maximum 'Atropurpureum'
Great Stonecrop Annual.
Annual that blooms in autumn, and has maroon leaves and greenish white flowers on stems 1 to 3 feet high.

S. sieboldii October Daphne Zones 4–5.
Blooms late summer into fall, 6 to 9 inches high; a bright pink that trails and is good for pot culture. Tolerates light shade. 'Ruby Glow' is a brilliant cultivar.

S. spectabile 'Autumn Joy' Stonecrop
Zones 3–10.
Extremely valuable for late summer and autumn color, often used in gardens of ornamental grasses, and for naturalizing. This cultivar starts blooming in light pink, turns to salmon, then to rosy russet. Attractive to butterflies and bees. About 1½ to 2 feet tall. Tolerates moisture.

SEE ALSO:
Platycodon grandiflorus 'Autumnalis', Balloon Flower, Flowers 12

Sedum spectabile 'Autumn Joy', Stonecrop. (McDonald)

Rudbeckia fulgida var. *sullivantii* 'Goldsturm', Cone-flower, Flowers 12
Solidago virgaurea 'Cloth of Gold', 'Golden Shower', Goldenrod, Herbs 8

ALTERNATES:
Aconitum carmichaelii, Aconite, Monkshood
Chrysanthemum nipponicum, Nippon Chrysan-themum
Chrysopsis villosa 'Golden Sunshine'
Eupatorium coelestrium, Mist Flower, Hardy Ageratum
Eupatorium maculatum, Joe-Pye Weed, Smokeweed
Polygonum cuspidatum 'Compactum', Japanese Fleece Flower

FALL PERENNIALS FOR SHADE

KIRINGESHOMA *kih-ring-gesh-oh-muh*
palmata Japanese Yellow Bells Zone 5.

Late-summer-blooming wildling, with yellow bell-flowers and bold, maple-shaped leaves. Plant root divisions in well-drained soil in spring. Not listed in all catalogs, but worth looking for.

MATURE HEIGHT: 3'
GROWTH RATE: slow
LIGHT: semi-sunny, shade
MOISTURE: roots moist, versatile

LIGULARIA *lig-yew-lay-ree-uh*

Formerly classified as Senecio and grown for its large, bold, leathery leaves and daisylike yellow flowers in summer and fall. Lovely with Japanese iris and large-leaved hostas. Set out root divisions in early spring, in well-drained soil. Thrives by the water and in moist borders.

Ligularia tussilaginea 'Aureo-maculata', Leopard Plant. (McDonald)

GROWTH RATE: medium
LIGHT: semi-sunny
MOISTURE: soil surface damp, versatile

L. dentata 'Desdemona' Bigleaf Ligularia
Zones 5–8.
Foliage green on top, mahogany-red on the under-side. Orange flowers. Height is 40 inches.

L. stenocephala Zones 4–8.
Deep yellow flowers in mid- and late summer, hand-some, coarsely toothed leaves and erect stems. The spikes stand well above the leaves, to 5 feet. 'The Rocket' is a lovely cultivar.

L. tussilaginea 'Aureo-maculata'
Leopard Plant Zones 8–10.
Leaves are blotched with yellow, white, or even pale pink. Often grown as a house plant.

SANGUISORBA *san-gwis-sorb-uh*
canadensis Canadian Burnet Zones 3–8.

Tall "bugbane" type of bloom, beginning well before frost. It is native to wet meadows of the North and

Sanguisorba canadensis, Canadian Burnet. (McDonald)

produces spikes of tiny white florets. Good for the wild garden or a moist border. Plant root divisions in early spring.

MATURE HEIGHT: 6'
GROWTH RATE: fast
LIGHT: semi-sunny
MOISTURE: soil surface damp

FLOWERS 15
DAYLILIES

The modern hybrids may not thrive as effortlessly as the old-fashioned daylily, yellow or pumpkin-colored and leggy, that is still found blooming by the roadside. But the delightful colors and varying growth habits of the new plants are the reasons for their growing popularity. Those named here are problem-free and have been known to the National Arboretum for some time. They are elite plants with beautiful flowers and high bud count, whose persistent foliage remains free of tip dieback.

COMPANION PLANTINGS
Allium; *Colchicum*; *Iris*; Spring bulbs; *Phlox*.

HEMEROCALLIS *hem-er-oh-kal-iss*
Daylily   Zones 3–9.
Daylilies produce many large, trumpet- or cup-shaped, reflexed or double blooms on stalks usually 3 to 4 feet tall. Flowers last about a day, but there are so many buds on each scape that the short flower life is not a problem. The daylily blooming period lasts many weeks, from early to late summer, when color is scarce. There are dwarfs 11 inches high, and big plants reaching to 6 feet. The colors of the modern hybrids are exciting solids or blends, ranging from creamy yellows to coral pinks and fiery reds. Someday there will be a white.

Breeders are working toward daylilies with longer blooming periods. So far, "extended bloom" in daylilies means about 18 hours. "Rebloomer" daylilies are plants that bloom again in late summer or early fall, or that continue blooming from summer until frost. Plants labeled "tetraploid" have twice as many chromosomes as "diploids." Tetraploids have richer, more intense colors, heavier petal texture, exceptional and unusual forms.

Daylilies are qualified as "evergreen," "semi-evergreen," or "dormant." Which kind to buy depends on your climate. With evergreen types, the arching, grasslike leaves continue through winter in frost-free climates, and the plants bloom again in their normal cycle. Choose these for warm regions.

The "dormants" require a dormant period brought on by frost in order to bloom, and tend to rot in frost-free climates. These are the plants for cooler regions.

"Semievergreens" are between the two, and may be evergreen in the warmer reaches of the cooler regions.

In small beds or big containers, plant rhizomes with the crown ½ to 1 inch below soil level, 1 foot apart, three to six together. To naturalize or use as a ground cover, mass the rhizomes 12 to 18 inches apart. Daylilies will crowd out the weeds and take care of themselves for years to come. To grow specimens in a mixed border, space them 3 to 6 feet apart to allow for interplanting.

Plant in spring or early autumn in bright sun or under tall trees. Plants prefer somewhat acid soil, and tolerate a range of conditions from wet to dry. Soil must be well drained and humusy. Daylilies benefit from a light mulch all season. The seasons of bloom indicated below vary a little with climate.

GROWTH RATE: medium
LIGHT: full sun, semi-sunny
MOISTURE: soil surface damp, versatile

EARLY
'Bertie Ferris', to 20 inches, 2½-inch flowers, deep persimmon, ruffled. Extended bloom. Dormant.
'Mary Todd', to 26 inches, 6-inch flowers, tetraploid, golden yellow. Semievergreen.

EARLY MIDSEASON
'Double Decker', to 30 inches, double golden yellow. Evergreen.
'Netsuki', to 20 inches, 3½-inch flowers, cream-pink blend. Semievergreen.
'Ruffled Apricot', to 28 inches, 7-inch flowers, apricot with lavender midribs and gold throat. Dormant.
'Stella de Oro', to 11 inches, dwarf miniature, 2¾-inch flowers, yellow with small green throat. Rebloomer. Extended bloom. Dormant.

Hemerocallis, Daylily. (Orndorff)

Hemerocallis 'Mary Todd', Early. (Orndorff)

Hemerocallis 'Ed Murray', Midseason. (Orndorff)

MIDSEASON

'Ed Murray', to 30 inches, 4-inch flowers, deep black-red with a green throat. Extended bloom. Dormant.

'Fragrant Light', to 30 inches, 6-inch flowers, light yellow with wide, ruffled petals, is chosen for its fragrance. Dormant.

'Pardon Me', to 18 inches, flowers 2¾ inches, bright red with yellow-green throat. Fragrant at night. Rebloomer. Dormant.

'Prairie Moonlight', to 28 inches; pale yellow flowers. Semievergreen.

MIDSEASON LATE

'Bountiful Valley', to 29 inches, 6-inch flowers, lemon yellow with lime throat. Prodigious bloomer. Rebloomer. Dormant.

'Ollalie Red', to 34 inches, 6¼-inch flowers, crimson-red with deeper halo and green throat. Tetraploid. Dormant.

'Sombrero Way,' to 24 inches, 5½-inch flowers in an orange-apricot blend with deeper throat. Rebloomer. Tetraploid. Dormant.

Hemerocallis 'Ruffled Apricot', Early Midseason. (Orndorff)

FLOWERS 16
PEONIES

Among the most beautiful spring flowers are the peonies—big, satiny globes with a fragrance particular to them. They thrive in cooler regions and are superb cut flowers.

COMPANION PLANTINGS
Spring bulbs; Annuals (see Flowers 17).

PAEONIA *pee-oh-ni-a*
Peony   Zones 3–8.

Peonies have been revered by Chinese gardeners and artists for more than 2,500 years, but they came to the West only two or three centuries ago. Thousands of elegant cultivars comprise the garden peonies of today. The colors range from creamy whites through pinks and blush pinks, to brilliant golds and dramatic crimsons. There are two major groups: herbaceous and tree peonies. Herbaceous peonies die back to the ground in fall; the woody structure of the tree peonies remains after the leaves fall. Both types bear a profusion of huge, many-petaled blooms in mid- to late spring.

Peonies require full sun, generous planting holes, and rich, humusy, well-drained soil. Maintain moisture in midsummer. They are more successful in neutral or slightly alkaline soils, but tolerate a range of acidity. Add a handful of dolomitic limestone to each planting hole, and a pound of bonemeal. Do not use manure for peonies. Dress with fertilizer in late fall and scratch it into the soil in early spring. Fall and spring dressings of ash from wood fires enhance performance. Peonies can live a century or more, but most require at least a year or two to become established. Do not place competitive plants near them. Avoid invasive ground covers, and keep the area free of weeds.

Peonies are magnificent cut flowers, but pick only a few and remove seedheads the first season or so until the plants are well established.

HERBACEOUS PEONIES

Huge blooms in mid- to late spring on 2- to 3-foot shrubby plants that die to the ground in fall. The foliage is a strong green, attractive, and in the North stays handsome through summer. Peonies are used in snow country for low hedges; the foliage dies away in fall, leaving space for snow to be removed from drives and walks. Partial shade is preferred in the warmer reaches of the growing region. Cut to the ground in fall and burn the foliage. Divide peonies only after they become dormant in fall; plant dormant roots. Root clumps have eyes; plant these so the eyes are between 1 and 2 inches under the soil.

The most popular peonies today are the many-petaled Doubles, but interest is growing in Single and Japanese peonies.

DOUBLE

Intensely double flowers. The petals unfold and unfold; the center is a big puff of petals.

'Alice Harding', classical blush, fragrant.

'Bowl of Cream', creamy white, a huge, bowl-shaped blossom, at midseason.

Late Double Peony cultivar. (McDonald)

Paeonia 'Midnight Sun', Single Peony. (Thomson)

Paeonia 'Renkaku', Chinese Peony. (Thomson)

Paeonia 'Thunderbolt', Saunders Hybrid Peony. (Thomson)

'Dinner Plate', light pink.
'Felix Supreme', light red. Superb cut flower.
'Karl Rosenfield', dark red, fragrant, very double.
'Rare China', semidouble, white.

JAPANESE AND SINGLE
Big flowers with a great mound of silky anthers in the center surrounded by a row of satiny petals.
'Krinkled White', typical of the large-flowered Japanese peonies, with broad, pure white petals like crinkled paper, and a golden central mound.
'Flame', a brilliant orange single.
'Midnight Sun', very dark red single. An attention-getter.

P. tenuifolia Fern-leaved Peony Zones 3–8.
Dark red with dense, ferny foliage, and only 12 to 15 inches high, for the front of the border. The beauty of the foliage remains to grace the border after the flowers have finished blooming. Mark the plant's location when it dies down to avoid destroying it in spring. There are single and double flower forms. Rubra Flora Plena is a catalog name given to a later-blooming lovely double.

TREE PEONIES

Tree peonies grew in Japan in the 7th century. They are shrubby, about 4 feet tall, equally wide, and have woody stems. Unlike the herbaceous peonies, they do not die to the ground after the leaves fall. Up to 75 flowers bloom in mid- or late spring. They are enormous, 6 to 10 inches across, single or double flowers. Improved modern cultivars bloom for 4 weeks or more.

The tree peonies are slow-growing and slow to recover from transplanting. But they are easy plants, beautiful as the focus of formal beds. At least 6 hours of direct sun is necessary and shelter from noon sun is profitable. Plant in early fall. Mulch the first winter. Set each plant with the graft point 6 inches below the soil line.

Paeonia tenuifolia, Fern-leaved Peony. (McDonald)

CHINESE, OR EUROPEAN
Large, double blooms, resembling herbaceous peonies.
'Godaishu', large globelike flowers, semidouble, pure white with a gold center. Prolific bloomer.
'Renkaku' (Flight of Cranes), large white, yellow center.

JAPANESE
These have satiny, crinkled petals, and narrow foliage.
'Rimpon', double, brilliant purple with yellow center.
'Hatsi Garashu', single, dark red with yellow center.

SAUNDERS HYBRIDS
'Age of Gold', spectacular double with a central rosette of creamy gold anthers. Blooms at an early age and is fragrant.
'Thunderbolt', black crimson, single.

FLOWERS 17
ANNUALS, BIENNIALS, AND TENDER PERENNIALS

Summer's great tender perennials, biennials, and annuals bring quick, vivid color to garden spaces left empty by the fading of spring-flowering bulbs and perennials. In cold climates these plants do not survive winter, with the exception of the Sweet Violet. However, several will self-sow.

Sow seeds in the garden in mid-spring, or start seeds in flats indoors 4 weeks before the last frost. Or plant seedlings from local garden centers. In very warm regions, the seasons reverse: tender perennials, biennials, and annuals are planted in fall to flower in winter.

Most of these plants prefer soil in the neutral range, grow rapidly in rich, well-drained, well-worked loam, and require sustained moisture to produce the summer-long show of flowers for which they are famous.

Most may be cut for bouquets, but some will last better as cut flowers than others. Cutting back to the nearest set of leaves makes the plant branch and improves flowering in most cases. Pinch out the leader (or growing tip) after planting to encourage branching. Remove spent blossoms to keep flowers

Antirrhinum majus, Snapdragon. (McDonald)

coming. In midseason shear back long-branched plants, such as petunias, to encourage a new round of flowers. Many of the plants here will go on blooming indoors if trimmed back by one-third and potted up before frost.

COMPANION PLANTINGS
All spring and fall bulbs.
Shrubs: Azalea (*Rhododendron*) cvs.; *Potentilla fruticosa,* Shrubby Cinquefoil; *Rosa,* Miniature Roses. Perennials: All, but particularly *Boltonia asteroides* 'Snowbank'; *Chrysanthemum* cvs.; *Dicentra,* Bleeding-heart; *Iris.*

AGERATUM aj-er-**ray**-tum
houstonianum Flossflower

Summer into fall color, with good green leaves, and fuzzy flower heads in shades of purple-blue, purple-pink, or white. Good in hanging baskets, or as an edger for borders. The ageratum's blue picks up the pinks in the border. Compact and taller sorts also available. Browns in heat but comes back into bloom with cooler weather. 'Blue Bedder' is a beautiful cultivar.

MATURE HEIGHT:	6"–12"
GROWTH RATE:	medium
LIGHT:	full sun, semi-sunny
MOISTURE:	roots moist, versatile

ANCHUSA an-**kew**-suh
capensis Bugloss, Flossflower

Biennial with small, red-edged, white-centered blue flowers in bloom from late spring into midsummer. Often self-sows. Nice massed or in containers. Sow seeds in mid-spring outdoors in well-worked soil.

MATURE HEIGHT:	1½'–3'
GROWTH RATE:	medium
LIGHT:	full sun
MOISTURE:	versatile

ANTIRRHINUM an-tihr-**rye**-num
majus Snapdragon

Spring-through-fall spires covered with bright flowers in all colors but blue. Fine hybrids include 'Tom Thumb', 6 to 9 inches; 'Intermediate', 12 to 18 inches; and 'Giant', 2 to 4 feet. Tender perennial that may winter over with protection and often self-sows. Pinch out leaders early to encourage bushiness and deadhead throughout the season to keep the flowers coming. Long-lasting cut flowers. Plant outdoors when the ground has warmed, in well-drained, rich, humusy soil in neutral range.

GROWTH RATE:	fast
LIGHT:	full sun
MOISTURE:	roots moist

CELOSIA sel-**loh**-shee-uh
argentea Woolflower

Woolly all-summer bloomer and lasting cut flower in dazzling reds and interesting forms, either crested or plumed. With hybridizing there are compact plants and a widening range of colors including apricot, bronze, and yellow. Sow seeds directly in rich, well-drained soil as soon as it has warmed.

MATURE HEIGHT: 2'–3'
GROWTH RATE: fast
LIGHT: full sun
MOISTURE: roots moist

CLEOME *klee-oh-mee*
hassleriana Spider Flower

Tall summer-to-frost bloomer that bears airy white, pink, or lavender flowers. Excellent filler for back of the border. Sow seeds in the garden when the ground warms. Self-sows freely.

MATURE HEIGHT: 3'–5'
GROWTH RATE: fast
LIGHT: full sun
MOISTURE: roots moist

CONSOLIDA *kon-sol-id-uh*
ambigua Rocket Larkspur

Showy annual delphinium (formerly classified as Delphinium ajacis) grown from seed planted in early spring. The height is 1 to 3 feet, and the large, full flower spikes, often double, bloom in white, pink, blue, or purple. In warmer areas, plant seeds in fall where they are to bloom. Or plant seedlings in spring, when the ground has warmed. Most successful in cool climates and well-drained soil that is well supplied with ground limestone, bone meal, and superphosphate. The perennial delphinium is described in Flowers 19.

MATURE HEIGHT: 1'–3'
GROWTH RATE: medium
LIGHT: full sun
MOISTURE: soil surface damp

COSMOS *kos-mose*

Tall single and double daisylike flowers with wide petals and feathery foliage, willowy and windblown, to mass at the back of the border. The colors are pale

Cleome hassleriana, Spider Flower. (McDonald)

Cosmos bipinnatus. (McDonald)

yellow, pink, magenta, white, or purple, with yellow or pink centers. Blooms from seed in 8 to 10 weeks; in the North, sow seeds indoors and transplant when the ground has warmed. May need staking.

GROWTH RATE: slow/medium
LIGHT: full sun
MOISTURE: versatile

C. bipinnatus
Blooms from midsummer to fall, with flowers 4 to 6 inches across on 4-foot plants. Single, double, and crested forms available in pinks, white, and crimsons.

C. sulphureus Yellow Cosmos
Golden yellow flowers with dark-tipped centers. Klondyke Dwarfs are under 3 feet, small-flowered, bushy, and early-blooming.

DAHLIA *dahl-yuh*
× *hybrida*

Tender, tuberous-rooted, with daisylike semidouble or double flowers late summer to frost. Flowers come in all colors but blue, in many sizes and striking forms. Unwin hybrids have smaller flowers but bloom from seed the same season if seeds are started indoors 6 to 8 weeks before the last frost is expected. New dwarf dahlias from Holland have exquisite form and are lovely in the border and as container specimens. After the last spring frost, plant tuberous roots 6 inches deep and 3 feet apart, in light, well-drained, moist loam, with lots of fertilizer. Provide a strong stake for each plant. Disbud for larger blooms. May winter over in Zones 9–10, but elsewhere lift and store tubers in a cool, dry place over winter.

MATURE HEIGHT: 2'–8'
GROWTH RATE: medium
LIGHT: full sun
MOISTURE: soil surface damp

Dahlia. (McDonald)

IMPATIENS *im-pay-shee-enz*

Succulent tender perennials and annuals with delicate, pointed leaves and bright flowers in pastels and bright colors. Indispensable for shaded porches, patio corners, and under garden shrubs and small trees. After the air has warmed, plant seedlings in light, rich soil. Most successful in very light shade, but tolerates direct sun if the soil is well supplied with humus and moisture is constant. Excellent for baskets, boxes, and borders.

MATURE HEIGHT: 1'–2'
GROWTH RATE: fast
LIGHT: semi-sunny, versatile
MOISTURE: roots moist

I. balsamina Garden Balsam
Leafy, upright succulent annual for the border, to 2½ feet high. Flowers may be white, red, or yellow, with some bicolors, and there are double-flowered varieties.

I. wallerana Zanzibar Balsam, Busy Lizzy
Much hybridized, valuable plant for quick color and lightly shaded situations. The succulent, branching stems are covered from early summer until frost with small flowers in sparkling colors from dark red and hot pink to intense coral, orchid, and white. There are bicolors and hybrids with variegated leaves. Height to 3 feet; compacts reach 6 to 8 inches. The New Guinea type have larger flowers and can tolerate more sun. Set out container-grown seedlings only after the last frost. Can be brought indoors to winter but generally succumbs to white fly.

NICOTIANA *nik-oh-shee-ay-nuh*
alata Flowering Tobacco

Semi-reclining, luxuriant large-leaved foliage with pretty tubular white flowers that open after sun-

Impatiens. (McDonald)

down and are quite fragrant. Blooms toward mid-summer and continues until frost. Modern hybrids such as 'Nikki White' have better branching habits than the species and bloom sooner. Flowers well in partial sun and tolerates damp situations. Tender perennial usually grown as an annual. It often self-sows.

MATURE HEIGHT: 3'
GROWTH RATE: medium
LIGHT: full sun, semi-sunny
MOISTURE: roots moist

PELARGONIUM *pel-ahr-goh-nee-um*
× *hortorum* Fish Geranium,
Zonal Geranium, House Geranium

Geranium is a common name for some species of the genus *Pelargonium*. *Geranium* also is a genus name of a group whose common name is Cranesbill or Hardy Geranium (see Flowers 10). *Pelargonium* is summer's windowbox favorite, the zonal geranium, a tender perennial with woody stems and flowers in clear shades of red, pink, white, purple, and shocking pink. There are bicolors and beautiful leaf variegations. Blooms from spring until frost and is indispensable for borders as well as boxes and baskets. (See also Flowers 18 and Herbs 6.) Wintered indoors on a sunny sill, it flowers sparsely on branch tips. Plants may be preserved for the next season if hung bare-root in a cool room. Tip cuttings root easily in late winter, spring, and summer. Set out rooted cuttings or plants after weather has warmed. Or sow seeds indoors 10 to 12 weeks before planting time. Prefers well-drained, sandy, not-too-fertile soil, on the dry side.

GROWTH RATE: medium
LIGHT: full sun
MOISTURE: rather dry

Portulaca grandiflora, Rose Moss. (McDonald)

PETUNIA *pet-tew-nee-uh*
× *hybrida*

Summer-long profusion of trumpet-shaped flowers on drooping stems, in every shade except blue. There are singles and doubles; forms with fringed, ruffled, or picotee petals; multifloras with smaller flowers but masses of them; and grandifloras with fewer but very large flowers. Bedding varieties are good filler plants in the border; cascading types are superb in hanging baskets. Slow to bloom from seed. Start seed indoors 6 to 10 weeks before the last frost, or buy nursery-grown seedlings to plant in well-drained, humusy soil when temperatures warm. Pre-

fers pH between 6.0 and 7.0. Pinch out the central stem tip at 6 inches, then every 4 inches until the plant is many-branched. Pick dead blooms and trim plants back by one-third at mid season to encourage late blooming. Fair as cut flowers.

GROWTH RATE: slow
LIGHT: full sun
MOISTURE: roots moist

PORTULACA *port-yew-lay-kuh*
grandiflora Rose Moss

Succeeds even on hot, dry slopes, a trailing plant with needle leaves and a profusion of single or double roselike blooms in red, pink, yellow, coral, or white. Cultivars stay open through the day; species blooms tend to close after bees have visited. Sow seeds in mid-spring in well-drained soil where plants are to bloom. Often self-sows and is a good basket plant.

MATURE HEIGHT: 8"
GROWTH RATE: fast
LIGHT: full sun
MOISTURE: versatile

TAGETES *ta-jeet-eez* Marigold

Tall or small, for hot, sunny borders, low hedges, or containers—fluffy, ruffled globes of gold, pumpkin-orange, or bicolors including mahogany. Blooms quickly from seed sown indoors 4 to 6 weeks before the weather warms and goes on blooming until after a few frosts. Easy-care, tolerant of drought and neglect. One of few annuals that bloom in southern Florida summers. Pungent scent. Long-lasting cut flowers. Some types self-sow.

GROWTH RATE: fast
LIGHT: full sun
MOISTURE: versatile

T. erecta African Marigold
For the back of the border, tall plants 2 to 3 feet high, with big, ruffled, clear yellow or orange blooms.

Pelargonium, Geranium, with *Salvia farinacea*, Mealycup Sage. (McDonald)

Verbena × *hybrida*, Garden Verbena. (McDonald)

Several forms have been introduced, semidouble and double, flat, quilled. There are also dwarfs.

T. patula French Marigold
Short bushy plants for edgings or window boxes, 1½ feet high, with big, full flowers in yellow or orange. Some strains have mahogany markings. Many forms.

T. tenuifolia Signet Marigold
Stocky plants to 2 feet with yellow flowers. Dwarfs of the species are popular for edgings. Self-sows.

VERBENA *ver-bee-nuh*
× *hybrida* Garden Verbena

Drought-resistant summer-to-frost bloomer that covers itself with heads of small florets in white, reds, pinks, yellows, purples. Vigorous, low-growing, excellent for carpeting the border and for hanging baskets. Good by the sea. Sow seeds indoors and plant out when the air warms, or sow seeds outdoors in early spring. Tender perennial grown as an annual. See also Ground Covers 5.

GROWTH RATE: fast
LIGHT: full sun
MOISTURE: versatile

VIOLA *vye-oh-luh*

The perennial violet and the more ephemeral pansies and Johnny-jump-ups are included in this genus of low-growing plants usually grown as biennials and annuals. The lasting foliage is attractive under small trees and tall shrubs, in rock gardens and naturalized plantings. They bloom in spring, some continuing into summer, need sustained moisture, and prefer cool weather. In good cultural conditions, they self-sow.

GROWTH RATE: medium
LIGHT: semi-sunny
MOISTURE: soil surface damp

V. odorata Sweet Violet   Zones 6–9.
Low-growing perennial about 8 inches high, with small, pansylike flowers in spring. Heart-shaped, dark green leaves half hide flowers that are blue-purple, white, sometimes pink or bicolor. Two choice cultivars are 'Royal Robe', with dark violet-blue, fragrant flowers on 6-inch stems, and 'White Czar', which has very large, fragrant white flowers on 4-inch stems. Succeeds in sun as well as semi-shade, and multiplies year after year. Plant seeds or root divisions in fall or early spring.

V. tricolor Johnny-jump-up   Zones 4–8.
Very small, pansylike flowers in yellow, white, and

Viola × *wittrockiana*, Pansy. (McDonald)

blue, 6 to 12 inches high. Short-lived perennial usually treated as an annual, and planted in the wild or rock garden. Often self-sows.

V. × *wittrockiana* Pansy
Low, cool-weather plants with fresh green foliage that bloom in the cool of a mild autumn or in spring. They have many faces—some marked with velvet-black, deep brown, or blue. Modern strains include some taller solid-color pansies in melting shades of coral, peach, orange, lavender, or yellow. Usually grown as annuals or biennials, and set out already blooming in mid-fall or spring. If spent flowers are removed, pansies will continue blooming into and even through summer.

ZINNIA *zinn-ee-uh*
elegans Zinnia

Blooms from summer to frost in red, pink, orange, magenta, yellow, white, and bicolors. Carefree flowers, they hold their color even in hot sun. Sizes range from 4-inch Thumbelinas for edging to 4-footers with blooms 8 inches in diameter. There are dahlia-flowered types, cactus-flowered forms, and ruffled blooms. 'Pumila' is one of many compact plants with names like 'Liliput' or 'Tom Thumb'. 'Peter Pan' zinnias are small plants with big flowers. 'Small World' has large flowers that begin when the plants are 4 inches high. 'Fantastic Light Pink' has strawberry-pink double flowers on 14-inch plants. All last well as cut flowers when placed in a roomy vase. Sow seeds indoors and set out when temperatures warm. Or sow outdoors when the air warms. Subject to mildew in late summer; space the plants well apart in well-drained soil, and water the soil, not the plants. Early in the season, pinch out the lead tip to force branching.

GROWTH RATE: fast
LIGHT: full sun
MOISTURE: roots moist

Zinnia elegans. (McDonald)

SEE ALSO:
Begonia semperflorens-cultorum, Bedding Begonia, Wax Begonia, Flowers 3
Browallia speciosa 'Major', Sapphire Flower, Flowers 18
Cheiranthus cheiri, Wallflower, Flowers 20
Coleus blumei, Painted Nettle, Flowers 18
Cuphea ignea, Cigar Flower, Flowers 18
Dianthus chinensis, Rainbow Pink, Flowers 20
Lobelia erinus, Edging Lobelia, Flowers 13
Lobularia maritima, Sweet Alyssum, Flowers 20
Papaver nudicaule, Iceland Poppy, Flowers 12
Rudbeckia hirta, Black-eyed Susan, Flowers 12
Salvia farinacea, Mealycup Sage, Flowers 14
Salvia splendens, Scarlet Sage, Flowers 14

ALTERNATES:
Agrostemma gracilis, Corn-cockle
Alternanthera ficoidea 'Versicolor', Snowball, Copper Alternanthera
Bellis perennis, English Daisy
Calendula officinalis, Pot Marigold
Callistephus chinensis, China Aster
Catharanthus roseus, Madagascar Periwinkle
Kochia scoparia, Summer Cypress
Lavatera trimestris, Tree Mallow
Lisianthus, dwarf cvs.
Nigella damascena, Love-in-a-mist
Phlox drummondii, Annual Phlox
Sanvitalia procumbens, Trailing Sanvitalia
Schizanthus pinnatus, Butterfly Flower
Senecio cineraria, Dusty Miller
Torenia fournieri, Bluewings

FLOWERS 18
BULBS FOR CONTAINERS AND FORCING

Spring- and fall-flowering bulbs and lilies thrive in well-drained, well-fertilized containers provided moisture is maintained and the light is right. In below-zero regions, they may not survive winter outdoors unless they are moved to a sheltered location. Plants that droop or trail add grace to container gardens filled with upright plants. Several of the Companion Plantings suggested here add fragrance as well as a trailing habit.

These flowering bulbs bloom successfully indoors or outdoors.

COMPANION PLANTINGS
Foliage plants: *Mentha spicata*, Spearmint; *Origanum majorana*, Sweet Marjoram, Annual Marjoram; *Petunia × hybrida*, Hybrid Petunia; *Rosmarinus officinalis* 'Prostratus', Rosemary; *Thymus × citriodorus* 'Aureus', Golden Lemon Thyme; *Vinca minor*, Periwinkle.

AGAPANTHUS *ag-ap-panth-us*
orientalis Lily-of-the-Nile   Zones 8–9.

Tall, summer-flowering bulb bears dense clusters of single or double blue or white funnel-shaped flowers. Specimen plant for large containers or the border in frost-free regions. 'Peter Pan', a 15-inch dwarf, is suited to small planters. Succeeds when partially submerged in soil. Plant in rich, moist soil with generous space for the roots. Winter indoors or provide protection.

MATURE HEIGHT: 3'
GROWTH RATE: medium
LIGHT: semi-sunny
MOISTURE: soil surface damp

ALLIUM *al-lee-um*
neapolitanum Daffodil Garlic,
Flowering Onion   Zones 7–9.

Beautiful flowering onion that bears fragrant, starry white blooms in spring. Plant in containers in spring for bloom that same season. Use a well-drained commercial planting mix. Withhold water in late fall and store in a cool room indoors for the winter. Begin watering again as temperatures warm and day length increases.

MATURE HEIGHT: 12"–14"
GROWTH RATE: medium
LIGHT: full sun
MOISTURE: soil surface damp

CHIONODOXA *kye-oh-nod-dox-uh*
Glory-of-the-snow

Very early spring bulbs with grassy leaves and spikes of blue flowers with white centers. Plant in containers in well-drained, sandy, humusy soil in early fall, and protect through winter.

GROWTH RATE: medium
LIGHT: full sun, semi-sunny
MOISTURE: roots moist

C. luciliae   Zones 4–8.
Starry flowers in violet-blue on 8-inch stalks. There are white and lavender cultivars, and some large-flowered varieties.

C. sardensis   Zones 4–8.
Similar to *C. luciliae* but the flowers are darker blue and arranged more loosely on the stem.

CLIVIA *klye-vee-uh*
× *cyrtanthiflora* Kaffir Lily   Zone 10.

Evergreen, deep green sword-shaped leaves topped by a tall stem bearing 5-inch flower heads in brilliant orange. Good in the border in mild climates—it can stand a little frost. In cool regions, it blooms in spring indoors and may rebloom outdoors later. Best when pot bound. Plant in fall in peaty soil and keep moist and fertilized. Dry down slightly after blooming. In Florida *C. miniata*, the scarlet kaffir lily, is grown in a well-drained border and blooms in spring.

MATURE HEIGHT: 2'
GROWTH RATE: medium
LIGHT: semi-sunny
MOISTURE: soil surface damp

FREESIA *free-zee-uh*
× *hybrida*   Zone 9.

Extraordinarily fragrant funnel-shaped flowers, about 8 on each 1½-foot-long slender stem, growing from bulblike corms. Colors are subtle combinations of red, orange, yellow, white, or pink. Modern doubles are as fragrant as singles. They are forced indoors or planted for bloom in boxes and planters outdoors in spring. Staking may be necessary. Plant 10 to 12 corms 2 inches deep in each container, from October through December—they bloom in 12 to 14 weeks. Water after planting, and not again until they have sprouted, then move to a sunny, cool windowsill. After blooming, maintain foliage as it ripens, then dry down, and store in a cool dry place for reuse. Prefers well-drained, somewhat acid soil.

MATURE HEIGHT: 1½'
GROWTH RATE: medium
LIGHT: full sun
MOISTURE: roots moist

SEE ALSO:
Crocus spp., Flowers 5
Hyacinthus orientalis var. *albulus*, Roman Hyacinth, Flowers 1
Muscari azureum, Grape Hyacinth, Flowers 1

Chionodoxa luciliae, Glory-of-the-snow. (McDonald)

Narcissus 'Tete-a-Tete', Cyclamineus Hybrids,
 Flowers 6
Scilla siberica, Siberian Squill, Flowers 1

FLOWERS FOR BASKETS AND WINDOW BOXES

These trailing perennials are among the most colorful for hanging baskets and window boxes. Flowering or variegated trailing ground covers, such as *Vinca minor* and small-leaved ivy, are good choices. Small upright plants that bloom profusely all season can be included in a mixed basket, but the main feature usually is one or more plants that droop or trail. Several of these succeed indoors.

ACHIMENES *ak-kim-in-eez*

Summer-to-fall basket plants, with bronzy foliage and tubular flowers in blue, crimson, lavender, pink, purple, scarlet, violet, white, yellow, or bicolor. Summer in part-shade on a porch or in a lath house. In early spring, plant rhizomes 1 inch apart, 1 inch deep in well-drained, sandy loam that contains some leaf mold; move outdoors when night temperatures are 55° F. Fertilize often. Keep growing tips pinched out until plants are well branched. Dry off in fall and store indoors for the winter.

MATURE HEIGHT: 1'–2'
GROWTH RATE: medium
LIGHT: semi-sunny
MOISTURE: soil surface damp

BROWALLIA *broh-wall-lee-uh*
speciosa 'Major' Sapphire Flower

Annual that blooms in filtered sun, producing small, tubular, lavender-blue flowers all summer. Start seeds indoors in late winter and keep plants pinched until they are well branched. Plant in well-drained,

Browallia speciosa 'Major' with coleus. (McDonald)

humusy soil and keep in filtered light outdoors for the season. For winter indoors, maintain on the dry side.

MATURE HEIGHT: 2'
GROWTH RATE: fast
LIGHT: semi-sunny
MOISTURE: roots moist

COLEUS *koh-lee-us*
blumei Painted Nettle

Foliage with almost infinite variegations of mahogany, green, yellow, white, blue, and rose. The insignificant, pale blue flowers are best pinched out. Excellent basket, pot, or border plant for filtered light outdoors, or semi-sun indoors. Cuttings root readily

and grow in water. Plant in well-drained soil but maintain moisture. The perennial species, *C. pumilus*, is a many-branched, creeping or trailing plant attractive in hanging baskets.

MATURE HEIGHT: 3'
GROWTH RATE: medium
LIGHT: semi-sunny
MOISTURE: roots moist

CUPHEA *kew-fee-uh*
ignea Cigar Flower

Tender perennial grown as an annual. It has attractive foliage and produces brilliant red blooms that resemble tiny cigars. There are dwarfs and hybrids in addition to the species. In spring, plant seeds indoors in well-drained, rich, humusy soil, and move to partial shade outdoors when the weather has warmed.

MATURE HEIGHT: 3'
GROWTH RATE: medium
LIGHT: semi-sunny
MOISTURE: roots moist

FUCHSIA *few-shuh*
× *hybrida* Zones 9–10.

Most beautiful of all basket plants, with pendulous flowers in many combinations of creamy white with cerise-red, purple, or pink. They bloom on new wood and will keep blooming if tips are pinched back often to encourage bushy growth. Rest plants through winter in a cool place, giving just enough water to keep wood from drying. In spring, cut back severely before new growth begins. Repot in well-drained, humusy loam. Prefers soil in the acid range, pH 6.0 to 7.0.

MATURE HEIGHT: 3'–5'
GROWTH RATE: slow
LIGHT: semi-sunny
MOISTURE: roots moist

Achimenes. (McDonald)

Fuchsia × *hybrida.* (McDonald)

LANTANA *lan-tay-nuh*

These are semitropical, woody or herbaceous plants with pretty crinkled leaves and rounded or flat-topped flower heads made up of small, tubular florets. Some species are used as ground cover, annual in the North, year-round in warm regions. The species here are superb basket plants and often are used by the seashore. Plant in early spring in rich garden soil.

GROWTH RATE: medium
LIGHT: full sun
MOISTURE: versatile

L. camara
Zones 8–10.
Shrub 2 to 6 feet tall, its flowers are first yellow, then change to orange and red, often having all three colors at the same time. Good pot plant for terraces and patios. May be trained as a container tree but must winter indoors.

L. montevidensis
Weeping Lantana, Trailing Lantana.
Zone 10.
A trailing shrub with pendant stems 2 to 3 feet long and pinkish purple flower clusters. In the North, this species flourishes as an annual ground cover and in hanging baskets. It often is used by the seashore.

PELARGONIUM *pel-ahr-goh-nee-um*
peltatum Ivy Geranium
Zone 10.

Geranium is a common name for some species of the genus *Pelargonium*. *Geranium* also is a genus name for a group whose common names are Cranesbill or Hardy Geranium (see Flowers 10). This very hand-

Pelargonium peltatum 'Sybil Holmes', Ivy Geranium. (McDonald)

some species is evergreen and trailing with stiff, waxy, ivy-shaped leaves. Blooms less profusely than zonal geraniums (see Flowers 17), from late winter to early fall. Blooms are white to deep rose with darker markings. Winter indoors in a cool, sunny place; water moderately in winter, but don't allow to dry out. Root cuttings in spring. Prefers well-drained soil. There are charming compacts. See also Herbs 6 for other geraniums that do well in containers.

GROWTH RATE: medium
LIGHT: full sun
MOISTURE: roots moist

SEE ALSO:
Begonia × *tuberhybrida* Pendula, Tuberous Begonia, Flowers 3
Bougainvillea , Vines 1
Impatiens wallerana, Zanzibar Balsam, Busy Lizzy, Flowers 17
Lobelia erinus, Edging Lobelia, Flowers 13
Petunia × *hybrida,* Flowers 17
Portulaca grandiflora, Rose Moss, Flowers 17
Rosa, Miniature Roses, Shrubs 19
Thunbergia alata, Black-eyed Susan Vine, Vines 7
Tropaeolum, Nasturtium, climbing varieties, Herbs 4
Verbena × *hybrida,* Garden Verbena, Flowers 17

ALTERNATES:
Oxalis cv.

FLOWERS 19
FLOWERS TO ATTRACT BEES, BIRDS, AND BUTTERFLIES

Holly Shimizu, first curator of the American Herb Garden at the U.S. National Arboretum, advises against the use of strong insecticides in gardens, especially where wildlife is present. They destroy useful insects as well as those that are a nuisance.

Lantana camara. (McDonald)

Angelica archangelica. (Shimizu)

Ms. Shimizu found the help given by beneficial insects outweighed the problems presented by the others—including Japanese beetles. If chemical control is necessary, use a mild insecticidal soap. Leave the plant skeletons in place at season's end so birds can eat the ripe seeds.

COMPANION PLANTINGS

Background plants: *Buddleia*, Butterfly Bush; *Campsis radicans*, Trumpet Creeper, Trumpet Vine. *Chionanthus retusus*, Fringe Tree.
Herbs: many, particularly *Lavandula angustifolia* 'Hidcote', English Lavender.
Annuals: *Petunia* × *hybrida*, and many others.

ANGELICA *an-jell-ik-uh*
archangelica Zones 4–8.

Tall, handsome, perennial or biennial, celerylike and aromatic plant that attracts beneficial insects and wasps. Large heads of florets bloom in summer. Perennial if flower heads are removed before they go to seed. Sow seeds in well-drained soil where plants are to grow, and thin to 6 inches apart.

MATURE HEIGHT: 4'–6'
GROWTH RATE: medium
LIGHT: semi-sunny
MOISTURE: roots moist

ASCLEPIAS *ass-kleep-ee-ass*

Showy, somewhat invasive perennial wildflowers related to common milkweed and beautiful when naturalized. Difficult to transplant but may be grown from seed. Drought-resistant. Plants are slow to break dormancy, so mark them well. Sow seed in late summer or spring, or plant root divisions in well-drained, sandy soil.

GROWTH RATE: medium
LIGHT: full sun
MOISTURE: roots moist, versatile

Asclepias tuberosa, Butterfly Weed. (McDonald)

A. currasavica Bloodflower Zones 7–8.
Even more attractive to butterflies than Butterfly Weed. Tender perennial grown as an annual, about 2½ feet high with bottle-green, willowlike foliage, and flat umbels of orange-scarlet florets from summer until frost. Excellent pot plant.

A. tuberosa Butterfly Weed Zones 3–9.
Butterflies and bees love the bright orange flowers that bloom over a long period in summer, followed by attractive seedheads. Hybrids available in yellows and bicolors. Grows to 3 feet.

Daucus carota, Queen-Anne's-lace. (McDonald)

DAUCUS *daw-kus*
carota Queen-Anne's-lace, Wild Carrot Zones 3–8.

Attractive to swallowtails and other butterflies. Tall, airy wildflower with pungent, ferny foliage and a broad, green-white seedhead with a tiny, purple-red central floret. Long lasting and beautiful in fresh or dried arrangements. Invasive, best in a wild garden. Sow seed of this biennial in well-drained soil in early fall or spring; it flowers the following year.

MATURE HEIGHT: 2'–3'
GROWTH RATE: slow
LIGHT: full sun
MOISTURE: versatile

DELPHINIUM *del-fin-ee-um*
elatum Candle Larkspur Zones 3–8.

Attractive to bees and butterflies. Summer-blooming, tall, spectacular flower spikes densely covered with beautiful blooms in intense shades of blue and contrasting pale pinks, lavenders, and white. The Pacific Giant series is one of many magnificent strains. Most successful in cooler climates, especially along the West Coast. Can be treated as annual or biennial in hot, humid areas. In warm climates, the annual Rocket Larkspur, *Consolida ambigua* (syn. *Delphinium ajacis*), is grown. Needs staking, but is a superb flower for fresh or dried arrangements. Stake in the back of the border or center in island beds. Plant root divisions in early spring in rich, humusy, well-drained soil supplied with lime. Remove spent flowers to encourage rebloom. Fertilizer essential.

MATURE HEIGHT: 4'–6'
GROWTH RATE: medium
LIGHT: full sun
MOISTURE: roots moist

Delphinium elatum, Candle Larkspur. (McDonald)

Gaillardia, Blanket Flower. (McDonald)

GAILLARDIA *gay-lard-ee-uh*
Blanket Flower

Attractive to butterflies and has interesting seed-heads. The showy, yellow-tipped red flowers bloom through summer if spent heads are removed. Tolerates drought and heat; needs well-drained soil. May bloom the first year from seed. Or plant root divisions in early spring.

GROWTH RATE: medium
LIGHT: full sun
MOISTURE: versatile

G. aristata 'Goblin'   Blanket Flower
                                   Zones 5–8.
Compact, mounded perennial, 1 foot high, with 2- to 3-inch flowers. Nice for the rock garden or the front of the border. Blooms all summer.

G. pulchella   Painted Gaillardia   Annual.
Showy annual to 2 feet high, it bears colorful flowers all summer. Many large, beautiful cultivars in brilliant colors.

GENTIANA *jen-shee-ay-nuh*
asclepiadea   Gentian

One of several low-growing species attractive to hummingbirds, with beautiful flowers in late summer and fall, often in vibrant shades of blue. Hardy, but zones are not available. Requires humusy, well-drained, somewhat acid, cool soil. Best started from seed; avoid transplanting.

MATURE HEIGHT: 1½'–2½'
GROWTH RATE: slow
LIGHT: semi-sunny
MOISTURE: roots moist

Helianthus annuus, Sunflower. (McDonald)

HELIANTHUS *hee-lee-anth-us*
Sunflower

Late-blooming, very tall, coarse plants with bold, sunny yellow flowers, for the vegetable patch or wild garden. They thrive in poor soil and tolerate drought. Sow seeds where the plants are to grow. Or set out tubers or root divisions in early spring.

GROWTH RATE: fast
LIGHT: full sun
MOISTURE: versatile

H. annuus   Annual.
This is an annual, the huge-headed sunflower with the big central disk whose seed is a staple for birds and health-food enthusiasts. Height to 12 feet, and flower heads may be 1 foot in diameter. Blooms from midsummer to frost. Birds will come to eat the seeds if the plants are far enough away from people traffic.

H. salicifolius   Willow-leaved Sunflower
                                   Zones 3–8.
Native to the Western Plains, about 7 feet tall, with daisylike yellow flowers in fall. Attractive in big borders or naturalized.

H. tuberosus   Jerusalem Artichoke
                                   Zones 3–8.
Small, fluffy flower heads on plants to 12 feet high. The edible root was a staple food of the American Indians. Invasive unless the tubers are dug and reduced every fall.

HESPERIS *hess-per-iss*
matronalis Dame's Rocket Zones 3–8.

Goldfinches love this tall, sprawling, invasive plant that bears fragrant phloxlike flowers in late spring and early summer. Colors are white and shades of pink, magenta, and lavender; flowers can be single or double. Best to naturalize. Perennial to −10° F, biennial or annual farther north. Sow seeds or plant root divisions in early spring in rich, moist soil.

MATURE HEIGHT: 2'–3'
GROWTH RATE: fast
LIGHT: versatile
MOISTURE: soil surface damp

KNIPHOFIA *nip-hoh-fee-uh*
uvaria Red-hot Poker Zones 6–8.

Especially attractive to hummingbirds, poker-shaped scarlet racemes that yellow as they age stand high above sword-shaped foliage from September to November. Combines well with low edgers in contrasting colors, like *Coreopsis lanceolata* 'Goldfink' (see Flowers 12). The smaller *K. tucki*, which blooms in summer, is yellow edged with red. Plant root divisions in early spring in sandy, well-drained soil.

MATURE HEIGHT: 2½'–3½'
GROWTH RATE: medium
LIGHT: semi-sunny
MOISTURE: roots moist

MYOSOTIS *mye-oh-soh-tiss*
Forget-me-not

Attractive to birds, little blue flowers with dainty foliage are beautiful when naturalized in drifts or planted around spring-flowering bulbs. Self-sows once established. Prefers acid soil. Plant root divi-

Myosotis, Forget-me-not. (McDonald)

Scabiosa caucasica, Pincushion Flower. (McDonald)

sions in early spring in moist, lightly shaded situations.

GROWTH RATE: medium
LIGHT: shade
MOISTURE: soil surface damp

M. alpestris Garden Forget-me-not
                              Zones 3–8.
The cultivar 'Victoria' is a mound-forming plant 6 to 8 inches tall, with intense blue flowers. Excellent edger.

M. scorpioides var. *semperflorens* Zones 3–8.
Vibrant little blue flowers with yellow eyes in bloom from spring until hot weather sets in; 8 inches high.

SCABIOSA *skay-bee-oh-suh*
caucasica Pincushion Flower Zones 4–8.

Attractive to butterflies, a large, showy perennial with ferny grayish foliage and pale blue, white, or lavender flowers from summer until frost. Good cutting flower. 'Blue Perfection' and 'Alba', a white, bloom profusely. Sow seeds in early spring or plant root divisions in well-drained soil with a pH in the neutral range. May bloom from seed the first season. Provide a light, dry winter mulch.

MATURE HEIGHT: 2'
GROWTH RATE: fast
LIGHT: full sun
MOISTURE: soil surface damp

VERBASCUM *ver-bask-um*
thapsus Mullein, Flannel Plant Zones 3–8.

Goldfinches harvest the ripe seeds from these tall plants with woolly, yellowing gray foliage and bright yellow flower clusters. Good subject for the back of the wild garden. The less hardy *V. chaixii* cultivar 'Album' produces beautiful spires of red-eyed white flowers, suitable for the summer border. Plant seeds or root divisions in well-drained soil in spring. Self-sows.

MATURE HEIGHT: 3'–5'
GROWTH RATE: medium
LIGHT: full sun
MOISTURE: versatile

SEE ALSO:
Allium tuberosum, Chinese Chives, Flowers 20
Asters, Flowers 14
Chrysanthemum, Flowers 14
Clematis, Vines 1
Coreopsis, Tickseed, Herbs 2
Dahlia × *hybrida*, Flowers 17
Fuchsia × *hybrida*, Flowers 18
Gladiolus, Corn Flag, Sword Lily, Flowers 2
Lantana montevidensis, Weeping Lantana, Trailing Lantana, Flowers 18
Lavandula, Lavender, Herbs 6
Liatris, Gay-feather, Flowers 14
Lobelia cardinalis, Cardinal Flower, Flowers 13
Lobularia maritima, Sweet Alyssum, Flowers 20
Monarda didyma, Bee Balm, Herbs 5
Nicotiana alata, Flowering Tobacco, Flowers 17
Paeonia, Peony, Flowers 16
Papaver, Poppy, Flowers 12
Passiflora spp., Passionflower, Vines 1
Phlox paniculata, Flowers 12
Portulaca grandiflora, Rose Moss, Flowers 17
Reseda odorata, Mignonette, Flowers 20
Rosmarinus officinalis, Rosemary, Herbs 9
Salvia elegans, Pineapple Sage, Flowers 14
Sedum spectabile, Stonecrop, Flowers 13
Viola odorata, Herbs 4
Zinnia elegans, Flowers 17

ALTERNATES:
Aconitum, Aconite, Monkshood
Anemone, Windflower
Aquilegia, Columbine
Arabis caucasica, Wall Rock Cress

Verbascum hybrid. (Thomson)

Browallia speciosa 'Major', Sapphire Flower
Helleborus orientalis, Lenten Rose
Hepatica, Liverleaf
Iberis sempervirens, Evergreen Candytuft
Malva, Mallow
Primula, Primrose
Ranunculus, Buttercup
Verbena, Vervain

FLOWERS 20
FRAGRANT FLOWERS

There are fragrant flowers in many sections of this book—including roses, daffodils, lilies, and tulips. The handful of flowering plants here are all loved for their perfume.

COMPANION PLANTINGS
Galium odoratum, Woodruff, Sweet Woodruff; *Hosta plantaginea* 'Grandiflora', Fragrant Hosta; *Lavandula angustifolia*, English Lavender; *Santolina chamaecyparissus*, Lavender Cotton. Many herbs also make good companions.

ALLIUM *al-lee-um* Ornamental Onion

Ornamental onions produce strikingly handsome flowers from tufts of dark green foliage. A few are very fragrant. The most distinctive species top slender stems with perfectly round heads of flowers. Plant bulbs in late fall or early spring in well-drained soil; fertilize generously during growth. Attractive to butterflies. Don't plant in a windswept border.

GROWTH RATE:	fast
LIGHT:	full sun
MOISTURE:	soil surface damp

A. giganteum Giant Onion   Zones 5–8.
Big, round, lilac-blue, 4-inch flower heads on stalks 4 feet tall. Striking accent for the back of the summer border. Larger yet is the Persian Onion, *A. christophii*, with 8- to 10-inch flower heads.

A. moly Lily Leek   Zones 3–8.
About 1 foot tall, with gray green leaves and loose heads of yellow flowers in mid-spring. Used as an edger, nice massed. Good companion to *Veronica latifolia*, 'Crater Lake Blue'. Thrives in light shade.

A. neapolitanum Daffodil Garlic,
Flowering Onion   Zones 7–9.
Beautiful flowering onion 12 to 14 inches high that bears fragrant, starry white blooms in spring. Plant in border or containers in spring for bloom that same season. In containers, use a commercial planting mix; withhold water in late fall, and store in a cool room indoors for the winter. Begin watering again as temperatures warm and day length increases. Good cut flowers.

A. rosenbacnianum Rosenbach Onion
    Zone 5.
Elegant round heads in a strong purplish violet, bloom for 4 to 6 weeks in midsummer. Reach a height of 2 to 3 feet. One of the best for drying.

A. sphaerocephalum Round-headed Garlic,
Drumsticks   Zone 5.
Foliage is pungent, like wild garlic, but the small, perfectly round reddish lavender heads are useful contrast in the midsummer border. Combines well with Aurelian Lilies like 'First Love'. To 2 feet tall.

Cheiranthus cheiri, Wallflower. (McDonald)

A. tuberosum Chinese Chives, Garlic Chives
    Zone 4.
Ornamental, 18 inches tall, in spreading clusters. In late summer, bears fragrant white flowers with a green midriff. Attractive to bees and excellent in dried arrangements.

CHEIRANTHUS *kye-ranth-us*
cheiri Wallflower

In early spring, bears sweetly fragrant flower heads similar to stock in every shade of yellow and orange, ranging to mahogany-red. Needs a cool, moist climate to last as a perennial. Plant seeds in summer for bloom the following spring. Treated as an annual where summers are hot.

MATURE HEIGHT:	1′–1½′
GROWTH RATE:	medium
LIGHT:	semi-sunny
MOISTURE:	soil surface damp

DIANTHUS *dye-an-thus*

Very fragrant genus, including superb low-growing edgers and ground covers like 'Tiny Rubies' (see Ground Covers 6) and the big florist's carnation. Gray green foliage is evergreen in warm climates. Old-fashioned species are most fragrant, but there are some fragrant newer cultivars, too. Plant root divisions in early fall or spring in well-drained, sandy, humusy soil in the neutral range. Withstands high heat.

GROWTH RATE:	medium
LIGHT:	full sun
MOISTURE:	roots moist, versatile

Allium species, Ornamental Onion. (Thomson)

D. × *allwoodii* Allwood Pink Zones 3–8.
About 8 to 15 inches high, with fluffy little carnations 2 to 2½ inches across, in blends of pink, red, and white, very fragrant. Blooms in early summer; remove spent flowers to encourage rebloom. Tolerates heat and drought.

D. barbatus Sweet William Zones 3–9.
Taller and less fragrant, provides strong color accents in late spring and early summer. Plants are 1 to 1½ feet high. Colors range through white, pink, rose, red-violet, and scarlet, with blends. Good cutting flowers. Perennial treated as a biennial.

D. caryophyllus Carnation, Clove Pink
Zones 8–9.
Florist's carnation, large-headed, and very fragrant, on plants 1 to 3 feet high. Demanding to grow, but rewarding. Must be staked. Local greenhouses may have hardy varieties. 'Golden Sun' is outstanding.

D. chinensis Rainbow Pink
Very fragrant, with 1-inch-wide flowers in white, red, or lilac, in loose clusters on plants 6 to 12 inches high. 'Heddewigii' blooms early from seed. Tender perennial grown as an annual. Start seeds in early spring indoors, transplant later in spring.

D. plumarius Cottage Pink, Grass Pink
Zones 3–9.
Beautiful gray green foliage, and 2 or 3 charming 1½-inch single or double flowers per stem in spring and early summer. Shades of salmon, rose, white, red. Fragrant.

Dianthus barbatus, Sweet William. (McDonald)

LOBULARIA *lob-yew-***lay***-ree-uh maritima* Sweet Alyssum

Sweet-scented flower for summer and early fall; low-growing mounds covered with tiny white or lavender florets. Good as an edger and in rock gardens and window boxes. Shear spent blooms to keep flowers coming. Tender perennial grown as an annual. Sow seeds as soon as soil has warmed, where plants are to bloom, and be patient. Self-sows. Thrives near the sea. Requires soil in the neutral range.

MATURE HEIGHT: 9"–12"
GROWTH RATE: fast
LIGHT: full sun
MOISTURE: versatile

Lobularia maritima, Sweet Alyssum. (McDonald)

POLIANTHES *pol-ee-anth-eez*
tuberosa   Tuberose   Zone 9.

Tender, tuberous-rooted perennial with loose flower spikes to 4 feet tall, from July into early fall. Flowers are white, bell-shaped, long-lasting, and extraordinarily fragrant at night from July into early fall. Double-flowered forms are preferred. Plant in groups of 6 at the back of the border or in large containers. Set tubers 3 inches deep in rich, well-drained soil with plenty of moisture. Plant in early summer or late spring in 4 weekly batches, for a succession of blossoms into early autumn. May be hardy with lots of winter protection farther north. The smaller *P. geminiflora*, Florida's Twin Flower, has a red bloom but is not noted for its fragrance.

MATURE HEIGHT: 4'
GROWTH RATE: slow
LIGHT: full sun, semi sunny
MOISTURE: roots moist

RESEDA *res-seed-uh*
odorata   Mignonette   Annual.

Low-growing annual, attractive to butterflies and very fragrant. It has long-lasting, heavy spikes of tiny greenish yellow flowers. Hybrids are less fragrant than the species. Sow seeds in early spring in rich, alkaline soil where the plants are to bloom, and thin to 8 inches apart. Sow again in late spring to prolong the season.

MATURE HEIGHT: 6"
GROWTH RATE: medium
LIGHT: semi-sunny
MOISTURE: soil surface damp

VALERIANA *vall-eer-ee-ay-nuh*
officinalis   Valerian, Garden Heliotrope
                                  Zone 3.

Stately, profuse bloomer with ferny foliage and flat, dense clusters of tiny florets, creamy white with

Reseda odorata, Mignonette. (McDonald)

strong, sweet scent of heliotrope. Blooms late spring through summer. The roots are used in making perfume. Sow seed in early spring or plant root divisions in well-drained soil. Self-sows and can be invasive.

MATURE HEIGHT: 2'–4'
GROWTH RATE: fast
LIGHT: full sun
MOISTURE: soil surface damp

SEE ALSO:
Acidanthera bicolor var. *murieliae*, Peacock Orchid, Flowers 2
Freesia × *hybrida*, Flowers 18
Lilium candidum, Madonna Lily, Herbs 5
Nicotiana alata, Flowering Tobacco, Flowers 17
Verbena platensis, Vervain Ground Covers 5

Polianthes tuberosa, Tuberose. (McDonald)

Small ornamental pool edged with flowering annuals and perennials. (Lilypons Water Gardens)

AQUATIC PLANTS

AQUATIC PLANTS

The U.S. National Arboretum Aquatic Garden surrounding the administration building is bigger and deeper than the average home reflecting pool, but it is composed of the same elements. Spires of water spill gently among the lilies, aerating the sinuous windings of the fish—multi-hued gold, silver, and orange Koi. Sculptural stands of bog plants unfold with the passing seasons. The water is so clear and dark it reflects the sky.

Water lilies, lotuses, and the lovely bog foliage plants are a water garden's ornaments. The other elements, in balanced quantities, are required to keep a pool or pond from losing its sparkle to algae and muddy accumulations. The Koi, along with submerged plants (oxygenating grasses), snails, water plants, and several man-made elements, work together to create and maintain the wholesome ecological balance represented by clear water.

POOL ECOLOGY

The following formula is given by the National Arboretum as a general guideline for a well-balanced pool:

For each square yard of pool surface
4 to 9 bunches of submerged plants
12 snails
2 fish 6 inches long
1 medium-size water lily

This combination will bring balance to a turgid pool in 4 to 8 weeks and will maintain the pool's clarity. Once balance is achieved, the pool should stay healthy for many years. The brief attacks of algae in spring last only until the seasonal growth of the ornamentals gets under way.

Algicides can be used to improve the look of a pool, but they do not change the basic conditions that encourage algae. The effect of algicides is temporary, and their use has to be continued to maintain clear water. Potassium permanganate is successful when used correctly, but available only by prescription. Copper sulfate also is successful but is not recommended because it can overdose and kill fish and pond plants. Neither is recommended for use by nonprofessionals. Algicides gardeners can safely use for both plants and fish are sold by aquatic nurseries.

The secret to the velvety black, reflective surface of the aquatic gardens at the National Arboretum is a black vegetable dye. It doesn't harm fish or plants and is generally available.

Among available "oxygenating grasses," now more correctly called submerged plants, are *Cabomba caroliniana*, Washington Grass; *Elodea canadensis* var. *gigantea*, Waterweed; *Myriophyllum*; and *Vallisneria americana*, Wild Celery or Water Celery. When submerged, these grasses compete with algae for dissolved nutrients, trap debris in their foliage, and provide spawning media for fish. Plant them in the soil in the bottom of the pool, or in containers 6 or more inches under the water surface. Several bunches may be planted together in a container: 6 bunches per 5-quart pail or 12 bunches per 10-quart pan. Submerged plants should be planted at the rate of 1 to 2 bunches per square foot of surface area. Do not fertilize. Bury the stems 1 to 2 inches deep.

Snails are the pool's housekeepers. They feed primarily on dead plant material and algae covering water surfaces. *Viviparis malleatus,* Japanese snails, are the most beneficial. They are available from aquatic nurseries.

Fish help control insect and mosquito larvae, and they produce carbon dioxide and nutrients needed by the plants. Several varieties of goldfish, including Shubunkins (*Carassius auratus*), comets, and Japanese fantails, survive year-round in outdoor pools, as do the big, handsome Koi (*Cyprinus carpio*) from Japan. In regions where pond surfaces may be frozen solid for long periods, it is necessary to keep the ice open to allow the escape of gases harmful to the fish. Aquatic

Nymphaea 'Texas Shell Pink', fragrant night-blooming water lily. (L. Thomas III)

nurseries sell small de-icing units that will maintain a frost-free area.

Water lilies and other ornamentals also help to maintain a pool's ecological balance. They provide shade for the fish and block out sunlight that encourages algae. For small backyard pools, it is recommended that 50 to 75 percent of the water surface be covered with plant material. In large landscapes and parks, coverage of a third of the pool is enough.

When giving sizes of water plants, nurseries generally indicate the footage ornamentals will cover with foliage and flowers. Large growers are plants covering 10 to 12 square feet. Plants covering 5 to 10 square feet are called medium growers. Small growers cover 4 to 6 square feet or less.

CULTURE

The ideal location for a water garden is in full sun for a minimum of 3 hours daily. As a rule, aquatic plants do not perform well in shade. Those that succeed in partial shade will do better in full sun.

Water garden plants grow in soil, under the water. Water lilies and lotuses usually are rooted in containers placed at depths that put their tops 8 to 18 inches under the surface. The hardy bog plants are set into soil, or containers filled with soil, so the tops of their rootstocks are up to 12 inches under the surface of the water, depending on the plant. Backyard ornamental pools usually are 15 inches to 3 feet deep. In deeper pools, blocks and bricks are used to bring containers to the desired depth.

Containers must be at least 4 inches deep, even for the smallest plants. Containers for frost-hardy perennial and frost-tender perennial water lilies should hold a minimum of 10 quarts of soil for each plant; for dwarf lotuses, 10 to 15 quarts; for regular-size lotus, 20 to 30 quarts. Most aquatic plants are not deep-rooting; the surface area of the pool (as described above), rather than room for root development, is the limiting factor in plant selection.

A rich, heavy garden soil is necessary to nourish the foliage and flowers produced annually by an aquatic plant. Lilies and lotuses are fertilized by the monthly addition of nutrient pellets. Fertilize the vigorous bog plants at half the rate for water lilies. Unimproved soil in the average backyard is suitable for aquatics, as is heavy, fibrous loam. Do not add peat, vermiculite, or sand to the soil. Do not add manures of any sort. Commercial potting mixtures contain additives and are not suitable for aquatic culture. Hold the planting medium in place with egg-sized rocks.

Water plants are tolerant of soils with a pH of 6.0 to 8.0. Optimum pH, according to research by the staff at Lilypons Water Gardens, is 6.5 to 7.5.

HARDINESS IN REGIONS WHERE THERE IS FROST

Perennial, or hardy, water plants winter-over in the pool successfully as long as the roots do not freeze—which they won't if they winter below the freeze line for water. In pools 15 to 24 inches deep with an average annual minimum temperature of 0° F, even hardy perennials must be lifted. In pools 3 to 4 feet deep, lilies can be kept in the filled pool: their containers may be lowered for the winter to depths where the pool water doesn't freeze.

More information about wintering procedures is given with the plant lists that follow.

There are water gardens in small home landscapes in all 50 states, even in areas where summers are short—southern Canada, Minnesota, the Great Lakes region, New Hampshire, and Vermont. Colorado has active water garden societies. There are even a few water gardens in Alaska. The majority of the continent's water gardens, however, are in the mid-Atlantic and southern states, including New York, Florida, and Texas. On the West Coast, water gardens range from Vancouver Island southward to Baja California and east to Texas.

Plantings in these cooler regions focus on frost-hardy perennials, the water lilies, and bog plants which can be brought to maturity early enough in summer to make the water garden worthwhile. But gardeners in Denver successfully grow frost-tender perennial lilies: they are planted in June and reach full bloom in August.

Water lilies and lotuses fill aquatic gardens with handsome pads and exquisite flowers. The frost-hardy perennial water lilies and lotuses bloom during the three summer months—June, July, and August—in most of the country. Many are fragrant, and the fragrance is unusual. Many last well as cut flowers if they are picked on the first day of opening.

COMPANION PLANTINGS FOR
SURROUNDING GROUNDS
Ground covers: *Chrysogonum virginianum*, Golden Star; *Juniperus horizontalis*, Creeping Juniper; *Zanthorhiza simplicissima*, Yellowroot.
Perennials: *Astilbe × arendsii* cvs., Spiraea; *Coreopsis verticillata* 'Golden Showers', Tickseed, Threadleaf Tickseed; *Platycodon grandiflorus* var. *mariesii*, Dwarf Balloon Flower.
Annuals: *Ageratum houstonianum*, Flossflower; *Begonia semperflorens-cultorum* Hybrids, Bedding Begonia or Wax Begonia; *Petunia × hybrida*, Hybrid Petunia.
Submerged plants: *Cabomba caroliniana*, Washington Grass; *Elodea canadensis* var. *gigantea*, Waterweed; *Myriophyllum*; *Vallisneria americana*, Wild Celery or Water Celery.

NYMPHAEA *nim-fee-uh*   Water Lily
Zones 3–10.

The water lilies described here are frost-hardy perennials. Frost-tender water lilies, which are grown as annuals, are described in Aquatics 2. The two types are similar but not related closely enough to cross-breed. The frost-hardy water lilies open in April in Texas and continue until November; in Maryland they begin blooming in late May and continue until early September.

The hardy lilies have smooth-edged leaves called "pads," which float on the water surface. In a crowded pool, the pads will stand above the surface.

The flowers range in size from as small as a pocket watch to twice as big as a hand. White, pink, red, and yellow are the colors. Characteristically, they have yellow centers. The unusual "changeables" open yellow and shade toward red as they mature. The juvenile leaves of some red and yellow lilies (including changeables) are handsomely mottled or flecked.

The flower of the hardy perennial water lily grows from a thick rootstock, or crown, resembling an iris rhizome. It is planted in soil under the water, usually in a container. Each crown sends roundish leaves to the surface, and, one or more at a time, flower buds float or rise above the water and bloom for three to four days. They are open from mid-morning to mid-afternoon.

Nurseries ship water lilies already growing, at the right time for planting in your area. Most supply good planting instructions with their shipments. See the introduction to Aquatic Plants for general information on containers, soil, and growing aquatics.

Pool water must be warm enough to work in comfortably, about 55–60° F, before the lilies are set

Nymphaea 'James Brydon'. (L. Thomas III)

out. The container tops should be 8 to 18 inches under the surface. If the pool is too deep for this, put blocks under the containers to bring them to the right height. A few water lilies described here succeed when planted 3 feet deep; these are the hardiest lilies. The plants require about 2 weeks to adjust after planting, then they begin to produce new foliage, followed by buds.

The rhizomes of the perennial lilies can stay in the pool all winter, but must not freeze. Their hardiness is determined not by air temperatures but by water

Nymphaea 'Attraction', frost-hardy perennial water lily. (Lilypons Water Gardens)

temperatures. In areas where pool water freezes to the level of the soil containers, in the fall lower the containers to below the winter freeze line. If the pool isn't deep enough, lift the containers and store them in a cool but not freezing area—a heated garage or cool cellar, for instance. Cover containers with damp cloth or newspapers and a plastic trash bag to keep in moisture. The rhizomes must not dry out.

In spring, when danger of frost is past, return the containers to their previous positions in the pool. The lilies will begin to bloom when daytime air temperatures are steady in the 70s or above.

Water lilies are fast and vigorous growers. During the growing season, the monthly addition of a fertilizer pellet to the soil of each lily can increase the number of blooms. They need full sun and rich soil, and multiply without help in a fertile environment.

RED WATER LILIES
N. 'Attraction', medium-large, is a classic deep red lily that blooms freely in water up to 3 feet deep, even in the South. It is slightly fragrant, prefers full but tolerates partial sun.
N. 'Escarboucle', medium-large, has brilliant deep red flowers and somewhat pointed petals. It is fragrant. Prefers full sun.
N. 'James Brydon', medium. The fragrant, red, double, cup-shaped flowers are borne in profusion on a plant grown in a tub garden or a large pool. Full or partial sun.

PINK WATER LILIES
N. 'Fabiola', small-medium, is an excellent bloomer that produces slightly fragrant, shell pink flowers with gold centers, several at a time over a long season. Good for beginners.
N. 'Pink Sensation', medium, has large, fragrant, light pink flowers that remain open into the afternoon. Full sun.

N. 'Hollandia', medium-large, bears a profusion of slightly fragrant, large double flowers. Good for cutting. Full sun.

YELLOW WATER LILIES

N. 'Chromatella', small-medium, yellow, suited to tubs and small pools. Full or partial sun.

N. 'Comanche', medium, is one of the "changeables." The slightly fragrant flowers open nearly yellow, then shade to rose-apricot, then to coppery bronze as they mature. The mature leaves are handsomely speckled. Good cut flower. Full or partial sun.

N. 'Sioux', medium, "changeable" with more pointed petals and more russet color than 'Comanche'. Full or partial sun.

N. 'Sunrise', medium-large, slightly fragrant, produces large yellow flowers that are borne over a long season. Flowers remain open later in the afternoon than those of other frost-hardy varieties.

WHITE WATER LILIES

N. 'Virginalis', medium-large, excellent bloomer, slightly fragrant, is one of the largest whites. Grows in water to 3 feet deep and has a long bloom season. Full sun.

N. 'Gladstone', medium-large, slightly fragrant, is pure white with a yellow center. This is a robust plant that can be grown in water to 3 feet deep. Needs full sun.

ALTERNATES:

Nymphaea 'Charlene Strawn', yellow
N. 'Masaniello', pink
N. 'Splendida', red
N. 'Marliac Carnea', light pink
N. 'William Falconer', red

AQUATICS 2
FROST-TENDER PERENNIAL WATER LILIES

The frost-tender perennial water lilies bloom more profusely, have bigger flowers, and offer a broader range of colors than the frost-hardy. They are excellent cut flowers and very fragrant. In areas where there are frosts, they are grown as tender perennials or annuals.

COMPANION PLANTINGS FOR
SURROUNDING GROUNDS

Shrubs: *Cotoneaster dammeri*, Bearberry Cotoneaster; *Forsythia × intermedia* 'Arnold Dwarf'; *Spiraea japonica* 'Alpina', Dwarf Japanese Spiraea.
Ground covers, perennials: *Deutzia gracilis* 'Nikko', Slender Deutzia; *Iberis sempervirens*, Evergreen Candytuft.
Annuals: *Ageratum houstonianum*, Flossflower; *Lantana ovatifolia* var. *reclinata*, Dwarf Lantana; *Lobularia maritima*, Sweet Alyssum.
Submerged plants: *Cabomba caroliniana*, Washington Grass; *Elodea canadensis* var. *gigantea*, Waterweed; *Myriophyllum*; *Vallisneria americana*, Wild Celery or Water Celery.

Nymphaea 'Comanche'. (Lilypons Water Gardens)

Nymphaea 'Virginalis'. (Williams)

NYMPHAEA *nim-fee-uh*   Water Lily

Tropical water lilies do everything on a bigger scale than the perennials in Aquatics 1. The foliage requires half again to twice as much pool space. They have more blooms, more fragrance, more petals, and thrive on heat. The foliage may be smooth, toothed and crimped, or fluted at the edge. The flowers stand well above the water on long stems, and are good for cutting.

One group blooms during the day. The flowers have a heady, sweet fragrance. Another group blooms only at night: their scent is sharper.

The colors range from rich magenta-red to pink and white, yellow, rosy yellow, violet, deep purple, and periwinkle blue. Tender perennials have time to come into bloom in Zones 3 to 10. In Texas they begin to bloom in late May; in Maryland they begin to bloom in June. They continue flowering until severe frost. They can winter over in the water garden only in frost-free areas. Elsewhere they are grown as annuals.

Tropicals are shipped by nurseries as growing plants. They are timed to arrive when water temperatures in the area have reached a constant 70° F. Plant them at once. See the introduction to Aquatic

Nymphaea 'Yellow Dazzler'. (L. Thomas III)

Plants for general information on containers, soil, and culture for aquatics. In about 2 weeks the plants will start growing again, and will begin to bloom in 2 to 4 weeks, depending on weather.

The solid black tuber of the frost-tender day-blooming lily is the size of a horse chestnut. Night-blooming tubers are twice as large. Wait a week or two after a killing fall frost before you begin to lift the tubers for winter storage. Wash the tubers carefully and store them at 55° F for the winter, in a sealed jar of damp sand. If water accumulates in the bottom of the jar, you have too much water. Keep the sand moist but not soggy. Replant the tubers in spring when the water temperature reaches a constant 70° F, nights as well as days. The lilies will come into bloom 2 to 3 months later.

To get earlier flowering, start the tubers in containers indoors in March in a tubful of water—an improvised pool. Return the containers to the outdoor pool when temperatures are holding at 70° F.

Frost-tender water lilies need full sun and rich soil, and multiply without help in a fertile environment.

Nymphaea 'Red Flare', a night-blooming tender water lily. (L. Thomas III)

Nymphaea 'Marian Strawn'. (Williams)

DAY BLOOMERS—FRAGRANT

N. 'General Pershing', medium-large with mottled foliage, has large pink blooms that open early in the morning and close at dusk. Blooms well until late in the season. Prefers full sun, but succeeds in partial sun.

N. 'Yellow Dazzler', medium-large with speckled foliage. The flowers are a strong yellow and remain open until almost dusk. Prefers full sun.

N. 'Marian Strawn', small-medium, has foliage that is flecked with black, and large, stately white blooms held well above the water surface. Prefers full sun, but succeeds in partial sun.

N. 'Blue Beauty', medium-large with speckled foliage, spectacular blue flowers, and an excellent blooming habit. Full sun.

N. 'Panama Pacific', small to large according to the space given it, with speckled foliage and blue-purple flowers. It is suited to all water gardens, from large ponds to small tubs. This is a viviparous water lily: it bears offspring, complete with foliage and buds, from an umbilicus in the center of mature leaves. Prefers full sun, but succeeds in partial sun.

NIGHT BLOOMERS—VERY FRAGRANT

N. 'Red Flare', medium-large with maroon foliage. The spectacular flowers have dark red petals and deep maroon stamens. Prefers full sun.

N. 'Texas Shell Pink', medium-large with green foliage and a profusion of frosty pink flowers. Prefers full sun, but succeeds in partial sun.

N. 'Emily Grant Hutchings', medium-large with bronzy foliage, and glowing frosty pink flowers. A superb bloomer that often produces flowers in clusters. Prefers full sun, but succeeds in partial sun.

ALTERNATES:
Nymphaea 'Aviator Pring', day bloomer
N. 'Leopardess', day bloomer
N. 'H. C. Haarstick', night bloomer

Nymphaea 'Emily Grant Hutchings'. (Williams)

AQUATICS 3
LOTUSES

Lotuses are perhaps the most spectacular plants growing in the National Arboretum Aquatic Garden. First cousins of the water lily, they require more space and effort to bring into bloom than water lilies.

COMPANION PLANTINGS
Water lilies and bog plants: *Marsilea mutica,* Australian Water Clover; *Nymphaea* 'Blue Beauty', Water Lily: *N.* 'Chromatella', Water Lily; *Thalia dealbata,* Water Canna; *Typha angustifolia,* Narrow-leaved Cattail.
Submerged plants: *Cabomba caroliniana,* Washington Grass; *Elodea canadensis* var. *gigantea,* Waterweed; *Myriophyllum*; *Vallisneria americana,* Wild Celery or Water Celery.

NELUMBO *nee-lum-boh*
nucifera   Sacred Lotus, East Indian Lotus
Zones 5–9.

Sacred to the ancient Hindi, revered by the Assyrians, Persians, and early Egyptians, the lotus is sometimes described as a big perennial water lily. The flowers have similarities, but the plants have distinct differences.

The big, showy, water-lily-like bloom may be 8 to 12 inches in diameter. It opens and closes over a period of 3 days. On the third day, the petals begin to fall away. Some lotuses are powerfully fragrant, and the fragrance has a hint of anise. They stand 2 to 5 feet above the water, and blooms range through shades of white, pink, and red. There are also yellows and creams. The flower is followed by a unique seedpod that looks like the spout of a watering can, and is striking in dried arrangements. Rhizomes and seeds are food crops in the East.

Lotus leaves are as extraordinary as the flowers. Between 2 and 3 weeks after planting, the lotus will put up leaves that float on the water. The next leaves stand high above the water and are shaped like wide, open, very shallow bowls. The leaves of miniature lotuses are 6 to 16 inches across; those of regular lotuses can be 3 feet wide and 6 feet above the water line. A thin layer of wax covering the leaf surface causes drops of water to roll around on it and sparkle in the sunlight.

The lotus grows from a large, banana-shaped tuber, 8 to 18 inches long. Plant the tuber in rich, porous soil in a container about 16 to 20 inches in diameter and 9 to 10 inches deep. The rootstock can grow to 10 or 15 feet in a season unless restricted by its container, and the resulting plant covers more surface than a small pool can afford. Set the tuber 2 inches beneath the soil with ½ inch of its growing tip showing above the soil. Weight the tuber with a flat rock to prevent it from floating, but don't cover the growing tip. Fill the container with pool water, and place it in the pool at a depth that puts 2 to 4 inches of water over the top of the growing tip. As the stem grows, move the container deeper. Established plants have 6 to 12 inches of water overhead. In deeper pools, set containers on blocks that bring the growing tips to the desired height.

In ponds whose water never freezes to the bottom, lotuses may be planted directly in soil. They will develop in the direction of deeper water as frost approaches, and can bloom from a depth of 3 to 4 feet. Where the water garden freezes to the bottom, handle lotuses as frost-hardy water lilies (Aquatics 1).

See the introduction to Aquatic Plants for general information on containers, soil, and culture for aquatic plants.

The lotus requires at least several weeks of sun with temperatures in the 80s to develop blooms. Order early and plant promptly. Every day of delay reduces the likelihood of blooming the first year. Planted by the 10th of May in climates similar to that

Nelumbo 'Mrs. Perry D. Slocum', Sacred Lotus. (Lilypons Water Gardens)

at the National Arboretum, lotuses will probably flower that year, but this is not guaranteed. Lotuses may be set out in water whose temperature is in the 40s or 50s.

Charles Thomas of Lilypons Water Gardens, one of the National Arboretum suppliers, recommends the following lotuses to new water gardeners with limited space.

N. nucifera 'Momo Botan Minima' is a pink dwarf double that shades to white, with leaves only 6 to 12 inches in diameter. It is excellent for smaller ponds and pools. Full sun.
N. 'Mrs. Perry D. Slocum', a changeable, is semidouble with very large flowers that start out pink, then turn creamy yellow. Leaves 20 inches in diameter.

ALTERNATE:
Nelumbo nucifera 'Alba Grandiflora', Sacred Lotus

AQUATICS 4
FROST-HARDY PERENNIAL BOG PLANTS

Water lilies and lotuses are the center of attention in an aquatic garden. The perennial bog plants here provide the setting, the contrast in form, foliage, and flower. Bog plants also are known as marginal plants, or plants for pool margins. They are planted with up to 12 inches of water overhead, either in the soil of the pond or in submerged containers. They can winter-over in water gardens in the zones stated for each species. See the introduction to Aquatic Plants for general information on culture of water plants.

COMPANION PLANTINGS FOR
SURROUNDING GROUNDS
Shrubs: *Juniperus horizontalis* 'Wiltonii', Blue Rug Creeping Juniper; *Mahonia aquifolium,* Oregon Grape.
Perennials: *Astilbe* × *arendsii* cvs., Spiraea; *Hemerocallis* 'Hyperion', Daylily; *Ligularia dentata* 'Desdemona'; *Lythrum salicaria* 'Morden's Pink', Purple Loosestrife; *Rudbeckia fulgida* var. *sullivantii* 'Goldsturm', Coneflower; *Sedum spectabile* 'Autumn Joy'.
Annuals: *Lobularia maritima,* Sweet Alyssum; *Petunia* × *hybrida,* Hybrid Petunia.
Submerged plants: *Cabomba caroliniana,* Washington Grass; *Elodea canadensis* var. *gigantea,* Waterweed; *Myriophyllum*; *Vallisneria americana,* Wild Celery or Water Celery.

ACORUS *ak-or-us*
calamus   'Variegatus'
Variegated Sweet Flag   Zones 4–10.

Upright, slender, lemon-scented irislike leaves, 2½ to 3 or 4 feet tall, with cream stripes and small, long-lasting greenish yellow flowers in short spikes, spring and summer. The rootstock, dried and ground, is used in confections and dry perfumes. Plant root divisions in early spring, up to 6 inches underwater in full or partial sun.

Acorus calamus, Sweet Flag. (Shimizu)

EQUISETUM *ek-wih-zee-tum*
hyemale Scouring Rush, Horsetail
Zones 3—9.

Upright, jointed, rushlike clumps of stems 3 to 4 feet tall, without leaves or flowers. Good contrast plant and bank holder. Evergreen in warm climates. May be poisonous to livestock. Prefers some shade, but tolerates full sun if growing in water and a cool climate. Plant divisions in spring or fall in wet soil, up to 6 inches underwater. Best grown in containers; the plant spreads rapidly.

IRIS *eye-riss*
pseudacorus Yellow Iris Zones 5—8.

Also known as Water Iris. Tall, 3 to 4 feet, with brown-veined, bright yellow flowers in late spring and early summer. Grows vigorously, developing stately clumps of 1-inch-wide leaves. Plant root divisions in full sun at water's edge or in containers up to 10 inches underwater in early spring or fall. Soil should be heavy, humusy, and slightly acid. Naturalized in the northeastern United States. There is also a variegated form and a beautiful double-flowered variety. Both grow to 24 inches when planted up to 4 inches underwater. Siberian and Japanese iris also thrive in wet soil (see Flowers 7).

MARSILEA *mar-sill-ee-uh*
mutica Australian Water Clover Zones 6—10.

An aquatic or marshy fern with floating four-part leaves that resemble clover. The leaves, to 3 inches across, are strikingly patterned and more decorative than the European Water Clover. Charming contrast to the big pads of the water lilies. Plant divisions in spring, 3 to 12 inches underwater in full or partial sun, or shade.

NYMPHOIDES *nim-foy-deez*
Floating-heart

Floating, heart-shaped leaves that bear little flowers in their axils. Spreads rapidly and is best grown in containers. Plant divisions in fall or spring, 3 or 4 to 12 inches underwater in full or partial sun.

N. cristatum Water Snowflake Zones 6—10. Also called White Snowflake. Floating leaves, with fragrant white flowers ¾ inch in diameter produced abundantly spring through fall.

N. geminata Yellow Snowflake Zones 6—10. Floating, chocolate brown leaves patterned with green veins, and bright yellow flowers from spring to fall.

N. peltata Yellow Floating-heart
Zones 6—10.
Floating green and maroon variegated leaves, 3 inches in diameter, and five-petaled yellow flowers held slightly above the water from spring to fall.

ORONTIUM *oh-ron-tee-um*
aquaticum Golden-club Zones 6—10.

Oval, floating or aerial, dark green leaves a foot or more long and 4 inches wide, topped by white spikes tipped with brilliant yellow florets in spring and early summer. Plant in early spring, up to 6 inches underwater in partial sun.

PONTEDERIA *pon-ted-deer-ee-uh*
cordata Pickerel Weed, Pickerel Rush
Zones 3—9.

Upright, to 30 inches or taller, each shoot having one long, oval to heart-shaped leaf. Forms handsome clumps and bears spikes of blue or pink flowers, sometimes with two yellow spots on the upper lip.

Iris pseudacorus, Yellow Iris. (McDonald)

Blooms spring to early fall. Good cut flowers. There is a white-flowered form. Plant up to 12 inches underwater in full or partial sun.

SAGITTARIA *saj-it-tay-ree-uh*

Among the best foliage aquatics, tuberous-rooted plants have arrow-shaped leaves and white flowers in summer. Plant divisions in late fall or early spring in full sun, up to 6 or 7 inches underwater.

S. lancifolia Arrowhead Zones 5—10. Upright, to 24 inches tall with 3-petaled white flowers.

S. sagittifolia 'Flore Pleno'
Double Oldworld Arrowhead. Zones 7—10. Similar, but tolerates up to 7 inches of water overhead and has attractive white double flowers.

SCIRPUS *sir-puss*
albescens White Bullrush Zones 5—10.

Upright, cylindrical leaves are 4 to 6 feet tall and nearly white. There are white flowers in summer. A good accent plant. Set out in boggy or wet soil, up to 6 inches underwater.

TYPHA *tye-fuh* Cattail

Reedy, upright swamp plants with long, narrow, stiff leaves borne on tall, unbranched stems. The characteristic velvety brown "cattail," several inches tall, tops slender stalks in summer and early fall. Good as tall accents, background plants, and for screening. Smaller when container-grown. Naturalizes quickly and is invasive when grown in the open ground. Plant root divisions in early fall or spring, up to 12 inches underwater in full or partial sun.

T. angustifolia Narrow-leaved Cattail
Zones 2—10.
To 6 feet tall. The leaves are narrow and the cattails light brown.

Pontederia cordata, Pickerelweed. (Lilypons Water Gardens)

Typha latifolia var. *variegata*, Variegated Cattail.

T. latifolia var. **variegata**   Variegated Cattail
Zones 5–10.
Dramatic variegated form grows to 5 feet tall. Plant
up to 6 inches underwater.

ALTERNATES:
Dulichium arundinaceum, Dwarf Bamboo
Iris kaempferi, Japanese Iris
Iris sibirica, Siberian Iris
Iris versicolor, Wild Iris, Blue Flag
Thalia dealbata, Water Canna

AQUATICS 5
TROPICAL BOG PLANTS

Some of the bog plants here are prized for their
foliage, others for their flowers. They are grown as
tender perennials and annuals as far north as Zone 3
and may winter successfully outdoors in warmer
zones, as noted below. Growers ship at planting time,
so set the plants out as soon as possible after they
arrive. If they are to be grown as annuals, plant in
containers; in fall, lift the containers and store for the
winter at 55° F, maintaining slight soil moisture. For
more information on the culture of aquatics, see the
introduction to Aquatic Plants.

COMPANION PLANTINGS FOR
SURROUNDING GROUNDS
Shrubs: *Pinus* dwarfs, Dwarf Pines; *Rosa*, Miniature
Roses.
Perennials: *Astilbe*, Spiraea; *Hosta*; *Ligularia dentata* 'Desdemona'; *Lysimachia punctata*, Yellow
Loosestrife; *Osmunda*; *Perovskia atriplicifolia*, Russian Sage; *Polystichum acrostichoides*, Christmas
Fern; *Rudbeckia fulgida* var. *sullivantii* 'Goldsturm',
Coneflower.
Annuals: *Lobularia maritima*, Sweet Alyssum; *Salvia
farinacea* 'Victoria', Mealycup Sage; *Tagetes patula*,
French Marigold.

Submerged plants: *Cabomba caroliniana*, Washington Grass; *Elodea canadensis* var. *gigantea*, Waterweed; *Myriophyllum*; *Vallisneria americana*, Wild
Celery or Water Celery.

CANNA *kan-nuh*
✕ *hybrida*   Water Canna   Zones 7–9.

Hybrid tropical canna adapted to water gardens.
They are handsome, bold, upright plants, to 4 feet
tall, with big red or yellow irislike flowers in summer.
Set out in containers in full sun in early spring, up to
6 inches underwater. These are tender perennials
hardy only in Zones 7 to 9: elsewhere, they are
grown as annuals, lifted in the fall, stored in containers for the winter, and replaced in the water in
the spring. Cultivars in the National Arboretum
Aquatic Garden include *C.* 'Endeavour', *C.* 'Erebus',
C. 'Ra', and *C.* 'Taney'.

COLOCASIA *kol-oh-**kay**-see-uh*
esculenta   Taro   Zones 9–10.

Also commonly called kalo and dasheen, the edible
tubers are made into poi, a starchy food of the tropics.
On this continent, taro is grown in water gardens for
its big, bold, heavily veined upright leaves; they grow
to 3½ feet tall. Plant tubers up to 12 inches underwater in full or partial sun.

CRINUM *krye-num*
americanum   Southern Swamp Crinum,
Bog Lily   Zones 8–10.

Plant has curved leaves 2 inches wide and up to 4 feet
long; in summer, a cluster of fragrant, narrow-petaled, beautiful white flowers with greenish
throats blooms on a 2-foot stalk. Grown primarily for
the flowers. Plant in spring, up to an inch underwater
in full sun. Tolerates partial sun.

CYPERUS *sye-**peer**-us*

Grown for the foliage: many narrow, grassy leaves
that radiate outward like the ribs of an exquisite

umbrella are borne on slender, upright stems. Green
inflorescence likely to interest only botanists. Plant
in spring, up to 6 inches underwater in full or partial
sun, or shade. In cooler regions, winter indoors as a
houseplant, keeping soil moist.

C. alternifolius   Umbrella Plant,
Umbrella Palm   Zones 9–10.

Upright to 5 feet tall, good for screening and accents
for the larger pond.

C. haspans   Dwarf Papyrus   Zones 9–10.

Attractive, airy clumps of foliage to 30 inches tall, for
smaller water gardens. Charming houseplant for indoor water garden.

HYDROCLEYS *hye-droh-klyss*
nymphoides   Water Poppy   Zones 9–10.

Small, decorative, floating, ovalish green leaves with
pretty, slightly raised, 3-petaled yellow flowers 2 to
2½ inches across in summer. Plant 4 to 12 inches
underwater in full or partial sun. In cool areas, winter
indoors in an aquarium placed in a sunny window.

HYMENOCALLIS *hye-men-ok-**kal**-liss*
liriosme   Spider Lily   Zones 8–10.

Upright plant to 2 feet tall, grown for the large,
narrow-petaled, very fragrant flowers in spring and
summer. Plant up to 6 inches underwater in full or
partial sun.

THALIA *thay-lee-uh*
geniculata   Red-stemmed Thalia
Zones 9–10.

In summer, small violet flower spikes are held airily
above large, bold leaves with red or purple stems to 5
feet tall. Grows in clumps, but isn't invasive. Plant in
spring, up to 6 inches underwater in full sunlight.

ALTERNATE:
Colocasia esculenta var. *fontanesii*, Violet-stemmed
Taro

Colocasia can be seen in the background of this water garden. (Lilypons Water Gardens)

Allium schoenoprasum, Chives, seedheads appear after flowers have gone. (McDonald)

HERBS

HERBS

The 2-acre National Herb Garden, founded in 1980, was a gift to the American people by the Herb Society of America. Its inviting paths and pungent plants evoke a time when the home garden was medicine chest as well as perfumery, spiritual center, supermarket, and social gathering place.

The Knot Garden is a modern interpretation with pruned plants and curving paths of intricate design fashionable in 16th-century England. The Historic Rose Garden is fragrant in season with wonderful old roses that parented the modern rose, America's national floral emblem. The herbs in the Dioscorides Garden have been used since first recorded by the famous Greek physician in A.D. 60. There are collections of dye herbs, early American and Indian herbs, medicinal and culinary herbs, industrial and fragrance herbs, Oriental herbs, and beverage herbs. In the center there are herbal trees and shrubs.

The lists that follow are recommended as the most useful and ornamental by Holly Shimizu, first curator of the National Herb Garden. Ms. Shimizu defines an herb as any plant with herbal use; roses, for instance, have long been a source of flavor as well as fragrance.

The Herb Society of America currently favors the silent H in pronouncing "herb."

GROWING HERBS

Trees and shrubs with herbal uses have the same cultural requirements as other woody plants. Some tender woody herbs, such as eucalyptus and gardenia, are grown in pots in cooler regions and wintered indoors. Not all succeed as houseplants, but some last several years if kept in a relatively cool room and misted often.

Most herbaceous herbs thrive anywhere sunny in well-drained soil with a pH of 6.5 to 7.0. The casual herb gardener tucks them in among perennials and food plants, in

Belamcanda ucchinensis, Blackberry Lily. (McDonald)

flower boxes or pots, or handy to the chef by the kitchen door. Many herbs require little fertilizing and can stand drought.

The gardener looking for a more formal presentation will find inspiration in the historic designs at the National Herb Garden.

The easy way to start perennial herbs is to set out container plants after the soil has dried and warmed in mid-spring. Soak the root ball briefly in water to which a soluble fertilizer has been added, pour a little of the water into the planting hole, and plant higher than the plant was growing in its container.

Annual and biennial herbs of the Umbillifer, or carrot, family are best grown from seed sown directly in the garden where they will grow, as they have a taproot and transplant badly. The flowers of these herbs resemble Queen-Anne's-lace. Dill is the best-known example.

Seeds that are slow germinators, such as parsley, thyme, sweet marjoram, and lemon balm, should be started indoors or bought as container plants. Some perennials and biennial seeds, such as catnip, borage, and caraway, can be planted in the fall and will overwinter and germinate the following spring. Woody plants and herbs that are slow germinators, for instance lavender, are best set out as container plants.

HARVESTING

Pick culinary herbs that will be used fresh just before they are needed. Rinse only if necessary. Choose tender sprig tips. Never strip a plant of all its foliage; it is needed to continue the growth process. In summer's high heat, especially in warm regions, herbs go into semi-dormancy; pick from the plants sparingly at this season as they are unable to replace missing foliage.

Aromatic herb foliage—parsley, oregano, lavender—is a delightful addition to fresh flower arrangements.

Pick flower heads of herbs as they appear to keep the plants from going to seed, which will slow foliage production. The flowers make pretty gourmet bouquets.

Pick fresh, fragrant leaves from herbal trees and shrubs as needed. Leaves that are naturally stiff and rather dry, like bay and lemon verbena, are readily preserved by drying the traditional way on screens (as described below for herbal seeds), or dry whole branch tips by hanging them upside down on a clothesline. Leaves and petals are used in potpourris, branches in dried arrangements.

Rose petals and fragrant, tender leaves for storing are picked in the early morning and dried on screens for as many days as needed to lose all moisture.

At season's end culinary herbs can be harvested and dried, or preserved in other ways. Parsley and parsleylike leaves (cilantro, for instance) keep well when finely chopped and frozen.

But most tender, moist leaves—basil, oregano, and

Petroselinum crispum, Parsley. (McDonald)

screens lined with paper towels for 5 days in an airy, dark, warm place. Thresh by rubbing the seedheads between your palms over a bowl. Gently blow away the chaff. Dry the seeds for another 10 days. Bottle in glass and cap tightly. If there's any sign of moisture in the next few days, oven-dry the seeds for 2 hours at 150° F. Label and date the jars. Herbs retain their color longer when stored away from light.

If you are growing herbs for winter arrangements, plant everlastings, especially sea lavender, as companion plants. The traditional way of preparing branches of herbs for dried arrangements is to tie loosely together cut branches 18 to 24 inches long, for tall arrangements, 8- to 12-inch stalks for tussie-mussies (small dried bouquets). Dry them hanging upside down from a clothesline in an airy, hot, dry place. Depending on flower and stem thickness, they become crisp in about 2 weeks. Store them in boxes lined with tissue paper. Or follow the manufacturer's manual instructions for drying flowers and herbs in a microwave oven.

tarragon for instance—darken when frozen. Rinse and dry small, fragrant leaves or short tip ends of these herbs, pack them into a large jar, and cover with good olive oil. Both leaves and oil are used in cooking, and the oil is good in salads.

Dill fern and other ferny herbs are snipped and dried like seeds.

Harvest leaves for preserving early in the morning, after they have dried from the night's dew, but before the sun reaches them and disperses the volatile fragrant oils.

To harvest the seeds of anise, dill, and fennel, allow the plants to bloom toward the end of summer. Harvest the seeds after the flowers show signs of yellowing or browning, and before the seeds are fully ripe and the seedheads dry. Once fully ripe, the seeds will disperse.

Before harvesting seeds, place a paper bag under the seedhead. Use a sharp knife or pruning shears to cut the seedheads and let them fall into the bag. Dry the heads on

HERBS 1
TREES AND SHRUBS FOR HERB GARDENS

These are some of the herbal trees and shrubs among the important foundation plants in the National Herb Garden at the Arboretum. Those not-hardy in the climate are grown in portable tubs and wintered indoors.

COMPANION PLANTINGS
Low foliage plants: *Artemisia absinthium* 'Lambrook Silver', Wormwood; *Mentha suaveolens* 'Variegata', Variegated Apple Mint; *Salvia farinacea* 'Victoria', Mealycup Sage, and *S. officinalis* 'Purpurea', Garden Sage.

LAURUS *law-rus*
nobilis   Grecian Laurel, Sweet Bay
Zones 7–9.

Wreaths of the evergreen laurel crowned the heroes of ancient Greece and Rome, and scented Victorian dry perfumes. The leaves are indispensable to the cuisines of many countries. Laurel is a handsome, columnar tree for gardens in mild climates and a superb pot plant for regions where it must winter indoors. It is shearable. At the Arboretum it is trained as standards and grown in terra-cotta pots set out in spring. Do not confuse it with the California Bay or Oregon Myrtle, *Umbellularia californica*. Prefers soil in the neutral range.

MATURE HEIGHT: 30'
GROWTH RATE: slow
LIGHT: full sun, semi-sunny
MOISTURE: roots moist

Laurus nobilis, Sweet Bay, in pot. (Shimizu)

Magnolia virginia, Sweet Bay. (McDonald)

MAGNOLIA *mag-no-lee-uh*
virginiana   Sweet Bay
Zones 5–9.

The flowering magnolia had herbal uses for the Indians. It is a magnificent tree whose white blooms fill the air with lemony fragrance for several weeks in spring. Evergreen in the South, it succeeds from Massachusetts to Florida. Prefers somewhat acid soil.

MATURE HEIGHT: 25'–60'
GROWTH RATE: medium
LIGHT: full sun
MOISTURE: soil surface damp

MESPILUS *mes-pill-us*
germanica   Medlar
Zone 5.

The medlar is a small tree related to the Hawthorn, and loved for its herbal history. It is mentioned in the Bible and was grown in medieval monasteries. Small pink flowers in mid-spring are followed by applelike, tiny fruit which, harvested after the first frost, have a pleasing acidity. The medlar responds well to pruning and shaping.

MATURE HEIGHT: 15'
GROWTH RATE: medium
LIGHT: full sun
MOISTURE: roots moist

MYRICA *mye-rik-uh*
pensylvanica   Bayberry
Zones 2–6.

Bayberry is a beautiful big shrub with gray green, semievergreen leaves that are aromatic when crushed. It flourishes in the coastal Northeast, and was a source of fragrance and dye for Indians and colonists. The small, wax-coated fruit still is used to scent candles. Bayberry can be trained as a small standard. Look for container-grown nursery plants: wildlings don't transplant well unless a sturdy root-ball can be provided. Requires acid-range soil.

MATURE HEIGHT: 9'
GROWTH RATE: fast
LIGHT: full sun, semi-sunny
MOISTURE: soil surface damp

PRUNUS *proo-nus*
mume   Japanese Apricot
Zones 6–9.

Very fragrant pink or white flowers bloom on this lovely little tree in February, even in snowstorms. In Japan, it is a symbol of endurance. Efforts to breed this quality into other flowering trees are underway at the National Arboretum. There are white and pink double-flowered cultivars. In Japan, the 1-inch apricot- or plumlike fruits are made into Mume liqueur, and pickles, eaten with herbs and salt.

MATURE HEIGHT: 30'
GROWTH RATE: fast
LIGHT: full sun
MOISTURE: roots moist

Vaccinium corymbosom, Highbush Blueberry. (McDonald)

Vitex agnus-castus, Chaste Tree. (McDonald)

SASSAFRAS *sass-a-fras*
albidum   Sassafras   Zones 4–8.

Distillations of the roots and bark were credited with medicinal properties by colonists and Indians and still retain that reputation in the South. The leaves are fragrant when crushed. A handsome container tree, but hard to transplant, sassafras is not carried by many nurseries. The red-orange fall foliage is so desirable that sassafras is an ongoing subject of research pertaining to transplanting. Prefers somewhat acid soil.

MATURE HEIGHT: 50'
GROWTH RATE: medium
LIGHT: full sun, semi-sunny
MOISTURE: soil surface damp

VACCINIUM *vak-sin-ee-um*   Blueberry

The blueberry species are distributed all over North America. They are twiggy shrubs with small, pale pink flowers in spring followed by blueberries, whose size depends on species, variety, and growing conditions. They are planted in gardens for their brilliant fall foliage and for fruit. In spring, plant containerized shrubs in well-drained, acid soil rich in humus. The Indians used dried blueberries as a food and condiment. Birds love the berries.

GROWTH RATE: medium
LIGHT: full sun, semi-sunny
MOISTURE: soil surface damp

V. angustifolium   Lowbush Blueberry
                                      Zones 2–7.
This is the 8-inch-high, mat-forming blueberry that grows wild on sandy and rocky slopes all over the northeastern United States and southeastern Canada. The fruit is smaller than the highbush species, but the foliage is just as brilliantly colored in the fall. Excellent ground cover.

V. corymbosum   Highbush Blueberry
                                      Zones 3–7.
This is the large-fruited blueberry most often found in commerce. U.S.D.A. research has resulted in many large-fruited varieties that bear very early, early, midseason, late, and very late. State agriculture extension services can recommend the varieties that grow best locally. Plants reach 6 to 12 feet high at maturity. The species shrubs in the Indian Garden at the National Arboretum are prized for their 2-month fruiting season and brilliant autumn foliage.

VITEX *vy-tex*
agnus-castus   Chaste Tree   Zones 6–7.

This small tree with aromatic silvery leaves produces extremely fragrant blue flowers in midsummer when little else blooms. Lovely for dried arrangements and in potpourris. The Romans used the dried, ground fruit as a substitute for black pepper. They also believed a branch kept under a wife's pillow ensured chastity in her husband's absence. Prefers neutral-range soil.

MATURE HEIGHT: 9'
GROWTH RATE: fast
LIGHT: full sun
MOISTURE: roots moist

ZIZYPHUS *zy-ziff-us*
jujuba   Jujube, Chinese Date   Zones 9–10.

A small tree with glossy green leaves, *Zizyphus* is grown for its datelike fruit and the white flowers which bloom in late spring and smell like grape soda. They are even more fragrant dried. It flourishes in hot, dry regions, and is self-fertile. Prefers neutral-range soil.

MATURE HEIGHT: 30'
GROWTH RATE: fast
LIGHT: full sun
MOISTURE: roots moist

SEE ALSO:
Aloysia triphylla, Lemon Verbena, Herbs 5
Crataegus phaenopyrum, Washington Thorn, Trees 12
Lavandula angustifolia 'Hidcote', English Lavender, Herbs 6
Rosa, Old Garden Roses, Herbs 7

ALTERNATES:
Actinidia arguta, Bower Actinidia, Tara Vine
Aristolochia serpentaria, Virginia Snakeroot
Cephalanthus occidentalis, Buttonbush
Cladrastis lutea, American Yellowwood
Comptonia peregrina, Sweet Fern
Cornus officinalis, Japanese Cornelian Cherry
Cotinus coggygria, Smoke Tree, Smokebush
Eucalyptus citriodora, Lemon-scented Gum
Hamamelis virginiana, Witch Hazel
Lindera benzoin, Spicebush
Magnolia stellata, Star Magnolia
Mahonia aquifolium, Oregon Grape
Nerium oleander, Oleander, Rose-bay
Osmanthus heterophyllus, Holly Olive, Chinese Olive

Zizyphus jujuba, Chinese Date. (Shimizu)

HERBS 2
FLOWERING HERBS

The flowers of the most strongly scented and flavored herbs generally are rather insignificant. But the flowers and fruit of the herbs in this group brighten the whole border.

COMPANION PLANTINGS
Colorful annuals and tender perennials: *Carthamus tinctorius*, Safflower; *Catharanthus roseus*, Madagascar Periwinkle; *Helianthus annuus*, Sunflower; *Heliotropium arborescens*, Heliotrope; *Lantana montevidensis* 'Alba', Trailing Lantana; *Nigella damascena* 'Miss Jekyll', Love-in-a-mist; *Pelargonium graveolens*, Rose Geranium and other scented geraniums; *Verbena canadensis* 'Apple Blossom', Rose Verbena; *Viola*, especially 'Prince Henry' and *V. tricolor*, Johnny-jump-up.

BELAMCANDA *bel-am-can-duh*
chinensis Blackberry Lily   Zone 5.

Belamcanda belongs to the Iris Family and bears red-spotted orange flowers in summer, followed in autumn by fruits that burst open to reveal black seeds. The pods are prized for dried arrangements. Plant seeds or tubers in early spring.

MATURE HEIGHT: 3'
GROWTH RATE: fast
LIGHT: full sun
MOISTURE: versatile

CARYOPTERIS *ka-ree-op-ter-is*
✕ *clandonensis* Bluebeard   Zone 7.

This subshrub has aromatic gray foliage and bears airy blue flower clusters on new wood in midsum-

Colchicum 'Waterlily', Autumn Crocus. (McDonald)

mer. Foliage and flowers are used in fresh and dried bouquets. Severe pruning in early spring improves the flowers. Prefers soil in the neutral range.

MATURE HEIGHT: 4'
GROWTH RATE: fast
LIGHT: full sun
MOISTURE: roots moist

COLCHICUM *kol-chik-um*
autumnale Autumn Crocus,
Meadow Saffron   Zone 4.

Autumn Crocus foliage appears in the spring, and the flowers bloom in the fall. Plant the corms in late summer for fall bloom and in late fall for spring bloom. 'Albo-plenum' has double white blooms.

'Pleniflorum' has double, lavender-tinged pink blooms. *Colchicum* is used in some modern medicines.

MATURE HEIGHT: 6"
GROWTH RATE: medium
LIGHT: full sun, semi-sunny
MOISTURE: roots moist, versatile

COREOPSIS *ko-ree-op-sis* Tickseed

Sunny, yellow, summer bloomer with a daisylike face, that flowers profusely for months. A wonderful cut flower. *C. tinctoria* is the annual type that is used as a dye. Airy, attractive foliage and small but long-lasting, showy yellow flowers. It is one of the easiest perennials to grow, and a staple of any low-maintenance garden. Plant seeds or root divisions 15 to 18 inches apart in spring in somewhat acid soil.

GROWTH RATE: fast
LIGHT: full sun
MOISTURE: roots moist

C. grandiflora 'Sunray'   Zones 4–10.
Fluffy, double-flowered, sturdy, compact plants to 20 inches tall. Very heat tolerant and adapts to drought.

C. lanceolata 'Goldfink'   Zones 4–10.
Handsome dwarf, 9 inches tall, with the broad flower head typical of *C. l.* 'Grandiflora', and perfect for the front of the border. Blooms from early summer until frost.

C. verticillata Threadleaf Tickseed
     Zones 7–9.
Taller, to 30 inches, lemon yellow flowers in late spring and summer; beautiful fernlike foliage. The cultivar 'Moonbeam' grows to about 18 inches and is light yellow. 'Golden Showers', to 18 inches, is a strong yellow.

CROCUS *kro-kus*
sativus Saffron Crocus   Zone 6.

The flowers appear in fall, and are purple with red and yellow anthers. The stigma, dried, is the saffron

Belamcanda chinensis, Blackberry Lily. (McDonald)

Coreopsis grandiflora 'Sunray'. (Burpee Co.)

Dianthus species. (McDonald)

Gypsophila paniculata 'Bristol Fairy', Baby's-breath. (Shimizu)

of Southeast Asian cuisines. In colonial times it flavored wedding foods and was an important source of yellow dye. Plant the bulbs in late summer, 4 inches deep in well-drained sandy soil. See Flowers 5.

MATURE HEIGHT:	3″–6″
GROWTH RATE:	medium
LIGHT:	semi-sunny
MOISTURE:	versatile

DIANTHUS *dye-an-thus*
caryophyllus Carnation, Clove Pink
Zones 8–9.

Carnations are one of the edible clove-scented flowers—"clove-gilly flowers"—used in ancient stillroom recipes. The gray green foliage is evergreen in mild climates. Old-fashioned species tend to be the most fragrant, but there are fragrant cultivars. 'Golden Sun' is outstanding. Plant root divisions in early fall or spring in soil in the neutral range. See Flowers 20.

MATURE HEIGHT:	1′
GROWTH RATE:	medium
LIGHT:	full sun
MOISTURE:	roots moist, versatile

FILIPENDULA *fil-i-pen-dew-luh*
ulmaria Queen-of-the-meadow Zone 2/3.

The foliage is delicately cut and whitish beneath, and the flowers of this tall, late spring bloomer are wintergreen-scented, beautiful white feathery plumes. It was one of Queen Victoria's favorite strewing herbs and a source of greenish yellow dye. *F. purpurea* is smaller and blooms in summer. Plant seeds or root divisions in spring in soil in the neutral range.

MATURE HEIGHT:	4′
GROWTH RATE:	medium
LIGHT:	full sun
MOISTURE:	soil surface damp

GYPSOPHILA *jip-soff-ill-uh*
paniculata Baby's-breath Zone 2/3.

Baby's-breath knits together bouquets, fresh or dried, and the border it blooms in. The tiny, roselike white flowers are borne profusely on airy branches from June to mid-July. 'Bristol Fairy' is a good double-flowered white. 'Pink Fairy' is an almost-white pink. *G. repens*, Creeping Gypsophila, is a delightful rock and ground cover. Plant rooted cuttings in spring in well-drained, rather dry soil in the neutral to alkaline range, at the back of the border or center of island beds. It needs space.

MATURE HEIGHT:	3′
GROWTH RATE:	slow
LIGHT:	full sun
MOISTURE:	roots moist

Filipendula ulmaria, Queen-of-the-meadow. (McDonald)

Perovskia atriplicifolia, Russian Sage. (McDonald)

PEROVSKIA *pehr-roff-skee-uh*
atriplicifolia Russian Sage Zone 4.

Russian sage has tall, beautiful, aromatic silvery foliage with grayish down. Graceful 2- to 3-foot spikes of silky blue flowers bloom from July to September. The foliage gives off a sagelike aroma when crushed. Breathtaking when naturalized and in mass plantings, and often used with ornamental grasses. Plant rooted softwood cuttings in early spring in soil in the neutral range.

MATURE HEIGHT:	3′
GROWTH RATE:	medium
LIGHT:	full sun
MOISTURE:	versatile

SEE ALSO:
Hemerocallis minor, Dwarf Yellow Daylily, Herbs 5
Lilium candidum, Madonna Lily, Herbs 5

Pulmonaria saccharata 'Mrs. Moon', Bethlehem
  Sage, Flowers 11
Rosa, Old Garden Roses, Herbs 7
Salvia elegans, Pineapple Sage, Flowers 14
Santolina virens, Green Santolina, Herbs 5

ALTERNATES:
Alcea rosea, Hollyhock
Anthemis tinctoria, Golden Marguerite
Cheiranthus cheiri, Wallflower
Iris kaempferi, Japanese Iris
Lychis flos-jovis, Flower-of-Jove
Pulmonaria officinalis, Jerusalem Sage
Punica granatum 'Nana', Dwarf Pomegranate
Teucrium chamaedrys, Germander
Valeriana officinalis, Valerian, Garden Heliotrope

HERBS 3
POPULAR CULINARY HERBS

Here are the most valuable cooking herbs. The
next list, Herbs 4, describes some that are less commonly used. In spring and summer, harvest as
needed for cooking and to add fragrance to bouquets
and centerpieces. In high heat the plants are semi-
dormant; take only tips of sprigs. Pick just before
using. At season's end, harvest stems and seeds to dry
for potpourris, dried arrangements, and winter seasoning.

COMPANION PLANTINGS
Edible flowers: *Borago officinalis*, Borage; *Calendula officinalis,* Pot Marigold; *Chrysanthemum cor-
onarium*, Crown Daisy; *Dianthus caryophyllus*, Carnation, Clove Pink; *Hemerocallis fulva*, Orange
Daylily; *Tropaeolum majus*, Nasturtium.

ALLIUM al-*lee*-um   Onion

There are *Allium* species for eating (onions) and
species grown for their big, perfectly round flower

Allium tuberosum, Garlic Chives. (Thomson)

Anethum graveolens, Dill.

heads. The National Arboretum herb garden includes chives, bunching onions, and other edible and
ornamental species. Plant bulbs in early spring; fertilize generously during growth.

GROWTH RATE:	fast
LIGHT:	full sun, semi-sunny
MOISTURE:	versatile

A. fistulosum   Japanese Bunching Onion,
Ciboule   Zone 4.
Handsome clumps 24 inches high that bear white
flowers. The pungent, strongly flavored bulb clumps
are dug, a portion reserved for pickles, cooking, or
salads, and the rest replanted. They quickly multiply.
Plant clumps anytime during the growing season.

A. schoenoprasum   Chives   Zone 2/3.
Hardy, decorative clumps 10 to 12 inches high, of
onion-flavored, thin tubular leaves harvested for salads, soups, and garnishes. Pick small, edible, lilac-
colored flowers in spring to prevent formation of
seedheads. Plant clumps in early spring.

A. tuberosum   Chinese Chives, Garlic Chives
                                             Zone 4.
Ornamental, 18 inches tall, in spreading clusters. Flat
leaves have mild garlic flavor. In late summer, fragrant white flowers with a green midriff. Attractive
to bees and excellent in dried arrangements. Plant
bulbs in late fall or early spring.

ANETHUM an-*neeth*-um
graveolens   Dill   Annual.

Beautiful, fernlike, gray green leaves and seeds are
important herbs in northern Europe, excellent with
potatoes, green beans, salads, soups. The airy flower
heads are edible. Sow seeds periodically to keep
young dill coming. Tends to be short-lived, especially
in warm climates. Harvest and dry leaves and seeds
for winter seasoning. Sow seeds in spring where dill
is to grow. The taproot makes transplanting success
doubtful. Prefers soil in the somewhat acid range.
Plants often self-sow.

MATURE HEIGHT:	1'–2'
GROWTH RATE:	fast
LIGHT:	full sun
MOISTURE:	soil surface damp, versatile

ARTEMISIA art-em-*miz*-ee-uh
dracunculus var. *sativa*
Tarragon   Zones 5–9.

Narrow, fragrant leaves, somewhat trailing, used
fresh or dried in vinegars, salads, sauces; excellent
with chicken or fish. Dried leaves scent potpourris
and toilet water. Test plants for pungent flavor before

Mentha species, Mint. (McDonald).

buying. Plant in early spring. Prefers well-drained soil in the neutral range. See Ground Covers 7.

MATURE HEIGHT: 1′–2′
GROWTH RATE: medium
LIGHT: full sun
MOISTURE: roots moist

MENTHA *menth-uh*

spicata Spearmint   Zone 3.

Extremely fragrant, crinkly green leaves, used dried and fresh as flavoring, medicinally, and for scent, in potpourris and bouquets. Small, edible, purplish flower spikes in summer. Spearmint is best for flavoring desserts, jellies, confections, Indian and Middle Eastern foods. Peppermint, *M.* × *piperita*, is used more as a medicine but also for herbal teas and potpourris. *M.* × *piperita* var. *citrata*, Bergamot Mint or Lemon Mint, also is used for teas. The creeping mint, *M. requienii*, grows rapidly and is a ground cover. *M. suaveolens* 'Variegata', Apple Mint, has beautiful variegated foliage and a flavor between apple and pineapple. *M. arvensis* var. *piperescens*, Japanese Mint, grows in the Medicinal and Oriental sections of the National Arboretum Herb Garden. Mint is hardy and easily propagated by root division almost any time; certain types are invasive once established. Confine to container growing unless naturalizing is the goal. Fertilize and water often. Mints prefer soil in the somewhat acid range.

MATURE HEIGHT: 1′–2′
GROWTH RATE: fast
LIGHT: versatile
MOISTURE: soil surface damp

OCIMUM *oss-im-um*

basilicum Basil   Annual.

Fragrant, fresh green leaves with a flavor between mint and licorice, a major Mediterranean culinary herb for tomatoes, roast lamb, and pesto sauce. Sow seeds in spring or set out seedlings. Pinch early to encourage branching and to keep flower spikes from forming. Lemon basils are available; 'Spicy Globe' is a flavorful miniature. The purple basils, ruffled or plain, have presence but less flavor. At summer's end, store leaves in olive oil in the refrigerator or make the harvest into pesto sauce and freeze. Dried basil is used in potpourris and cooking. Prefers well-drained soil in the somewhat acid range.

MATURE HEIGHT: 18″–24″
GROWTH RATE: fast
LIGHT: full sun
MOISTURE: versatile

ORIGANUM *o-rig-an-num*

Valuable Mediterranean herbs whose spicy, fragrant leaves flavor salads, sliced tomatoes, tomato sauces, and ratatouille. Small, sometimes woolly, on graceful stalks, charming as a garnish and in small bouquets and centerpieces. Keep the edible, pinkish purple or white flower spikes pinched out. Good basket plants. Prefer soil that is well-drained and slightly alkaline.

MATURE HEIGHT: 1′–2′
GROWTH RATE: fast
LIGHT: full sun
MOISTURE: roots moist

Ocimum basilicum 'Spicy Globe', Basil. (McDonald)

Origanum 'Aureum', Gold-leaved Marjoram. (McDonald)

O. majorana Sweet Marjoram,
Annual Marjoram   Annual.
This species is closely related to *O. vulgare* but usually is grown as an annual. Sow seeds in early spring or set out seedlings.

O. vulgare Marjoram, Pot Marjoram,
Oregano   Zones 3–9.
A perennial grown as Italian oregano. Set out root divisions in early spring. Don't confuse this species with Mexican Oregano, *Lippia graveolens*, a tender perennial sometimes used as an oregano flavor in hot regions where it tends to grow well.

PETROSELINUM *pet-roh-sel-lye-num*
crispum Parsley   Biennial, Zone 3.

A major French herb and universal garnish, pretty in kitchen bouquets and with red geraniums. It ties together other flavors and gives character to stews, soups, salads, and fish. The many small branches end in dark green leaves, flat or curly; curly types are easiest to mince. Small, crisp, edible green-yellow flowers appear the second year; keep them picked. Harvest all the branches before winter, mince, and freeze. A biennial, it goes to seed rapidly the second year. Sow seeds early every spring. Prefers well-drained soil in the neutral range.

MATURE HEIGHT: 1′
GROWTH RATE: slow
LIGHT: versatile
MOISTURE: soil surface damp

SEE ALSO:
Laurus nobilis, Grecian Laurel, Sweet Bay, Herbs 1
Rosmarinus officinalis 'Arp', Rosemary, Herbs 9
Salvia officinalis, Sage, Herbs 9
Satureja hortensis, Summer Savory, Herbs 10
Satureja montana, Winter Savory, Herbs 10
Thymus × *citriodorus* 'Doone Valley', Lemon Thyme, Herbs 10

ALTERNATES:
Capsicum annuum (Grossum Group), Sweet Peppers, Pimientos

HERBS 4
UNUSUAL CULINARY HERBS

With the rising interest in foods of other times and other lands, herb gardens are becoming more exotic. The plants here are a modest first step for the culinary explorer.

COMPANION PLANTINGS
Colorful annuals and tender perennials: *Helianthus annuus*, Sunflower; *Nigella sativa*, Black Cumin; *Tagetes tenuifolia*, Signet Marigold.
For herbal teas: *Matricaria recutita*, Sweet False Chamomile; *Thymus* 'Doone Valley', a lemon-scented thyme.

ANTHRISCUS *an-thris-us*
cerefolium Chervil   Annual.

Chervil is parsleylike but flatter, with a hint of anise. It is used in Italian cooking, salads, and egg dishes. In

Anthriscus cerefolium, Chervil. (McDonald)

late fall or early spring sow seeds where the plants are to grow. Branches of spring-sown plants will be ready for harvest 6 to 8 weeks later. Plants may self-sow. Harvest at season's end, chop finely, and freeze. Will not tolerate extreme heat. Prefers somewhat acid soil.

MATURE HEIGHT: 12″–18″
GROWTH RATE: medium
LIGHT: full sun
MOISTURE: soil surface damp

CORIANDRUM *koh-ree-and-rum*
sativum Coriander, Chinese Parsley,
Cilantro   Annual.

Coriander's foliage is the Cilantro in Latin American recipes and the Chinese Parsley of the Orient. The flavor is similar to a mix of parsley and chopped celery leaves, but more pungent. The dried seeds are chewed in the Far East as an after-dinner mouth freshener, and ground for use in curries, cookies, cakes, pastries, lentil and pea soup, and after-dinner coffee. Sow seeds in early spring or fall where the plants are to grow. Plants may self-sow. At summer's end allow the small white flowers to go to seed and harvest these when they are tan-white and dry. Prefers soil in the neutral range.

MATURE HEIGHT: 1′–2′
GROWTH RATE: medium
LIGHT: full sun
MOISTURE: versatile

CYMBOPOGON *sim-bo-poe-gone*
citratus Lemongrass   Zone 10.

Lemongrass grows in tall, dense clumps. The plant is gorgeous because of its grassy texture, and leaves resemble onion stems but are bigger and tougher. Peeled to the tender core, it is chopped and used to give a lemon flavor to curries, stews, rice, sweets, and tea. Chopped lemongrass also is dried for winter seasoning. In the National Arboretum Herb Garden, lemongrass is grown in pots which winter indoors. Plant root divisions in spring. Prefers neutral-range soil.

MATURE HEIGHT: 3′
GROWTH RATE: fast
LIGHT: full sun
MOISTURE: roots moist

FOENICULUM *fee-nik-yew-lum*
vulgare Fennel   Annual.

Tall ribbed stalks and exquisite, ferny foliage, both anise-flavored. The foliage is minced over omelets, tomatoes, salads, and fish sauces. The thicker stalks of *F. v.* var. *dulce*, Finocchio, and var. *piperitum*, Carosella, are eaten cooked, or raw with dips. Fennel produces flattish flowers similar to Queen-Anne's-lace; keep them pinched out, or save to harvest seeds for cooking and tea. Biennial grown as an annual.

Cymbopogon citratus, Lemongrass. (Shimizu)

Foeniculum vulgare var. *dulce*, Finocchio. (McDonald)

Sow seeds in mid-spring, where the plants are to grow. Prefers limy soil.

MATURE HEIGHT: 4'–6'
GROWTH RATE: fast
LIGHT: full sun
MOISTURE: roots moist

LEVISTICUM *lev-iss-tik-um*
officinale Lovage   Zones 5–7.

Tall, beautiful lovage, every part of which smells like celery, was among the most prized herbs of the

Tropaeolum majus, Nasturtium. (McDonald)

Middle Ages. The roots and seeds seasoned meats and broths, the stems and leafstalks flavored teas, and the aromatic seeds went into confections and liqueurs. Almost tropical in appearance, lovage looks attractive in the back of the flower or herb border. Sow seeds in fall or plant root divisions in spring or fall. Prefers somewhat acid and moist loam.

MATURE HEIGHT: 6'
GROWTH RATE: medium
LIGHT: full sun, semi-sunny
MOISTURE: roots moist

POTERIUM *poh-teer-ee-um*
sanguisorba Burnet   Zone 3.

Burnet is a small perennial whose leaves are used fresh to add a cucumber flavor to green salads. When harvesting, cut leaves to the base of the stem; new leaves will follow. Sow seeds as they ripen in the fall or plant root divisions in spring. Salad burnet is especially beautiful after a rain when drops glisten on the leaves. Prefers neutral-range soil.

MATURE HEIGHT: 2'
GROWTH RATE: medium
LIGHT: full sun
MOISTURE: roots moist

TROPAEOLUM *trop-pee-ol-um*
Nasturtium

Pungent-scented, showy annuals and perennials, some climbing, twining vines with single or double-spurred flowers in sparkling warm colors. Carefree in cool regions and beautiful in hanging baskets but they don't transplant easily. Sow seeds outdoors where they are to grow or indoors in plantable peat pots. The tuberous-rooted types may be propagated by root division. Poor, dry soil gives the best results. Nasturtiums attract bees and hummingbirds.

GROWTH RATE: fast
LIGHT: full sun, semi-sunny
MOISTURE: roots moist

T. majus   Annual.
One to 4 feet high, with bright flowers all summer in combinations of yellow, red, and orange. The flowers and the round, fresh green foliage add the bite of watercress to salads, sandwiches, and vegetable and fruit platters. The soft green seeds, pickled, are a substitute for capers, *Capparis spinosa*.

T. peregrinum Canary-bird Flower,
Canary Creeper   Annual.
Fast-growing climber that can reach 8 to 10 feet in a season and makes an excellent screen. The flowers are small, light yellow, and have long green spurs.

T. polyphyllum Wreath Nasturtium
     Zones 7–10.
Perennial, tuberous-rooted climber with grayish blue leaves and yellow and red or yellow and orange flowers.

VIOLA *vye-oh-luh*
odorata Sweet Violet   Zones 6–9.

The sweet-scented violet was grown extensively to flavor confections and make perfumes. The edible flowers, candied, make exotic bonbons and pastry

Viola odorata, Sweet Violet. (McDonald)

garnishes and are dried for potpourris and sachets. Buds are served sprinkled over salad greens and dressed with oil and vinegar. Heart-shaped, dark green leaves half hide flowers that may be white or blue-purple, sometimes pink. Two choice cultivars are 'Royal Robe' and 'White Czar'. Plant seeds or root divisions in fall or early spring. Easily naturalized. See also Flowers 17.

MATURE HEIGHT: 8"
GROWTH RATE: medium
LIGHT: semi-sunny
MOISTURE: soil surface damp

SEE ALSO:
Aloysia triphylla, Lemon Verbena, Herbs 5
Crocus sativus, Saffron Crocus, Herbs 2
Lavandula angustifolia 'Hidcote', English Lavender, Herbs 6
Pelargonium crispum, Lemon Geranium, Herbs 6
Pelargonium graveolens, Rose Geranium, Herbs 6
Pelargonium odoratissimum, Apple Geranium, Herbs 6
Rosa rugosa, Japanese Rose, Herbs 7

ALTERNATES:
Galium odoratum, Woodruff, Sweet Woodruff
Melissa officinalis, Bee Balm, Lemon Balm

HERBS 5
FRAGRANT HERBS FOR DRYING

These herbal plants have strongly scented parts that retain their aroma even after drying. They are among the most useful for dry perfumes and arrangements. See also Herbs 6 and Herbs 7. The Companion Plantings below are useful as dried flowers but are not necessarily fragrant.

COMPANION PLANTINGS
Flowers for drying: *Achillea filipendula* 'Coronation Gold', Fern-leaved Yarrow; *Centaurea cyanus,* Bach-

elor's-button; *Consolida ambigua*, Annual Larkspur; *Lavandula angustifolia*, English Lavender; fragrant *Rosa* cultivars; everlastings.

ALOYSIA *al-loy-see-uh*
triphylla   Lemon Verbena   Zones 8–10.

This is a big, usually deciduous shrub, with bright green leaves strongly scented of lemon. The dried foliage is added to potpourris and herbal teas, and used to flavor beverages and foods. Bears small white flowers from summer to autumn. In cool climates lemon verbena is pot-grown and summered outdoors, wintered inside. Prune vigorous seasonal growth to keep the plant a manageable pot size. Lemon Verbena is also known as *Lippia citriodora*.

MATURE HEIGHT: 5′–8′
GROWTH RATE: medium
LIGHT: full sun
MOISTURE: roots moist

HEMEROCALLIS *hem-er-oh-kal-iss*
minor   Dwarf Yellow Daylily   Zone 2/3.

The lemon-yellow blooms of this old-fashioned daylily are fragrant and edible. (Buds of *H. fulva*, the orange-flowered wild daylily or Tawny Daylily, are the "golden needles" of Oriental dishes.) Like most daylilies, *H. minor* thrives in sun or semi-shade, along roadsides, on slopes and banks, and naturalizes rapidly enough to be used as ground cover. The blooms last hardly more than a day, but appear over many weeks. Set out container plants in early spring or plant root divisions anytime during the growing season. Prefers somewhat acid soil.

MATURE HEIGHT: 2′
GROWTH RATE: medium
LIGHT: full sun, semi-sunny
MOISTURE: soil surface damp

Lilium candidum, Madonna Lily. (McDonald)

Matricaria recutita, Sweet False Chamomile. (McDonald)

LILIUM *lil-ee-um*
candidum   Madonna Lily   Zones 4–8.

This lily's hauntingly perfumed pure white flowers bloom in clusters in late spring and early summer. Since antiquity they have been symbols of purity and healing. The dried blooms are used in winter arrangements. Plant tubers in fall, no more than 1 inch below the soil surface. Unlike most lilies, it prefers well-drained soil that is somewhat alkaline. See Flowers 8.

MATURE HEIGHT: 3′–5′
GROWTH RATE: fast
LIGHT: full sun
MOISTURE: roots moist

MATRICARIA *mat-rik-kay-ree-uh*
recutita   Sweet False Chamomile   Annual.

Sometimes called German chamomile, this species is the best for chamomile tea. The leaves and flowers have the fresh, sweet smell of apple or pineapple, lovely dried in potpourri. Will self-sow and naturalize readily. Sow seeds in early spring; in 6 to 8 weeks the plants reach 2 feet, bloom, and after flowering, die. Prefers neutral-range soil.

MATURE HEIGHT: 1½′–2½′
GROWTH RATE: fast
LIGHT: full sun
MOISTURE: versatile

MELISSA *mel-liss-uh*
officinalis   Lemon Balm, Bee Balm
                                    Zones 4–8.

Bee balm is another lemon-scented herb used in teas, dry perfumes, and arrangements. Nicely textured leaves give off a strong lemon scent when crushed or steeped in water. A hardy perennial, *Melissa* produces small, delicate white florets in July and August. Plant root divisions anytime in spring or fall. Bee balm naturalizes readily. It attracts bees, as does another plant called bee balm, *Monarda didyma*, below. Prefers neutral-range soil.

MATURE HEIGHT: 1′
GROWTH RATE: fast
LIGHT: full sun
MOISTURE: soil surface damp

MONARDA *mon-nard-uh*
didyma   Bee Balm   Zones 4–8.

The fresh or dried leaves of this and certain other *Monarda* species are sun-steeped to make herbal teas. 'Croftway Pink' is one cultivar featured at the Arboretum. The Indians made a "sweating tea" of *M. punctata*, Horsemint, which produces fragrant, yellow-spotted blooms and beautiful pink bracts in

Melissa officinalis, Lemon Balm, variegated. (McDonald)

Monarda didyma 'Croftway Pink', Bee Balm. (McDonald)

summer. *M. didyma*'s shaggy, summer-long, red, pink, white, or purple blooms attract hummingbirds, butterflies, and bees. Plant root divisions in spring or autumn. Bee balm spreads and may need restraining. Prefers soil with a pH between 6.0 and 7.0.

MATURE HEIGHT: 2'–3'
GROWTH RATE: fast
LIGHT: full sun, semi-sunny
MOISTURE: roots moist, versatile

SANTOLINA *san-toh-lye-nuh*
chamaecyparissus Lavender Cotton
Zones 6–9.

A low-growing, shrubby, evergreen plant as multi-branched as coral, with cool-looking blue-gray foliage that appears silvery in moonlight, lavender cotton is often included in knot gardens and herb collections. Small, pale yellow, buttonlike flowers bloom above the foliage in late spring and summer. *S. virens*, Green Santolina, is smaller, to 15 inches. The fragrant leaves and flowers are dried for wreaths, winter arrangements, and sachets to repel moths. The flowers are a fixative for the fragrance in potpourris. May be grown as a clipped hedge and succeeds easily in poor, sandy soil in the neutral range and by the sea. Suffers sometimes in hot summers where humidity is a problem. Plant root divisions in spring.

MATURE HEIGHT: 1½'–2'
GROWTH RATE: medium
LIGHT: full sun
MOISTURE: roots moist

TANACETUM *tan-uh-seet-um*
vulgare var. *crispum* Fern-leaf Tansy
Zone 3.

Tansy's lacy leaves and buttonlike, bright yellow flowers with their strong, sharp aroma were once a

Santolina chamaecyparissus, Lavender Cotton. (McDonald)

cure-all. Tansy flavored roast lamb before mint sauce became popular; flavored puddings, pancakes, cakes, and teas; was applied with buttermilk to improve the complexion; and was dried for potpourris and winter arrangements. The colonists planted it by their front doors to repel insects. Today the species grows wild by the roadside in the Northeast. The leaves are somewhat toxic in large amounts. Plant root divisions in spring.

MATURE HEIGHT: 2'–3'
GROWTH RATE: medium
LIGHT: full sun, versatile
MOISTURE: versatile

SEE ALSO:

Artemisia abrotanum, Southernwood, Ground Covers 7
Artemisia annua, Sweet Wormwood, Ground Covers 7
Gardenia jasminoides, Gardenia, Cape Jasmine, Herbs 9
Laurus nobilis, Grecian Laurel, Sweet Bay, Herbs 1
Lavandula angustifolia, English Lavender, Herbs 6
Mentha × *piperita* var. *citrata,* Bergamot Mint, Lemon Mint, Herbs 3
Pelargonium, scent-leaf types, Herbs 6
Rosa gallica 'Officinalis', Apothecary Rose, Herbs 7

Tanacetum vulgare, Tansy. (McDonald)

Rosmarinus officinalis, Rosemary, Herbs 9
Thymus herba-barona, Caraway Thyme, Herbs 10
Zizyphus jujuba, Jujube, Chinese Date, Herbs 1

ALTERNATES:
Borago officinalis, Borage
Chamaemelum nobile, Chamomile, Russian Chamomile
Iris × germanica var. *florentina*, Orris Root
Nepeta cataria, Catnip

HERBS 6
FRAGRANT HERBS FOR THE GARDEN

The flowers and foliage of these plants are among the most fragrant in the garden. Set them near patios, porches, and windows that are open in summer, and where you will brush against them often.

COMPANION PLANTINGS
Colorful annuals and perennials: *Artemisia abrotanum*, Southernwood; *Consolida ambigua* (syn. *Delphinium ajacis*), Rocket Larkspur; *Salvia farinacea* 'Victoria', Mealycup Sage; *Tagetes tenuifolia*, Signet Marigold; *Zinnia*, 'Peter Pan' types.

EUCALYPTUS *yew-kal-lip-tus*
citriodora Lemon-scented Gum
Zones 8–10.

The eucalyptus are very aromatic, evergreen, fast-growing trees common in California. In cool climates they are grown as pot plants and wintered indoors. They quickly become too big for pot culture but the foliage is so desirable, fresh or dried, that the effort involved in growing them is worthwhile. This species has attractive bark and lemon-scented leaves.

Heliotropium arborescens, Heliotrope. (McDonald)

Harvest young branch tips for bouquets, wreaths, or potpourri baskets. See also Trees 4.

MATURE HEIGHT: 50'
GROWTH RATE: fast
LIGHT: full sun
MOISTURE: roots moist

HELIOTROPIUM *hee-lee-oh-troh-pee-um* arborescens
Heliotrope, Cherry Pie
Zone 10.

From May to September, heliotrope in bloom fills the air with a fragrance like vanilla or cherry pie. It is a tender perennial of modest size with flat clusters of flowers in darkest purple, palest lavender, or white that are excellent for fresh or dried bouquets. Look for container-grown plants whose fragrance you can check. Heliotrope may be trained to standard, or tree, form. In cool regions, grow it in a pot and bring it inside for the winter. Pinch young plants to encourage bushiness and bloom. *Valeriana officinalis*, Valerian, has a similar fragrance and is known as Garden Heliotrope, but they are different plants.

MATURE HEIGHT: 15"
GROWTH RATE: medium
LIGHT: full sun
MOISTURE: roots moist

LAVANDULA *lav-van-dew-luh* Lavender

Lavender belongs in every garden. A low-growing shrub or subshrub, its needle-narrow, gray green foliage fills the air with fragrance when brushed. Lovely growing among roses, the 6- to 10-inch flowering stems bear very fragrant tiny lavender-blue florets in spring and again in fall if cut back after each blooming. Dried lavender buds go into sachets, perfumes, confections, teas, and sauces. In old England, small fruits and sweets were served on dried, stripped lavender sticks. In contemporary Provence, the buds flavor salads and cooked foods. Set out container plants in early spring. Prefers well-drained, neutral-range soil.

MATURE HEIGHT: 2'–3'
GROWTH RATE: slow
LIGHT: full sun
MOISTURE: roots moist

L. angustifolia English Lavender Zones 5–9.
This species is the one seen most often in herb gardens. Florets bloom on upright stems that look good in the front of the border and as a low, clipped hedge. The dark blue-lavender flowers of 'Hidcote' are better than those of the species. There's also a white cultivar. Oil of lavender is distilled from this species and *L. stoechas*.

L. dentata French Lavender Zones 6–9.
Less hardy, this species often is grown in pots and wintered indoors. It can be trained as a standard.

L. stoechas subsp. *pedunculata*
Spanish Lavender Zones 7–9.
Tender, but has especially lovely flowers and is an excellent basket plant.

NARCISSUS *nar-siss-us* Daffodil

Favorite spring-flowering bulbs in combinations of gold, white, salmon pink, or ivory, or gold and glowing orange, white, and coral. The bloom periods of most species and cultivars range from early to late spring. See Flowers 6.

GROWTH RATE: medium
LIGHT: full sun, semi-sunny
MOISTURE: soil surface damp

N. poeticus Poet's Narcissus,
Pheasant's-eye Zone 4.
Poet's narcissus has been grown for its exquisite fragrance since before the time of Elizabeth I. It blooms in mid-spring in the northern states but not until June in Maritime Canada.

N. × odorus Campernelle Jonquil Zone 6.
This extremely fragrant hybrid has a short tube and

Lavandula angustifolia, English Lavender. (Shimizu)

two to four yellow flowers on each stalk. It blooms in early spring and can be forced indoors.

PELARGONIUM *pel-ahr-goh-nee-um*
Geranium

Geranium is a common name for some species of the genus *Pelargonium. Geranium* also is a genus name of a group whose common names are Cranesbill or Geranium (Flowers 10). *Pelargonium* species are excellent plants for bedding, borders, pots, and baskets, and are appreciated for the very aromatic foliage rather than for the flowers. They summer outdoors, winter indoors except for frost-free areas, where they are perennial. Tip cuttings root easily in late winter, spring, and summer. Set out rooted cuttings or plants after danger of frost is past. Heights vary.

GROWTH RATE: medium
LIGHT: full sun
MOISTURE: roots moist

P. crispum   Lemon Geranium,
Finger Bowl Pelargonium   Zone 10.
The small crinkly leaves have a lemony aroma. Crushed or rubbed between the fingers, they scent the hands and the air. They are dried for potpourris. The flowers have two tones of pink.

P. graveolens   Rose Geranium   Zone 9.
Rose geranium leaves exude a sweet scent. They were included, one to a jar, in apple and other clear jellies, flavored cakes, and tea. The flowers are rose with a dark purple spot in the middle of the upper petal.

P. odoratissimum   Apple Geranium,
Nutmeg Pelargonium   Zone 10.
The leaves are small, velvety, and ruffled; the flowers white. The fragrance is sweet and nice for flavoring cakes.

P. tomentosum   Peppermint Geranium,
Woolly Pelargonium   Zone 10.
The large, soft, woolly leaves are peppermint-scented. The flowers are white, spotted red. Excellent texture plant.

Pelargonium tomentosum, Peppermint Geranium. (McDonald)

SEE ALSO:
Aloysia triphylla, Lemon Verbena, Herbs 5
Citrus × *limonia (otaitensis),* Otaheite Orange, Herbs 9
Gardenia jasminoides, Gardenia, Cape Jasmine, Herbs 9
Laurus nobilis, Grecian Laurel, Sweet Bay, Herbs 1
Ocimum basilicum, Basil, Herbs 3
Rosa damascena, Damask Rose, Herbs 7
Viola odorata 'Royal Robe', Sweet Violet, Herbs 4

ALTERNATES:
Acorus calamus, Sweet Flag
Cedronella canariensis, Canary Balm
Cheiranthus cheiri, Wallflower
Comptonia peregrina, Sweet Fern
Dianthus caryophyllus, Carnation, Clove Pink
Hemerocallis minor, Dwarf Yellow Daylily
Hesperis matronalis, Sweet Rocket, Dame's Violet
Melissa officinalis, Bee Balm, Lemon Balm
Nepeta × *faassenii,* Persian Ground Ivy

Nicotiana 'Nikki White'
Perovskia atriplicifolia, Russian Sage
Pimpinella anisum, Common Anise
Salvia sclarea, Clary
Santolina chamaecyparissus, Lavender Cotton
Thymus × *citriodorus,* Lemon Thyme
Valeriana officinalis, Valerian, Garden Heliotrope

HERBS 7
OLD GARDEN ROSES

Old Garden Rose is the American Rose Society's official classification for historic species of this beautiful flowering shrub which evolved from roses known in the East before the Great Wall of China was built or Cleopatra strewed perfumed petals at Anthony's feet. During the Dark Ages a few of the fragrant early species survived in the herb gardens of the Franciscan monasteries. The Crusaders brought more from Persia. The Elizabethans flavored sweets and scented toiletries with roses. Later the China traders brought two of the ancestors of the modern rose—the exquisite tea-scented Tea Rose, *Rosa* × *odorata,* and the China Rose, *Rosa chinensis.* Both these roses had a characteristic that the wonderful old (and hardier) species lacked: they bloomed all season long, not just in spring. Napoleon's Empress Josephine and her gardeners at Malmaison were among the many growers whose love for these new roses contributed to the development of the modern hybrid tea rose.

The beautiful, historic Old Garden Roses included here grow in the National Arboretum Herb Garden. Among them are many of the fragrant roses originally used in potpourris and dry perfumes. Most flower for 4 weeks in early or mid-spring; a few repeat bloom. Some are plants trained to trellises, where they grow 2 or 3 feet taller than the heights given below, which are for free-standing plants. Curator Holly Shimizu found that once they were established in good soil in full sun, these old roses succeeded without requiring a great deal of chemical pest and disease control. Where zone hardiness is not given, the plant probably is winter-hardy down to about 0° F if protected by mulch or soil mounds and windbreaks. In regions of subzero winters, Styrofoam or other insulated covers are necessary for winter survival.

Modern hybrids bred for long-season bloom and hardiness are named in Shrubs 6; roses for hedges are found in Shrubs 19; and climbing roses in Vines 2.

See Shrubs 6 for an overview on rose culture.

COMPANION PLANTINGS
Low-growing foliage plants, fragrant herbs, bulbs: *Artemisia abrotanum,* Southernwood; *Chrysanthemum parthenium,* Double Feverfew; *C. p.* 'Aureum', Golden Feverfew; *Hosta* 'Krosso Regal' interplanted with pink tulips; *Iberis sempervirens,* Evergreen Candytuft; *Lavandula angustifolia* 'Hidcote', English Lavender; *Pennisetum alopecuroides* 'Purpurascens', Purple Pennisetum; *Rosmarinus officinalis* 'Arp', Rosemary; *Salvia farinacea* 'Victoria', Mealycup Sage; *S. officinalis* 'Purpurea', Garden Sage; *Teucrium chamaedrys,* Germander.

ROSA *roh-zuh*
× *alba* White Rose of York   Zone 4.

A superb hybrid is 'Celestial', whose very fragrant, delicate, blush-pink flowers are perfectly complimented by the blue-green foliage. Blooms in spring. Decorative hips. Height: 4–5 feet.

R. × *borboniana* Bourbon Rose
Extremely fragrant cupped blooms in spring, repeated occasionally in summer, made this rose a Victorian favorite. It was a forerunner of the hybrid perpetual roses. 'La Reine Victoria' (1872) is a stunning medium pink with strong fragrance. The Bourbons can be trained against a wall, but are not really climbers. Height: 5–6 feet.

R. *centifolia* Cabbage Rose   Zone 5.
These big, multi-petaled pink roses were painted by the Dutch masters. There are many very fragrant, very double blooms in spring. An excellent cultivar is 'Fantin Latour'. Height: 5 feet.

Rosa gallica 'Officinalis', Apothecary Rose.

R. c. 'Muscosa' Moss Rose
The hardy moss roses have an attractive, often fragrant, mossy growth on the sepals and calyx. 'Gloire des Mousseuses' is a very fragrant pink double.

R. c. 'Cristata' Crested Rose,
Chapeau de Napoleon
This rose is just touched with moss and has dark pink, very double, very fragrant flowers. 'William Lobb', a vigorous, very fragrant plant, is a dark crimson purple. To 6 feet.

R. *chinensis* China Rose   Zone 7.
With slight fragrance and not very hardy, but everblooming and resistant to insects and diseases, the

Rosa 'La Reine Victoria', Bourbon Rose. (McDonald)

China rose is an ancestor of modern hybrid teas. A descendant of the original species from China still sold by nurseries is 'Old Blush' (grown since before 1700), a two-tone pink that will flower from May to December (in warmer regions) if deadheaded. Another China rose, 'Mutabilis', is unique in that the single pink blooms change to orange-yellow as they mature on maroon stems. Height: 3 feet. Good for pot culture. Hardy to 10° F.

R. *damascena* Damask Rose   Zone 4.
A favorite of the ancient Romans. In spring the winter-hardy damask roses produce extremely fragrant clusters of huge, flattish flowers with a quartered effect, in white, pale pink, or red. The cultivar 'Autumn Damask' is pink, and its flowering is recurrent. 'Madame Hardy' is a winter-hardy fragrant white with a green button eye, described as one of the most beautiful white roses in the world. Height: 5–5½ feet.

R. *eglanteria* Eglantine, Sweet Briar
Zone 4.
The leaves smell of sweet pippin apples and in fall there are beautiful orange-scarlet hips. Shakespeare described this species. Victorians planted it by windows so breezes could sweep the fragrance indoors. The flowers appear in spring; they are single and pink, rather like apple blossoms. To 6 feet.

R. *gallica* 'Officinalis' Apothecary Rose
Zone 5.
The oldest cultivated form of *R. gallica*. This extremely fragrant spring-blooming rose was commercially cultivated near Provins, France, in the 18th century. The essential oils and dried petals were shipped all over the world in conserves and perfumes. The apothecary rose is unique in that the petals are more fragrant after drying. The species reaches about 5 feet and is subject to mildew. *R. g.* var. *versicolor*, Rosa Mundi (1581), is a hardy, very fragrant, white, pink, or red, with spectacular blooms in spring. A spreading plant, 3 to 4 feet high.

R. *glauca* (probably *rubrifolia*)
A beautiful specimen plant, loved for its reddish mauve foliage. The flowers are small and single, pink or blush pink streaked with red, followed in fall by scarlet hips. Especially attractive interplanted with *Digitalis* (Foxglove), *Iberis* (Candytuft), *Verbena hastata* (Blue Verbena), and *Alchemilla vulgaris* (Lady's Mantle). Height: 5 feet.

R. × *harisonii* Harison's Yellow   Zone 4.
This very fragrant, semidouble, deep golden yellow rose naturalized on the frontier and is believed to be the inspiration for "The Yellow Rose of Texas." It takes care of itself and resents all but minimum care. Blooms profusely in spring. A lovely specimen plant. Arching canes 5–7 feet tall.

HYBRID PERPETUAL ROSES
The famous American Beauty Rose, with its deep pink flowers and long stems, belongs in this group that evolved from the Bourbon rose. The big, fragrant flowers bloom profusely in spring, with some repeat bloom in summer and fall. 'Paul Neyron' (1851) is a hardy, strongly fragrant, clear rose-pink with huge blooms 4½ to 5½ inches across. 'General Jacqueminot' is a bold red, and 'Reine des Violettes', a mauve. Height: 5–6 feet.

Rosa × harisonii, Harison's Yellow. (McDonald)

R. × noisettiana   Noisette Rose
An American cross between the musk and China roses, in spring clusters of as many as 100 exquisite buds open into small, fragrant flowers. Bloom repeats in summer. The original cultivar, 'Champney's Pink Cluster', a lovely light pink, is in the Arboretum rose garden. Noisettes are very tender, and where there is frost tips may die back and plants don't grow as large, but in frost-free regions they may grow to 7 feet or more.

R. × odorata   Tea Rose   Zone 7.
In the late 1700s, China traders brought home to Europe the first of these tea-scented roses with their pointed buds, disease resistance, and ever-blooming habit. The species became, with the other everbloomer, *Rosa chinensis*, the China rose, one of the ancestors of the modern hybrid tea. The tea rose is tender to cold, but often is evergreen in frost-free regions. 'Niphetos' is a beautiful white, 3 to 4 feet tall; 'Mrs. Dudley Cross' is peach and pink, 3 feet tall.

R. rugosa   Japanese Rose   Zone 2.
Rugosas are very hardy and disease-resistant; they bear lots of single, fragrant flowers in white, pink, or red. The plants work well as specimens, in hedges, on sandy slopes, and for naturalizing. The surest roses for seaside gardens. Spring-blooming; if deadheaded, some repeat in summer. The big, orange-red hips are excellent for making teas and jams. 'Frau

Rosa × noisettiana, 'Champney's Pink Cluster'.

Dagmar Hartopp' has silvery pink flowers; 'Blanc Double de Coubert' is a lovely double white. To 6 feet.

R. virginiana   Virginia Rose   Zone 3.
The Indians used the long-lasting, bright red hips of this vigorous native species to flavor foods and make tea. In spring, there are beautiful single, bright magenta-to-pink blooms borne in clusters or individ-ually. The autumn foliage is brilliant. Grows to about 6 feet, but with pruning stays to 3 feet. Good choice for naturalizing and succeeds by the seashore. Extremely hardy.

SEE ALSO:
Climbing Roses, Vines 2
Roses for Hedges and Edging, Shrubs 19
Modern Shrub Roses, Shrubs 6

European colonists brought to their new land herbal lore dating back to antiquity. The Indians taught them the plant secrets of the new continent. The National Arboretum has both an Early American Garden and an American Indian Garden devoted to herbs and other plants grown by our ancestors.

COMPANION PLANTINGS
Colorful annuals and biennials: *Angelica archangelica*; *Calendula officinalis*, Pot Marigold; *Catharanthus roseus*, Madagascar Periwinkle; *Matricaria recutita*, Sweet False Chamomile; *Nigella damascena*, Love-in-a-mist; *Ruta graveolens*, Rue; *Salvia officinalis*, Sage; *Symphytum officinale*, Comfrey.

ASARUM *ass-uh-rum* Wild Ginger

Low woodland perennials with large heart-shaped leaves and stems that arch above small, almost-hidden purplish brown flowers. They aren't spectacular but are delightful, easy, fast-growing ground covers for shady places. Used as a substitute for ginger. Plant root divisions in early spring. Prefers slightly acid soil.

GROWTH RATE:	fast
LIGHT:	shade
MOISTURE:	soil surface damp

A. caudatum   Zones 4–8.
This species is just 3 to 6 inches tall, with evergreen leaves, and purplish flowers that bloom in late spring.

A. europaeum European Wild Ginger
     Zones 6–8.
European wild ginger was used medicinally by the ancient Greeks and Romans. It is a low-growing woodland perennial with beautiful, crisp, heart-shaped, glossy evergreen leaves, a handsome ground cover and superb ornamental. In early spring, small

purple-brown flowers appear. Plant root divisions in early spring. Excellent for the wild garden or shaded border.

CEPHALANTHUS *sef-al-**lanth**-us*
occidentalis Buttonbush   Zones 5–10.

The Indians used the bark of this shrub to relieve toothaches. It grows wild in swampy woodlands and is pretty in summer when the small, ball-shaped, fragrant, creamy white flowers are in bloom. Not sold by all nurseries and successful only in truly moist situations. Plant root divisions during the growing season or sow seeds as soon as ripe. Prefers somewhat acid soil.

MATURE HEIGHT:	5′–15′
GROWTH RATE:	medium
LIGHT:	full sun, semi-sunny
MOISTURE:	soil surface damp

ECHINACEA *ek-in-**nay**-shee-uh*
purpurea Purple Coneflower   Zone 3.

Sturdy, rather coarse perennial the Indians used against cancer. Valuable in herb gardens, wild gardens, and formal borders for the July and August display of bright, daisylike, cone-centered, long-lasting purple or pink flowers. 'Bright Star' is an attractive maroon cultivar to 30 inches tall. Excellent for fresh bouquets and for drying. Plant root divisions in early spring in somewhat acid soil.

MATURE HEIGHT:	3′–4′
GROWTH RATE:	medium
LIGHT:	full sun
MOISTURE:	roots moist

GAULTHERIA *gol-**theer**-ee-uh*
procumbens Wintergreen, Checkerberry
     Zone 4.

Indians drank tea made from wintergreen berries and leaves for relief from rheumatism and fevers. It is a beautiful creeping, evergreen ground cover that

Echinacea purpurea, Purple Coneflower. (McDonald)

grows wild in the woods of the Northeast. Waxy, white bell-like flowers appear under the leaves in spring, followed by edible red berries with a distinctive, refreshing flavor. Plant container-grown plants in early spring, or sow seeds in sandy peat and keep under glass until growing. Prefers soil in the acid range.

MATURE HEIGHT:	3″–6″
GROWTH RATE:	medium/slow
LIGHT:	shade
MOISTURE:	soil surface damp

MAHONIA *muh-**hoh**-nee-uh*
aquifolium Oregon Grape   Zone 6.

Oregon grape is also called holly barberry. The mahonias are decorative shrubs with coarse-textured, shiny evergreen leaves resembling those of holly. They bear fragrant clusters of yellow flowers in late winter or early spring, followed by blue-black grapelike fruit with a silvery bloom. Fruit and stems were sources for yellow dye for the Navajo. The leaves turn bronze-purple in fall. 'Atropurpureum' is purple in winter. 'Charity' is an early bloomer. Keep pruned to about 3 feet or the plants become awkward. Look for asexually propagated plants with shiny leaves and set them out in late fall or very early spring. *M. repens* is a shiny, hardy, low-growing native evergreen species about 10 inches tall. It makes an excellent ground cover for shade.

MATURE HEIGHT:	3′–6′
GROWTH RATE:	medium
LIGHT:	semi-sunny
MOISTURE:	soil surface damp

MATTEUCCIA *mat-**tew**-shee-uh*
pensylvanica Ostrich Fern   Zones 3/4–8.

The coiled fronds of the emerging leaves of this and other ferns are called "fiddleheads." The American

Asarum species, Wild Ginger. (McDonald)

Mahonia aquifolium, Oregon Grape. (Shimizu)

listed in catalogs, include 'Cloth of Gold' and 'Golden Shower'.

MATURE HEIGHT: 3'
GROWTH RATE: medium
LIGHT: full sun
MOISTURE: roots moist

SEE ALSO:
Arctostaphylos uva-ursi, Bearberry, Ground Covers 3
Colchicum autumnale, Autumn Crocus, Herbs 2
Crocus sativus, Saffron Crocus, Herbs 2
Dianthus caryophyllus, Carnation, Clove Pink, Herbs 2
Monarda punctata, Horsemint, Herbs 5
Stachys byzantina, Woolly Betony, Lamb's-ears, Ground Covers 2

ALTERNATES:
Acorus calamus, Sweet Flag
Arisaema triphyllum, Jack-in-the-pulpit
Comptonia peregrina, Sweet Fern
Cornus sericea (syn. *stolonifera*), Red-osier Dogwood

Indians gathered and ate them in spring, and they are still an early spring treat in New England. The ostrich fern grows wild on moist wooded slopes and in swamps. It is one of the tallest native ferns and easy to grow—in sun with ample moisture, or in shade. Fronds of the species *M. struthiopteris* (offered by nurseries as ostrich fern) reach 3 to 5 feet. Plant root divisions in late fall or early spring. Versatile and attractive in many situations.

MATURE HEIGHT: 3'–6'
GROWTH RATE: medium
LIGHT: versatile
MOISTURE: soil surface damp

RUSCUS *rusk-kus*
aculeatus   Butcher's Broom, Box Holly
Zone 8.

Low-growing shrub with evergreen hollylike leaves. Green flowers bloom in the middle of the leaflike stems and are followed by bright red berries. The ancient Greeks drank a wine made from the leaves and fruit as a cure for hepatitis and headaches. In cool regions it is pot-grown to summer outdoors and winter indoors. Plant root divisions in fall or early spring; both a male and a female plant are required for good fruiting. The plant attracts birds and does well by the seashore.

MATURE HEIGHT: 2'–3'
GROWTH RATE: medium/slow
LIGHT: versatile
MOISTURE: roots moist

SOLIDAGO *sol-id-day-goh*
odora   Sweet Goldenrod   Zones 3–9.

Easily grown perennial used by American Indians for medicinal teas and smoking materials. Fragrant yellow plumes bloom for 3 or 4 weeks in late summer. Lovely as a filler in the border and in fresh or dried bouquets. This plant is not the species often believed to cause hayfever. Dig wild plants in early spring. Cultivars of another species, *S. virgaurea*,

Solidago cultivar, Goldenrod. (McDonald)

Lilium candidum, Madonna Lily
Mentha arvensis var. *piperescens*, Japanese Mint
Myrica pensylvanica, Bayberry
Valeriana officinalis, Valerian, Garden Heliotrope

HERBS 9
HERBS FOR BASKETS AND POTS

Many beautiful and fragrant herbs from warm regions are grown in cooler climates in containers that can be wintered indoors. Rosemary and several other creeping and long-stemmed herbs make good basket and container plants.

COMPANION PLANTINGS
Flowering basket plants: *Catharanthus roseus*, Madagascar Periwinkle; *Portulaca grandiflora*, Rose Moss; *Verbena tenuisecta*, Moss Verbena; *Vinca major*, Greater Periwinkle; *Zinnia* 'Liliput' and 'Tom Thumb'.

CITRUS *sit-rus*

The genus includes lemons, grapefruits, and limes. The fragrant flowers and aromatic rind, particularly orange rind, have been used in perfumes and potpourris for centuries. Garden trees in the South, in cooler regions they are small but fruitful pot plants to summer outdoors in the sun and winter indoors. The small, thornless Calamondin, or Panama Orange, formerly C. mitis reclassed as × *Citrofortunella* var. *mitis*, whose 1-inch sour oranges are used for marmalade or in place of lemon, is a familiar house or greenhouse plant in the North. Prefers somewhat acid soil. See also Trees 16.

GROWTH RATE:	slow
LIGHT:	full sun
MOISTURE:	roots moist

Gardenia jasminoides. (McDonald)

Myrtus communis, Myrtle. (McDonald)

C. aurantium   Sour Orange   Zone 10.
A 30-foot garden tree but smaller in pot culture, the sour orange has long, blunt spines and large, very fragrant, waxy flowers. The rough-skinned fruit makes good marmalade.

C. × limonia (otaitensis)   Otaheite Orange
                                           Zone 10.
This is a tree 2 to 3 feet tall with fragrant purple-tinged white flowers. The 2-inch fruits are orange to deep yellow.

C. limon   Lemon   Zone 10.
In southern gardens the lemon tree grows to 20 feet. It is spiny and has lemon-tasting winged leaves that

can be used in cooking. 'Ponderosa' has waxy white flowers and large pear-shaped fruits.

GARDENIA *gar-deen-ee-uh*
jasminoides   Gardenia, Cape Jasmine
                                       Zones 8–10.

The velvety white flowers of these glossy-leaved evergreen shrubs are among the most fragrant in the world. They have grown in the South since colonial times. The fruit is a source of yellow dye in Japan. In the North, gardenias are grown in pots, summered outdoors in semi-sun, wintered indoors in a southern exposure. They bloom from early spring through summer. *G. j.* 'Fortuniana' is a double-flowered form. Prefers acid-range soil.

MATURE HEIGHT:	6'
GROWTH RATE:	medium
LIGHT:	semi-sunny
MOISTURE:	roots moist

MYRTUS *mert-us*
communis   Myrtle   Zones 8–9.

An evergreen shrub, the flowering myrtle was believed in ancient times to be the luckiest plant to have in one's garden. The very aromatic dark green leaves are used in potpourris. Myrtle thrives as a pot plant—summered out, wintered in—and is a favorite for training to standard or topiary forms. The flowers, beautiful creamy white puff balls, bloom for 5 or 6 weeks in summer, followed by bluish black berries. It grows well near the seashore and makes an excellent clipped hedge. *Vinca minor*, Periwinkle, also is called Running Myrtle, but *M. communis* is the true myrtle known since ancient times. Prefers neutral-range soil.

MATURE HEIGHT:	over 6'
GROWTH RATE:	medium
LIGHT:	full sun, semi-sunny
MOISTURE:	roots moist

Nerium oleander, Oleander. (McDonald)

NERIUM *neer-ee-um*
oleander Oleander, Rose-bay Zones 9–10.

The oleanders are evergreen shrubs or small trees, with showy spring-through-summer clusters of single or double blooms in white, yellow, red, pink, or lilac. There are sweet-scented types, notably a double-flowered red. Oleander can be clipped and shaped. It withstands droughts and in hot, dry climates, is used as a street and hedge plant. In cool regions it grows in pots, summered outdoors in the sun, wintered indoors in a bright window. Like some other medicinal herbs, oleander is very poisonous and not recommended where there are children.

MATURE HEIGHT: 20'
GROWTH RATE: medium
LIGHT: full sun
MOISTURE: roots moist

ROSMARINUS *ross-muh-rye-nus*
officinalis Rosemary   Zones 7–9.

The lasting mint-pine fragrance of rosemary's needlelike evergreen leaves, fresh or dried, is a symbol of fidelity. Colonists placed sprigs in wedding bouquets, and made rosemary tea, wine, toilet waters, and dry perfumes. A Mediterranean native, it is used to flavor soups, stews, and roasts, particularly lamb and pork. In cooler regions, rosemary is a popular pot plant, summered outdoors, wintered indoors in a bright, cool room. Lovely light blue edible flowers bloom in clusters in late winter and early spring. Rosemary may be pruned and is a good bonsai subject. The hardy cultivar 'Arp' survives winters in the National Arboretum herb garden. Nice filler for bare spots in walls or the rock garden. Spreading varieties are used as ground cover where they are hardy: *R. o.* var. *humilis* is hardy to New Jersey; *R. o.* 'Prostratus' in southern California. Prefers neutral-range soil.

Rosmarinus officinalis, Rosemary. (McDonald)

Salvia officinalis 'Aurea', Golden Sage. (McDonald)

MATURE HEIGHT: 2'–4'
GROWTH RATE: medium
LIGHT: full sun
MOISTURE: roots moist

SALVIA *sal-vee-uh*
officinalis Sage   Zones 4–9.

Sage is an erect subshrub or woolly herb with violet, blue, or white flower spikes in summer and sharply aromatic, downy foliage. *Salvia* means health, and sage teas and wines have traditionally been taken to improve longevity, wisdom, and patience. Sage flavors stuffings for pork, poultry, and fish; dishes of eggplant and tomato; and soups, sauces, meat loaf, chowders, and marinades. 'Ictarina' is an attractive cultivar with golden variegated leaves. Plant rooted

cuttings in spring. Prefers neutral-range soil. Prune sage every 2 or 3 years as needed to maintain a good shape. Ornamental salvias are discussed in Flowers 14.

MATURE HEIGHT: 2'–3'
GROWTH RATE: medium
LIGHT: full sun
MOISTURE: roots moist

SEE ALSO:
Cymbopogon citratus, Lemongrass, Herbs 4
Laurus nobilis, Grecian Laurel, Sweet Bay, Herbs 1
Lavandula dentata, French Lavender, Herbs 6
Lavandula stoechas subsp. *pedunculata*, Spanish Lavender, Herbs 6
Mentha spicata, Spearmint, Herbs 3
Origanum majorana, Sweet Marjoram, Annual Marjoram, Herbs 3
Thymus × *citriodorus* 'Aureus', Golden Lemon Thyme, Herbs 10
Thymus herba-barona, Caraway Thyme, Herbs 10
Thymus praecox subsp. *arcticus* 'Albus', 'Coccineus', 'Splendens', Herbs 10
Tropaeolum, Nasturtium, climbing varieties, Herbs 4

ALTERNATE:
Zingiber officinalis, Ginger

HERBS 10
HERBS FOR NOOKS AND CRANNIES

These versatile herbs are small plants to tuck into tiny spaces. They are sturdy and drought-resistant, successful in crannies and stone walls. A few even flourish between stones in garden paths.

ACHILLEA *ak-il-lee-uh*
tomentosa Woolly Yarrow Zones 2/3–8/9.

Yarrow was associated with incantations and witches in medieval Europe; tea made of yarrow roots, leaves, and flowers still is taken for colds and rheu-

Achillea tomentosa, Woolly Yarrow.

Chamaemelum nobile, Chamomile.

matism by devotees of herbal medicine. In spring and summer, long-blooming cultivars produce single or double flowers in shades of white, pink, or yellow. For drying for winter arrangements, cut stems while still in bud. The plant is semievergreen and tough, a mat-forming, long-lived perennial with ferny, woolly, aromatic foliage. Planted at the base of rocks and stone walls, it makes a graceful transition to the lawn. It tolerates light foot traffic and is sometimes used as a lawn substitute. Yarrow flourishes in full sun and in sandy soil by the sea. Plant root divisions in early spring. See Flowers 12 for ornamental cultivars. Prefers neutral-range soil.

MATURE HEIGHT: 6"–12"
GROWTH RATE:　medium
LIGHT:　full sun
MOISTURE:　roots moist

CHAMAEMELUM *kam-muh-mee-lum*
nobile　Chamomile, Russian Chamomile
Zones 4–9.

This charming but tough, hardy little perennial produces yellow flowers in late spring. The leaves are lacy, semievergreen and smell slightly of apples when crushed. In mild areas, chamomile is planted as a ground cover to be walked on and mowed. In Elizabethan times, chamomile-covered banks and mounded earth made pleasant resting places called "chamomile seats." Today, the major herbal use is for teas and hair rinses; sweet false chamomile, *Matricaria recutita*, makes better chamomile tea. Sow seeds or plant root divisions in early spring. Chamomile formerly was known as Anthemis nobilis. Prefers soil in the neutral range.

MATURE HEIGHT: 1'
GROWTH RATE:　medium
LIGHT:　full sun
MOISTURE:　roots moist, versatile

GALIUM *gay-lee-um*
odoratum　Woodruff, Sweet Woodruff
Zones 4–9.

Woodruff has aromatic green leaves and beautiful white flowers in spring. The Victorians made moth-repellent sachets with mixtures of dried woodruff flowers and leaves, herbs, and spices. It also is used to flavor May wine and as a fixative for dry perfumes. A hardy perennial, it naturalizes in moist, woodsy, or shady places and can take over a border unless con-

trolled. Plant root divisions or seeds in early spring. Sweet woodruff has been returned to the *G. odoratum* classification after a period as Asperula odorata. Prefers acid-range soil.

MATURE HEIGHT: 6"
GROWTH RATE:　fast
LIGHT:　semi-sunny, shade
MOISTURE:　soil surface damp

SATUREJA *sat-yew-reej-uh*
montana　Winter Savory　　　　Zones 4–9.

Winter savory is a low, woody evergreen, once used to treat liver and lung problems. The crushed leaves taste of pepper and are said to relieve the pain of a bee sting. In summer, there are tiny white or pink flowers that are long-lasting and attract bees. It is a decorative little plant for nooks and crannies, borders, and edgings. Plant rooted cuttings or seedlings in early spring. Very similar is Summer Savory, *S. hortensis*, an annual.

MATURE HEIGHT: 1'
GROWTH RATE:　medium
LIGHT:　full sun
MOISTURE:　roots moist

SEDUM *seed-um*
sieboldii　October Daphne　　　Zones 3–9.

A low-growing succulent, sedum has evergreen, almost circular blue-green leaves with a narrow red edge. In late summer, there are dense clusters of small, star-shaped pink to lavender flowers. There are also golden-splotched varieties. Sedum survives wet or dry soil, sun or shade, and is ideal for nooks and crannies, rock gardens, pockets in rocks and walls, by steps, and in the flower border. It often self-sows and grows readily from root divisions set out in early spring.

Galium odoratum, Sweet Woodruff. (Shimizu)

MATURE HEIGHT: 6"–9"
GROWTH RATE: fast/medium
LIGHT: full sun, semi-sunny
MOISTURE: versatile

THYMUS *tye-mus*   Thyme

The thymes are mostly low, attractive, evergreen plants whose intensely aromatic leaves are among the most useful of the herbs. It was a personal fragrance of the Greeks, an antidepressant to the Romans, and a favorite ingredient in Victorian tussie-mussies, sachets, rubbing vinegars, and bath lotions. Today it flavors tea, gumbo, and bouillabaisse, and is used extensively in French, Italian, and many other cuisines. Parisians sprinkle dried thyme on steaks before broiling them. Because of its tolerance for heat and drought (it grows wild on hillsides in the Mediterranean area), thyme is used to carpet rocky slopes and in crevices in stone walks and walls. Trailing types are excellent pot and basket plants. Plant root divisions in early spring in well-drained soil in the neutral range.

MATURE HEIGHT: 2"–8"
GROWTH RATE: medium
LIGHT: full sun
MOISTURE: roots moist

T. × citriodorus   Lemon Thyme   Zones 3–9.
The lemon-scented leaves combine lemon and thyme flavors and are good for seasoning. An excellent plant for hanging baskets. 'Aureus' is a cultivar with gold-variegated leaves. 'Doone Valley' has golden highlights.

T. herba-barona   Caraway Thyme
Zones 4–9.
A low-growing, matted, trailing thyme with purple flowers in July, and wonderfully tough tiny green leaves that combine the flavors of caraway and thyme.

Thymus vulgaris, Thyme. (McDonald)

T. praecox subsp. arcticus   Creeping Thyme
Zones 3–9.
This species is excellent for walkways because it can stand abuse. Attractive as a pot plant, especially 'Albus' (white-flowered), 'Coccineus' (crimson), and 'Splendens' (red).

T. vulgaris   Zones 4–9.
This is the species preferred for seasoning, an erect, aromatic subshrub with white-haired stems and small spikes of lilac or purple flowers in May and June. The two cultivars used as cooking herbs are *T. v.* 'English', and *T. v.* 'French', which has narrow leaves. There is quite a lot of variety among the French thymes. The cultivar 'Argenteus', Silver Thyme, is an ornamental, not a cooking thyme.

SEE ALSO:
Rosmarinus officinalis 'Prostratus', Rosemary, Herbs 9

ALTERNATES:
Artemisia ludoviciana, Western Mugwort, White Sage
Artemisia stellerana, Dusty-miller
Asarum europaeum, European Wild Ginger
Lysimachia nummularia, Moneywort, Creeping Jennie, Creeping Charlie

Slender, nodding foxtails of a mass planting of Pennesetum dance in every breeze. (Oehme)

ORNAMENTAL GRASSES

ORNAMENTAL GRASSES

Ornamental grasses are the context, or framing, for a landscape design often called the "new naturalism" and the "New American Garden" style, a direction backed by the scientists and curators at the National Arboretum. It combines grasses that sway, flow, and bend with the wind and wild-seeming flowering perennials, trees, and shrubs.

The National Arboretum's New American Garden fronts the Activity Building. The building and lot are intended as a prototype of an average ranch house with a one-third-acre front yard. The garden design was a gift of Washington-based landscape architects Wolfgang Oehme and James van Sweden, whose firm is identified with the new direction in landscaping. To the grass gardens of Europeans in the 1920s, Oehme and van Sweden have added trees and shrubs to increase form and texture—they are used as sculpture is used—and color in bold sweeps, massing bulbs and perennials by the hundreds.

The garden is intended to function as an urban meadow, which, typically, is mowed yearly after flowering. In the New American Garden, the plants are allowed to develop throughout the year without pruning, staking, spraying, or deadheading. In late winter they are cut back to the ground, mulched, and, as new foliage begins to emerge, fertilized with 10–6–4 that is half organic at the rate of 5 pounds per 100 square feet. Watering is by underground or surface irrigation system. Seedheads are allowed to ripen and stand through fall and winter, and there are lots of fruiting and berrying plants. The design and maintenance plan promotes a healthy ecological balance that encourages birds and does not exclude insects. The majority of insects are beneficial when a garden includes a variety of plants and somewhat resembles a naturally evolved ecosystem.

Color, texture, and unfolding growth are present in all four seasons. In spring, naturalized flowering bulbs carpet spaces between the cut-back ornamental grasses. Tulips in exotic forms, with narcissus and species iris, work wonderfully well here. In summer, masses of black-eyed Susan, Russian sage, and other flowering perennials that take care of themselves bloom along the walks and among the half-grown grasses. From early summer to fall, the dominant grasses mature, lifting tall, light-catching inflorescences to the wind. The tallest grasses and a few hollies shield the annex from the

View of the New American Garden at the U.S. National Arboretum. (Oehme)

road. Smaller grass species are set closer to the building. A few well-placed trees and flowering or fruiting shrubs mimic a meadow's variety. Additional seasonal color comes from big tubs of annuals, vegetables, and herbs.

In fall, sweeps of sedum turn russet-pink-coral, then fade to brown, and the fruiting trees color red and orange. With cold weather, ornamental grasses come into their own—rustling, tossing in the wind, and eventually binding a carpet of snow at their feet.

Through all its seasons, broad paths and comfortable stopping places invite meditation. For the birds there are banquets of seeds, insects, and worms, as well as nesting spaces and materials in this garden where chemical controls are never needed.

DESIGNING WITH GRASSES

Gardens designed around ornamental grasses adapt to many situations. Many ornamental grasses flourish by the shore, a visual bridge to native reeds. Their year-round beauty is not meant to be forever perfectly in bloom. The eye learns to appreciate their wind-tossed freedom from restraint.

Create no lines or borders in this kind of garden. Let spaces flow, tied together by the trees, ground covers, flowering perennials, and grasses. Plant clumps of medium-size grasses as islands with curved borders. Avoid straight lines in pathways. Vary heights, mixtures, and widths of flower beds to avoid any formal sense. Present plants to be viewed from all sides. Intermix groupings of different species.

To achieve romantic effects include conventional foliage, bark, and stem forms that contrast with the linearity of the grasses. Include small and medium-size native trees such as *Chionanthus retusus*, Fringe Tree; *Cornus kousa* var. *chinensis*, Chinese dogwood; *Franklinia alatamaha*, Franklin Tree; *Ilex*, Holly; *Lagerstroemia* in all colors, Crape Myrtle; *Tsuga*, Hemlock; *Hamamelis*, Witch hazel; and *Magnolia virginiana*, Sweet Bay. The trees capture the drama of the fourth season—the rain, ice, and snow that darken, lighten, and encrust bark and bare branches with changing textures.

Use evergreens sparingly as counterpoints to change and as foils to the dramatic effects of dried umbels and grasses in the winter landscape.

Plant bright perennial flowers by the hundreds. Grasses are colored buff and tan, sea green and green, gold and pale gold—perfect counterpoints for the bright spires, rounds, and clumps of flowers.

The Companion Plantings on the lists that follow include many bulbs and flowering perennials that Oehme and van Sweden combine with ornamental grasses. Among those used often are hardy low-maintenance coreopsis, sedum, yarrow, and daylilies, as well as brilliant tulips with exotic forms. Work for year-round appeal, from shoot to flowers and unfolding inflorescences. Choose flowers for textural contrast as well as color, counting on dried forms to present strong

contrast with the grasses in the third season, autumn.

Grasses are seen in many Washington, D.C., in-ground municipal plantings. And even to the unaccustomed eye, the summer and fall aspect of tall grasses in giant street containers is pleasing. After a snowfall, a big cement urn filled with drying golden grasses, standing at the foot of a wall of cement and marble, recalls winter fields in New England.

PLANTING GRASSES

Planting ornamental grasses in the home garden requires thought, or the garden will look unkempt. Plan with care. Expect to use half flowering perennials and half ornamental grasses—tall for sculptural effects, screening, and to replace time-consuming espaliers against bare walls; medium and small for edging.

Choose plants that will thrive with a minimum of stress in the site and create the illusion of always having grown there. Choose only plants that flourish without staking or pruning. Add native rocks to the design.

Ornamental grasses are planted as are other perennials, rather high in the ground, in well-drained soil unless otherwise specified, to which 25 to 50 percent organic matter has been added. Do not fertilize immediately after planting. Grasses must be planted fairly closely together to discourage weeds, but with enough room for growth. At the National Arboretum a sprayer with a fine mist of nonselective brush killers was used early in spring. Once the area was established, little additional weeding was required.

Wolfgang Oehme believes working in masses makes a small space look larger: "Several should be planted together rather than just one," he says. "They will have better impact." In their larger designs, Oehme and van Sweden mass perennials in minimums of 50 and routinely set out 120,000 plants. Every inch of the soil is filled up. For smaller gardens, they recommend planting perennials in clusters of no less than 6.

Like perennials, grasses don't fill out until the second season. Once installed, they are not expected to require division for at least 5 to 10 years. Ultimately, all perennials and grasses must be lifted, divided, and replanted in well-prepared soil.

ORNAMENTAL GRASSES 1
GRASSES FOR COLOR AND TEXTURE

Late in the growing season, many of the ornamental grasses raise feathery flowers on tall, wiry stems. Usually the flowers are straw-encased seeds called "inflorescences." The shades are subtle—silvery, bronze, beige-gold, dun. The color in ornamental grasses is primarily in the leaves—blues and blue-greens, fresh greens, solid golds, gold with stripes, the red of Japanese Blood Grass, *Imperata cylindrica* 'Red Baron'. Movement is the gift of all the ornamental grasses, tall and small; movement and music—the whisper of wind in the grass.

COMPANION PLANTINGS
Trees: *Hamamelis mollis,* Chinese Witch Hazel.
Shrubs: *Amelanchier laevis*, Shadblow Serviceberry.
Bulbs: *Eremurus stenophyllus,* Foxtail Lily; Lily-flowered Tulips; Red Parrot Tulips.
Flowers: *Rudbeckia fulgida* var. *sullivantii* 'Goldsturm', Coneflower; *Sedum spectabile* 'Autumn Joy', Stonecrop.

BOUTELOUA *boot-el-loo-ah*
gracilis Mosquito Grass   Zones 4–9.

Fine-leaved, open, upright clumps whose July flowers are flat-topped and one-sided, dark red to purple, as ephemeral as mosquitoes flitting above the nodding foliage. Good drainage is essential. Plant in spring, in sun, in small groups.

MATURE HEIGHT: 1'–2'
GROWTH RATE: medium
LIGHT: full sun
MOISTURE: roots moist

Cortaderia selloana, Pampas Grass. (Oehme, van Sweden)

Erianthus ravennae, Ravenna Grass. (Oehme)

BRIZA *brye-tza*
subaristata Quaking Grass   Zones 7–8.

This is a slender, delicate, clump-forming, knee-high meadow grass that moves all the time. It blooms early in May—short, light, puffy panicles that quake and tremble in the breeze. There are colored fruit clusters in fall. *Briza* is a tender perennial grown as an annual. Tolerates drought. Set out in masses, in spring or fall, in well-drained soil.

MATURE HEIGHT: 2'–3'
GROWTH RATE: medium
LIGHT: full sun
MOISTURE: versatile

Festuca mairei, Fescue. (Oehme)

CORTADERIA *kor-ta-deer-ee-uh*
selloana 'Pumila' Compact Pampas Grass
Zones 8–10.

Compact variety of a magnificent tall, clump-forming, upright grass with bluish leaves, for warm regions. In late summer the female flowers are spectacular, silky white plume-panicles, 3 feet long on some species. There are silvery, variegated, and pink cultivars offered. Popular specimen plant on the West Coast and in Florida. Plant in full sun in spring.

MATURE HEIGHT: 4'–6'
GROWTH RATE: medium
LIGHT: full sun
MOISTURE: versatile

ERIANTHUS *air-ee-anth-us*
ravennae Ravenna Grass   Zones 6–9.

A magnificent architectural plant, 9 to 12 feet tall, with broad, arching, silvery leaves. In late summer 3-foot silvery purple flower heads appear. Like the pampas grass it resembles, but hardier, it is a specimen and demands lots of space. Often seen in West Coast landscapes. In spring, plant in well-drained soil in full sun.

MATURE HEIGHT: 9'–12'
GROWTH RATE: fast
LIGHT: full sun
MOISTURE: roots moist

FESTUCA *fes-tew-kuh* Fescue

This genus includes familiar lawn grasses as well as big, handsome ornamentals. They form tufts of fine wiry leaves, which are rolled in some species. The summer flowers are the elegant narrow panicles of lawns gone to seed, green-white or purplish. Well-drained soil in the neutral range is a requirement. Regionally proven varieties are best.

GROWTH RATE: fast
LIGHT: full sun
MOISTURE: roots moist

Helictotrichon sempervirens, Blue Oat Grass. (Oehme)

F. amethystina var. superba
Blue Sheep's Fescue   Zones 4–8.
A good, durable grass, to 3 feet tall; the cultivar 'Rainbow Fescue' is particularly attractive.

F. cinerea 'April Grun'
Olive-Green Sheep's Fescue   Zones 4–8.
Ornamental fescue only 8 inches high, whose leaves are a beautiful green. Popular from coast to coast for small gardens. The narrow panicles are purplish. Mass in sun or light shade. Some tolerance for moist conditions. Plant in spring or fall.

F. mairei   Maire's Fescue   Zones 5–9.
A handsome tufting grass with cascading grayish foliage about 2 feet tall. Use in clumps or masses—it isn't bold enough to be a specimen. There's an insignificant flower. Plant in full sun, in spring.

HELICTOTRICHON *hel-lik-toe-try-con*
sempervirens   Blue Oat Grass   Zones 4–8.

Shining 2-foot puffs of wiry gray blue leaves. In May exquisitely delicate, narrow, golden, oatlike flowers

Pennisetum alopecuroides, Rose Fountain Grass.

sway far above the foliage on tall stems. Hardy and semievergreen. Plant in groups or masses. Lovely next to Russian Sage, *Perovskia atriplicifolia*. Must have good drainage. Set out clumps in spring or fall.

MATURE HEIGHT: 2′
GROWTH RATE: medium
LIGHT: full sun
MOISTURE: roots moist

IMPERATA *im-puh-ray-tuh*
cylindrica 'Red Baron'
Japanese Blood Grass   Zones 6–9.

A fairly new grass. The leaves are erect and pointed, with bloodred tips. Most successful when planted in groups or massed in sun or light shade where the sun will backlight the leaves. In this setting blood grass

glows a brilliant red. Hardy and does well in poor soil, reaching 1 to 2 feet in height. Grows very well in Dallas, Texas, and similar climates. Set out in spring. The light required depends on the region: in hot regions like Dallas, it grows best in semi-sun; in cooler places it needs full sun.

MATURE HEIGHT: 1′–2′
GROWTH RATE: medium
LIGHT: full sun, semi-sunny
MOISTURE: roots moist

PENNISETUM *pen-nis-seet-um*
alopecuroides   Rose Fountain Grass
                                 Zones 6–9.

Fountains of very fine, arching leaves grow 3 to 4 feet high. Then in July, stems rise above the leaves, bearing slender, rose tan, nodding foxtails at the tips of flowering spikelets. Fountain grass needs lots of space. Set out in groups or masses in sunny places. Excellent on the West Coast, as is the beautiful, less hardy *P. setaceum* (Zones 8–10). Plant in spring.

MATURE HEIGHT: 3′–4′
GROWTH RATE: medium
LIGHT: full sun
MOISTURE: soil surface damp

STIPA *stye-puh*
gigantea   Giant Feather Grass   Zones 7–9.

One of the most decorative landscape grasses. It is especially successful on the West Coast, difficult on the East Coast. Opens to upright tufts 6 feet high, with slender, feathery, very airy panicles to 2 feet long, purplish, then turning to gold. Lovely when the wind catches the plants. Use as a specimen or in a small group. Plant in sun in spring. Good drainage is essential, and soil in the neutral range is preferred.

MATURE HEIGHT: 6′
GROWTH RATE: medium
LIGHT: full sun
MOISTURE: roots moist

Imperata cylindrica 'Red Baron', Japanese Blood Grass. (Oehme)

SEE ALSO:

Hakonechloa macra 'Aureola', Golden Variegated Hakonechloa, Ornamental Grasses 5

Miscanthus sinensis 'Purpurascens', Red Silver Grass, Ornamental Grasses 3

Sesleria autumnalis, Autumn Moor Grass, Ornamental Grasses 6

ALTERNATES:

Festuca ovina var. *glauca*, Blue Fescue
Koeleria lobata, Blue Hair Grass
Sesleria caerula, Blue Moor Grass
Sesleria heuflerana

ORNAMENTAL GRASSES 2
GRASSES FOR NATURALIZING AND SLOPES

Ornamental grasses are planted with the expectation that they will naturalize and care for themselves. In addition, the plants here are good soil stabilizers. Many spread irresistibly and need space.

COMPANION PLANTINGS

Trees: *Juniperus virginiana,* Eastern Red Cedar.
Shrubs: *Cotoneaster multiflorus* or *Cotoneaster bullatus* forma *floribundus*; *Cornus alba* 'Sibirica', Siberian Dogwood.
Bulbs: *Camassia quamash,* Indian Lily; *Eremurus stenophyllus,* Foxtail Lily; Botanical or Species Tulips hybrids, *Tulipa fosterana,* 'White Emperor', 'Red Emperor', 'Yellow Emperor'; *Tulipa sylvestris, Tulipa turkestanica.*
Flowers: *Hemerocallis fulva,* Orange or Tawny Daylily; *Lysimachia punctata,* Yellow Loosestrife; *Perovskia atriplicifolia,* Russian Sage; *Rudbeckia fulgida* var. *sullivantii* 'Goldsturm', Coneflower.

Carex flacca, Blue Sedge. (Oehme)

Miscanthus sacchariflorus, Silver Banner Grass. (Oehme, van Sweden)

CAREX *kah-rex* Sedge

These are rather small grasses, with narrow, delicate leaves, some arching, others upright. The clumps are well defined. Many species prefer shade, or some shade (see Ornamental Grasses 5), though some succeed in sun. They spread and need space. Excellent for holding slopes.

GROWTH RATE:	fast
LIGHT:	full sun, versatile
MOISTURE:	roots moist

C. flacca Blue Sedge Zones 5–9.
A dense sedge with not much of a flower, but beautiful blue foliage about 12 inches high. Like a reed, it spreads rapidly; massed in big spaces it can take over. Soil can be wet or dry, and the location sunny or lightly shaded. Plant in spring or fall.

C. glauca Blue Sedge Zones 5–9.
This lovely blue-gray sedge is hardier to cold and spreads more slowly than *C. flacca*. Smaller (to 6 inches) and neater, it is a good choice for modular gardens and flower borders. Plant in sun or light shade, in wet or dry soil, spring or fall.

C. humilis Zones 5–9.
A grassy clump-former new in this country, this small species reaches 6 to 8 inches. Well suited as a ground cover for naturalized areas of the rock garden. It hugs the ground, holds the soil, and has great charm. Suited for sun or shade. Set out in spring or fall.

MISCANTHUS *mis-kanth-us*
sacchariflorus Silver Banner Grass
Zones 5–9.

The wonderfully useful *Miscanthus* species are big, clump-forming, perennial grasses with broad, grassy leaves. A variety of species appear in different categories in this section of the book. This 4- to 6-foot species is a spreading grass that must be used boldly, in large spaces. Tall, silky, silvery tan plumes sway above the foliage in late summer and fall. Plant in spring or fall, in groups or masses, in sun or partial shade or by the water's edge.

MATURE HEIGHT:	4'–5'
GROWTH RATE:	fast
LIGHT:	semi-sunny, versatile
MOISTURE:	versatile

PENNISETUM *pen-nis-seet-um*
incomptum Fountain Grass Zones 6–9.

Arching, 3- to 4-foot, very fine leaves rise in a fountain-like clump; starting in July, tannish flower spikelets with conspicuous bristles rise above the leaves. Fountain grass spreads at a run and needs lots of space. A wonderful ground cover. Plant in masses in full in sun in spring.

MATURE HEIGHT: 3'–4'
GROWTH RATE: fast
LIGHT: full sun, semi-sunny
MOISTURE: versatile

SPODIOPOGON *spoh-dee-oh-poe-gone sibiricus* Silver Spike   Zones 5–9.

A very architectural clump-forming grass. Green, reedlike foliage 4 to 5 feet tall first turns red, then golden as autumn approaches. In July and August stately, upright silvery flower spikes appear and remain through winter. Feature as a specimen, or naturalize in small groups. Plant in spring or fall. It thrives in full sun but can tolerate light shade.

MATURE HEIGHT: 4'–5'
GROWTH RATE: medium
LIGHT: versatile
MOISTURE: versatile

Pennisetum incomptum, Fountain Grass. (Oehme)

Spodiopogon sibiricus, Silver Spike. (Oehme, van Sweden)

SEE ALSO:
Hakonechloa macra, Ornamental Grasses 5
Spartina pectinata, Prairie Cord Grass, Ornamental Grasses 7
Uniola paniculata, Sea Oats, Ornamental Grasses 4

ALTERNATES:
Chasmanthium latifolium, Northern Oats, Wild Oats
Elymus glaucus, European Dune Grass

ORNAMENTAL GRASSES 3
GRASSES FOR RAPID GROWTH AND SUMMER SCREENING

These are very tall grasses that gain their height rapidly and change through the seasons. They provide live screening for summer and a fascinating progression of colors from green to gold as summer turns to fall.

COMPANION PLANTINGS
Trees: *Sophora japonica*, Japanese Pagoda Tree; *Zelkova serrata*, 'Village Green', Japanese Zelkova.
Shrubs: *Viburnum sieboldii*, Siebold Viburnum.
Flowers: *Inula magnifica*, Elecampane; *Lythrum salicaria* 'Morden's Pink', Purple Loosetrife; *Macleaya cordata,* Plume Poppy.

ARUNDO *ar-run-do* Reed

These tall perennnial reeds form large clumps 8 to 20 feet high, depending on the location. They have naturalized in the Southeast, particularly along the coast, but produce their magnificent feathery panicles only in warm regions. Good drainage is required.

GROWTH RATE: fast
LIGHT: full sun
MOISTURE: soil surface damp

Arundo donax, Giant Reed. (van Sweden)

A. donax   Giant Reed   Zones 7–10.
A bold, upright clump 7 to 12 feet high, spreading quickly by means of large rhizomes. Woody stems develop wide, flat leaves, like corn leaves, and big tassels of 1- to 2-foot-long flowers and seeds appear late in summer. Spreads slowly but increases steadily to make a masssive clump that lives for decades. As screening it is tough, long-lasting, and effective. Cut back to the ground annually. Use as a specimen and give it space. Thrives in moist, well-drained soil and full sun. Plant in spring.

Miscanthus floridulus, Giant Silver Grass. (Oehme)

A. donax 'Versicolor'   Giant Stripe,
Striped Giant Reed   Zones 8–10.
This is one of the tallest of the variegated grasses, 3 to 7 feet high. A bold, upright clump, the leaves are striped white and green. Thrives in moist, well-drained soil but isn't quite as hardy as the species. Plant in full sun in spring. This is a selection of the variety *variegata*.

CALAMAGROSTIS *kal-amuh-gros-tis*
C. acutiflora 'Stricta'   Feather Reed Grass
Zones 5–9.

A sun-loving, clump-forming grass, 5 to 7 feet tall and tightly upright, this is one of the first ornamental grasses to bloom. The fluffy bluish panicles come out in June and turn into beautiful golden tan reeds full of light. They remain until the following spring. In the New American Garden at the National Arboretum, Oehme, van Sweden and Associates massed feather reed grass to create an effective light screen separating the gift shop from the road. The seeds are sterile, so the grass is never invasive. Plant in groups in spring or fall. 'Karl Foerster', a beautiful, sturdy cultivar, is a little smaller than 'Stricta', 5 to 6 feet at maturity, and blooms even earlier.

GROWTH RATE: fast
LIGHT: full sun
MOISTURE: roots moist

MISCANTHUS *mis-kanth-us*
Silver Grass

The several *Miscanthus* species are big, perennial grasses with broad, grassy, gracefully arching leaves. They are best used boldly, in big spaces. Tall, silky, silvery tan plumes stand above the foliage in late summer and fall. Excellent in groups or masses, in full sun. *Miscanthus* species appear on several Ornamental Grasses lists as they are valuable in a variety of situations and have differing cultural requirements. Some, for instance, thrive only at water's edge—see Ornamental Grasses 7.

GROWTH RATE: fast
LIGHT: full sun
MOISTURE: roots moist

M. floridulus   Giant Silver Grass Zones 5–9.
This is one of the tall grasses, 8 to 10 or 12 feet, somewhat coarse but full of silvery light when the wind catches it. It has arching, wide leaves and an architectural form that changes with the seasons. Winter blows the leaves away but the canes remain. In a sunny spot in moist soil or at the water's edge it grows jungle-thick and makes a dense screen. The plant won't thrive if it dries out. Use as a specimen or plant a serrated line for screening. Set out in spring. It was formerly known as *M. sinensis* var. *giganteus*.

Calamagrostis, Feather Reed Grass. (Oehme)

M. sinensis Japanese Silver Grass
Zones 5–9.
One of the most desirable and versatile of the landscape grasses, this is a robust, open-upright, dense clump of silver grass 6 to 8 feet tall, which develops slowly into dense, effective screening. The drooping, pale pink to red flower clusters open on panicles up to 1 foot long. Plant in groups or masses in sun or partial shade. Set out plants in spring.

M. sinensis 'Gracillimus' Maiden Grass
Zones 6–9.
An upright-arching cultivar 4 to 6 feet tall, with fine texture. The ¼-inch-wide, long, curly leaves have a prominent white midvein. The flowers are at first reddish pink to red, then turn silvery white in autumn on curly, branching panicles. Considered by some to be the most elegant of all the grasses, it is a frequent subject of Japanese artists. In masses it makes colorful screening. Set out in a sunny location in spring.

M. sinensis 'Purpurascens' Red Silver Grass
Zones 7–9.
This more compact species reaches 3 to 4 feet and is prized for its color and early bloom. In July silvery reddish panicles grow high above the foliage, then as summer wanes, the foliage turns reddish to deep purple. Flowers and foliage last through winter. Dramatic enough for specimen or group planting, and excellent for screening. Plant in spring in full sun.

M. sinensis 'Yaku Jima' Zones 6–9.
This compact dwarf from the island of Yaku Jima reaches 2 to 3 feet in height and has a very narrow and delicate leaf. The flower is a plume that stands high above the foliage in early August. Use as a specimen or in groups, and for screening. Plant in spring in full sun.

SEE ALSO:
Sinarundinaria nitida, Blue Clump Bamboo, Ornamental Grasses 5
Spodiopogon sibiricus, Silver Spike, Ornamental Grasses 2

ALTERNATES:
Chasmanthium latifolium, Northern Oats, Wild Oats
Miscanthus sacchariflorus, Silver Banner Grass
Spartina pectinata, Prairie Cord Grass
Spartina pectinata 'Aureo-marginata', Variegated Cord Grass

ORNAMENTAL GRASSES 4
GRASSES FOR SEASHORE GARDENS

Many ornamental grasses thrive in well-drained, rather sandy soil. The ones described here do more—they handle a salty atmosphere and are recognized dune stabilizers.

COMPANION PLANTINGS
Trees: *Elaeagnus angustifolia,* Russian Olive; *Magnolia virginiana,* Sweet Bay; *Pinus thunbergiana,* Japanese Black Pine.
Shrubs: *Buddleia alternifolia,* Fountain Buddleia; *Lavandula angustifolia* 'Hidcote', English Lavender; *Rosa rugosa,* 'Sir Thomas Lipton', Japanese Rose.
Flowers: *Achillea filipendula* 'Coronation Gold', Fern-leaved Yarrow; *Cleome spinosa* 'Pink Queen'; *Dicentra spectabilis,* Bleeding-heart; *Digitalis purpurea,* Foxglove; *Echinacea purpurea,* Purple Coneflower; *Liriope platyphylla* 'Majestic', Lilyturf; *Perovskia atriplicifolia,* Russian Sage; *Sedum spectabile* 'Autumn Joy', Stonecrop; *Viola odorata* 'Royal Robe', Sweet Violet.

AMMOPHILA *am-moff-il-uh*
Beachgrass

These perennial grasses are very valuable for ground cover in dry, sandy soils, especially along the seacoast. The plants survive salt spray and spread quickly on creeping rootlets. Excellent for preventing wind erosion on beaches and dunes.

GROWTH RATE:	medium
LIGHT:	full sun
MOISTURE:	roots moist

A. arenaria European Beachgrass
Zones 3–6.
Grows wild along the coasts and is a great beach binder and dune stabilizer from Washington to northern California. Naturalized, it reaches 4 to 5 feet in height, with leathery leaves about 1 foot long and a spiky inflorescence. It is easily propagated by division of the creeping rootstock in early spring, and for that reason isn't easily found in nurseries.

A. breviligulata American Beachgrass
Zones 3–8.
Native beachgrass, similar to but slightly larger than *A. arenaria,* the European plant; grows 7 to 8 feet high. It grows wild along the Great Lakes and the Atlantic Coast from Newfoundland to North Carolina. Highly desirable as a sand stabilizer and easily propagated by division of the creeping rootstock. Plant in spring.

ELYMUS *ee-lim-us*
glaucus European Dune Grass Zones 3–9.

(In Europe, *E. arenarius.*) A successful sand binder, this is an upright, knee-high, bold, clumping plant with flat, grasslike leaves and dense 8-inch terminal spikes of tiny flowers. The leaves are blue-green, ⅝ inch wide, 1 foot long on a plant 2 to 3 feet high. Rapid spreader on a rhizomatous rootstock and attractive enough to be in the garden. Plant groups or

Miscanthus sinensis 'Purpurascens', Red Silver Grass. (Oehme van Sweden)

Elymus glaucus, European Dune Grass. (Oehme, van Sweden)

masses in full sun, in spring or fall.

MATURE HEIGHT: 2'–8'
GROWTH RATE: medium
LIGHT: full sun
MOISTURE: versatile

PHRAGMITES *frag-mye-tees*
australis Reed   Zones 4–10.

An enormous reed, to 19 feet high, that grows wild in wetlands, brackish or fresh—everywhere. The fluffy tannish seedheads swaying in the wind on their rigid golden stalks are a familiar sight in fall, sought after for winter arrangements. The plant is easily established and readily becomes rampant in moist areas. Plant in full sun in moist ground, in spring or fall.

MATURE HEIGHT: 12'–19'
GROWTH RATE: medium
LIGHT: full sun
MOISTURE: roots moist

UNIOLA *yew-nee-oh-luh*
paniculata Sea Oats   Zone 6.

A native of coastal dunes from Virginia to Texas, sea oats is an excellent soil and dune stabilizer. It is also a beautiful plant whose leaves and fruiting panicles are dried for winter arrangements. The flat, oatlike fruit spikes may be 1 inch wide and 2 inches long, and are borne in drooping clusters. The plant reaches 8 feet and is suitable only for large spaces. Plant in spring.

MATURE HEIGHT: 8'
GROWTH RATE: fast
LIGHT: full sun
MOISTURE: roots moist

SEE ALSO:
Sinarundinaria nitida, Blue Clump Bamboo, Ornamental Grasses 5
Spartina pectinata, Prairie Cord Grass, Ornamental Grasses 7

Spartina pectinata 'Aureo-marginata', Variegated Cord Grass, Ornamental Grasses 7

ALTERNATES:
Carex flacca, Blue Sedge
Panicum virgatum, Switch Grass
Spodiopogon sibiricus, Silver Spike
Molinia caerulea subsp. *arundinacea*, Purple Moor Grass

ORNAMENTAL GRASSES 5
GRASSES FOR SHADE

Here are plants that will flourish in semi-shade at the edge of woodlands, and in the shadow of tall buildings and plants, though they succeed with more sun, too. Tall grasses with their stately inflorescences are as handsome as espaliers against a stark, modern masonry wall, but require far less maintenance.

Phragmites (right) with *Spodiopogon* (left), *Miscanthus* (front), and daylilies. (van Sweden)

Carex morrowii 'Variegata', Japanese Sedge. (Oehme)

94

Trees: *Amelanchier laevis*, Shadblow, Serviceberry; *Cornus kousa* var. *chinensis* 'Rosabella', Chinese Dogwood; *Hamamelis vernalis*, Witch Hazel.
Shrubs: *Ilex* 'Sparkleberry', Holly; *Mahonia aquifolium*, Oregon Grape.
Flowers: *Aralia racemosa*, Spikenard; *Astilbe* × *arendsii* 'Fanal', Spiraea; *Bergenia cordifolia*; *Hosta* 'Honeybells'; *Ligularia dentata*, 'Desdemona'; *Lysimachia punctata*, Yellow Loosestrife.

CAREX *kah-rex*   Sedge

This genus has gracefully arched leaves and forms well defined, neat, rounded clumps. The species here flourish in light shade, spread rapidly, and demand little attention. Some species successful in full sun appear in Ornamental Grasses 2.

GROWTH RATE: fast
LIGHT: semi-sunny
MOISTURE: roots moist

C. buchananii   Fox Red Curly Sedge
Zones 5–10.
An upright, wiry sedge, architectural and well defined, 2 to 3 feet high. It is reddish bronze, and the blades curl at the tips. Beautiful when planted next to black Mexican smooth rock. Set out as a specimen or in groups in spring.

C. morrowii 'Variegata'   Japanese Sedge
Zones 5–9.
A pretty, clumping, low-growing, evergreen ground cover 1 to 2 feet tall. The color is a fresh green marked by a bright silver stripe down the center. Often seen as an edging plant in California. Plant in partial shade to full sun, in spring or fall.

C. muskingumensis   Palm Sedge Grass
Zones 4–9.
An interesting, low, clumping grass, 2 to 3 feet high, upright but arching in a manner reminiscent of the individual leaves of a palm frond. Nicely textured and a good, bright green. Pretty brown seedheads in summer, just a little taller than the leaves. Mass in

Chasmanthium latifolium, Wild Oats. (Oehme)

partial shade. Plant in spring or fall. Needs constant moisture.

CHASMANTHIUM *kass-manth-ee-um*
latifolium   Northern Oats, Wild Oats
Zones 5–9.

Narrow, upright, then arching fresh green leaves 3 to 5 feet high that turn bronze in fall. The flat fruit heads may be 1 inch wide and 1 inch long, held like spangles on slender drooping stems that stand well above the foliage. They shimmer in the breeze. The plant is lovely at the edge of woods. Plant in groups or masses, in shade or partial shade, in spring.

MATURE HEIGHT: 3'–5'
GROWTH RATE: fast
LIGHT: semi-sunny, versatile
MOISTURE: roots moist

DESCHAMPSIA *des-shamp-see-uh*

Knee-high, dense, tufted grasses with very narrow leaves that are an excellent dark green nearly all winter. In early summer, slender stems raise clouds of light-catching, drooping, very fine open panicles. Two species and several cultivars are grown, both shade loving but adaptable to partial sun.

MATURE HEIGHT: 2'–3'
GROWTH RATE: medium
LIGHT: semi-sunny, versatile
MOISTURE: roots moist, versatile

Carex muskingumensis, Palm Sedge Grass. (Oehme, van Sweden)

Deschampsia caespitosa, Tufted Hair Grass. (Oehme)

Sinarundinaria nitida, Blue Clump Bamboo. (Oehme)

D. caespitosa Tufted Hair Grass Zones 4–9.
Almost evergreen in California, this is the most popular species. There are a number of yellow cultivars. A 2- to 3-foot fountainy tuft of narrow leaves rises in spring; then in May or early summer, clouds of very fine, feathery, light-catching, drooping and nodding open panicles soar above the leaves. The flowers are light green or purplish spikelets to 10 inches long. They dance in every breeze. Cut the flower stalks in late summer. The leaves remain evergreen almost all winter. They grow again in early spring. Rapidly spreading plant that requires lots of space and consistently moist soil, in sun or partial shade. Plant in groups or masses in spring or fall.

D. caespitosa var. *vivipara*
Viviparous Hair Grass Zones 5–9.
'Fairy's Joke' is a favorite cultivar. Much planted in California and the most delicate member of the genus, growing to 3 feet tall. Clouds of very fine panicles move with the winds. It is slightly more tender to cold than the species, and spreads rapidly. Plant in groups or masses, in sun or partial shade, in consistently moist soil. Set out in spring or fall.

HAKONECHLOA *hakun-eh-**clo**-uh*
macra Zones 4–9.

A cascading, lovely light green grass, 2 feet tall. 'Aureola', Golden Variegated Hakonechloa, is a yellow-gold, like goldenrod, striped with green; it is hardy in Zones 7–9, grows 1 to 2 feet tall. The species and cultivar are attractive planted together and with *Imperata cylindrica* 'Red Baron', Japanese Blood Grass. In spring, plant clumps in semi-shade.

MATURE HEIGHT: 2′
GROWTH RATE: slow
LIGHT: semi-sunny
MOISTURE: roots moist

LUZULA *loo-**zul**-ah*
nivea Snowy Wood Rush Zones 4–9.

A delicate, cascading, tufting grass to 2 feet high, with dainty clusters of white-green flowers that nod on arching stems above the plant in spring and early summer. It spreads rapidly. Plant in groups or masses, in shade or partial shade in spring. Very tolerant of drought.

MATURE HEIGHT: 2′
GROWTH RATE: slow
LIGHT: semi-sunny
MOISTURE: versatile

SINARUNDINARIA *sin-ah-rund-in-**ay**-ee-ah* nitida
Blue Clump Bamboo Zones 8–10.

A magnificent sculptural evergreen bamboo for warm regions. The elegant arching leaves are fresh green on one side, bluish on the other. Mature height is to 20 feet. Never needs cutting back and isn't invasive, though it eventually makes a good-sized clump. This plant requires patience but is rewarding. Plant in semi-shade, in spring.

MATURE HEIGHT: 20′
GROWTH RATE: slow
LIGHT: semi-sunny
MOISTURE: roots moist

SEE ALSO:
Imperata cylindrica, Japanese Blood Grass, Ornamental Grasses 1

Pennisetum incomptum, Fountain Grass, Ornamental Grasses 2
Sesleria autumnalis, Autumn Moor Grass, Ornamental Grasses 6

ALTERNATES:
Carex comans, New Zealand Hair Sedge
Festuca gigantea, Giant Fescue

ORNAMENTAL GRASSES 6
GRASSES FOR SUNNY, DRY URBAN AREAS

In their search for plants that tolerate drought, heat, neglect, and are interesting in all four seasons, gardeners are turning more and more to grasses. They are planted in street-side pocket parks in combination with other ornamentals like the familiar Companion Plantings below, and also in big tubs and planters in front of municipal buildings.

COMPANION PLANTINGS
Trees: *Elaeagnus angustifolia*, Russian Olive; *Magnolia virginiana*, Sweet Bay; *Sophora japonica*, Japanese Pagoda Tree; *Zelkova serrata*, 'Village Green', Japanese Zelkova.
Shrubs: *Euonymus alata* 'Compacta', Dwarf Winged Spindle Tree; *Syringa reticulata* (syn. *amurensis* var. *japonica*), Japanese Tree Lilac.
Bulbs: *Allium giganteum*, Giant Onion; *Camassia quamash*, Indian Lily; *Eremurus stenophyllus*, Foxtail Lily; *Tulipa fosterana*, 'Orange Emperor', 'Red Emperor', Emperor Tulip; *Tulipa Kaufmanniana*, 'Westpoint', Water Lily Tulip; *Tulipa greigii* 'Sweet Lady', 'Goldwest', Greigii Tulips; Red Parrot Tulips; Species Tulips.
Flowers: *Achillea filipendula* 'Coronation Gold', Fern-leaved Yarrow; *Ceratostigma plumbaginoides*, Blue Ceratostigma, Plumbago; *Coreopsis verticillata* 'Golden Showers', Threadleaf Tickseed; *Sedum* 'Ruby Glow'; *Stachys byzantina*, Woolly Betony, Lamb's-ears; *Yucca filamentosa*, Adam's-needle.

Panicum virgatum, Switch Grass. (Oehme)

Molinia cultivar. (Oehme, van Sweden)

CHONDROPETALUM *kon-dro-pet-al-lum*
tectorum   Zones 8–10.

A new grasslike plant from South Africa, gaining popularity in California. It forms a strong clump, and is reedy with an interesting jointed linear structure similar to that of *Equisetum*, that makes a handsome accent. Of particular appeal is the fresh, very green color, which persists. Plant in full sun, in spring. The plant can stand summer drought, but needs spring rain. Prefers well-drained soil in the neutral range.

MATURE HEIGHT: 3'–4'
GROWTH RATE: medium
LIGHT: full sun
MOISTURE: roots moist, versatile

FESTUCA *fes-tew-kuh*
cinerea   Blue Fescue   Zone 4.

A low-growing, fine-textured, tufting grass with many slender stems. Many varieties have blue foliage. Leaves about 6 to 10 inches tall, but the fruiting heads reach to 2 feet. Handsome with succulents and dramatic specimens such as the swordlike New Zealand flax. Good ground cover for well-drained dry slopes and rock gardens. Plant in spring or fall.

MATURE HEIGHT: 10"
GROWTH RATE: fast
LIGHT: full sun
MOISTURE: roots moist

MOLINIA *moh-lye-nee-uh*
caerulea subsp. *arundinacea*
'Transparent'   Tall Purple Moor Grass
                          Zones 5–8.

Fine-textured, wiry, fountaining tufts of very tall grass, rather compact compared to the species. In July, red- to violet-tinted, delicate, wispy seedheads rise on purplish 5- to 8-inch panicles high above the leaves and move constantly in the wind. In fall they turn golden yellow. Successful in full sun or partial shade, dry or wet soils. Set out as a specimen or plant in groups, in spring. 'Karl Foerster' is slightly taller, 6 to 7 feet.

MATURE HEIGHT: 5'–6'
GROWTH RATE: fast
LIGHT: full sun
MOISTURE: roots moist

PANICUM *pan-ik-um*
virgatum 'Haense Herms'   Red Switch Grass
                          Zones 5–9.

The finely cut leaves turn red in late summer and remain all winter, making this one of the best overall red landscape grasses in fall. Lovely naturalized with purple asters. The clump is upright, narrower at the base, 3 to 4 feet tall, and spreads quickly. Clouds of fine blooms stand above the leaves beginning in July. Plant in full sun in groups, in spring or fall.

MATURE HEIGHT: 3'–4'
GROWTH RATE: fast
LIGHT: full sun
MOISTURE: roots moist, versatile

PENNISETUM *pen-nis-seet-um*
orientale   Oriental Fountain Grass
                                    Zones 7–9.

Tufted, mound-forming clumps of narrow, ribbony leaves grow 2 to 3 feet high. In summer masses of fuzzy, tasseled cattails bloom above the leaves on rigid stems that sway in the wind. A rapid grower, it needs space. In spring, plant in groups or masses in full sun. Requires well-drained soil.

MATURE HEIGHT: 2'–3'
GROWTH RATE: fast
LIGHT: full sun
MOISTURE: surface soil dry

SESLERIA *sess-lair-ee-uh*
autumnalis   Autumn Moor Grass
                                    Zones 5–8.

Moor grass never suffers from drought and is a good city subject. Low-growing, about 1½ feet, the attractive, chartreuse-green tufts bloom in fall—pale airy flowers that lighten the whole plant. Useful to edge shrubs and in the rock garden as a specimen. Plant in spring or fall.

MATURE HEIGHT: 1½'
GROWTH RATE: fast
LIGHT: semi-sunny
MOISTURE: roots moist

SEE ALSO:

Calamagrostis × *acutiflora* 'Stricta', Feather Reed Grass, Ornamental Grasses 3
Carex flacca, Blue Sedge, Ornamental Grasses 2
Miscanthus sinensis 'Gracillimus', Maiden Grass, Ornamental Grasses 3
Pennisetum incomptum, Fountain Grass, Ornamental Grasses 2
Spodiopogon sibiricus, Silver Spike, Ornamental Grasses 2

Sesleria autumnalis, Autumn Moor Grass. (Oehme)

ORNAMENTAL GRASSES 7
GRASSES FOR WET CONDITIONS

The plants here perform reliably in wet conditions. Some may also grow in drier situations—Audrey Teasdale, botanist with Monrovia Nursery Company in California, reports seeing miscanthus growing well in dry places.

COMPANION PLANTINGS

Trees: *Acer rubrum* 'Red Sunset', Red Maple, Swamp Maple; *Cornus kousa* var. *chinensis* 'Summer Stars', Chinese Dogwood; *Magnolia* 'Galaxy'.

Shrubs: *Mahonia aquifolium*, Oregon Grape.
Flowers: *Astilbe* × *arendsii* cvs,; Spiraea; *Hemerocallis* 'Hyperion', Yellow Daylily; *Hosta plantaginea* 'Grandiflora', Fragrant Hosta; *Lysimachia punctata*, Yellow Loosestrife.
Aquatic plants: *Iris pseudacorus*, Yellow Iris; *Pontederia cordata*, Pickerel Weed, Pickerel Rush; *Sagittaria lancifolia*, Arrowhead; *Scirpus albescens*, White Bullrush; *Thalia dealbata*, Water Canna; *Typha angustifolia*, Narrow-leaved Cattail; Tropical Water Lilies: 'General Pershing', 'Texas Shell', 'Dauben', 'Mrs. Martin E. Randig', 'Marion Strawn', 'Woods White Knight', 'Maroon Beauty', 'Red Flair', 'Eldorado'.

ACORUS *ak-or-us*
gramineus 'Variegatus'
Variegated Grassy-leaved Sweet Flag
                                    Zones 5–9.

A native of marshy places with irislike leaves, it is an ancient fragrance herb loved for its sweet lemony scent. Greenish flowers are borne on small spikes in June. This species is a white-striped dwarf. Though not strictly an ornamental grass, it is included in bog gardens and is much used on the West Coast. 'Ogon' is a gold-variegated, slightly taller cultivar. Plant in sun, spring or fall.

MATURE HEIGHT: 8"
GROWTH RATE: fast
LIGHT: full sun
MOISTURE: roots moist

CAREX *kah-rex*
pendula   Drooping Sedge Grass
                                    Zones 5–9.

A 2-foot, arching, drooping sedge to mass as a ground cover with lots of space in which to grow. Very handsome in fall. Almost evergreen, but in late winter it browns. There's an insignificant bloom in spring. Set out in spring, in partial shade where moisture is assured. Prefers somewhat acid soil but is versatile.

Pennisetum orientale, Oriental Fountain Grass. (Oehme, van Sweden)

MATURE HEIGHT: 2'
GROWTH RATE: fast
LIGHT: semi-sunny
MOISTURE: roots moist

MISCANTHUS *mis-kanth-us*
Japanese Silver Grass

Most of the *Miscanthus* species on these pages are big, bold plants with broad, grassy, gracefully arching leaves. They are characterized by the appearance in late summer or fall of silky, silvery plumes that stand high above the foliage. They clump rapidly and are most attractive when used boldly in big spaces, either in groups or massed. The species here succeed by the water's edge in sun or partial shade. Plant clumps in spring or fall.

GROWTH RATE: fast
LIGHT: full sun
MOISTURE: roots moist

M. sinensis 'Variegatus'
Variegated Japanese Silver Grass
Zones 5–10.

There are many forms of this beautiful species, a robust, open-upright or dense, clump-forming grass growing 6 or 8 to 13 feet tall. The silvery flowers are pale pink to red and open silvery white, on open panicles to 1 foot long. Plant in spring, in sun or partial shade at water's edge, with lots of room to spread.

M. sinensis 'Zebrinus' Zebra Grass
Zones 5–10.

This striking upright species is a big plant, 6 to 8 feet tall, whose leaves sport horizontal yellow bands like a zebra. Plant as a specimen, in sun, with room to spread. Thrives by the water's edge. It may be less hardy than some other *M. sinensis* species. Set out in spring.

Spartina pectinata, Prairie Cord Grass. (Oehme)

PANICUM *pan-ik-um*
virgatum Switch Grass Zones 4/5–9.

This 3- to 6-foot grass is upright and narrow with fast-spreading, rhizomatous roots. Beginning in July, dense clouds of dark red to purple spikelets on open panicles to 2 feet long stand above the leaves. In fall the finely cut leaves turn bright yellow and remain on the plant all winter. Good choice when a big, fast-spreading plant is wanted for a moist or wet site. Plant in full sun in groups, in spring or fall.

MATURE HEIGHT: 3'–6'
GROWTH RATE: fast
LIGHT: full sun
MOISTURE: roots moist

SPARTINA *spar-ti-nuh*
pectinata Prairie Cord Grass Zones 5–9.

A gracious, spreading grass 4 to 6 feet high with a drooping habit that shows off well when plants are massed on a slight incline or at water's edge. It forms a dense clump, narrow at the base, of wide leaves so tough they can almost be used for cord. Spreads quickly, especially in moist soil. The leaves of the taller—5 to 7 feet—variegated cultivar, 'Aureo-marginata', are edged with yellow. Plant in masses or groups in sun at water's edge, in spring or fall.

MATURE HEIGHT: 4'–6'
GROWTH RATE: fast
LIGHT: full sun
MOISTURE: roots moist

SEE ALSO:

Calamagrostis × *acutiflora*, Feather Reed Grass, Ornamental Grasses 3
Deschampsia caespitosa, Tufted Hair Grass, Ornamental Grasses 5
Miscanthus sacchariflorus, Silver Banner Grass, Ornamental Grasses 2
Molinia caerulea subsp. *arundinacea*, Tall Purple Moor Grass, Ornamental Grasses 6

ALTERNATES:

Arundo donax, Giant Reed
Arundo donax 'Versicolor', Giant Stripe
Elymus glaucus, European Dune Grass

Carex pendula, Drooping Sedge Grass. (Oehme)

Naturalized Ajuga is a sea of blue in spring. (McDonald)

GROUND COVERS

GROUND COVERS

Any plant can be considered as ground cover, but the most resistant and useful are the plants on the lists that follow—low-growing forms that naturalize and multiply, keeping everything else out. Once ground covers were used only to soften untended slopes and fill shady places under old trees where they competed successfully with tree roots. But in this new era of gardening, ground covers are looked to as replacement for the time-consuming, water-guzzling lawn and as an alternative to paving.

In the naturalized New American Garden, ground covers are grouped in richly varied combinations rather than in single-species displays—plains of English ivy or pachysandra. A typical combination that has everything—flowers, fresh foliage, and fall color—is *Viola odorata*, Sweet Violet, and *Vinca minor*, Periwinkle, with *Pachysandra terminalis*, Japanese Pachysandra, *Artemisia stellerana*, Dusty-miller, and *Ceratostigma plumbaginoides*, Blue Ceratostigma or Plumbago. It includes plants for shade, some for semi-shade under tall trees, some for full sun. Among the most beautiful

to naturalize in light shade are the ferns, listed in Ground Covers 4, which flourish under trees and along shady walls, and are ideal for damp spots in light woodlands.

When the classic ground covers are used—*Hedera helix*, English Ivy, *Pachysandra*, low-growing *Juniperus* species, *Liriope*, *Hosta*—now they are interplanted, as though they had occurred in nature, with daffodils and other bulbs, ornamental grasses tall and small, summer-flowering shrubs, and perennial flowers. Favorite flowers for this purpose are natives, such as *Aquilegia, Asclepias, Coreopsis, Echinacea, Liatris, Phlox, Rudbeckia, Solidago, Stokesia*, and *Yucca*. More exotic flowers, such as *Gypsophila, Iris, Peonia*, and *Sedum*, are used sparingly.

The summer-flowering shrubs planted with the ground covers—*Hydrangea, Lagerstroemia, Caryopteris, Buddleia*—are set 12 to 16 inches apart, allowed to flower on current growth, and cut back to the ground each spring.

In a ground cover design, try to include one or more of the lovely flowering ground covers. Among them are roses—

Juniperus procumbens 'Nana', Dwarf Japanese Garden Juniper. (Neumann)

Deutzia gracilis 'Nikko', Slender Deutzia. (Neumann)

no-maintenance *Rosa rugosa,* Japanese Rose, and *Rosa virginiana,* Virginia Rose (see Herbs 7), which flourish in neglect by the seashore. The ground-hugging Memorial Rose, *Rosa wichuraiana,* is a good choice for erosion control of slopes. *Forsythia × intermedia* 'Arnold Dwarf' is another delightful plant that flourishes when naturalized on highway slopes and in rocky fields in full sun. There are many more in the list that follows.

PLANTING GROUND COVERS

Since the intention is to avoid high maintenance, choose plants that will flourish in the site and soil as it is, especially when a large piece of ground is to be covered. Test the soil for fertility and pH. Choose acid-loving plants for acidic soils. Check drainage, and if it is poor, choose plants from Ground Covers 10.

When a smaller area is involved, the soil can be modified to give the ground cover a good start. In fall or early spring, after the soil has dried, till 8 inches deep three times over a 2-week period. Cover the area with 2 or 3 inches of compost or decomposed leaves, and mix it in. For every 1,000 square feet, add 80 pounds each of limestone and gypsum. Mix that in. Put on 2 inches of mulch and plant through the mulch. Plan on at least 2 years for the plants to grow enough to cover completely: most will require more time unless very closely planted.

Practice a fairly regular fertilization program. In the early years, in late winter and again in late spring, apply a complete fertilizer at half the rate recommended.

GROUND COVERS 1
FLOWERING GROUND COVERS

Plant the flowering ground covers where they will be seen from the house, and if you use the house primarily during certain seasons, choose species that will bloom when you are there. Combine flowering ground covers with ground covers that have colorful foliage to create richly textured views.

CERATOSTIGMA *ser-at-oh-stig-muh*
plumbaginoides
Blue Ceratostigma, Plumbago   Zones 5–9.

Vigorous plants that form low mats spreading to 18 inches, of almost evergreen, glossy, dark green leaves. From midsummer to cold weather electric blue flowers appear, then the foliage turns bronze—in California almost red. Excellent as ground cover, edger, in rock and wall gardens. Stays in top form when sheared annually with a lawn mower set high. Set out root divisions in spring. Listed in some catalogs as Plumbago larpentae.

MATURE HEIGHT: *6″–12″*
GROWTH RATE: moderate
LIGHT: versatile
MOISTURE: versatile

COTONEASTER *ko-toh-nee-ass-ter*

Handsome shrubs with interesting branching and showy fall displays of bright red or orange berries. The cold-hardy types tend to be deciduous, and the evergreens are hardy only in warmer regions. The flowers are small, white or pinkish, and bloom in spring and summer. There are both low-growing and tall species. They require well-drained soil, in the neutral range, but are versatile, full sun or light shade. To ensure successful transplanting, in spring

Cotoneaster horizontalis, Rock Cotoneaster. (Neumann)

set out container or balled-and-burlapped plants. Birds are attracted by the fruits.

GROWTH RATE: medium
LIGHT: full sun, semi-sunny
MOISTURE: versatile

C. adpressus Creeping Cotoneaster
Zones 4–7.
A beautiful slow-growing, dense dwarf with showy red fruit. The height is 12 to 18 inches and the spread 4 to 6 feet. It often roots where branches touch the soil. White or pink flowers appear in summer. An early variety, *C. a. praecox*, grows more quickly, has lovely foliage and larger fruits.

C. dammeri Bearberry Cotoneaster
Zones 5–8.
This prostrate species makes a solid, glossy, evergreen carpet beautiful on banks, massed, and as a border. Vigorous grower. White flowers in summer, followed by red berries.

C. horizontalis Rock Cotoneaster
Zones 4/5–7.
Outstanding species with flat, layered branches 2 to 3 feet high and a spread of 5 to 8 feet. Rich foliage, bright red fruits. The dainty leaves of the cultivar 'Variegata' are edged with white, a lovely slow-growing shrub.

Ceratostigma plumbaginoides, Plumbago. (McDonald)

Lantana montevidensis, Trailing Lantana. (McDonald)

Deutzia gracilis 'Nikko', Slender Deutzia. (Neumann)

C. microphyllus Small-leaved Cotoneaster
Zones 6–7.
Evergreen species 2 to 4 feet high, that can spread to 15 feet across. Pink flowers followed by scarlet berries.

C. salicifolius var. repens
Willowleaf Cotoneaster Zones 6–8.
Evergreen to semievergreen, rapidly spreading variety which forms a dense carpet. Small, narrow leaves and profuse clusters of small red berries. 'Scarlet Leader', Zones 5–7, is 6 to 12 inches tall and spreads to 6 feet.

DEUTZIA *dewt-see-uh*
gracilis 'Nikko' Slender Deutzia Zones 4–8.

'Nikko' gives a lavish late April display of exquisite white flower clusters and has burgundy foliage in fall. The plant is a compact, low-spreading cultivar introduced from Japan by horticulturist Sylvester G. March and former National Arboretum director Dr. John L. Creech. Plant in spring or fall in soil in the neutral range.

MATURE HEIGHT: 2′
GROWTH RATE: medium
LIGHT: full sun, semi-sunny
MOISTURE: versatile

LANTANA *lan-tay-nuh*

These are semitropical woody or herbaceous plants with pretty crinkled leaves and year-round clusters of small, tubular flowers in warm climates south of Washington, D.C. The two species below, resistant to salt and drought, are prime ground covers for open areas, banks, slopes, and the seashore. Plant in early spring in rich garden soil.

GROWTH RATE: medium
LIGHT: full sun
MOISTURE: versatile

L. montevidensis Weeping Lantana,
Trailing Lantata Zones 8–10.
A trailing shrub with pendant stems 2 to 3 feet long and pinkish purple flower clusters. Outstanding ground cover for frost-free regions where it can be perennial. In the North, this species flourishes as an annual ground cover and in hanging baskets. It is often planted in seashore gardens.

L. ovatifolia var. reclinata Dwarf Lantana
Zones 8–10.
Less than a foot high, this variety offers a year-round display of flowers in yellow, orange, or red. It tolerates some salt, a lot of drought, and in central and southern Florida is planted on banks, slopes, and open areas.

PHLOX *flox*
subulata   Moss Pink, Moss Phlox
Zone 2/3.

Semievergreen, mat-forming perennial to 6 inches high with needlelike foliage and, in early spring, masses of tiny pink flowers. There are lovely lavender-blue cultivars and whites as well. 'Chattahoochee' is a beautiful lavender-blue with a red eye. Ideal for the tops of rock walls, rock gardens, and cultivated slopes in sun. Carefree and multiplies in well-drained soil mixed with generous amounts of leaf mold and peat moss. Plant root divisions in early fall or spring and divide every few years.

MATURE HEIGHT: 6″
GROWTH RATE: medium
LIGHT: full sun
MOISTURE: versatile

SPIRAEA *spye-ree-uh*
japonica   Japanese Spirea Zones 3–8.

An upright shrub to 6 feet that bears flat clusters of pink flowers in summer, an excellent tall ground cover. Easy to grow, it thrives in almost any soil and situation, but is most beautiful growing in moist soil

Phlox subulata, Moss Pink.

and full sun. Prune lightly in early spring to encourage more flowering growth. *S. j.* 'Alpina' is a low-growing type with pink flowers; the species *S. nipponica*, Tosa Spirea, has white flowers. Prefers neutral-range soil.

MATURE HEIGHT: 6′
GROWTH RATE: medium
LIGHT: versatile
MOISTURE: versatile

TULBAGHIA *tul-bag-ee-uh*
violacea   Society Garlic Zones 9–10.

A clump-forming, cormous herb with showy purple, urn-shaped flowers in huge rounded clusters spring, summer, and fall. Flourishes in open, sunny areas of California and Florida and is grown as a pot plant in the North. The flowers and foliage are faintly scented of garlic. Plant seed or divisions of offsets in light, sandy soil in spring.

MATURE HEIGHT: 16″–24″
GROWTH RATE: medium
LIGHT: full sun
MOISTURE: roots moist, versatile

SEE ALSO:
Ajuga genevensis, Geneva Bugle, Ground Covers 2
Chelone obliqua, Turtlehead, Snakehead, Ground Covers 10
Cytisus spp., Broom, Ground Covers 7
Epimedium × *rubrum,* Red Alpine Epimedium, Ground Covers 6
Forsythia × *intermedia* 'Arnold Dwarf', Ground Covers 9
Galax urceolata, Ground Covers 10
Genista pilosa 'Vancouver Gold', Broom, Ground Covers 9
Genista sagittalis, Arrow Broom, Ground Covers 9
Hosta plantaginea 'Grandiflora', Fragrant Hosta, Ground Covers 8
Hypericum buckleyi, Blue Ridge St.-John's-wort, Ground Covers 9
Hypericum calycinum, Aaron's Beard, Creeping St.-John's-wort, Ground Covers 9
Hypericum × *moseranum,* Gold Flower, Ground Covers 9
Iberis sempervirens, Evergreen Candytuft, Ground Covers 6
Lamium maculatum 'Variegatum', Spotted Dead Nettle, Ground Covers 10
Liriope platyphylla, Lilyturf, Ground Covers 5
Liriope spicata, Creeping Lilyturf, Ground Covers 5
Potentilla tridentata, Three-toothed Cinquefoil, Ground Covers 6
Ruellia makoyana, Monkey Plant, Ground Covers 10
Vinca major, Greater Periwinkle, Ground Covers 3
Vinca minor, Periwinkle, Ground Covers 3
Zephyranthes spp, Rain Lily, Ground Covers 5

ALTERNATES:
Calluna vulgaris, Heather, Scotch Heather
Campanula carpatica, Tussock Bellflower, Carpathian Bellflower
Chaenomeles japonica, Lesser Japanese Quince
Convallaria majalis, Lily-of-the-valley
Erica spp., Heath
Hemerocallis 'Aztec Gold', Yellow Daylily
Sedum, Stonecrop, Orpine

GROUND COVERS 2
GROUND COVERS WITH DECIDUOUS FOLIAGE

Breeders yearly add to the popular ground covers. Like fashions, these new cultivars come and go; the proven performers remain. Here are some of the best.

AEGOPODIUM *ee-go-poh-dee-um*
podagraria 'Variegatum'   Bishop's Weed
Zones 3–9.

White edges on 6-inch-high silvery green leaves make this vigorous grower colorful. In any soil—in sun or shade—it spreads to 3 feet in a couple of years; in good soil it can be invasive. In late spring insignificant white flowers similar to Queen-Anne's-lace appear and persist. Sow seeds or plant root divisions in early spring.

MATURE HEIGHT: 6″
GROWTH RATE: fast
LIGHT: versatile
MOISTURE: versatile

AJUGA *aj-yew-guh*
reptans   Carpet Bugle   Zones 2–3.

Semievergreen, low-growing, upright, leafy stems densely carpet the ground and in spring cover themselves with flowers of blue, purple, or white. Spreads rapidly. 'Burgundy Glow' has variegated burgundy

Aegopodium podagraria 'Variegatum', Bishop's Weed.

foliage and 8-inch-high blue flowers. *A. genevensis,* Geneva Bugle, makes a better floral show and grows less vigorously. The cultivar 'Atropurpurea' has bronze-purple foliage and purple flowers; 'Rubra' has dark purple leaves, purple-red flowers; 'Variegata's' leaves are mottled with creamy white. In the north *Ajuga* succeeds in full sun, but in the South it prefers some shade. Set out root divisions in early spring.

MATURE HEIGHT: 4″–10″
GROWTH RATE: fast
LIGHT: versatile
MOISTURE: versatile

ARTEMISIA *art-em-miz-ee-uh*
ludoviciana var. *albula*   Silver-king Artemisia
Zones 5–9.

Drought-resistant herbs, to 3 feet tall, with airy, frosty-looking foliage that is fragrant, valuable for edging, in borders, and as ground cover in larger landscapes. There are tiny grayish white florets. The plant is easily grown in well-drained garden soil and can tolerate full sun. Plant root divisions in early spring.

MATURE HEIGHT: 3′
GROWTH RATE: medium
LIGHT: full sun
MOISTURE: versatile

PAXISTIMA *pax-ist-im-uh*
canbyi   Cliff Green, Mountain Lover
Zones 3–8.

An evergreen shrub, about 12 inches high with a spread of about 3 feet and leathery leaves that turn bronze in cool weather. Small reddish flowers bloom on slender stems in mid-spring. Excellent for naturalizing, in rock gardens, or as edging. In well-drained, sandy, peaty soil it thrives in full sun or shade. Plant container-rooted divisions in spring.

MATURE HEIGHT: 12″
GROWTH RATE: slow
LIGHT: versatile
MOISTURE: roots moist

PILEA *pye-lee-uh*
microphylla   Artillery Plant   Zone 10.

A short-lived perennial about 1 foot tall with tiny, ferny green leaves and insignificant green flowers in

Ajuga reptans, Carpet Bugle. (McDonald)

Paxistima canbyi, Cliff Green.

summer, fall, and winter. It discharges pollen in a fashion that has earned it its common name. In Florida it is used as ground cover in full sun, under trees, and in shaded places. Moderately tolerant of salt, drought, and light conditions. Plant root divisions in spring.

MATURE HEIGHT: 1'
GROWTH RATE: medium
LIGHT: versatile
MOISTURE: versatile

STACHYS *stay-kiss*

Attractive filler for the border and handsome ground cover with small violet or white flowers that stand above the woolly, grayish leaves from midsummer until frost. Sow seeds in spring or plant root divisions in early fall or early spring.

GROWTH RATE: medium
LIGHT: full sun, semi-sunny
MOISTURE: roots moist

Stachys byzantina, Lamb's-ears. (Shimizu)

S. byzantina   Woolly Betony, Lamb's-ears
Zone 4.
Perennial 1 to 1½ feet tall, with large, semievergreen, gray leaves that are very woolly and almost luminous in moonlight. Good edger for the border. Small purple flowers bloom from July to frost, lovely in fresh bouquets and dried arrangements. May be listed (incorrectly) as S. olympica and S. lanata. This species once was used to bandage cuts.

S. officinalis   Betony   Zone 4.
Grows to about 1–2 feet high and was prized by the Romans and during the Middle Ages. It was drunk as tea, also made into a green salve and a preserve taken for every ill of the head and to keep away "witches and evil spirits." The colonists drank a bitter tonic made of it. The purple flowers appear in July and August and are quite ornamental.

SEE ALSO:
Achillea tomentosa, Woolly Yarrow, Herbs 10
Arctostaphylos uva-ursi, Bearberry, Ground Covers 3
Artemisia stellerana, Dusty-miller, Ground Covers 7
Athyrium goeringianum 'Pictum', Japanese Silver Painted Fern, Ground Covers 4
Euonymus fortunei, Vines 8
Gaultheria procumbens, Wintergreen, Checkerberry, Herbs 8
Hedera canariensis 'Variegata', Variegated Algerian Ivy, Ground Covers 3
Hedera helix 'Argenteo-variegata', 'Aureo-variegata', Variegated English Ivy, Ground Covers 3
Hosta spp., Ground Covers 8
Juniperus spp., Juniper, Ground Covers 3
Pachysandra procumbens, Allegheny Pachysandra, Ground Covers 8
Pachysandra terminalis 'Green Carpet', Japanese Pachysandra, Ground Covers 8
Pachysandra terminalis 'Variegata', Silver Edge Pachysandra, Ground Covers 8
Santolina chamaecyparissus, Lavender Cotton, Herbs 5
Vinca minor 'Variegata', Variegated Periwinkle, Ground Covers 3
Zebrina pendula, Wandering Jew, Ground Covers 8

GROUND COVERS 3
GROUND COVERS WITH EVERGREEN FOLIAGE

The most versatile ground covers are plants that are interesting in every season—they offer textured new growth in spring, flowers and fruit in summer, and autumn color. The plants listed here all have four-season appeal. Some of the ground covers on other lists also are evergreen, as are many of the ferns in Ground Covers 4.

ARCTOSTAPHYLOS *ark-toh-staff-il-os*
uva-ursi   Bearberry   Zones 2–8.

A prostrate, creeping plant that forms evergreen mats of bright green leaves that turn bronze in winter. In late spring and early summer, pink-tinted urn-shaped flowers bloom; they are followed by lustrous red fruit attractive to birds. Bearberry thrives in poor, sandy soil, in hot sun, and tolerates salt spray. 'Massachusetts' is an improved cultivar. Vigorous and trouble-free. Set out potted plants in early spring, in soil with a pH in the acid range.

MATURE HEIGHT: 6"–1'
GROWTH RATE: slow
LIGHT: full sun, semi-sunny
MOISTURE: rather dry, versatile

HEDERA *hed-er-uh*   Ivy

Vigorous and evergreen, ivy succeeds under trees and in hot, dry city conditions. In the mature form, it is shrublike. As a climbing vine it reaches 25 to 50 feet. As a ground cover it is 6 to 8 inches high. Interesting features are the two distinct stages of leaf development; creeping along the ground or beginning to climb, ivy produces "juvenile" foliage which never flowers. The "adult" stage comes when ivy climbs a support: small, green clusters of petalless flowers are borne at the tips, followed in autumn by black fruit. Ivy throws many "sports," shoots dif-

Arctostaphylos uva-ursi, Bearberry. (Neumann)

Hedera helix, English Ivy.

ferent from the parent. Plant rooted divisions in early spring and keep damp until established. Shear every 3 or 4 years to maintain foliage density.

MATURE HEIGHT: 6″–8″
GROWTH RATE: fast
LIGHT: versatile
MOISTURE: versatile

H. canariensis Algerian Ivy   Zones 9–10.
A large-leaved ivy with burgundy red twigs and petioles. 'Variegata' leaves are edged in yellowish white. Excellent at seaside, under trees, on banks and slopes, and in open areas. Grows better in central and northern Florida than in the southern part of the state.

H. helix English Ivy   Zones 5–9.
Stands 6 to 8 inches high and the strands can stretch to 90 feet. A vigorous grower that competes well with tree roots. There are hundreds of cultivars, varying in hardiness and coloration. Popular on the West Coast is 'Baltic', which is hardier than the species; hardier yet is 'Bulgaria'; 'Wilson' is hardy to Zone 4. *H. h.* 'Aureo-variegata' is variegated yellow; *H. h.* 'Argenteo-variegata' is variegated white.

JUNIPERUS *joo-nip-er-us* Juniper

This woody, evergreen genus includes 60-foot trees, shrubs, and ground-hugging plants a few inches to 2 feet high with a spread of 4 to 8 feet. The low-growing junipers have long, elegant, highly textured, gracefully layered branches. Foliage colors range from gray blue and green-blue to light green tipped with gold. Some take on purple hues in winter. The species below are superb evergreen ground covers that thrive even in sunny, hot, dry locations, and in almost any well-drained soil. A spreading root system makes junipers easy to transplant. Some blight exists; choose blight-resistant cultivars recommended by local nurseries. Set out container plants in spring or fall.

tinted purple in winter, and blue fruit. Stands up to hot sun in southern California, where it is considered the finest of the prostrate junipers. 'Douglasii', Waukegan Juniper, a good choice for sandy soils, has steel blue foliage that gradually turns purple in fall. The species prefers soils in the acid range, pH 5.0 to 6.0.

J. × *media**   Zones 3–9.
The cultivar 'Sea Spray', a sport of 'Pfitzerana Glauca', has blue-green foliage, is under 1 foot tall, hardy to −20° F, and resists blight and root rots. 'Pfitzerana Compacta', a dwarf Pfitzer Juniper, grows 1 to 3 feet tall and is gray green. The branch tips of 'Pfitzerana Aurea' are tipped with gold when new.

J. procumbens 'Nana'
Dwarf Japanese Garden Juniper   Zones 4–9.
This 6-inch-high dwarf ground cover grows 6 to 8 inches per year. The dense growth is mosslike in appearance, with branches one on top of another and foliage that is generally blue-green.

J. sabina Savin Juniper   Zones 3–7.
About 12 to 15 inches high, and notable for upward-reaching branches and an informal elegance. Choose blight-resistant cultivars such as 'Broadmoor', a soft grayish green; 'Moor-Dense' is a compact Broad-

Juniperus horizontalis 'Wiltonii', Blue Rug Creeping Juniper.

GROWTH RATE: medium
LIGHT: full sun
MOISTURE: versatile

J. chinensis var. *sargentii* Sargent's Juniper   Zones 3–9.
Mound-forming juniper about 2 to 3 feet high, with a spread of 8 to 10 feet. The cultivar 'Glauca' has feathery blue-green leaves. It succeeds even in limestone soils. Also listed by authorities as *J. sargentii* and *J. sargentii* 'Glauca'.

J. conferta Shore Juniper   Zones 5–9.
Vigorous, trailing juniper 12 to 28 inches high, with dense bluish green foliage and black fruits. It hugs the ground and flourishes in full sun, sandy soils, and harsh seaside conditions. 'Emerald Sea' is an excellent cultivar, free of the tendency to dieback typical of some. Set out container plants in spring.

J. horizontalis 'Wiltonii'
Blue Rug Creeping Juniper   Zones 3–9.
A flat, trailing juniper 6 inches high that grows 8 to 12 inches per year, and has intense silver-blue foliage

moor; 'Skandia', pale grayish green; or 'Tamariscifolia No Blight', bluish green.

J. squamata Singleseed Juniper   Zones 4–8.
'Blue Star', more mounded in habit, is 1½ to 2 feet high, an improved variety, slow-growing, with foliage that is a rich silvery blue. A favorite ground cover in northern California and similar climates. 'Variegata' is a prostrate, spreading variety under 12 inches high with cream-colored new growth. Good in the South but won't tolerate the heat of the Southwest.

MICROBIOTA *mye-kroh-bye-ot-uh decussata* Siberian Carpet Cypress   Zones 2–8.

A textured, mat-forming evergreen like juniper, it is about 2 feet high, with a spread of as much as 15 feet.

---

*Juniperus × *media* is not listed in *Hortus Third*. It is a cross between *Juniperus chinensis* and *Juniperus sabina*. 'Pfitzerana' is Pfitzer Juniper.

Vinca minor, Periwinkle. (Neumann)

The plumed foliage is graceful and thrives in shade where it remains green all year. It may be grown in sun and will turn copper in winter. Easy to care for, hardy, and drought-resistant. Set out container-grown plants in spring in well-drained soil.

MATURE HEIGHT: 2′
GROWTH RATE: medium
LIGHT: versatile
MOISTURE: versatile

OPHIOPOGON *off-ee-oh-poh-gon*
japonicus Lilyturf, Mondo Grass
Zones 5–10.

Tufts of rich green, grassy evergreen leaves 6 to 12 inches high. Resembles *Liriope platyphylla*, Lilyturf, which tolerates stronger sun. It is a preferred soil binder for banks and a turf substitute in southern Florida. Tolerates salt spray and drought. Easy to grow in shade or sun. Most successful in sandy, humusy soil. Plant in spring.

MATURE HEIGHT: 6″–12″
GROWTH RATE: medium
LIGHT: semi-sunny, versatile
MOISTURE: versatile

VINCA *vin-kuh* Periwinkle

A fast-spreading very low plant or ground cover with trailing stems 2 to 3 feet long, and with small, pretty, shiny, dark green leaves. Lavender-blue, purple, rose, or white flowers in spring. An elegant ground cover, it naturalizes in well-drained, rich soil with lots of organic matter. Thrives under trees, as a lawn alternative, and on lightly shaded banks. The plants must not dry out, especially the first season. Plant root divisions in early spring or fall.

GROWTH RATE: fast
LIGHT: semi-sunny
MOISTURE: roots moist

V. major Greater Periwinkle Zones 7–9.
Very vigorous and fast growing, with paler, larger leaves than *V. minor*, this species is about 10 inches high and forms a carpet in sun or shade. A top ground cover on the West Coast. Blue or white flowers stand above the foliage for many weeks in spring and summer. 'Variegata' has crisply variegated leaves, spreads rapidly, and blooms in mid-spring.

V. minor Periwinkle Zones 5–9.
A low-growing plant (3 to 6 inches high) with small, beautiful, dark green leaves and lavender-blue flowers. The cultivar 'Alba' has white flowers; 'Variegata' has variegated leaves. Deep watering in droughts and shearing every 2 or 3 years keeps vinca in top form.

SEE ALSO:
Cotoneaster dammeri, Bearberry Cotoneaster, Ground Covers 1
Euonymus fortunei, Wintercreeper, Vines 8
Galax urceolata, Ground Covers 10
Iberis sempervirens, Evergreen Candytuft, Ground Covers 6
Pachysandra terminalis, Japanese Pachysandra, Ground Covers 8
Paxistima canbyi, Cliff Green, Mountain Lover, Ground Covers 2
Potentilla tridentata, Three-toothed Cinquefoil, Ground Covers 6
Sedum acre, Golden-carpet, Gold Moss, Ground Covers 6
Vaccinium angustifolium, Lowbush Blueberry, Herbs 1

ALTERNATES:
Calluna vulgaris, Heather, Scotch Heather
Erica carnea, Spring Heath, Snow Heather
Gaylussacia brachycera, Box Huckleberry
Mahonia repens, Oregon Grape
Shortia galacifolia, Oconee-bells

GROUND COVERS 4
FERNS FOR GROUND COVER

Ferns are strikingly beautiful specimen plants for the wild garden. They multiply in the proper habitat—the partially shaded, moist woodlands to which most are native. Some species are evergreen. Ferns thrive in somewhat acid, moist, humus-rich soil (an ideal soil is half loam, half peat, fertilized with composted cow manure), and they are partial to deep shade. Most can stand some drought if shaded, and some sun if the soil is well supplied with moisture, such as along the banks of a stream or drainage ditch. Most ferns are propagated by rhizome division in early spring. Keep the rhizomes well moistened until vigorous growth is evident.

Some of the ferns on this list are not easy to find in the trade and are being decimated in the wild by thoughtless collectors. It is unfortunate, because ferns tend to die at high rates when taken from the wild, whereas they are easy to handle if nursery grown. More catalogs are offering ferns now.

LIGHT: semi-sunny, shade
MOISTURE: roots moist

ADIANTUM *ad-ee-an-tum*
pedatum Maidenhair Fern Zones 3–8.

Delicate, bright green fronds to 1 foot across are borne at the forked ends of wiry, strong, black-purple stems that dance in the wind. Airy, beautiful, and hardy enough for the rocky north woods. Prefers shade under tall trees and rich, well-drained soil in

Adiantum pedatum, Maidenhair Fern. (Wayside Gardens)

Dennstaedtia punctilobula, Hay-scented Fern.
(Wayside Gardens)

the pH 6.0–8.0 range. Must be kept moist. Deciduous.

ATHYRIUM *a-theer-ee-um*

One of the easiest ferns to grow. Deciduous, tall, graceful, light green, with lance-shaped fronds that have many leaflets. Successful in partial shade almost anywhere.

A. felix-femina Lady Fern   Zones 3–8.
Spreads at a moderate rate in moist conditions. Tolerant of fairly dry soils. The finely divided fronds can reach 12 to 20 inches and are produced throughout the growing season.

A. goeringianum 'Pictum'
Japanese Silver Painted Fern   Zones 3–8.
A vigorous grower to 18 inches at least, with a gray silver central stripe on green fronds, wine-red stems, and a weeping habit. It tolerates competitive conditions.

A. thelypteroides Silvery Spleenwort
                                    Zones 5–8.
Similar to Lady Fern and tolerates difficult conditions. Excellent ground cover.

CYRTOMIUM *ser-toh-mee-um*
falcatum Holly Fern, Japanese Holly Fern
                                    Zones 9–10.

Evergreen in warm regions, the form is upright to spreading, 1 to 2 feet high with hollylike, glossy, dark green leaves 8 inches wide and to 2½ feet long. It spreads slowly, tolerates some salt and drought, and prefers well-drained, moist, somewhat acid soil. In Florida it is used as a ground cover under trees and on partially shaded banks and slopes.

DENNSTAEDTIA *den-stet-ee-uh*
punctilobula Hay-scented Fern Zones 2–8.

Hardy and deciduous, the delicate, beautifully cut, arching fronds of this fern grow 20 to 32 inches long and form solid masses. They are fragrant when crushed. With ample moisture, this fern grows vigorously all over North America, in sun or shade, in

Athyrium goeringianum 'Pictum', Japanese Silver Painted Fern. (Wayside Gardens)

Dryopteris erythrospora, Japanese Shield Fern. (Wayside Gardens)

rocky fields or pastures. It spreads rapidly and is an excellent choice for naturalizing, but not wise for small gardens.

DRYOPTERIS *drye-opp-ter-iss*

Deciduous and evergreen species that are big and beautiful, with delicate, much-divided fronds rising gracefully to form symmetrical groups or nice clumps. Many are found wild in our woodlands and are among the easiest ferns to grow. Light shade and moisture for the roots are essential.

D. erythrospora Japanese Shield Fern
                                    Zones 5–9.
An attractive, conspicuous, deciduous species from Japan, outstanding for its color. The fronds are 2 to 3 feet tall and have rounded red spores.

D. marginalis Marginal Shield Fern,
Leather Wood Fern   Zone 3.
Generally evergreen, a dozen or so 15- to 20-inch fronds form a handsome individual plant. The fronds are upright in the growing season but may lie flat during winter. Not a rapid spreader.

Osmunda cinnamomea, Cinnamon Fern. (Wayside Gardens)

NEPHROLEPIS nef-frol-ep-iss
Sword Fern   Zone 10.

A genus of tropical ferns that form dense crowns of long, narrow fronds 1 to 3 feet long, arching or drooping. In Florida they are used as ground cover under trees, and on shady banks and slopes.

OSMUNDA os-mund-uh
cinnamomea   Cinnamon Fern   Zones 3–8.

The young fiddleheads of this big, deciduous fern are covered with cinnamon-colored felt and turn to dark green as they grow into fronds 8 inches wide and, in cultivation, 3 feet long. Spreads slowly, in acid soil, in wet swampy places or shady sites.

POLYPODIUM pol-ip-poh-dee-um
virginianum   Rock Polypody,
American Wall Fern   Zones 3–8.

A low, spreading, evergreen fern whose vertical or horizontal frond stalks rise from creeping rhizomes. In partial shade it can become a dense ground cover. Tolerates well-drained soils.

POLYSTICHUM pol-list-ik-um

A large genus of narrow ferns with lustrous green leaves that grow in circular, arching clusters from a central rootstock. Most are evergreen, excellent for damp, shady places where soil is rich in humus.

P. acrostichoides   Christmas Fern
                                              Zones 3–8.
A very handsome and agreeable evergreen fern with deep, rich green, leathery fronds growing as large as 2 feet long and 5 inches wide. It can tolerate more sun than many ferns if given adequate moisture.

P. braunii   Shield Fern, Braun's Holly Fern
                                              Zones 3–8.
Extremely handsome, graceful, arching, evergreen fern 2 to 3 feet tall, with twice-divided pinnae covered with bristles along the edges. Prefers cool,

moist, deeply shaded soil and may require a mist of water in hot weather.

RUMOHRA rue-mow-ruh
adiantiformis   Leatherleaf Fern   Zones 9–10.

The 1½- to 3-foot long, dark green, leathery fronds make beautiful cut foliage; in Florida it is used as ground cover under trees and on partially shaded banks and slopes. Growth rate is medium. It tolerates some salt and drought. Deciduous.

THELYPTERIS thel-lip-ter-iss

Deciduous, hardy ferns with good color and bold foliage, excellent for shady situations and acid soils. They spread rapidly in moist humus-rich soils with some shade.

T. hexagonoptera   Beech Fern,
Broad Beech Fern   Zones 3–9.
Broadly triangular fronds grow 10 to 24 inches long. This species spreads quickly if given rich, moist conditions, and provides a bright green ground cover for shady places.

T. novboracensis   New York Fern   Zones 2–8.
Plants with finely divided 12- to 24-inch fronds spread rapidly in moist, humus-rich soil.

SEE ALSO:
Lygodium palmatum, Hartford Fern, Vines 4
Matteuccia struthiopteris, Ostrich Fern, Herbs 8

ALTERNATE:
Dryopteris spinulosa, Fancy Fern, Spinulose Wood Fern, Shield Fern

GROUND COVERS 5
LAWN ALTERNATIVES

Here are some good lawn alternatives, but there are more. Many of the ground covers in other sections of this book may be planted as lawn alternatives. English Ivy (*Hedera helix*), for instance, is wonderfully tough in the city. Also consider some of the durable spreading plants recommended for naturalizing in Ground Covers 9.

LIRIOPE lihr-rye-oh-pee   Lilyturf

Top ground cover: a charming, low growing, round, clump-forming plant with arching, dark green, grassy leaves that are evergreen. There are small spikes of showy white or lavender flowers in summer. Useful under trees, as edging for borders, and in rock gardens. Succeeds in sun or shade and can be lawn material for a small space. Plant root divisions in early spring.

MATURE HEIGHT: 12"–18"
GROWTH RATE: medium
LIGHT: versatile
MOISTURE: versatile

L. platyphylla   Zones 6–10.
Described by the University of Florida as the best turf substitute in southern Florida; also an excellent plant for erosion control. Some tolerance to salt spray and drought. Full sun to light shade. Cultivars offer green or bluish leaves, and red, lavender, blue, white, or purple flowers. 'Variegata' has yellow-edged leaves and blue flowers. Excellent under trees, as edging,

Liriope platyphylla, Lilyturf. (Neumann)

Verbena species. (McDonald)

on banks and slopes. 'Christmas Tree' is a fine cultivar, with white and blue flowers standing above the foliage in midsummer and fall.

L. spicata Creeping Lilyturf   Zones 6–10.
Covers faster than other species and is lower to the ground, with narrow green leaves and purple or white flowers. Prefers light shade.

LYSIMACHIA *lye-sim-may-kee-uh*

Perennials that produce small yellow flowers in summer and flourish in moist open places. Can become invasive. Easily propagated in spring or fall by root division. Prefers soil in the neutral range.

GROWTH RATE:	fast
LIGHT:	versatile
MOISTURE:	soil surface damp, versatile

L. nummularia Creeping Jennie,
Creeping Charlie   Zones 3–8.
Creeping Jennie is vigorous and low-growing, 1 to 2 inches high, with round, dark green leaves, and abundant bright yellow, cup-shaped flowers in summer. It prefers waterside locations but succeeds in drier sites, in sun or light shade, as long as moisture is maintained. *L. n.* 'Aurea' is a golden-leaved form for wet, difficult places.

L. punctata Yellow Loosestrife   Zones 5–8.
Tall plant, to 3 feet, that bears whorls of yellow flowers in summer. Prefers shade and naturalizes readily. Often combined with ornamental grasses in large landscapes as a lawn alternative.

VERBENA *ver-bee-nuh*   Vervain

Vigorous, low-growing, creeping plant covered with flowers all summer long. Some species are scented, notably *V. platensis*, which is fragrant at night. Colors range through every shade of red and blue. Stem-rooted spreader with solid, matlike growth, and an outstanding lawn substitute in warm regions such as Arizona. Provide full sun and rich garden soil in the neutral range. Sow seeds outdoors in early spring.

GROWTH RATE:	fast
LIGHT:	full sun
MOISTURE:	roots moist

V. canadensis Rose Verbena Zones 6–10.
A plant about 18 inches high, with pink and purple blooms; it thrives throughout the Southwest and Mexico. Wonderful ground cover and lawn substitute.

V. rigida   Zones 6–10.
Between 12 and 18 inches high, this species has narrow, sharply toothed leaves 2 to 3 inches long, and purple flowers in dense spikes. It blooms the first year from seed. A cultivar, 'Flame', grows to 4 inches tall, and makes a brilliant carpet of flowers. Excellent edger and ground cover.

ZEPHYRANTHES *zeff-er-ranth-eez*
Zephyr Lily, Rain Lily, Fairy Lily

Charming grassy plants that grow from bulbs and produce crocuslike blooms after rain, 2 to 3 inches

across, 6 inches high, in pink, purple, white, orange, or red. There's also a yellow sold as sulphurea. In Florida and other frost-free areas, the species sold locally are good lawn substitutes, perennial edging for borders, or seashore ground covers. Where winter temperatures drop below 25° F, grow as tender perennials. Constant moisture is essential.

MATURE HEIGHT:	6″–12″
GROWTH RATE:	slow
LIGHT:	full sun, part shade
MOISTURE:	soil surface moist

Z. candida Autumn Zephyr Lily   Zone 9.
Leaves are narrow, stiff, and up to 12 inches high, appearing in late summer and lasting until the following spring in frost-free areas. The flowers are white, about the same height as the leaves, sometimes pink outside. They bloom in late summer and autumn.

Z. rosea Cuban Zephyr Lily   Zone 10.
This species grows to 12 inches with spreading, flat leaves. The flowers are rose red, about an inch long, and bloom in fall.

ZOYSIA *zoy-zee-uh*
tenuifolia Zoysia Grass   Zones 6–10.

Tough, thick, bright green creeping turf grass for hot summers. Needs 2 years to become established, then needs little care other than mowing. Hardy in southern Connecticut, but turns beige with the first frost and stays beige until growth resumes in late spring. Tolerates salt and drought, sun or light shade, and once established, is hard to eliminate. Provide rich, well-prepared, well-drained loam that holds moisture. In early spring, set out zoysia plugs and keep watered until growth resumes.

MATURE HEIGHT: 3″–4″
GROWTH RATE: slow
LIGHT: full sun
MOISTURE: versatile

SEE ALSO:
Arctostaphylos uva-ursi, Bearberry, Ground Covers 3
Ceratostigma plumbaginoides, Blue Ceratostigma, Plumbago, Ground Covers 1
Dichondra micrantha, Ground Covers 10
Euonymus fortunei, Wintercreeper, Vines 8
Hedera helix, English Ivy, Ground Covers 3
Hypericum calycinum, Aaron's Beard, Creeping St. John's-wort, Ground Covers 9
Juniperus, Juniper, Ground Covers 3
Ophiopogon japonicus, Lilyturf, Mondo Grass, Ground Covers 3
Pachysandra spp., Ground Covers 8
Vinca minor, Periwinkle, Ground Covers 3

ALTERNATES:
Achillea tomentosa, Woolly Yarrow
Coronilla varia, Crown Vetch

GROUND COVERS 6
GROUND COVERS FOR NOOKS AND CRANNIES

These rugged and beautiful plants can stand neglect and drought. They will thrive in hot pockets between stones and rocky outcroppings, on top of stone walls, or along walks. Their easy-care beauty is ideal for use in small spaces and for low-maintenance sites.

ARABIS *ar-ab-iss*
caucasica Wall Rock Cress   Zone 6.

Silver-green tufts of leaves covered in spring with a froth of sweet-scented small white flowers. Beautiful spilling over the top of a rock wall and in rock gardens. Thrives even in the poor soil of rocky slopes. There are rose-pink cultivars. Gritty, well-drained soil and full sun are essential. Sow seeds or plant root divisions in fall. The similar but smaller *A. alpina,* Mountain Rock Cress, stays in bloom longer but is not easy to find in cultivation.

MATURE HEIGHT: 12″
GROWTH RATE: medium
LIGHT: versatile
MOISTURE: roots moist

AURINIA *aw-rin-ee-uh*
saxatilis Basket-of-gold, Goldentuft
Zones 3–8.

In spring this mat-forming perennial is a carpet of small yellow flowers. Wonderful on slopes or in rock gardens combined with other flowering ground covers such as *Iberis sempervirens,* Evergreen Candytuft (below), *Phlox subulata*, Moss Pink (see

Ground Covers 1), and pink *Aubrieta.* 'Compacta' is denser and clumpier. Sow seed in early spring in full sun in any well-drained soil. *A. saxatilis* is the new scientific name for Alyssum saxatile. Don't confuse this with sweet alyssum, *Lobularia maritima* (see Flowers 20).

MATURE HEIGHT: 6″
GROWTH RATE: medium
LIGHT: full sun
MOISTURE: roots moist, versatile

DIANTHUS *dye-anth-us*
'Tiny Rubies'   Zones 3–8.

Dianthus is the clove-scented genus that includes large florists' carnations and several species of grass or cottage pinks. 'Tiny Rubies' is one of many cultivars in brilliant colors. The flowers are small and red—bright as rubies in light—fragrant, and 6 to 10 inches tall. They bloom in spring, and if deadheaded, through summer and into fall. The plant is a compact, silver-green, grassy tuft that is virtually evergreen. Perfect for nooks and crannies in the garden and rock garden. Thrives in well-drained, sandy soil in the neutral range; withstands high heat. Set out root divisions in fall or spring.

MATURE HEIGHT: 6″–10″
GROWTH RATE: medium
LIGHT: full sun
MOISTURE: versatile

EPIMEDIUM *ep-im-meed-ee-um*
grandiflorum Long-spur Epimedium
Zones 3–8.

Dainty, semievergreen plant with graceful sprays of charming, irregular bicolored flowers—pink, yellow, white, violet—in May. Cut flowers last well. Thrives in moist, peaty loam that is well drained. 'Rose Queen' is a lovely, durable rose. Plant root divisions in spring in soil in the acid range. *E. × rubrum,* Red

Epimedium species. (McDonald)

Alpine Epimedium, is a hybrid that has red and yellow or white flowers in June and red-bronze leaves that turn green with a red edge as the season advances.

MATURE HEIGHT: 10″–12″
GROWTH RATE: medium
LIGHT: semi-sunny
MOISTURE: versatile

IBERIS *eye-beer-iss*
sempervirens Evergreen Candytuft
Zones 4–8.

Low-growing, narrow-leaved, evergreen plant about 10 inches high with a large spread, useful in rock and

Iberis sempervirens, Evergreen Candytuft. (Neumann)

Potentilla tridentata, Three-toothed Cinquefoil. (Neumann)

wall gardens and as edging for spring borders. In mid-spring it is blanketed with dense heads of white flowers. Often reblooms if clipped back after flowering. Thrives without care in full or semi-sun and somewhat acid soil. Plant root divisions in early spring. Bees love it. 'Snowflake' has larger flowers. 'Autumn Snow', an excellent edger, blooms again in fall.

MATURE HEIGHT: 9"–1'
GROWTH RATE: medium
LIGHT: full sun, versatile
MOISTURE: versatile

POTENTILLA *poh-ten-till-uh*
tridentata Three-toothed Cinquefoil
Zones 2–7.

Low-growing mat of evergreen leaves delightful in wild gardens, rock gardens, nooks and crannies, as edging or ground cover. Small blooms, like strawberry flowers, in May and June. Not showy, but dear. It needs little care once established in an open, sunny site. Succeeds by the seashore. Prefers acid-range soil, pH 4.5–5.0. Set out plants in early spring.

MATURE HEIGHT: 10"
GROWTH RATE: medium
LIGHT: full sun
MOISTURE: versatile

SEDUM *seed-um*
acre Golden-carpet, Gold Moss Zones 4–9.

Low, creeping, mat-forming semi-succulent with tiny, pale green evergreen leaves on trailing stems; good for filling corners in stone steps, rock gardens, and walls. Bears bright yellow flowers in late spring and early summer. The stems root where they touch moist soil, are tough, heat- and drought-resistant. Succeeds in poor, dry soils. Plant root divisions after blooming in any well-drained soil. See also Flowers 14.

MATURE HEIGHT: 2"
GROWTH RATE: medium
LIGHT: full sun
MOISTURE: versatile

Sedum species. (McDonald)

SEMPERVIVUM *sem-per-vye-vum*
tectorum Hen-and-chickens Zone 4.

Evergreen perennial whose rootstock forms tightly clustered 12-inch-high rosettes of fleshy, bright green leaves with red-purple pointed tips. Clusters of soft pink, purple, white, or yellow flowers grow from the center in summer. Excellent for dry, poor soils, rocky pockets, between stepping stones. Withstands high heat and multiplies steadily. Primarily grown for foliage, it thrives in neutral-range soil and any well-drained situation in full sun or light shade. Plant rooted offsets in spring.

MATURE HEIGHT: 1'
GROWTH RATE: medium
LIGHT: versatile
MOISTURE: versatile

SEE ALSO:
Arctostaphylos uva-ursi, Bearberry, Ground Covers 3
Chamaemelum nobile, Chamomile, Russian Chamomile, Herbs 10
Hedera helix, English Ivy, Ground Covers 3
Heuchera sanguinea, Coralbells, Flowers 10
Vinca major, Greater Periwinkle, Ground Covers 3

ALTERNATES:
Cerastium tomentosum, Snow-in-summer
Mentha requienii, Creeping Mint
Rosmarinus officinalis 'Prostratus', Rosemary

GROUND COVERS 7
GROUND COVERS FOR SEASHORE GARDENS

Ground covers recommended for the seashore have the ability to bind sandy soils, withstand salt, and hold up in heavy weather. In addition to the plants listed here, some plants in Ornamental

Grasses 4 flourish by the sea, as will some bog plants, Aquatics 4 and 5. *Rosa rugosa*, Japanese Rose (see Shrubs 19), is another good seashore plant and the hybrids are quite beautiful.

ARTEMISIA *art-em-miz-ee-uh*
Sagebrush, Mugwort

Drought-resistant herbs with gray white foliage and insignificant flowers. Some species are particularly good ground covers, others are strongly scented herbs, and all are valued for their foliage. Several species often used in flower borders are included

Artemisia stellerana, with Cardinal Flower. (McDonald)

Cytisus, Broom. (Oehme)

here. All are easily grown in well-drained garden soil and do best in full sun. Plant root divisions in early spring.

GROWTH RATE: medium
LIGHT: full sun
MOISTURE: versatile

A. abrotanum Southernwood Zones 5–9.
Perennial to 4 feet tall, with very aromatic threadlike leaves used as a moth repellent. There are tiny, pale yellow flowers in drooping clusters. Cut back severely in spring or it gets weedy.

A. annua Sweet Wormwood
Annual 1 to 5 feet tall, very fast growing with fragrant, lacy foliage, and small flowers in late summer. Good background plant for flowers.

A. ludoviciana var. albula
Silver-king Artemisia Zones 5–9.
This airy, frosty-looking, 3-foot-tall foliage plant is fragrant, valuable for edging, borders, and as ground cover in larger landscapes. There are tiny grayish white florets in summer.

A. stellerana Dusty-miller Zones 3–9.
Perennial 2- to 3-foot herb native to the northeastern coast where its thick, woolly white leaves thrive on sandy beaches above the high-tide line. Striking as edging, in borders, and as ground cover by the seashore. There are tiny yellow flowers in early summer.

CYTISUS *sit-iss-us* Broom

Nearly leafless evergreen or deciduous shrubs, rounded with long weeping stems, that flourish by the shore on both coasts and in dry, sandy soils in between. Masses of pealike flowers in spring and summer. Once established they care for themselves, but should be set out as small plants, since they don't transplant easily. Set out container plants from a nursery in spring or fall in sandy soil.

GROWTH RATE: fast
LIGHT: full sun
MOISTURE: versatile

C. albus Portuguese Broom Zones 5–8.
A beautiful broom with white to pale yellow flowers; grows to about 1 foot high and spreads.

C. × kewensis Kew Broom Zones 6–7.
This hybrid is a creeping shrub about 1 foot high with small, creamy white flowers in mid-spring.

ILEX *eye-lex*
vomitoria 'Schellings Dwarf'
Dwarf Yaupon Holly Zones 7–10.
Extremely compact, evergreen holly 1 to 3 feet high, with rich dark green foliage that is red when new. Excellent for the seashore, under trees, and in open areas. Insignificant white flowers appear in spring. This is a male clone, so there is no fruit. Set out

container-grown plants in early spring or fall in well-drained soil.

MATURE HEIGHT: 1'–3'
GROWTH RATE: medium
LIGHT: full sun
MOISTURE: versatile

IPOMOEA *eye-poh-mee-uh*
pes-caprae Beach Morning-glory,
Railroad Vine Zones 9–10.

Fast-growing creeper with strands to 60 feet, and a superb sand binder for dry banks, coastal slopes, and in open areas in subtropical and tropical climates. The flowers are purple, white, blue, pink, or red, showy, blooming in summer and fall. In early spring sow seeds in well-drained, enriched soil; soak seeds overnight before planting.

MATURE HEIGHT: 4"–6"
GROWTH RATE: fast
LIGHT: full sun
MOISTURE: versatile

LEIOPHYLLUM *lye-oh-fill-um*
buxifolium Sand Myrtle Zone 5.

Small, evergreen, spreading shrub, lustrous dark green in summer and bronzy in cool weather. In

Leiophyllum buxifolium, Sand Myrtle. (Neumann)

spring to early summer clusters of dainty, waxy buds open to white flowers. It isn't easy to establish, and must have moist soil, but flourishes without care once growing and is particularly useful for southeastern coastal areas. In spring set out containerized plants in moist, sandy, acid soil enriched with peat and organic matter.

MATURE HEIGHT: 1'–3'
GROWTH RATE: slow
LIGHT: full sun, semi-sunny
MOISTURE: soil surface damp

MYOPORUM *my-pore-um*
'Pacifica' Zones 9–10.

Extraordinarily fast-spreading, shrubby hybrid with branches to 30 feet across, used in California and other dry, warm regions for binding soil and sandy coastal slopes. Fire-resistant and water-conserving. One of these 2- to 3-foot-tall plants develops an 8-foot mat in just a year. The branches root where they touch the soil. Its attraction is interesting evergreen foliage dotted with translucent spots that are visible when viewed against the light. Plant container-grown root divisions in early spring.

MATURE HEIGHT: 2'–3'
GROWTH RATE: fast
LIGHT: full sun
MOISTURE: versatile

SESUVIUM *se-suh-vee-um*
portulacastrum Sea Purslane Zones 9–10.

A native, mat-forming, seastrand plant of Florida, where it is grown by the shore as a sand binder. It grows medium-fast to about 1½ feet and has showy pink flowers year-round. Set out root divisions in early spring.

MATURE HEIGHT: 1½'
GROWTH RATE: medium
LIGHT: full sun
MOISTURE: versatile

WEDELIA *wuh-deel-yuh*
triloba Zone 10.

Fast-growing creeper with showy yellow blooms all year, and branches to 6 feet long or more, rooting at the nodes. Considered one of the best ground covers and edgers in Florida. It thrives under trees, at the seashore, on banks and slopes, in open areas. It tolerates salt and drought. Plant root divisions in early spring.

MATURE HEIGHT: 6"–8"
GROWTH RATE: fast
LIGHT: full sun
MOISTURE: versatile

SEE ALSO:
Arctostaphylos uva-ursi, Bearberry, Ground Covers 3
Hypericum calycinum, Aaron's Beard, Creeping St.-John's-wort, Ground Covers 9
Juniperus conferta, Shore Juniper, Ground Covers 3
Lantana montevidensis, Weeping Lantana, Trailing Lantana, Ground Covers 1
Potentilla tridentata, Three-toothed Cinquefoil, Ground Covers 6
Rosa rugosa, Japanese Rose, Shrubs 19
Rosa virginiana, Virginia Rose, Herbs 7

ALTERNATE:
Armeria maritima, Thrift

GROUND COVERS 8
GROUND COVERS FOR SHADE

These easy-care ground covers will flourish in light to deep shade. Several prefer somewhat acid soils and require sustained moisture.

CONVALLARIA *kon-val-lay-ree-uh*
majalis Lily-of-the-valley Zones 2–7.

Delicate green spears 4 to 8 inches high unfurl pointed leaves and through them rise stems bearing small, creamy white bells whose fragrance is part of a famous perfume, Joy. The plants grow from pips (roots) set out in early spring. In well-drained, humusy, moist soil in shaded locations they will multiply indefinitely. Prefers acid-range soil with a pH between 5.0 and 6.0. Lovely ground cover for under trees or tall shrubs, and for the wild garden. Plant pips in fall. Deciduous.

Convallaria majalis, Lily-of-the-valley. (Neumann)

Hosta in bloom. (Neumann)

MATURE HEIGHT: 6″–8″
GROWTH RATE: medium
LIGHT: shade
MOISTURE: versatile

HOSTA *hoss-tuh*

Clump-forming ground cover and foliage plant for shade. Tall lavender or white flower spikes rise above the foliage in summer and early fall. The big leaves are bold, sometimes wavy-edged, in rich shades of green, blue-green, gold, and variegated combinations. Sizes range from compact dwarfs to giant clumps 5 feet across. They need 3 years to develop into handsome specimens. Culture is easy. Set out container plants in spring, late summer, or early fall, in well-drained soil rich in humus.

GROWTH RATE: slow
LIGHT: semi-sunny, shade
MOISTURE: soil surface damp

H. 'Honeybells' Zones 3–9.
Grass-green leaves, and in July and August, 3-foot lavender-lilac fragrant flower spikes.

H. lancifolia var. *albomarginata*
Narrow-leaved Hosta Zones 3–9.
Narrow leaves brushed with white, to 2 feet, and lavender blooms in August and September.

H. montana 'Aureo-marginata' Zones 3–9.
Large green leaves irregularly margined in yellow which turns to cream as the season progresses. The clumps get wide and stand more sun than other hostas.

H. plantaginea 'Grandiflora' Fragrant Hosta
Zones 3–9.
White flowering, 20 inches high, this is a fragrant hosta that blooms in late summer. The light green leaves are large, 10 inches long and 6 inches wide. One of the most beautiful and useful for the flower border.

H. sieboldiana 'Frances Williams' Zones 3–9.
Also known as 'Gold Edge' or 'Gold Circle', the plant forms 4-foot clumps with very large puckered leaves—like seersucker—blue green with broad golden margins that deepen with the season. Foliage-height soft lilac flowers in late spring and early summer. The bold foliage remains to envelop bare-legged late bloomers like *Lycoris,* the beautiful Magic or Resurrection Lily (see Flowers 3), planted in the same bed.

H. tardiflora Zones 3–9.
Narrow, dark green leaves form a clump 12 inches high. The pale purple flowers bloom late at about foliage height and hold their flowers until well into fall. Needs moist, organically rich soil in partial shade.

H. undulata Zones 3–9.
Wavy green leaves with white centers, and lavender flowers in late spring and early summer. Foliage enhances the early summer blooms of *Allium gigan-teum* and *A. rosenbachianum* (see Flowers 20). Best color develops in plants growing in shade.

PACHYSANDRA *pak-iss-**sand**-ruh*

Elegant evergreen ground cover and lawn alternative for shaded places and under trees and shrubs. Upright rosettes of dark green, scalloped leaves flush light green with spring growth and produce interesting but not showy green-white flowers. It thrives in rich, moist, somewhat acid soil and in light to heavy shade. Where sunlight hits pachysandra in winter it yellows, and those same places may die back in high heat and drought during summer. Competes well with tree roots. Set out root divisions in fall or early spring.

MATURE HEIGHT: 6″–12″
GROWTH RATE: moderate
LIGHT: shade
MOISTURE: roots moist, versatile

P. procumbens Alleghany Pachysandra
Zones 4–9.
Native to the Southeast, where it is evergreen, growing in rounded clumps. It is the most successful species for warmer regions. In spring white-purple flower spikes reach to 5 inches high.

P. terminalis Japanese Pachysandra
Zones 3–8.
One of the most elegant ground covers and lawn substitutes for cooler regions, where it flourishes under shrubs and small trees. 'Green Carpet' is a deep green, improved cultivar. 'Variegata', Silver Edge Pachysandra, is beautifully edged with white, but doesn't grow quite as vigorously as the species.

SARCOCOCCA *sar-koh-**kok**-uh*
hookerana var. *humilis* Sweet Box
Zones 5–8.

Spreading evergreen shrub about 2 feet tall, with lustrous, dark green leaves, and in early spring, small, fragrant, whitish flowers followed by fleshy, berrylike

Pachysandra terminalis, Japanese Pachysandra.

Sarcococca hookerana, Sweet Box.

fruit. Spreads slowly to form a dense, shiny green mat. Shade is necessary, but the plants tolerate competition from trees and dripping eaves. Plant root divisions in early spring.

MATURE HEIGHT: 2′
GROWTH RATE: slow
LIGHT: shade
MOISTURE: versatile

ZEBRINA *zeb-rye-nuh*
pendula Wandering Jew   Zone 10.

Trailing plant that roots at the joints, it is grown for its broad, pointed, strikingly striped leaves with bands of white above and purple below. Year-round, there are charming but not showy, tiny, red-purple flower clusters. Known in the Northeast as a basket house-plant, in tropical Florida it is used as colorful ground cover under trees, but can be invasive.

MATURE HEIGHT: 6″–1′
GROWTH RATE: fast
LIGHT: semi-sunny, shade
MOISTURE: roots moist

SEE ALSO:
Ajuga reptans, Carpet Bugle, Ground Covers 2
Arctostaphylos uva-ursi, Bearberry, Ground Covers 3
Asarum caudatum, Wild Ginger, Herbs 8
Ceratostigma plumbaginoides, Blue Cerastostigma, Plumbago, Ground Covers 1
Epimedium grandiflorum, Long-spur Epimedium, Ground Covers 6
Euonymus fortunei, Wintercreeper, Vines 8
Ferns, Ground Covers 4
Hedera helix, English Ivy, Ground Covers 3
Lamium maculatum 'Variegatum', Spotted Dead Nettle, Ground Covers 10
Liriope spicata, Creeping Lilyturf, Ground Covers 5
Mahonia repens, Creeping Oregon Grape, Herbs 8
Microbiota decussata, Siberian Carpet Cypress, Ground Covers 3

Ophiopogon japonicus, Lilyturf, Mondo Grass, Ground Covers 3
Paxistima canbyi, Cliff Green, Mountain Lover, Ground Covers 2
Pilea microphylla, Artillery Plant, Ground Covers 2
Potentilla tridentata, Three-toothed Cinquefoil, Ground Covers 6
Vinca minor, Periwinkle, Ground Covers 3
Xanthorhiza simplicissima, Yellowroot, Ground Covers 10

ALTERNATES:
Hemerocallis, Daylily
Viola odorata, Sweet Violet

GROUND COVERS 9
FAST-GROWING GROUND COVERS FOR SLOPES AND EROSION CONTROL

Some of these plants grow so quickly and vigorously they aren't suited to small gardens. In the right situation and given room to spread, they protect the soil and reward the eye throughout the seasons.

BACCHARIS *bak-kar-iss*
pilularis Dwarf Baccharis, Coyote Brush, Chaparral Broom   Zones 7–9.

Low-growing, evergreen shrub native to the dry, sunny soils and slopes of Oregon and California. Described as a soil stabilizer that survives droughts and conserves water, it is used as a sand binder on coastal bluffs. The cultivar 'Twin Peaks', about 1 foot high and 10 feet across, is fire-resistant. Set out container plants in spring.

MATURE HEIGHT: 1′
GROWTH RATE: fast
LIGHT: full sun
MOISTURE: versatile

COMPTONIA *komp-toh-nee-uh*
peregrina Sweet Fern   Zones 2–8.

Deciduous, aromatic shrub with fernlike foliage, useful for covering banks and successful in peaty or dry, sandy soils where it reaches about 5 feet. Often listed in catalogs as Myrica asplenifolia. The leaves are sometimes dried and used to make tea. Doesn't transplant easily. Plant clump divisions in early spring in soil with a pH in the acid range.

MATURE HEIGHT: 5′
GROWTH RATE: fast
LIGHT: versatile
MOISTURE: versatile

CORONILLA *ko-roh-nill-uh*
varia Crown Vetch   Zone 3.

Dense, bushy plant, 1 to 2 feet high, with clusters of pealike pink-white flowers in summer and fall. Valuable as quick cover for roadside slopes, steep, dry, rocky banks, and to prevent erosion in large spaces. Too vigorous for the home garden. Plant root divisions in spring or fall. Prefers soils in the neutral range. The variety 'Penngift' succeeds in sun or shade.

MATURE HEIGHT: 1′–2′
GROWTH RATE: fast
LIGHT: full sun
MOISTURE: versatile

FORSYTHIA *for-sith-ee-uh*
× *intermedia* 'Arnold Dwarf'   Zones 5–8.

Low-growing dwarf of a deciduous shrub whose yellow-gold flowers appear before the leaves to herald the coming of spring. This 3-foot species with a 5-foot spread flowers sparsely even when mature, but the gracefully arching branches root where they touch, binding the soil of sunny banks and rocky slopes. Requires little or no care. Plant root divisions in early spring in well-drained soil.

Coronilla varia, Crown Vetch. (Neumann)

MATURE HEIGHT: 3'
GROWTH RATE: fast
LIGHT: full sun
MOISTURE: versatile

GENISTA *jen-nist-uh* Broom

Semievergreen shrub that bears showy, pealike yellow flowers, thrives in poor, dry, sandy soils and makes a lovely display on sunny slopes. Set out container-grown plants in well-drained soil in spring. Takes time to establish but is carefree once growing.

GROWTH RATE: slow
LIGHT: full sun
MOISTURE: versatile

G. pilosa 'Vancouver Gold' Zones 6–8.
A slow-growing shrub about 1 foot high, with small hairy leaves and short clusters of yellow flowers in spring and summer. Excellent in rock gardens.

G. sagittalis Arrow Broom Zones 4–8.
About 12 inches high, with spreading branches; in spring there is a profusion of yellow, pealike flowers. A superior ground cover for hot sun and sandy soil.

HYPERICUM *hye-pehr-ik-urn* St.-John's-wort

Small, dense shrubs that throughout summer bear masses of silky, buttercup-yellow flowers resembling single roses with gold or red stamens. The evergreen species are good ground covers for rocky slopes and a variety of dry soils. Mowing or shearing in early spring encourages masses of blooms. Set out container-grown plants in early spring.

GROWTH RATE: medium
LIGHT: full sun, semi-sunny
MOISTURE: versatile

H. buckleyi
Blue Ridge St.-John's-wort Zones 5–8.
A 1-foot-high, round, ground-hugging mat, with flowers slightly smaller than *H. calycinum*. It doesn't

Hypericum species, St.-John's-wort. (Neumann)

spread as rapidly, and is a good choice for smaller gardens and southern climates.

H. calycinum Aaron's Beard,
Creeping St.-John's-wort Zones 5–8.
Rapidly spreading, semievergreen shrub growing 12 to 18 inches high with a spread of 18 to 24 inches. The flowers, 2 to 3 inches across, are borne on new wood all summer. Fast, effective cover.

H. × *moseranum* Gold Flower Zones 7–8.
Compact, tufting shrub, 2 feet high, with flowers to 2½ inches across that bloom all summer. On the West Coast it often is used as ground cover under *Eucalyptus* trees (see Trees 4). It requires practically no attention.

RHOEO *ree-oh*
spathacea Oyster Plant Zones 9–10.

Beautiful foliage plant naturalized in Florida. The leaves are up to 1 foot long and 3 inches wide, purple on the underside and dark green on top. White

flowers nearly buried in a pair of boat-shaped umbels bloom year-round, and are the source of some common names for this plant, among them Moses-on-a-raft and Two-men-in-a-boat. A less invasive, non-flowering dwarf, 'Vittata', is recommended as ground cover under trees, on banks and slopes, by the seashore, and in open areas. Plant rhizome divisions in early spring.

MATURE HEIGHT: 1'–2'
GROWTH RATE: fast
LIGHT: full sun, semi-sunny
MOISTURE: versatile

ROSA *roh-zuh*
wichuraiana Memorial Rose Zone 5.

Prostrate rose with small white flowers in late summer followed by reddish fruits. It is a strong grower with trailing branches. They root when they touch moist soil, producing thick mats of glossy foliage that often is evergreen. Excellent ground cover for banks and slopes. Set out container-grown plants in early fall or spring. Prefers soil in the neutral range.

MATURE HEIGHT: 2"
GROWTH RATE: fast
LIGHT: full sun
MOISTURE: roots moist

RUELLIA *rew-ell-ee-uh*
brittoniana Mexican Bluebell Zones 9–10.

Small shrub with attractive leaves and showy flowers in branching clusters. There are two species used as ground cover in climates like that of southern Florida: the one that flourishes in wet soils is discussed in Ground Covers 10. The species described here has beautiful bluish lavender flowers in spring and summer, can stand some salt, is very tolerant of drought and poor soil, and naturalizes readily. It is used as a flowering ground cover for open areas and requires pruning to stay in good form. Plant root divisions in early fall or spring.

MATURE HEIGHT: 1½'–2'
GROWTH RATE: medium
LIGHT: semi-sunny
MOISTURE: versatile

Rosa wichuraiana, Memorial Rose. (Neumann)

SEE ALSO:
Arctostaphylos uva-ursi, Bearberry, Ground Covers 3
Euonymus fortunei, Wintercreeper, Vines 8
Hedera canariensis, Algerian Ivy, Ground Covers 3
Hedera helix, English Ivy, Ground Covers 3
Jasminum spp., Jasmine, Vines 5
Juniperus, Juniper, Ground Covers 3
Liriope platyphylla, Lilyturf, Ground Covers 5
Liriope spicata, Creeping Lilyturf, Ground Covers 5
Ophiopogon japonicus, Lilyturf, Mondo Grass,
  Ground Covers 3
Ruellia makoyana, Monkey Plant, Ground Covers 10
Trachelospermum jasminoides, Star Jasmine, Con-
  federate Jasmine, Vines 8
Vinca, Periwinkle, Ground Covers 3
Xanthorhiza simplicissima, Yellowroot, Ground
  Covers 10
Zephyranthes spp., Rain Lily, Ground Covers 5

GROUND COVERS 10
GROUND COVERS FOR WET CONDITIONS

The bog plants in Aquatics 4 are, in some instances, suitable ground covers for wet places. See
also Ornamental Grasses 7.

CHELONE *kee-loh-nee*
obliqua Turtlehead, Snakehead Zones 4–9.

Hardy native perennial that grows wild in moist
woodlands and marshes. In September and October,
rigid spikes to 2 feet tall bear lilac-pink flowers
shaped like a turtle's head or a snapdragon bloom.

Chelone obliqua, Turtle's Head. (Wayside Gardens)

Chrysogonum virginianum, Golden Star. (Wayside Gardens)

The dark green basal foliage extends up the stems,
setting off the flowers handsomely. In spring, plant
root divisions in semi-shade. Prefers somewhat acid
soil.

MATURE HEIGHT: 2'
GROWTH RATE: medium
LIGHT: semi-sunny, shade
MOISTURE: soil surface damp

CHRYSOGONUM *kriss-og-on-num*
virginianum Golden Star   Zones 5–9.

Low, fast-spreading plant bright with starry golden-
yellow flowers from early spring into autumn. The
foliage is attractively scalloped and bright green. It is
native to the eastern United States and thrives in
rich, humusy soil well supplied with moisture, in full
sun or part shade. Plant in early spring. Prefers somewhat acid soil, with a pH between 6.0 and 7.0.

MATURE HEIGHT: 8"
GROWTH RATE: fast
LIGHT: full sun, semi-sunny
MOISTURE: soil surface damp

DICHONDRA *dye-kond-ruh*
micrantha   Zone 10.

Beautiful, emerald green, cushiony, creeping, turf-
forming plant with minute curved leaves, used in

warm regions as a lawn alternative, particularly in places difficult to mow. Popular in the Southwest, particularly California. It will not thrive if it dries out and requires more watering than turf grasses, but tolerates light foot traffic. Set out plugs, or sow seeds in early spring in well-dug soil supplied with plenty of organic material. Audrey Teasdale, horticulturist at Monrovia Nurseries, recommends full sun though the plant is also successful in partial light under trees.

MATURE HEIGHT: 3″
GROWTH RATE: medium
LIGHT: full sun, semi-sunny
MOISTURE: soil surface damp

GALAX *gay-lax*
urceolata   Zone 3.

Handsome evergreen perennial, about 1 foot high, with beautiful, thick, heart-shaped basal leaves which are used by florists in arrangements. The leaves turn bronze in autumn. Small white flowers on slender stems blossom in late spring and early summer. It is an excellent ground cover, most successful in moist, peaty loams in shady portions of a rock or wild garden. Plant root divisions in early spring in soil in the acid range, with a pH of 4.0 to 5.0.

MATURE HEIGHT: 1′
GROWTH RATE: medium/slow
LIGHT: semi-sunny
MOISTURE: soil surface damp

LAMIUM *lay-mee-um*
maculatum 'Variegatum'
Spotted Dead Nettle   Zone 3.

Herbaceous perennial that has trailing stems 6 to 8 inches high, and dark green oval leaves blotched with white along the midrib. Light purple-red flowers bloom throughout the summer. The beautifully variegated silver leaves of the cultivar 'Beacon Silver' are edged with a narrow band of green. Fast-growing

ground cover for moist, shaded locations. May be kept within bounds for use as an edger if it is cut back often. Plant seeds or root divisions in spring. For light, calcareous soils in rigorous climates.

MATURE HEIGHT: 6″–8″
GROWTH RATE: fast
LIGHT: shade
MOISTURE: soil surface damp

RUELLIA *rew-ell-ee-uh*
makoyana Monkey Plant   Zone 10.

Small shrub with beautiful leaves and showy flowers in branching clusters. Two species are used as ground covers in warm regions: the one for dry situations appears in Ground Covers 9. The species described here grows to about 1½ feet tall, with dark green, leathery leaves veined with white and purple beneath. The flowers are purple and bloom all year. It is good for moist, shady sites, where it reseeds readily—under trees, in open areas, as an edger—but requires good soil to flourish. Plant root divisions in early fall or spring.

MATURE HEIGHT: 1½′
GROWTH RATE: medium
LIGHT: semi-sunny
MOISTURE: soil surface damp

SELAGINELLA *sel-uh-jin-nell-uh*

Selaginellas are foliage plants—pretty, lacy, fernlike perennials used as ground cover under trees, and on banks and slopes in tropical and subtropical regions. Moist, shady situations are essential. Plant root divisions in spring.

LIGHT: semi-sunny, shade
MOISTURE: soil surface damp

S. involvens Erect Selaginella   Zone 10.
This species reaches 8 to 12 inches, grows slowly, and has green foliage. It may be used as an edger and as a ground cover.

S. uncinata Peacock Moss, Rainbow Fern,
Blue Selaginella   Zone 10.
Fast-growing species too vigorous to be an edger, this selaginella is 1 to 2 feet tall and has beautiful blue-green foliage.

XANTHORHIZA *zanth-oh-rye-zuh*
simplicissima Yellowroot   Zones 3–9.

Low, deciduous shrub that spreads rapidly in moist, shady places, and is an excellent tall ground cover. Lacy leaves turn orange-gold in fall, and in early spring there are interesting though not showy drooping clusters of small, brown-purple flowers. The inner bark and roots are yellow. It is tolerant of both dry sandy soil and heavy soil, but thrives in well-drained, moist, somewhat acid soil. Plant root divisions in spring or fall.

MATURE HEIGHT: 2′–3′
GROWTH RATE: medium
LIGHT: versatile
MOISTURE: roots moist

SEE ALSO:
Lysimachia nummularia, Creeping Jennie, Creeping Charlie, Ground Covers 5

Lamium maculatum, Spotted Dead Nettle. (Wayside Gardens)

Clematis 'Betty Corning', a long-blooming introduction of Dr. T. R. Dudley, of the National Arboretum. (Corning)

VINES

INTRODUCTION TO

VINES

A vine is defined as a plant needing support to develop. Most popular ornamental vines are woody, but the fast-growing herbaceous vines are among the quickest ground covers and screening. Dr. Theodore Dudley, National Arboretum Research Botanist who introduced the new and beautiful late-flowering 'Betty Corning' clematis, describes vines as valuable plants for those following the new naturalism.

Vines combine beauty and practicality. Deep-rooted, vigorous growers, they are relatively drought-resistant, achieve huge effects, and require little help once established. They occupy small in-ground space, grow successfully in large planters if there's no ground available, and have modest watering needs for the foliage produced. In return they bloom or fruit, give shade, soften and cover stark modern walls, beautify fences, hide unsightly posts and drains, smother stumps, dead trees, and dilapidated buildings, and screen out unattractive views. Southern Californians'

gardens, which are on the edge of the desert, lead in vine use. In small condominium and garden apartment spaces, they are especially valuable.

SUPPORTING VINES

To include a vine in the garden, start by taking stock of the available man-made structures—and choose a vine whose support can be supplied. The way a vine climbs dictates the support needed. There are three ways: One group climbs by twining stems around a narrow support. Typical of this type are *Ipomoea hederacea*, Ivy-leaved Morning-glory, and *Lonicera*, Woodbine or Honeysuckle. For such vines, the support can be a wooden post, a pipe, a few wires or strings. Other vines climb by twining tendrils or leaf petioles; *Clematis* is an example. These require a structure of wires, or wire mesh. The last group climbs by aerial rootlets that secrete an adhesive glue. Examples are *Hedera helix*, English Ivy, and *Parthenocissus quinquefolia*, Virginia Creeper or

Pyrostegia venusta, Flame Vine, a spectacular warm-climate flowering vine, and close-up on facing page. (Meerow)

Woodbine. These need only an unbroken but rather rugged surface, such as a brick or stucco wall, or a rough, unpainted fence.

Vines that will eventually be big, for instance *Wisteria* and *Celastrus orbiculatus*, Oriental Bittersweet, require supports built of heavy timbers.

In all cases where wood is used for support, it must be pressure treated with a wood preservative. Avoid growing vines against wooden buildings, as the plants hold moisture that can cause rot. Allow at least a 3-inch air space between foliage and house walls. Vines are healthier when there is air circulating all around them.

Don't plant vines that climb by tendrils near trees or large shrubs.

PLANTING VINES

Provide well-drained, well-prepared soil and a generous planting hole. Test for drainage, and plant as directed for woody plants in Section Two. Most vines aren't difficult about pH, except some clematis.

Plant a vine about 6 inches away from the wall or support it is to climb, so there will be air space behind the foliage when it matures. Maintain a 3-inch mulch, especially in summer to keep roots cool. Fertilize lightly in spring before growth begins. Water well when young. If the vine is sheltered from rain, water the foliage occasionally with the garden hose, but not when it is coming into or in bloom.

Keep dead, extraneous, or weak wood pruned out. Some large, vigorous species, such as *Wisteria*, require severe pruning almost every season, and can overwhelm and damage shutters and other wooden structures, and kill trees, unless kept in bounds.

PRUNING

Pruning time is according to purpose. Flowering vines that bloom on current year's growth are pruned in winter.

Flowering plants that bloom in spring on 1-year-old wood are pruned when the flowers fade.

Winter-prune deciduous plants during dormancy, just after the coldest part of the season and until growth begins. Summer-prune when seasonal growth is complete. Avoid fall pruning; wounds heal more slowly and the late growth stimulated by this pruning may be damaged by the first frosts.

It is not necessary to paint, tar, or otherwise cover a pruning cut or wound. Find the ring or collar from which each branch grows. Cut back just to it, but do not damage it. From there the plant will develop an attractive, healthy covering for the wounded area.

VINES 1
FLOWERING VINES

The number of flowering vines in cultivation tells us how much they are enjoyed. This section presents some favorites, each interesting in many ways. The woody vines are slower to grow, but soon enough the gnarled, twisting trunks acquire the timeless aura of ancient bonsai—well worth a few years of patience. For the most beautiful flower show, when blooming is over lightly prune the old vines of those plants that bloom on last year's wood; in very early spring prune those that bloom on the current year's growth. Pruning stimulates growth and provides more new branches for blooming.

ALLAMANDA *al-lam-mand-uh*
cathartica Allamanda, Golden-trumpet
Zone 10.

Rambling, fast-growing, evergreen climber, with large leathery leaves on thick stems, excellent for screening and ground cover in warm climates. Fragrant, tubular, golden yellow flowers bloom spring, summer, and fall. Needs strong support, and rich, well-drained soil. Tolerates some drought. Prune when the leaves drop. Plant container-grown plants in early spring.

GROWTH RATE: fast
LIGHT: full sun
MOISTURE: versatile

ANTIGONON *an-tig-oh-non*
leptopus Coral Vine   Zones 9–10.

Beautiful, fast-growing vine for screening, trellises, and fences. It climbs by twisting tendrils and needs support and pruning after it has flowered. Bright coral pink flowers in summer (in fall in Florida). Some tolerance for drought. Plant container-grown plants in early spring.

Allamanda cathartica. (Meerow)

GROWTH RATE: fast
LIGHT: full sun
MOISTURE: versatile

BOUGAINVILLEA *boog-in-vill-ee-uh*
many hybrids and cultivars   Zone 10.

A rambling vine for arbors, fences, and trellises with showy red, pink, orange, purple, or white flowers. Good basket plant. Spiny, evergreen, drought-resistant, it blooms on new growth, year-round, but most profusely in summer. It has some tolerance for salt and thrives in well-drained soil with high humus content. Plant container-grown plants in spring. On the West Coast the variegated dwarf cultivars are preferred: 'Crimson Jewel', which combines crim-

Bougainvillea.

son, pink, and orange, and the new, very purple, 'Oo-la-la'. There are a great many named cultivars with different flower colors and growth habits.

GROWTH RATE: medium
LIGHT: full sun
MOISTURE: versatile

CLEMATIS *klem-at-iss*

Very beautiful flowering vines. The species described here are famous for their extraordinary flowers, some 5 to 9 inches across. Others are vigorous plants that quickly will screen stone walls, arbors, trellises, and fences, and have small but fragrant blooms. They grow by attaching leaf stalks to the support provided or by scrambling over other vegetation. Among species often used for quick screening are: *C. balearica,* a pale yellow; *C. cirrhosa,* an evergreen with yellow-white flowers; *C. flammula,* Virgin's Bower, a white, fall-blooming species hardy south of Pennsylvania; *C. rehderana,* a deciduous climber with nodding, pale yellow flowers. *C. recta,* a fragrant white in flower from June to September, is one of the hardiest. In cold areas look for locally grown, large-flowered cultivars.

The genus is easy to grow once established, but needs deeply dug, light, moist soil, enriched with leaf mold and sweetened with lime. Some do well in acidic soils also. Plant where the vines can be in full sun and the roots in some shade, or mulch well. For those species that flower on old wood, thin old stalks lightly after flowering. Those that flower on new wood are pruned to the ground when dormant.

MATURE HEIGHT: variable with years
GROWTH RATE: variable with species
LIGHT: semi-sunny
MOISTURE: roots moist

C. armandii Armand Clematis   Zones 7–8.
Lovely, with very showy clusters of white or pink fragrant flowers 2 to 3 inches across in spring, and evergreen, dark green, leathery leaves. Especially vigorous in the Pacific Northwest and southeastern United States. Blooms on old wood, so prune after flowering. There are pink cultivars.

C. dioscoreifolia Japanese Clematis
Zones 9–10.
For north and central Florida and warm climates. It has fragrant, showy white flowers, summer and fall, grows medium fast and tolerates some drought and a wide range of soils. Prune in winter.

C. × jackmanii Jackman Clematis
Zones 3–8.
These are fast-growing hybrids with extraordinary, perfect, purplish violet blooms 4 to 7 inches across. Many large-flowered clematis are not vigorous, but these hybrids are the best for rapid screening. They flower from summer to frost on new growth. There is a large number of cultivars in varying colors and combinations.

C. maximowicziana (syn. *paniculata*)
Sweet Autumn Clematis   Zones 4–9.
For quick screening of slopes, rocky outcroppings, or city fences. Lustrous foliage, and a profusion of 1-inch white flowers in fall. Blooms on new wood.

Clematis × jackmanii, Jackman Clematis. (Dudley)

C. montana　Anemone Clematis　Zones 6–10.
Vigorous white-flowered species to train on a fence
or grow as a ground cover, with medium flowers of
white or pink, in late spring, on the previous season's
growth. The hardier var. *rubens* has fragrant rosy
pink flowers, and new foliage is reddish. It is very
hardy and grows north of Boston and Albany.

C. tangutica　Golden Clematis　Zones 3–8.
Masses of beautiful, bell-shaped, soft yellow flowers
2 to 4 inches across appear in June, intermittently in
summer, and profusely again in late summer and
early autumn. Unusually hardy and will come back
the same season if winter-killed. Best in full sun.
Flowers on new wood.

C. texensis　Scarlet Clematis　Zones 4–8.
Better density for screening than most clematis. Nodding, scarlet, bell-shaped flowers borne profusely on
new wood, summer till frost. The hybrid 'Duchess of
Albany' has large pink-purple flowers streaked with
white.

C. viticella　Zones 4–8.
This species can grow 6 feet in one year. It has dainty
hanging blue or purple flowers on long upright stalks
in mid- and late summer. 'Betty Corning' blooms
over a longer period than the species. It is best in full
sun, mulched heavily. Very hardy hybrids, such as
'Huldine', are available. Blooms on new wood. Every
several years can be cut back to the ground in winter.

Clematis 'Betty Corning'. (Dudley)

CRYPTOSTEGIA *krip-toh-steej-ee-uh*
madagascariensis
Madagascar Rubber Vine   Zone 10.

Climbing evergreen vine used as specimen or dense cover for fences, trellises, and trees in subtropical and tropical Florida. Lavender flowers summer and fall, and beautiful leaves veined in red. Prune after the flowering period. Needs a sturdy support. Some salt tolerance. Plant container-grown plants spring or summer.

GROWTH RATE:	medium
LIGHT:	full sun, semi-sunny
MOISTURE:	versatile

DISTICTIS *dis-tik-tis*

Woody evergreens that climb by tendrils, grown in southern California for their handsome foliage and long-blooming, showy, trumpet-shaped flowers. Specimen vines for trellises, arbors, and patios. Tolerates hot sun. Set out container-grown plants in spring, in well-drained soil.

GROWTH RATE:	medium
LIGHT:	full sun, semi-sunny
MOISTURE:	versatile

D. buccinatoria   Blood-trumpet Zones 9–10.
The flowers are bloodred with a yellow base, and the large leaves are evergreen.

D. 'Rivers'   Zones 9–10.
Very showy late fall bloomer in the South, with mauve to purple trumpets with yellow throats and handsome evergreen foliage. Sometimes called the 'Royal Trumpet Vine'.

PASSIFLORA *pass-if-floh-ra*

Mostly evergreen, fast-growing, climbing vines that attach themselves by tendrils, and have exotic, sweet-scented flowers and fruits, some edible. Hardy species will grow as far north as New York, but the genus is commonly planted for screening and fruit only in warm regions such as southern Florida. Needs staking and plenty of water, but tolerates some drought. Plant container-grown plants in early spring.

GROWTH RATE:	fast
LIGHT:	full sun
MOISTURE:	roots moist

P. caerula   Blue Passionflower   Zone 10.
Slender, vigorous vine with slightly scented, large, complex flowers, pale pink with white and purple crown. Fruits are egg-shaped, yellow, to 2 inches long.

P. coccinea   Red Passionflower   Zone 10.
Outstanding, fast-growing, free-flowering vine with exotic vivid red flowers to 5 inches wide, summer and fall, against rich green evergreen leaves. The flowers last only a day but are prolific. Used in subtropical and tropical regions to cover trellises and fences.

P. edulis   Passion Fruit   Zone 10.
Handsome foliage. This species is grown for its fruit, known as "granadillo" in Latin America, as well as for the fragrant purple and white flowers that bloom all year. Many cultivars are available.

PYROSTEGIA *pye-roh-steej-ee-uh*
venusta (syn. *ignea*)   Flame Vine   Zone 10.

Quick-growing evergreen vine, with spectacular fiery orange flowers from October through Christmas. In hot climates such as southern California and Florida, it is grown as cover for trellises, fences, and masonry. Prune severely after flowering. Set out container-grown plants in early spring. Needs well-drained soil with pH in the neutral range.

GROWTH RATE:	fast
LIGHT:	full sun
MOISTURE:	versatile

Tecomaria capensis, Cape Honeysuckle. (Meerow)

SCHIZOPHRAGMA *shye-zoh-frag-muh*
hydrangeoides   Japanese Hydrangea Vine
Zones 5–8.

High-climbing deciduous vine with large, roundish leaves and, in midsummer, white flower clusters to 9 inches across. It has clinging rootlike holdfasts, and resembles climbing hydrangea (see Vines 8). Handsome clinging to walls and old tree trunks. Prune in winter, only if needed. It thrives in moist, fertile soil, if well supported, and tolerates a wide range of light. Soil may be acid to neutral. Plant container-grown plants in early spring.

GROWTH RATE:	slow
LIGHT:	versatile
MOISTURE:	roots moist

TECOMARIA *tek-oh-may-ree-uh*
capensis   Cape Honeysuckle   Zones 9–10.

Fast-growing evergreen woody vine or sprawling shrub to 6 feet or more, with pink, orange-red, or scarlet flowers summer and fall. There are yellow-flowered and variegated cultivars. It has some tolerance for salt and drought, grows well in sandy soil, and may be sheared as a shrub. Plant container-grown plants in early spring.

GROWTH RATE:	fast
LIGHT:	full sun
MOISTURE:	roots moist, versatile

WISTERIA *wiss-teer-ee-uh*

Wisteria in full bloom are breathtaking—a fragrant spring show of long, drooping flower clusters in various colors that burst forth just as new foliage emerges. However, these fast-growing, twining vines can invade and damage attics and destroy trees. Confine wisteria to pergolas, controlled "green roofing" for porches, stone walls. In winter prune back vigorous old growth to 3 or 4 buds. Limit nitrogen in fertilizer; too much will inhibit flowering to the advantage of lush foliage. Set out container-grown cultivars in early spring and pamper until growth begins. Prefers acid-range soil. 'Alba' is a very fragrant white; 'Purpurea' is purplish violet.

Passiflora caerulea, Blue Passionflower. (Dunselman)

Wisteria floribunda, Japanese Wisteria. (Dudley)

GROWTH RATE:	fast
LIGHT:	full sun
MOISTURE:	roots moist

W. floribunda Japanese Wisteria Zones 4–9.
This species and *W. sinensis*, Chinese Wisteria, (see Vines 9) are grown in northern gardens for their large, fragrant flower clusters, 9 to 20 inches long, pink, white, or lilac, single or double. Double-flowered selections may flower erratically and not hold up well in wet weather.

W. macrostachya Kentucky Wisteria
Zones 5–8.
A lovely vine that blooms after the foliage develops, providing a modest but later show of fragrant flower clusters 10 inches long in lilac-purple. Another late wisteria, *W. frutescens,* American Wisteria, blooms June to August in the South. It is a less vigorous vine that produces short but dense clumps of fragrant blush-violet flowers on new wood.

Trachelospermum jasminoides, Star Jasmine. (Longwood Gardens)

SEE ALSO:
Aristolochia durior, Dutchman's-pipe, Vines 8
Bignonia capreolata, Cross Vine, Vines 7
Campsis × *tagliabuana* 'Madame Galen', Vines 6
Gelsemium sempervirens 'Pride of Augusta', Yellow Jasmine, Carolina Yellow Jasmine, Vines 4
Hydrangea anomala subsp. *petiolaris*, Climbing Hydrangea, Vines 8
Lathyrus odoratus, Sweet Pea, Vines 7
Lonicera × *brownii* 'Dropmore Scarlet', Brown's Honeysuckle, Trumpet Honeysuckle, Coral Honeysuckle, Vines 5
Lonicera × *heckrottii*, Everblooming Honeysuckle, Vines 5
Lonicera sempervirens 'Superba', 'Magnifica', 'Sulfurea', Trumpet Huneysuckle, Coral Honeysuckle, Vines 5
Pileostegia viburnoides, Tanglehead, Vines 4
Trachelospermum jasminoides, Star Jasmine, Confederate Jasmine, Vines 8

ALTERNATES:
Akebia quinata, Five-leaf Akebia
Campsis grandiflora, Chinese Trumpet Creeper
Campsis radicans, Trumpet Creeper
Clematis balearica
Clematis cirrhosa
Clematis flammula
Clematis recta, Ground Clematis
Clematis rehderana, Rehder's Clematis
Clerodendrum thomsoniae, Tropical Bleeding-heart
Jasminum officinale, Poet's Jasmine
Petrea volubilis, Queen's Wreath
Polygonum aubertii, China Fleece Vine, Silver Lace Vine

VINES 2
FLOWERING VINES: ROSES

Climbing roses put forth long canes that may be trained to rise against a trellis or wall, or to ramble along a fence. "Training" means being tied—roses don't climb on their own. For aficionados of tree form and standard roses, large-flowered or miniature, the climbing roses here are excellent material, along with Floribundas such as 'Europeana', a 2- to 2½-foot bush that produces huge panicles of rich red rosettes 3 inches across.

There are Large Climbing Roses (CL) and Miniature Climbing Roses (MCL). The large types are usually included as backdrop for rose gardens—trained to an arch, a pergola, or a wall. The miniatures require little space at the base and succeed in containers with winter protection. They are ideal for small condominium patios and porches.

A climbing rose can handle only 5 or 6 heavy canes. Every year or so remove one of the oldest canes, then new shoots will develop. Save only 2 or 3 of these for flowering next year. After the flowers fade, prune this year's flowering canes back to a dormant eye on the outside. Often they'll throw out another stem that will bloom. See Shrubs 6 for an overview on rose culture.

Old Garden Roses appear in Herbs 7; Polyantha and Miniature roses, and roses for hedges in Shrubs 19, shrub roses in Shrubs 6.

COMPANION PLANTINGS
Tall spring-flowering bulbs, such as early Darwin Hybrid Tulips.
Perennials and annuals: *Lavandula angustifolia* 'Hidcote', English Lavender; *Salvia farinacea*, 'Blue Bedder', Mealycup Sage; *S. officinalis* 'Albiflora', White Garden Sage.
Miniature roses for hanging baskets: 'Anita Charles', pink blend (M); 'Green Ice', white (M); 'Orange Honey' (M); 'Red Cascade' (MCL).
Miniatures roses for boxes and planters, 10- to 14-inch compact bushy cultivars: 'Centerpiece', red; 'Cinderella,' white; 'Cupcake', pink; 'Rainbow's End', yellow blend; 'Sequoia Gold', yellow; 'Toy Clown', red blend.
Roses for ground cover, steep banks, retaining walls: *Rosa wichuraiana*, Memorial Rose.

ROSA *roh-zuh* Rose

The climbing characteristic has been bred into almost all classes of roses. Some are ramblers, with dense clusters of small flowers on pliant canes formed annually from the base. Others have stiffer canes and large flowers borne singly or in clusters. The most plentiful and beautiful flowers are produced by climbers that are pruned every year. It is generally true that climbing roses trained horizontally produce flowers more abundantly than those trained to grow upward.

Like other roses, climbers require a minimum of 6 hours of full sun daily for maximum bloom production. With 4 or 5 hours of sun, flowers will be sparse. Climbers flower well with some shade on the base, as long as most of the plant is in the sun. Most climbing hybrid tea roses are less winter-hardy than the modern, large-flowered climbers, which are bred for hardiness, disease-resistance, and prolific, long-season bloom. A few are fragrant.

Dr. H. Marc Cathey, Director of the National Arboretum, plants climbing roses in spring, shrub roses in spring or fall. His favorite climber is 'Climbing Peace', a magnificent, slightly fragrant rose which usually requires 2 to 3 years to get established before it will bloom.

Some of the Old Garden Roses (*Albas*, Bourbons, and Hybrid Perpetuals) growing at the National Arboretum were trained to trellises—and grew 2 to 3 feet taller than when planted as free-standing, or self-supporting, specimens.

CLIMBING MINIATURES

'Hi-Ho' (MCL). Popular climbing miniature, charming little plant for limited space. The flowers are 1½ inches in diameter, light red or deep pink, double, in abundant clusters. Blooming repeats well through the season. Canes 6 to 7 feet.

'Little Girl' (MCL). Outstanding climbing miniature that bears clusters of exceptionally lovely, 1½-inch, pink blend formal blooms all season. Canes grow 4 to 5 feet.

LARGE-FLOWERED CLIMBERS

'America' (CL). Medium-tall climber, 9 to 12 feet. Magnificent flowers of exhibition quality, strongly fragrant, elegant and formal—big 4-inch blooms in beautiful salmon pink. Prolific in spring, with fair repeat bloom. Disease-resistant, winter-hardy.

'Blaze' (CL). Very vigorous, hardy, with canes 12 to 15 feet long, and bearing large clusters of 2- to 3-inch semidouble, cupped, slightly fragrant, bright scarlet flowers. The foliage is leathery and dark. It

Rosa 'Hi-Ho', and 'Starina'. (Bell)

Rosa 'Little Girl'. (Bell)

Rosa 'New Dawn' (right) with *R.* 'City of York'. (McDonald)

blooms heavily in spring with some recurrent bloom during the season. It has been grown successfully everywhere in the country, is easy to care for and dependable. It also is versatile, rambling along fences and climbing garages, pergolas, and posts with equal ease.

'Dortmund' (Kordesii CL). Profuse bloomer in spring, with excellent repeat bloom throughout the season. Fragrant, 4-inch, crimson red flowers with white eyes are borne in large clusters. Big, vigorous shrubs, 8 to 10 feet; disease-free and winter-hardy.

'Golden Showers' (CL). Former AARS (All-American Rose Selections) winner, hardiest of climbing yellows and most rewarding. Magnificent daffodil-yellow flowers open into 5- to 5½-inch blooms that are fragrant, and produced abundantly and repeatedly until late fall. The plant is upright, between 8 and 10 feet, but can reach to 15 feet.

'New Dawn' (CL). Very tall, winter-hardy plant that grows vigorously and needs lots of room—the canes grow 15 to 20 feet. It produces slightly fragrant, medium-size, blush-pink, lavish double blooms repeatedly throughout the season.

'Viking Queen' (CL). Climber introduced by the University of Minnesota. Disease-resistant and hardier than most climbing roses, able to withstand winters in the cold top tier of the country with minimal protection. The 3- to 4-inch flowers are very fragrant, medium to deep pink, and borne repeatedly in large clusters. The canes reach 10 to 12 feet.

SEE ALSO:

Hedge, and Polyantha and Miniature Roses, Shrubs 19
Old Garden Roses, Herbs 7
Roses for flowers, Shrubs 6

Rosa 'Blaze'. (McDonald)

VINES 3
VINES FOR FOLIAGE: DECIDUOUS

Here are vines with exceptionally handsome foliage. Some also have attractive flowers. Those that bear male and female flowers on separate plants (dioecious) will fruit profusely only if plants of both sexes are present.

ACTINIDIA *ak-tin-nid-ee-ah*

Fast-growing, deciduous, twining vines that give excellent cover for sturdy trellises and arbors and have lustrous, dense foliage and, in some species, fragrant flowers and luscious little fruits. Male and female flowers are borne on separate plants. Set out container-grown plants in well-drained soil in spring.

GROWTH RATE:	fast
LIGHT:	full sun, semi-sunny
MOISTURE:	versatile

A. arguta   Bower Actinidia, Tara Vine
Zones 4–8.
Most rampant grower of the genus and very adaptable. Can also be used as a ground cover. Long, lustrous leaves to 5 inches. Insignificant summer flower clusters are followed by greenish yellow berrylike fruits.

A. deliciosa (syn. *chinensis*)
Chinese Gooseberry, Kiwi Fruit, Kiwi
Zones 7–9.
Vigorous though not rampant, this species is grown for the luscious, tart-sweet kiwi fruit. The leaves are long and heart-shaped, velvety white underneath, with reddish hairs on stems and twigs. Bears fragrant flowers and fruits on short branches of year-old wood; in the warmer reaches of its range, a male plant ensures the female plant will produce the popular, brown-to-green-skinned, green-fleshed kiwis.

A. kolomikta   Zones 4–8.
The male vine is highly ornamental, variegated with white and pink coloration. The small, fragrant, white, female flowers bloom in late spring and are followed by small, greenish yellow, edible fruits in fall. Needs well-limed soil and good light to color brightly. Give extra attention until well established.

A. polygama   Silver Vine   Zone 4.
Less vigorous, with silver-white to yellow markings on the leaves of male plants. The small white flowers are fragrant. The small fruits are edible.

AMPELOPSIS *am-pel-lop-siss*

Vigorous vines, climbing by tendrils, excellent for fast cover of trellises, arbors, walls, fences, slopes. Colorful berries in autumn. Tolerant of urban conditions. Provide strong support. Plant container-grown plants in spring.

GROWTH RATE:	fast
LIGHT:	full sun, semi-sunny
MOISTURE:	versatile

A. arborea   Pepper Vine   Zones 7–10.
Rather weedy evergreen vine in the South, used in wild gardens or for fast coverage of fences. It has some tolerance for drought, prefers full sun.

A. brevipedunculata   Porcelain Ampelopsis
Zones 4–9.
Strong, invasive climber with bright green, handsomely textured leaves, striking in summer and fall when the berries appear in a color range of porcelain blue, green, purple, and pink. Attracts birds. 'Elegans' grows more slowly and has smaller leaves than the species, and is beautifully variegated with white and pink. Interesting for specimen use. Fruit colors best in full sun.

PARTHENOCISSUS *parth-en-oh-siss-us*   Woodbine

Woody climbers famous for brilliant scarlet color in autumn in the deciduous species. Plants produce clusters of small greenish flowers, followed by dark berries and then the glorious fall color. Attract birds. Give beauty to large blank walls, but can damage

Parthenocissus tricuspidata, Boston Ivy. (Dudley)

masonry; even after removal, the traces remain. Excellent ground covers and tolerate urban conditions, drought, partial shade. Plant container-grown plants in spring.

GROWTH RATE: medium
LIGHT: versatile
MOISTURE: versatile

P. henryana   Zones 7–9.
Most beautiful of the woodbines; leaves are bluish green marked with white on the veins, and purplish underneath. Color is brightest in partial shade. In fall it turns a strong purplish red. Flower clusters slender and to 6 inches long. Blue berries. Choice ground cover for slopes.

P. quinquefolia   Virginia Creeper, Woodbine
                                  Zones 3–9.
Vigorous climber hard to keep in bounds, but has attractive reddish new growth, blue berries, and brilliant scarlet color in the fall. Color is best when growing in full sun. It tolerates urban conditions, is an excellent ground cover for slopes. Attractive to birds.

P. tricuspidata   Boston Ivy   Zones 4–8.
Rampant vine, like Virginia Creeper, with lustrous leaves, blue-black berries, and brilliant orange-red color in fall, the species often chosen for clinging to stonework. Color is best in full sun. 'Lowii' and 'Veitchii' have smaller leaves and are less vigorous. Attracts birds.

SEE ALSO:
Aristolochia durior, Dutchman's-pipe, Vines 8
Epipremnum aureum, Pothos, Vines 8
Hydrangea anomala subsp. *petiolaris*, Climbing Hydrangea, Vines 8
Menispermum canadense, Yellow Parilla, Moonseed, Vines 8

ALTERNATES:
Schisandra chinensis, Magnolia Vine
Vitis cognetiae, Crimson Glory Vine

VINES 4
VINES FOR FOLIAGE: EVERGREEN

Some vines that are deciduous or treated as annuals in cool regions are evergreen when growing farther south. But there are hardy evergreen vines as well. This section contains both hardy and tender vines that are evergreen in warm climates, and grown primarily for their foliage.

CLYTOSTOMA *klye-tost-om-uh*
callistegioides Argentine Trumpet Vine
                                  Zones 9–10.

Vigorous, evergreen climbing shrub, 30 to 60 feet, that roots where it touches soil. The leaves are glossy and dark green, and delicate lavender trumpet-shaped flowers, 3 inches long, bloom in pairs for about 2 months in late spring into summer. Some salt and drought tolerance. In moist climates prune back

Clytostoma callistegioides, Argentine Trumpet Vine. (Meerow)

annually. Set out container-grown plants in early fall or spring in rich, well-drained but moist loam.

GROWTH RATE: fast
LIGHT: full sun, semi-sunny
MOISTURE: roots moist, versatile

FICUS *fye-kus*
pumila   Creeping Fig   Zones 9–10.

A vigorous creeping or climbing evergreen fig that covers itself with dainty green leaves an inch long or slightly longer. The erect fruiting branches produce much coarser, larger leaves and are pruned off to maintain the dainty appearance of the vine. The little figs are not edible. 'Variegatus' has small, white-edged leaves. Beautiful on masonry walls, which it climbs by means of rootlets. Tolerates drought well and some salt exposure. Plant container-grown plants in spring in sun or partial shade. Too much sun, especially in the South, can burn out the foliage. Can be grown as a houseplant in the North.

GROWTH RATE: fast
LIGHT: full sun, semi-sunny
MOISTURE: versatile

GELSEMIUM *jel-seem-ee-um*
sempervirens   Yellow Jasmine,
Carolina Yellow Jasmine   Zones 7–9.

A vigorous, dense, twining evergreen with long, slender, reddish stems. It climbs and also makes an excellent ground cover. Masses of large, fragrant, funnel-shaped yellow flowers appear in spring, with some repeat in fall. 'Pride of Augusta' is a beautiful double-flowered cultivar. Does well on dryish fence rows along roadsides. Grows faster in full sun in moist, well-drained soils rich in organic matter but tolerates shade. Plant container-grown plants in early spring.

GROWTH RATE: fast
LIGHT: versatile
MOISTURE: versatile

HEDERA *hed-er-uh*   Ivy

Vigorous and evergreen, ivy succeeds under trees and in hot, dry city conditions. In the mature form, it is shrublike. As a climbing vine it reaches 25 to 50 feet. As a ground cover it is 6 to 8 inches high. Interesting features are the two distinct stages of leaf development; creeping along the ground or beginning to climb, ivy produces "juvenile" foliage which never flowers. The "adult" stage comes when ivy climbs a support: small, green clusters of petalless flowers are borne at the tips, followed in autumn by black fruit. Ivy throws many "sports," shoots different from the parent, and there are literally hundreds of cultivars and selections. Plant rooted divisions in early spring and keep damp until established. Shear back every 3 or 4 years to maintain foliage density.

MATURE HEIGHT: 6"–8"
GROWTH RATE: fast
LIGHT: versatile
MOISTURE: versatile

H. canariensis   Algerian Ivy   Zones 9–10.
A large-leaved ivy with burgundy red twigs and petioles. 'Variegata' leaves are edged in yellowish white. Excellent at seaside, under trees, on banks and slopes, and in open areas. Grows better in central and northern Florida than in the southern part of the state.

H. helix   English Ivy   Zones 5–9.
Stands 6 to 8 inches high and the strands can stretch to 90 feet. A vigorous grower that competes well with tree roots. There are hundreds of cultivars, varying in hardiness and coloration. Popular on the West Coast is 'Baltic', which is hardier than the species; hardier yet is 'Bulgaria'; 'Wilson' is hardy to Zone 4. *H. h.* 'Aureo-variegata' is variegated yellow; '*H. h.* 'Argenteo-variegata' is variegated white.

LAPAGERIA *lap-aj-jeer-ee-uh*
rosea   Chilean Bellflower   Zones 9–10.

Tall, showy, evergreen vine with many slender, branched, twining stems; often seen in the South and Southeast. Bell-shaped, rose red flowers bloom in the leaf axils in summer and fall, and are long-lasting when cut. Good container plant. 'Albiflora' is a beautiful white-flowered variety. It prospers in well-drained, rich, sandy loam. Set out container-grown plants in spring; prefers soil in the alkaline range.

GROWTH RATE: medium
LIGHT: semi-sunny, shade
MOISTURE: roots moist

LYGODIUM *lye-goh-dee-um*
palmatum   Hartford Fern   Zones 6–9.

Graceful, climbing, feathery ferns most often seen in greenhouses (*L. scandens* for instance), but this species is hardier. It has long, twining evergreen fronds with ivylike leaves, lovely in a wild or fern garden. With wire support, can be trained to 6 feet high. Needs moist, humusy soil with enough sand for good

Macfadyen unguis-cati, Cat's-claw. (Meerow)

Solandra guttata, Goldcup. (Meerow)

drainage and a somewhat acid pH. Plant root divisions in spring.

GROWTH RATE: medium
LIGHT: semi-sunny, shade
MOISTURE: soil surface damp

MACFADYENA *mak-fad-dee-ain-uh*
unguis-cati Cat's-claw   Zones 8–10.

Semievergreen climbing vine with delicate foliage and large, to 4-inch-long, yellow, funnel-shaped flowers in clusters of 2 or 3 in spring. The name comes from the resemblance of its climbing tendrils to the claws of a cat. Once established, drought-tolerant. Set out container-grown plants in spring or early fall.

MATURE HEIGHT: 25'–30'
GROWTH RATE: fast
LIGHT: full sun
MOISTURE: versatile

MANDEVILLA *man-dev-vill-uh*
splendens Pink Allamanda   Zones 9–10.

There are many hybrids of this choice twining evergreen with showy pink flowers in summer. In Florida it is grown on fences and trellises. It tolerates some salt and drought and flourishes in well-drained sandy soil to which lots of peat moss has been added. Plant container-grown plants in spring.

GROWTH RATE: fast
LIGHT: full sun
MOISTURE: versatile

MONSTERA *mon-ster-uh*
deliciosa Ceriman   Zones 9–10.

Spectacular, 3-foot-long, lobed and perforated leaves and creamy white flower spathes followed by aromatic, delicious fruit (tasting like a cross between bananas and pineapple) make this a favorite evergreen climber in Florida. One common name for it is

Mandevilla splendens, Pink Allamanda. (Meerow)

"windowleaf"—it is that large. In the North it is a popular houseplant for shade, sometimes listed as Philodendron pertusum. Planted at the foot of a tree, *Monstera* climbs high, dangling cordlike roots. It succeeds outdoors as well as indoors with almost no light; in good light it is magnificent but too much sun can burn the leaves. Prefers well-drained, humusy soil. Set out container plants in spring.

GROWTH RATE: medium
LIGHT: versatile
MOISTURE: soil surface damp

PILEOSTEGIA *pye-lee-oh-stee-jee-uh*
viburnoides Tanglehead   Zones 8–9.

One of the best evergreen climbers, resembling the elegant climbing hydrangea (see Vines 8) in its manner of attachment but it doesn't have the large,

showy flower bracts. The small flowers are born on terminal panicles. Leathery, dark green, glossy leaves to 5 inches long. Thrives in shade. Plant container-grown plants in early spring.

GROWTH RATE: medium to slow
LIGHT: semi-sunny, shade
MOISTURE: versatile

SOLANDRA *sol-land-ruh*
guttata Goldcup, Chalice Vine   Zones 9–10.

Vigorous, partly climbing, shrubby plant, with broad evergreen leaves to 6 inches long. In winter or early spring, it bears large, single, fragrant white or yellow flowers to 9 inches long, spotted purple. Yearly pruning helps keep the plants in good condition. Strong support is required for the woody stems to climb. Tolerates salt spray and thrives in well-drained, sandy loam, with plenty of moisture in winter, less in the hot months.

MATURE HEIGHT: 20'
GROWTH RATE: fast
LIGHT: full sun
MOISTURE: roots moist

STAUNTONIA *ston-toh-nee-uh*
hexaphylla Japanese Staunton Vine
Zones 8–9.

Tall, woody, evergreen twining vine with attractive dark green foliage. It produces fragrant clusters of whitish male flowers as well as purplish female blooms on the same plant. Choice for warm climates as a screen or trained on an arbor. Flourishes in rich, moist, well-drained soil with lots of leaf mold and somewhat acid pH. Plant container-grown plants in spring.

GROWTH RATE: slow
LIGHT: shade
MOISTURE: soil surface damp

SEE ALSO:
Bignonia capreolata, Cross Vine, Vines 7
Clematis armandii, Armand Clematis, Vines 1
Epipremnum aureum, Pothos, Vines 8
Euonymus fortunei, Vines 8
Kadsura japonica, Scarlet Kadsura, Vines 6
Passiflora coccinea, Red Passionflower, Vines 1
Passiflora edulis, Passion Fruit, Vines 1
Tecomaria capensis, Cape Honeysuckle, Vines 1
Trachelospermum jasminoides, Star Jasmine, Confederate Jasmine, Vines 8

ALTERNATES:
Polygonum aubertii, China Fleece Vine, Silver Lace Vine
Rosa wichuraiana, Memorial Rose

VINES 5
VINES WITH FRAGRANT FLOWERS

These are the vines whose very names evoke fragrance. A few other highly scented vines appear in other sections of the book—the fragrant clematis species and wisterias can be found in Vines 1, Flowering Vines. Look for other fragrant vines on the See also list, below.

HOLBOELLIA *hole-bowl-lee-uh*
grandiflora Zones 7–10.

High-climbing, woody, evergreen twining vine, and vigorous grower once established. In late spring through early summer it bears inch-long, open-face, white with violet flowers that are very fragrant. The fruit is purple, fragrant, delicious, long, like tiny bananas, several in a cluster. Set out container-grown plants in early spring in well-drained soil.

MATURE HEIGHT: 30'–35'
GROWTH RATE: medium
LIGHT: full sun, versatile
MOISTURE: roots moist

Jasminum species. (Neumann)

JASMINUM *jass-min-um*

Vigorous deciduous or evergreen rambling shrubs or vines with small, very fragrant, white, pink, or yellow densely clustered flowers spring and summer. Set out as ground cover, the species form 2- to 6-foot mounds of stems that trail or climb to 20 feet, rooting where they touch moist soil. Shear to 6 inches every 3 to 5 years. Many jasmines are hardy in Florida—and invasive. For ground cover the evergreen or semievergreen *J. humile* var. *glabrum* 'Revolutum', Italian Jasmine, and *J. mesnyi*, the beautiful Japanese, Primrose, or Yellow Jasmine, are used on banks and slopes, in open areas, and under trees, as is the scentless *J. multiflorum*, Downy Jasmine, which has showy flowers. 'Revolutum' is fragrant. Set out container plants fall or spring.

GROWTH RATE: medium
LIGHT: versatile
MOISTURE: versatile

J. officinale Poet's Jasmine Zones 7–10.
This is the semievergreen jasmine most commonly grown—a fragrant, white-flowered species. In Florida it blooms in the spring, summer, and fall, but farther north, in summer only. 'Grandiflorum' has large, purple-tinged flowers.

J. polyanthum Pink Jasmine Zones 8–10.
Dense clusters of fragrant, pale pink flowers bloom freely on this fast-growing species, spring through summer. Rich green foliage.

J. × stephanense Stephan Jasmine
Zones 7–10.
A hybrid with fragrant pink flowers.

LARDIZSABALA *lahr-diz-ah-bay-luh*
biternata Zone 9–10.

Evergreen, dioecious climbers with dark green, glossy leaves, and for a long period in spring, purple and white flowers 1 inch across. Potent fragrance, very sweet, quite unusual. Sweet, edible, and fra-

grant fruits follow. They are oblong, dark purple, and 2 to 3 inches long. Plant container-grown plants in spring. May be difficult to find, but a valuable plant.

MATURE HEIGHT: 35'
GROWTH RATE: medium
LIGHT: full sun, semi-sunny
MOISTURE: roots moist

LONICERA *lon-iss-er-uh* Honeysuckle

Vigorous climbing and twining vines or tall shrubs, most with very fragrant flowers and bright berrylike fruits attractive to many types of birds, which disperse the seeds. The shrubby types can be trained as tall or low hedges. The vines grow easily to 12 to 20 feet. Prefer soil in the neutral range, pH 6.0–8.0. Most species thrive in full sun; *L. pileata*, Privet Honeysuckle, a shrub honeysuckle that does well by the seashore, tolerates some shade. Some vigorous species become rampant and hard to get rid of in warmer regions. An example is the shade-tolerant *L. japonica* 'Halliana', Hall's Honeysuckle, which is almost evergreen and has very fragrant flowers.

GROWTH RATE: medium
LIGHT: full sun
MOISTURE: versatile

L. × brownii Brown's Honeysuckle
Zones 3–8.
The beautiful cultivar 'Dropmore Scarlet' bears a profusion of red flowers from June through late fall and is fairly hardy. It is choice for blooming, but not for fragrance. A climbing vine.

L. caprifolium Italian Woodbine Zones 6–9.
Twining vine to 20 feet, with beautiful, fragrant, yellowish white flowers in whorls, beginning in late spring or early summer. The fruit is orange-red.

L. etrusca 'Superba' Cream Honeysuckle
Zones 7–9.
Vigorous deciduous or semievergreen twining vine with large, fragrant, yellowish flowers produced in summer. The fruit is red.

L. × heckrottii Everblooming Honeysuckle
Zones 4–8.
The most beautiful of the twining, climbing types.
The fragrant flowers are carmine, opening to yellow
then changing to pink, from late spring to fall. The
fruit is red, not as profuse as some other species.

L. periclymenum Woodbine Zones 5–9.
Grows to 8 feet, and is a good choice for smaller
gardens. It is a climbing, twining vine with grayish
green leaves, fragrant yellow-white flowers, from
summer till frost. The fruits are red. 'Graham
Thomas' will grow to 40 feet and is very fragrant.
Pruning back in early summer encourages bloom.

L. pileata Privet Honeysuckle Zones 5–9.
This is a low evergreen shrub rather than a vine, and
is a good ground cover or edger tolerant of seashore
conditions. It grows up to 1½ feet high, is often
prostrate with long stems that can have a 4-foot
spread. The dark green leaves are glossy. Small, fragrant white flowers are borne in spring, and violet to
amethyst translucent fruits in late summer. Tolerates
light shade, especially when young.

L. sempervirens Trumpet Honeysuckle,
Coral Honeysuckle Zones 4–8.
Scentless but hardy, with long-lasting fruits attractive
to birds, including hummingbirds, this species has
glossy green foliage and showy flowers; especially
'Magnifica', a late bloomer with bright red flowers;
'Superba', bright scarlet flowers; 'Sulfurea' true,
clear yellow blooms, repeats till frost. Popular on
both coasts.

SEE ALSO:
Actinidia deliciosa (syn. *chinensis*), Chinese Goose-
berry, Kiwi Fruit, Kiwi, Vines 3
Actinidia polygama, Silver Vine, Vines 3
Clematis maximowicziana (syn. *paniculata*), Sweet
Autumn Clematis, Vines 1
Clematis montana var. *rubens,* Anemone Clematis,
Vines 1
Clematis rehderana, Rehder's Clematis, Vines 1

Lonicera sempervirens, Trumpet Honeysuckle. (Dudley)

Gelsemium sempervirens, Yellow Jasmine, Carolina
Yellow Jasmine, Vines 4
Lathyrus odoratus, Sweet Pea, Vines 7
Rosa, Rose, Vines 2
Stauntonia hexaphylla, Japanese Staunton Vine,
Vines 4
Trachelospermum jasminoides, Star Jasmine, Con-
federate Jasmine, Vines 8
Wisteria sinensis, Chinese Wisteria, Vines 1

ALTERNATES:
Akebia quinata, Five-leaf Akebia
Clematis armandii, Armand Clematis
Clematis balearica
Clematis cirrhosa
Clematis flammula
Dolichos lablab, Hyacinth Bean

VINES 6
VINES ATTRACTIVE TO BIRDS

Fruiting plants—especially vines—attract birds.
They provide perches for gathering and feeding, shelter for nests, and berries for food. Some fruiting
plants are dioecious—that means male and female
flowers are produced on different plants (though
there are exceptions) and must grow near each other
for the female to produce the best fruit. Remember
when acquiring vines for feathered friends that they
drop seeds everywhere. That makes some beautiful
and vigorous vines potentially pesky weeds; as a
result, some end up on the Alternates list (for instance, *Berchemia*).

CAMPSIS *kamp-siss* Trumpet Creeper

Vigorous, deciduous, woody climbing vines whose
showy orange or scarlet trumpet-shaped flowers attract hummingbirds. The vines climb by means of
aerial rootlets and will need additional support. Rich
soil and full sun give best results. Tolerate urban
conditions. Set out container-grown plants in early
spring. Flowers are produced on new growth. Prune
early every spring to encourage flowering sprouts.

GROWTH RATE: fast
LIGHT: full sun, semi-sunny
MOISTURE: versatile

C. grandiflora Chinese Trumpet Creeper
Zones 7–9.
Clinging, climbing vine that gives a late summer
show of large, vivid scarlet-orange flushed with pink,
and pastel flowers, but is less cold-hardy than *C. radicans*, below.

C. radicans Trumpet Creeper, Trumpet Vine
Zones 4–9.
Fast-growing, dense, woody vine that grows into
roof-high foliage cover, and bears deep orange flowers
in summer and fall. Provides quick, large-scale summer screening the birds love; tolerates urban conditions and drought.

C. × tagliabuana 'Madame Galen'
Zones 4–9.
Vigorous hybrid between *C. radicans* and *C. grandiflora* with the hardiness of the former and the
larger flowers of the latter, in orange and scarlet.

CELASTRUS *se-last-rus* Bittersweet

Vigorous, twining, deciduous vines, some rampant
and invasive, planted for their brilliant red-orange
berries surrounded by woody orange capsule seg-
ments—fall food for birds. Usually dioecious, so
plant an occasional male to ensure maximum fruit.
They grow almost anywhere, easily, but fruit best in
full sun. Good ground cover for rocky slopes and wild
places, but can smother trees. Tolerates urban conditions, some drought. Prune old wood in early spring
to improve fruiting. Plant container-grown plants in
spring.

GROWTH RATE: fast
LIGHT: full sun, versatile
MOISTURE: versatile

C. orbiculatus Oriental Bittersweet
Zones 5–8.
Vigorous, fast-covering vine with large, glossy leaves
and bunches of brilliant capsules, yellow on the
inside with scarlet seeds. Excellent for erosion control, slope planting, and dry places. Grows to 30 or
40 feet and is choice for rapid ground cover and
screening.

C. scandens American Bittersweet,
Climbing Bittersweet Zones 3–8.
Grows to 25 feet or taller, in sun or partial shade, and
is somewhat easier to contain than *C. orbiculatus*.
The fruit is yellow-orange with crimson seeds.

COCCULUS *kok-yew-lus*
carolinus Carolina Moonseed Zones 6–8.

Elegant, twining, deciduous and dioecious vine that
grows to 15 feet. Greenish white flowers are followed
by very heavy, drooping clusters of bright red fruit on
female plants if a male plant is nearby. Plant container-grown plants in spring. Can be invasive.

GROWTH RATE: medium
LIGHT: versatile
MOISTURE: versatile

KADSURA *kad-soor-uh*
japonica Scarlet Kadsura Zones 7–9.

Evergreen or semievergreen twining shrub to 12 feet
high, with yellowish white flowers June to September. The flowers are 1 inch or more across, very
attractive, on stalks 2 to 3 inches long. They are
followed in the fall by showy, pendulous clusters of
orange-scarlet berries. A vigorous vine, useful for
screening and fence cover. Dioecious, and both male
and female plants are necessary for good fruiting.
Male flowers are somewhat smaller. Plant container-
grown plants in early spring.

GROWTH RATE: fast
LIGHT: full sun
MOISTURE: versatile

SMILAX *smye-lax* Greenbrier

Fast-growing and good for slopes and erosion control.
Dioecious and either deciduous or evergreen vines
that climb by tendrils, and have prickly stems and
greenish yellow flowers. If a male plant is nearby, the
female bears red or blue-black berries which attract
birds. Some species are thornless. A good filler plant

for a large area. This is not the florists' smilax *(Asparagus asparagoides)*. Smilax flourishes in any soil, tolerates shade, and easily turns into a thicket. Can become a pernicious weed. Plant container-grown plants in early spring.

GROWTH RATE:	fast
LIGHT:	versatile
MOISTURE:	versatile

S. megalantha Coral Greenbrier Zones 7–9.
Evergreen climber, to 20 feet, with sturdy spines on angled stems. The leaves are narrow, shiny, and about 5 inches long. The berries are brilliant coral-red.

S. rotundifolia Zones 4–8.
Deciduous, wiry vine with creeping, quickly spreading rootstock that soon turns into a thorny thicket. Vigorous soil binder even in very poor soils. The leaves grow to 6 inches long, and the berries are black.

S. smallii (syn. *lanceolata*) Small's Brier Zones 7–9.
High-climbing, woody evergreen vine with almost spineless stems, glossy leaves 3½ inches long, and showy fruit that is red to brown. The leaves often appear variegated with lighter green. Very adaptable to all conditions.

S. walteri Red-berried Bamboo Zones 7–9.
Superb berrying vine which often appears as a scrambling or scandent shrub—slender, heavily fruiting, woody, and deciduous. Very showy fruits last through the winter if not eaten by birds. Birds will eat other smilax berries when very hungry, but the berries of this species are choice food for them.

VITIS *vye-tiss* Grape Vine

Woody, tendril-climbing, deciduous, grape-producing vines with beautiful big leaves which, in the ornamental species, turn a brilliant red in fall. The fruit on the species mentioned below is loved by birds but is not suitable for table use. The leaves of grapes are food for Japanese beetles, which attack roses, so don't plant these if roses are in the landscape. Under the right conditions *Vitis* species naturalize readily, are excellent for slopes and erosion control. Grapes are particular about drainage and pH: discuss your potential for growing grapes with the U.S.D.A. Extension Service (see Appendix). Plant year-old vines, in spring or fall, with some protection in cold areas.

GROWTH RATE:	fast
LIGHT:	full sun, part shade
MOISTURE:	roots moist

V. aestivalis Summer Grape Zones 5–9.
Tall, vigorous climber that produces berry-sized fruit in clusters to 7 inches long, much loved by birds.

4*V. cognetiae* Crimson Glory Vine Zones 5–8.
Highly ornamental, tendril-climbing, with ropy stem, and dense, heavy foliage; grows very quickly to 50 feet or more. Roundish leaves up to a foot long turn bright crimson in fall. Fruits are tiny. Excellent quick cover for slopes and pergolas. Needs moist, well-drained soil in sun or part shade and must be pruned annually.

V. labrusca Fox Grape Zones 5–8.
Strong, high climber with short, wide clusters of tiny

grapes. Birds flock to fox grapes. It is the parent of the 'Concord' grape, the best source for jelly.

SEE ALSO:
Ampelopsis brevipedunculata, Porcelain Ampelopsis, Vines 3
Campsis radicans, Trumpet Creeper, Vines 9
Clematis cvs., Vines 1
Euonymus fortunei, Vines 8
Lonicera caprifolium, Italian Woodbine, Vines 5
Lonicera etrusca 'Superba', Cream Honeysuckle, Vines 5
Lonicera × *heckrotii*, Everblooming Honeysuckle, Vines 5
Lonicera periclymenum 'Graham Thomas', Woodbine, Vines 5
Lonicera sempervirens, Trumpet Honeysuckle, Coral Honeysuckle, Vines 5
Parthenocissus quinquefolia, Virginia Creeper, Woodbine, Vines 3
Parthenocissus tricuspidata, Boston Ivy, Vines 3

ALTERNATES:
Berchemia scandens, Supplejack
Menispermum canadense, Yellow Parilla, Moonseed

VINES 7
VINES FOR RAPID GROWTH OR SCREENING

Some annual, biennial, perennial, and tender perennial vines grow a splendid 10 to 30 feet in a season, providing quick cover for screening, slopes, and erosion control. Because of their rapid growth, many tender perennials listed here can be grown as annuals in cold climates. The plants here can also overwhelm a small garden if given optimum conditions. A short growing season and poor soil restrain their exubérance. For rich garden soils and a long warm season, choose slower-growing woody vines.

ADLUMIA *ad-loo-mee-uh*
fungosa Climbing Fumatory Zones 3–9.

Exquisite little deciduous climbing vine that in summer fairly drips with delicate, pendulous, slightly fragrant, blush-pink flowers like smaller bleeding-hearts. A rapid grower, it never becomes an obnoxious weed. It is biennial and will seed itself, growing to 15 feet in its second year. The fruit is a small capsule that splits to release a seed, which can be gathered and sown in early spring where plants are wanted. Prefers somewhat acid-range soil with lots of humus. Roots must be cool and moist but not wet. Mulch against summer heat.

MATURE HEIGHT:	14'–15'
GROWTH RATE:	fast
LIGHT:	semi-sunny, shade
MOISTURE:	roots moist

ASARINA *ass-ah-reen-uh*

Tender perennials that climb to about 6 feet by means of coiling leafstalks, and have showy flowers like

snapdragons in blue, purple, pink, and white. Lovely as trellis cover in warm climates. Start seeds indoors and plant out after all danger of frost is past. Formerly classed as Maurandya.

GROWTH RATE:	fast
LIGHT:	full sun
MOISTURE:	roots moist

A. barclaiana Zones 8–10.
Vigorous, twining perennial climber that produces very showy purple flowers. It blooms from late summer through fall and grows about 10 feet in a season. There are white and rose cultivars.

A. erubescens Creeping Gloxinia Zones 8–10.
Tender perennial vine with attractive grayish green foliage and beautiful rose pink flowers.

A. procumbens Zones 6–10.
Somewhat tender, with creamy white to pinkish flowers through much of the summer. This one is hardier than the other species described.

A. scandens Zones 8–10.
Similar to the species above, but the flowers are two shades of lavender.

CARDIOSPERMUM *kard-ee-oh-spermum* halicacabum
Balloon Vine, Heart Vine Zones 9–10.

Woody perennial in warm climates, self-sowing biennial elsewhere, either valued for its dense foliage and as a quick screen, or uprooted as a pesky weed. It grows to 10 feet in a season. Insignificant white flowers appear year-round, followed by balloon-shaped black fruits spotted with a white heart. Sow seeds in early spring where the plants are to grow.

GROWTH RATE:	fast
LIGHT:	full sun
MOISTURE:	roots moist

CLITORIA *klye-toh-ree-uh*
ternatea Atlantic Pea Zone 10.

Slender climber to 15 feet with small leaves and a summer-long profusion of clusters of two-tone blue flowers with yellow markings. Long lasting as a cut flower. Usually grown as a biennial, from seed started every spring. Or set out container-grown plants.

GROWTH RATE:	fast
LIGHT:	full sun
MOISTURE:	roots moist

COBAEA *koh-bee-uh*
scandens Mexican Ivy,
Cup-and-saucer Vine Zone 9.

Fast-screening vine with showy, graceful, bell-shaped, usually purple-lavender flowers that bloom for many months. Good cover for porches and trellises. It is a big, woody perennial in warm climates, often grown as an annual in the North from seeds started indoors. In warm regions, sow seeds directly outdoors in early spring in moist, not too rich, sandy soil.

Cobaea scandens, Cup-and-saucer Vine. (Meerow)

MATURE HEIGHT: 25'
GROWTH RATE: fast
LIGHT: full sun
MOISTURE: roots moist

DOLICHOS *dol-ik-oss*
lablab   Hyacinth Bean   Annual.

Twining vine with dark green leaves. Grows rapidly to 15 or 20 feet in a season, useful for quick summer screening. Graceful clusters of purple or white flowers, followed by large purple seedpods. Usually grown as an annual. In spring, sow seeds where they are to grow, in rich, light loam. Provide support for climbing.

GROWTH RATE: fast
LIGHT: full sun
MOISTURE: roots moist

IPOMOEA *eye-poh-mee-uh*
Morning Glory

The morning glories are annual or perennial vines. They have wide-open, colorful, trumpet-shaped flowers, and provide fast screening if given wire supports. Some are useful as ground cover. In the North they are grown as annuals that bloom from late spring through summer; in Florida, many are evergreen and bloom all year. They have some tolerance for salt and moderate drought resistance. In hospitable climates, volunteers become weedy pests, hard to eradicate. In late winter or early spring, plant seeds indoors in peat pots or outdoors where they are to grow; soak the seeds overnight first.

GROWTH RATE: fast
LIGHT: full sun, semi-sunny
MOISTURE: roots moist

I. alba   Moonflower   Zones 9–10.
Formerly classified as Calonyction aculeatum, this is

a robust, tender perennial climber with 8-inch leaves, cultivated for the large, fragrant nighttime flowers. Very weedy in southern Florida.

I. coccinea   Red Morning-glory   Annual.
Twining vine with large, heart-shaped leaves that grows 10 to 15 feet in a season and bears long clusters of yellow-throated red flowers.

I. hederacea   Ivy-leaved Morning-glory
                                          Annual.
Tender annual twining vine, with showy pale blue or purple flowers. 'Grandiflora' and 'Superba' are improved forms. Can be invasive. Blooms May to September.

I. nil   Imperial Japanese Morning-glory,
White Edge Morning-glory   Zone 10.
Fast-growing perennial vine with excellent cultivars. The flowers may be violet, purple, blue, rose, or multicolored, fluted, fringed, or double. In the North it is grown as an annual. It succeeds in pots in rich soil with a high nitrogen content and lots of humus.

I. purpurea   Annual.
Fast-growing to 10 feet, a hardy annual with bright scarlet flowers summer and early fall. Many improved varieties are available. It grows wild in the South, where it can be invasive.

I. setosa   Brazilian Morning-glory
                                       Zones 7–10.
Tender twining perennial with leaves to 10 inches long, and small, rose-lavender flowers on long, hairy stems.

I. tricolor   Annual.
Twining perennial or tender annual. The leaves are to 10 inches across, and it bears large tricolor flowers that are red, white, and purplish blue. There are many cultivars.

LATHYRUS *lath-ihr-us*
odoratus   Sweet Pea   Annual.

Old-fashioned favorite annual for light screening, loved for its cut flowers—very fragrant, delicate, pealike blooms in every pastel shade. Quick-growing, twining, the tendrils need training strings or wires. Many cultivars are offered, both late and early bloomers, and there are some dwarfs. Cool air, plenty of moisture, and deadheading are essential. Grows easily from seed in ordinary garden soil. Start seeds indoors early and plant out as soon as the frost is out of the ground.

GROWTH RATE: fast
LIGHT: full sun
MOISTURE: roots moist

MOMORDICA *mom-mord-ik-uh*

Quick-growing annual or tender perennial vines that climb by means of tendrils and bear bright flowers and fruit. The blooms are yellow with black centers. The bitter, bright yellow or orange fruits are cooked and eaten in Asia, and the seeds are used in Chinese medicine. Plant seeds outdoors after danger of frost in rich soil where the plants are to grow.

GROWTH RATE: fast
LIGHT: full sun
MOISTURE: roots moist

M. balsamina   Balsam Apple   Annual.
Fast-growing to 20 feet in a season, with attractive, pale green leaves. The flowers are yellow with black centers. The fruits are round, with ballooned centers, and burst when fully ripe.

M. charantia   Balsam Pear,
Bitter Cucumber   Annual.
Grows quickly to 12 to 18 feet and bears yellow flowers. When the fruit splits open it shows bright red seed.

PHASEOLUS *fas-see-ol-us*
coccineus   Scarlet Runner Bean   Annual.

Twining perennial vine that grows to 15 feet in a season, usually grown as an annual. Brilliant red flowers are beautiful, and the plant also produces excellent edible green beans. Needs training wires, and often is used as a cover for trellises and porches. There are white-flowered varieties. Plant seeds in early spring in rich, well-drained soil with a pH in the acid range.

GROWTH RATE: fast
LIGHT: full sun
MOISTURE: roots moist

THUNBERGIA *thun-berj-ee-uh*

The species here are twining vines, grown as basket plants in the North and perennials in the South, for the summer-long show of small, trumpet-shaped flowers in shades of yellow, purple, blue, or white. They need rich soil and ample moisture. Start seeds indoors in early spring and plant when danger of frost is gone.

GROWTH RATE: fast
LIGHT: full sun
MOISTURE: roots moist

Momordica charantia, Balsam Pear. (Longwood Gardens)

T. alata   Black-eyed Susan Vine   Zones 9–10.
Twining perennial with dense, heart-shaped leaves and a big show of colorful flowers, yellow, orange, or cream-colored, with purple-black centers. Quick screen, but support must be given.

T. fragrans   Sweet Clock Vine   Zones 9–10.
Twining, woody evergreen vine with showy, often fragrant, white flowers summer and fall. It self-sows and can become weedy.

T. grandiflora   Blue Trumpet Vine,
Bengal Clock Vine   Zone 10.
Twining evergreen that must be pruned to keep the sprays of big blue or white flowers in view. Blooms summer and fall. Very aggressive.

T. gregorii   Zone 10.
Twining vine with glossy leaves and bright orange flowers that thrives in southern California. Formerly *T. gibsonii*. Often grown as an annual.

SEE ALSO:
Actinidia arguta, Bower Actinidia, Tara Vine, Vines 3
Actinidia deliciosa (syn. *chinensis*), Chinese Gooseberry, Kiwi Fruit, Kiwi, Vines 3
Ampelopsis brevipedunculata, Porcelain Ampelopsis, Vines 3
Antigonon leptopus, Coral Vine, Vines 1
Aristolochia durior, Dutchman's-pipe, Vines 8
Campsis radicans, Trumpet Creeper, Trumpet Vine, Vines 6
Celastrus orbiculatus, Oriental Bittersweet, Vines 6
Celastrus scandens, American Bittersweet, Vines 6
Epipremnum aureum, Pothos, Golden Pothos, Vines 8
Kadsura japonica, Scarlet Kadsura, Vines 6
Menispermum canadense, Yellow Parilla, Moonseed, Vines 8
Passiflora caerula, Blue Passionflower, Vines 1
Passiflora coccinea, Red Passionflower, Vines 1
Passiflora edulis, Passion Fruit, Vines 1
Pyrostegia venusta (syn. *ignea*), Flame Vine, Vines 1
Tecomaria capensis, Cape Honeysuckle, Vines 1
Tropaeolum peregrinum, Canary-bird Flower, Herbs 4
Tropaeolum polyphyllum, Wreath Nasturtium, Herbs 4
Vitis cognetiae, Crimson Glory Vine, Vines 6

ALTERNATE:
Clematis × jackmanii, Jackman Clematis

FOR SLOPES AND EROSION CONTROL

AKEBIA *ak-kee-bee-uh*
quinata   Five-leaf Akebia   Zones 4–9.

Lovely, slender, woody vine with airy foliage and fragrant, small, dark purple flowers in spring, followed by 2- to 4-inch purple-violet, delicious clusters of fruits in fall. Grows rapidly to 30 feet or more, evergreen in warm climates. Good ground cover. Thrives in well-drained soil and sun. Set out container plants in early spring.

GROWTH RATE:	fast
LIGHT:	full sun
MOISTURE:	versatile

ARGYREIA *ar-joh-ree-uh*
splendens   Silver Morning-glory   Zone 10.

An uncommon, beautiful, tall, twining, evergreen perennial vine related to Morning-glory, but grown for its showy silvery foliage. The flowers are a pinky rose and bloom throughout summer. Some drought resistance. Plant container-grown plants in early spring.

GROWTH RATE:	fast
LIGHT:	full sun
MOISTURE:	versatile

BIGNONIA *big-noh-nee-uh*
capreolata   Cross Vine   Zones 7–9.

Highly desirable, colorful, vigorous vine climbing to 50 feet with tendril supports, beautiful as wall or ground cover. The foliage is dense, and in spring, the plant bears clusters of bright yellow-red tubular flowers. Plant container-grown plants in early spring.

MATURE HEIGHT:	50′
GROWTH RATE:	fast
LIGHT:	full sun, semi-sunny
MOISTURE:	roots moist

POLYGONUM *pol-lig-on-um*
aubertii   China Fleece Vine, Silver Lace Vine

Zones 4–8.

Lovely, fast-to-rampant vine that twines up to 20 feet. It has heavy foliage and small, fragrant, pinkish white flowers in fleecy clusters in late summer into fall. Thrives even in the city. Must be pruned severely in small gardens. Plant container-grown plants in early spring.

Epipremnum aureum, Golden Pothos. (Meerow)

MATURE HEIGHT:	20′
GROWTH RATE:	fast
LIGHT:	versatile
MOISTURE:	versatile

SEE ALSO:
Ampelopsis, Vines 3
Celastrus orbiculatus, Oriental Bittersweet, Vines 6
Celastrus scandens, American Bittersweet, Vines 6
Clematis maximowicziana (syn. *paniculata*), Sweet Autumn Clematis, Vines 1
Euonymus fortunei, Vines 8
Hedera helix, English Ivy, Vines 4
Menispermum canadense, Yellow Parilla, Moonseed, Vines 8
Parthenocissus quinquefolia, Virginia Creeper, Woodbine, Vines 3
Periploca graeca, Grecian Silk Vine, Vines 9
Rosa wichuraiana, Memorial Rose, Ground Covers 9
Smilax rotundifolia, Greenbrier, Vines 6
Vitis, Grape Vine, Vines 6

VINES 8
VINES THAT GROW IN SHADE

Vines grow toward the sun, but many don't mind if their feet are cool and shaded. In fact, some vines prefer it—the beautiful flowering Clematis, for instance, in Vines 1. The vines described here are even more accommodating—they flourish in partial shade.

ARISTOLOCHIA *ar-ist-oh-loh-kee-uh*
durior   Dutchman's-pipe   Zones 4–8.

Deciduous twining vine often planted for porch cover, with foot-long, heart- or kidney-shaped leaves. It can screen a trellis or wire frame in a single season. The common name describes the small, brownish yellow flowers profusely borne in late spring. Thrives in ordinary, well-drained soil, in sun or shade; tolerates urban conditions. Plant container-grown plants in early spring.

GROWTH RATE:	fast
LIGHT:	full sun, semi-sunny
MOISTURE:	versatile

EPIPREMNUM *e-pi-prem-num*
aureum   Pothos, Golden Pothos   Zone 10.

Vigorous, evergreen, perennial vine, 20 to 40 feet tall, with big, bright green leaves beautifully splotched with yellow or white. It climbs by attaching aerial rootlets to rough bark or masonry and may need tying. Handsome cascading over walls. 'Marble Queen' has elegant white and gray green variegations. In the North, pothos is an almost indestructible, but much smaller, vine that flourishes indoors with little light. Grows well in deep shade, but needs light for best variegation. High tolerance to drought. Plant container-grown plants any time in early spring. Formerly classified as Scindapsus aureus.

GROWTH RATE: fast
LIGHT: semi-sunny, shade
MOISTURE: versatile

EUONYMUS *yew-on-im-us*
fortunei Wintercreeper   Zones 4–9.

The genus includes deciduous trees and shrubs with brilliant fall foliage. There are also evergreen shrubby forms, climbers, and ground covers, like this species. Fruits appear in fall and persist, bright pinkish orange capsules which open to expose seeds that are orange-red and attractive to birds. The species *fortunei* is the hardiest of the evergreen vines used as climbers and ground covers and has several white-veined, tiny-leaved selections. 'Erecta' is a catchall term for climbing types. 'Emerald Leader' and 'Emerald Beauty' are upright to 5 or 6 feet, and beautifully fruited. Euonymus succeeds on dry, rocky slopes and in shady places, and many variegated, fruitful cultivars are useful ground covers. Early spring shearing encourages compactness. Set out container-grown plants in early spring in well-drained soil. Euonymus is a very valuable ornamental, in spite of a vulnerability to scale. Always ask for scale-resistant plants.

GROWTH RATE: fast
LIGHT: versatile
MOISTURE: versatile

HEDERA *hed-er-uh*   Ivy

Vigorous and evergreen, ivy succeeds under trees and in hot, dry city conditions. In the mature form, it is shrublike. As a climbing vine it reaches 25 to 50 feet. As a ground cover it is 6 to 8 inches high. Interesting features are the two distinct stages of leaf development; creeping along the ground or beginning to climb, ivy produces "juvenile" foliage which never flowers. The "adult" stage comes when ivy climbs a support: small, green clusters of petalless flowers are born at the tips, followed in autumn by black fruit. Ivy throws many "sports," shoots different from the parent. Plant rooted divisions in early spring and keep damp until established. Shear every

3 or 4 years to maintain foliage density. Prefers soils in the pH 6.0–8.0 range.

MATURE HEIGHT: 6"–8"
GROWTH RATE: fast
LIGHT: versatile
MOISTURE: versatile

H. canariensis Algerian Ivy   Zones 9–10.
A large-leaved ivy with burgundy red twigs and petioles. 'Variegata' leaves are edged in yellowish white. Excellent at seaside, under trees, on banks and slopes, and in open areas. Grows better in central and northern Florida than in the southern part of the state.

H. helix English Ivy   Zones 5–9.
Stands 6 to 8 inches high and the strands can stretch to 90 feet. A vigorous grower that competes well with tree roots. There are hundreds of cultivars, varying in hardiness and coloration. Popular on the West Coast is 'Baltic', which is hardier than the species; hardier yet is 'Bulgaria'; 'Wilson' is hardy to Zone 4. *H. h.* 'Aureo-variegata' is variegated yellow; *H. h.* 'Argenteo-variegata' is variegated white.

HYDRANGEA *hye-drain-jee-uh*
anomala subsp. *petiolaris*
Climbing Hydrangea   Zones 5–7.
A beautiful twining, climbing vine, woody and impressive in maturity, slow-growing until established and very hardy. Magnificent in bloom. The small, fragrant flowers and their showy white bracts are borne in clusters in late spring and early summer, and the leaves are dark green and lustrous. Needs rich, moist soil, and can tolerate salt air, shade, and urban conditions. Can become invasive when mature; prune after flowering, as needed. Plant container-grown plants in early spring and take good care of them until established. Formerly known as H. petiolaris. Shade tolerant, though flowering is reduced significantly.

GROWTH RATE: slow
LIGHT: full sun, semi-sunny
MOISTURE: roots moist

Hydrangea anomala subsp. *petiolaris*, Climbing Hydrangea. (Thomas)

LAPAGERIA *lap-aj-jeer-ee-uh*
rosea   Chilean Bellflower   Zones 9–10.

Beautiful evergreen vine to 20 feet tall for tropical regions, with dark, leathery leaves and long, waxy, rose red flowers. It thrives on sandy loam in partial to full shade. Flowers come in late summer and fall and last well as cut flowers. Good tub specimen. Drainage and loose soil are essential. Plant container-grown plants in early spring.

GROWTH RATE: fast/medium
LIGHT: semi-sunny, shade
MOISTURE: roots moist

MENISPERMUM *men-iss-sperm-um*
canadense   Yellow Parilla, Moonseed
          Zones 5–8.

Dense, twisting vine to 12 feet or more, with lustrous, dark green, distinctly lobed leaves, and attractive clusters of yellow or white florets in spring, followed by clusters of small berrylike, blue-black fruits. Adds interest to the landscape and gives good, fast cover for slopes. Plant container-grown plants in early spring. Attracts birds.

GROWTH RATE: fast
LIGHT: semi-sunny, shade
MOISTURE: versatile

TRACHELOSPERMUM *trak-el-oh-sperm-um* *jasminoides*
Star Jasmine, Confederate Jasmine
          Zones 8–10.

Low-growing, evergreen, twining or climbing shrubby vine whose branches have holdfast roots. In the southeastern United States and California, it is

Euonymus fortunei. (Neumann)

Lapageria rosea, Chilean Bellflower. (Longwood Gardens)

loved for the fragrance of its clusters of star-shaped white flowers that bloom in spring and are followed by seedpods up to 7 inches. It has some drought tolerance and resists trampling. Good for slopes and banks. Plant container-grown plants in fall or spring. There are many cultivars, some with variegated foliage, small, differently shaped leaves, and reduced growth habit.

GROWTH RATE: medium
LIGHT: full sun
MOISTURE: roots moist, versatile

SEE ALSO:
Adlumia fungosa, Climbing Fumatory, Vines 7
Celastrus scandens, American Bittersweet, Vines 6
Ficus pumila, Creeping Fig, Vines 4
Gelsemium sempervirens, Yellow Jasmine, Carolina Yellow Jasmine, Vines 4
Lapageria rosea, Chilean Bellflower, Vines 4
Lygodium palmatum, Hartford Fern, Vines 4
Parthenocissus henryana, Woodbine, Vines 3
Pileostegia viburnoides, Tanglehead, Vines 4
Smilax megalantha, Coral Greenbrier, Vines 6
Stauntonia hexaphylla, Japanese Staunton Vine, Vines 4
Thunbergia grandiflora, Blue Trumpet Vine, Bengal Clock Vine, Vines 7

ALTERNATES:
Actinidia arguta, Bower Actinidia, Tara Vine
Ampelopsis
Decumaria barbara, Climbing Hydrangea
Hibbertia scandens, Snake Vine, Gold Guinea Plant
Schizophragma hydrangeoides, Japanese Hydrangea Vine

VINES 9
VINES FOR URBAN CONDITIONS

These vines aren't more successful in urban conditions than elsewhere, but where there is environmental stress and pollution, they will perform well.

One of the most valuable vines for urban situations is English ivy, *Hedera helix*, which appears in Vines 4 and Vines 8. Several of the vines here appear on other lists.

AMPELOPSIS *am-pel-lop-siss*

Vigorous vines that climb by tendrils, excellent for fast cover of trellises, arbors, walls, fences, slopes. Colorful berries in autumn. Provide strong support. Plant container-grown plants in spring.

GROWTH RATE: fast
LIGHT: full sun, semi-sunny
MOISTURE: versatile

A. arborea Pepper Vine   Zones 9–10.
Rather weedy evergreen vine in the South, used in wild gardens or for fast coverage of fences. It has some tolerance for drought, prefers full sun.

A. brevipedunculata Porcelain Ampelopsis
Zones 4–9.
Strong, invasive climber with bright green, handsomely textured leaves, striking in summer and fall when the berries appear in a color range of porcelain blue, green, purple, and pink. Attracts birds. 'Elegans' grows more slowly and has smaller leaves than the species, and is beautifully variegated with white and pink. Interesting for specimen use. Fruit colors best in full sun.

ARISTOLOCHIA *ar-ist-oh-loh-kee-uh*
durior Dutchman's-pipe   Zones 4–8.

Deciduous twining vine often planted for porch cover, with foot-long, heart- or kidney-shaped leaves. It can screen a trellis or wire frame in a single season. The common name describes the small, brownish yellow flowers profusely borne in late spring. Thrives in ordinary, well-drained soil, in sun or shade. Plant container-grown plants in early spring.

GROWTH RATE: fast
LIGHT: full sun, semi-sunny
MOISTURE: versatile

CAMPSIS *kamp-siss*
radicans Trumpet Creeper, Trumpet Vine
Zones 4–9.

Fast-growing, dense, woody climbing vine that climbs by means of aerial rootlets and will need support. It produces deep orange flowers in summer and fall and affords large-scale summer screening the birds love. Attracts hummingbirds. Flowers appear on new growth; prune early every spring to encourage flowering sprouts. Plant container-grown plants in early spring.

GROWTH RATE: fast
LIGHT: full sun, semi-sunny
MOISTURE: versatile

CLEMATIS *klem-at-iss*
maximowicziana (syn. *paniculata*)
Sweet Autumn Clematis   Zones 4–9.

Very beautiful flowering vine for quick screening of slopes, rocky outcroppings, or city fences. Lustrous foliage and a profusion of 1-inch white flowers in fall. Needs deeply dug, light, moist soil, enriched with leaf mold and sweetened with lime. Plant so the vine can be in full sun and the roots in shade. Mulch well. Blooms on new wood; prune to the ground when dormant.

GROWTH RATE: fast
LIGHT: full sun, semi-sunny
MOISTURE: roots moist

HYDRANGEA *hye-drain-jee-uh*
anomala subsp. *petiolaris*
Climbing Hydrangea   Zones 5–7.

A beautiful twining, climbing vine, woody and impressive in maturity, slow-growing until established and very hardy. Magnificent in bloom. The small, fragrant flowers and their showy white bracts are borne in clusters in late spring and early summer, and the leaves are dark green and lustrous. Needs rich,

Campsis radicans, Trumpet Creeper. (Neumann)

moist soil, and can tolerate salt air and shade. Can become invasive when mature; prune after flowering, as needed. Plant container-grown plants in early spring and take good care of them until established. Formerly known as H. petiolaris. Shade tolerant, though flowering is reduced significantly.

GROWTH RATE:	slow
LIGHT:	full sun, semi-sunny
MOISTURE:	roots moist

MUEHLENBECKIA *mew-len-bek-ee-uh*
complexa Wire Vine Zones 9–10.

Sprawling, twining plant with slender, wiry green stems that bear both male and female flowers. It tolerates seashore conditions and is a popular basket plant indoors and in warm climates. Best in full sun. Plant container-grown plants in early fall in warmer regions.

GROWTH RATE:	medium
LIGHT:	versatile
MOISTURE:	roots moist

PARTHENOCISSUS *parth-en-oh-siss-us* Woodbine

Woody climbers famous for brilliant scarlet color in autumn in the deciduous species. Plants produce clusters of small greenish flowers, followed by dark berries and then the glorious fall color. Attract birds. Give beauty to large blank walls, but can damage masonry; even after removal, its traces remain. Excellent ground covers and tolerate drought and partial shade. Plant container-grown plants in spring.

GROWTH RATE:	medium
LIGHT:	versatile
MOISTURE:	versatile

Wisteria sinensis, Chinese Wisteria. (Neumann)

P. quinquefolia Virginia Creeper, Woodbine
Zones 3–9.

Vigorous climber hard to keep in bounds, but has attractive reddish new growth, blue berries, and brilliant scarlet color in the fall. Color is best when growing in full sun. It is an excellent ground cover for slopes. Attractive to birds.

P. tricuspidata Boston Ivy Zones 4–8.
Rampant vine, like Virginia Creeper, with lustrous leaves, blue-black berries, and brilliant orange-red color in fall; the species is often chosen for clinging to stonework. Color is best in full sun. 'Lowii' and 'Veitchii' have smaller leaves and are less vigorous. Attracts birds.

PERIPLOCA *per-rip-lok-uh*
graeca Grecian Silk Vine Zones 6–8.

Woody vines growing vigorously, with persistent though deciduous dark green, glossy, oval leaves 5 inches long. The greenish flowers are brown-purple inside, and produced in clusters of 8 to 12, followed by 5-inch-long seedpods in pairs. Weedy if not controlled. Plant root divisions in early spring in well-drained soil.

MATURE HEIGHT:	20'–30'
GROWTH RATE:	fast
LIGHT:	full sun
MOISTURE:	roots moist

POLYGONUM *pol-lig-on-um*
aubertii China Fleece Vine, Silver Lace Vine
Zones 4–8.

Lovely fast-to-rampant vine that twines up to 20 feet. It has heavy foliage and small, fragrant, pinkish white flowers in fleecy clusters in late summer into fall. Must be pruned severely in small gardens. Plant root divisions in early spring.

GROWTH RATE:	fast
LIGHT:	versatile
MOISTURE:	versatile

WISTERIA *wiss-teer-ee-uh*
sinensis Chinese Wisteria Zones 4–9.

Vigorous vine with delicate foliage which offers a magnificent spring show of fragrant, lilac flower clusters 9 to 20 inches long. Wisteria in full bloom is breathtaking, but this fast-growing, twining vine can invade and destroy attics and trees. Confine to pergolas, controlled "green roofing" for porches, stone walls. In winter prune back vigorous old growth to 3 or 4 buds. Limit nitrogen in fertilizer; too much will inhibit flowering to the advantage of lush foliage. Set out container-grown cultivars in early spring and pamper until growth begins. Prefers acid-range soil. 'Alba' is a very fragrant white cultivar; 'Purpurea' is purplish violet.

GROWTH RATE:	fast
LIGHT:	full sun
MOISTURE:	roots moist

SEE ALSO:
Hedera helix, English Ivy, Vines 4

Azaleas bloom in spring in the dappled shade of young pink and white dogwoods. (Miller)

SHRUBS

INTRODUCTION TO

SHRUBS

The new naturalism leaves behind the rigid landscape inherited from Europe, with its clipped, pruned, and pinched flowering and evergreen shrubs and small trees in a high-maintenance wall-to-wall carpet of grass. Symmetrical foundation plantings that repeat a neighborhood formula are not recommended. Monoculture promotes pests and diseases: the street overrun with roses soon is overrun with Japanese beetles.

Greater variety is more exciting as well as potentially sounder ecologically. There's year-round appeal in combinations of shrubs and small trees chosen for contrast in texture, scale, form, foliage, flowers, fruit, color, bark. Scour the nurseries for newly domesticated native shrubs. They already have adapted to your yard. Plant berried shrubs that attract birds: they'll control insects. Tolerate a normal quota of insects. When the shrubs are disease-resistant, there are more friendly insects than enemies in the garden. New summer growth covers over even the depredations of the terrifying gypsy moth. Let summer's flowers become berries and seeds for the birds.

Keep abreast of research on natural controls. *Euonymus* specimens at the National Arboretum are now free of scale insects, pests that can cause a never-ending battle. Scales on the insects' back literally protect them from insecticides. U.S.D.A. scientists found predator beetles in Korea that attack and control the pest at the Arboretum without the aid of insecticides. Insects proven beneficial, such as ladybugs and praying mantises, are hard to keep at home, but this is the hope for the future.

Introduce shrubs that bloom in late winter, summer, late summer, fall. The spring is overly lavish with attention-getting flowers. Fill spaces waiting for next season's show with naturalized flowering bulbs, the little ones that pop before the snow has quite gone, as well as the familiar brave crocuses and the later daffodils, irises, brilliant tulips and alliums. Plant for color in the months when the family lives outdoors and let winter be wholesomely unkempt, unpruned, a garden for the birds.

Place shrubs as nature landscapes, in clumps of varied species, asymmetrically balancing columnar evergreens with

A mature Spiraea vanhouttei, Bridal-wreath, in full flower. (Neumann)

spreading flowering species and plants whose fall foliage will glow. Bind them with a rich variety of naturalized ground covers that never need mowing. Screen with groups rather than regiments.

Small shrubs can be grown successfully in a nonsuitable soil because their roots are small enough for effective long-term soil modification. Be aware that mulch (compost included) for acid-loving plants must be acid—shredded pine bark is the choice of some researchers, but peat moss is often recommended. Add acid fertilizer to a compost pile intended for use with acid-loving plants.

Give back to the shrubs some of the advantages of life as understory plants in the forest. They have built-in fail-safe systems that respond beneficially to reasonable stress—dormancy is one that takes over in hot, dry summers as well as in cold winters. Most plants can adapt to some drought and suffer most when they are watered daily, shallowly, and forced to be lush when the weather isn't supporting lush growth. Feed the soil as the forest does, with fallen leaves. Gather, shred, compost, and return to the garden in the form of compost every fallen leaf and every scrap of healthy organic debris.

See Section Two for specific instructions on planting time, planting, and maintenance of woody plants. Be sure to plant shrubs high. Do not raise mulches beyond 2 or 3 inches, and keep them away from the main stem. Too-deep mulch can suffocate shallow-rooted plants and cause roots and stem to rot. Rough up or score the root ball of container-grown plants. The instructions for planting trees apply generally to shrubs—dig a large, shallow hole, prepare the soil, water the first season or two.

Do not fertilize at planting time. Almost invariably, container-grown shrubs have been lavishly fertilized to encourage growth, and their soil has as much as it can handle for the first season or two.

Fertilize well-established shrubs once annually, in late fall after the first heavy frost, for very early blooming types, and early spring for others. Do not allow the product to come into contact with the plant. Use a light application of 10–6–4 fertilizer that is 50 percent organic for non-acid-loving plants, and an acid fertilizer that is 50 percent organic for evergreens, azaleas, rhododendrons, and other acid-loving plants.

Under-use fertilizer consistently. Apply only nonpolluting fertilizers and biodegradable controls. The new gardening ethic accepts blemishes rather than planting shrubs dependent on frequent applications of pesticides. Decades of experience at the National Arboretum have shown that healthy plants properly handled will withstand and recover from many pests and develop few diseases.

Select dwarf and slow-growing cultivars, and prune only once a year, just after flowering, or just as growth resumes each spring, according to flowering process. Shrubs that bloom on new wood may be pruned in late winter or early spring before growth begins. Those that bloom on old wood should be pruned immediately after flowering, which is just before bud initiation begins for the next season.

Prune young developing shrubs during active growth. Succulent shoots cut in half immediately begin to grow lateral shoots. When the plants have reached the desired height, prune after new growth has developed fully for the season. Extend pruning back slightly into the old wood.

Pines can be made to branch by cutting back the candles approximately by half in early summer. Other conifers can be made to branch by pruning branch ends almost any time of the year except the dormant period. To encourage dense branching to the ground, begin pruning conifers when the plants are 3 to 5 years old to establish the desired shape early in the plants' development.

SHRUBS 1
FLOWERING SHRUBS FOR EARLY AND MID-SPRING

Witch hazels and forsythia are early spring favorites. Try viburnum as a follow-on; many beautiful new cultivars and hybrids have brilliant berries in summer, and colorful fall foliage in addition to their spring blossoms.

COMPANION PLANTINGS
Bulbs: *Chionodoxa luciliae*, Glory-of-the-snow; *Crocus*; *Eranthis hyemalis*, Winter Aconite; *Narcissus* × *odorus*, Campernelle Jonquil; *N. poeticus*, Poet's Narcissus, Pheasant's-eye; Species Tulips.
Perennials: *Campanula carpatica*, Tussock Bellflower; *Potentilla fruticosa*, Shrubby Potentilla.

CHAENOMELES *kee-nom-ee-lees*
speciosa   Japanese Quince,
Flowering Quince   Zones 4–8.

Thorny shrub with brilliant and beautiful single or double early spring flowers followed by glossy green leaves. Among many lovely cultivars: 'Nivalis' is a white; 'Apple Blossom', white-pink; 'Phyllis Moore', pink, semidouble; 'Cardinalis', red, double; 'Rubra Grandiflora' has large, single, deep crimson-red flowers. Branches force easily in late winter. The fragrant, 2-inch, waxy, yellowish fruits in fall are used for preserves.

MATURE HEIGHT:	10'
GROWTH RATE:	medium/slow
LIGHT:	full sun, semi-sunny
MOISTURE:	roots moist

FORSYTHIA *for-sith-ee-uh*
× *intermedia*   Golden-bells   Zones 5–8.

Spreading (to 12 feet wide), almost indestructible shrub covered with perky yellow flowers in late winter to early spring. May bloom in a mild winter.

Forsythia. (Neumann)

Does not bloom reliably north of Zone 5. The graceful arching varieties spread rapidly. Tall-growing varieties should be allowed to grow naturally but may be sheared for hedges and espalier. Good bank holder and useful for erosion control. This species is a border forsythia. 'Arnold Giant' is the hardiest. 'Lynwood' has the best flowers. 'Nana', 5 to 8 feet tall, is a slow-growing dwarf that roots where it touches and is a good ground cover; see also Ground Covers 9. Prefers soil in the neutral range, pH 6.0 to 8.0. Branches force easily in late winter.

MATURE HEIGHT:	8'–10'
GROWTH RATE:	fast
LIGHT:	full sun
MOISTURE:	versatile

Chaenomeles species, Flowering Quince. (Neumann)

HAMAMELIS *ham-am-ee-liss*
Witch Hazel

Small deciduous tree or tall shrub, whose branches bear yellow ribbonlike flower petals, often fragrant, in fall, late winter, or earliest spring—usually the first shrub to bloom. Grows well under tall trees in deciduous woods. Good in the East and Midwest for screens and hedges, and makes an excellent container plant. Brilliant fall color in leaves and bark. Prefers soil in the acid range, well drained.

GROWTH RATE:	medium/slow
LIGHT:	semi-sunny
MOISTURE:	roots moist

H. × *intermedia*   Witch Hazel   Zones 5–8.
'Arnold Promise' has large, deep yellow, fragrant flowers. Height to 20 feet. Autumn color of 'Diane' is exceptionally rich orange-red.

H. mollis   Chinese Witch Hazel
                                    Zones 5/6–8.
A large shrub or small tree, to 30 feet; it has the largest flowers and they are very fragrant. The fall color is orange-yellow. It is the least hardy of the witch hazels.

H. virginiana   Witch Hazel   Zones 4–8.
Height to 15 feet. This is the last woody plant to bloom in fall in New England. The narrow yellow flowers appear just when the leaves drop. Fruit comes the following fall before the flowers. Succeeds in woodsy light shade, but is showier in full sun in the North.

MAGNOLIA *mag-nohl-ee-uh*

Deciduous and evergreen shrubs and trees that flower in early to mid-spring. Most shrub magnolias have single, semidouble, or double blooms from white to pink to dark reddish purple before the leaves

Hamamelis virginiana, Witch Hazel. (Neumann)

appear. The flowers of some shrubs—*M. stellata*, Star Magnolia, for instance—are vulnerable in areas where spring weather is variable, but I've seen magnolias succeed in sheltered locations as far north as southern Connecticut. Prefer soil pH of 5.0 to 6.0. See also Trees 2 and Trees 3.

GROWTH RATE: medium/slow
LIGHT: full sun, semi-sunny
MOISTURE: roots moist

M. × loebneri 'Merrill'   Zones 4–8.
A cultivar of the cross between *M. kobus* and *M. stellata*, it is earlier to bloom and reaches mature height, about 25 feet, much sooner. Easy to grow and has fragrant blooms with usually 15 petals.

M. stellata Star Magnolia   Zones 5–9.
Tall, single-stemmed, deciduous semishrub with silvery bark and large, starry, narrow-petaled white flowers in early to mid-spring. Flowers are single, semidouble, or double and bloom before the leaves appear. Give protection from wind where spring climate is variable: buds may be killed in cold spells of Zone 5. Mature height, 15 to 20 feet. Prefers fertile, loamy soil that holds moisture well. Transplant in early spring while dormant and take care of it until established. Among several lovely cultivars are the many-petaled pinks, 'Centennial', 'Royal Star',

Magnolia 'Susan'. (Neumann)

and 'Rosea'; National Arboretum introductions 'Susan', a pink, and 'Betty', to 10 feet, one of the best dark-flowered magnolias; 'June', pale lavender outside, white inside; 'Dandy', dark lavender outside, white inside.

MALUS *may-lus*
sargentii   Sargent Crab Apple   Zones 4–8.

Smallest crab apple, a low, rounded, bush form, covered in spring with highly fragrant small single flowers, red in bud, opening to white. In fall, birds flock to the tiny red fruits. There are many lovely flowering crabs, but some have problems that are hard to control. This species spreads to 16 feet, and is fairly resistant. Crab apples prefer well-drained, somewhat neutral soil, pH 6.0 to 8.0. See also Trees 2.

MATURE HEIGHT: 8'
GROWTH RATE: slow
LIGHT: full sun
MOISTURE: roots moist

PIERIS *pye-eer-iss*

Valuable, hardy, evergreen shrubs or small trees with showy buds all winter and drooping clusters of urn-shaped flowers in spring. New foliage is bronzy. Most beautiful where there is some protection from wind and full sun. Prefer well-drained acid soil, pH 4.0 to 5.0, with lots of organic matter.

GROWTH RATE: slow
LIGHT: semi-sunny
MOISTURE: roots moist

P. floribunda   Fetterbush, Mountain Andromeda   Zones 5–8.
Shapely, pendulous shrub with upright pearly buds in late winter, unfolding to white or pink in mid-spring. Showy leaves. Good as a specimen and in foundation plantings.

P. japonica 'Red Mill'   Lily-of-the-valley Bush   Zones 5–8.
Tall species, to 9 feet. New foliage is red, fading to green as the season advances. Needs several hours of sun for full flowering.

VIBURNUM *vye-burn-um*

Spring-flowering deciduous, semievergreen, or evergreen shrubs or small trees, interesting in all seasons. Valued for adaptability and reddish buds that open to white or pink flowers. Fine green foliage and colorful fall fruits and foliage. Many are delightfully fragrant. The leaves do not tolerate sulfur sprays or dusts. Prefer well-drained, slightly acid soils. Donald Egolf of the National Arboretum has selected several of the superior cultivars named here.

GROWTH RATE: slow
LIGHT: full sun, semi-sunny
MOISTURE: roots moist

V. × *burkwoodii* 'Mohawk'   Zones 5–8.
Compact, to 6 to 8 feet, with abundant dark red buds that open to white flowers with red-blotched reverse. Mid-spring bloom. Strong spicy clove fragrance. Glossy, semi-persistent foliage holds green late into fall, and in warmer regions sometimes turns wine red.

V. × *carlcephalum* 'Cayuga'   Zones 5–8.
Blooms before 'Mohawk', but not really early, producing abundant pink buds that open to white. Compact growth to about 5 feet, and good, heavy, dark green foliage that persists in the South. Clove-scented and has brilliant fall color. Fruits are black. Excellent choice for small gardens.

V. carlesii   Zones 5–8.
Small deciduous shrub, rounded in form, and pinkish red buds opening to white flowers, intensely fragrant. Red fruits turn black in late summer. Loved for its fragrance, but is being replaced by the new cultivars, which often are showier and healthier.

V. 'Chesapeake'   Zones 5–8.
Deciduous, compact shrub with glossy, dark green foliage that turns red to orange in fall. Abundant pink buds in mid-spring open to lovely white flowers. Most successful in heavy loam with a pH of 6.0 to 6.5.

V. × *juddii*   Judd Viburnum   Zones 4–7.
Full, rounded plant that reaches to 15 feet and is a good choice for cooler areas and larger landscapes. Very fragrant, semi-snowball pinkish white flowers in mid-spring. Fruits are black. Blooms when it reaches 6 feet. Deciduous.

V. prunifolium   Black Haw   Zones 4–8.
Large shrub or small tree with horizontal branches, to 15 feet, that blooms in mid-spring. Pendant black fruits persist often until the following late winter. The autumn foliage is rich wine red. 'Holden' is a weeping form; 'Gladwyne' is a large-fruited form. Deciduous.

V. rufidulum   Southern Black Haw   Zones 5–8.
Blooms at the same season as the black haw, but reaches to 30 feet at maturity. It has velvety, dark brown winter buds and dark glossy green foliage that turns deep bloodred in fall. Branching is horizontal. Deciduous.

SEE ALSO:
Camellia japonica, Shrubs 23
Camellia sasanqua, Shrubs 23
Fothergilla gardenii, Dwarf Witch Alder, Shrubs 12
Fothergilla major, Shrubs 12

ALTERNATES:
Ceanothus, Redroot
Cytisus, Broom
Daphne mezereum, February Daphne
Erica carnea, Spring Heath, Snow Heather
Genista, Broom
Kerria japonica, Japanese Rose
Mahonia, Oregon Grape
Spiraea × *arguta* 'Compacta', Compact Spiraea

Viburnum carlesii in bloom.

Viburnum carlesii.

SHRUBS 2
AZALEAS (*RHODODENDRON*)

The plants here are examples of the many azalea cultivars—past, present, and future. Some are comparatively new and may not yet be common in the retail trade. Others are quite old and rare. This list of regionally grouped plants will afford beginners an overview of an enormous subject, and provide some idea of cultivars that will thrive in their climate. Local chapters of the Azalea Society of America (ASA) welcome inquiries and can be reached through the National Arboretum, or by writing to The Azalea Society of America, Box 6244, Silver Spring, MD 20906. They can help find cultivars not offered by local nurseries.

COMPANION PLANTINGS
Background plants: *Acer palmatum* 'Crimson Queen', Threadleaf Japanese Maple; *Ilex* 'Nellie R. Stevens', Holly; *Magnolia stellata* 'Royal Star'.
Bulbous plants: *Begonia grandis*, Hardy Begonia; *Eranthis hyemalis*, Winter Aconite; *Galanthus elwesii*, Giant Snowdrop; *Narcissus*, Daffodil, cvs.
Perennials: *Ajuga reptans*, Carpet Bugle; *Dicentra spectabilis*, Bleeding-heart; *Hosta* spp.

AZALEA *a-zay-lee-uh*

Azaleas are evergreen or deciduous members of the genus *Rhododendron* (see Shrubs 3). Thousands of beautiful cultivars have been developed. Azaleas aren't just smaller rhododendrons; they are botanically distinct from one another. Rhododendron leaves may have scales on the undersides; azalea leaves are hairy. Rhododendron flowers usually have ten stamens, azaleas five. Rhododendron flowers frequently are bell-shaped; azalea blossoms are funnel-shaped.

Azaleas generally bloom somewhat earlier than rhododendrons, but the season extends from early spring to late summer. Within that context, the cultivars here are labeled Early, Mid-season, or Late bloomers. Many azaleas flower during the first months of spring, but some flower in fall and these are gaining attention.

The blooms are beautiful single, semidouble, or double forms. Colors and color combinations include various hues of white, yellow, pink, orange, purple, and red. White-flowered plants tend toward yellow foliage in fall, while the leaves of red, purple, and pink cultivars redden or bronze for a variable but unadvertised off-season extra benefit.

Azaleas may be divided into four size groups: Very low, up to 18 inches; Low, up to 3 feet; Medium, up to 6 feet; and Tall, over 6 feet.

The growth rate is given where figures are available. It is variable: some plants achieve 4 feet in 5 or 6 years, which is fast. Others take 25 or 30 years to reach 4 feet, and that is slow. Slow growers are recommended for under a window or in the front of a border. However, azaleas respond well to pruning, so potential size is not an absolute deterrent.

Azaleas do well in cities. In fact, they do well everywhere their modest cultural requirements are met. Cultivars that originated in your region are apt to be the easiest to grow in your own garden, though they are not limited to their place of origin by any means.

Azaleas and rhododendrons are handled similarly. Buy balled-and-burlapped or container plants already in bloom—that guarantees the color.

The ideal site for azaleas and rhododendrons is one in which the soil is moderately acid (pH 4.5–6.0), well drained, high in organic matter, and beneath a tall canopy of trees which permit plenty of filtered sunlight. Since few sites are perfect, the gardener's task is to determine what is lacking and then to provide soil amendments that alter the pH, increase the organic content, and improve the drainage as necessary. In difficult cases, it is often easier to grow the plants in raised beds.

Your local office of the Extension Service of the U.S.D.A. (see Appendix) will explain how to bring soil to the desired pH level, either by adding ground sulfur or ferrous sulfate if it is too alkaline, or lime if it is too acidic.

To improve a bed for planting, spread over the site for each plant 3 to 6 inches of sphagnum peat, finely ground pine bark or fibrous, acid compost. Add 2 to 4 inches of coarse yellow-brown builder's sand, or perlite, and a generous handful of gypsum. Mix all this in to a depth of 12 to 18 inches.

Set the plants slightly higher in their holes than the level at which they were growing, and never put a $15 plant in a 50 cent hole. Make sure the hole is big enough to accommodate expanding roots, and anticipate settling. Never cultivate near azaleas, as they are shallow rooted. Mulch with any organic material except sphagnum peat moss, which has a tendency to harden. Pine needles or bark, very old sawdust, acid compost of oak leaves or pine needles, or any of the bagged ground barks are all suitable mulches. Replenish the mulch as necessary to maintain 2 to 4 inches of mulch through summer heat.

Water azaleas every 5 to 7 days during dry spells, especially new plantings. Keep the soil damp but never soggy.

Use fertilizer sparingly. If you must fertilize, use any acid preparation—4-12-10, for instance—designed for the purpose, and do not exceed the rate of application indicated. Those who prefer organic fertilizers may use cottonseed meal at the rate of 1 cupful around the base of a 3-foot plant. Never fertilize at planting time; new plants almost invariably have been heavily fertilized when you get them. Never fertilize prior to blooming, as that will stimulate growth during the period when you want the plants to put their energy into blooming. The optimum time to fertilize is after flowering ends but before July 4. The season's new growth must be given an opportunity to harden in preparation for winter.

Prune only to remove unhealthy branches and to keep the plants shapely and within the desired size limits. Do it after the last bloom has faded in spring. Never prune after midsummer; next season's flowers are in those branches. Note that azalea "sprays" in bloom make exceptional cut flowers for the table.

EVERGREEN AZALEAS

BELGIAN INDIAN AZALEAS
Tender cultivars originally of European origin, these plants are suitable only for the warmest parts of the deep South, and are most often seen as potted florist gift plants to be discarded after a few weeks. They are large-flowered, single and double, medium or tall azaleas, in a full range of colors, with many variegated forms.
'Albert-Elizabeth', 3-inch, double, white flower with an irregular reddish orange border. Medium height. Late.

Glenn Dale and Kurume azaleas thrive in dappled shade. (Miller)

'Kehr's White Rosebud'. (Harding)

'Vervaeneana', 3½-inch, double, rose salmon flower, with an irregular white border. Medium height. Late.

SOUTHERN INDIAN AZALEAS

A subset of the Belgian Indian group, tolerant of southern climates. Grown as far north as the mid-Atlantic region, where they may fail. A protected location or warmer microclimate improves performance in areas where the climate is marginally suitable. In the South, older plants grow to 6 or 7 feet high and 8 or 9 feet wide. They are smaller farther north.

'Formosa', 3-inch, single, deep purplish red flower with a darker blotch. Medium to tall. Mid-season.

'George L. Tabor', 3½-inch, single, white flower flushed with a purplish pink hue and darker blotch. Medium to tall. Mid-season.

'Mrs. G. G. Gerbing', 3½-inch, single, white flower; inconspicuous blotch. Medium to tall. Mid-season.

PENNINGTON AZALEAS

Developed by Ralph Pennington of Covington, Georgia, these azaleas are great for the South, and presumed suited to the Southwest. Diverse as to size.

'Beth Bullard', 3½-inch, single, salmon pink flower. Low- and slow-growing. Late.

'Pennington White', 2-inch, single, white flower with an inconspicuous blotch. Eventually 4 to 5 feet tall and slightly wider. Early.

KEHR AZALEAS

A select group of five hybrids, all particularly attractive double-flowered forms, developed by Dr. August Kehr, Hendersonville, North Carolina. The examples below are low-growers, hardy to − 10° F.

'Anna Kehr', 1¾-inch, double, purplish pink flower. In 10 years, grows to 2 feet tall and 2½ feet wide. Mid-season.

'Kehr's White Rosebud', 1¾-inch, double, white flower with a green throat. In 10 years, grows to 2 feet tall and 2½ feet wide. Mid-season.

GLENN DALE AZALEAS

Some 454 very good hybrids developed at the U.S.D.A. Glenn Dale Station by B. Y. Morrison, first director of the U.S. National Arboretum, for the mid-Atlantic states. In 1947, the National Arboretum established masses of seedlings of Glenn Dale azaleas on Mount Hamilton. Cultivars from this group have been successfully grown all over the U.S. and abroad. Variable as to size. Some do not exceed 2 feet; others reach 10 to 12 feet in 30 years.

'Martha Hitchcock', 3-inch, single, white-throated flower with a reddish purple margin. May exceed the 4 to 5 feet generally predicted as its mature height. Mid-season.

'Glacier', 3-inch, single, white flower with a faint green tone. Admired for its fine dark green foliage. Medium-grower. Early.

BELGIAN–GLENN DALE AZALEAS

Five cultivars introduced in the early 1960s, the result of crossing a Belgian Indian hybrid with a Glenn Dale hybrid. Marginal in the Washington, D.C. area; better in the South.

'Pink Ice', 3-inch, double, light reddish purple flower with occasional purple flecks. Upright, medium height. Mid-season.

'Green Mist', 2½-inch, semidouble, white flower with a greenish blotch. Upright, medium height. Mid-season.

KURUME AZALEAS

Of Japanese origin, these azaleas were introduced to America in 1917, and are suited to Zones 7–9. Compact form with single or double smaller flowers and leaves, often delicate pink to scarlet. The much-overused 'Snow' is an example of a white Kurume. There are lavender and purple Kurumes as well. Stands pruning well.

'Coral Bells', 1¼-inch, single, pink flower. Medium-grower. Early.

'Pink Pearl', 2-inch, single, pink flower with lighter center and rose blotch. Medium-grower. Early.

BACK ACRES AZALEAS

A continuation of the Glenn Dale hybrids. These were developed by Ben Morrison, in retirement at Pass Christian, Mississippi. Satisfactory in the Washington, D.C., area, with exceptions, but not reliable farther north.

'Margaret Douglas', 2¾-inch, single flower with a light pink center and yellowish pink margin. Low-grower. Late.

'Marian Lee', 2½-inch, single flower with a pink-tinted white center and a red border. Medium-grower. Late.

NORTH TISBURY AZALEAS

Introduced by Polly Hill, Martha's Vineyard, Massachusetts, in the 1970s. Ideal for small yards and rock gardens. Tight little mounds that are only marginally successful at the Arnold Arboretum, Massachusetts, but are recommended for warmer climates. They are beautiful in hanging baskets.

'Alexander', 2½-inch, single, reddish orange flower

'Nancy of Robinhill'. (Miller)

Glenn Dale and Kurume hybrid azaleas. (Miller)

'Indian Summer', a Gable hybrid azalea. (Miller)

with a darker blotch. After 16 years, plants grow 15 inches high and 6 feet wide. Late.

'Marilee', 2¼-inch, single, red flower with a purple blotch. After 17 years, 2 feet tall and 6 feet wide. Late.

KAEMPFERI AZALEAS

European hybrids introduced here in the 1920s. They are suitable for all but the very coldest regions, but may be hard to find. More recently, selected forms of the species itself (Japanese) have become popular. Some of them, the so-called "fall bloomers," exhibit the tendency to bloom a second time in the fall. In time, to 8 feet tall.

'Louise', 1¼-inch, single, red flower. Very upright, tall. Mid-season.

'Willy', 2-inch, single, pink flower. Very upright, tall. Mid-season.

ROBIN HILL AZALEAS

Developed by Robert Gartrell, Wyckoff, New Jersey, and grown extensively in the East, South, and West. This group is suited to all but the coldest areas.

'Betty Anne Voss', 3-inch, double, purplish pink flower. After 5 years, grows to 14 inches tall and 28 inches wide. Late.

'Nancy of Robinhill', 3½-inch, double, light purplish pink flower with an occasional light red blotch. Low-growing. Late.

LINWOOD AZALEAS

Developed by Albert Reid, Linwood, New Jersey, and introduced in the mid-1960s. Typically compact with double or semidouble flowers. Being grown in all but the coldest regions.

'Hardy Gardenia', 2½-inch, double, white flower. In 8 years, grows to 14 inches tall and 30 inches wide. Mid-season.

'Garden State Garnet', 2¼-inch, single, purplish red flower. In 6 years, grows to 30 inches high and 40 inches wide. Mid-season.

GIRARD AZALEAS

Developed by Peter Girard, Sr., Geneva, Ohio, and among the hardiest azaleas available. Low-growers.

'Girard's Scarlet', 2½-inch, single, deep red flower. In 5 years, grows to 18 inches high by 24 inches wide. Mid-season.

'Girard's Hot Shot', 2½-inch, single, dark reddish orange flower. In 5 years, grows to 18 inches tall and 24 inches wide. Mid-season.

GABLE AZALEAS

Developed by Joseph Gable, Stewartstown, Pennsylvania, and growing all over the country. Among the hardiest available, to Zone 5 (but not completely evergreen that far north). There are pink, rose, white, purple, lavender, and assorted red shades.

'Louise Gable', 2¼-inch, semidouble, pink flower

with a darker blotch. Medium-grower. Late.

'Purple Splendor', 2-inch, single, reddish purple flower. Medium-grower. Mid-season.

SHAMMARELLO AZALEAS

Well established and of recognized hardiness, developed by Tony Shammarello, South Euclid, Indiana. Medium- to low-growers.

'Elsie Lee', 2½-inch, semidouble, light reddish flower. In 15 years, grows to 3 feet high and equally wide. Mid-season.

'Helen Curtis', 2½-inch, semidouble, white flower. In 15 years, grows to 2 feet high and 3 feet wide. Late.

SCHROEDER AZALEAS

Relatively new hybrid group developed by H. R. Schroeder, Evansville, Indiana. Proven reliable in the Midwest. Among the hardiest and should prove useful in the colder regions. Mostly low-growers.

'Carrie Amanda', 2-inch, single, white-throated with a magenta-rose border. In 10 years, grows to 15 inches high and 2 feet wide. Mid-season.

'Hoosier Sunrise', 1½-inch, double, bright pink flower. In 10 years, grows to 15 inches high and 18 inches tall. Mid-season.

GREENWOOD AZALEAS

Comparatively new group of lovely low and medium height azaleas, developed by Bill Guttormsen, Canby, Oregon, from crosses involving Kurume, Glenn Dale, and Gable hybrids. They are expected to perform well outside the Northwest.

'Greenwood Orange', 2½-inch, double, reddish orange flower. After 10 years, grows to 2½ feet high and 2 feet wide. Mid-season.

'Pink Cloud', 3¾-inch, double, pink flower. After 10 years, grows to 3 feet high and 2 feet wide. Mid-season.

HARRIS AZALEAS

New Group developed by James Harris, Lawrenceville, Georgia, from crosses involving Satsuki, Glenn Dale, and Back Acres hybrids. The group is not uniformly reliable in the D.C. area, but some are extremely hardy. Medium- to low-growers.

'Parfait', a Harris hybrid azalea. (Miller)

Satsuki azaleas. (Miller)

'Parfait', 2-inch, single, white flower with a variable purplish pink flush and a conspicuous darker blotch. After 10 years, grows to 3½ feet tall and as wide. Early.

'Fascination', 4-inch, single, light pink flower with a red border. After 9 years, grows to 2½ feet tall and 3 feet wide. Late.

SATSUKI AZALEAS
Large-flowered late bloomers typically of Japanese origin and including *R. indicum* and *R. tamurae*. Low- and slow-growing, many of the cultivars date back to the 17th century and are comparatively new to America, having first appeared in the 1930s. Valuable for bonsai but not recommended for landscape use in colder regions or where there are rabbits.

'Macrantha Purple', 2-inch, single, light purple flower. Medium-grower. Late.

'Shinnyo-no-tsuki', 3-inch, single, white-centered flower with a purplish red margin. Low-grower. Late.

DECIDUOUS AZALEAS

GHENT AZALEAS
The 19th-century product of European crosses of American native azaleas. Prefer a cool climate and are very hardy, to Zone 4. Not widely available and not indicated for the South or Southwest due to low heat tolerance. White, yellow, orange, pink, or red, single or double flowers in mid-spring.

'Coccinea Speciosa', 1½-inch, single, yellowish pink flower with an orange blotch. Upright and tall. Late.

'Daviesi', 2½-inch, single, pale yellow flower fading to white with a conspicuous yellow blotch. Upright and tall. Late.

MOLLIS AZALEAS
This group was developed in the last century in Europe. They are slightly less hardy than the Ghents, to Zone 5, and not for regions where temperatures run high in summer. May be hard to find. Whites, yellows, oranges, pinks, reds, and many combina-

tions. Bloom in late spring.

'Koeningin Emma', 2½-inch, single flower, light orange-yellow to strong orange, with a suffusion of yellowish pink and an orange blotch. Upright, tall. Late.

'Koster's Yellow', 3½-inch, single flower, orange-yellow with an orange blotch. Upright, tall. Late.

OCCIDENTALE AZALEAS
R. occidentale, the Western Azalea, is an American native. Several groups based on the Western Azalea are known as Occidentale Azaleas. They are most successful in the cool, stable climate of the Northwest. Not suited to the temperature extremes, heat or cold, of the North, South, or East.

'Irene Koster', 2½-inch, single, white flower, with a flush of pink. Upright, tall. Mid-season.

'Foggy Dew', 2-inch, single, white flower with a pink and yellow tone. Upright, tall. Mid-season.

KNAP HILL AND EXBURY AZALEAS
The group includes the Knap Hill, Exbury, Slocock, Ilam, and Windsor hybrids introduced after World

Mollis azalea. (Miller)

Rhododendron 'Mary Fleming'. (Beaudry)

War II. Progress is being made on the domestic front as evidenced by the following hybrid groups: Bovee Knap Hill, Carlson Exbury, Girard (deciduous), and Slonecker. These plants cannot stand extremes of heat; they are more successful in the cooler northern areas. Many gorgeous azaleas with large, mostly single flowers in brilliant colors. There may be 28 to 30 flowers in a single cluster. White, yellow, cream, pink, orange, red. Hardy to Zones 5–6.
'Gibraltar', 2½-inch, single, vivid burnt orange flower with fringed petals, in very large trusses. Hardy, fragrant. Tall, columnar. Mid-season.
'George Reynolds', 2¾-inch, single, yellow flower with a hint of green in the throat and a conspicuous yellow blotch. Medium, spreading. Mid-season.

AMERICAN NATIVE AZALEAS
In recent years there has been a renaissance of interest in developing hybrids from the known native American azaleas. In addition, selections are being introduced from species discovered in the field or grown from random seed. Examples of some established hybrid groups include Abbott, Chinquapin Hill, Leach, and Weston hybrids, which extend the range and versatility of these azaleas. With the exception of *R. occidentale*, the Western Azalea, natives seem adaptable to many situations.
'Galle's Choice', 1¾-inch, single, light yellow flower that has a white throat and light pink tips. Tall. Mid-season. Hardy to 0° F.
'Marydel', 1¾-inch, single, white flower with a deep purplish pink margin. In 10 years, grows to 3 feet

tall and equally wide. Hardy to −10° F. Mid-season.

R. arborescens Sweet Azalea Zones 5–9.
Red fall foliage, a vigorous grower, to 9 feet, that blooms late in spring through early summer, and is unusually fragrant. White with a reddish eye and pink to red filaments.

R. austrinum Florida Flame Azalea
Zones 5–9.
Fragrant, predominant yellow and orange to orange-red flowers appearing very early. Versatile as to light and moisture. Spreads by underground runner. 'My Mary' has 2½-inch, single, fragrant yellow flowers. Medium. Hardy to −10°F. Early.

R. vaseyi Pink-shell Azalea Zones 4–9.
Native to North Carolina and hardy in New England in moist soil. It blooms in mid-spring. 'Pinkerbell' has a 2-inch, deep pink, single flower. Tall. Hardy to −15° F. Mid-season.

ROYAL AZALEA
Hardy native of Korea and Manchuria, its very fine flower and distinctive leaf have made it exceptionally popular.

R. schlippenbachii Royal Azalea
Zones 5–8.
Very early bloomer to 4 or 5 feet tall, with big, showy clusters of fragrant, 3-inch pink flowers. Small leaves with down on the underside. Deciduous leaves with some color in fall.

SHRUBS 3
RHODODENDRONS

Here are some beautiful, established *Rhododendron* cultivars and species for the various regions of the United States where these plants thrive. The Northwest has the ideal climate but rhododendrons succeed in many other places. The list below is a fair representation of those commercially available. Azalea species belong to this genus, and are described in the preceding list, Shrubs 2.

COMPANION PLANTINGS
Trees: *Cornus* cvs., Dogwood; *Pinus*, Pine.
Shrubs: Azalea (*Rhododendron*) cvs.; *Kalmia latifolia*, Mountain Laurel; *Mahonia aquifolium*, Oregon Grape; *M. bealei*, Leatherleaf Mahonia; *Tsuga canadensis* 'Pendula', Weeping Canadian Hemlock. Ground covers: Ferns; *Hosta*; *Pachysandra*.
Flowers: *Iris danfordiae*, Danford Iris; *I. reticulata*, Netted Iris.

RHODODENDRON roh-doh-**den**-dron

There are over 900 species and thousands of evergreen and deciduous rhododendron cultivars. In regions where they succeed, these tall shrubs with their huge, airy globes of exquisite flowers are the most valued for spring or early summer display. The pink, rose, lavender, purple, white, or yellow flowers often are flushed, splotched, or spotted with another shade or color. These are understory plants that thrive in good light under tall trees. They reach 20 feet and more in the wild, but in cultivation most mature at 6 or 8 feet. There are also dwarfs. Small-leaved rhododendrons are better able to stand temperature extremes than the large-leaved types, but both are planted in all regions where they succeed.

Buy young container-grown or balled-and-burlapped plants from reliable, preferably local, nurseries. Consider plants' mature size. Be conservative in estimating rhododendron hardiness. A rhododendron beyond its hardiness range may survive and bud, but never bloom. Set plants out in mid-fall or very early spring.

Site plants so they have some shelter from winter winds. The site, soil, and culture recommendations for azaleas on the preceding list apply to rhododendrons.

Full morning sun and afternoon shade are preferred over morning shade and full afternoon sun. North- and east-facing sites are better than south- and west-facing. Provide part sun for large-leaved evergreen types. Filtered or dappled sun under tall trees is best. Small-leaved and deciduous types generally can handle full sun all day where fog and cloudy skies are frequent. In hot, dry climates all need protection from noonday sun. Rhododendrons generally grow rather slowly and flower best when spent heads are removed. Prune back ungainly branches after flowering.

The American Rhododendron Society (ARS) has chapters all over the country; they welcome questions on cultivar choices and cultural practices. For information, contact the U.S. National Arboretum.

The cultivars here are grouped according to regions where they are successful.

MID-ATLANTIC REGION
'Mary Fleming', yellow-pink, to 3 or 4 feet, early mid-season, small leaf, hardy to −15° F.
'Ben Moseley', purple with a pink blotch, to 6 feet, mid-season, large leaf, hardy to −15° F.

Rhododendron 'Scintillation'. (Beaudry)

'Caroline', orchid and pink, to 8 feet, mid-season, large leaf, hardy to −15° F.
'Janet Blair', light pink, to 8 feet, mid-season, large leaf, hardy to −15° F.
'Nova Zembla', red, to 5 feet, mid-season, large leaf, hardy to −25° F.
'Parker's Pink', dark pink and white bicolor, to 5 feet, mid-season, large leaf, hardy to −20° F.
'Holden', rose-red, to 4 feet, mid-season, large leaf, hardy to −15° F.
'Roseum Elegans', rose-lilac, to 6 feet, mid-season, large leaf, hardy to −25° F.
'Scintillation', pink, to 8 feet, mid-season, large leaf, hardy to −10° F. Hardy and vigorous, very versatile.
'Cadis', light pink, 10 to 12 feet, mid-season to late, large leaf, hardy to −15° F.

R. dauricum   Zones 4–8.
Deciduous or semievergreen, very early, to 4 or 5 feet tall, with purple, pink, and white flowers. Small leaf, hardy to −25° F. The variety *sempervirens* tends to be evergreen.

R. fortunei   Fortune's Rhododendron
Zones 5–8.
Evergreen, to 12 feet, early to mid-season, with fragrant pink flowers. Large leaf, hardy to −15° F. Many of the cultivars popular in Boston and southward were bred from this species.

R. makinoi   Zones 6–8.
Evergreen, to 5 or 6 feet, mid-season to late. Flowers are soft pink, often spotted with crimson. Large leaf, hardy to −10° F.

R. mucronulatum   Zones 4–7.
Deciduous, 5 to 8 feet tall, very early, with dark pink and white flowers. Small leaf, hardy to −15° F. The leaves appear after the flowers and color vividly in autumn. 'Cornell Pink' is a phlox-pink cultivar.

R. yakusimanum   Zones 5–8.
Evergreen foliage covered beneath with woolly indumentum (covering of hair), 3 to 4 feet tall and as wide, mid-season. Flowers bright rose, opening to white. Large leaf, hardy to −25° F. 'Yaku Princess'

(Yakusimanum hybrid) has apple-blossom pink flowers conspicuously blushed. Sun or partial shade.

SOUTHERN UNITED STATES
'Lenape', pale yellow, to 6 feet, early, small leaf, hardy to −10°.
'P. J. M.', lavender-purple, to 4 feet, early, small leaf, hardy to −25° F.
'Mary Fleming', yellow-pink, to 3 or 4 feet, early to mid-season, small leaf, hardy to −15° F.
'Tom Koenig', pink, to 4 feet, early to mid-season, small leaf, hardy to −10° F.
'Windbeam', pink, to 4 feet, early to mid-season, small leaf, hardy to −25° F.
'Caroline', orchid and pink, to 8 feet, mid-season, large leaf, hardy to −15° F.
'Carolina Rose', pink *Azaleodendron* (cross between an azalea and a rhododendron), to 4 feet. mid-season, small leaf, hardy to −10° F.
'Janet Blair', light pink, to 8 feet, mid-season, large leaf, hardy to −15° F.
'Nova Zembla', red, to 5 feet, mid-season, large leaf, hardy to −25° F.
'Olin O. Dobbs', red and purple, to 4 feet, mid-season, large leaf, hardy to −15° F.
'Rochelle', rose with a pink blotch, to 6 feet, mid-season, large leaf, hardy to −10° F.
'Roseum Elegans', rose-lilac, to 6 feet, mid-season, large leaf, hardy to −25° F.
'Scintillation', pink, to 8 feet, mid-season, large leaf, hardy to −10° F.
'Tom Everitt', pink, to 6 feet, mid-season, large leaf, hardy to −15° F.
'Wheatley', pink, to 8 feet, mid-season, large leaf, hardy to −15° F.
'Cadis', light pink, to 10 to 12 feet, mid-season to late, large leaf, hardy to −15° F.

R. yakusimanum   Zones 5–8.
Evergreen foliage covered beneath with woolly indumentum (covering of hair), 3 to 4 feet tall and as wide, mid-season. Flowers bright rose, opening to white. Large leaf, hardy to −25° F. 'Yaku Princess' (Yakusimanum hybrid) has apple-blossom pink flowers conspicuously blushed. Sun or partial shade.

Rhododendron 'Tom Everitt'. (Beaudry)

GREAT LAKES REGION

'Llenroc', light pink with yellow eye, to 5 feet, early, small leaf, hardy to −15° F.

'Vernus', light pink, to 5 feet, early, large leaf, hardy to −25° F.

'Weston's Pink Diamond', light fuchsia, to 5 feet, early, small leaf, hardy to −10° F.

'Olga Mezitt', pink, to 3 feet, early, small leaf, hardy to −15° F.

'Ben Moseley', purple with a pink blotch, to 6 feet, mid-season, large leaf, hardy to −15° F.

'Brown Eyes', pink with brown blotch, to 8 feet, mid-season, large leaf, hardy to −15° F.

'Catawbiense Album', Catawba Rhododendron, white, to 6 feet, mid-season, large leaf, hardy to −25° F.

'English Roseum', rosy pink, to 6 feet, mid-season, large leaf, hardy to −25° F.

'Janet Blair', light pink, to 8 feet, mid-season, large leaf, hardy to −15° F.

'Lodestar', large white flowers in extra large trusses with a bronze-gold flare, to 6 feet, mid-season, large leaf, hardy to −20° F. Award winner.

'Nova Zembla', red, to 5 feet, mid-season, large leaf, hardy to −25° F.

R. × laetevirens   Wilson Rhododendron
Zones 4–8.
Often offered as Wilsonii. Evergreen and low-growing to 2 to 3 feet and wider, mid-season. Pink to purplish flowers. Small leaf, hardy to −15° F.

R. mucronulatum   Zones 4–7.
Deciduous, 5 to 8 feet tall, very early, with dark pink and white flowers. Small leaf, hardy to −15° F. The leaves appear after the flowers and color vividly in autumn. 'Cornell Pink' is a phlox-pink cultivar.

PACIFIC NORTHWEST

'Elizabeth', red, to 3 feet, early, large leaf, hardy to 0°.

'Hallelujah', fluorescent pink, to 4 feet, mid-season, large leaf, hardy to −15° F.

'Loder's White', white, to 12 feet, mid-season, large leaf, hardy to 0° F.

'Mrs. Furnival', light rose-pink blotched deeper pink, to 6 feet, mid-season, large leaf, hardy to −10° F. Award winner.

'The Honorable Jean Marie de Montague', classic red, to 5 feet, mid-season, large leaf, hardy to −5° F. Emerald green foliage and long-lasting flowers. Very sun-tolerant. Slow growing.

'Trude Webster', pink, to 5 feet, mid-season, large leaf, hardy to −10° F.

'Unique', ivory, to 4 feet, mid-season, large leaf, hardy to −5° F.

'Van Ness Sensation', light orchid-pink, to 5 feet, mid-season to late, large leaf, hardy to −5° F.

'Vulcan's Flame', red, to 6 feet, mid-season, large leaf, hardy to −15° F.

'Gomer Waterer', white, to 6 feet, mid-season to late, large leaf, hardy to −15° F.

'Anna Rose Whitney', rose, to 6 feet, mid-season to late, large leaf, hardy to −5° F.

R. augustinii   Zones 7–9.
Evergreen, to 8 feet tall, early. The flowers are blue to lavender-rose. Small leaf, hardy to 5° F.

R. yakusimanum   Zones 5–8.
Evergreen foliage covered beneath with woolly indumentum (covering of hair), 3 to 4 feet tall and as

Rhododendron 'The Hon. Jean Marie de Montague'.

wide, mid-season. Flowers bright rose, opening to white. Large leaf, hardy to −25° F. 'Yaku Princess' (Yakusimanum hybrid) has apple-blossom pink flowers conspicuously blushed. Sun or partial shade.

NEW ENGLAND REGION

'Ramapo', pink-violet, to 2 feet, early, small leaf, hardy to −25° F.

'Besse Howells', burgundy-red, to 4 feet, early mid-season, large leaf, hardy to −20° F.

'Harold Amateis', red, to 5 feet, early mid-season, large leaf, hardy to −15° F.

'Mary Fleming', yellow-pink, to 3 or 4 feet, early mid-season, small leaf, hardy to −15° F.

'Windbeam', pink, to 4 feet, early to mid-season, small leaf, hardy to −25° F.

'Apple Blossom', pink, to 8 feet, mid-season, large leaf, hardy to −15° F.

'Brown Eyes', pink with brown blotch, to 8 feet, mid-season, large leaf, hardy to −20° F.

'Cadis', light pink, 10 to 12 feet, mid-season, large leaf, hardy to −15° F.

'Rochelle', rose-pink with deep red blotch, to 6 feet, mid-season, large leaf, hardy to −10° F.

'Scintillation', pink, to 8 feet, mid-season, large leaf, hardy to −10° F.

'Westbury', pink, to 8 feet, mid-season, large leaf, hardy to −15°F.

'Wheatley', pink, to 8 feet, mid-season, large leaf, hardy to −15°F.

R. brachycarpum   Fujiyama Rhododendron
Zones 6–8.
Evergreen, to 10 feet tall, very late. White flowers are flushed pink and spotted yellow. Large leaf, hardy to −25° F.

R. fortunei   Fortune's Rhododendron
Zones 5–8.
Evergreen, to 12 feet, early to mid-season, with fragrant pink flowers. Large leaf, hardy to −15° F. Many of the cultivars popular in Boston and southward were bred from this species.

R. metternichii   Leatherleaf Rhododendron
Zones 5–9.
Evergreen, to 8 feet, mid-season. Flowers are rose, spotted with darker rose. Large leaf, hardy to −15° F.

R. smirnowii   Smirnow Rhododendron
Zones 5–8.
Evergreen to 6 feet tall and as broad, early bloomer. Flowers are white, rosy red, or lavender-pink. Large leaf, hardy to −15° F. The leaves are felted on the underside.

Rhododendron 'Harold Amateis'. (Beaudry)

SHRUBS 4
FLOWERING SHRUBS FOR LATE SPRING

Many of these lovely shrubs have very fragrant blossoms. Try a viburnum if you have any space at all for a flowering spring shrub. Azaleas, rhododendrons, and roses are on lists Shrubs 2, 3, 6, and 19.

COMPANION PLANTINGS
Spring-flowering bulbs: *Hyacinthus orientalis* 'Blue Magic', Dutch Hyacinth; *Muscari azureum* 'Heavenly Blue', Grape Hyacinth; *M. a.* 'Album', White Grape Hyacinth; *Narcissus asturiensis*; *Scilla siberica* 'Spring Beauty', Siberian Squill; *Tulipa* Kaufmanniana, Water-lily Tulip; *T. greigii*; *T. pulchella* 'Violacea'.
Perennials: *Ajuga reptans*, Carpet Bugle; *Galium odoratum*, Woodruff, Sweet Woodruff.

CHIONANTHUS *kye-oh-nanth-us*
retusus Fringe Tree Zones 5–9.

Large deciduous bush that in late spring bears panicles of small fringelike flowers in white or greenish white, on the current year's growth. Female plants (only) follow with persistent, purple fruit in late summer that contrasts nicely with the yellow fall foliage and attracts birds. Bark is an attractive gray. Good as a specimen plant, or in groups, and near buildings. Tolerant of air pollution. Prefers acid-range, well-drained soil. Dioecious-polydioecious and may need companion to fruit well. See also Trees 11.

MATURE HEIGHT: 15'
GROWTH RATE: slow
LIGHT: full sun
MOISTURE: soil surface damp

Chionanthus retusa, Fringe Tree.

Kalmia latifolia, Mountain Laurel.

KALMIA *kal-mee-uh*
latifolia Mountain Laurel Zones 4–9.

Handsome evergreen shrub to 15 feet or more in the wild, usually found under tall trees. Leathery leaves and a profusion of lovely white, pink, or variegated blooms in late spring. Prefers moist, well-drained, acid-range, organic soils. In nutrient-deficient soils and full sun it develops leaf spot. Remove faded flowers at once. Mulch to maintain moisture. 'Ostbo Red' is a red-budded clone, considered the best. May be easier to find in West Coast nurseries.

MATURE HEIGHT: 7'
GROWTH RATE: slow
LIGHT: semi-sunny
MOISTURE: roots moist

MAGNOLIA *mag-nohl-ee-uh*
liliiflora Lily Magnolia Zones 5–8.

The species is a rounded, shrubby magnolia almost as wide as it is tall. A cross made at the National Arboretum resulted in a series called 'The Little Girl Hybrids', named 'Betty', 'Jane', 'Jody', and so on. They bloom later than the Star Magnolia, avoiding damage from inclement weather. Flowers open before the leaves and make a superb display. Sporadic flowering in summer. Their range is Zones 3 to 8. Prefers rich, slightly acid, loamy soil that holds moisture well but is well drained. 'Ann' is recommended by Dr. Michael A. Dirr.

MATURE HEIGHT: 8'–12'
GROWTH RATE: slow
LIGHT: full sun, semi-sunny
MOISTURE: roots moist

SYRINGA *sihr-rin-guh* Lilac

In Canada and New England, lilac is the fragrance of spring. The lilacs are tall shrubs or small, multi-stemmed trees, with fresh green leaves and many-flowered panicles of lilac-colored, purple, or white flowers, some double. They came to America with the earliest settlers and were being hybridized in

France in the late 1700s. Some gardeners still call the hybrids "French lilacs." The many cultivars range through white, pink, red-purple, rich purple, and blue, but not all are as fragrant as the common lilac, *S. vulgaris*. They make fine specimens and hedges, sometimes called "lilac walks." Mildew is almost inevitable, particularly on lower leaves in crowded plantings, but is minimal in dry, airy, cool regions, and with some species and cultivars. Efforts are being made through breeding programs to improve the quality of the foliage in summer and to add attractive fall color. Sucker shoots are freely produced at the base; remove suckers from grafted cultivars, and thin them to one or two replacement shoots on other lilacs. Newly planted lilacs sometimes fail to bloom for a few years. Be patient. Lilacs grow best in moist, nearly neutral soil. They must have good air circulation, generous mulching, and periodic pruning. Remove dead blooms. For tree lilac, see Trees 3.

GROWTH RATE:	slow
LIGHT:	full sun
MOISTURE:	versatile

S. meyeri — Zones 3–7/8.
Shrub, to 8′ spreading to 12′, rounded, with violet-purple flowers. Mildew-resistant, particularly in the Midwest and the East. 'Palabin' is a compact cultivar that begins to flower when only a foot high. Good for the shrub border, with an evergreen background.

S. patula 'Miss Kim'   Manchurian Lilac — Zones 3–8.
Upright little lilac to 9′, with purple buds that open to fragrant icy blue flowers in panicles 4 to 6 inches long, often in pairs. Blooms later than ordinary lilacs. May develop fairly good fall color. Mildew resistant.

S. vulgaris — Zones 3–8.
This species came to America with the colonists and grows easily almost everywhere in the temperate zone. There are hundreds of cultivars. Flowers mid-spring, and is sweetly fragrant. Height to 20 feet. There are lilac-colored flowers, and whites, pinkish colors, magentas, yellow-whites, and double-flowered forms. Ask for mildew-resistant cultivars from local nurseries. 'Sensation' has picotee-edged flowers.

VIBURNUM *vye-**burn**-um*

Flowering deciduous, semievergreen, or evergreen shrubs or small trees, with interest in four seasons. Valued for adaptability and reddish buds that open in spring and late spring to white or pink flowers. The plants here bloom in late spring. Fine green foliage and colorful late summer and fall fruits. The foliage can be spectacular red-purple and persists into late fall. The flowers of many viburnums are delightfully fragrant. The leaves do not tolerate sulfur sprays or dusts. Prefer well-drained, slightly acid soils.

GROWTH RATE:	slow
LIGHT:	full sun, semi-sunny
MOISTURE:	roots moist

V. dilatatum 'Catskill' — Zones 4/5–7.
Blooms late. Deciduous, with creamy flowers in May, and early June on new growth. Prized for heavy show of fruit beginning in late summer and persisting until winter, and for good orange-red autumn color. A compact plant to 5 feet, good choice for small gardens. National Arboretum introduction.

V. odoratissimum   Sweet Viburnum — Zone 10.
Evergreen, with small white flowers. Grows to 12 or 15 feet at a moderate pace, and is used in southern Florida as an informal hedge. Prefers acid soil.

V. 'Oneida' — Zones 4/5–7.
Creamy white flowers in abundance in mid-spring and again sporadically in summer. Fruits are glossy, dark red, and persist until late winter. Foliage is yellow and orange-red. Upright plant to 15 feet and almost as wide. Deciduous. National Arboretum introduction.

V. plicatum var. tomentosum
Double File Viburnum — Zones 4–8.
Twin rows of flower clusters with sterile flowers around the outside. Horizontal branches. Blooms in late May, early June. Red fruits develop in fall from the small fertile flowers in the center. 'Mariesii' grows to 9 feet, a graceful plant with large sterile florets. Fruits are red, maturing to black. The cultivar 'Shasta' is about 6 feet by 10 feet. Tolerant of many exposures and soils, it does best in sun in the North, light shade in the South. The white flowers are followed by red, upright fruits, maturing to black. As a specimen or in masses, it makes a striking silhouette in winter. 'Shasta' is considered by the National Arboretum scientist who introduced it, Dr. Donald R. Egolf, to rival the dogwood in beauty. Deciduous.

V. sargentii 'Susquehanna' — Zones 4–8.
Select upright plant that reaches 12 to 15 feet, with a heavily branched, corky trunk and leathery leaves. In late spring it produces masses of large, flat clusters of white flowers ringed with sterile flowers. Striking when red fruits appear in late summer and early fall. Deciduous.

SEE ALSO:
Azalea (*Rhododendron*) cvs., Shrubs 2
Rhododendron cvs., Shrubs 3
Rosa, Rose, Shrubs 6

ALTERNATES:
Arctostaphylos uva-ursi, Bearberry
Buddleia alternifolia, Fountain Buddleia
Ceanothus ovatus, Redroot
Cotinus coggygria, Smoke Tree, Smokebush
Kolkwitzia amabilis, Beautybush
Leucothoe fontanesiana, Drooping Leucothoe
Pernettya mucronata
Skimmia reevesiana
Spiraea prunifolia, Bridal Wreath
Spiraea × vanhouttei, Bridal Wreath
Weigela florida 'Variegata'

Viburnum dilatatum.

SHRUBS 5
FLOWERING SHRUBS FOR SUMMER AND FALL

Treasured for color in the hot months when few shrubs bloom. Many will continue to flower until frost. Some shrubs known for early spring bloom in cooler regions begin to bloom in the South as early as October—camellias, for instance. See Shrubs 23.

COMPANION PLANTINGS
Annuals and perennials: *Ageratum houstonianum* 'Blue Bedder', Flossflower; *Chrysanthemum × morifolium* cvs. 'Grandchild', 'Illusion'; *Lantana montevidensis*, Trailing Lantana; *Lavandula angustifolia* 'Hidcote', English Lavender; *Nigella damascena*, Love-in-a-mist; *Sanvitalia procumbens*, Trailing Sanvitalia; *Tagetes patula*, French Marigold.

ABELIA *ah-**beel**-ee-uh*
× *grandiflora* 'Edward Goucher' — Zones 5–9.

Dense, rounded, multi-stemmed shrub that bears a profusion of purple-pink flowers through summer until frost. Long-lasting leaves turn purplish bronze

Abelia × grandiflora. (Neumann)

in late fall. Semievergreen except in the South where leaves may persist through winter. Good bank cover and hedge. Prefers well-drained soil in the acid range, but is versatile as to pH. Prune winter-killed growth in spring; blooms on new growth.

MATURE HEIGHT: 5'
GROWTH RATE: fast/medium
LIGHT: full sun, semi-sunny
MOISTURE: roots moist

BUDDLEIA *bud-lee-uh*
davidii Summer Lilac   Zones 6–9.

Large deciduous shrub with narrow gray green leaves to 10 inches long. Valued for fragrant lavender flowers with an orange eye, in dense 1-foot spikes from July to fall. Cultivar colors range from white to dark purple. Attracts bees, hummingbirds, and butterflies. For best bloom and height control, prune to the ground each spring; blooms on new wood, and bushes quickly recover. Thrives in fertile, well-drained, neutral-range soil.

MATURE HEIGHT: 20'
GROWTH RATE: fast
LIGHT: full sun
MOISTURE: versatile

ERICA *ehr-ik-uh*
vagans Cornish Heath   Zones 5–9.

Low, spreading, evergreen shrub with needlelike leaves. Bears tiny tubular flowers from July to October in pinkish clusters to 6 inches long. Best massed; good ground cover for border corners and rock garden. Flourishes in well-drained, acid-range soil, pH 5.0 to 6.0, with high organic content. Some well-established cultivars are 'Alba' and 'Lyonesse', white; 'Mrs. D. F. Maxwell', cherry red; 'St. Keverne', deep pink.

MATURE HEIGHT: 1'
GROWTH RATE: fast
LIGHT: full sun, semi-sunny
MOISTURE: roots moist

HIBISCUS *hye-bisk-us*

Tall, deciduous and evergreen shrubs that bear a profusion of short-lived flowers. Need well-drained sandy loam, pH 5.5 to 7.0, with high organic content. Good container and espalier subjects.

LIGHT: full sun, semi-sunny
MOISTURE: soil surface moist

H. rosa-sinensis Chinese Hibiscus
Zones 9–10.
For warm regions of Texas, Florida, and California. Fast-growing evergreen 6 to 8 feet tall, with very showy year-round flowers in red, yellow, orange, white, sometimes with a contrasting eye and a variety of shadings, to 6 inches in diameter, single or double. Used as specimen and for hedges. Requires full sun and frequent fertilization. The flowers last only one day, but appear constantly. Container plant

Buddleia davidii, Summer Lilac.

in the North, where it is wintered indoors in a sunny window.

H. schizopetalus Japanese Hibiscus,
Fringed Hibiscus   Zones 9–10.
Gorgeous fringed, pendant flowers and a weeping habit. Fast-growing evergreen 8 to 12 feet tall, for specimen use.

H. syriacus 'Diane' Rose-of-Sharon,
Shrub Althaea   Zones 5–8.
Erect shrub to 8 feet tall and 5 feet wide. Flowers are pure white, 4 to 6 inches in diameter, with waxy, heavily ruffled petals crinkled on the margin. Specimen plant, or use in groups as background or hedge. Strong, dense branching makes it attractive in winter. 'Helene' and 'Minerva' are good newcomers. Hardy farther north in a protected corner.

HYPERICUM *hye-pehr-ik-um*
prolificum Broombrush,
Shrubby St.-John's-wort   Zones 4–8.

Small woody shrub or ground cover, valued for summer-long golden yellow flowers resembling small

Hibiscus 'Diana'. (Neumann)

single roses. 'Hidcote' has larger flowers, but may die to the ground in winter in unprotected places. Does well in dry, rocky soil, and tolerates some alkalinity. Set out container plants. Early spring shearing encourages masses of blooms.

MATURE HEIGHT: 3'–5'
GROWTH RATE: medium
LIGHT: full sun, semi-sunny
MOISTURE: versatile

LAGERSTROEMIA *lay-gur-streem-ee-uh* indica Crape Myrtle   Zones 7–9.

Southern, deciduous, small, multi-stemmed, very wide, flowering trees or large shrubs. The bark of this species is mottled light tan to gray, and very smooth. In late summer branches are tipped with big upright flowering panicles. The beautiful, newly disease- and mildew-resistant hybrids of *indica* × *fauriei* are white through melting tones of pink, lavender, and melon, to red and purple and have exfoliating bark, cinnamon to brown. Some have colorful foliage in fall. To limit height, some gardeners cut the plants to the ground in early spring, sacrificing the bark. Crape myrtles leaf out late in spring, especially when new. They prefer moist, heavy loam and clay soils in the acid range, pH 5.0 to 6.5. Provide a moisture-retaining mulch: do no late season (fall) watering. If killed back by frosts, they are likely to send up new shoots in succeeding years. Magnificent massed, and good for informal hedges or specimen planting. Small and medium-size crape myrtles are good container plants for outdoors.

In coming years look for the many exquisite, mildew-resistant shrubby or treelike crape myrtles introduced by Donald Egolf, and released to the nursery trade by the National Arboretum. They were made possible by hybridization of *L. indica* with *L. fauriei*, a species collected by Dr. John Creech, former director of the National Arboretum, from a cold site 1,200 feet above sea level in the mountain forests above Kurio, Yakushima, Japan. The plants described

Lagerstroemia indica, Crape Myrtle. (Neumann)

here are all hybrids of *L. indica* × *L. fauriei*, shrublike in growth.

GROWTH RATE: fast/medium
LIGHT: full sun
MOISTURE: roots moist

'Apalachee': dense branching, bark exfoliates exposing cinnamon to chestnut brown bark; light lavender flowers. Fall foliage from green through orange and russet to dark red. Slow grower, just 12 feet in 12 years.

Among introductions now with nurserymen are: 'Catawba', 6 to 8 feet tall and as wide, purple; 'Cherokee', to 12 feet, red; 'Powhatan', 6 by 6 feet, medium purple; 'Seminole'; to 8 feet, 7 wide, clear pink; 'Tuscarora', to 15 feet, coral pink flowers, orange-red leaves in fall, and striking bark.

In a few years look for semi-dwarfs combining mildew resistance, fine, textured foliage brilliantly colored in autumn, and densely branched, compact growth. They are named 'Acoma', 'Hopi', 'Pecos', 'Potomac', and 'Zuni'; their flowers are white, clear light pink, medium pink, and medium lavender. Heights from 7 to 9 or 10 feet. 'Scarlett O'Hara' is darker red and shorter. For taller cultivars, see Trees 1 and Trees 3.

POTENTILLA *poh-ten-till-uh* fruticosa Shrubby Cinquefoil   Zones 2–7.

Almost indestructible low bush and ground cover, valued for small, bright yellow blooms, like big buttercups, June through frost. Needs little care once established in an open, sunny site. Profits from occasional pruning. Some established cultivars are: 'Coronation Triumph', a 4-foot shrub bearing many yellow flowers. Does well in Midwest. 'Katherine Dykes', fine 3-foot shrub that arches and spreads, and has lemon yellow flowers 1 inch across; 'Knaphill', dense, low mounded form, that bears a profusion of small yellow flowers. Rated highly for the Midwest. Tolerates some drought.

MATURE HEIGHT: 10"–4'
GROWTH RATE: medium
LIGHT: full sun

SEE ALSO:
Camellia, Shrubs 23
Hydrangea arborescens 'Grandiflora', Hills-of-snow, Shrubs 22
Hydrangea macrophylla, Bigleaf Hydrangea, French Hydrangea, Shrubs 11
Hydrangea paniculata 'Grandiflora', Peegee Hydrangea, Shrubs 22
Hydrangea quercifolia, Oak-leaved Hydrangea, Shrubs 22
Lonicera tatarica, Tatarian Honeysuckle, Shrubs 15
Osmanthus × *fortunei*, Shrubs 15
Osmanthus heterophyllus, Holly Olive, Chinese Olive, Shrubs 15

ALTERNATES:
Aesculus parviflora, Buckeye, Bottlebrush Buckeye
Caryopteris × *clandonensis*, Bluebeard
Nerium oleander, Oleander
Spiraea × *bumalda* 'Anthony Waterer', 'Froebellii', Spiraea
Spiraea × *vanhouttei*, Bridal-wreath
Tamarix ramosissima, Tamarisk, Salt Cedar

SHRUBS 6
SHRUB ROSES

The rose was designated by Congress as the nation's floral emblem in 1987. The extraordinary beauty and spring-to-fall blooming period of the modern rose have made it the most popular flower in America. The roses here are hardy and as free of problems as roses ever are—really quite disease-resistant and low in maintenance needs.

Polyantha and miniature roses, and roses for hedges are discussed in Shrubs 19; Climbers in Vines 2; Old Garden Roses in Herbs 7.

COMPANION PLANTINGS
Spring-flowering bulbs: *Narcissus* × *odorus,* Campernelle Jonquil; *N. poeticus,* Poet's Narcissus, Pheasant's-eye; fringed white Parrot Tulip, such as 'Madonna'; Peony-flowered Tulips (late, double), such as 'Angelique'; large, pink single late tulips, such as 'Pink Diamond'.
Perennials and annuals: *Lavandula angustifolia* 'Hidcote', English Lavender; *Salvia farinacea* 'Blue Bedder', Mealycup Sage; *S. officinalis* 'Albiflora', White Garden Sage.
Edging annuals: *Zinnia*, 'Peter Pan', 'Lilliput', or 'Tom Thumb', gold and white; 'Small World Pink' or 'Fantastic Light Pink'.

ROSA *roh-zuh* Rose

The wonderful everblooming characteristic of modern roses is the gift of hybridizers who crossed fragrant, hardy, Old Garden Roses that bloom only in spring with roses from warm regions of China that bloom all season. In extensive field tests conducted by the American Rose Society, the varieties listed here have performed well in all regions of the United States. They are winter-hardy down to about 0° F when protected by mulch or soil mounds and windbreaks. In regions of subzero winters, Styrofoam or other insulated covers are necessary for winter survival. The varieties listed here that won "The All-American Rose Selections Award" in the American Rose Society trials are identified by the letters "AARS" and year of the award.

There are two classifications of roses here: the large-flowered, exquisite Hybrid Teas (HT), which bloom singly or in small clusters on long stems; and the showy Floribundas (FL) which produce masses of somewhat smaller roses in clusters. All have been bred for all-season blooming, but production slows in the hottest months.

Rose culture varies according to region. The following is very general information that will benefit by instruction from a local rose society or informed nurseryman.

All roses require well-drained, deeply prepared (18 inches deep at least), rich organic soil, ample fertilizer in early spring and throughout the early summer, and moist soil around the roots. At least 6 hours of full sun are essential for maximum flower production; with only 4 to 5 hours of sun, blooming is sparse.

Prepare a planting hole the size of a bushel basket. Set hybrid roses so the bud union is 2 inches above the soil level. Apply mulch almost to the stem. Every 7 to 10 days and after every heavy rainfall apply an all-purpose rose spray that controls insects and dis-

Rosa 'Pascali'. (McDonald)

well throughout the summer. Very hardy and disease-resistant.

'Touch of Class' (HT) AARS 1986
Very elegant rose for the gardener interested in flower exhibitions and garden shows. The slightly fragrant tricolored flower is huge, 4½ to 5 inches across, pink, coral, and cream. Sturdy, upright shrub, well shaped and reaches 4 to 5 feet. Hardy and considerably resistant to disease.

FOR FRAGRANCE

'Fragrant Cloud' (HT)
Strikingly colorful coral-red blossoms, famous for their strong fragrance. Many, many large, well-formed blooms all season on erect, shapely shrubs 3 to 4 feet tall. Hardy, disease-resistant.

'Miss All-American Beauty' (HT) AARS 1968
Big, eye-catching, very fragrant, many-petaled, deep pink flowers. The plant is bushy and vigorous, 4 to 5 feet tall, winter-hardy and disease-resistant.

'Double Delight' (HT) AARS 1977
Has everything a rose can offer, including exceptional spicy fragrance, long stems, and season-long bloom. In bud the rose is urn-shaped. It opens into a magnificent 5-inch flower, white brushed with rich red. The broad, 3½- to 4-foot plant is upright and

ease. They're sold in atomizers that are easy to use. Once a week drench each plant with a gallon of water mixed with ¼ teaspoon of houseplant fertilizer. Continue until the middle of August, then stop feeding so they can harden up for winter.

When cutting roses for bouquets, leave a 5-leaf, outward-facing sprig on each shoot as a base for the new shoots. Remove all suckers growing from below the bud union as soon as they appear.

Make all cuts ½ inch above the bud eye or sprig.

Spring-flowering roses bloom on side shoots that develop from wood maturing in late summer. Those are the growing points that through winter will be forming flowers. Do any pruning right after blooming ends, but not later.

Roses that bloom all season or on new wood are pruned after real cold settles in in late fall. Remove weak canes and cut back healthy canes to 2 feet. In spring when the buds are breaking, prune back to 12 to 18 inches.

BEAUTIFULLY FORMED ROSES FOR CUTTING

Hybrid Tea roses are long-stemmed roses growing on leggy plants 3 to 6 feet high. They don't flower as freely as other classifications. Perfection in each bloom is their main feature. Growers often disbud to increase the size of remaining blooms.

'Olympiad' (HT) AARS 1984
Medium-size plant, 4 to 5 feet tall, with lovely foliage that is dark green and glossy. The slightly fragrant flower is bright red and very large, 4 to 4½ inches across. Lasts well on the plant and when cut. Exceptionally disease-resistant and hardy.

'Pascali' (HT) AARS 1969
This famous white rose blooms on an upright shrub 3½ to 4 feet tall and has large, glossy, dark green leaves. The long-lasting many-petaled rose flower is exquisite in bud and perfect in form. 'Pascali' blooms

Rosa 'Touch of Class'. All-America Rose Selections.

Rosa 'Miss All-American Beauty'.

winter-hardy. In areas where mildew is prevalent, the plant will need mildew protection.

'Sunsprite' (FL)
Compact, with masses of very fragrant, long-lasting, deep yellow flowers throughout the season. The plant is upright, 2½ to 3 feet tall at maturity, and very hardy and disease-resistant.

FOR MASSES OF COLOR
Floribunda means "abundantly flowering." The flower form varies: some floribundas are shaped like tea roses, and others like cabbage roses. The flowers generally are smaller than those of the teas. Good for bouquets, but mainly for garden show.

'Showbiz' (FL) AARS 1985
Low, spreading plant, 2½ to 3 feet tall, with quite lovely foliage that is dark green and glossy. The roses are plentiful all season, long lasting, medium red, borne in clusters. Winter-hardy and disease-resistant.

'Redgold' (FL) AARS 1971
Compact, medium plant, 3 to 4 feet tall, with a continuous show of brilliant orange-pink flowers exquisitely edged with gold from June until frost. The blooms are 3 inches across, moderately double.

'Trumpeter' (FL)
For a long period in spring, 'Trumpeter' glows with masses of bright orange red roses borne in clusters; good repeat blooming in summer and fall. Compact

plant, 3½ to 4½ feet, well shaped and sturdy. Disease-resistant and winter-hardy.

SEE ALSO:
Climbing Roses, Vines 2
Hedge, and Polyantha and Miniature Roses, Shrubs 19
Old Garden Roses, Herbs 7

SHRUBS 7
BROADLEAVED AND NEEDLED EVERGREEN SHRUBS

Here are the great evergreen shrubs. Combine needled and broadleaved evergreens to give rich variety to the garden. Some especially suited to hedges are described in Shrubs 18. The beautiful flowering rhododendrons and azaleas are in Shrubs 2 and Shrubs 3. Evergreens aren't really green forever: they drop and replace foliage but in very long cycles, 18 months to several years in the case of hemlock. Many evergreens prefer soils in the acid range.

COMPANION PLANTINGS
Background plant: *Betula papyrifera,* Canoe Birch, White Birch, Paper Birch.
Shrubs: *Heliotropium arborescens,* Heliotrope; *Hibiscus rosa-sinensis*, Chinese Hibiscus; *Rosa canina,* Dog Rose.
Flowers: *Achillea filipendula* 'Coronation Gold', Fern-leaved Yarrow; *Centaurea cyanus,* Cornflower, Bachelor's-button; *Consolida ambigua* (syn. *Delphinium ajacis)*, Rocket Larkspur.
Ground cover: *Pachysandra terminalis*, Japanese Pachysandra.

Rosa 'Showbiz'. All-America Rose Selections.

Aucuba japonica 'Crotonifolia'. (Neumann)

AUCUBA *aw-kew-buh*
japonica 'Variegata'   Gold-dust Tree
Zones 6–8.

Dioecious, rounded, evergreen shrub successful in shade, even deep shade. It has large bright green leaves which are flecked with yellow in 'Variegata', a female; 'Maculata' has leaves blotched yellow-white and is male. The female produces large red berries that persist into winter. Prefers well-drained soil with high organic content. Two other established cultivars are 'Crotonifolia', whose leaves are dusted with white spots, and 'Picturata', which has deep green leaves with a large yellow blotch in the centers.

MATURE HEIGHT: 6'–10'
GROWTH RATE: medium
LIGHT: semi-sunny, shade
MOISTURE: roots moist

BERBERIS *ber-ber-iss*
verruculosa   Barberry   Zones 6–8.

Compact and delicate, with glossy dark green leaves that are whitish underneath. Golden yellow flowers in early spring followed by blue-black fruit with bloom. Turns bronze in fall. Excellent for banks and edging. Prefers neutral-range soils, pH 6.0 to 8.0.

MATURE HEIGHT: 3'
GROWTH RATE: slow
LIGHT: full sun, semi-sunny
MOISTURE: roots moist

BUXUS *bux-us*   Box, Boxwood

Superb little-leaved formal evergreens from low shrubs to small trees, valuable as foundation plants or specimens, and excellent for group plantings and hedges. They are slow growing, long lived, and transplant very easily. Used in nearly all formal and knot gardens, herb plantings, and estate landscapes. Boxwood takes pruning particularly well and is a favorite subject for topiary treatment. Prefers well-drained

soil and can grow in semi-sun. Mulch with peat moss or leaf mold to keep the roots cool. Do not cultivate around the plants as the roots are near the surface. Prefers neutral-range soils, pH 6.0 to 8.0.

GROWTH RATE: slow
LIGHT: full sun, semi-sunny
MOISTURE: roots moist

B. microphylla   Japanese Box   Zones 6–9.
Natural height is 3 to 4 feet, with an equal spread. 'Compacta' is especially low. 'Tide Hill' grows to 2 feet and is likely to be more than twice as wide. 'Morris Midget' is a compact edger.

B. sempervirens 'Suffruticosa'   Edging Box,
Dwarf Box   Zones 5–9.
Some 150-year-old plants are only 3 feet high. This plant may be pruned to just a few inches high, but left alone will grow to 4 or 5 feet after a number of years.

Buxus sempervirens 'Suffruticosa', Edging Box.

The small leaves are quite aromatic. It has been valued since colonial times.

CEANOTHUS *see-an-nohth-us*
× *delilianus*   Zones 7–9.

The genus is lilaclike, including flowering deciduous and evergreen shrubs and small trees hardy in mild climates, from British Columbia to southern California. This hybrid is an evergreen shrub to 3 feet tall, valued for its dark to pale blue flowers in April. Look for established cultivars such as 'Gloire de Versailles', pale blue, and 'Gloire de Plantieres', dark blue. This is a hybrid of *C. americanus*, which prefers slightly acid soil. Prune deciduous species in spring to maintain compact, attractive growth. Successful in any well-drained soil and withstands droughts. Good espalier plant.

GROWTH RATE: medium
LIGHT: full sun
MOISTURE: roots moist, versatile

CHAMAECYPARIS *kam-ee-sip-ar-iss*
obtusa 'Nana Aurea'
Dwarf Golden Hinoki Cypress   Zones 5–9.

A genus of tall evergreen trees, but there are useful slow- and low-growing forms. This cultivar is a compact semi-dwarf under 10 feet, with golden foliage. 'Nana Gracilis' has deep green, lustrous foliage, and reaches to 4 to 6 feet. 'Pygmaea' is a lovely dwarf with bronzy green leaves that grows very slowly to about 3 feet.

GROWTH RATE: slow
LIGHT: full sun
MOISTURE: roots moist

ELAEAGNUS *el-ee-ag-nus*
pungens 'Maculata'   Thorny Elaeagnus
Zones 7–9.

Medium to large shrub whose leaves have a deep yellow blotch of variable size. The flowers are silvery

Elaeagnus pungens, Thorny Elaeagnus. (Neumann)

white, with a fine fragrance, and appear in October. Fruit in spring. If the leaves on branches fail to variegate, cut these branches out at once. Useful for highway plantings, to naturalize on banks, and as barriers and tall hedges. Requires pruning to maintain an attractive shape when used as a specimen. Tolerates exposure at the seashore and poor soils. Thrives in light, sandy loam.

MATURE HEIGHT: 10'–12'
GROWTH RATE: fast
LIGHT: full sun
MOISTURE: versatile

ILEX eye-lex Holly

Hollies are beautiful evergreen or deciduous shrubs and trees (*I. latifolia,* Luster-leaf Holly, reaches 60 feet). Valued for brilliant fall and winter display of red fruit attractive to robins and other birds. Most are hardy only in Zones 4 to 7 and south. Leaf form varies from small, smooth, and shiny to large and very spiny—like the hollies that are a symbol of Christmas. Leaf color is green, except in some beautifully variegated clones of English holly (*I. aquifolium* 'Argenteo-marginata', 'Aureo-marginata', Trees 6). Some have red berries, some have yellow or black. Hollies are dioecious and most require a pollinator. Need well-drained soil and are best in semi-sun. See also Shrubs 11, 14, and 16.

GROWTH RATE: medium
LIGHT: full sun, semi-sunny
MOISTURE: roots moist

I. cornuta 'Burfordii' Burford's Chinese Holly, Burford Horned Holly Zones 7–9.
Cultivar to 10 feet tall with fine foliage that has one or two "teeth"; the small, round, long-lasting fruits are glossy red and can occur without pollination. Handsome specimen for foundation planting. 'China Girl' is an evergreen with glossy, rich green foliage and an abundance of red fruits in fall; 'China Boy' is the

male pollinator; both are hardy to Zone 5. Height 5 to 6 feet. See also Shrubs 11. The variety *rotunda* slowly grows to 5 feet and has an excellent globe form that needs no pruning.

I. crenata Japanese Holly Zones 5–8.
Black-berried species that grows slowly to 4 feet though some can reach 25 feet, and some just 12 inches. Among cultivars 1 to 4 feet tall is 'Helleri', a bushy, slow-growing dwarf female, excellent for edgings, rock gardens, driveway borders, or foundation plantings. *I. c.* 'Golden Heller' is golden. 'Glory', a small male plant, is a good pollinator. 'Tiny Tim' is considered hardier than these. 'Convexa' has small leaves, is hardy, takes pruning, and makes a good formal hedge. It is a female clone and produces fruits in profusion.

I. 'Nellie R. Stevens' Zones 6–9.
Best holly for hedges, a tall evergreen shrub or small, pyramidal tree 15 to 25 feet high with pretty leaves and red berries. It can be pollinated by any nearby male of the species that flowers at a similar time. 'Edward J. Stevens' is a large male clone useful for pollinating Nellie.

I. vomitoria 'Gulftide' Yaupon Holly Zones 7–10.
Low-growing improved cultivar with beautiful scarlet berries borne in profusion. To 5 feet. Established cultivars excellent for southern gardens are 'Emily Brunner' and its pollinator 'James Swann', both introduced by Shadow Nurseries.

JUNIPERUS joo-nip-er-us Juniper

Mostly small conifers, with needlelike or scalelike leaves. The male cones are yellow, like catkins, and the female fruits are berries. It is a woody, evergreen genus including 60-foot trees, shrubs, and ground-hugging plants a few inches to 2 feet high with a spread of 4 to 8 feet. The low-growing junipers have long, elegant, highly textured, gracefully layered branches. Foliage colors range from gray blue, green-blue, to light green tipped with gold. Some take on purple hues in winter. The species below are superb evergreen ground covers that thrive even in sunny, hot, dry locations and in almost any well-drained soil. A spreading root system makes junipers easy to transplant. Some blight exists: choose blight-resistant cultivars recommended by local nurseries. Set out container plants in spring or fall. See also Trees 4.

GROWTH RATE: medium
LIGHT: full sun
MOISTURE: versatile

J. chinensis var. **sargentii** Sargent's Juniper Zones 3–9.
Mound-forming juniper about 2 to 3 feet high, with a spread of 8 to 10 feet. The cultivar 'Glauca' has feathery blue-green leaves. It succeeds even in limestone soils. Also listed by authorities as *J. sargentii* and *J. sargentii* 'Glauca'.

J. conferta Shore Juniper Zones 5–9.
Vigorous, trailing juniper 12 to 28 inches high, with dense bluish green foliage and black fruits. It hugs the ground and flourishes in full sun, sandy soils, and harsh seaside conditions. 'Emerald Sea' is an excellent cultivar, free of the tendency to dieback typical of some. Set out container plants in spring.

Ilex cornuta 'Burfordii', Burford Chinese Holly.

Ilex crenata, Japanese Holly. (Neumann)

Juniperus horizontalis 'Wiltonii', Blue Rug Creeping Juniper. (Neumann)

J. horizontalis 'Wiltonii'
Blue Rug Creeping Juniper   **Zones 3–9.**
A flat, trailing juniper 6 inches high that spreads 8 to 12 inches per year, and has intense silver-blue foliage tinted purple in winter, and blue fruit. Stands up to hot sun in southern California, where it is considered the finest of the prostrate junipers. There are some slightly taller cultivars: 'Douglasii', Waukegan Juniper, has steel blue foliage that gradually turns purple in fall and is a good choice for sandy soils. 'Bar Harbor' is a low-growing form about 1 foot tall, that spreads to 6 to 8 feet. It has gray green foliage tinted purple in winter, and blue fruit. The species prefers soils in the acid range, pH 5.0. Effective among rocks and good under seashore conditions.

J. × media   Juniper Hybrid   Zones 3–9.
The cultivar 'Sea Spray', a sport of 'Pfitzerana Glauca', Blue Pfitzer Juniper, has blue-green foliage, is under 1 foot tall, hardy to −20° F, and resists blight and root rots. 'Pfitzerana Compacta', Dwarf Pfitzer

Juniper, grows 1 to 3 feet tall and is gray green. The branches of 'Pfitzerana Aurea', Golden Pfitzer Juniper, are tipped with gold when new.

J. sabina   Savin Juniper   Zones 3–7.
About 12 to 15 inches high, and notable for upward-reaching branches and an informal elegance. Choose blight-resistant cultivars such as 'Broadmoor', a soft grayish green; 'Moor-Dense', a compact Broadmoor; 'Skandia', pale grayish green; or 'Tamariscifolia No Blight', bluish green.

J. squamata   Singleseed Juniper   Zones 4–8.
'Blue Star', more mounded in habit, is 1½ to 2 feet high, an improved variety, slow-growing, with foliage that is a rich silvery blue. A favorite ground cover in northern California and similar climates. 'Variegata'

is a prostrate, spreading variety under 12 inches high with cream-colored new growth. Good in the South but won't tolerate the heat of the Southwest.

KALMIA   *kal-mee-uh*

The laurels are handsome evergreen understory shrubs most successful in moist, well-drained, acid soils rich in organic matter. They bear lovely white, pink, or variegated blooms in mid- to late spring. Remove faded flowers at once. Mulch to maintain moisture. Prefer acid-range soils, pH 5.0 to 6.0.

GROWTH RATE: slow
LIGHT: full sun, semi-sunny
MOISTURE: roots moist

K. angustifolia   Sheep Laurel   Zones 2–8.
Small, to 2 feet tall, with blue-green leaves and rose pinjto purplish crimson flowers late spring to early summer. It grows on rocky barrens and in old pastures, often in semi-shade. There is a white-flowered form.

K. latifolia   Mountain Laurel   Zones 4–9.
Tall, handsome evergreen shrub, 7 to 8 feet tall in cultivation. It has leathery leaves and produces a profusion of lovely white, pink, or variegated blooms in late spring. Prefers moist, well-drained, acid-range, organic soils. In nutrient-deficient soils and full sun it develops leaf spot. Remove faded flowers at once. Mulch to maintain moisture. 'Ostbo Red' is a red-budded clone, considered the best of all. May be easier to find in West Coast nurseries. 'Elf', a dwarf form to 3 feet high, is evergreen and bears a profusion of lovely dark pink blooms in late spring.

MAHONIA   *muh-hoh-nee-uh*
Oregon Grape

The mahonias are handsome shrubs with coarse-textured, hollylike, shiny evergreen leaves good in light shade. They bear fragrant clusters of small yellow flowers in late winter or early spring, followed by blue-black grapelike fruit with a silvery bloom.

Juniperus conferta, Shore Juniper. (Neumann)

Kalmia latifolia, Mountain Laurel. (Neumann)

Mahonia bealei, Leatherleaf Mahonia.

The leaves bronze in fall. Keep pruned to about 3 feet or the plants become awkward.

MATURE HEIGHT: 3'–6'
GROWTH RATE: medium
LIGHT: semi-sunny
MOISTURE: soil surface damp

M. aquifolium   Zones 5–8.
The dark evergreen leaves turn a beautiful bronze in autumn. Ask for asexually propagated plants, which are sure to have shiny leaves. The species height is to 3 feet, but there are dwarfs.

M. bealei Leatherleaf Mahonia Zones 6–8.
Yellow fragrant flowers appear in spikes followed by blue, grapelike fruits. The hollylike leaves of this species don't bronze in fall but it is an excellent choice for shade.

M. repens Creeping Oregon Grape
                                              Zones 5–8.
Shiny, hardy, low-growing native evergreen species about 10 inches tall that makes an excellent ground cover for shade.

NANDINA *nan-dye-nuh*
domestica Heavenly Bamboo Zones 6–9.

Airy, graceful shrub whose long narrow leaves remain evergreen. Loose clusters of whitish florets appear in spring, followed in autumn by brilliant red berries in drooping clusters. They are showier than those of holly and remain all winter. Dense enough for good screening, and a specimen plant. When grown in sunny situations, leaves color maroon to orange-red in cold weather. Lovely with *Betula papyrifera*, Canoe Birch (see Trees 1) and *Juniperus* ground covers (see Ground Covers 3). 'Fire Power', 'Harbor Dwarf', and 'Woods Dwarf' are resistant cultivars that grow to about 3 feet and have good winter color. Good container plant.

MATURE HEIGHT: 8'
GROWTH RATE: fast/medium
LIGHT: full sun, semi-sunny, shade
MOISTURE: roots moist

Nandina domestica, Heavenly Bamboo. (Neumann)

PICEA *pye-see-uh* Spruce

Tall needled evergreens with the aromatic, rigid needles and form associated with Christmas trees. Pyramidal with whorled branches. There are a few shrub-size forms. They thrive in open situations, in well-drained but not-too-dry soil. Prefer soils in the acid range, pH 5.0 to 6.0.

GROWTH RATE: medium/slow
LIGHT: full sun
MOISTURE: roots moist

P. abies 'Nidiformis' Bird's Nest Spruce
                                              Zones 2–8.
Slow-growing cultivar reaches 3 to 6 feet tall after 24 years.

P. glauca 'Conica' White Spruce Zones 3–8.
Slow-growing dwarf from 10 to 15 feet with compact pyramidal habit and light bluish green needles.

P. pungens 'Fat Albert'
Colorado Blue Spruce   Zones 3–8.
Reaches 10 feet in 10 years; needles are bright blue in summer and hold their color throughout the year.

Thrives in well-drained soil and tolerates some drought. 'R. H. Montgomery' is silver-blue and under 5 feet at maturity.

PIERIS *pye-eer-iss*

Valuable, hardy, evergreen shrubs or small trees with showy buds all winter and drooping clusters of urn-shaped flowers in spring. New foliage is bronzy. Most beautiful where it has some protection from wind and full sun. Prefers well-drained acid soil, pH 4.0 to 5.0, with lots of organic matter.

GROWTH RATE: slow
LIGHT: semi-sunny
MOISTURE: roots moist

P. floribunda Fetterbush,
Mountain Andromeda   Zones 5–8.
Shapely, pendulous shrub with upright pearly buds in late winter, unfolding to white or pink in mid-spring. Showy leaves. Good as a specimen and in foundation plantings.

P. japonica 'Red Mill' Lily-of-the-valley Bush
                                              Zones 5–8.
Tall species, to 9 feet. New foliage is red, fading to green as the season advances. Needs some sun for full flowering. 'Variegata' is an attractive cultivar.

PINUS *pye-nus*
mugo var. *mugo* Mugho Pine Zones 2–8.

A slow-growing conifer known for its persistent, long, needlelike leaves sheathed in bundles, one of the few shrublike pines. It can reach 8 to 10 feet in height and is broad-spreading. It is a superior landscape plant but may be subject to scale; buy resistant cultivars. The pines will grow in dry, sandy soils where little else grows, but they are sensitive to air pollution. Most require somewhat acid soil, pH 5.0 to 6.0.

Pieris japonica, Lily-of-the-valley Bush. (Neumann)

GROWTH RATE: medium/slow
LIGHT: full sun
MOISTURE: roots moist, versatile

SKIMMIA *skim-ee-uh*

Dwarf, shade-loving evergreen shrubs whose leaves are aromatic when crushed. In early spring, or fall and winter in warm regions, there are clusters of small, somewhat fragrant flowers in upright panicles, followed by berrylike, inedible fruit. Some species are dioecious. Good urban and pot plants. Prefer moist, acid, sandy soil with lots of peat but will survive in alkaline conditions.

GROWTH RATE: slow
LIGHT: semi-sunny, shade
MOISTURE: roots moist

S. japonica   Zones 7–9.
Slow-growing, densely branched shrub 3 to 5 feet high, with yellowish white flowers borne by the female plant. Male flowers are larger and very fragrant. The species is dioecious and requires a male nearby to produce its bright red berries.

S. reevesiana   Zones 7–9.
Smaller plant, to 2 feet, with white flowers that are bisexual. One plant alone will fruit. Requires a rich, moist, acid soil.

TAXUS *tax-us* Yew

Stately trees and vigorous shrubs with narrow, needlelike leaves, used since the Roman times as lawn specimens, for hedges, and massing. It is considered the finest needled evergreen for landscaping. May be sheared and pruned repeatedly to maintain size and to shape topiaries and espaliers. Prefer alkaline soil, so are not good with azaleas and rhododendrons. Succeed in sun or shade, in moist, well-drained soil but need protection from strong winds. Usually dioecious. The female bears seeds with a fleshy red aril.

GROWTH RATE: fast
LIGHT: versatile
MOISTURE: roots moist, versatile

T. baccata 'Nana' Dwarf English Yew
                                                    Zones 6–8.
This dwarf form has darker needles than the species and grows to a compact pyramid, about 3 feet high. 'Pygmaea ' remains at something under 2 feet. 'Repandens' is wide with arching branches, 2 to 4 feet tall, and 12 to 15 wide. It is hardy to Zone 5.

T. baccata 'Standishii' Standish English Yew
                                                    Zones 6–7.
The best golden yew for small gardens; a fastigiate form. Grows to 25 feet, but slowly and may be kept small by shearing. Another cultivar, 'Washingtonii', to 15 feet and as wide, has open branches and leaves a rich gold that fades to yellow-green. Usually dioecious. Prefers moist, well-drained sandy loam. There are variegated and yellow forms that grow well in the Northwest and on the West Coast.

T. cuspidata 'Nana' Dwarf Japanese Yew
                                                    Zones 4–8.
One of the best varieties, it grows very slowly to 6 feet, usually is female, dense and compact. 'Densa' has very dense and wide-spreading branches, and an

old plant may be 4 feet by 20 across. It is a little lower than 'Nana'.

T. × media 'Brownii' Brown's Yew Zones 4–7.
Valuable, dense male clone that grows to about 9 by 12 feet in 20 years. Most shrub sizes are wider than they are tall, and many slow-growers have been named. 'Densiformis', the most dense, reaches 6 to 8 feet tall. 'Hatfieldii' grows to about 12 feet in 20 years. 'Hicksii', to 20 feet high after 15 to 20 years, is naturally columnar. 'Wardii' is dense, wide and flat, about 6 by 19 feet in 20 years. 'Kelseyi' grows to about 12 by 9 feet in 20 years and fruits early.

THUJA *thew-juh* Arborvitae

Lacy-leaved evergreen shrubs for foundation planting, specimens, and tall hedges and windbreaks. Formal, dense, clippable, and easy to grow. Height can be 40 to 60 feet, but more often is 12 to 15 feet. Best growth is on fertile, moist, well-drained soil. Choose established cultivars known to maintain good color in winter. Best-looking plants are in full sun, though they tolerate some shade.

GROWTH RATE: medium/slow
LIGHT: full sun, semi-sunny
MOISTURE: roots moist

T. occidentalis American Arborvitae
                                                    Zones 2–7/8.
In the North it can grow to 40 or 60 feet but is usually seen under 25. Needs lots of moisture and tolerates limestone soils. 'Wareana' is a handsome, hardy, slow-growing plant. Among several small cultivars, 'Hetz Junior' or 'Hetz Midget' is a rounded dwarf between 2 and 5 feet at maturity. Among golden forms are 'Rheingold', slow-growing to 10 feet, with golden yellow needlelike juvenile foliage, and 'Nigra', an improved compact strain with darker winter color. National Arboretum curator Sue Frost Martin recommends 'Emerald Green' for good winter color.

T. orientalis (listed as *Platycladus orientalis*)
Oriental Arborvitae   Zones 6–9.
Successful in the Southeast and Southwest. Smaller species, usually 18 to 25 feet high in cultivation, with grass green foliage when young, changing to a darker green as it matures. Needs less moisture than American arborvitae.

TSUGA *tsoo-guh*
canadensis 'Pendula'
Weeping Canadian Hemlock   Zones 3–7.

Feathery, dark-needled, graceful, slow-growing weeping hemlock that stays at shrub height, 10 to 20 feet. Twice as wide as it is tall. Shallow-rooted like other hemlocks, and easy to transplant and grow. Needs moisture and doesn't do well in hot dry summers. Prefers somewhat acid soil.

GROWTH RATE: slow
LIGHT: full sun, semi-sunny
MOISTURE: roots moist

SEE ALSO:
Azalea (*Rhododendron*) cvs., Shrubs 2
Camellia japonica, Shrubs 23
Camellia sasanqua, Shrubs 23

Gardenia jasminoides, Gardenia, Cape Jasmine, Shrubs 23
Laurus nobilis, Grecian Laurel, Sweet Bay, Herbs 1
Ligustrum japonicum (texanum) 'Silver Star', Waxleaf Privet, Japanese Privet, Shrubs 18
Ligustrum lucidum, Glossy Privet, Shrubs 18
Nerium oleander, Oleander, Rose-bay, Shrubs 18
Osmanthus × fortunei, Devil-weed, Shrubs 15
Osmanthus fragrans, Tea Olive, Sweet Olive, Shrubs 15
Osmanthus heterophyllus 'Gulftide', Holly Olive, Chinese Olive, Shrubs 15
Paxistima canbyi, Cliff Green, Mountain Lover, Ground Covers 2
Pyracantha coccinea, Fire Thorn, Shrubs 16
Rhododendron, Shrubs 3
Viburnum odoratissimum, Sweet Viburnum, Shrubs 4

ALTERNATES:
Calluna vulgaris, Heather
Cotoneaster salicifolius 'Autumn Fire', Willowleaf Cotoneaster
Daphne cneorum, Garland Flower
Daphne odora 'Aureo-marginata', Winter Daphne
Erica vagans, Cornish Heath
Euonymus fortunei
Gaultheria procumbens, Wintergreen, Checkerberry
Gaultheria veitchiana
Lonicera pileata, Privet Honeysuckle
Pernettya mucronata
Photinia × fraseri, Fraser's Photinia
Pittosporum tobira, Japanese Pittosporum
Prunus lauroc.erasus, Cherry Laurel
Ruscus aculeatus, Butcher's Broom, Box Holly
Santolina
Sarcococca hookeriana var. *humilis*, Sweet Box

SHRUBS 8
SHRUBS WITH RED FOLIAGE ALL SEASON

A few shrubs start the season red and remain red. The best are described here. But with the high heat of summer even these fade somewhat toward green before turning brilliant red in the fall. The very best cultivars are a beautiful crimson, breathtaking when the sun shines through new leaf tips. Some require full sun to achieve their color potential.

COMPANION PLANTINGS
Trees: *Acer rubrum* 'October Glory', Red Maple; *Sophora japonica*, Japanese Pagoda Tree.
Shrubs: *Chionanthus retusus*, Fringe Tree; Dwarf white azaleas.
Spring bulbs: *Crocus* cvs., blue and white; *Tulipa fosterana*, 'White Emperor', 'Red Emperor'; white Parrot tulips.
Flowers: *Ceratostigma plumbaginoides*, Blue Ceratostigma, Plumbago; *Chrysanthemum*, white and gold; *Impatiens*, white; *Veronica spicata*, 'Sunny

Borders', Speedwell.
Herb: *Lavandula angustifolia* 'Hidcote', English Lavender.

ACER *ay-ser*
palmatum 'Dissectum Atropurpureum'
Threadleaf Japanese Maple   Zones 5/6–8.

Valuable, elegant, deciduous ornamental with beautiful leaves. It is grown as a bonsai, tub plant, and specimen. The species includes trees that reach to 50 feet in the wild on the East Coast, as well as shrub-size plants. Some cultivars are green-leaved and become brilliant red or orange in fall; others, very red in spring, fade toward green in summer. The leaves of those known as "dissectum" are very fine and deeply cut. At maturity, this cultivar is a sculptural, rounded mound 6 to 8 feet tall, with pendulous branches and exquisitely cut leaves that are bloodred in spring, hold their color better than others in summer, and color again brilliantly when cold comes. Requires fairly constant moisture, and well-drained soil. In warm regions, leaves may burn in full sun: afford some protection. 'Crimson Queen' is just 4 to 6 feet tall, an unusual and attractive dwarf weeping form with excellent summer color. Prefers acid-range, well-drained soil. 'Dissectum Variegatum' is a weeping variegated form. There are many variegated green, pink, and white. Established cultivars with yellow foliage include 'Osakazuki', whose leaves turn bloodred in autumn.

GROWTH RATE:	medium/slow
LIGHT:	full sun, semi-sunny
MOISTURE:	roots moist

BERBERIS *ber-ber-iss*
Barberry thunbergii 'Crimson Pygmy'
Japanese Barberry   Zones 5–8.

A low, dense plant 3 to 6 feet tall and often wider than it is tall, with brilliant fall color especially when growing in full sun. One of the first to leaf out in spring. Superb hedge plant. Deciduous.

Berberis thunbergii 'Crimson Pygmy'. (Neumann)

GROWTH RATE:	slow
LIGHT:	full sun, semi-sunny
MOISTURE:	roots moist

CORYLUS *kor-il-us*
maxima 'Purpurea'   Purple Giant Filbert
Zones 4–7.

Tall deciduous shrub grown for its dark purple leaves, to 6 inches long. Color fades toward green in high heat. Prefers rich, well-drained soil, and some protection from north winds. Colors best when grown in full sun.

MATURE HEIGHT:	15'
GROWTH RATE:	medium
LIGHT:	full sun
MOISTURE:	roots moist

Cotinus coggygria, Smoke Tree.

COTINUS *kot-tine-us*
coggygria   Smoke Tree, Smokebush
Zones 4/5–9.

Tall shrubs whose size, color, and leaf form harmonize with the barberries. Effective specimens almost as wide as they are tall, often planted as tall hedges. Leaves are pink-purple turning to yellow and orange in fall, and there are purplish red fruits. In summer it is enveloped in pink-gray fruiting panicles 6 to 10 inches long. Bark at maturity is corky and beautiful. Fall foliage is brilliant orange-red. Interesting cultivars include 'Royal Purple', whose foliage unfolds from red to a rich purple that doesn't fade, and 'Notcutt's Variety' (synonym *rubrifolium*), a lighter purple.

MATURE HEIGHT:	15'
GROWTH RATE:	medium/slow
LIGHT:	full sun
MOISTURE:	versatile

PHORMIUM *form-ee-um*
tenax   New Zealand Flax   Zone 9.

Warm-climate ornamental, tender, with striking, tough, 9- by 5-inch-wide leathery leaves which separate at the apex and are red or orange on the margins. Clusters of angular-stemmed red flower spikes rising to 7 feet are held above the foliage. Prefers well-drained soil but tolerates moisture. Good at the seashore.

MATURE HEIGHT:	4'–5'
GROWTH RATE:	fast
LIGHT:	versatile
MOISTURE:	versatile

PRUNUS *proon-us*
spinosa var. *purpurea*   Blackthorn, Sloe
Zones 4–8.

Spiny shrub of dense growth with handsome bronzy red foliage. Good as specimen and in hedges and grows well in poor soils. Profusion of small pink flowers in early spring, and shiny black fruits in fall. 'Plena' is double-flowered. Thrives in well-drained sandy loam.

MATURE HEIGHT:	12'
GROWTH RATE:	medium
LIGHT:	full sun
MOISTURE:	roots moist

ALTERNATES:
Berberis × *ottawaensis* 'Purpurea', Barberry
Corylopsis pauciflora, Winter Hazel

SHRUBS 9
SHRUBS WITH YELLOW FOLIAGE ALL SEASON

Shrubs with yellow foliage add vibrant color to the garden, especially in spring. The best of them look from a distance as though they are covered with yellow flowers. The yellow may fade toward green in summer's high heat and return in fall.

Trees: *Acer macrophyllum*, Oregon Maple, Big-leaf Maple; *A. palmatum* 'Okushimo', Japanese Maple; *Parrotia persica*, Persian Parrotia.

Bulbs: *Crocus chrysanthus* 'E. A. Bowles'; *C.* 'Peter Pan'; *C. vernus* 'Remembrance'; *Galanthus nivalis*, Snowdrop; *Hyacinthus* cvs., white, yellow, blue; *Narcissus* cvs., white and yellow; *Tulipa* cvs., white Parrot Tulips.

Flowers: *Chrysanthemum* cvs., white, russet, red; *Hemerocallis minor*, Dwarf Yellow Daylily; *Impatiens* cvs., white; *Lobelia erinus*, Edging Lobelia.

BERBERIS *ber-ber-iss*
thunbergii 'Aurea'   Yellow Japanese Barberry
Zones 4–8.

Slow-growing, low, dense plant 2 to 4 feet tall with truly citron-yellow foliage, except when growing in shade. One of the first plants to leaf out in spring. Best in moist, well-drained soil but tolerates urban conditions and drought. Deciduous.

GROWTH RATE:	slow
LIGHT:	full sun
MOISTURE:	roots moist

CHAMAECYPARIS *kam-ee-sip-ar-iss*

A genus of tall evergreen trees—to 120 feet—but there are cultivars that have a low, spreading habit useful in rock gardens, for accents, and for specimen planting. The leaves are interesting, small, compressed, usually green above and white beneath. Prefer moist, loamy, well-drained soil, a humid climate and open conditions.

GROWTH RATE:	medium
LIGHT:	full sun
MOISTURE:	roots moist

C. obtusa 'Crippsii'
Cripp's Golden Hinoki Cypress   Zones 5–9.
Valuable slow-growing dwarf with rich golden yellow foliage. Form is dense and pyramidal. It reaches 8 to 10 feet, and may grow to 30 feet in time.

C. obtusa 'Nana Aurea'
Dwarf Golden Hinoki Cypress   Zones 5–9.
A compact semi-dwarf under 10 feet, with golden foliage. 'Nana Gracilis' has thick, dark green foliage and slowly grows into a pyramid about 6 feet high.

C. pisifera 'Filifera Aurea'
Golden Thread Sawara Cypress   Zones 3–8.
The branch tips are very golden in spring, but may turn toward green in late summer or fall. Foliage texture is fine. Reaches 6 to 8 feet after 15 years. It prefers some acid in the soil.

JUNIPERUS *joo-nip-er-us*
chinensis 'Gold Coast'   Chinese Juniper
Zones 3–9.

Woody, evergreen genus including 60-foot trees, shrubs, and ground-hugging plants a few inches to 2 feet high with a spread of 4 to 8 feet. The low-growing cultivars have long, elegant, highly textured, gracefully layered branches. This cultivar is compact, about 4 by 4 feet at maturity, with leaves that are medium green, tipped with a good yellow color. The cultivar 'Old Gold' is similar, but the leaves

are bronzy yellow and hold their color through winter. The junipers thrive even in sunny, hot, dry locations, and in almost any well-drained soil. A spreading root system makes transplanting easy.

GROWTH RATE:	medium
LIGHT:	full sun
MOISTURE:	versatile

LIGUSTRUM *lig-gust-rum*
× *vicaryi*   Vicary Golden Privet   Zones 5–9.

The privets are vigorous, tall evergreen or deciduous shrubs that are most often used as trimmed hedges. The leaves are small, like boxwood, but the shrubs grow faster than boxwood and are very tolerant. They give off a particular and not always popular odor when the small green-white flowers are in bloom. This species is evergreen, grows slowly to 10 to 12 feet, and has many erect branches covered with bright golden foliage. Needs full sun to color well, and looks best when untrimmed. The 'Storzinger Strain' is said to be hardier. Succeeds in dry urban situations and by the seashore.

GROWTH RATE:	slow
LIGHT:	versatile
MOISTURE:	versatile

PHYSOCARPUS *fiss-oh-kar-pus*
opulifolius 'Dart's Gold'   Eastern Ninebark
Zones 2–8.

Small, upright deciduous shrub with dense branching, used as a rapid-growing filler and background. It bears small white or pink flower clusters in late spring. Early in the season it looks like a mass of yellow flowers. The new leaves are golden, and through the season turn first lime green, then dark green. Reddish to brown fruit capsules redden in the fall, adding interest. May be cut back, for it regrows well.

MATURE HEIGHT:	5'–9'
GROWTH RATE:	fast
LIGHT:	full sun, semi-sunny
MOISTURE:	versatile

SPIRAEA *spye-ree-uh*
× *bumalda* 'Limemound'   Spiraea
Zones 3–8.

Small deciduous mounding shrub that is a good filler and low massing plant. Dense, slender branches that are lemon yellow with a russet tinge in spring, blending to lime green when mature. Light pink flowers in summer. In fall the foliage becomes orange-red on red stems. Prefers good, moist soil, but is tolerant of every soil but very wet. Prune in early spring before growth starts.

MATURE HEIGHT:	2'–3' × 3'–5'
GROWTH RATE:	fast
LIGHT:	full sun
MOISTURE:	versatile

TAXUS *tax-us*   Yew
baccata 'Standishii'   Standish English Yew
Zones 6–7.

The best golden yew for small gardens. Grows to 25 feet, but may be kept small by shearing. Another

cultivar, 'Washingtonii', to 15 or more feet and almost as wide, has a more open form. Branches are yellow-green, with leaves a rich gold that fades to yellow-green as the season develops. Usually dioecious. Prefers moist, well-drained, sandy loam. There are variegated forms that grow well in the Northwest and on the West Coast.

GROWTH RATE:	fast
LIGHT:	full sun, semi-sunny, versatile
MOISTURE:	roots moist, versatile

SEE ALSO:
Acer palmatum 'Osakazuki', Threadleaf Japanese Maple, Shrubs 8

ALTERNATES:
Calluna vulgaris 'Gold Haze', Heather, Scotch Heather
Calluna vulgaris 'Robert Chapman', Heather, Golden Heather
Chamaecyparis obtusa 'Nana Aurea', Golden Hinoki Cypress
Ilex crenata 'Golden Heller', Japanese Holly
Juniperus × *media* 'Pfitzerana Aurea', Golden Pfitzer Juniper
Lonicera nitida 'Baggesen's Gold', Honeysuckle
Pittosporum tenuifolium 'Warnham Gold', Tawhiwhi
Sambucus canadensis 'Aurea', Golden American Elder, Sweet Elder
Thuja occidentalis 'Rheingold', American Arborvitae

SHRUBS 10
SHRUBS WITH BLUE, GRAY, AND SILVER FOLIAGE

Silver or gray foliage in the background heightens flower colors. The romantic blues soften surrounding greens. Blue also brings out the rose in pink flowers and reinforces nearby blues and lavenders. Blue, gray, and silver foliage draws the eye. One of these special plants in a small landscape is beautiful—and enough. The color generally is brightest with new growth in spring.

COMPANION PLANTINGS
Tree: *Malus sieboldi* 'Fuji', Toringo Crab Apple.
Vines: *Clematis viticella* 'Betty Corning'; *Rosa* 'America' (CL), Climbing Rose.
Bulbs: *Crocus* 'E. A. Bowles'; *C.* 'Blue Pearl'; *C. tomasinianus; C.* 'Whitewell Purple'.
Shrubs and flowers: *Dicentra spectabilis* cvs. 'Adrian Bloom', 'Bountiful', 'Pantaloons', Bleeding-heart; *Lavandula angustifolia* 'Hidcote', English Lavender; *Paeonia officinalis* cvs. 'Alice Harding', 'Rare China', 'Felix Supreme', 'Karl Rosenfield', Peony; *P. tenuifolia*, Fern-leaved Peony.
Annuals and tender perennials: *Aster* × *frikartii* 'Wonder of Staffa'; *Chrysanthemum* cvs., white and red; *Impatiens* cvs., white and rose; *Salvia farinacea*, 'Blue Bedder', Mealycup Sage.

ARTEMISIA art-em-**miz**-ee-uh
ludoviciana var. *albula*   Silver-king Artemisia
                                    Zones 5–9.

Airy, frosty looking foliage plant, fragrant, valuable for edging, borders, and as ground cover in larger landscapes. There are tiny grayish white florets. Tolerates drought and full sun, and is easily grown in well-drained garden soil. Plant container-grown plants in early spring. See also Ground Covers 7.

MATURE HEIGHT: 3′
GROWTH RATE: medium
LIGHT: full sun
MOISTURE: versatile

CHAMAECYPARIS kam-ee-**sip**-ar-iss
pisifera 'Boulevard' (syn. 'Cyanoviridis')
Sawara Cypress   Zones 3–8.

Cypresses are tall, narrow conifers with flat scalelike foliage that is white on the undersides, and a dark, dramatic silhouette; some have handsome, fissured bark. This cultivar is an exquisite compact form of medium height. It has feathery foliage, silvery green in summer, grayish blue in winter, and grows into a rounded cone. Prefers moist, loamy, well-drained soil, a humid climate, and open conditions.

MATURE HEIGHT: 10′
GROWTH RATE: medium
LIGHT: full sun
MOISTURE: roots moist

ELAEAGNUS el-ee-**ag**-nus

Tall, deciduous, and sometimes evergreen shrubs or small trees with gray green willowlike leaves silvery beneath. Fragrant cream-yellow flowers in spring are followed by sweet and mealy fruit that is yellow or orange with silvery scales. Self-sow and can become pests, but excellent for naturalizing and erosion control. Good tall hedge. Withstand heavy pruning and difficult conditions, including drought, and may be better in dry climates than moist. Tolerate exposure at the seashore and poor soils. Thrive in light, sandy loam.

GROWTH RATE: fast/medium
LIGHT: full sun
MOISTURE: versatile

E. angustifolia   Russian Olive   Zones 2–7.
Deciduous, 12 to 15 feet, but can reach 30 and 40 feet. Open, airy, branching, silver to gray green in summer. Fragrant but small flowers appear in mid-spring. Useful for hedges, highway plantings, and as a specimen in a large landscape.

E. philippinensis   Zones 9–10.
Evergreen in tropical and subtropical climates. Between 8 and 15 feet at maturity, it is known in Florida as Lingaro. Small, fragrant, yellowish white flowers. Weeping habit and sprawling, but may be kept compact by shearing. Prefers acid soils.

FEIJOA fay-**joh**-uh
sellowiana   Pineapple Guava, Feijoa
                                    Zone 8–10.

For warmer regions, a gray green evergreen shrub or small tree with interesting, handsome, asymmetrically branching foliage. In spring, delicate, showy, cup-shaped flowers, white and purplish with a cluster of dark red stamens. They are followed by small, tasty fruit in late summer and early fall. May require cross-pollination to set fruit. Among self-fruiting selections are 'Pineapple Gem', 'Beachwood', and 'Coolidge'. Full sun is needed for good fruit production. Prefers well-drained, loamy soil. Flowers are produced on current season's growth. Can be pruned after fruiting to form an attractive hedge.

MATURE HEIGHT: 10′–18′
GROWTH RATE: fast
LIGHT: full sun, semi-sunny
MOISTURE: roots moist

Eleagnus angustifolia, Russian Olive. (Neumann)

JUNIPERUS joo-**nip**-er-us   Juniper

Mostly small conifers, with needlelike or scalelike leaves. The male cones are yellow, like catkins, and the female fruits are berries. The genus includes 60-foot trees, shrubs, and ground-hugging plants a few inches to 2 feet high with a spread of 4 to 8 feet. The low-growing junipers have long, elegant, highly textured, gracefully layered branches. Foliage colors range from gray blue and green-blue, to light green tipped with gold. Some take on purple hues in winter. The species below are superb as ground covers, thriving even in sunny, hot, dry locations, and in almost any well-drained soil. A spreading root system makes junipers easy to transplant. Some blight exists: choose blight-resistant cultivars recommended by local nurseries. Set out container plants in spring or fall.

GROWTH RATE: medium
LIGHT: full sun
MOISTURE: versatile

J. chinensis var. *sargentii* 'Glauca'
Blue Sargent's Juniper   Zones 3–9.
Mound-forming juniper about 2 to 3 feet high, with a spread of 8 to 10 feet. The cultivar 'Glauca' has feathery blue-green leaves. It succeeds even in limestone soils.

J. horizontalis 'Bar Harbor'   Zones 3–9.
Low-growing form about 1 foot tall that spreads to 6 to 8 feet. It has gray green foliage tinted purple in winter and blue fruit. The species prefers soils in the acid range, pH 5. Effective among rocks and good under seashore conditions.

PICEA pye-**see**-uh
pungens ' Fat Albert'   Colorado Blue Spruce
                                    Zones 3–8.

Big conifers with the aromatic, rigid needles, large cones, and pyramidal form associated with Christmas trees. This species is a tall evergreen tree of the cool North and Northwest. The cultivar grows slowly, about 10 feet in 10 years, and has needles that are bright blue in summer and hold their color throughout the year. Thrives in well-drained soil, and tolerates some drought. 'R. J. Montgomery', under 5 feet at maturity, is another silver-blue compact.

MATURE HEIGHT: 10′
GROWTH RATE: slow
LIGHT: full sun
MOISTURE: roots moist

SEE ALSO:
Euonymus fortunei, Wintercreeper, Vines 8

ALTERNATES:
Buddleia alternifolia 'Argentea', Silver Fountain Buddleia
Calluna vulgaris 'Silver Queen', Heather, Scotch Heather
Erica tetralix 'Alba Mollis', Dwarf White Cross-leaved Heath, Dwarf White Bog Heather
Perovskia atriplicifolia, Russian Sage
Potentilla davurica 'Beesii', Bush Cinquefoil
Potentilla fruticosa 'Abbotswood', 'Primrose Beauty', Shrubby Cinquefoil
Salix elaeagnos, Rosemary Willow, Hoary Willow

SHRUBS WITH VARIEGATED FOLIAGE

A variegated shrub strikes a clear, crisp note, like a starched collar and cuffs. It can brighten a shady corner (many prefer some protection from noon sun, especially in warm regions), lightens the green of shrub borders, and makes a handsome, sophisticated specimen plant.

COMPANION PLANTINGS
Background: *Chamaecyparis pisifera* 'Boulevard' (syn. 'Cyanoviridis'), Sawara Cypress; *Juniperus* × *media* 'Pfitzerana Compacta', Dwarf Pfitzer Juniper. Bulbs: *Crocus* spp.; *Eranthis hyemalis*, Winter Aconite; *Galanthus nivalis*, Snowdrop; *Narcissus* cvs., white and gold; *Tulipa* Double Early 'Peach Blossom', Tulip; *T.* cvs., Parrot Tulips, white and red. Annuals, biennials, perennials: *Aster* × *frikartii* 'Wonder of Staffa'; *Salvia farinacea* 'Victoria', Mealy-cup Sage; *S. officinalis* 'Albiflora', White Garden Sage; *Stokesia laevis*, Stokes' Aster; *Tagetes* 'Fireworks', Marigold; *Zinnia elegans* 'Persian Carpet Mix'.

AUCUBA aw-kew-buh
japonica 'Variegata'   Gold-dust Tree
Zones 6–8.

Rounded, medium-size evergreen shrub successful in shade, even deep shade. Excellent background plant with large, bright green leaves flecked with yellow in 'Variegata', a female. 'Maculata' has leaves blotched yellow-white and is male. Females produce large, persistent, red berries. Plant both sexes for best fruiting. Thrives under heavy-rooted trees, like birches and lindens, where grass won't grow. Prefers well-drained soil with high organic content. Good houseplant in a cool room. 'Crotonifolia' has leaves dusted with white spots, and 'Picturata', deep green leaves with a large yellow blotch in the center.

Euonymus fortunei 'Gracilis'. (Neumann)

MATURE HEIGHT:	6'–10'
GROWTH RATE:	medium
LIGHT:	semi-sunny, shade
MOISTURE:	roots moist

CODIAEUM koh-dih-ee-um
variegatum Croton   Zones 9–10.

The most colorful variegated foliage shrub of all, it grows to about 6 feet outdoors in warm regions and has evergreen leaves streaked and splotched with carmine-red and bright yellow. Very popular container plant for terraces, greenhouses, and indoor gardens. There are hundreds of cultivars with varying leaf color patterns. Colors best in full sun and tolerates drought. Good informal hedge plant for warm regions.

MATURE HEIGHT:	4'–7'
GROWTH RATE:	medium
LIGHT:	full sun
MOISTURE:	versatile

Aucuba japonica 'Variegata', Gold-dust Tree.

CORNUS korn-us
alba 'Argenteo-marginata'
Variegated Tartarian Dogwood   Zones 2–8.

Showy, medium-size, deciduous shrub with four-season interest. In spring, white flower clusters appear; through late spring and summer, irregular creamy white leaf margins add a cool accent; in autumn and winter the stems turn bright red, lovely in a dusting of snow. Beautiful massed and naturalized or as a single accent plant in a landscape. At the National Arboretum it is planted in big white tubs on one of the terraces. Prefers moist, well-drained soil. New growth has the most brilliant winter stem color; rigorous spring pruning will force strong new growth. Especially appreciated in the West and in southern Canada. 'Spaethii' borders its leaves with yellow.

MATURE HEIGHT:	8'–10'
GROWTH RATE:	fast
LIGHT:	full sun, semi-sunny
MOISTURE:	roots moist

ELAEAGNUS el-ee-ag-nus
pungens 'Maculata'   Thorny Elaeagnus
Zones 7–9.

Popular evergreen shrub with medium to large leaves that have a deep yellow blotch of variable size. Fragrant silvery white flowers in October. Fruits in spring. Leaves on some branches may fail to variegate; cut out these branches at once. Useful for highway plantings, to naturalize on banks, and as barriers and tall hedges. For specimen use it will require pruning.

MATURE HEIGHT:	10'–12'
GROWTH RATE:	fast
LIGHT:	full sun
MOISTURE:	versatile

EUONYMUS yew-on-im-us

The genus includes deciduous trees and shrubs with brilliant fall foliage, evergreen upright shrubs, climbers, and ground covers. In fall persistent, bright pinkish orange capsules open exposing seeds that are orange-red and attractive to birds. Succeed on dry, rocky slopes and in shady places. Early spring shearing encourages compactness. Set out container-grown plants in early spring in well-drained soil. Very valuable ornamental, in spite of vulnerability to scale in some species.

GROWTH RATE: fast
LIGHT: versatile
MOISTURE: versatile

E. fortunei 'Emerald 'n Gold' Wintercreeper
Zones 5–8.
Low-growing, evergreen, white-veined form, 1 to 1½ feet high, with glossy, dark green tiny leaves with yellow margins. The foliage of 'Golden Prince', which forms a mound, is gold-tipped when new. This is one of the hardiest of the variegated forms. See also Vines 8.

E. japonica 'Aurea-variegata'
Golden Variegated Spindle Tree,
Golden Variegated Japanese Spindle Tree
Zones 6–9.
Best variegated euonymus for the South. Evergreen, compact, upright, usually 5 to 10 feet high and half as wide. Handsome little leaves with well-defined dark green margins, blotched with yellow. Excessive fertility, according to Dr. Michael A. Dirr, encourages reversion from the variegated form to plain green. Withstands heavy pruning. Subject to scale.

HYDRANGEA hye-drayn-jee-uh
macrophylla 'Variegata'
Variegated Bigleaf Hydrangea,
French Hydrangea   Zones 6–9.

Medium-size deciduous shrub with large green leaves edged white or cream, attractive in three seasons. The big, showy flower heads, in which the small fertile flowers are surrounded by rings of much larger sterile flowers, are called "lace cap" hydrangeas, and appear in mid- to late summer. (The big globe-shaped hydrangea form is known as "hortensia".) Color depends on soil pH. Available aluminum in acid soil ensures blue. A pH of 5.0 to 5.5 results in a soft blue color. To maintain pink color, the soil pH must be in the range of 6.0 to 6.5 or slightly higher. Great seashore plant. Prefers humusy, well-drained soil and flowers best in full sun. Valuable in dried arrangements. Flowers in this species form from previous season's growth; do any necessary pruning as soon as blooms fade.

MATURE HEIGHT: 3'–6'
GROWTH RATE: fast
LIGHT: full sun, semi-sunny
MOISTURE: roots moist

ILEX eye-lex
cornuta 'O'Spring' Chinese Holly,
Horned Holly   Zones 7–9.

Brightly variegated shrub-size cultivar of a genus with an enormous range of forms and sizes, from compact foot-high dwarfs to 70-foot trees. The fine leaves are evergreen, curled and toothed, and the small, round, long-lasting fruits are glossy red. Handsome specimen for foundation planting. Hollies are dioecious, but this species bears fruit without normal

Weigela florida 'Rosea'.

cross-pollination. Needs well-drained, somewhat acid soil and does best in semi-sun.

MATURE HEIGHT: 10'
GROWTH RATE: medium
LIGHT: full sun, semi-sunny
MOISTURE: roots moist

LIGUSTRUM lig-gust-rum
L. japonicum texanum 'Silver Star'
Wax-leaf Privet, Japanese Privet   Zones 7–9.

Evergreen variegated privet, whose leaves are deep green with creamy silver edges. It is a compact, slow-growing cultivar, erect, and of medium height.

GROWTH RATE: fast
LIGHT: versatile
MOISTURE: versatile

PIERIS pye-er-iss
japonica 'Variegata'
Variegated Andromeda   Zones 5–8.

Upright broadleaved evergreen with trim, dark green leaves margined white but tinged pink in spring. In early spring, slightly fragrant, white, urn-shaped flowers are borne in drooping 3- to 6-inch panicles. Good foundation plant, interesting in all seasons. Prefers well-drained soil in the acid range, pH 4.0 to 5.0. Prune after flowering, if needed.

MATURE HEIGHT: 10'–12'
GROWTH RATE: medium/slow
LIGHT: full sun, semi-sunny
MOISTURE: roots moist

WEIGELA wye-jeel-uh

Adaptable, deciduous flowering shrubs with clusters of showy flowers in late spring. Pruning is done after

flowering. Not very exciting when the blooms fade, but easy to grow, and the variegated cultivars are attractive in three seasons. Prefer well-drained soil and a winter mulch.

MATURE HEIGHT: 3'
GROWTH RATE: slow
LIGHT: full sun
MOISTURE: roots moist

W. florida 'Variegata Nana'
Variegated Dwarf Weigela   Zones 4–8.
One of the best deciduous variegated shrubs for the border. The new growth is soft green edged with creamy white, and the plant is compact and rounded. In late spring soft pink flowers appear. Prefers well-drained soil.

W. praecox 'Variegata' Variegated Weigela
Zones 4–6.
This species is the earliest to bloom. The nodding flowers are deep rose and the leaves are edged pale yellow to creamy white. Usually a compact 4 to 6 feet tall.

SEE ALSO:
Acer palmatum 'Dissectum Variegatum', Variegated Threadleaf Japanese Maple, Shrubs 8
Cotoneaster horizontalis 'Variegata', Variegated Rock Cotoneaster, Ground Covers 1
Euonymus fortunei, 'Gracilis', 'Silver Queen', Vines 8
Osmanthus heterophyllus 'Aureo-marginatus', 'Aureus', 'Variegatus', Holly Olive, Chinese Olive, Shrubs 15

ALTERNATES:
Acanthopanax sieboldianus 'Variegatus'
Kerria japonica 'Picta', Japanese Rose
Thujopsis dolabrata 'Variegata', Variegated Hiba Arborvitae

SHRUBS 12
SHRUBS WITH RED, ORANGE, AND YELLOW FOLIAGE IN FALL

These are shrubs whose fall colors light up the whole garden. Autumn color is strongest when the shrubs have 6 hours of full sun daily.

COMPANION PLANTINGS
Trees: *Betula nigra*, River Birch; *Chamaecyparis pisifera* 'Boulevard' (syn. 'Cyanoviridis'), Sawara Cypress.
Ground covers: *Juniperus* cvs.
Shrubs: Azalea (*Rhododendron*) Glenn Dale cvs.; *Rosa rugosa* cvs., Japanese Rose; *R. virginiana*, Virginia Rose.
Spring bulbs: *Crocus*; *Eranthis hyemalis*, Winter Aconite; Species Tulips.
Perennials and tender perennials: *Coreopsis lanceolata* 'Goldfink', Tickseed; *C. verticillata* 'Golden Showers', Tickseed, Threadleaf Tickseed; *Paeonia tenuifolia*, Fern-leaved Peony; *Papaver nudicaule*, Iceland Poppy.

ACER *ay-ser* Maple

Very valuable deciduous trees and elegant shrubs with beautiful leaves, used as specimens and tub plants. Maples whose leaves are always red are discussed in Shrubs 8. Need fairly constant moisture and prefer well-drained soil with a pH in the acid range.

GROWTH RATE: medium/slow
LIGHT: full sun, semi-sunny
MOISTURE: roots moist

A. palmatum 'Osakazuki'   Japanese Maple
Zones 4–8.
Many of the green-leaved Japanese maples color brilliantly in fall. The cultivar 'Osakazuki' is a small tree or large shrub with large leaves, yellow to light green in summer, that turn a stunning fluorescent red in fall. In warm regions, leaves may burn in full sun; afford some protection. Its height is to 15 feet.

A. p. 'Sangokaku'   Coral Bark Maple
Zones 5–9.
A small multi-branched tree or large shrub whose delicate light green foliage turns bright yellow in fall. A most unusual characteristic is that the bark turns brilliant coral-red in winter; it is striking standing in snow. Handsome container plant. Pruning out unwanted limbs enhances this plant's beauty. Height 10 to 15 feet.

ARONIA *ar-roh-nee-uh*
arbutifolia 'Brilliantissima'   Chokeberry
Zones 5–9.

A splendid, compact, deciduous shrub that has white flowers in spring, followed in autumn by long-lasting, glossy red berries and leaves. Beautiful massed along a road, in light woods, or in the border. Prefers acid-range soils. The species is perhaps best in moist situations.

MATURE HEIGHT: 6'–8'
GROWTH RATE: medium
LIGHT: full sun, semi-sunny
MOISTURE: roots moist

BERBERIS *ber-ber-iss* Barberry

Wide-ranging group of slow-growing deciduous and evergreen thorny shrubs, adaptable and handsome year-round. They make impenetrable hedges and offer a three-season display. Most produce pinkish or reddish new leaves in late spring that turn to green in summer, and then color orange, yellow, and red in fall. Small, attractive, yellow flowers in mid-spring, rather hidden by foliage in most species. Red, purplish, or bluish black fruits appear in late summer. Tolerant of soil and moisture. The evergreens are a little less hardy than the deciduous types and adapt to considerable shade. Deciduous barberries color best in rich, moist soils in the neutral range, and full sun.

GROWTH RATE: slow
LIGHT: full sun, semi-sunny
MOISTURE: roots moist

B. × *gladwynensis* 'William Penn'   Zones 5–9.
Low, spreading habit, 2 to 3 feet at maturity, adaptable and vigorous. Fall color is superb. Good low hedge.

Aronia arbutifolia 'Brilliantissima', Chokeberry. (Neumann)

B. koreana Korean Barberry   Zones 5–9.
Tall, to 6 feet, deciduous, valuable for fall color. The spring flowers are tiny, yellow, and borne in pendant clusters. The fruits are brilliant red, and the autumn color is excellent.

CORNUS *korn-us* Dogwood

The best-known dogwoods are the lovely spring-flowering trees, but the genus also includes the red-stemmed tall shrubs described here, valued for their unusual cold-weather color. Dogwoods prefer a moist, well-drained situation.

GROWTH RATE: fast
LIGHT: full sun, semi-sunny
MOISTURE: roots moist

C. alba 'Sibirica' Siberian Dogwood,
Red Twig Dogwood   Zones 2–8.
Medium-size, multi-stemmed, vase-shaped deciduous shrub with rounded dark green leaves. In spring, it bears the white flowers typical of dogwood trees, but smaller, followed by blue-white berries in fall. In winter, the bark turns a vivid coral-red and brightens the garden all winter long. The color is best when the shrub is cut back in late winter to encourage the production of young shoots. Handsome in pots. Height 8 to 10 feet. Prefers moist soil and supports wet situations. Better north of Zone 8.

C. sericea (syn. *stolonifera*)
Red-osier Dogwood   Zones 2–8.
Very like *alba* in every respect though the winter red of *alba* may be better. White flowers in late spring are followed by white or bluish fruit. Good bank holder. Most attractive naturalized and massed. 'Flaviramea', Golden-twig Dogwood, is similar, but the stems are yellow.

Fothergilla gardenii, Dwarf Witch Alder. (Neumann)

COTONEASTER *kot-toh-nee-ass-ter*
salicifolius 'Autumn Fire'
Willowleaf Cotoneaster   Zones 6–8.

One of a group of handsome shrubs with interesting branching and showy fall displays of bright red or orange berries. They require well-drained soil in the neutral range, but are versatile, tolerating full sun or understory light. This cultivar is small, 2 to 3 feet high, with silver-backed leaves. It is semievergreen or evergreen in the South, and one of the best for that region. Glossy leaves are purplish in winter, and a profusion of scarlet fruits persist. To ensure suc

Euonymus alata 'Compacta', Dwarf Winged Spindle Tree. (Neumann)

cessful transplanting, in spring set out container or balled-and-burlapped plants. See also Ground Covers 1.

GROWTH RATE: medium
LIGHT: full sun, semi-sunny
MOISTURE: versatile

EUONYMUS *yew-on-im-us*
alata 'Compacta' Dwarf Winged Spindle
Tree   Zones 3–8.

Small deciduous tree or tall shrub, and one of the best for brilliant fall color. It fairly flames in shades of pink-scarlet. Its tidy but full growth is valuable for hedges, municipal plantings, and specimen display. The corky bark "wings" are treasured by flower arrangers. Colors in full sun or part shade. Prefers well-drained soil.

MATURE HEIGHT: 10'–12'
GROWTH RATE: slow
LIGHT: full sun, semi-sunny
MOISTURE: roots moist

FOTHERGILLA *foth-er-gill-uh*

Valuable deciduous shrubs attractive in three seasons, from the showy white flower spikes that are borne through spring to the brilliant yellow and orange-red fall color. Require well-drained soil in the acid range, and prefer sandy loam with lots of peat moss added. Color is best when grown in full sun.

GROWTH RATE: fast
LIGHT: full sun
MOISTURE: roots moist

F. gardenii Dwarf Witch Alder   Zones 5–8.
Low, bushy shrub to 3 or 4 feet tall and as wide or wider. Bears fragrant white flowers throughout spring.

F. major (syn. *monticola*)   Zones 4–8.
Upright landscape plant 6 to 10 feet tall, valued for its honey-scented, long-blooming spring flowers and handsome, dark green foliage that colors bright yellow to orange and scarlet in fall.

Nandina domestica, Heavenly Bamboo.

NANDINA nan-**dye**-nuh
domestica Heavenly Bamboo Zones 6–9.

Airy, graceful shrub whose long narrow leaves remain evergreen. Loose clusters of whitish florets appear in spring, followed in autumn by brilliant red berries in drooping clusters. They are showier than hollies and remain all winter. Dense enough for good screening and nice as a specimen plant. When growing in sunny situations, leaves color maroon to orange-red in cold weather. Lovely with *Betula nigra*, River Birch (See Trees 1) and *Juniperus* ground covers (see Ground Covers 3). 'Fire Power', 'Harbor Dwarf', and 'Woods Dwarf' are disease-resistant cultivars that grow to about 3 feet and have good winter color.

MATURE HEIGHT: 8'
GROWTH RATE: fast/medium
LIGHT: full sun, semi-sunny
MOISTURE: roots moist

SEE ALSO:
Cotinus obovatus, American Smoke Tree, Chittamwood, Trees 7
Hamamelis × intermedia 'Diane', Witch Hazel, Shrubs 1
Hamamelis mollis, Chinese Witch Hazel, Shrubs 1
Itea virginica, Sweetspire, Shrubs 25
Mahonia repens, Creeping Oregon Grape, Herbs 8
Viburnum × burkwoodii 'Mohawk', Shrubs 1
Viburnum × carlcephalum 'Cayuga', Shrubs 1
Viburnum nudum, Smooth Withe-rod, Swamp Haw, Shrubs 25

ALTERNATES:
Azalea (*Rhododendron*) 'Hinodegiri'; Glenn Dale cvs.
Azalea (*Rhododendron*) viscosa, Swamp Azalea
Berberis atropurpurea 'Red Bird', Barberry
Cotoneaster apiculatus, Cranberry Cotoneaster
Photinia villosa

Rhus aromatica (syn. *canadensis*), Fragrant Sumac
Rhus typhina, Staghorn Sumac

SHRUBS 13
DWARF AND SLOW-GROWING SHRUBS

Very many low- or slow-growing forms of the most valuable shrubs are available from local nurseries. A few outstanding performers are described here. Several more are discussed on the evergreens list, Shrubs 7. "Dwarf" isn't a particular height; it refers to plants markedly smaller than the species or variety. Some slow-growing forms take so many decades to attain significant height that they can be used as dwarfs in landscaping.

Calluna vulgaris, Heather.

COMPANION PLANTINGS
Bulbs: *Begonia grandis*, Hardy Begonia; *Crocus* cvs.; *Eranthis hyemalis*, Winter Aconite; *Tulipa*, Species Tulips.
Perennials: *Achillea taygetea* 'Moonshine', Yarrow; *Dianthus × alwoodii*, Allwood Pink; *Hibiscus moscheutos*, Rose Mallow; *Viola × wittrockiana*, Pansy.
Annuals: *Ageratum houstonianum*, Flossflower; *Zinnia* 'Small World Pink', 'Fantastic Light Pink'.

CALLUNA kal-**lew**-njuh
vulgaris Heather Zones 4–6.

Low-growing evergreen shrub effective as low cover for roadsides, borders, corners, and in mass plantings on sunny, sandy slopes. Wide-spreading branches with tidy, overlapping scalelike leaves. Bears a profusion of small, nodding, pink to purple flowers in dense clusters to 10 inches long in late summer. There are very many cultivars. 'Gold Haze' has yellow leaves. 'Foxii Nana' makes a very dense mound to 6 inches tall. Flowers of 'Alba' cultivars are white, double, and larger. Annual pruning improves flowering. Good filler for bouquets, and excellent for drying. Prefer lean, porous, acid soils with a pH 6.0 or less, and protection from wind. Flowers best in full sun.

MATURE HEIGHT: 3'
GROWTH RATE: slow
LIGHT: full sun, semi-sunny
MOISTURE: roots moist

HYPERICUM hye-**pehr**-ik-um
St.-John's-wort

Low, woody shrubs or ground covers, evergreen or semievergreen, valued chiefly for summer-blooming bright yellow flowers that are like single roses with conspicuous gold or red stamens. They do well in poor soil, tolerating some alkalinity. The less hardy will die to the ground in winter but grow to flower well the following season. Useful for the shrub border and rock garden.

GROWTH RATE: medium
LIGHT: full sun, semi-sunny
MOISTURE: versatile

Skimmia japonica. (Neumann)

H. × moseranum Gold Flower Zones 6–8.
To 2 feet tall, shrubby and globelike with persistent foliage and arching red stems. The dark gold flowers are set off by bright orange stamens. Blooms through the hot summer months. Effective in large groups.

H. prolificum Broombrush,
Shrubby St.-John's-wort Zones 4–8.
Small, woody shrub or ground cover with evergreen leaves, 3 to 5 feet tall, valued for its summer-long golden yellow flowers shaped like small single roses. 'Hidcote' has larger flowers, but may die to the ground in winter in unprotected places. Does well in dry, rocky soil, and tolerates some alkalinity. Set out container plants. Early spring shearing encourages masses of blooms.

SANTOLINA *san-toh-lye-nuh*

Gray-leaved, low, evergreen shrubs with aromatic leaves and inconspicuous flowers. The silvery color adds a cool note to rock gardens, knot gardens, and borders, and beautifully sets off roses. Handsome in container gardens. Good drainage is essential.

GROWTH RATE:	medium
LIGHT:	full sun
MOISTURE:	roots moist

S. chamaecyparissus Lavender Cotton
Zones 6–9.
Low-growing, evergreen, shrubby plant 1½ to 2 feet tall, as multi-branched as coral. It has cool-looking blue-gray foliage that appears silvery in moonlight. Small, pale yellow, buttonlike flowers bloom above the foliage in late spring and summer. Used in dried arrangements and valued for continuing fragrance.

S. virens Green Santolina Zones 7/6–9.
Smaller than lavender cotton, to 15 inches. May be grown as a clipped hedge. Succeeds easily in poor, sandy soil in the neutral range, and by the sea. Suffers in hot summers where humidity is a problem. The flowers are a creamy color. Less hardy than the species above.

SKIMMIA *skim-ee-uh*

Dwarf, shade-loving evergreen shrubs whose leaves are aromatic when crushed. In early spring, or fall and winter in warm regions, there are clusters of small, somewhat fragrant flowers in upright panicles, followed by inedible berrylike fruit. Some species are dioecious. Good urban and pot plants. Prefer moist, acid, sandy soil with lots of peat but will survive in alkaline conditions.

GROWTH RATE:	slow
LIGHT:	semi-sunny, shade
MOISTURE:	roots moist

S. japonica Zones 7–9.
Slow-growing, densely branched shrub 3 to 5 feet high; yellowish white flowers borne by the female plant. Male flowers are larger and very fragrant. The species is dioecious and requires a male nearby to produce its bright red berries.

S. reevesiana Zones 7–9.
Smaller plant, to 2 feet, with white flowers that are bisexual. One plant alone will fruit. Requires a rich, moist, acid soil.

SEE ALSO:
Azalea (*Rhododendron*), low and slow-growing, Shrubs 2
Berberis julianae 'Nana', Dwarf Wintergreen Barberry, Shrubs 18
Berberis thunbergii 'Crimson Pygmy', Japanese Barberry, Shrubs 8
Buxus microphylla 'Compacta', 'Morris Midget', 'Tide Hill', Compact Box, Compact Boxwood, Shrubs 18
Buxus sempervirens 'Suffruticosa', Edging Box, Dwarf Box, Shrubs 18
Chamaecyparis obtusa 'Nana gracilis', 'Pygmaea Dwarf Hinoki Cypress, Shrubs 7
Cotoneaster horizontalis, Rock Cotoneaster, Ground Covers 1
Ilex cornuta var. *rotunda*, Dwarf Chinese Holly, Shrubs 7
Ilex crenata 'Helleri', 'Tiny Tim', Japanese Holly, Shrubs 7
Ilex vomitoria 'Gulftide', Yaupon Holly, Shrubs 7
Juniperus × media 'Pfitzerana Compacta', Dwarf

Hypericum species, St.-John's-wort.

Nandina 'Harbor Dwarf', Heavenly Bamboo. (Monrovia Nursery Co.)

Pfitzer Juniper, Shrubs 7
Kalmia latifolia 'Elf', Mountain Laurel, Shrubs 7
Nandina 'Harbor Dwarf', 'Woods Dwarf', Heavenly Bamboo, Shrubs 12
Picea pungens 'Fat Albert', Colorado Blue Spruce, Shrubs 10
Rosa wichuraiana, Memorial Rose, Ground Covers 9
Taxus baccata 'Nana', 'Pygmaea', 'Repandens', Dwarf English Yew, Shrubs 7
Taxus × media 'Brownii', 'Densiformis', Yew, Shrubs 7

ALTERNATES:
Erica, Heath
Forsythia × intermedia 'Arnold Dwarf'
Fuchsia magellanica 'Tom Thumb', Hardy Fuchsia
Ilex cornuta 'O'Spring', Chinese Holly, Horned Holly

SHRUBS 14
SHRUBS FOR TOPIARY AND ESPALIER

Topiaries and espaliers take years to develop; choose resistant and climate-hardy plants, and those that respond well to pruning. Evergreen foliage plants with small leaves are preferred for topiary training—box and yew for instance. Also popular are shrubby perennials, such as rosemary. Look for plants whose natural form is suited to the topiary form intended.

Fruit trees are the traditional choice for espalier, but plants with bold foliage or striking flowers are increasingly popular. Those recommended here will suggest other potential subjects.

BUXUS *bux-us* Box, Boxwood

Superb small-leaved formal evergreens whose slow growth and acceptance of pruning makes them ideal for topiary. Used in nearly all formal and knot gardens, herb plantings, and estate landscapes. Most successful growing in well-drained, neutral-range soil, They adapt to semi-sun. Mulch with compost or leaf mold to keep the roots cool. Do not cultivate around the plants as the roots are on the surface. Easy to transplant.

GROWTH RATE:	slow
LIGHT:	full sun, semi-sunny
MOISTURE:	roots moist

B. microphylla Box, Boxwood Zones 6–9.
Natural height is 3 to 4 feet, with an equal spread. 'Green Beauty' and 'Compacta' are established cultivars often used for topiary. 'Tide Hill' grows to 2 feet and more than twice as wide. 'Morris Midget' is a compact edger.

B. sempervirens 'Suffruticosa' Edging Box, Dwarf Box Zones 5–9.
Some 150-year-old plants are only 3 feet high. Pruning can keep this cultivar just a few inches tall, but left alone it will grow slowly to 4 or 5 feet. The small leaves are quite aromatic. It has been valued since Colonial times. 'Myrtifolia' is a low cultivar, 4 to 5 feet tall.

CAMELLIA *kam-meel-ee-uh*

Spectacular southern shrub or small tree grown for its large, lustrous leaves and showy, waxy flowers in fall, winter, and/or early spring. Where temperatures go below freezing, buds may be killed or delayed if the camellias are in exposed positions. Makes an interesting espalier. There are semidouble and double forms in shades of white, pink, rose, or purple-red. A few cultivars are fragrant. Select with the assistance of a reliable local nursery. Prefers well-drained, humus-rich soil in the acid range. The National Arboretum's first camellia plantings were started in Cryptomeria Valley with a gift in 1949—a collection of the fall-blooming *Camellia sasanqua* planted along trails leading to the nearby dogwood collection. 'Frost Queen' and 'Cinnamon Cindy' are among introductions that came from research conducted on this group.

GROWTH RATE:	slow
LIGHT:	semi-sunny
MOISTURE:	soil surface damp

C. japonica Zones 7–8.
Widely grown in the warm South and California. It can be a shrub 10 to 15 feet tall or a small tree, depending on the cultivar. Suitable for espalier, though the species below is more often used. Flowers are large, up to 5 inches across, and bloom in late winter and early spring. Monrovia Nursery Company offers tree-form and espalier camellias.

C. sasanqua Zones 7–8.
Small shrub, to 12 feet, and except for certain hybrids, generally hardier than the other species and earlier to bloom. Leaves and flowers are smaller—

Buxus sempervirens 'Suffruticosa', Edging Box.

Camellia japonica.

flowers to 2 inches in diameter—with a profusion of fragrant blooms. Many semidouble and double forms. Among established cultivars are 'Showa-no-Sakae', 'Jean May', and 'Flower Girl', which has vibrant pink blooms all along the branches in late fall and winter. This is the one most used for espaliers.

CEANOTHUS *see-an-nohth-us*
× *delilianus*   Zones 7–9.
Evergreen shrub to 3 feet tall, valued for its dark to pale blue flowers in April. Look for established cultivars such as 'Gloire de Versailles', pale blue, and 'Gloire de Plantieres', dark blue. Spring-prune deciduous species to maintain compact, attractive growth.

Successful in any well-drained soil and withstands droughts. Good espalier plant for the West Coast. Hybrid of *C. americanus* which prefers slightly acid soil.

GROWTH RATE:	medium
LIGHT:	full sun
MOISTURE:	roots moist, versatile

FORSYTHIA *for-sith-ee-uh*
× *intermedia*   Zones 5–8.

Spreading to 12 feet wide, an almost indestructible deciduous shrub covered with perky yellow flowers

Forsythia × *intermedia*. (Neumann)

in late winter/early spring. Tall-growing varieties (to 8 feet) may be sheared for espalier. 'Arnold Giant' is the hardiest. 'Lynwood' has the best flowers. 'Nana', 5 to 8 feet tall, is a slow-growing dwarf that roots where it touches. Branches force easily in late winter.

MATURE HEIGHT:	8'–10'
GROWTH RATE:	fast
LIGHT:	full sun
MOISTURE:	versatile

HIBISCUS *hye-bisk-us*

Tall deciduous and evergreen shrubs that bear a profusion of short-lived flowers. Need well-drained sandy loam, pH 5.5 to 7.0, with high organic content. Good container and espalier subjects.

GROWTH RATE:	medium
LIGHT:	full sun, semi-sunny
MOISTURE:	soil surface moist

H. rosa-sinensis   Chinese Hibiscus
                                       Zones 9–10.
Fast-growing, handsome shrub 6 to 8 feet tall, with very showy year-round flowers in red, yellow, orange, white, sometimes with a contrasting eye and a variety of shadings, to 6 inches in diameter, single or double. Requires full sun and frequent fertilization. The flowers last only one day, but appear constantly.

H. schizopetalis   Japanese Hibiscus,
Fringed Hibiscus   Zones 9–10.
Gorgeous fringed, pendant flowers and a weeping habit. Fast-growing evergreen 8 to 12 feet tall, for specimen use.

ILEX *eye-lex*   Holly

Beautiful evergreen or deciduous shrubs and trees (*I. latifolia*, the Luster-leaf Holly, reaches 60 feet) valued for brilliant green leaves and fall berries. Most can stand a lot of pruning; low, small-leaved types like the species below are good for topiary. Dioecious: most require a pollinator. Need well-drained soil and are best in semi-sun.

GROWTH RATE:	medium
LIGHT:	full sun, semi-sunny
MOISTURE:	roots moist

I. crenata 'Repandens'
Spreading Japanese Holly   Zones 5–8.
Black-berried species that grows slowly to 4 feet, though some can reach 25 feet. 'Repandens' is a spreading form whose leaves are closely spaced, thin, and flat. Among cultivars 1 to 4 feet tall is 'Helleri', a bushy, slow-growing dwarf female. *I. c.* 'Golden Heller' is golden. 'Glory', a small male plant, is a good pollinator. 'Tiny Tim' is considered hardier than these. 'Convexa' has small leaves, is hardy, takes pruning. It is a female clone and produces fruits in profusion.

I. vomitoria 'Gulftide'   Gulftide Yaupon Holly
                                       Zones 7–10.
Low-growing, improved cultivar with beautiful scarlet berries borne in profusion. To 5 feet. Established cultivars excellent for southern gardens are 'Emily Brunner' and its pollinator 'James Swann', both introduced by Shadow Nurseries. The species was much used in Williamsburg for topiary.

Pyracantha espalier. (Neumann)

MYRTUS *mert-us*
communis Myrtle   Zone 8.

Shrub with very aromatic dark evergreen leaves. Thrives as a pot plant, and is a favorite for training to standard or topiary forms. The flowers bloom for 5 or 6 weeks in summer, beautiful creamy white puffballs, followed by bluish black berries. Prefers neutral-range soil.

MATURE HEIGHT: 6' +
GROWTH RATE: medium
LIGHT: full sun, semi-sunny
MOISTURE: roots moist

PYRACANTHA *pye-ruh-kanth-uh*
coccinea Fire Thorn   Zones 6–9.

Handsome, evergreen, thorny shrub valued for its fine foliage and attractive flowers in mid-spring followed by clusters of brilliant scarlet fruit in fall. Takes pruning well, makes a delightful bonsai, and often is espaliered against a wall—there's a lovely example near the entrance to the National Arboretum Administration Building. Transplants with difficulty, so handle with care until established. Look for cultivars resistant to scale and fire blight. Among these are 'Mohave', an upright shrub 8 to 10 feet tall with masses of orange-red berries; 'Navajo', about 6 feet tall by 7½ feet wide; 'Shawnee', yellow fruits; 'Teton', a strong grower to 16 feet and as wide, is very hardy. Prefers well-drained soil, tolerates being dry in summer, and fruits best in full sun; pH 5.5 to 7.5.

GROWTH RATE: fast/medium
LIGHT: full sun, semi-sunny
MOISTURE: roots moist

ROSMARINUS *ross-muh-rye-nus*
officinalis Rosemary   Zone 7.

Lastingly fragrant, needlelike, evergreen leaves, used in dry perfumes and cooking. Lovely light blue edible flowers bloom in clusters in late winter and early spring. Rosemary may be pruned and is a good bonsai subject. The hardy cultivar 'Arp' survives winters in the National Arboretum herb garden. Nice filler for bare spots in walls or the rock garden. The variety *humilis* is hardy to New Jersey; *R. o.* 'Prostratus' is much used in southern California. Prefers neutral-range soil.

MATURE HEIGHT: 2'–4'
GROWTH RATE: medium
LIGHT: full sun
MOISTURE: roots moist

TAXUS *tax-us* Yew

Vigorous needled evergreens highly tolerant of pruning and shearing, much used for topiary. Grow well in sun or shade, in moist, well-drained soil. The female bears seeds with a fleshy red aril. Usually dioecious. Prefer alkaline soil, so not really good in a bed with azaleas and rhododendrons.

GROWTH RATE: fast
LIGHT: versatile
MOISTURE: roots moist

T. baccata 'Nana' Dwarf English Yew
Zones 6–8.
Dwarf form with darker needles than the species, it grows to a compact pyramid, about 3 feet high. 'Pygmaea ' remains at under 2 feet. 'Repandens' is wide with arching branches, 2 to 4 feet tall and 12 to 15 wide. It is hardy to Zone 5.

T. baccata 'Standishii' Standish English Yew
Zones 6–7.
The best golden yew for small gardens; a fastigiate form. Another cultivar, 'Washingtonii', to 15 feet and as wide, has open branches and rich gold leaves that fade to yellow-green. Usually dioecious.

T. cuspidata 'Nana' Dwarf English Yew
Zones 4–8.
One of the best varieties, a female, dense and compact. It grows very slowly to 6 feet. 'Densa' has very dense and wide-spreading branches—an old plant may be 4 feet by 20 across. It is a little lower than 'Nana'.

T. × media 'Brownii' Brown's Yew
Zones 4–7.
Valuable, dense male clone that grows to about 9 by 12 feet in 20 years. 'Densiformis' is similar, but a little smaller—to 5 feet high. Some taller established cultivars are: 'Hatfieldii', about 12 feet tall; 'Hicksii', taller than it is wide; 'Wardii', dense, wide, and flat, about 6 feet tall; 'Kelseyi', to about 12 by 9 feet.

SEE ALSO:
Azalea (*Rhododendron*), Kurume hybrids, Shrubs 2
Eugenia aromatica (syn. *Syzygium aromaticum*), Shrubs 18
Eugenia brasiliensis, Brazil Cherry, Shrubs 18
Eugenia myrtifolia (syn. *Syzygium paniculatum*) 'Globulus', Dwarf Brush Cherry, Shrubs 18
Eugenia uniflora, Surinam Cherry, Shrubs 18
Laurus nobilis, Grecian Laurel, Sweet Bay, Herbs 1

ALTERNATES:
Juniperus, many
Ligustrum lucidum, Glossy Privet
Ligustrum japonicum (Texanum) 'Silver Star', Privet
Ligustrum × vicaryi, Vicary Golden Privet
Pittosporum tobira, Japanese Pittosporum
Tsuga canadensis 'Pendula', Weeping Canadian Hemlock

SHRUBS 15
SHRUBS WITH FRAGRANT FLOWERS

A garden with fragrance planned for every season is truly a delight. Plant these shrubs beside outdoor living areas, porches, and entrances and where they will be brushed against frequently. The most fragrant flowers are often modest—but they are among the most rewarding.

COMPANION PLANTINGS
Background: *Ligustrum amurense*, Amur Privet; *Rhododendron fragrantissimum*.
Ground covers: *Hosta plantaginea* 'Grandiflora', Fragrant Hosta; *Verbena platensis*.
Many flowers and herbs, including *Cheiranthus cheiri*, Wallflower; *Galium odoratum,* Woodruff, Sweet Woodruff; *Lobularia maritima*, Sweet Alyssum; *Nicotiana alata* 'Grandiflora', Flowering Tobacco.

CALYCANTHUS *kal-ik-kanth-us*
floridus Carolina Allspice   Zones 4–9.

Medium-tall shrub with maroon flowers 2 inches across in mid-spring or early summer, followed by 2-inch-long seed clusters that are aromatic when crushed. The flower fragrance is fruity. Leaves turn yellow in autumn. Plant becomes leggy in too much shade. Grows anywhere, but best in rich, well-drained soil.

MATURE HEIGHT: 4'–9'
GROWTH RATE: slow
LIGHT: versatile
MOISTURE: roots moist

Lonicera fragrantissima, Winter Honeysuckle. (Neumann)

CHIMONANTHUS *kye-moh-nanth-us*
praecox Wintersweet   Zones 7–9.

Tall, wide, deciduous shrub. In late winter before the leaves appear, it bears wonderfully fragrant yellow flowers in the axils of the previous season's wood. In frost-free climates, it blooms all winter. The lustrous green leaves are up to 10 inches long. Needs good drainage and flourishes in sandy loam with leaf mold added.

MATURE HEIGHT: 10'
GROWTH RATE: slow
LIGHT: full sun, semi-sunny
MOISTURE: roots moist

DAPHNE *daff-nee*

Attractive, low, wide, semievergreen to evergreen shrubs famous for their profusion of fine-textured flowers with superb fragrance. Valued for rock gardens and small borders. Prefer well-drained sandy loam with lots of leaf mold added and near neutral soil—pH 6.0—but are versatile. Mulch to protect from summer heat and drought, and cover with branches in winter. Transplanting is difficult—buy container-grown plants and handle with care until new growth is evident. Worth the effort to get them established.

GROWTH RATE: slow
LIGHT: full sun
MOISTURE: roots moist

D. × burkwoodii   Zones 4–8.
'Somerset' is semievergreen, to 3 or 4 feet high and 6 feet wide. In late spring and often again in summer, it bears masses of star-shaped, delightfully fragrant, pale pink flowers. 'Carol Mackie' has leaves edged with a gold band.

D. cneorum Garland Flower   Zones 4–7.
Dense evergreen about 1 foot high and twice as wide. The rosy pink flowers cover the plant with very fragrant blossoms in mid-spring and sometimes again in summer. 'Variegata' has cream-edged leaves. 'Pygmaea' has pink flowers on prostrate branches.

D. odora 'Aureo-marginata'   Winter Daphne
Zones 8–10.
Evergreen, very fragrant, and the easiest of the daphnes to grow; in very early spring, deep crimson buds open to dense heads of white flowers. Leaves have light margins of yellow. Slowly grows to 4 or 5 feet high.

LONICERA *lon-iss-er-uh* Honeysuckle

Vigorous climbing and twining vines or tall shrubs, most with very fragrant flowers and bright berrylike fruits. They are attractive to many types of birds that disperse the seeds. The shrubby types can be trained as tall or low hedges. Prune to maintain control. Prefer soil in the neutral range, pH 6.0 to 8.0. Most species thrive in full sun. See also Vines 5.

GROWTH RATE: medium
LIGHT: full sun
MOISTURE: versatile

L. fragrantissima   Winter Honeysuckle
Zones 4–8.
Exceptionally fragrant, creamy white blooms begin in late winter and early spring. They are lemon-scented and last a month or so, followed by bright red berries that persist through early summer. Pendulous branches. Grows to about 8 to 10 feet tall by 10 feet wide.

L. tatarica Tatarian Honeysuckle   Zones 3–8.
Taller than Winter Honeysuckle, to 10 feet or more and as wide, and it blooms later, with pink to white very fragrant flowers followed by red or yellow fruits. Among established cultivars are 'Arnold Red,' darkest red and resistant to aphids; 'Grandiflora', white; 'Morden Orange', pale pink flowers, orange fruit, and hardy; 'Virginalis', large rose pink flowers.

MICHELIA *mye-keel-ee-uh*
figo (syn. *fuscata*) Banana Shrub
Zones 8–10.
Densely branched evergreen to 15 feet, with handsome glossy leaves. Creamy yellow flowers edged with purple bloom in spring and repeat. Powerful scent of bananas. Suited only to southern gardens. Cold-hardy to 10° F.

MATURE HEIGHT: 15'
GROWTH RATE: slow
LIGHT: full sun
MOISTURE: roots moist

OSMANTHUS *os-manth-us* Devil-weed

Shapely evergreen shrubs or small trees, with dark green hollylike foliage and small, very fragrant blooms in spring or fall. Tolerate shearing and heavy pruning. Prefer well-drained, rather acid soil, but can stand some alkalinity.

Osmanthus heterophyllus, Holly Olive. (Neumann)

MATURE HEIGHT:	8'–10'
GROWTH RATE:	medium/slow
LIGHT:	full sun, semi-sunny
MOISTURE:	roots moist

O. × fortunei   Zones 8–9.
Reaches 15 to 20 feet at maturity but may be kept to a smaller size by pruning. Dark green leathery leaves and very fragrant flowers in mid-fall.

O. fragrans   Tea Olive, Sweet Olive
                                    Zones 8–9.
Large shrub or small tree, 20 to 30 feet tall, with extremely fragrant small white flowers in spring.

O. heterophyllus   Holly Olive, Chinese Olive
                                    Zones 7–9.
Not as handsome as the hybrid above, but hardier, with exceedingly fragrant white flowers September or October into early November. Among excellent cultivars is 'Gulftide', 10 to 15 feet high, with very glossy foliage. 'Aureo-marginatus' has leaves margined with yellow, as does 'Aureus.' *O. heterophyllus* 'Variegatus' is often seen in nurseries. It is about 8 feet tall, an erect evergreen shrub whose dark green leaves are edged with creamy white.

PHILADELPHUS *fil-ad-**delf**-us*
Mock Orange

Deciduous shrubs whose beautiful white flowers and delicious fragrance are an unforgettable part of northern springtimes. A one-season plant, indicated only for gardens with space to spare. Vigorous growers, they succeed almost anywhere they are hardy, thriving in well-drained soil rich in organic matter. Remove old wood after flowering. Some uncategorized cultivars are particularly hardy and fragrant, among them 'Minnesota Snowflake', to 6 feet, and 'Miniature Snowflake', a double under 3 feet.

GROWTH RATE:	fast
LIGHT:	versatile
MOISTURE:	versatile

P. × limonei   Zones 5–8.
Upright shrub to 6 feet tall that bears very fragrant flowers in late spring and early summer. 'Avalanche' has single flowers and grows to 4 feet high. 'Frosty Morn', to 3 feet, is double flowered. 'Innocence' is one of the most fragrant and grows to 8 feet.

P. × virginalis   Zones 5–8.
Grows to 9 feet and has single flowers 2 inches across. 'Glacier' is under 6 feet and has double flowers. 'Bouquet Blanc' is under 6 feet with single flowers.

SEE ALSO:
Chionanthus retusus, Fringe Tree, Shrubs 4
Clethra alnifolia, Sweet Pepperbush, Shrubs 23
Hamamelis mollis, Chinese Witch Hazel, Shrubs 1
Itea virginica, Sweetspire, Shrubs 25
Lavandula angustifolia, English Lavender, Herbs 6
Paeonia, Peony, many, Flowers 16
Rosa, Rose, many, Shrubs 6, Herbs 7
Syringa meyeri 'Palabin', Lilac, Shrubs 4
Syringa patula 'Miss Kim', Manchurian Lilac, Shrubs 4
Syringa vulgaris, Lilac, Shrubs 4
Viburnum × burkwoodii 'Mohawk', Shrubs 1
Viburnum × carlcephalum 'Cayuga', Shrubs 1

Viburnum carlesii, Shrubs 1
Viburnum × juddii, Judd Viburnum, Shrubs 1

ALTERNATES:
Azalea (*Rhododendron*) 'Irene Koster', 'White Lights'
Azalea (*Rhododendron*) *poukhanensis,* Korean Azalea
× *Citrofortunella mitis,* Calamondin Orange
Pittosporum tobira
Rhododendron, several

SHRUBS 16
SHRUBS ATTRACTIVE TO BIRDS

Birds adopt gardens that provide shelter, water, and food. They love berries, including those the gardener intends for the table. The ornamental shrubs described here are especially attractive to birds, but don't overlook those on the See also list at the end of the section. Birds also gather fine pine

Ilex 'Sparkleberry', a National Arboretum introduction.

needles and the fruits of some conifers in Shrubs 7. Remember that fruiting shrubs that bear male and female flowers on separate plants (dioecious) will fruit profusely only if plants of both sexes are present.

COMPANION PLANTINGS
As background: *Arbutus unedo*, Strawberry Tree; *Carpinus caroliniana*, American Hornbeam; *Malus floribunda*, Showy Crab Apple.
Perennials: *Heuchera sanguinea*, Coralbells; *Monarda didyma*, Bee Balm.

ELAEAGNUS *el-ee-ag-nus*
umbellata Autumn Olive   Zones 3–8.

Tall shrub, 12 to 18 feet, valued for its silvery young foliage, and covered in fall with silvery berries that turn red as they mature. The fragrant, funnel-shaped, silvery white flowers are borne in late spring. Adapts to exposure at the seashore and poor soils. Thrives in light, sandy loam.

GROWTH RATE:	fast/medium
LIGHT:	full sun
MOISTURE:	versatile

ILEX *eye-lex* Holly

Hollies are beautiful evergreen or deciduous shrubs and trees (*I. latifolia*, Luster-leaf Holly, reaches 60 feet). Valued for brilliant fall and winter display of red fruit attractive to robins and other birds. Most are hardy only in Zones 4 to 7 and south. Leaf form varies from small, smooth, and shiny to large and very spiny—like the hollies that are a symbol of Christmas. Leaf color is green, except in some beautifully variegated clones of English holly (*I. aquifolium* 'Argenteo-marginata' and 'Aureo-marginata', Trees 6). Some have red berries, some have yellow or black. Hollies are dioecious, and most require a pollinator. Need well-drained soil and are best in semi-sun. See also Shrubs 7, 11, and 14.

Pyracantha 'Mohave'.

Pyracantha 'Shawnee'.

GROWTH RATE:	medium
LIGHT:	full sun, semi-sunny
MOISTURE:	roots moist

I. cornuta Chinese Holly, Horned Holly   Zones 7–9.
'Burfordii' is a well-established cultivar to 10 feet tall, or more. The fine leaves are evergreen, with one or two "teeth"; the masses of small, round, long-lasting fruits are glossy red and can occur without pollination. A handsome specimen for foundation planting. 'China Girl' is an evergreen with glossy, rich green foliage and an abundance of red fruits in fall; 'China Boy' is the male pollinator. Both are hardy to Zone 5. Their height is about 5 to 6 feet.

I. 'Dr. Kassab'   Zones 7–9.
Handsome pyramidal evergreen holly, 15 to 20 feet tall, with excellent red fruits in dense clusters. This is a female and depends on a male in the area for pollination.

I. 'Lydia Morris' and 'John Morris' Zones 6–8.
Evergreen, pyramidal shrubs to 12 or 15 feet and as wide, with very handsome spiny, dark green foliage. The female produces an abundance of red berries. The male is its pollinator.

I. 'Sparkleberry'   Zones 5–8.
Large, upright deciduous shrub to 18 feet introduced by Gene Eisenbeiss and William Kosar of the National Arboretum, and outstanding for its bright, very long-lasting, shiny red fruit. The best show of fruit is after the leaves fall. Wonderful in floral decorations and against a snowfall. This is one of the best female clones. Easy to grow. Its pollinator is *I.* 'Apollo'.

PYRACANTHA *pye-ruh-kanth-uh*
coccinea Fire Thorn   Zones 6–9.

Also called Scarlet Fire Thorn, this is a handsome, evergreen, thorny shrub valued for its fine foliage and clusters of brilliant scarlet fruit in fall. Robins love them. The attractive flowers appear in mid-spring. Takes pruning well, makes a delightful bonsai, and is good espaliered against a wall—there's a lovely ex-

ample near the entrance to the National Arboretum Administration Building. Good specimen and hedge plant. Transplants with difficulty, so handle with care until established. Look for cultivars resistant to scale and fire blight. Among established cultivars are 'Mohave', an upright shrub 8 to 10 feet tall with masses of orange-red berries; 'Navajo', about 6 feet tall by 7½ feet wide; 'Shawnee', yellow fruits; and 'Teton', a strong grower to 16 feet and as wide, and very hardy. Prefers well-drained soil, tolerates being dry in summer, and fruits best in full sun. pH 5.5 to 7.5.

GROWTH RATE:	fast/medium
LIGHT:	full sun, semi-sunny
MOISTURE:	roots moist

SAMBUCUS *sam-bew-kus*
canadensis American Elder, Sweet Elder   Zones 3–9.

Tall, deciduous, somewhat untidy shrub grown for sweet edible fruit which is very attractive to song sparrows and other birds. Good for roadsides, naturalizing, wet areas. In late spring and early summer, it bears white flowers in flat clusters to 10 inches across, followed by small, bluish black berries that make good elderberry jelly. The flowers, dried, were used to make tea and for flavoring. The plant suckers profusely and needs pruning to stay in good shape. Prefers moist soils but adapts to some drought. Among cultivars worth noting is 'Aurea', which has yellow foliage and cherry-red fruits.

MATURE HEIGHT:	12′
GROWTH RATE:	fast
LIGHT:	full sun, semi-sunny
MOISTURE:	soil surface damp, versatile

VIBURNUM *vye-burn-um*
dentatum Arrowwood, Southern Arrowwood   Zones 3–9.

Deciduous shrub 6 to 15 feet tall that bears white flowers with yellow stamens in late spring, followed

Viburnum dentatum, Arrowwood.

in fall by blue or black fruit very attractive to birds. Good in hedges, groupings, massed, the shrub border, and for screening. It is versatile and adapts to salt spray. Prefers well-drained soil and, when growing well, requires pruning to stay in shape.

GROWTH RATE: slow
LIGHT: full sun, semi-sunny
MOISTURE: roots moist

SEE ALSO:
Cornus, Dogwood, Shrubs 12
Lonicera tatarica 'Arnold Red', 'Grandiflora', 'Morden Orange', 'Virginalis', Tatarian Honeysuckle, Shrubs 15
Malus sargentii, Sargent Crab Apple, Shrubs 1
Myrica pensylvanica, Bayberry, Herbs 1
Rosa rugosa and hybrids, Japanese Rose, Shrubs 19
Vaccinium corymbosum, Highbush Blueberry, Herbs 1

ALTERNATES:
Ilex aquifolium 'Amber', 'Bacciflava', English Holly
Rhamnus frangula, Alder Buckthorn

SHRUBS 17
DECIDUOUS SHRUBS FOR HEDGES, EDGING, AND SCREENING

These handsome flowering and foliage shrubs make excellent hedges, edgers, and screening for summer. For evergreen hedges, turn to Shrubs 18; for rose hedges, see Shrubs 19. There is pruning information in Shrubs 18, and in the introduction to Shrubs.

COMPANION PLANTINGS
Ground covers and/or edgers: *Lamium maculatum* 'Beacon Silver' and 'Nancy', Spotted Dead Nettle; or any of the low-growing ground covers in Ground Covers 1–10.

ABELIA *ah-beel-ee-uh*
× *grandiflora* 'Edward Goucher'   Zones 5–9.

Dense, rounded, multi-stemmed shrub that bears a profusion of slightly fragrant purple-pink flowers through summer until frost. Long-lasting leaves color purplish bronze in late fall. Semievergreen except in the South, where leaves may persist through winter. Good bank cover and hedge. Prefers well-drained soil in the acid range, but it is versatile as to pH. Prune winterkill in spring; blooms on new growth.

MATURE HEIGHT: 5'
GROWTH RATE: medium
LIGHT: full sun, semi-sunny
MOISTURE: roots moist

BERBERIS *ber-ber-iss*   Barberry

Slow-growing deciduous and evergreen thorny shrubs, adaptable and handsome year-round. They make impenetrable hedges and offer a three-season display. Most produce pinkish or reddish new leaves in late spring that turn to green in summer, and then color orange, yellow, and red in fall. Small attractive yellow flowers in mid-spring, rather hidden by foliage in most species. Red, purplish, or bluish black fruits appear in late summer. Tolerant of soil and moisture. The evergreens are a little less hardy than the deciduous types and adapt to considerable shade (Shrubs 18). Deciduous barberries color best in full sun and rich, neutral-range, moist soils.

GROWTH RATE: slow
LIGHT: full sun, semi-sunny
MOISTURE: roots moist

B. koreana   Korean Barberry   Zones 5–9.
Deciduous, tall, to 6 feet. The spring flowers, borne in pendant clusters, are tiny and yellow; the fruits are brilliant red, and the autumn color is excellent.

B. thunbergii 'Crimson Pygmy'
Japanese Barberry   Zones 5–8.
A low, dense plant 3 to 6 feet tall and often wider than it is tall, with brilliant fall color especially when growing in full sun. One of the first to leaf out in spring. Superb hedge plant. Deciduous.

DEUTZIA *dewt-see-uh*
gracilis 'Nikko'   Slender Deutzia   Zones 4–8.

Compact, low-spreading with lavish late-April display of exquisite white flower clusters; burgundy foliage in fall. Attractive low hedge. The cultivar was introduced from Japan by National Arboretum hor-

Abelia × *grandiflora* hedge in the dogwood area of the National Arboretum.

ticulturist Sylvester G. March and former director Dr. John L. Creech. Plant in spring or fall in soil in the neutral range.

MATURE HEIGHT: 2'
GROWTH RATE: medium
LIGHT: full sun, semi-sunny
MOISTURE: versatile

EUONYMUS *yew-on-im-us*
alata 'Compacta'
Dwarf Winged Spindle Tree   Zones 3–8.

Small deciduous tree or tall shrub, and one of the best for brilliant fall color. It fairly flames in shades of pink-scarlet. Tidy but full growth is useful for hedges, municipal plantings, and specimen display. The corky bark "wings" are treasured by flower arrangers. Colors in full sun or part shade. Prefers well-drained soil.

MATURE HEIGHT: 10'–12'
GROWTH RATE: slow
LIGHT: full sun, semi-sunny
MOISTURE: roots moist

HAMAMELIS *ham-am-ee-liss*
Witch Hazel

Small deciduous trees or tall shrubs, whose branches are covered with yellow, ribbonlike flower petals, often fragrant, in fall, late winter, or earliest spring, usually the first shrubs to bloom. Grow well in deciduous woods. Good in the East and Midwest for screens and hedges, and excellent as container plants. Brilliant fall color in leaves and bark. Provide well-drained soil in the acid range.

GROWTH RATE: medium/slow
LIGHT: semi-sunny
MOISTURE: roots moist

H. × intermedia   Zones 5–8.
'Arnold Promise' has large, deep yellow, fragrant flowers. Height to 20 feet. Autumn color of 'Diane' is exceptionally rich orange-red.

Hamamelis × intermedia, Witch Hazel, and privet hedge.

H. mollis   Chinese Witch Hazel   Zones 5/6–8.
A large shrub, to 30 feet, or small tree; it has the largest flowers and they are very fragrant. The fall color is orange-yellow.

HIBISCUS *hye-bisk-us*   Hibiscus

The old-fashioned shrub hibiscus are hardy and adaptable, with good deciduous foliage and a profusion of short-lived flowers. They require well-drained sandy loam, pH 5.5 to 7.0, with high organic content. Good subjects for espalier.

MATURE HEIGHT: 8'
GROWTH RATE: medium
LIGHT: full sun, semi-sunny
MOISTURE: soil surface moist

Kolkwitzia amabilis, Beautybush.

H. rosa-sinensis   Chinese Hibiscus
                                                Zones 9–10.
For warm regions of Texas, Florida, and California. Fast-growing handsome shrub 6 to 8 feet tall, with very showy year-round flowers in red, yellow, orange, white, sometimes with a contrasting eye and a variety of shadings, to 6 inches in diameter, single or double. Hybrids may be ruffled or fringed. Used as specimen and for hedges. Requires full sun and frequent fertilization. The flowers last only one day, but appear constantly. Grown as a container plant in the North and wintered indoors in a sunny window.

H. syriacus 'Diane'   Rose-of-Sharon,
Shrub Althaea   Zones 5–8.
Erect shrub to 8 feet tall and 5½ feet wide. Flowers are pure white, 4 to 6 inches in diameter, with waxy, heavily ruffled petals crinkled on the margin. Good specimen plant, or use in groups as background or hedge. Strong, dense branching makes it attractive in winter. 'Helene' is a related form, hardy farther North in a protected corner.

KOLKWITZIA *kol-kwits-ee-uh*
amabilis   Beautybush   Zones 6–9.

Fast-growing, tall, deciduous shrub lovely in bloom when it is covered with showy pink bell-shaped flowers with yellow throats. Useful in larger landscapes as a tall, naturalized screen and windbreak. Needs well-drained soil. Flowers on last year's wood. Cut older stems after flowering as needed to keep the plant attractive.

MATURE HEIGHT: 10'
GROWTH RATE: fast
LIGHT: full sun
MOISTURE: roots moist

LIGUSTRUM *lig-gust-rum*   Privet

Tall evergreen or deciduous shrubs very useful as specimens and especially valued for hedges. Have small leaves like boxwood but are much easier plants to grow. Growth is vigorous, and pruning is required. Tolerant of almost any condition.

GROWTH RATE: fast
LIGHT: versatile
MOISTURE: versatile

L. × ibolium   Zones 4–7.
Deciduous, fast-growing to 8 or 10 feet, and has glossy, dark green foliage. The leaves of 'Variegatum' have a soft creamy yellow edge. Excellent hedge plants. Clippable.

L. obtusifolium   Zones 3–7.
Deciduous, to 10 or 12 feet tall, and the best privet for screen and background planting or hedge. The variety *regelianum*, Regel's Privet, is lower, to 4 or 5 feet. The flowers are white, and to some, unpleasantly fragrant; the fruit that appears in early fall is blue-black and persistent.

SPIRAEA *spye-ree-uh*
× vanhouttei   Zones 4–8.

Beautiful deciduous flowering plant with graceful branches arching to the ground. It covers itself with showy small white flowers in mid-spring. Makes a good formal hedge. Don't clip this one. Prefers moist soil but is very versatile.

MATURE HEIGHT: 6′
GROWTH RATE: fast
LIGHT: full sun
MOISTURE: versatile

SEE ALSO:
Berberis thunbergii 'Aurea', Yellow Japanese Barberry, Shrubs 9
Chaenomeles speciosa, Japanese Quince, Flowering Quince, Shrubs 1
Cotinus coggygria, Smoke Tree, Smokebush, Shrubs 8
Elaeagnus angustifolia, Russian Olive, Shrubs 10
Forsythia × *intermedia*, Shrubs 1

Ilex verticillata 'Winter Red', Winterberry, Shrubs 25
Lagerstroemia indica, Crape Myrtle, Shrubs 5
Ligustrum japonicum texanum 'Silver Star', Waxleaf Privet, Japanese Privet, Shrubs 11
Lonicera, Honeysuckle, Shrubs 15
Osmanthus, Devil-weed, Shrubs 15
Prunus spinosa var. *purpurea*, Blackthorn, Sloe, Shrubs 8
Rosa, Rose, Shrubs 19
Syringa, Lilac, Shrubs 4
Viburnum 'Chesapeake', Shrubs 1

ALTERNATES:
Paeonia, Peony
Rhamnus frangula 'Columnaris', Tallhedge Alder Buckthorn
Tagetes, Marigold
Yucca filamentosa, Adam's-needle

SHRUBS 18
EVERGREEN SHRUBS FOR HEDGES, EDGING, AND SCREENING

Evergreen hedges are more costly and slower growing than deciduous hedges, but they are attractive year-round, more enduring, and generally need less pruning. Clippable hedges are best for formal landscapes. Thorny plants are indicated when the aim is to keep out intruders, tall or small, like dogs and cats. See also Shrubs 7. Buy young 18- to 24-inch plants that are well branched. They will make new growth from the base when pruned, ensuring a dense hedge that is well branched to the ground. Prune to keep the base slightly wider than the top—especially important with evergreens, which drop their needles when shaded by a wider top and don't regrow. Prune young developing hedges and shrubs during active growth. Succulent shoots cut in half immediately begin to grow lateral shoots. For infor-

mation on pruning evergreens, see the introduction to Shrubs.

COMPANION PLANTINGS
Ground covers: *Hedera helix*, English Ivy; *Pachysandra terminalis*, Japanese Pachysandra; *Vinca minor*, Periwinkle.

BERBERIS *ber-ber-iss*   Barberry

The species here are evergreen shrubs, attractive in three seasons. They make impenetrable hedges. Most produce pinkish or reddish new leaves in late spring that turn green later. Small attractive yellow flowers in mid-spring, rather hidden by foliage in most species. Red, purplish, or bluish black fruits appear in late summer. Versatile as to soil and moisture. The evergreens are somewhat less hardy than deciduous types and adapt to considerable shade. Barberry prefers neutral-range soil, pH 6.0 to 8.0.

GROWTH RATE: slow
LIGHT: full sun, semi-sunny
MOISTURE: roots moist

B. buxifolia 'Nana'   Zones 6–9.
Slow-growing plant to 2 feet that makes a dense mound and a handsome low hedge. Abundant yellow flowers in early spring are followed by purple-blue berries. New growth has reddish tinge.

B. julianae Wintergreen Barberry Zones 5–9.
Grows medium-fast to about 8 feet. Very attractive broad, spiny leaves that turn purplish bronze in winter. Conspicuous yellow flowers, followed by black berries with a silvery bloom. 'Nana' is a good dwarf but hard to find.

B. × mentorensis   Zones 5–8.
Fast-growing to 5 to 7 feet. Evergreen or near evergreen with stiff upright branches and heavy, thick, dark foliage that turns yellow-orange and red in late fall. The berries are dull, dark red. Tolerates heat and drought. Handsome if not pruned. Good hedge plant for the West.

B. verruculosa Barberry   Zones 6–8.
To 3 feet tall. Compact and delicate, with glossy dark green leaves that are whitish underneath. Golden

Spiraea × *vanhouttei*, Bridal-wreath. (Neumann)

Berberis julianae, Wintergreen Barberry.

yellow flowers. Blue-black fruit with bloom. Turns bronze in fall. Excellent for banks and edging.

BUXUS *bux-us* Box, Boxwood

Superb small-leaved formal evergreens from low shrubs to small trees, valued as foundation plants, specimens, in group plantings and hedges. Slow-growing, long-lived, they appear in most knot gardens, formal herb borders, and estate landscapes. Accept pruning well and are a favorite topiary subject. Well-drained soil is needed. Mulch with peat moss or leaf mold to keep roots cool; cultivate shallowly. Transplant easily.

GROWTH RATE: slow
LIGHT: full sun, semi-sunny
MOISTURE: roots moist

B. microphylla   Zones 4–9.
Natural height is 3 to 4 feet, with an equal spread. Adapts to considerable shade. 'Compacta' is especially low. 'Tide Hill' grows to 2 feet and is more than twice as wide. 'Morris Midget' is a compact edger.

B. sempervirens 'Suffruticosa'   Edging Box, Dwarf Box   Zones 5–9.
A dwarf valued since colonial times—150-year-old plants can be 3 feet high. With pruning, can be kept under 1 foot; unchecked it will grow to 4 or 5 feet. Aromatic leaves. Many variegated cultivars. The species is a tall shrub or small tree.

EUGENIA *yew-jeen-ee-uh*

Mostly tall evergreen plants widely used for hedges in Florida and California. Attractive leaves, white flowers, and colorful berrylike fruits, edible in some species. Cloves are the dried buds of *E. aromatica* (syn. *Syzygium aromaticum*).

GROWTH RATE: medium/slow
LIGHT: full sun, semi-sunny
MOISTURE: roots moist

E. brasiliensis Brazil Cherry   Zones 9–10.
Tall shrub, to 10 or 15 feet in Florida, with showy white flowers followed by edible cherrylike fruit in spring. Needs lots of light, but is an excellent specimen and informal hedge plant.

E. myrtifolia (syn. *Syzygium paniculatum*) 'Globulus' Dwarf Brush Cherry   Zone 10.
Dwarf form of a small tree. Dense, vivid bronze-amber color of emerging foliage is retained throughout the year. Clip to suitable size. Bears white flowers; its rose-purple fruit is used to make jelly.

E. uniflora Surinam Cherry   Zones 9–10.
Reaches 4 to 15 feet, has fragrant white flowers and dark crimson fruit with a spicy flavor that is used in making jams. Grown as a hedge, formal and informal, and for fruit. Can be pruned to any size.

LIGUSTRUM *lig-gust-rum* Privet

Vigorous-growing evergreen or deciduous shrubs for tall, dense hedges. Small leaves like boxwood but an easier plant to grow. May be sheared or trained as topiary, but it can grow out of bounds if untended. Insignificant white-green flowers in spring, and an odor some find objectionable. Trimming is necessary

Photinia × fraseri, Fraser Photinia. (Monrovia Nursery Co.)

or privet becomes scraggly in a few years. Tolerant of almost any condition.

GROWTH RATE: according to species
LIGHT: tolerant
MOISTURE: tolerant

L. amurense Amur Privet   Zones 3–8.
Deciduous or semievergreen according to climate, this is the hardiest of the hedge privets and holds its olive green foliage longer than others. To 14 or 16 feet.

L. japonicum (texanum) 'Silver Star'
Wax-leaf Privet, Japanese Privet   Zones 7–9.
The leaves are deep green in the center and have creamy silver edges. Compact, slow-growing cultivar, erect, medium height. Shearable. Nearly perfect tall hedge.

L. lucidum Glossy Privet   Zones 8–10.
Evergreen privet for warmer regions valued for its glossy leaves. It generally grows rapidly to 20 or 25 feet. Good tall screen.

L. ovalifolium California Privet   Zones 5–8.
Evergreen or semievergreen according to climate. Glossy green foliage and dense growth make this a very popular hedge plant. To 10 or 15 feet. Dull white, heavily scented flowers are produced in terminal panicles in summer. The fruits are black. There are variegated cultivars.

L. × vicaryi Vicary Golden Privet   Zones 4–9.
Evergreen, to 10 or 12 feet tall, with many erect branches covered with bright golden foliage. Needs full sun to color well and looks best when untrimmed. The 'Storzinger Strain' is said to be hardier. Succeeds in dry urban situations and by the seashore.

NERIUM *neer-ee-um*
oleander Oleander, Rose-bay   Zones 9–10.

Evergreen shrubs or small trees with showy spring-through-summer clusters of single or double blooms in white, yellow, red, pink, or lilac. There are sweet-scented types, notably a double-flowered red. Oleander can be clipped. It withstands drought and in hot, dry climates is used as a street and hedge plant. Good shore specimen. In cool regions it is grown in pots, summered outdoors, and wintered indoors in a bright window.

MATURE HEIGHT: 12'–15'
GROWTH RATE: medium
LIGHT: full sun
MOISTURE: roots moist

PHOTINIA *foh-tin-ee-uh*

Excellent ornamental shrubs or small trees with showy white flowers in clusters in summer, followed by berrylike fruit. Excellent tall hedges, screening, and windbreaks. Prefer well-drained soil and do best in airy locations. Avoid where fire blight is prevalent, for they are highly susceptible; elsewhere, plant only resistant cultivars.

Nerium oleander, Oleander. (Neumann)

P. × fraseri Fraser's Photinia Zones 6–9.
Medium-size white flower in spring and new foliage that is an eye-catching, glistening coppery red on bright red stems. 'Indian Princess' is a dwarf form with orange-copper new growth.

P. glabra Japanese Photinia Zones 7–9.
Small for the genus, 10 or 12 feet high, and useful for flowering hedges and screening. Showy flowers in flat clusters in midsummer, followed by red berries.

TSUGA *tsoo-guh* Hemlock

Feathery, graceful, fast-growing (usually), pyramidal, needled evergreen trees, with shallow roots that make transplanting at any age easy. They respond beautifully to clipping and shearing. In the Northeast, one of the most widely used evergreens for hedges and screening. They need moisture and don't do well in hot, dry summers.

GROWTH RATE: fast
LIGHT: full sun
MOISTURE: roots moist

T. canadensis Canada Hemlock Zones 4–8.
This is the species which is planted young, then trimmed and maintained in hedge form. May also be sheared as a topiary. Somewhat intolerant of city conditions. There is a weeping form, 'Pendula'.

T. caroliniana Carolina Hemlock Zones 4–8.
Similar to the species above, but said to be more tolerant of urban conditions.

T. heterophylla Western Hemlock
Zones 6–8.
The choice for the cool Northwest, from Alaska to northern California. It has short narrow branches.

Tsuga canadensis, Canadian Hemlock. (Neumann)

Rosa 'Starina'. (Bell)

T. mertensiana Mountain Hemlock
Zones 6–8.
Beautiful in its native region, Alaska to California. The leaves of 'Argentea' are bluish green.

TEUCRIUM *tewk-ree-um*
chamaedrys Germander Zones 3–8.

Evergreen subshrub and herb that makes a neat low hedge or edging and often is used in place of boxwood where the latter isn't hardy. It is dense, about 1 foot high, with toothed leaves and loose spikes of redpurple to rose flowers in summer. The variety *prostratum* is lower and flowers more heavily. Welldrained soil is very important.

MATURE HEIGHT: 1′
GROWTH RATE: medium
LIGHT: full sun
MOISTURE: roots moist

SEE ALSO:
Berberis × gladwynensis 'William Penn', Barberry, Shrubs 12
Elaeagnus pungens 'Maculata', Thorny Elaeagnus, Shrubs 11
Ilex cornuta 'O'Spring', Chinese Holly, Horned Holly, Shrubs 11
Ilex, Holly, Shrubs 16, Shrubs 7
Lavendula angustifolia, English Lavender, Herbs 6
Lonicera tatarica, Tatarian Honeysuckle, Shrubs 15
Myrtus communis, Myrtle, Shrubs 14
Osmanthus heterophyllus 'Gulftide', Holly Olive, Chinese Olive, Shrubs 15
Pittosporum tobira, Japanese Pittosporum, Shrubs 21
Pyracantha coccinea cvs., Fire Thorn, Shrubs 14
Santolina chamaecyparissus, Lavender Cotton, Shrubs 13
Taxus cvs., Yew, Shrubs 7
Thuja cvs., Arborvitae, Shrubs 7
Viburnum × burkwoodii 'Mohawk', Shrubs 1
Viburnum × carlcephalum 'Cayuga', Shrubs 1

ALTERNATES:
Chamaecyparis obtusa cvs.
Chamaecyparis pisifera cvs.
Nandina domestica, Heavenly Bamboo
Prunus laureocerasus, Cherry Laurel
Raphiolepis umbellata, Yedda Hawthorn

SHRUBS 19
ROSES FOR HEDGES AND EDGING

Roses, with their lovely flowers and daunting thorns, have been planted as hedges since the days of Sleeping Beauty. Those named here are vigorous and showy, superb plants for edgings and hedges, tall and small. Any of them is beautiful enough to stand alone. If not entirely problem-free, all are very resistant, hardy, and easy to grow.

Climbing Roses are described in Vines 2; Shrub Roses, Shrubs 6; Old Garden Roses, Herbs 7.

ROSA *roh-zuh* Rose

Best for edging are small Miniatures (M) and Polyanthas (POL); for hedges, large Floribundas (FL) and Rugosas. All require 6 hours of sun a day to flower fully.

The miniature roses are hybrid descendants of 'Rouletti', a selection of *Rosa chinensis* 'Minima', the Fairy Rose, which blooms all season. Some are climbers. They flower freely from June to frost, and are 12 to 18 inches high with flowers less than 1¾ inches in diameter, often shaped like tiny hybrid teas or cabbage roses. Too small to be effective in a rose garden, but delightful as edging plants in rock gardens and containers. Miniature roses will bloom for a time indoors on a very sunny windowsill. They also flourish in containers set in sun on patio or porch, but should winter out of the wind near a house wall, with some protection.

The original Polyantha roses came from natural crosses of the China Rose and a dwarf sport of *Rosa multiflora*, Baby Rose, which is the understock for rose cultivars grown as hedges or "living fences." The modern hybrids are low—less than 30 inches high—and flower freely throughout the season, bearing clusters of charming little flowers under 2 inches. They grow vigorously and are very hardy.

Floribundas are larger Polyanthas. They combine the qualities of the vigorous, small-flowered Polyanthas with those of hybrid tea roses, whose blooms are big and often fragrant. Floribunda roses are 2 to 3½ or 4 inches in diameter, produced in clusters over a long season. They are sometimes called "cluster roses," and are so showy and so reliable that they are widely used to landscape roadsides and parks in Europe.

Rugosa is the name of a *Rosa* species and also of a rose classification, Rugosa rose. The common name, however, is Japanese Rose. These big plants send out their sweet-scented, single or double flowers in spring with some repeat, and can take care of themselves. Colors include white, pink, and red. The tall, stiff, spiny canes make superb hedges. The plants are very hardy and have been used to tie down sandy slopes. The best adapted rose for seashore planting. Has decorative, edible rose hips.

See Shrubs 6 for an overview on rose culture.

ROSES FOR LOW BORDERS AND EDGINGS

'Centerpiece' (M). Outstanding performer; red, high-centered, double roses in profusion, on compact, bushy, 12- to 16-inch plants with dark green leaves.

'China Doll' (POL)
This exquisite Polyantha bears a profusion of large clusters of 1½-inch light pink, semidouble blooms throughout the warm season. Compact plant, 12 to 18 inches high, rounded, very vigorous and hardy. Disease-resistant.

'Cupcake'(M)
Compact, bushy little plant, 12 to 16 inches high, with soft, clear pink, fully double, small tea roses throughout the season. Good cut flower.

'Lavender Jewel' (M)
Rare soft lavender edged with magenta and the perfect form of double tea roses, just 1¼ inches in diameter. Lavish bloom through the growing season on spreading plants 12 to 16 inches high.

'Rise 'N Shine' (M)
Lovely little plants that cover themselves with beautiful, clear yellow roses the form of full-size hybrid teas. Good fragrance. Compact, erect, bushy plants 15 inches high. Recipient of the American Rose Society Award of Excellence.

'Snow Bride' (M)
Exquisite, well-formed, fully double little hybrid tea, creamy white with a slight fragrance; abundant blooms all season. Slightly spreading plant, but compact and bushy, 12 to 16 inches high.

'Starina' (M)
Beautifully formed little rose, excellent for specimen planting, hedges, and cutting, brilliant orange-red touched with yellow at the base. Some fragrance. Blooms all season on bushy, compact plants 12 to 16 inches tall.

'The Fairy' (POL)
Superb Polyantha hybrid shrub rose, with abundant clusters of small, charming, very full, slightly fragrant, seashell-pink blooms, from early summer until frost. Long-lasting cut flower. Compact plant, 24 to 30 inches high, beautiful low hedge.

FOR HIGH HEDGES

'Betty Prior' (FL). Prolific bloomer from spring through fall in a hardy hedge. Deep carmine-pink

Rosa 'The Fairy'. (Bell)

Rosa 'Betty Prior' planted as a hedge. (Bell)

Rosa rugosa 'Rubra'. (McDonald)

single flower turns a richer color in cool weather, borne in full, beautiful clusters. Plant grows to 4 or 5 feet, good foliage and a nice upright, bushy, spreading form.
'Meidomonac' (SHRUB)
Lovely, everblooming shrub rose; soft pink blooms 2½ to 3½ inches across. Between 3 and 5 feet tall, very vigorous, hardy and disease-tolerant.
'Simplicity' (FL). Excellent Floribunda, 3 to 3½ feet high; colorful hedge, with medium-pink, semi-double, 3- to 4-inch flowers in clusters through the season. Disease-resistant, winter-hardy.

R. rugosa and hybrids   Japanese Rose
Any Rugosa makes a beautiful spring-flowering hedge, with red-orange rose hips in fall that last through winter. If spent blooms are removed, many Rugosas repeat bloom; for instance, the hybrid 'Sir Thomas Lipton' produces masses of large, double, fragrant white flowers in spring and blooms again in fall. Very hardy plant, 4 to 5 feet tall.

SEE ALSO:

Climbing Roses, Vines 2
Old Garden Roses, and species roses, Herbs 7
Roses for cutting, Shrubs 6

SHRUBS 20
SHRUBS FOR CITY STREETS AND DRY PLACES

These shrubs thrive even in dry urban situations. Many more appear on the See also list below. All benefit from good soil preparation.

COMPANION PLANTINGS
Tree: *Gingko biloba* 'Magyar', Maidenhair Tree.
Shrub: *Scaevola* 'Mauve Clusters'.
Flowers: *Pelargonium* × *hortorum*, House Geranium; *Petunia* × *hybrida*, single and double Hybrid Petunia; *Portulaca grandiflora*, Rose Moss; *Sedum spectabile* 'Autumn Joy', Stonecrop; *Tagetes patula*, French Marigold.

ARTEMISIA *art-em-miz-ee-uh*
ludoviciana var. albula   Silver-king Artemisia
Zones 5–9.

This airy, frosty looking foliage plant is fragrant, valuable for edging, in borders, and as ground cover in larger landscapes. There are tiny grayish white florets. Tolerates drought and full sun, and is easily grown in

well-drained garden soil. Plant container-grown plants in early spring. See also Ground Covers 7.

MATURE HEIGHT: 3'
GROWTH RATE: medium
LIGHT: full sun
MOISTURE: versatile

LIGUSTRUM *lig-gust-rum*
× vicaryi   Vicary Golden Privet   Zones 5–9.

Vigorous, tall evergreen often used for a trimmed hedge. The leaves are small, like boxwood, but the shrub grows faster than boxwood and is very tolerant. Has a particular and not always popular odor when the small green-white flowers are in bloom. This species grows slowly to 10 to 12 feet, and has many erect branches covered with bright golden foliage. Needs full sun to color well and looks best when untrimmed. Succeeds in dry urban situations and by the seashore. The 'Storzinger Strain' is noted as hardier.

GROWTH RATE: slow
LIGHT: versatile
MOISTURE: versatile

KERRIA *kehr-ree-uh*
japonica 'Pleniflora'   Japanese Rose
Zones 5–8.

Vigorous, upright, bushy plant that bears a profusion of 1- to 2-inch golden blooms in spring. The flowers resemble tiny mums and are long-lasting when cut. The branches stay green in winter. Thin old stems after flowering. The species is smaller, needs less pruning, and gives some repeat bloom in summer.

MATURE HEIGHT: 6'
GROWTH RATE: medium
LIGHT: full sun, semi-sunny
MOISTURE: roots moist, versatile

PINUS *pye-nus*
mugo var. mugo   Mugho Pine   Zones 2–7.

Slow-growing conifer known for its persistent, long, needlelike leaves sheathed in bundles. One of the few shrublike pines. It can reach 8 to 10 feet in height, and is broad-spreading. It is a superior landscape plant but may be subject to scale; buy resistant cultivars. The pines will grow in dry, sandy soils where little else grows but they are sensitive to air pollution. Most require somewhat acid soil, pH 5.0 to 6.0.

GROWTH RATE: medium/slow
LIGHT: full sun
MOISTURE: roots moist, versatile

POTENTILLA *poh-ten-till-uh*
fruticosa   Shrubby Cinquefoil   Zones 2–7.

Almost indestructible low bush and ground cover valued for small, bright yellow blooms, like big buttercups, June through frost. Needs little care once established in an open, sunny site. Profits from occasional pruning. Some established cultivars are: 'Coronation Triumph', a 4-foot shrub bearing many yellow flowers, does well in Midwest; 'Katherine Dykes', fine 3-foot shrub that arches and spreads, and

Pittosporum tobira, Japanese Pittosporum. (McDonald)

has lemon yellow flowers 1 inch across; 'Knaphill', dense, low mounded form, that bears a profusion of small yellow flowers. Rated highly for the Midwest. Tolerates some drought.

MATURE HEIGHT: 10"–4'
GROWTH RATE: medium
LIGHT: full sun
MOISTURE: versatile

RHAMNUS *ram-nus*
frangula 'Columnaris'
Tallhedge Alder Buckthorn Zones 2–7.

Deciduous shrub to 12 feet or more with shiny, dark green leaves that turn bright yellow in fall. The flowers are inconspicuous and the berrylike fruits change from red to black. The seeds are spread by birds and can become a nuisance. Good screen, hedge, and windbreak, requiring little trimming. Grows in almost any soil and withstands difficult conditions.

MATURE HEIGHT: 15'
GROWTH RATE: medium
LIGHT: full sun, semi-sunny
MOISTURE: versatile

SKIMMIA *skim-ee-uh*

Dwarf, shade-loving evergreen shrubs whose leaves are aromatic when crushed. In early spring, or fall and winter in warm regions, they bear clusters of small, somewhat fragrant flowers in upright panicles followed by inedible berrylike fruit. Often flowers and fruit are on the shrub at the same time. Some species are dioecious. Good urban and pot plants. Prefer moist, acid, sandy soil with lots of peat, but will survive in alkaline conditions.

GROWTH RATE: slow
LIGHT: semi-sunny, shade
MOISTURE: roots moist

S. japonica Zones 7–9.
Slow-growing, densely branched shrub 3 to 5 feet high, with yellowish white flowers borne by the female plant. Male flowers are larger and very fragrant. The species is dioecious and requires a male nearby to produce its bright red berries.

S. reevesiana Zones 7–9.
Smaller plant, to 2 feet, with white bisexual flowers. One plant alone will fruit. Requires a rich, moist, acid soil.

SEE ALSO:

Azalea (*Rhododendron*), Shrubs 2
Berberis × *mentorensis*, Barberry, Shrubs 18
Berberis thunbergii 'Aurea', Yellow Japanese Barberry, Shrubs 9
Berberis thunbergii 'Crimson Pygmy', Japanese Barberry, Shrubs 8
Ceanothus × *delilianus*, Shrubs 7
Chaenomeles speciosa, Japanese Quince, Flowering Quince, Shrubs 1
Chionanthus retusus, Fringe Tree, Shrubs 4
Forsythia × *intermedia* cvs., Shrubs 1
Hibiscus rosa-sinensis, Chinese Hibiscus, Shrubs 5
Hibiscus syriacus cvs., Rose-of-Sharon, Shrub Althaea, Shrubs 5
Hydrangea cvs., Shrubs 22
Hydrangea macrophylla 'Variegata', Variegated Bigleaf Hydrangea, Shrubs 11
Juniperus cvs., Juniper, Shrubs 7
Lagerstroemia indica, Crape Myrtle, Shrubs 5
Ligustrum cvs., Privet, Shrubs 18
Lonicera fragrantissima, Winter Honeysuckle, Shrubs 15
Lonicera tatarica, Tatarian Honeysuckle, Shrubs 15
Myrica pensylvanica, Bayberry, Shrubs 22
Nerium oleander, Oleander, Rose-bay, Shrubs 18
Picea pungens 'Fat Albert', Colorado Blue Spruce, Shrubs 7
Pittosporum tobira, Japanese Pittosporum, Shrubs 21
Rhododendron cvs., Shrubs 3
Symphoricarpos orbiculatus, Indian Currant, Coralberry, Shrubs 24
Tsuga caroliniana, Carolina Hemlock, Shrubs 18
Yucca filamentosa 'Bright Edge', 'Gold Sword', Adam's-needle, Shrubs 22

ALTERNATES:
Elaeagnus angustifolia, Russian Olive
Elaeagnus philippinensis
Kolkwitzia amabilis, Beautybush
Physocarpus opulifolius 'Dart's Gold', Eastern Ninebark
Rhus, Sumac
Sambucus canadensis, American Elder, Sweet Elder
Spiraea × *bumalda* 'Anthony Waterer', 'Froebellii'
Spiraea × *vanhouttei*, Bridal-wreath
Weigela florida 'Variegata nana', Variegated Dwarf Weigela

SHRUBS 21
SHRUBS FOR CONTAINER PLANTING

Plants seen in tree form (roses) and as topiaries (boxwood) and espaliers (camellias, rosemary) are good container material. So are many of the fragrant woody herbs in Herbs 1 (Trees and Shrubs for Herb Gardens) and flowering shrubs in Shrubs 1. Avoid containerizing plants that require constantly moist soil. Containers set in hot sun and wind dry out daily. Automatic watering systems are helpful for big container gardens. An 8-inch pot handles a young shrub, but it will eventually need a 14-, then an 18-inch pot. Lightweight planting mixes keep big containers easy to move indoors in winter. See also Trees 16.

COMPANION PLANTINGS
Flowers: *Browallia speciosa*, Sapphire Flower; *Lobelia* cv. 'Crystal Palace'; *L. erinus*, Edging Lobelia; *Pelargonium peltatum*, Ivy Geranium; *Vinca minor*, Periwinkle; *V. m.* 'Variegata', Variegated Periwinkle; *Viola* × *wittrockiana*, Pansy.

ACER *ay-ser* Maple

Maple shrubs have delicate and colorful foliage. They need fairly constant moisture and prefer well-drained, acid-range soil. Afford protection from direct sun in warm regions. Good container plants but not for indoors.

GROWTH RATE: medium/slow
LIGHT: full sun, semi-sunny
MOISTURE: roots moist

A. palmatum 'Dissectum Atropurpureum'
Threadleaf Japanese Maple Zones 5/6–8.
Sculptural, rounded mound 6 to 8 feet tall with deeply incised, fine leaves bloodred in spring, and again when cold comes. 'Crimson Queen', 4' to 6' feet tall, is an attractive dwarf weeping form, with excellent summer color.

A. p. 'Osakazuki' Japanese Maple
Zones 4–8.
Small tree or large shrub with large leaves, yellow to light green in summer, that turn a stunning fluorescent red in fall. Its height is to 15 feet.

A. p. 'Sangokaku' Coral Bark Maple
Zones 5–9.
Small multi-branched tree or large shrub whose delicate light green foliage colors bright yellow in fall.

189

Acer palmatum, Japanese Maple.

Acer palmatum 'Crimson Queen'. (Monrovia Nursery Co.)

Acer palmatum 'Dissectum'. (Monrovia Nursery Co.)

Valued for the bark, which turns brilliant coral-red in winter; plant is striking standing in snow. Handsome container plant. Pruning out unwanted limbs enhances this plant's beauty. Height 10 to 15 feet.

AUCUBA *aw-kew-buh*
japonica 'Variegata' Gold-dust Tree
Zones 6–8.

Evergreen background plant with large bright green leaves flecked yellow in 'Variegata', a female; 'Maculata' has leaves blotched yellow-white and is male. Females produce large persistent red berries. Plant both sexes for best fruiting. Makes a good houseplant in a cool room. 'Crotonifolia' has leaves dusted with white spots, and 'Picturata', deep green leaves with a large yellow blotch in the center.

MATURE HEIGHT: 6'–10'
GROWTH RATE: medium
LIGHT: semi-sunny, shade
MOISTURE: roots moist

Acer palmatum 'Burgundy Lace'. (Monrovia Nursery Co.)

× CITROFORTUNELLA
sit-roh-for-tew-nell-uh
mitis Calamondin Orange Zones 9–10.

Beautiful upright evergreen shrub with leathery bright green leaves, small, fragrant white flowers, and tiny juicy sour orange fruits that make excellent preserves and orangeade. In the North, this container plant should be wintered indoors. Needs well-drained soil.

MATURE HEIGHT: 3'–5'
GROWTH RATE: slow
LIGHT: full sun
MOISTURE: roots moist

CODIAEUM *koh-dih-ee-um*
variegatum Croton Zones 9–10.

The most colorful variegated foliage shrub of all, its big evergreen leaves are streaked and splotched with carmine red and bright yellow. Very popular container plant for terraces, greenhouses, and indoor gardens. There are hundreds of cultivars with varying leaf color patterns. Colors best in full sun and tolerates drought. Good indoors in strong light.

MATURE HEIGHT: 4'–15'
GROWTH RATE: medium
LIGHT: full sun
MOISTURE: versatile

CORNUS *korn-us* Dogwood

The best-known dogwoods are the lovely spring-flowering trees, but the genus includes the red-stemmed tall shrubs described here, valued for their unusual cold-weather color. Dogwoods prefer a moist, well-drained situation.

GROWTH RATE: fast
LIGHT: full sun, semi-sunny
MOISTURE: roots moist

C. alba 'Sibirica' Siberian Dogwood
Zones 2–8.
Medium-size, multi-stemmed, vase-shaped deciduous shrub with rounded dark green foliage. In spring, it bears the white flowers typical of dogwood trees, but smaller, followed by blue-white berries in fall. In winter, the bark turns a vivid coral-red and brightens the garden all winter long. The color is best when the shrub is cut back in late winter to encourage the production of young shoots. Handsome in pots. Height 8 to 10 feet. Prefers moist soil and supports wet situations. Better north of Zone 8.

C. sericea (syn. *stolonifera*)
Red-osier Dogwood Zones 2–8.
Very like *alba* in every respect though *alba*'s winter red may be better. White flowers in late spring are followed by white or bluish fruit. Good bank holders. Most attractive naturalized and massed. 'Flaviramea', Golden-twig Dogwood, is similar, but the stems are yellow.

COTONEASTER *kot-toh-nee-ass-ter*
salicifolius 'Autumn Fire'
Willowleaf Cotoneaster Zones 6–8.

Small, with silver-backed leaves, semievergreen or evergreen in the South, a handsome shrub with

Cotoneaster salicifolius, Willowleaf Cotoneaster. (Neumann)

interesting branching. Glossy leaves purplish in winter, and a profusion of scarlet fruits that persist. To ensure successful transplanting, in spring set out container or balled-and-burlapped plants in well-drained soil. Birds are attracted by the fruits. Good container plant but not one to bring indoors.

MATURE HEIGHT: 2'–3'
GROWTH RATE: medium
LIGHT: full sun, semi-sunny
MOISTURE: versatile

GARDENIA *gar-deen-ee-uh*
jasminoides Gardenia, Cape Jasmine
Zones 8–10.

Velvety white flowers of this glossy leaved evergreen shrub are among the most fragrant in the world. In the North it is pot-grown, summered outdoors in semi-sun, and wintered indoors in a cool sunny window, with high humidity. Blooms from early spring through summer. Prefers acid-range soil. *G. j.* 'Fortuniana' is a double-flowered form.

MATURE HEIGHT: 6'
GROWTH RATE: medium
LIGHT: semi-sunny
MOISTURE: roots moist

HAMAMELIS *ham-am-ee-liss*
Witch Hazel

Small deciduous trees or tall shrubs, whose branches are covered with yellow ribbonlike flower petals, often fragrant, in fall, late winter, or earliest spring. Usually the first shrubs to bloom. Excellent container plants for outdoors. Brilliant fall color in leaves and bark. Prefer soil in the acid range, well-drained. Place containers where fragrance can be appreciated.

GROWTH RATE: medium/slow
LIGHT: semi-sunny
MOISTURE: roots moist

H. × intermedia Zones 5–8.
'Arnold Promise' has large, deep yellow, fragrant flowers. Height to 20 feet. Autumn color of 'Diane' is exceptionally rich orange-red.

H. mollis Chinese Witch Hazel Zones 5/6–8.
A large shrub, to 30 feet, or small tree; it has the largest flowers and they are very fragrant. The fall color is orange-yellow. It is the least hardy.

H. virginiana Zones 4–8.
Height to 15 feet. This is the last woody plant to bloom in fall in New England. The narrow yellow flowers appear just when the leaves drop. Fruit comes the following fall before the flowers. Succeeds in woodsy light shade, but is showier in full sun in the North.

NANDINA *nan-dye-nuh*
domestica Heavenly Bamboo Zones 6–9.

Airy, graceful evergreen shrub. Loose clusters of whitish florets in spring are followed in autumn by showy red berries in drooping clusters, generally persistent through winter. When growing in sunny situations, leaves color maroon to orange-red in cold weather. Good container plant for outdoors. 'Fire Power', 'Harbor Dwarf', and 'Woods Dwarf' are disease-resistant cultivars that grow to about 3 feet and have superior winter color.

MATURE HEIGHT: 8'
GROWTH RATE: fast/medium
LIGHT: full sun, semi-sunny
MOISTURE: roots moist

NERIUM *neer-ee-um*
oleander Oleander, Rose-bay Zones 9–10.

Evergreen shrub or small tree with showy spring-through-summer clusters of single or double blooms in white, yellow, red, pink, or lilac. There are sweet-scented types, notably a double-flowered red. With-

stands drought. In cool regions it is grown in pots, summered outdoors, and wintered indoors in a bright window.

MATURE HEIGHT: 12'–15'
GROWTH RATE: medium
LIGHT: full sun
MOISTURE: roots moist

PITTOSPORUM *pit-os-por-um*
tobira Japanese Pittosporum Zones 9–10.

Handsome, spreading evergreen shrub to 10 or 12 feet, with leathery leaves and wonderfully fragrant greenish white flowers (like orange blossoms) in early summer. Good at the seashore and as a container plant; may be wintered indoors in cool regions. Prefers well-drained soil and has some tolerance to drought and salt spray. 'Variegata' has white-margined leaves. See also Trees 11.

MATURE HEIGHT: 10'–12'
GROWTH RATE: slow
LIGHT: full sun, semi-sunny
MOISTURE: roots moist

PODOCARPUS *poh-doh-karp-us*

Handsome evergreen shrubs and small trees with needlelike narrow leaves used as a specimen and hedge plant in warm regions. Young plants are good container subjects in the North but must winter indoors. Dioecious. Need well-drained soil and tolerate some shade.

GROWTH RATE: medium
LIGHT: semi-sunny
MOISTURE: roots moist, versatile

P. gracilior Weeping Fern Pine Zone 10.
Graceful medium-size evergreen with dense, pendant branches. Used as specimen in Florida and a pot plant in the North, to winter indoors. Height: 10 to 20 feet.

P. macrophyllus Southern Yew Zones 9–10.
Bears edible purple fruit; leaves resemble the yew. Height 8 to 25 feet. The variety *maki*, Chinese Podocarpus, is shrubby and smaller.

RHAPIS *ray-pis*
excelsa Lady Palm Zones 9–10.

Slow-growing, bushy, clump-forming palm with reed-like stems that is used as an informal hedge in Florida, and a pot plant to winter indoors in the North. Yellows in direct sun; has some drought tolerance.

MATURE HEIGHT: 6'–10'
GROWTH RATE: slow
LIGHT: semi-sunny
MOISTURE: roots moist

SANTOLINA *san-toh-lye-nuh*

Gray-leaved, low evergreen shrubs with aromatic leaves, handsome in container gardens and with roses. Not good indoors. Need well-drained soil.

GROWTH RATE: medium
LIGHT: full sun
MOISTURE: roots moist

Hibiscus in tree form. (Monrovia Nursery Co.)

S. chamaecyparissus   Lavender Cotton
                                      Zones 6–9.
Low evergreen to 1½ or 2 feet tall, as multi-branched as coral, with foliage that is silvery in moonlight. Small, pale yellow, buttonlike flowers bloom above the leaves in late spring and summer. Used in dried arrangements and valued for its continuing fragrance.

S. virens   Green Santolina   Zones 7–9.
Smaller than lavender cotton, to 15 inches. Succeeds easily in poor, sandy soil in the neutral range but not in hot summers and high humidity. The flowers are a creamy color.

SKIMMIA *skim-ee-uh*

Dwarf, shade-loving evergreen shrubs whose leaves are aromatic when crushed. In early spring, or fall and winter in warm regions, they bear clusters of small, somewhat fragrant flowers in upright panicles, followed by inedible berrylike fruit. Often flowers and fruit are on the shrub at the same time. Some species are dioecious. Good urban and pot plants. Prefer moist, acid, sandy soil with lots of peat but will survive in alkaline conditions.

GROWTH RATE:	slow
LIGHT:	semi-sunny, shade
MOISTURE:	roots moist

S. japonica   Zones 7–9.
Slow-growing, densely branched shrub 3 to 5 feet high, with yellowish white flowers borne by the female plant. Male flowers are larger and very fragrant. The species is dioecious and requires a male nearby to produce its bright red berries.

S. reevesiana   Zones 7–9.
Smaller plant, to 2 feet, with bisexual white flowers. One plant alone will fruit. Requires a rich, moist, acid soil.

SEE ALSO:
Azalea (*Rhododendron*), North Tisbury, Shrubs 2
Buxus, Box, Boxwood, Shrubs 7
Camellia japonica, Shrubs 14

Camellia sasanqua, Shrubs 14
Chamaecyparis obtusa 'Nova', Dwarf Golden Hinoki Cypress, Shrubs 7
Chamaecyparis pisifera 'Filifera Aurea', Golden Thread Sawara Cypress, Shrubs 9
Hibiscus rosa-sinensis, Chinese Hibiscus, Shrubs 14
Hibiscus schizopetalis, Japanese Hibiscus, Fringed Hibiscus, Shrubs 14
Ilex cornuta 'Burfordii', Burford's Chinese Holly, Burford Horned Holly, Shrubs 7
Juniperus, most, Juniper, Shrubs 7
Lagerstroemia indica cvs., Crape Myrtle, Shrubs 5
Myrtus communis, Myrtle, Shrubs 14
Pieris japonica 'Red Mill', Lily-of-the-valley Bush, Shrubs 1
Pinus mugo var. *mugo*, Mugho Pine, Shrubs 7
Rhododendron cvs., Shrubs 3
Rosmarinus officinalis, Rosemary, Shrubs 14
Thuja occidentalis 'Emerald Green', American Arborvitae, Shrubs 7

ALTERNATES:
Corylus maxima 'Purpurea', Purple Giant Filbert
Hydrangea arborescens 'Grandiflora', Hills-of-snow
Hydrangea macrophylla, French Hydrangea, Hortensia
Hydrangea paniculata 'Grandiflora', Peegee Hydrangea
Hydrangea quercifolia, Oak-leaved Hydrangea
Kalmia latifolia, Mountain Laurel
Leucothoe fontanesiana, Drooping Leucothoe
Leucothoe fontanesiana var. *nana*, Dwarf Drooping Leucothoe
Ligustrum × *vicaryi*, Vicary Golden Privet
Ligustrum × *vicaryi* 'Storzinger Strain', Vicary Golden Privet
Lonicera tatarica, Tatarian Honeysuckle
Mahonia bealei, Leatherleaf Mahonia
Magnolia × *soulangiana*, Chinese Magnolia, Saucer Magnolia
Magnolia stellata, Star Magnolia
Osmanthus fragrans, Fragrant Olive, Sweet Olive
Pyracantha coccinea, Fire Thorn

SHRUBS 22
SHRUBS FOR SEASHORE GARDENS

These plants are successful in sandy situations and tolerate salt spray. They also will succeed in sandy situations inland. Most require well-drained soil. For shrubs that thrive in wet soils, see Shrubs 25.

COMPANION PLANTINGS
As background: *Cupressus macrocarpa*, Monterey Cypress; *Cytisus multiflorus*, White Spanish Broom; *C.* × *praecox*, Warminster Broom.
Vine: *Polygonum aubertii*, China Fleece Vine.
Flowers: *Aurinia saxatilis*, Basket-of-gold, Golden Tuft; *Pelargonium* × *hortorum*, House Geranium.

BACCHARIS *bak-kar-iss*

Dioecious shrubs, deciduous or evergreen, found in the salt marshes of America. Conspicuous, tubular, white or yellowish flowers appear in summer.

GROWTH RATE:	fast
LIGHT:	full sun
MOISTURE:	roots moist

B. halimifolia   Groundsel-bush   Zones 4–9.
Deciduous, to 12 feet tall, with small heads of yellowish flowers in clusters, in summer, followed on the female plant by plumes of white, bristly seeds in fall. Good marsh plant, though it adapts to drier soil.

B. pilularis   Dwarf Baccharis, Coyote Brush, Chaparral Broom   Zones 7–9.
Low-growing, evergreen shrub native to the dry sunny soils and slopes of Oregon and California. Soil stabilizer that survives droughts and conserves water, used as a sand binder on coastal bluffs. The cultivar 'Twin Peaks', about 1 foot high and 10 feet across, is fire-resistant.

CYTISUS *sit-iss-us*   Broom

Nearly leafless evergreen or deciduous rounded shrubs with long weeping stems. They flourish by the shore on both coasts and in dry, sandy soils in between. Masses of pealike flowers in spring or summer. Established plants care for themselves. Set out young container-grown plants—they will transplant more easily.

GROWTH RATE:	fast
LIGHT:	full sun
MOISTURE:	versatile

C. albus   Portuguese Broom   Zones 5–8.
This beautiful broom grows to about 1 foot high and spreads. It covers itself with clouds of white to pale yellow flowers in early summer.

C. × **kewensis**   Kew Broom   Zones 6–7.
Creeping hybrid about 1 foot high with small, creamy white flowers in mid-spring.

C. scoparius   Scotch Broom   Zones 5–9.
To 6 feet tall, with masses of strongly colored yellow flowers in mid-spring. There are many handsome cultivars, some double, in colors ranging from crimson through lilac and apricot to tricolor.

HYDRANGEA *hye-drayn-jee-uh*

Medium-size deciduous shrub with large green leaves, attractive even after blooms dry. The big, showy, long-lasting heads of florets appear in mid- to late summer and may be "lace cap" types or "hortensias." "Lace cap" flower heads are composed of small fertile flowers surrounded by rings of much larger sterile flowers. "Hortensias" are big globe-shaped flowers composed of fertile florets. Color ranges from cream through rose to dark blue, and depends on soil pH. Available aluminum in acid soil ensures blue. A pH of 5.0 to 5.5 results in a soft blue color. To maintain pink color, soil must be in the pH range of 6.0 to 6.5 or slightly higher. Great seashore plants. Prefer humusy, well-drained soil, and flower best in full sun. *H. anomala* subsp. *petiolaris* is the lovely Climbing Hydrangea in Vines 8.

GROWTH RATE:	fast
LIGHT:	full sun, semi-sunny
MOISTURE:	roots moist

H. arborescens   Hills-of-snow   Zones 4–9.
Upright shrub to 6 feet with rounded leaves and big clusters of creamy flowers, few sterile. The cultivar

Cytisus scoparius 'Moonglow', Scotch Broom. (Neumann)

'Grandiflora' has huge, all-sterile flowers. 'Annabelle' produces 12-inch round flower heads from early to late summer, and grows to about 4 feet.

H. paniculata 'Grandiflora'
Peegee Hydrangea   **Zones 4–9.**
Tall treelike shrub to 20 feet, with smaller leaves, and in late summer mostly sterile flowers in conical clusters, creamy at first changing to rose then bronze. Benefits from a mulch of well-rotted manure.

H. quercifolia   Oak-leaved Hydrangea
     Zones 5–9.
Six-foot shrub with ornamental leaves 8 inches or longer. Blooms in late summer and through autumn. The cone-shaped showy flower heads have both sterile and fertile florets that change from cream to soft rose. Thrives in shade. Look for new cultivars with larger florets.

ILEX *eye-lex*   Holly
glabra   Gallberry, Inkberry   **Zones 5–7.**

Black-berried, usually evergreen shrub to 3 feet high found in swampy areas of the Northeast. Flat, leathery, glossy green leaves, sparingly toothed. The flowers are white. 'Compacta' is a heavily fruiting female clone. 'Leucocarpa' has white fruit. 'Viridis' has good winter color.

GROWTH RATE:	medium
LIGHT:	full sun, semi-sunny
MOISTURE:	roots moist

JUNIPERUS *joo-nip-er-us*   Juniper

Mostly small conifers, with needlelike or scalelike leaves; the male cones are yellow, like catkins, and the female fruits are berries. The species below thrive even in sunny, hot, dry locations, and in almost any well-drained soil. A spreading root system makes junipers easy to transplant. Some blight exists; choose blight-resistant cultivars recommended by local nurseries.

GROWTH RATE:	medium
LIGHT:	full sun
MOISTURE:	versatile

J. conferta   Shore Juniper   **Zones 5–9.**
Vigorous, trailing juniper 12 to 28 inches high, with dense bluish green foliage and black fruits. It hugs the

Prunus maritima, Beach Plum. (Neumann)

ground and flourishes in full sun, sandy soils, and harsh seaside conditions. 'Emerald Sea' is an excellent cultivar, free of the tendency to dieback typical of some.

J. × media   Pfitzer Juniper   **Zones 3–9.**
The cultivar 'Sea Spray', a sport of 'Pfitzerana Glauca', has blue-green foliage, is under 1 foot tall, hardy to −20° F and resists blight and root rots. 'Pfitzerana Compacta', a dwarf Pfitzer Juniper, grows 1 to 3 feet tall and is gray green. The branch tips of 'Pfitzerana Aurea' are tipped with gold when new.

MYRICA *mye-rik-uh*
pensylvanica   Bayberry   **Zones 2–6.**

Beautiful big shrub with gray green, semievergreen leaves that are aromatic when crushed. It flourishes in the coastal Northeast. The small, wax-coated fruit still is used to scent candles. Bayberry can be trained as a small standard. Look for container-grown nursery plants; wildlings don't transplant well unless a sturdy rootball can be provided. Requires acid-range soil.

MATURE HEIGHT:	9'
GROWTH RATE:	fast
LIGHT:	full sun, semi-sunny
MOISTURE:	soil surface damp

PRUNUS *proon-us*
maritima   Beach Plum   **Zones 4–9.**

Round bush that produces masses of small white blooms in clusters before the leaves appear. The dull purple or reddish fruit that follows in late summer is about 1 inch across, and is used to make delicious jams. There are many improved varieties. It grows wild along the coast and is especially useful for sandy marshes. Prefers somewhat acid soil.

MATURE HEIGHT: 6'
GROWTH RATE: medium
LIGHT: full sun
MOISTURE: roots moist

TAMARIX *tam-uh-rix*
ramosissima (syn. *pentandra*) Tamarisk, Salt Cedar   Zones 2–7.

Large shrub or small tree with long, slender branches that seem leafless, though there are delicate, scale-like leaves. The flowers bloom in feathery clusters in late summer on this year's wood. Prune before spring growth to maintain form. Excellent sand binder and very successful by the seashore and in sandy soils inland. Withstands both dry and wet situations.

MATURE HEIGHT: 10'
GROWTH RATE: fast
LIGHT: full sun
MOISTURE: soil surface damp, versatile

YUCCA *yukk-uh*

Bold rosette of big, swordlike leaves. In summer, established plants produce long-lasting, astonishing, 4- to 6-foot woody spikes of big white or purple, bell-shaped flowers 2 inches or more across. Good evergreen companions to cacti. In the fall or spring, plant in well-drained, preferably sandy soil, not too rich.

GROWTH RATE: fast
LIGHT: full sun
MOISTURE: rather dry

Y. filamentosa 'Bright Edge'   Adam's-needle
                                 Zones 5–10.
Specimen plant also useful in hedges. The floral spike rises to 5 feet and has creamy white flowers. The leaves are 15 inches long, 1 inch across, with shaggy threads along the edges. Another handsome cultivar of the species is 'Gold Sword', a 3-foot rosette of leaves with bright yellow centers and soft green margins.

Y. glauca   Soapweed   Zones 4–10.
Smaller, better for the Midwest, more tolerant of shade, and one of the hardiest of the genus. Narrow, white-edged, gray green leaves, 3 feet long and ½ inch wide. The flowers are greenish white on a 3-foot spike.

SEE ALSO:
Elaeagnus, Shrubs 10
Hydrangea anomala subsp. *petiolaris*, Climbing Hydrangea, Vines 8
Hydrangea macrophylla 'Variegata', Variegated Bigleaf Hydrangea, French Hydrangea, Shrubs 11
Juniperus horizontalis 'Bar Harbor', Juniper, Shrubs 10
Ligustrum ovalifolium, California Privet, Shrubs 18
Ligustrum × vicaryi, Vicary Golden Privet, Shrubs 18
Nerium oleander, Oleander, Rose-bay, Shrubs 18
Phormium tenax, New Zealand Flax, Shrubs 8
Pittosporum tobira, Japanese Pittosporum, Shrubs 21
Rosa rugosa, Japanese Rose, Shrubs 19
Santolina, Shrubs 13
Viburnum dentatum, Arrowwood, Southern Arrowwood, Shrubs 16

ALTERNATES:
Atriplex canescens, Four-wing Saltbush
Calluna vulgaris, Heather, Scotch Heather
Clethra acuminata, Sweet Alder, Summersweet
Lonicera pileata, Privet Honeysuckle

SHRUBS 23
SHRUBS FOR SHADE

No landscape shrubs grow in the full or deep shade found under low-branching trees or under evergreens. Only a few succeed in the semi-shade found next to tall buildings and under large shrubs which cast a shadow about half the day. But many shrubs, including some that flourish in full sun, also succeed in light shade. They are "understory" plants, plants native to the light shade and filtered sunlight under high-branched trees.

COMPANION PLANTINGS
Background: *Ilex* cvs., Holly; *Itea ilicifolia*, Hollyleaf Sweetspire; *Taxus baccata* 'Stricta', Irish Yew; *Vaccinium ovatum,* California Huckleberry.
Ground covers: *Lamiastrum galeobdolum*, Yellow Archangel; *Pachysandra*.
Flowers: *Clivia miniata,* Scarlet Kaffir Lily; *Impatiens; Myosotis sylvatica*, Garden Forget-me-not.

CAMELLIA *kam-meel-ee-uh*

Spectacular southern shrub or small tree grown for its lustrous large leaves and showy waxy flowers in fall, winter, and/or early spring. Semidouble and double forms in shades of white, pink, rose, or purple-red. A few cultivars are fragrant. The cultivars are too numerous to describe; select with the assistance of a reliable local nursery. Prefer well-drained, humus-rich soil in the acid range. Where temperatures go below freezing, buds may be killed or delayed if the camellias are in exposed positions. The

National Arboretum's first camellia plantings were started in Cryptomeria Valley with a gift in 1949—a collection of the fall-blooming *Camellia sasanqua* planted along trails leading to the nearby dogwood collection. 'Frost Queen' and 'Cinnamon Cindy' are among introductions that came from research conducted on this group.

GROWTH RATE: slow
LIGHT: semi-sunny
MOISTURE: soil surface damp

C. japonica cvs.   Zones 7–8.
Widely grown in the warm South and California. It can be a shrub 10 to 15 feet tall or a small tree,

Camellia japonica shrub in full flower.

Camellia japonica bloom.

Camellia sasanqua. (Neumann)

depending on the cultivar. Suitable for espalier, though the species below is more often used. Flowers are large, up to 5 inches across, and bloom in late winter and early spring. Monrovia Nursery Company offers tree form and espalier camellias.

C. sasanqua cvs.   Zones 7–8.
Small shrub, to 12 feet, and except for certain hybrids, generally hardier than the other species and blooms earlier. Leaves and flowers are smaller—flowers to 2 inches in diameter—with a profusion of fragrant blooms. Many semidouble and double forms. Among established cultivars are 'Showa-no-Sakae', 'Jean May', and 'Flower Girl', which has vibrant pink blooms all along the branches in late fall and winter. This is the one most used for espaliers.

CLETHRA *kleth-ruh*
alnifolia Sweet Pepperbush   Zones 3–9.

Easy to grow, superior shrub to 8 feet tall. It bears delightfully fragrant white flowers in upright panicles to 6 inches long for many weeks in summer on current season's growth. Excellent for heavy shade and wet areas. 'Paniculata' has white flowers and is a vigorous grower. The buds of 'Pink Spires' are pink to rose and open to pale pink. 'Rosea' is a beautiful shrub with dark, glossy green leaves, and pink buds that open paler.

GROWTH RATE:	medium/slow
LIGHT:	versatile
MOISTURE:	versatile

COTONEASTER *kot-toh-nee-ass-ter*
salicifolius Willowleaf Cotoneaster
Zones 7–8.

Evergreen to semievergreen, gracefully arching upright shrub to 15 feet tall, with white flowers in woolly clusters. Small narrow leaves and profuse clusters of small red berries. 'Autumn Fire' is a brilliant cultivar.

GROWTH RATE:	medium
LIGHT:	full sun/semi-sunny
MOISTURE:	versatile

FUCHSIA *few-shuh*
magellanica Hardy Fuchsia   Zones 4/5–8.

Much-branched shrub to 12 feet when trained on a wall or trellis. The lovely pendulous fuchsia flowers are an inch or more long, with red calyx and blue petals. Survives in northern New York with winter protection. Blooms on new wood. To encourage growth and maintain form, cut back severely in early spring after the leaf buds show. Prefers well-drained soil in the acid range, pH 6.0 to 7.0.

GROWTH RATE:	slow
LIGHT:	semi-sunny
MOISTURE:	roots moist

GARDENIA *gar-deen-ee-uh*
jasminoides Gardenia, Cape Jasmine
Zones 8–10.

The velvety white flowers of this glossy-leaved evergreen shrub are among the most fragrant in the world. It has been grown in the South since colonial times. In the North it is pot-grown, summered outdoors in semi-sun, wintered indoors in a sunny window. Blooms from early spring through summer. Prefers acid-range soil. *G. j.* 'Fortuniana' is a double-flowered form.

MATURE HEIGHT:	6'
GROWTH RATE:	medium
LIGHT:	semi-sunny
MOISTURE:	roots moist

LEUCOTHOE *lew-koth-oh-ee*
fontanesiana Drooping Leucothoe
Zones 4–8.

Handsome evergreen shrub to 6 feet tall, and just as wide, with arching, slender branches and shiny leaves to 7 inches long that become bronzed in fall. In early summer it bears small clusters of waxy, white urn-shaped flowers. Cut old stems after flowering to keep the plant vigorous. *Nana* is a dwarf to 2 feet tall that can spread to 6 feet wide. Prefers sandy, peaty soil in the acid range, pH 5.0 to 6.0., and partial shade. Nice with rhododendrons.

GROWTH RATE:	medium
LIGHT:	semi-sunny
MOISTURE:	roots moist

Clethra alnifolia, Sweet Pepperbush. (Neumann)

PRUNUS *proon-us*
laurocerasus   Cherry Laurel   Zones 6–8.

Evergreen shrub or small tree, vigorous, valued for its shiny leaves and fountaining form. Fragrant flowers are produced in clusters in spring, followed by small, dark purple fruit. An important landscape plant in the South. The variety *schipkaensis* is hardier than the species. Look for scale-resistant cultivars. 'Rotundifolia' is a bushy form recommended for hedges.

MATURE HEIGHT: 6'
GROWTH RATE: fast
LIGHT: semi-sunny
MOISTURE: roots moist

SEE ALSO:

Aucuba japonica 'Variegata', Gold-dust Tree, Shrubs 11
Azalea (*Rhododendron*) cvs., Shrubs 2
Berberis, evergreen species, Shrubs 18
Buxus microphylla, Boxwood, Shrubs 18
Ceanothus ovatus, Shrubs 24
Euonymus alata 'Compacta', Dwarf Winged Spindle Tree, Shrubs 17
Gaultheria procumbens, Wintergreen, Checkerberry, Herbs 8
Gaultheria veitchiana, Shrubs 25
Hamamelis × intermedia, Witch Hazel, Shrubs 1
Hamamelis mollis, Chinese Witch Hazel, Shrubs 1
Hamamelis virginiana, Witch Hazel, Shrubs 1
Hydrangea quercifolia, Oak-leaved Hydrangea, Shrubs 22
Ilex crenata 'Convexa', 'Helleri', Japanese Holly, Shrubs 7
Ilex glabra, Gallberry, Inkberry, Shrubs 22
Ilex verticillata 'Winter Red', Winterberry, Shrubs 25
Kalmia angustifolia, Sheep Laurel, Shrubs 7
Kalmia latifolia, Mountain Laurel, Shrubs 7
Laurus nobilis, Grecian Laurel, Sweet Bay, Herbs 1
Lindera benzoin, Spicebush, Shrubs 25
Lonicera pileata, Privet Honeysuckle, Vines 5
Mahonia aquifolium, Oregon Grape, Shrubs 7
Mahonia bealei, Leatherleaf Mahonia, Shrubs 7

Mahonia repens, Creeping Oregon Grape, Shrubs 7
Rhododendron cvs., Shrubs 3
Skimmia japonica, Shrubs 13
Skimmia reevesiana, Shrubs 13
Taxus baccata 'Repandens', Prostrate English Yew, Shrubs 7
Taxus cuspidata 'Densa', Japanese Yew, Shrubs 7
Viburnum × burkwoodii 'Mohawk', Shrubs 1

ALTERNATES:

Coprosma × kirkii
Daphne × burkwoodii 'Somerset'
Illicium floridanum, Purple Anise
Kerria japonica 'Pleniflora', Double Japanese Rose
Photinia × fraseri, Fraser's Photinia
Photinia glabra, Japanese Photinia
Pieris floribunda, Fetterbush, Mountain Andromeda
Pieris japonica 'Valley Valentine', 'Red Mill', Lily-of-the-valley Bush
Tsuga canadensis 'Pendula', Weeping Canadian Hemlock

Prunus laurocerasus bloom.

Prunus laurocerasus, Cherry Laurel. (Neumann)

SHRUBS 24
SHRUBS FOR SLOPES AND
EROSION CONTROL

For erosion control, look for plants that increase by underground rootstocks, or suckers. Natives to an area are often the best choices. For instance, excellent erosion controllers in California are the sages (*Artemisia* species and some of the salvias) that form much of the chaparral growth on hillsides. Here are some shrubs suited to the purpose. See also Ground Covers 9.

COMPANION PLANTINGS
Background: *Bergenia cordifolia*; *Forsythia suspensa*, Weeping Forsythia; *Rosa banksiae* 'Alba Plena', Banksia Rose.
Ground covers: *Genista pilosa* 'Vancouver Gold', Broom; *Ruellia brittoniana*, Mexican Bluebell.
Flowers: *Aquilegia*, Columbine; *Hemerocallis*, Daylily; *Sedum ewersii* 'Album', Ewers Stonecrop.

CEANOTHUS *see-an-nohth-us*
Redroot

Very handsome flowering deciduous and evergreen shrubs and small trees hardy in mild climates, from British Columbia to southern California. Considered the West Coast counterpart of the eastern lilac, but the foliage is more attractive. The flowers of the evergreens appear in spring; the deciduous in summer. Spring-prune deciduous species to maintain compact, attractive growth. Successful in any well-drained soil; withstand droughts. Good espalier plants.

GROWTH RATE: medium
LIGHT: full sun
MOISTURE: roots moist, versatile

C. × delilianus   Zones 7–9.
Evergreen shrub to 3 feet tall, valued for its dark to pale blue flowers in April. Look for established cultivars such as 'Gloire de Versailles', pale blue, and 'Gloire de Plantieres', dark blue. This is a hybrid of *C. americanus*, which prefers slightly acid soil.

C. ovatus   Zones 4–9.
Hardy deciduous landscape plant with white flowers, native to the Northeast. Not as showy as the species above but this is a good naturalizer, and it has handsome red fruit capsules in summer. Does well by the shore.

COMPTONIA *komp-toh-nee-uh*
peregrina   Sweet Fern   Zones 2–8.

Deciduous, aromatic shrub with fernlike foliage, useful for covering banks and successful in peaty or dry, sandy soils. Often listed in catalogs as Myrica asplenifolia. In dry, sandy soil, it grows to about 5 feet. The leaves are sometimes dried and used to make tea. Doesn't transplant easily. Prefers soil in the acid range.

MATURE HEIGHT: 5'
GROWTH RATE: fast
LIGHT: versatile
MOISTURE: versatile

COPROSMA *kop-ross-muh*
✕ *kirkii*　　　　　　　　　Zones 8–9.

Scrambling or suberect shrub that is dioecious and semievergreen. Grown on the West Coast for ornamental foliage and fruit. The flowers are white or greenish. Good sand binder, and successful in beach areas.

MATURE HEIGHT: 1½'
GROWTH RATE: fast
LIGHT: full sun
MOISTURE: roots moist, versatile

ECHIUM *ek-ee-um*　Viper's Bugloss

Annuals and biennials that are handsome, weedy, and persistent, with one-sided spikes of showy, often blue, flowers above rough, hairy leaves. Grow easily in any well-drained (even poor, dry) soil. Sow seeds in early spring.

GROWTH RATE: fast
LIGHT: full sun
MOISTURE: versatile

E. fastuosum　Pride of Madeira　Zones 9–10.
Shrubby and branching, to 6 feet tall, with hairy gray leaves and purple to dark blue flowers. Much used for slope planting in California.

E. vulgare　Blueweed, Blue-devil　Zones 3–8.
Biennial 1 to 3 feet tall. The flowers bloom in summer, pink at first and fading to blue. Considered a nuisance in fields, but it will flourish without care in dry soils.

ELAEAGNUS *el-ee-ag-nus*

Tall deciduous and sometimes evergreen shrubs or small trees with gray green willowlike leaves that are silvery beneath. There are fragrant cream-yellow flowers in spring, followed by sweet and mealy fruit

that is yellow or orange with silvery scales. Multiply readily and can become pests but are excellent plants for naturalizing and erosion control. Good tall hedge. Withstand heavy pruning and difficult conditions, including drought, and may be better in dry climates than moist. Tolerate exposure at the seashore and poor soils. Thrive in light, sandy loam.

GROWTH RATE: fast/medium
LIGHT: full sun
MOISTURE: versatile

E. angustifolia　Russian Olive　Zones 2–7.
Deciduous, 12 to 15 feet, but also can reach 30 to 40 feet. Open airy look, silver to gray green in summer and one of the most effective for gray foliage. Flowers appear in mid-spring and are fragrant but small. Useful for hedge, highway plantings, and as a specimen in large landscape.

E. philippinensis　　　　　Zones 9–10.
Evergreen in tropical and subtropical climates. Between 8 and 15 feet at maturity, it is known in Florida as Lingaro and has small, fragrant, yellowish white flowers. Weeping habit and sprawling, but may be kept compact by shearing. Prefers acid soils.

FORSYTHIA *for-sith-ee-uh*
✕ *intermedia* 'Arnold Dwarf'　　　Zones 5–8.

Low-growing dwarf of a deciduous shrub whose yellow-gold flowers appear before the leaves and herald spring. This 3-foot species with a 5-foot spread flowers sparsely even when mature, but the gracefully arching branches root where they touch, binding the soil of sunny banks and rocky slopes. Requires little or no care. Plant root divisions in early spring in well-drained soil.

MATURE HEIGHT: 3'
GROWTH RATE: fast
LIGHT: full sun
MOISTURE: versatile

RHUS *russ*　Sumac

The species of landscape value are planted primarily for their brilliant fall color and velvety red fruit clusters. Most effective massed in naturalized plantings on slopes. They are versatile as to soil, tolerate drought and pollution, and spread easily.

GROWTH RATE: fast
LIGHT: full sun
MOISTURE: roots moist, versatile

R. aromatica (syn. *canadensis*)
Fragrant Sumac　　　　　　　Zones 4–8.
Fast-spreading dense shrub to 3 feet with aromatic leaves. In early spring before the leaves appear there are yellow flowers in short spikes. Red berrylike fruits and brilliant leaf color in late summer and fall. Good for bank planting, slopes, and erosion control.

R. copallina　Dwarf Sumac, Shining Sumac
　　　　　　　　　　　　　　　Zones 5–8.
Tall shrub or small tree to 30 feet and a most ornamental sumac distinguished by winged leaf stalks. The foliage is glossy red in fall. In summer there are greenish flowers in dense clusters, followed by red fruit.

R. typhina　Staghorn Sumac　Zones 3–9.
Deeply divided foliage that turns gold, orange, and scarlet in fall. The greenish pyramidal flowers that appear in early summer are followed by crimson fruit clusters that persist and are attractive to many birds. 'Laciniata' is an established cultivar whose texture is finer than that of the species.

ROSA *roh-zuh*
virginiana　Virginia Rose　　　Zones 3–8.

Spreads very fast by underground runners and can be kept to 3 feet by pruning. Has three-season interest: Indians used the long-lasting, bright red hips of this vigorous native to flavor foods and make tea in summer; in spring, there are beautiful, single, bright magenta-to-pink blooms in clusters or alone; the autumn foliage is brilliant. Choice for naturalizing and succeeds by the seashore. Extremely cold-hardy. The flowers of 'Plena' are double.

MATURE HEIGHT: 6'
GROWTH RATE: fast
LIGHT: full sun
MOISTURE: roots moist

SYMPHORICARPOS *sim-for-ik-karp-os*
orbiculatus　Indian Currant, Coralberry
　　　　　　　　　　　　　　　Zones 3–8.

Shrub that bears small, yellow-white flowers in midsummer, followed by red berries that are strung along the stem and last well into winter. Lovely in autumn when fruit and foliage are brilliant. Spreads rapidly by underground suckers and is an excellent bank holder. Durable, deciduous, untidy shrub that grows in any soil or situation, and tolerates urban conditions.

MATURE HEIGHT: 6'
GROWTH RATE: fast
LIGHT: full sun, versatile
MOISTURE: roots moist, versatile

Rhus copallina, Dwarf Sumac, fall color.

SEE ALSO:

Berberis thunbergii 'Crimson Pygmy', Japanese Barberry, Shrubs 8

Calluna vulgaris, Heather, Shrubs 13

Cornus alba 'Argenteo-marginata', Variegated Tartarian Dogwood, Shrubs 11

Cornus alba 'Sibirica', Siberian Dogwood, Red Twig Dogwood, Shrubs 12

Cornus sericea (syn. *stolonifera*) 'Flaviramea', Golden-twig Dogwood, Shrubs 12

Cotoneaster adpressus, Creeping Cotoneaster, Ground Covers 1

Cotoneaster dammeri, Bearberry Cotoneaster, Ground Covers 1

Hypericum buckleyi, Blue Ridge St.-John's-wort, Ground Covers 9

Hypericum calycinum, Aaron's Beard, Creeping St.-John's-wort, Ground Covers 9

Juniperus chinensis var. *sargentii*, Sargent's Juniper, Shrubs 7

Juniperus horizontalis 'Wiltonii', Blue Rug Creeping Juniper, Shrubs 7

Taxus baccata 'Repandens', Prostrate English Yew, Shrubs 7

Vaccinium angustifolium, Lowbush Blueberry, Herbs 1

Vaccinium corymbosum, Highbush Blueberry, Herbs 1

ALTERNATES:

Cistus ladaniferus, Rock Rose

Cytisus, Broom

Erica vagans, Cornish Heath

Leocothoe fontanesiana, Drooping Leucothoe

Mahonia aquifolium, Oregon Grape

Mahonia repens, Creeping Oregon Grape

Myrica pensylvanica, Bayberry

Physocarpus opufolius 'Dart's Gold', Eastern Ninebark

Polygonum cuspidatum var. *compactum* (syn. *reynoutria*)

Prunus laurocerasus 'Zabelliana', Zabel Laurel

Clethra alnifolia, Sweet Pepperbush.

Rosmarinus officinalis, Rosemary

Viburnum dentatum, Arrowwood, Southern Arrowwood

Xanthorhiza simplicissima, Yellowroot

Yucca filamentosa, Adam's-needle

SHRUBS 25
SHRUBS FOR WET CONDITIONS

Only bog plants, Aquatics 4 and 5, succeed in bogs. The plants on this list thrive in moist spots—near a stream, for instance—but for most, the soil must be well drained. Many charming shrubs native to the Pacific Northwest are useful in similar climates.

COMPANION PLANTINGS

Tree: *Acer rubrum* 'October Glory', Red Maple, Swamp Maple.

Shrubs: *Salix babylonica* 'Crispa', Corkscrew Willow; *Zenobia pulverulenta.*

Perennials: *Astilbe* × *arendsii*, Spiraea; *Camassia leichtlinii*, Camass; *Equisetum hyemale,* Scouring Rush, Horsetail; *Iris pseudacorus*, Yellow Iris; *Lilium canadense*, Canada Lily, Wild Yellow Lily; *Lobelia cardinalis,* Cardinal Flower; *Lythrum salicaria* 'Morden's Pink', Purple Loosestrife; *Myosotis scorpiodes* var. *semperflorens*, Forget-me-not.

CLETHRA *kleth-ruh*   Sweet Alder,
Summersweet *alnifolia*
Sweet Pepperbush   Zones 3–9.

Easy to grow, superior shrub to 8 feet tall. In summer it bears delightfully fragrant white flowers in upright panicles to 6 inches long for many weeks on current season's growth. Excellent for heavy shade and wet

areas. The buds of 'Pink Spires' are pink to rose and open to pale pink. 'Rosea' is a beautiful shrub with dark, glossy green leaves, and pink buds that open paler. Grows in soils ranging from gravelly banks to wet spots, but does best in mildly acid soils with much organic material added.

GROWTH RATE:	medium/slow
LIGHT:	versatile
MOISTURE:	versatile

CORNUS *korn-us*   Dogwood

The best-known dogwoods are the lovely spring-flowering trees, but the genus includes the twiggy shrubs described here which are valued for their unusual fall color. Dogwoods prefer well-drained but moist soil.

GROWTH RATE:	fast
LIGHT:	full sun, semi-sunny
MOISTURE:	roots moist

C. alba 'Sibirica'   Siberian Dogwood
                                        Zones 2–8.
Medium-size, multi-stemmed, vase-shaped deciduous shrub with rounded, dark green foliage. In spring, it bears the white flowers typical of dogwood trees, but smaller, followed by blue-white berries in fall. In winter, the bark turns a vivid coral-red and brightens the garden all winter long. The color is best when the shrub is cut back in late winter to encourage the production of young shoots. Handsome in pots. Height 8 to 10 feet. Prefers moist soil and supports wet situations. Better north of Zone 8.

C. amomum   Silky Dogwood, Red Willow
                                        Zones 5–8.
Similar to *alba*. Grows to 8 to 10 feet, and has purple twigs in winter. Good for moist situations.

C. sericea (syn. *stolonifera*)
Red-osier Dogwood   Zones 2–8.
Very like *alba* in every respect though *alba*'s winter red may be better. White flowers in late spring are followed by white or bluish fruit. Good bank holder. Most attractive naturalized and massed. 'Flaviramea', Golden-twig Dogwood, is similar, but the stems are yellow.

GAULTHERIA *gol-theer-ee-uh*
veitchiana   Zones 7–9.

These evergreen shrubs are most often seen in West Coast gardens. Lustrous leaves and white to blush-pink bell-shaped flowers in mid-spring are followed by indigo-blue berries. Prefers moist soil in somewhat acid range.

MATURE HEIGHT:	3'
GROWTH RATE:	medium/slow
LIGHT:	shade
MOISTURE:	soil surface damp

ILEX *eye-lex*
verticillata 'Winter Red'   Winterberry
                                        Zones 4–8.

Established selection of a native deciduous holly that originated in swampy areas. Valued for brilliant fall and winter display (lasting into January) of red fruit attractive to robins and other birds. Good hedge plant. Dioecious— a male must be near the female to guarantee best fruiting. Fruits in shade. 'Chryso-carpa' has yellow fruits. 'Nana' has red fruits twice the size of the species and remains under 3½ feet tall.

MATURE HEIGHT: 8'–10'
GROWTH RATE: medium
LIGHT: full sun, semi-sunny
MOISTURE: soil surface moist

ITEA *it-ee-uh*
virginica Sweetspire   Zones 7–9.

Deciduous shrub with fragrant, showy white flowers in dense upright clusters to 6 inches long, spring to midsummer, depending on region. Foliage is bright green in summer, and turns brilliant, even fluorescent, red in autumn. Prefers moist fertile soils and will grow in wet places.

MATURE HEIGHT: 8'
GROWTH RATE: medium/slow
LIGHT: full sun, semi-sunny
MOISTURE: soil surface moist

LINDERA *lin-deer-uh*
benzoin Spicebush   Zones 4–8.

Shrub with aromatic leaves and good yellow flowers; flourishes without help and stays in bounds when naturalized. The fruits are a glossy red and persist after foliage is gone. The leaves are up to 5 inches long and turn a clear yellow in fall. Attractive to butterflies. Transplant in early spring and only when small. Thrives in light woods with well-drained, moist, humusy soil, but tolerates quite a lot of shade.

MATURE HEIGHT: 6'–8'
GROWTH RATE: slow
LIGHT: full sun, semi-sunny
MOISTURE: soil surface damp

PERNETTYA *per-nett-ee-uh*
mucronata   Zones 7–9.

Low evergreen with nodding white or pinkish flowers in early summer valued for its white to dark purple berries that last all winter. The variety *coccinea* has red fruit, and there are several other colorful varieties. Worth looking for, but ask the nursery to guarantee the cross-pollinators. Thrives in moist soil with good peat content.

MATURE HEIGHT: 2'
GROWTH RATE: medium
LIGHT: full sun
MOISTURE: soil surface damp

SAMBUCUS *sam-bew-kus*
canadensis American Elder, Sweet Elder
     Zones 3–9.

Tall, deciduous, somewhat untidy shrub grown for sweet edible fruit, which is very attractive to song sparrows and other birds. Good for roadsides, naturalizing, wet areas. In late spring and early summer, it bears white flowers in flat clusters to 10 inches across, followed by small, bluish black berries that make good elderberry jelly. The flowers, dried, were used to make tea and for flavoring. The plant suckers profusely and needs pruning to stay in good shape.

Prefers moist soils but adapts to some drought. Among cultivars worth noting is 'Aurea', which has yellow foliage and cherry-red fruits.

MATURE HEIGHT: 12'
GROWTH RATE: fast
LIGHT: full sun, semi-sunny
MOISTURE: soil surface damp, versatile

TAMARIX *tam-uh-rix*
ramosissima (syn. *pentandra*)
Tamarisk, Salt Cedar   Zones 2–7.
Large shrub or small tree with long, slender branches that seem leafless, though there are delicate, scalelike leaves. The flowers bloom in feathery clusters in summer on this year's wood. Prune before spring growth to maintain form. Excellent sand binder and very successful by the seashore and in sandy soils inland. Withstands both dry and wet situations.

MATURE HEIGHT: 10'
GROWTH RATE: fast
LIGHT: full sun
MOISTURE: soil surface damp, versatile

VIBURNUM *vye-burn-um*

Flowering deciduous, semievergreen, or evergreen shrubs or small trees, interesting in all seasons. Flowers, fine green foliage, and colorful fall fruits and foliage. Many are delightfully fragrant. They are particularly valued for their adaptability. The leaves do not tolerate sulfur sprays or dusts. The species here prefer well-drained, moist soils.

GROWTH RATE: slow
LIGHT: full sun, semi-sunny
MOISTURE: roots moist

V. cassinoides Withe-rod, Appalachian Tea
     Zones 2–8.
Deciduous viburnum native to the moist woodlands, and valued for its dependable show of red foliage and colorful fruit in cold weather. In late spring there are white flowers in 5-inch clusters. The fruit colors from green to reddish to black, often with all colors in the same cluster simultaneously. Prefers well-drained, slightly acid soil and stands up to either shade or sun.

V. nudum Smooth Withe-rod, Swamp Haw
     Zones 6–9.
Similar to the species above, but a better choice for southern gardens. Height is 10 feet or more. Lustrous large leaves that assume brilliant color in the fall.

SEE ALSO:
Aronia arbutifolia 'Brilliantissima', Chokeberry, Shrubs 12
Azalea (*Rhododendron*) *vaseyi*, Pink-shell Azalea, Shrubs 2
Rhododendron cvs., Shrubs 3
Thuja occidentalis, American Arborvitae, Shrubs 7
Vaccinium corymbosum, Highbush Blueberry, Herbs 1

ALTERNATES:
Andromeda polifolia, Bog Rosemary
Calycanthus floridus, Carolina Allspice
Cephalanthus occidentalis, Buttonbush
Comptonia peregrina, Sweet Fern
Rosa palustris, Swamp Rose
Salix caprea, Pussy Willow

An ancient flowering cherry in full bloom commands the view of a spring meadow at the U.S. National Arboretum. (Cathey)

TREES

TREES

The director of the U.S. National Arboretum, H. Marc Cathey, encourages every American to plant, now and in the next decades, as many trees as possible in the home garden and in the community. He urges the use of native trees, shrubs, and wildflowers for public parks and highway plantings. Native plants are adapted to the environment and flourish without chemical intervention. This is part of an evolving ethic called "the new naturalism."

Though scientists often disagree on the evidence of climate change, a majority believe the deforestation of the tropics, specifically the rain forest in the Amazon basin—a major source of oxygen for the planet—is raising carbon dioxide levels and adding to a "greenhouse" effect harmful to mankind. Every tree the home gardener plants decreases the carbon dioxide content of our atmosphere and lessens the greenhouse effect.

Dr. Alden Townsend, who contributed to the Trees section of this book, believes that gardeners can also measurably improve the environment by buying and planting only hardy, disease-free ornamentals, and by avoiding monoculture, the

Young apple tree in bloom.

repetition of a few popular species in every neighborhood garden. Aesthetically and physically, there's more life in contrast.

Even for small gardens, trees offers more landscaping opportunities than gardeners generally consider. Plan the early spring garden, which is too cold to live in, for the beauty of branches that will emerge in gold, red, and burgundy and keep their color all season—there's more to spring than flowering trees!

Position fall and winter events so they invite meditation. Stand a small tree whose structure is beautiful covered with snow where it can be seen from the residence. Even a small garden can feature a specimen with rugged or colorful exfoliating bark—let it shelter a big rock, a stand of golden grass, ferns, a few brilliant early tulips and narcissus.

The forester's definition of a tree is a plant having a single main trunk, and reaching not less than 10 to 20 feet at maturity. Some plants thought of as trees may be grouped here under shrubs—or under both. Lilacs, for instance, grow as, or may be trained/pruned to, single-stem tree form, and also in multi-stem shrub form. The Index indicates the pages on which each can be found.

Don't experiment with hardiness when planting trees. Failure is too visible and costly. Choose plants well within their cold hardiness range, especially flowering trees. Flower buds can be spoiled by late frosts even when foliage survives year after year. Don't count on the protection of microclimates created by sheltered locations when planting trees. At maturity, trees are too tall to shelter.

Choose trees that prefer or adapt to the local soil structure and pH. Adding masses of organic material to the earth in which a tree is to be planted has no lasting benefit since a tree's root system eventually extendes far beyond the improved soil of its planting hole. The feeder roots of a tree 80 feet tall reach 80 to 120 feet out from the drip line (the area circumscribed by the tree's outermost branches). There are few feeder roots within the drip line.

The current research view is that trees take hold more successfully and grow stronger and more resistant if subject to natural stress. Staking may not be helpful. A tree should be staked no longer than its first year to permit its root system to begin to knit into the ground. If winds are dangerous, erect a windbreak; remove it as soon as possible.

Current research suggests that annual fertilization and frequent watering of woody plants, especially trees, may stimulate rapid growth but results in plants that are more vulnerable to wind storms, frosts, droughts, extremes of temperature, pests, and diseases.

Deep root fertilization bypasses most of the feeder roots and may pollute the water table. Feeder roots are almost all in the top 8 to 18 inches of soil. Trees usually receive as much fertilizer as they need when the lawns in which they grow are treated.

Gotelli dwarf conifer collection is one of the most valuable at the National Arboretum. (Neumann)

Fertilize a tree only when lack of growth, or other specific signs, suggest a real need. Spread an all-purpose fertilizer over the soil or lawn surface from the drip line outward. The rule of thumb is that a tree has feeder roots extending a distance from the drip line up to half again its height.

Do not fertilize at planting time: plants are already heavily fertilized by growers to bring them to market size quickly.

Flowering trees that bloom on the current year's growth, such as crape myrtle, are pruned in late winter/early spring. Flowering trees that bloom in spring on one-year-old wood, such as dogwoods and the flowering fruit trees, are pruned when the flowers fade.

Winter-prune deciduous trees during dormancy, just after the coldest part of the season. If the tree bleeds when sap start to flow, do not be concerned. It will cease when the tree leafs out.

Summer-prune when seasonal growth is complete if the intention is to slow or dwarf the development. Reducing the leaf surface reduces the sugar synthesized and translocated to the roots and limits next year's growth.

Avoid fall pruning: wounds heal more slowly.

It is not necessary to paint, tar, or otherwise cover a pruning cut or wound. Find the ring or collar from which each branch grows. Cut back to just in front of it, but do not damage it. From there, the plant will develop an attractive, healthy covering for the wounded area.

Tree wrappings are a protection for the first months. But in time they constrict the trees and can cause cracking. Research on apple orchard trees has shown that a painted-on whitewash—calcium carbonate with resins in it—prevents the winter sun from injuring the young trunks.

See Section Two for specific instructions on planting time, planting, and maintenance of woody plants.

TREES 1
TREES WITH COLORFUL, EXFOLIATING, OR DISTINCTIVE BARK

In winter, beautiful bark comes into its own, a revelation of texture and color obscured during the leafy months. The chalky white bark of the paper birch standing against evergreens and stormy winter skies is a familiar treasure. But there are many lovely barks, some that peel away cyclically, exposing new bark whose color is a contrast. It's called "exfoliating" bark.

COMPANION PLANTINGS
Trees: Tall evergreens (Trees 4).
Shrubs: *Fothergilla major* (syn. *monticola*); *Rosa rugosa*, Japanese Rose.
Perennials: *Epimedium* × *rubrum,* Red Alpine Epimedium; *Helleborus orientalis*, Lenten Rose.

ACER *ay-ser* Maple

Large, important group of beautiful, deciduous ornamentals ranging from stately shade trees to colorful multi-branched plants described in the section on shrubs. The smaller types are successful container subjects. Most maple trees are slow-growing, adaptable, and flourish in well-drained, moist soil. In dry spells, water even mature maples deeply. They prefer somewhat acid soil. Colorful bark is a characteristic of several maples, including *A. palmatum* 'Sangokaku', the Coral Bark Maple in Shrubs 12.

GROWTH RATE:	slow/medium
LIGHT:	full sun
MOISTURE:	roots moist

Acer griseum, Paperbark Maple.

A. buergeranum Trident Maple Zones 4–8/9.
Nice medium-size shade tree for small patios, with decorative brown exfoliating bark. Tolerant of pollution and some drought. In late fall, the foliage turns yellow, orange, and red. Height to 20 to 25 feet.

A. davidii David Maple Zones 4–8/9.
Handsome bark striped white in winter. The fall color of the leaves is golden with orange. Height to 45 feet. Rarely seen outside arboreta, but worth mentioning because the bark is exceptionally interesting.

A. griseum Paperbark Maple Zones 4–8.
Outstanding for bark which peels away in strips like some birches, revealing a lovely cinnamon-brown interior. Interesting in all seasons. Vibrant red and orange leaves in fall. Open, rounded habit. Height to 25 feet.

A. pensylvanicum Striped Maple, Moosewood Zone 3.
A native tree with bark striped white on the trunks and branches, and good yellow foliage in autumn. Thrives in partial shade at the edge of the woods. To 36 feet.

ARBUTUS *arb-yew-tus*

Small broadleaved evergreen trees or large shrubs treasured in warmer areas for their fine flowers, fruits that attract birds, and ornamental exfoliating bark.

GROWTH RATE:	medium/slow
LIGHT:	full sun, semi-sunny
MOISTURE:	roots moist

A. menziesii Madrone, Pacific Madrone Zones 7–9.
Pacific Coast specimen tree to 50 or 100 feet. It has lustrous dark leaves, whitish underneath, and warm brown bark that sheds yearly, somewhat untidily. Lovely bell-shaped flowers in spring, followed by clusters of orange or orange-red berries. Good even in poor, somewhat acid dry soils. Can't stand drying winds, needs well-drained soil, and is most easily transplanted when young.

A. unedo Strawberry Tree Zones 8–10.
Lovely evergreen for the warm West Coast, to about 30 feet. The foliage is tinted amber. Masses of white flowers bloom in fall, followed by long-lasting red fruits, orange-red like strawberries. Requires acid soil and a dry climate to succeed. 'Compacta' is a 5-foot shrub, grown in containers in cooler regions and moved to shelter during cold weather.

BETULA *bet-yew-la* Birch

The birches are tall, slender trees valued for their graceful habit and silky bark, which is usually striped dark gray or black. Foliage is yellow to yellow-green in fall. Require well-drained, moist, humusy soil in the somewhat acid range. Birch borers are a real problem: plant resistant cultivars or spray.

GROWTH RATE:	medium
LIGHT:	versatile
MOISTURE:	versatile

B. nigra 'Heritage' River Birch Zones 4–9.
The handsome white outer bark of river birches exfoliates, exposing inner bark that may be salmon pink to grayish, cinnamon, or reddish brown. Grows medium fast, must have moist roots, and can stand periodic flooding. Nice in winter. Best in soil with a pH below 6.5. At the National Arboretum a good planting of this specimen separates the herb garden from the meadow. It is resistant to birch bark borer. To 30 feet.

B. papyrifera Canoe Birch, White Birch, Paper Birch Zones 2–6/7.
Indians made canoes of the chalky white bark which peels in big sheets and is striped dark grey or black. Outstanding in winter against evergreens and in the snow. Handsome yellow foliage in autumn. It reaches 50 to 70 feet.

B. platyphylla var. *japonica* 'Whitespire' Japanese White Birch Zones 2–6/7.
A superior birch introduction by John L. Creech, a former director of the National Arboretum. It has distinctive white bark with contrasting black triangles at the base of lateral branches. Slender pyramidal form. Grows slowly to 50 feet.

PINUS *pye-nus*
bungeana Lace-bark Pine Zones 4–8.

Evergreen recognized by the long, needlelike leaves sheathed in bundles which hold several years. Multitrunked, pyramidal specimen tree. With maturity, bark exfoliates in irregular plates exposing a light interior bark; worth waiting for. The young stems are green with white and brown mixed in. Needs well-drained soil. Pines grow in dry, sandy soils where little else grows, but are sensitive to air pollution. Most require somewhat acid soil, with a pH of 5.0 to 6.0.

MATURE HEIGHT:	30'–50'
GROWTH RATE:	slow
LIGHT:	full sun
MOISTURE:	roots moist

PRUNUS *proon-us*
maackii Amur Cherry Zones 2–6.

Small flowering cherry valued for very showy glossy red-brown exfoliating bark striped with black and gray like the white birch. It's a small tree, one of the hardy cherries, that produces 2- to 3-inch racemes of small white flowers, followed by black berries that attract birds. In 10 years, it reaches 15 feet tall and 12 feet wide.

MATURE HEIGHT:	15'
GROWTH RATE:	medium
LIGHT:	full sun
MOISTURE:	roots moist

SEE ALSO:
Acer palmatum 'Sangokaku', Coral Bark Maple, Shrubs 12
Clethra barbinervis, Japanese Clethra, Trees 11
Eucalyptus spp., Trees 4
Franklinia alatamaha, Franklin Tree, Trees 3
Lagerstroemia indica, Crape Myrtle, Trees 3
Platanus × *acerifolia*, London Plane, Trees 13

ALTERNATES:
Betula pendula, European White Birch

Pinus bungeana, Lace-bark Pine. (Neumann)

Carpinus carolinana (syn. *americana*), American Hornbeam
Crataegus marshallii, Hawthorn
Cryptomeria japonica, Japanese Cedar
Fagus grandifolia, American Beech
Parrotia persica, Persian Parrotia
Platanus occidentalis, Eastern Sycamore, American Plane
Stewartia pseudocamellia, Japanese Stewartia
Ulmus parvifolia 'Galaxy', Chinese Elm

TREES 2
TREES WITH FLOWERS IN EARLY AND MID-SPRING

All trees bloom—maples are edged with scarlet buds as winter warms, and in spring some weeping willows drip golden catkins. But not all trees flower conspicuously. Those listed here have been loved for centuries for their early, showy flowers . Later bloomers are described in Trees 3.

Long-time monoculture is associated with the many diseases and insects affecting these popular plants, but who in the Northeast could imagine spring without lilacs or flowering crab apples? In the wild, species are scattered; when masses of plants of the same family or genus grow in proximity, the insects and diseases that prey on them are reinforced. When plants are noted as susceptible to a problem, buy only resistant cultivars from responsible nurserymen. Diversity of plantings is also a defense against common plant problems.

COMPANION PLANTINGS
Background: Evergreens (Trees 4); *Hamamelis* × *intermedia* 'Arnold Promise', Witch Hazel.
Ground covers: *Juniperus horizontalis* 'Bar Harbor', Creeping Juniper; *Pachysandra* cvs.
Perennials: *Anemone pulsatilla* 'Rubra', Red Pasqueflower; *Pulmonaria saccharata* 'Mrs. Moon', Bethlehem Sage.

AESCULUS *ess-kew-lus*
× *carnea*   Red Horse Chestnut   Zones 3–7.

Beautiful medium-height shade tree with large deciduous leaves, and showy flesh-colored or red flowers in upright panicles in spring. Fruit is inedible and prickly. Leaves hold their color well into autumn. The well-established 'Briotii' is more compact, has larger panicles of double, deeper red, flowers and is recommended for lawns and streets—but it is a bit messy. Prefers soil in the neutral range.

MATURE HEIGHT: 30'–40'
GROWTH RATE: medium
LIGHT: full sun, semi-sunny
MOISTURE: roots moist

Cercis canadensis, Redbud. (Neumann)

CERCIS *ser-siss*   Redbud

Small native trees valued for early, showy red-purple buds that appear before or with the foliage, and open to rosy pink flowers. Reddish new foliage. Good naturalized in light woodlands, and especially nice in combination with dogwoods. Require well-drained, sandy soil. Transplant only young trees, and do it in early spring.

GROWTH RATE: medium
LIGHT: full sun, semi-sunny
MOISTURE: versatile

C. canadensis   Redbud, Eastern Redbud   Zones 5–9.
Multi-stemmed or low-branching tree with red-purple buds in spring before heart-shaped foliage appears. Fall foliage is yellow. Height is to 25 feet. The new foliage of 'Forest Pansy' is brilliant purple that dulls; hardy only to − 10° F. 'Royal' has the best white flowers. 'Silver Cloud' has variegated leaves. The flowers of 'Wither's Pink Charm' are light pink. 'Flame' has lasting double flowers.

C. occidentalis   Western Redbud   Zone 8.
Western form similar to *canadensis*, but smaller, to 15 feet. Hardy only to 10° F.

C. reniformis   Zone 8.
Small form, to 12 feet tall, with very glossy dark leaves.

CORNUS *korn-us*   Dogwood

Highly valued, small, lovely, flowering trees, native to light woodlands, and covered in spring with large star-shaped white flowers (pointed bracts) perched like big butterflies on layered branches. In fall there are bright red berries attractive to birds, and the foliage may turn a real red. The beautiful, much-planted, *C. florida*, Flowering Dogwood, and its pink and red cultivars are developing serious problems. Improved cultivars are in process but at this writing

Dogwoods at the National Arboretum. (Neumann)

none is recommended by National Arboretum's Dr. Frank Santamour. Dogwoods require well-drained, humusy soil. Flowering dogwoods donated by the Woman's National Farm and Garden Association are set among hemlocks and informal plantings of other dogwoods at the National Arboretum—among them are some weeping cultivars.

GROWTH RATE:	medium
LIGHT:	full sun, versatile
MOISTURE:	roots moist

C. capitata   Evergreen Dogwood
                                    Zones 8–9.

Grown in California, it reaches 40 feet, and has pale yellow bracts in late spring and early summer. The foliage is dark, lustrous, semi- or evergreen, and bronzes in winter.

C. kousa var. chinensis   Chinese Dogwood
                                    Zones 5–8.

Dr. Santamour recommends planting this dogwood in place of Flowering Dogwood. In tests for disease-resistant dogwoods from 20 geographic sources it came through best. The bracts are larger, come a few weeks later than those of *C. florida*, and are set facing up on branch tops—most beautiful when viewed from above. Research seeking to produce this species with flowers more visible from the ground should yield better cultivars in the next few years. It has interesting mottled bark and reddish leaves in autumn. Some drought-resistance and prefers well-drained soil in the acid range. Needs more light than *C. florida*. Height to 25 feet in cultivation. 'Milky Way' has large, pure white flowers, raspberrylike fruits that attract birds, and attractive bark. 'Summer Stars', an introduction by William Flemmer of Princeton Nurseries, blooms into August in the Washington, D.C., area and has very long-lasting flowers. *Kousa* is a good espalier plant. 'Elizabeth Lustgarten' is a beautiful weeping form selected at Lustgarten Nurseries, in Long Island, N. Y. Because the blooms are on weeping branches they are more visible from ground level.

C. mas   Cornelian Cherry, Sorbet   Zones 4–8.

Small, long-lived, multi-branching deciduous tree or tall shrub, not as showy as the later-blooming flowering dogwoods, but it flowers in early spring when there is little else blooming. Masses of long-lasting tiny clusters of yellow umbels, followed in late summer by scarlet fruit that is edible but acid and was once a food crop. Birds are attracted to the fruit. Good for the Midwest. Height to 25 feet. Prefers rich, well-drained soil.

Fall color of *Cornus kousa*, Chinese Dogwood. (Neumann)

Magnolia × *soulangeana*, Saucer Magnolia.

C. nuttallii Mountain Dogwood,
Pacific Dogwood   Zones 7–9.
West Coast version of Flowering Dogwood, *C. florida*; ranges from British Columbia to southern California. The showy bracts are white, then flushed pink. Height is to 75 feet. 'Corigo Giant' has bracts larger than the species. There are also varieties with variegated leaves.

MAGNOLIA *mag-nohl-ee-uh*

One of the planet's oldest trees. The genus includes tall, deciduous shrubs that bloom in early to mid-spring before the foliage appears, as well as majestic evergreen trees that bloom later. Provide humusy, acid soil, pH 5.0 to 6.0, and an acid mulch about 4 inches deep to maintain essential moisture. Well-drained soil is needed in cooler regions. Transplant with care before new growth begins in early spring.

GROWTH RATE: medium/slow
LIGHT: full sun
MOISTURE: roots moist

M. 'Galaxy'   Zones 5–9.
This superior hybrid is a National Arboretum introduction developed by Dr. F. A. Santamour. It is single-trunked, reaches about 40 feet; has an excellent branching habit, and handsome, saucer-type flowers, ruby red shading to magenta-rose toward the tip, and opening to a paler red-purple. It blooms early but late enough to escape most late frosts.

M. × soulangeana Chinese Magnolia,
Saucer Magnolia   Zones 5–9.
Lovely little tree whose perfect, up to 6-inch flowers appear before the leaves in late winter or early spring; they are usually purplish on the outside and cream to white inside. Height is 20 to 30 feet, and width about the same. Avoid planting it in warm, south-facing situations that will encourage bloom before frosts are really over. Provide well-drained, humusy soil with a pH of 5.0 to 6.0 or 6.5. Transplant with care before

new growth begins in early spring. Tolerates some pollution. 'Lennei', about 20 feet tall, has large, long-lasting purple sepals and blooms after the last frost; 'Lennei Alba' has big pure white flowers. Height 15 to 25 feet.

M. 'Spectrum'   Zones 6–9.
Similar to the above, but a later-blooming introduction by Dr. Santamour. The flowers are large, dark purple outside, white within.

MALUS *may-lus* Apple

The flowering crab apples belong to this genus, small—8 to 30 feet tall—trees with spreading branches covered in spring with masses of exquisite apple blossoms and in fall with small red fruits birds love. There are several weeping cultivars and a few fastigiate, or columnar, forms. Though susceptible to serious problems, their beauty has made them the most important small landscape trees through the northern U.S. and southern Canada. Of the 700 to 800 cultivars, many are susceptible to disease; buy from an established local nursery and insist on disease-resistant cultivars. Plant in well-drained soil. Those named here are among the most resistant, but there are many others.

GROWTH RATE: medium
LIGHT: full sun, semi-sunny
MOISTURE: roots moist

M. baccata Siberian Crab Apple Zones 2–7.
One of the tallest and hardiest flowering crab apples, in mid-spring it produces fragrant white flowers, followed by long-lasting orange and yellow fruits. The cultivar 'Jackii' is to 20 feet tall and as wide, with exceptionally bright red fruit and excellent disease resistance. One of the earliest to bloom.

M. 'Candied Apple' Weeping
Weeping Candied Crab Apple   Zones 4–8.
Valued for its weeping form and the hint of red in new foliage. To 15 feet and as wide. Flowers are

purplish pink; the fruits are red and persistent. There are other good weeping forms.

M. 'Dolgo' Crab Apple   Zones 2–7.
A big, to 40 feet, spreading tree with white flowers and red fruit. Suitable for shade and unusually cold-hardy.

M. floribunda
Japanese Flowering Crab Apple   Zones 4–7.
Height to 18 feet with a spread to 25 feet, and a fine winter silhouette of spreading branches. The flowers are particularly attractive—deep pink to red in bud, pink fading to white as they open. Fruit is yellow-red, effective in early fall.

M. hupehensis Tea Crab   Zones 4–7.
Most picturesque of all, the long, wandlike branches are covered with fragrant flowers that are pink in bud, and open to white. Follows the above species in bloom time. To 20 feet or more, with a spread to 25 feet. Fruits are greenish yellow to red. Excellent resistance to crab problems, except fire blight.

M. 'Louisa' Crab Apple   Zones 4–8.
Red-leaved upright, spreading crab apple with outstanding bright pink flowers and clean summer foliage. Yellow fruit, ½ inch long. The height is about 15 feet.

M. 'Narragansett' Crab Apple   Zones 4–8.
Early-blooming National Arboretum introduction that is disease-resistant and of superior landscape value. Long-lasting flower buds are first dark carmine, later bright red, opening to white flowers tinged with pink. Fruit is glossy cherry-red in pendulous clusters of 4 to 7, persisting until frost. Good tree for specimen planting in a small garden, and for massing along highways or in parks. It has been released to the nursery trade and should be available soon.

M. 'Parrsi' Pink Princess™ Crab Apple
                                    Zones 5–8.
Very low crab, 8 feet tall, spreading to 12 feet, with purple foliage turning bronze, rose pink flowers, and

Malus 'Naragansett', Crab Apple. (Cathey)

Malus sieboldii 'Fuji', Crab Apple.

deep red fruit. This is a naturally dwarf tree with excellent resistance.

M. 'Red Jade' Crab Apple   Zones 4–8.
A small tree—10 to 15 feet—with long, elegant, weeping branches. Glossy green foliage, and a profusion of white double flowers 1½ inches in diameter; outstanding bright red fruits that persist into winter. In some regions it has disease problems; follow the recommendations of a reliable local nurseryman.

M. sieboldi 'Fuji' Crab Apple   Zones 4–8.
National Arboretum selection by Roland M. Jefferson. Early spring flowers and fresh green foliage followed by orange fruit. The dark, deeply grooved trunk has gray platelets and a rugged look that is handsome in the winter landscape.

M. 'White Cascade' Crab Apple   Zones 4–8.
To 15 feet tall, with pink buds that open to single white flowers, and yellow fruit ⅜ inch long. It seems to be fairly resistant, but has not been long in culture.

PRUNUS *proon-us*

Small, hardy, early-flowering; among the most beautiful of all flowering trees. In this genus are included the edible stone fruits: plums, apricots, peaches, almonds, nectarines, cherries, and cherry laurels.

Prunus serrulata, Japanese Flowering Cherry.

The cherries, plums, and peaches bred for improved flowers are known as "flowering" plums, peaches, cherries, and so on. They have small fruits attractive to birds. Ornamental plums have maroon to purple leaves (see Trees 5). Some of the wild cherries are good naturalizers (see Trees 12). All thrive in well-drained, sandy loam and are subject to problems affecting roses. Buy resistant cultivars from responsible local nurserymen. These trees succeed in cities as long as they have room to spread and good growing conditions.

GROWTH RATE: fast/medium
LIGHT: full sun
MOISTURE: roots moist

P. × blireana Flowering Plum Zones 5–9.
Bright and early bloomer that reaches to about 20 feet. The foliage is reddish purple when new, fading to green-bronze in summer, and turning red-bronze in fall. The flowers are bright pink, double, about 1 inch in diameter.

**P. cerasifera 'Krauter Vesuvius'
Flowering Plum** Zones 9–10.
This is similar to the above, but a better choice for California.

P. 'Okame' Flowering Cherry Zones 5–9.
Dr. Henry Skinner, who was director of the National Arboretum in the 1930s, brought the first hybrid from England to America. It is a hardy, upright, branching cherry with a profusion of deep maroon buds that open into small, long-lasting bright pink blossoms. Young trees flower. Foliage is dark green, finely textured, and in fall it turns yellow, orange, and orange-red. Reaches 25 feet with a 20-foot spread. Thrives in any well-drained soil where moisture is maintained. Prune in midwinter or after flowering.

P. sargentii Sargent Cherry Zones 5–8.
Larger, early-flowering cherry with many assets—single, deep pink flowers in clusters, bronze-red foliage in fall, excellent cinnamon and chestnut brown bark. Upright with spreading branches, it gives good shade. Has exceptionally colorful fall foliage—bronze-orange and orange-red. Width almost equals height—30 to 50 feet. Very hardy. 'Columnaris' is an upright, narrow form useful for street planting. It has beautiful autumn color and handsome mahogany bark.

P. serrulata Japanese Flowering Cherry Zones 5–9.
Choose cultivars as opposed to species. Among the best are 'Kwanzan' (syn. 'Sekiyama'), which has dark green leaves that turn bronze-orange to orange-red in fall. Large clusters of double pink flowers make this the showiest cherry. It blooms later than plums. 'Shiro-fugan' is a vigorous grower with pink buds that open to white and fade back to pink with age. 'Shirotae' (syn. 'Mount Fuji') is small, to 15 feet and almost 20 wide, with glossy foliage that turns yellow in fall. Lovely pink buds open to large, fragrant, semidouble or double white flowers.

P. subhirtella 'Pendula' Higan Cherry,
Rosebud Cherry Zones 5–8.
One of the earliest, a weeping cherry with abundant single pink flowers hanging from graceful, drooping branches. Very popular. The fruits are black and inconspicuous. 'Pendula Plena Rosea', Double Weep-

Pyrus calleryana 'Bradford Pear', Callery Pear.

ing Cherry (syn. 'Yae-Shidare-Higan'), is a pink double; hardy to Zone 5. 'Autumnalis Roseae', Autumn Flowering Cherry, an upright spreading form with slender branches, has semidouble to double light pink flowers in spring and fall. The fall foliage color is yellow to bronze. Attractive branching pattern. Hardy to Zone 4.

P. 'Tai Haku' White Flowering Cherry Zones 4–8.
Vigorous tetraploid with clusters of white, saucer-shaped blooms 2½ inches across. New foliage is reddish bronze, fading to green.

P. yedoensis Yoshino Cherry Zones 5–8.
These are the Japanese trees famous for the early spring display at the Tidal Basin in Washington, D.C. Unfortunately, the blooms are rather short-lived. The form is upright and spreading, with single, fragrant, light pink blossoms that fade to white; yellow foliage in fall. Growth rate is medium and the height 40 to 50 feet. Prefers somewhat acid soil and adapts to a semi-sunny situation. 'Akebono' has true pink flowers; it is one of the finest flowering cherries. 'Shidare Yoshino' is called Weeping Yoshino Cherry. 'Ivensii' has fragrant white flowers on weeping branches.

PYRUS *pye-rus*
calleryana Bradford Pear, Callery Pear Zones 4–8.

Beautiful pyramidal tree to 40 feet or more, covered in early spring with clusters of small white blooms. The glossy green leaves turn an attractive wine red in fall. There' are a few small russet fruits in winter to attract birds. The original cultivar was 'Bradford', which tends to split. Two recent disease-resistant selections from the National Arboretum are stronger. The columnar 'Capitol' is a good choice for narrow sites and streets, and has persistent autumn foliage. 'Whitehouse', a tree for boulevards and parks, has a strongly developed central stem, abundant flowers

before the leaves, and beautiful red and purple leaves early in the fall. It is named for W. E. Whitehouse, a retired U.S.D.A. horticulturist. The callery pears withstand drought and succeed in soils with a pH of 5.5 to 7.5. They are good espalier subjects.

MATURE HEIGHT: 30'–50'
GROWTH RATE: medium
LIGHT: full sun
MOISTURE: versatile

TABEBUIA *tab-eb-bew-yuh*
impetiginosa Pink Trumpet Tree Zones 9–10.

One of several evergreen or briefly deciduous species popular in warm Florida and California; valued for their trumpet-shaped flowers in various colors, late winter or spring. This one is an excellent small semievergreen tree with dark green leaves and showy clusters of large, rosy pink flowers. Also called Purple Tabebuia. Needs staking until 6 or 8 feet tall; prune to a single trunk, then allow it to grow naturally. *T. chrysotricha* is similar but has golden flowers.

MATURE HEIGHT: 15'–25'
GROWTH RATE: fast
LIGHT: full sun
MOISTURE: versatile

SEE ALSO:
Malus 'Prairifire', 'Strawberry Parfait', Crab Apple, Trees 5
Prunus × blireana 'Moseri', Moser Flowering Purple-leaf Plum, Trees 5
Prunus cerasifera 'Atropurpurea', 'Newport', 'Mount St. Helens'™, 'Thundercloud', Cherry Plum, Trees 5

ALTERNATES:
Hamamelis × intermedia 'Arnold Promise', Witch Hazel
Prunus cerasifera 'Diversifolia', Cherry Plum
Prunus × cistena 'Big Cis', Purple-leaf Plum

TREES 3
TREES WITH FLOWERS IN LATE SPRING AND SUMMER

The flowering trees here usually bloom in late spring or early and midsummer. Some repeat, and a few flower in fall. The focus here is on species and cultivars that delight the eye even when the trees are not in bloom. See the comments about monoculture and flowering trees in the introduction to Trees 2.

COMPANION PLANTINGS
Background: *Ligustrum amurensis*, Amur Privet; *Nyssa sylvatica*, Pepperidge, Sour Gum; *Taxus baccata* 'Washingtonii', Washington English Yew; *T. b.* 'Pygmaea', Pygmy English Yew.
Perennials: *Aster × frikartii* 'Wonder of Staffa'; *A. novi-belgii*, New York Aster; *Solidago virgaurea* 'Cloth of Gold', 'Golden Shower', Goldenrod.

CATALPA *kat-tal-puh*
speciosa Western Catawba Zones 5–8.

Big flowering tree with showy clusters of flowers in summer when little else blooms, followed by long, slender pods. Short-lived, but imposing street and park tree that grows easily in difficult areas.

MATURE HEIGHT:	50'–60'
GROWTH RATE:	fast/medium
LIGHT:	full sun, semi-sunny
MOISTURE:	versatile

CLADRASTIS *klad-rast-iss*
lutea American Yellowwood Zones 4–9.

Slow-growing small tree—9 to 12 feet in 10 years—with silver bark, and brilliant orange-yellow autumn foliage. In late spring or early summer it produces foot-long pendulous clusters of fragrant white flowers resembling wisteria. Drought-resistant and trouble-free. Nice as a shade tree.

Koelreuteria paniculata, Golden-rain Tree.

MATURE HEIGHT:	30'–50'
GROWTH RATE:	slow
LIGHT:	full sun, semi-sunny
MOISTURE:	versatile

DAVIDIA *dav-vid-ee-uh*
involucrata Dove Tree Zones 6–8.

Broad, pyramidal specimen tree with interesting orange-brown scaly bark. The name derives from two showy white bracts of unequal length to 6 inches long that appear under the insignificant flowers in mid- to late spring. Also called "handkerchief tree." Slow to come into bloom. Good in the South; in colder regions it may survive but won't flower well. Rare, but worth looking for. The variety *vilmoriniana* is hardy to Zone 5.

MATURE HEIGHT:	20'–40'
GROWTH RATE:	medium/slow
LIGHT:	full sun, semi-sunny
MOISTURE:	roots moist

DELONIX *del-lon-ix*
regia Royal Poinciana, Flame Tree Zone 10.

Deciduous summer-flowering tree that makes a fantastic show; the range is limited to southern Florida, California, and Hawaii. Fernlike foliage and clusters of bright scarlet and yellow flowers to 4 inches wide are followed by flat pods to 2 feet long and 2 inches wide. Greenhouse or pot subject in cooler regions. Tolerates some salt and considerable drought.

MATURE HEIGHT:	25'–40'
GROWTH RATE:	fast
LIGHT:	full sun
MOISTURE:	roots moist

FRANKLINIA *frank-lin-ee-uh*
alatamaha Franklin Tree Zones 5–8.

Excellent small tree to show off for fragrant, white, camellialike flowers with yellow stamens, 3 inches across, in August to mid-fall. Bright green foliage turns orange-red in fall. Interesting ridged bark. Needs well-drained soil with lots of organic material, in the acid range, pH 5.0 to 6.0. Do not grow where cotton has been raised. Nice with fothergillas (see Shrubs 12).

MATURE HEIGHT:	10'–20'
GROWTH RATE:	medium
LIGHT:	full sun, semi-sunny
MOISTURE:	roots moist

KOELREUTERIA *kel-roo-teer-ee-uh*
paniculata Varnish Tree, Golden-rain Tree Zones 5–9.

Lovely small shade tree and ornamental for lawn or patio. In midsummer it bears upright panicles of

Cladrastis lutea, American Yellowwood. (Neumann)

bright saffron flowers to 15 inches long, followed by papery seedpods that change from green to yellow to brown. Attractive yellow fall foliage. Withstands drought, wind, pollutants, and poor and alkaline soils. *Hortus Third* names the genus Golden-rain Tree, which is a more appropriate name but might cause confusion with laburnums (see below) whose common name is Golden-chain Tree.

MATURE HEIGHT: 30'–40'
GROWTH RATE: medium
LIGHT: full sun
MOISTURE: versatile

LABURNUM *lab-burn-um*
× *watereri* 'Vossii'   Golden-chain Tree
Zones 5–7.

Airy, pretty, tall shrub or small tree with rich yellow wisterialike flower panicles 18 to 24 inches long in late spring or early summer. Easily grown in a protected spot in well-drained soil with high organic content. May be rather short-lived.

MATURE HEIGHT: 15'–25'
GROWTH RATE: medium
LIGHT: full sun, semi-sunny
MOISTURE: roots moist

LAGERSTROEMIA *lay-gur-streem-ee-uh*
indica   Crape Myrtle   Zones 7–9.

Southern, deciduous, multi-stemmed, very wide, flowering small trees or large shrubs. The bark of this species is mottled light tan to gray, and very smooth. In late summer, branches are tipped with big, upright, flowering panicles. In coming years look for the many exquisite, mildew-resistant, shrubby or tree-like crape myrtles introduced by Donald Egolf, and released to the nursery trade by the National Arboretum. They were made possible by hybridization of *indica* with *fauriei*, a species collected by Dr. John Creech, former Arboretum director, from a cold site 1,200 feet above sea level in the mountain forests above Kurio, Yakushima, Japan. The plants described here, all hybrids of *indica* × *fauriei*, bear flowers of white through melting tones of pink, lavender, and melon to red and purple and have exfoliating bark, cinnamon to brown. Some have colorful foliage in fall. To limit height, some gardeners cut the plants to the ground in early spring, sacrificing the bark. Crape myrtles leaf out late in spring, especially when new. They prefer moist, heavy loam and clay soils in the acid range, pH 5.0 to 6.5. Provide a moisture-retaining mulch and do no late season (fall) watering. If killed back by frosts, they are likely to send up new shoots in succeeding years. Magnificent massed, and good for informal hedges or specimen planting. Small and medium-size crape myrtles are good container plants for outdoors.

GROWTH RATE: fast/medium
LIGHT: full sun
MOISTURE: roots moist

'Apalachee': dense, branching, exfoliates exposing cinnamon to chestnut brown bark; light lavender flowers. Fall foliage from green through orange and russet to dark red. Slow grower, just 12 feet in 12 years.

Laburnum × *watereri*, Golden-chain Tree.

'Comanche': bark exfoliates to sandalwood-colored inner bark; coral pink flowers. Slow growing, 12 feet in 15 years, may eventually reach 18 feet.
'Lipan': bark exfoliates from near white to beige, to gray; medium lavender flowers in 4- to 8-inch panicles. Mature height 12 to 18 feet.
'Muskogee': attractive bark, light lavender flowers to 10 inches long. Especially mildew-resistant. To 30 feet tall.
'Natchez': lovely year-round and has exfoliating bark; pure white flowers. May reach 21 feet by 30 or more wide. Others in this size range include 'Tuskegee', 'Miami', 'Biloxi', 'Wichita'.
'Osage': mottled chestnut brown bark; clear pink flowers. The leaves turn red to dark red in fall. Slower growing, to 12 by 9 feet in 12 years.
'Sioux': bark is light to medium gray brown; flowers are dark pink. In fall, foliage is light maroon to bright red. Reaches 14 feet by 10 wide in 10 years.
'Yuma': bark is light gray and mottled; long-lasting lavender flower panicles may rebloom. Slower to grow, reaches 12 feet tall by 10 feet wide in 12 years.

MAGNOLIA *mag-nohl-ee-uh*

One of the planet's oldest trees. The genus includes tall, deciduous shrubs that bloom in early to mid-spring before the foliage appears, as well as majestic evergreen trees that bloom later. Provide humusy, acid soil, pH 5.0 to 6.0, and an acid mulch about 4 inches deep up to the trunk to maintain essential moisture. Well-drained soil is needed, especially in cooler regions. Transplant with care before new growth begins in early spring.

GROWTH RATE: medium/slow
LIGHT: full sun
MOISTURE: roots moist

M. grandiflora   Bull Bay, Southern Magnolia
Zones 7–9.
Symbol of southern plantation days, an imposing broadleaved evergreen flowering tree 60 to 80 feet and more, with handsome, stiff, glossy leaves to 8 inches long. Huge, wonderfully fragrant, creamy, waxy flowers are borne in spring and summer. Leaves of some have brown backs and are attractive in arrangements; brown-backed forms are believed hardier. Fruit cones to 4 inches long open to expose red seeds. Good choice for landscaping large buildings and for espalier. Prefers cool shade and loose soil that is moist, deep, and fertile. Requires protection north of Washington, D.C. 'Majestic Beauty'™ is pyramidal and has cup-shaped white flowers to 12 inches across in summer, and large, lustrous green leaves. 'Little Gem' is an outstanding compact with nice russet color and 6-inch flowers in spring; some rebloom in summer. 'Victoria', a very hardy 20-foot tree, is almost as wide as it is high. 'St. Mary's' is a choice compact, pyramidal in shape, that produces many full-size flowers while still young.

M. × 'Timeless Beauty'   Zones 6–9.
Believed to be a hybrid of the two species here, it is a dense evergreen tree, zone hardier due to *M. virginiana*. It has a unique flowering habit, large creamy white flowers blooming all during the growing season. Blooms terminally from vegetative growth, then produces another terminal bloom.

M. virginiana   Sweet Bay   Zones 5–9.
Lovely, graceful smallish tree for patio or garden, evergreen in warmer regions, deciduous farther north. Very fragrant lemon-scented creamy white rounded flowers appear with the leaves in late spring and early summer, and then sporadically to early fall. The fruit is dark red, to 2 inches long, and the leaves

silver-backed. Adjusts to considerable shade and wet or swampy soils. Height can be 25 to 60 feet. Growth rate is medium to fast.

STEWARTIA *stew-art-ee-uh*

Large shrubs or beautiful small trees attractive in all seasons. Creamy white summer-to-early-fall flowers with contrasting stamens. Handsome exfoliating bark, and autumn foliage is purple to vivid orange to orange-red. *Fothergilla gardenii* and *F. major* (see Shrubs 12) are good companions. Need well-drained, humusy soil, somewhat acid.

GROWTH RATE: fast/medium
LIGHT: full sun, semi-sunny
MOISTURE: roots moist

S. koreana   Zones 5–8.
Height 20 to 30 feet. The flowers have a wavy margin, and the bark is quite beautiful—flaky, with patches of contrasting gray brown, brown, and orange-brown.

S. ovata var. grandiflora   Mountain Camellia
Zones 5–9.
To 15 feet high and as wide, slow-growing, and a little difficult, so it is best planted young. *Grandiflora* has larger flowers than the species, and the foliage is a beautiful orange to scarlet in fall. Requires acid soil, pH 4.5 to 5.5. Grows along stream banks in the wild.

S. pseudocamellia   Japanese Stewartia
Zones 7–9.
The most popular species. Height is 30 to 40 feet. Flowers resemble camellias, and red bark is very colorful in winter. Brilliant fall foliage.

STYRAX *stye-rax*   Snowbell

Deciduous or evergreen tall shrubs or small trees, lovely specimens for lawn, patio or border. A profusion of white bell-shaped flowers appear in late spring or early summer, somewhat hidden by leaves. Most effective seen from below. Prefers well-drained, moist, somewhat acid soil rich in organic matter. Easiest to transplant when young. Good companion to azaleas, rhododendrons, and kalmias (Shrubs 2, 3, and 7). Notably trouble-free. Fissured bark is handsome.

GROWTH RATE: medium
LIGHT: full sun, semi-sunny
MOISTURE: roots moist

S. japonicus   Japanese Snowbell   Zones 5–9.
Dainty tree with a profusion of white, bell-shaped, pendant flowers in late spring and early summer. Height is 15 to 20 feet or more. There are weeping cultivars with clear pink flowers. Lovely in partial shade. Site for protection in cold climates.

S. obassia   Fragrant Snowbell   Zones 6–9.
Small tree with dense, upright branching, and fragrant, showy white flowers earlier than the species described above. Height 20 to 30 feet.

SYRINGA *sihr-rin-guh*   Lilac

The tree lilacs below are outstanding when in bloom. Lilacs grow best in moist, nearly neutral soil. They require generous mulching and periodic pruning. Good air circulation helps them withstand the ten-

dency to mildew. Remove dead blooms. The treasured late-spring bloomers do not have the enchanting fragrance of common lilac, *S. vulgaris*.

MATURE HEIGHT: 20'–30'
GROWTH RATE: medium
LIGHT: full sun
MOISTURE: versatile

S. × henryi   Henry Lilac   Zones 3–7.
Blooms earlier than the species below. The flowers of 'Lutece' are pale violet-pink.

S. reticulata (syn. amurensis var. japonica)
Japanese Tree Lilac   Zones 3–7.
One of the most trouble-free lilacs, an excellent small tree to use as a specimen, for street planting, or in groups. In late spring it produces large and extremely showy white flower panicles whose odor is somewhat like privet. Dr. Michael A. Dirr suggests slightly acid soil.

TABEBUIA *tab-eb-bew-yuh*
impetiginosa   Pink Trumpet Tree
Zones 9–10.

A small tree, deciduous or semievergreen, with showy purple-pink flowers in spring. In the warm regions of California and Florida it is seen in gardens, parks, as a street tree, and in median planting.

MATURE HEIGHT: 15'–20'
GROWTH RATE: slow
LIGHT: full sun
MOISTURE: versatile

SEE ALSO:
Arbutus menziesii, Madrone, Pacific Madrone, Trees 1
Arbutus unedo, Strawberry Tree, Trees 1
Oxydendrum arboreum, Sourwood, Sorrel Tree, Trees 7
Pittosporum undulatum, Victorian Box, Mock Orange, Trees 11

alternates:
Albizia julibrissin, Silk Tree, Mimosa
Cassia spp.
Cotinus obovatus, American Smoke Tree, Chittamwood
Liriodendron tulipifera, Tulip Tree
Robinia pseudoacacia 'Semperflorens', Black Locust
Sophora japonica, Japanese Pagoda Tree

TREES 4
TREES WITH EVERGREEN FOLIAGE

To get maximum impact, use both broadleaved and needled evergreen trees in the landscape—the combination is far richer than either type alone. The blue in conifers is prized, and as a result many cultivars with blue, blue-green, and silvery leaves have been developed; the text here names some of the most reliable. Use blue trees with discretion.

Evergreens aren't green forever; they do drop and replace foliage, but in very long cycles—18 months

to several years in the case of hemlocks. Many, but not all, evergreens prefer soils in the acid range. See Shrubs 7 for shrubby forms of the evergreens.

COMPANION PLANTINGS
Tree: *Acer rubrum* 'October Glory', Red Maple, Swamp Maple.
Shrubs: Evergreen Azalea (*Rhododendron*) and *Rhododendron*.
Flowers: *Hemerocallis* 'Stella De Oro', 'Double Decker', Daylily; *H. minor*, Dwarf Yellow Daylily; *Lilium* spp. and cvs., Lilies.

ABIES *ay-bih-eez*   Fir

Firs are needled conifers native to high altitudes. They are large, pyramidal forest trees distinguished from spruces, which are the favorites for Christmas, by their flatter needles—usually with two white bands beneath. The cones are erect and shatter soon after they mature. Firs suffer in hot, dry situations and thrive in moist, well-drained soil in the acid range, pH 5.0 to 6.0.

GROWTH RATE: fast/medium
LIGHT: full sun
MOISTURE: roots moist

A. concolor   White Fir   Zones 3–7.
Handsome native of the Rockies and the Southwest, 30 to 50 feet tall in cultivation. Has silvery bluish green needles, and green-purple 3- to 5-inch cones. Hardier and more resistant to city conditions and drought than most firs. Doesn't tolerate heavy clay soils. 'Conica' is slow-growing and more dwarf. 'Violacea' has silvery blue needles. Several blue cultivars are also available.

A. firma   Japanese Fir, Momi Fir   Zones 4–8.
Similar to the above species in many ways, but taller, and the needles are light green. Difficult to establish in cultivation but a much-loved Christmas tree in the West.

ARBUTUS *arb-yew-tus*

Small, flowering, broadleaved evergreens for warmer areas. The fruits attract birds, and the exfoliating bark is handsome.

GROWTH RATE: medium/slow
LIGHT: full sun, semi-sunny
MOISTURE: roots moist

A. menziesii   Madrone, Pacific Madrone
Zones 7–9.
To 50 feet and taller, with dark, lustrous leaves that are whitish underneath, and warm brown bark that sheds yearly and untidily. Lovely bell-shaped flowers in spring, followed by clusters of orange or orange-red berries. Adapts to poor, somewhat acid dry soils. Prefers well-drained situations, protection from drying winds, and is best transplanted when young.

A. unedo   Strawberry Tree   Zones 8–10.
Smaller, to about 30 feet, with amber-tinted foliage. Masses of white flowers bloom in fall, followed by long-lasting red fruits, orange-red like strawberries. Requires acid soil and a dry climate. 'Compacta' is a 5-foot shrub, grown in containers in cooler regions and moved to shelter during cold weather.

CALOCEDRUS *kal-oh-seed-rus*

decurrens   California Incense Cedar
Zones 6–8.

Stately conifer native to the Northwest; columnar, formal, with dark green aromatic, scalelike foliage. It resembles *Thuja occidentalis*, American Arbovitae (see below), but holds its color and is a better choice for warm climates. Small cones, and scaly, cinnamon-red bark. Hardy in southern New England, and beautiful in a landscape large enough to accommodate it. Requires well-drained soil and some shelter from sweeping winds.

MATURE HEIGHT: 70′
GROWTH RATE: medium/slow
LIGHT: full sun
MOISTURE: roots moist

CEDRUS *seed-rus*   Cedar

Large, handsome conifers with small, whorled, clustered needles, and large cones, graceful when young, impressive when mature, and demanding a large landscape. Long-lived and slow-growing. Prefer an open situation, but out of the wind, with well-drained and preferably somewhat acid soil.

GROWTH RATE: slow/medium
LIGHT: full sun, semi-sunny
MOISTURE: roots moist

C. atlantica 'Glauca'   Blue Atlas Cedar
Zones 7–8.
Lovely blue-needled pyramidal cultivar that grows quickly when young. Height is 40 to 60 feet. 'Glauca Pendula' has drooping branchlets. The species is light green to silvery blue. 'Fastigiata' is a narrow form with good blue needles. Makes a good bonsai.

C. deodara   Deodar Cedar   Zones 7–8.
The most graceful of the cedars, the branches are pendulous, and the height is 40 to 70 feet in 30 or 40

Cedrus atlantica, Atlas Cedar.

years. Color is light green, grayish green, or silver. Can be damaged by severe winters at the northern edge of its range. 'Pendula' is a beautiful weeping form.

C. libani   Cedar-of-Lebanon   Zones 5–7.
Celebrated in biblical times, this distinguished but charming evergreen is narrow when young, then becomes flat-topped. Needles are dark or bright green. Prefers well-drained soil, dry air, in an open situation, and does not tolerate shade or pollution. 'Pendula' is a drooping form created by grafting and staking.

CHAMAECYPARIS *kam-ee-sip-ar-iss*
False Cypress

Tall, pyramidal conifers with flat, scalelike foliage that is white on the undersides, and a dark, dramatic silhouette. Some have handsome, fissured bark. Grow best where humidity is high, in well-drained, sandy soil, and need shelter from strong winds and excess cold.

GROWTH RATE: slow
LIGHT: full sun
MOISTURE: roots moist

C. obtusa   Hinoki Cypress   Zones 5–8.
One of the best evergreens. Dark, glossy green foliage, slow-grower, 60 to 75 feet tall, with a compact pyramidal form. Prefers moist, loamy, well-drained soil, a humid climate, and open conditions. 'Crippsii', Cripp's Golden Hinoki Cypress, is a valuable medium-fast growing, dense and pyramidal form with rich, golden yellow foliage. It reaches 8 to 10 feet, 30 in time. Zones 4–8. 'Filicoides' is slow-growing, medium in size, with frondlike branches; a good container plant.

C. pisifera 'Boulevard' (syn. 'Cyanoviridis')
Sawara Cypress   Zones 4–8.
Small, exquisite, dwarf evergreen to 10 feet tall, with fine-textured plumelike, silvery blue foliage and a strikingly narrow pyramidal shape. The leaves are silvery green in summer, grayish blue in winter.

CRYPTOMERIA *krip-toh-meer-ee-uh*

japonica   Japanese Cedar   Zones 5–8.

Majestic, very beautiful, pyramidal conifer 50 to 60 feet tall in cultivation, with small needles, charming cones under an inch in length, and reddish, shredding bark. Pleasant cedarlike scent. Excellent for street plantings, allees, and large landscapes (such as the National Arboretum's bonsai garden and parking area). Prefers light, rich, somewhat acid soil, needs shelter from high winds and plenty of moisture. 'Yoshino' is an established cultivar, 30 to 40 feet tall. 'Lobbii' is a dense compact tree, to 60 feet tall. 'Compacta' has bluish green leaves and grows to 45 feet. Low forms have been developed, some 6 feet tall. 'Elegans', a bushy, juvenile form, has brownish red foliage in winter and reaches to 15 feet. A regular spray program may be required in your area—check with the local Agricultural Extension Service before planting.

GROWTH RATE: medium
LIGHT: full sun
MOISTURE: roots moist

CUPANIOPSIS *coo-pan-ee-op-siss*
anacardioides   Carrotwood Tree
Zones 9–10.

Small broadleaved evergreen, rounded, with beautiful, dark green leathery leaflets, used in warm parts of the West Coast and in Florida. A canopy of spreading branches gives dense shade. Mature trees may produce yellow-orange fruit. High tolerance to heat, drought, coastal winds. Prefers well-drained soil.

MATURE HEIGHT: 30′–40′
GROWTH RATE: slow
LIGHT: full sun
MOISTURE: versatile

CUPRESSUS *kew-press-us*   Cypress

Magnificent pyramidal conifers, dark and dramatic, with aromatic scalelike foliage under an inch long. Thrive in warm climates and sandy loam. Prefer to be well drained and withstand considerable drought.

GROWTH RATE: medium
LIGHT: full sun
MOISTURE: roots moist

C. arizonica   Arizona Cypress   Zones 6–9.
Tall, fast-growing, with varying green to gray green foliage. Height to 40 feet.

C. macrocarpa   Monterey Cypress
Zones 9–10.
Fascinating pyramidal cypress that thrives on the California coast but does not succeed inland. Most elegant when most windswept. Slow-growing, excellent windbreak. Pyramidal when young, rounding with maturity. 'Golden Pillar' is golden in full sun, lime green in shade.

C. sempervirens   Italian Cypress   Zones 7–9.
Very narrow, columnar tree that grows slowly to 50 to 60 feet. Dramatic effect, superb for formal allees and dramatic statements. There are blue and golden forms.

EUCALYPTUS *yew-kal-lip-tus*
Australian Gum, Ironbark

Important group of big, round- or oval-leaved evergreens from Australia. They are used in southern California and other warm regions in landscaping, as street trees, and for screening. Very aromatic fresh or dried foliage is a florist staple. Has colorful exfoliating bark, and fuzzy white or red flowers attractive to honeybees. A popular container plant in the North, wintered indoors. Tolerant of drought, but needs protection from cold wind.

MATURE HEIGHT: 30′–100′
GROWTH RATE: fast
LIGHT: full sun
MOISTURE: roots moist

E. cinerea   Silver-dollar Tree   Zones 8–10.
Small to medium-size tree with blue-green coin-shaped juvenile leaves, excellent for cut foliage. White flowers in spring.

E. citriodora   Lemon-scented Gum
Zones 8–10.
This fall-bloomer has attractive bark and lemon-scented leaves and flowers. White flowers in fall. Can stand close to a wall. To 50 feet.

E. globulus Blue Gum   Zones 9–10.
A big tree, once planted in wet areas to dry them up. Used as a windbreak around citrus groves in California. Handsome but messy, with exfoliating bark, leaves, and fruit, but a very fast grower.

E. leucoxylon White Ironbark   Zones 8–10.
A medium-size tree; the end branches with their spiraling, rounded, aromatic leaves are a popular florist's item. Best near the seacoast as it requires moist air to flourish. 'Rosea' has pink flowers.

FICUS *fye-kus*
retusa var. *nitida*   Indian Laurel Zones 9–10.

Small, broad-headed evergreen with weeping branches when mature, used widely in southern and central California as a shade and street tree. The leaves are leathery and a good green. 'Green Gem'™ PP 5900 is resistant to ficus problems and a dense grower. Popular container plants in the North, summered outside and wintered indoors. Must be well drained.

MATURE HEIGHT: 25'–40'
GROWTH RATE: medium
LIGHT: full sun, semi-sunny
MOISTURE: roots moist

JUNIPERUS *joo-nip-er-us* Juniper

Mostly small conifers, with needlelike or scalelike leaves. The male cones are yellow, like catkins, and the female fruits are berrylike cones. Genus includes 60-foot trees, shrubs, and ground-hugging plants a few inches to 2 feet high with a spread of 4 to 8 feet. A spreading root system makes junipers easy to transplant. Some blight exists; choose blight-resistant cultivars recommended by local nurseries. Set out container plants in spring or fall.

GROWTH RATE: medium
LIGHT: full sun
MOISTURE: versatile

J. chinensis Chinese Juniper   Zones 4–9.
Species includes tall forms 20 to 30 feet at maturity. 'Keteleeri' has green foliage and is a broadly pyramidal tree with blue fruits. 'Mas' and 'Spartan' are good columnar forms. 'Kaizuka' (syn. 'Torulosa') has a rustic, twisted form, and is much used in Hollywood and along the California coast—to 20 or 30 feet. 'Kaizuka Variegated' is mottled yellow and grows to about 15 feet.

J. scopulorum Rocky Mountain Juniper
                                   Zones 3–7.
A narrow, pyramidal tree, 30 to 40 feet tall, successful from British Columbia to California. 'Blue Heaven' and 'Gray Gleam' are small trees known for their color. 'Skyrocket' stays 8 to 12 inches wide, and 20 to 35 feet tall.

J. virginiana Red Cedar   Zones 2–9.
A densely pyramidal tree, sometimes columnar, good specimen, that can be massed for windbreaks, and is used in hedges and for topiary. The leaves are scalelike, and the fragrant red wood is used for chests and cabinets. The cultivar 'Burkii', about 30 feet tall, is a good blue that colors purple in winter. 'Canaertii' is very hardy, yellow-green in spring, dark green in winter.

Juniperus chinensis, Chinese Juniper. (Neumann)

MAGNOLIA *mag-nohl-ee-uh*

One of the planet's oldest, this genus includes tall, deciduous shrubs that bloom in early to mid-spring before the foliage appears, as well as majestic evergreen trees that bloom later. Provide humusy, acid soil, pH 5.0 to 6.0, and an acid mulch about 4 inches deep up to the trunk to maintain essential moisture. Well-drained soil is needed, especially in cooler regions. Transplant with care before new growth begins in early spring.

GROWTH RATE: medium/slow
LIGHT: full sun, semi-sunny
MOISTURE: roots moist

M. acuminata Cucumber Tree   Zones 3–8.
Big tree—50 to 80 feet—with leaves to 10 inches long, that has greenish and not very showy flowers high up in early to mid-spring. Recommended where a big, wide-spreading shade tree is needed. Prefers somewhat acid soil and grows rather quickly.

M. grandiflora Bull Bay, Southern Magnolia
                                   Zones 7–9.
Symbol of southern plantation days, an imposing broadleaved evergreen flowering tree 60 to 80 feet and more, with handsome, stiff, glossy leaves to 8 inches long. Huge, fragrant, creamy, waxy flowers are borne in spring and summer. The leaves of some have brown backs, lovely when tossed by the wind and attractive in arrangements; brown-backed forms are believed hardier. Fruit cones to 4 inches long open to expose red seeds. A good choice for landscaping large buildings and for espalier. Prefers cool weather and shade, and loose soil that is deep and fertile. Requires protection north of Washington, D.C. 'Majestic Beauty'™ is pyramidal and has cup-shaped white flowers to 12 inches across in summer, and large, lustrous green leaves. 'Little Gem' is an outstanding compact with nice russet color and 6-inch flowers in spring; some rebloom in summer. 'Victoria', a very hardy 20-foot tree, is almost as wide

as it is high. 'St. Mary's' is a choice compact, pyramidal in shape, that produces many full-size flowers while still young.

M. virginiana Sweet Bay   Zones 5–9.
Lovely, graceful, smallish tree for patio or garden, evergreen in warmer regions, deciduous farther north. Very fragrant, creamy white, rounded flowers appear with the leaves in late spring and early summer, and then sporadically to early fall. The fruit is dark red, to 2 inches long, and the leaves silver-backed. Adjusts to considerable shade and wet or swampy soils. Height can be 25 to 60 feet. Growth rate is medium to fast.

PICEA *pye-see-uh* Spruce

Big conifers with the aromatic, rigid needles, large cones, and pyramidal form associated with Christmas trees. There are a few shrub-size forms. Spruces thrive in cool regions, open situations, and well-drained, humusy soil in the acid range, pH 5.0–6.0.

GROWTH RATE: medium/slow
LIGHT: full sun
MOISTURE: roots moist

P. abies Norway Spruce   Zones 2–7.
Fast-growing, 40 to 60 feet tall; a good quick windbreak or tall screen. Less attractive when older. There are attractive cultivars with weeping or mounding branches.

P. glauca White Spruce   Zones 2–6.
Strong windbreak useful in cold parts of the Midwest, very easy to grow and versatile. It has whitish leaves, and reaches 40 to 60 feet or more. These are superior evergreens for specimen use in the East.

P. omorika Serbian Spruce   Zones 4–7.
Narrow, pyramidal, graceful spruce, with a slender trunk and drooping branches. Good specimen and street tree for the Northeast. Not widely available. 'Pendula' is a slender tree with drooping, partially twisted branches.

Picea omorika, Serbian Spruce.

P. orientalis Oriental Spruce   Zones 5–8.
Beautiful at the National Arboretum, a slow grower to 60 feet, one of the best spruces for small properties. Short, green, glossy needles, and a tidy habit. 'Gracilis' is a slow-growing form, 15 to 20 feet tall, with bright green needles.

P. pungens 'Glauca'   Colorado Blue Spruce
Zones 3–8.
Stiff, formal pyramidal spruce with soft silvery blue-gray foliage when young; it later turns silver-gray to blue-green. Height after 30 years is about 30 feet. 'Moerheimii' is very blue, and the color is retained in winter. 'Hoopsii' is very silvery, one of the best cultivars for consistent color. More adaptable to urban situations than most other spruces.

PINUS *pye-nus*   Pine

Big, important group of conifers known for long, pointed, but usually rather soft needles sheathed in bundles and lasting two or more years. Pyramidal in youth, but most eventually are flat-topped. The cones are large. Pines succeed in dry, sandy soils where little else grows, but they are sensitive to air pollution. Most require well-drained, somewhat acid soil, pH 5.0 to 6.0. Transplant with care in early spring. There are dwarf forms of many species.

GROWTH RATE: medium/slow
LIGHT: full sun
MOISTURE: roots moist, versatile

P. bungeana Lace-bark Pine   Zones 4–8.
Beautiful, multiple-stemmed in youth. In maturity, has superb mottled bark which becomes chalk white and exfoliates. The young stems are a mixture of green with white and brown. Height is 30 to 50 feet.

P. cembra Swiss Stone Pine, Russian Cedar
Zones 4–8.
Upright and relatively narrow with blue-green needles, 35 to 40 feet tall, very handsome and slow-growing. One of the best.

P. halepensis Aleppo Pine, Jerusalem Pine
Zones 8–9.
Rugged pine with irregular, upward-reaching branches in maturity, good at the seashore, and thrives in hot, dry, and windy places. Somewhat smaller tree.

P. nigra Austrian Pine, Austrian Black Pine
Zones 4–7.
Rich, dark green, vigorous, dense with stiffer needles than white pine, more interesting structure with age.

Pinus bungeana, Lace-bark Pine. (Neumann)

Can live in the city and at the seashore, and can stand wind and adverse conditions as long as the soil is well drained and moist. Resists heat and drought. Succeeds in containers. Height is 60 to 70 feet. Prone to disease in the Midwest.

P. strobus White Pine   Zones 2–8.
Tall—50 to 80 feet—rapid grower, excellent property divider, screen, specimen, and windbreak. Wind sweeping through tall white pines is a lovely sound. One of the best pines for the East. 'Pendula's' drooping branches sweep the ground. 'Fastigiata' is a beautiful columnar form with ascending branch tips.

P. thunbergiana Japanese Black Pine
Zones 4–8.
Picturesque, to 30 or more feet tall, choice for bonsai, container growing, informal accents; prunable and adapts to semi-sunny situations. Outstanding salt tolerance and a great seashore plant. Requires fertile soil and more moisture than most other pines. 'Majestic Beauty' PP 5078, is offered as resistant to smog damage.

PLATYCLADUS *plat-ik-klay-dus*
orientalis (syn. *Thuja orientalis*)
Oriental Arborvitae   Zones 6–9.
A plant reclassification has transferred the well-known Oriental Arborvitae to this genus but the plant may continue to be listed as *Thuja* for some time. It thrives in the Southeast and Southwest. It is a small tree with grass green foliage when young, changing to a darker green as it matures. Needs less moisture than American arborvitae, *Thuja occidentalis* (see below). Choose among the many excellent cultivars.

MATURE HEIGHT: 18'–25'
GROWTH RATE: medium/slow
LIGHT: full sun, semi-sunny
MOISTURE: roots moist

Pinus thunbergiana, Japanese Black Pine. (Oehme)

Platycladus orientalis, Oriental Arborvitae.

PSEUDOTSUGA *soo-doh-tsoo-guh*
menziesii Douglas Fir   Zones 4–6.

Towering to 250 or 300 feet in the wild, this soft-needled conifer forms an open, airy pyramid and becomes bluer as it matures. Large pendulous cones are 4 ½ inches long. Dramatic landscape ornamental and an important timber tree in its native Northwest. Not suited to dry, windy areas. Prefers neutral or just slightly acid, well-drained soil and moist air. A smaller variety, *P. m.* var. *glauca*, Rocky Mountain Douglas Fir, grows more slowly and is long-lasting as a Christmas tree.

> MATURE HEIGHT: 40'–80'
> GROWTH RATE:　medium
> LIGHT:　　　　full sun
> MOISTURE:　　roots moist

SCIADOPITYS *sye-ad-dop-it-iss*
verticillata Umbrella Pine,
Japanese Umbrella Pine   Zones 5–8.

Small conifer distinguished by its long, dark, glossy green needles and unusual texture. It stays under 30 feet for 20 years and more. Excellent lawn specimen worth searching out. Easy to establish in rich, moist, but well-drained, acid soil with some protection from wind.

> MATURE HEIGHT: 20'–30'
> GROWTH RATE:　slow
> LIGHT:　　　　full sun, semi-sunny
> MOISTURE:　　roots moist

SEQUOIA *see-kwoy-uh*
sempervirens Redwood   Zone 7.

Striking, long-lived conifer native to the coastal Northwest and reaching 300 feet and more in the wild, with a trunk 25 feet across, and fibrous red bark. Height is much less in cultivation. Succeeds when young in other regions with adequate rainfall.

(Closely related to *Sequoiadendron giganteum*, the very ancient Giant Sequoia; trees in the few remaining groves are believed many centuries old.) Fire-resistant and grows by streambeds and on hillsides. 'Santa Cruz' has soft, pale green foliage. 'Soquel', a smaller pyramidal tree, has dark green foliage that's blue on the underside.

> MATURE HEIGHT: 70'–90'
> GROWTH RATE:　fast
> LIGHT:　　　　full sun, semi-sunny
> MOISTURE:　　soil surface damp

TAXUS *tax-us* Yew

Stately trees and vigorous shrubs with short, stiff, narrow, needlelike leaves, used since Roman times as lawn specimens, for hedges, and massing. May be sheared and pruned repeatedly to maintain size or to shape topiaries and espaliers. Prefer alkaline soil, so are not good with azaleas and rhododendrons. Succeed in sun or shade, in moist soil with excellent drainage, but need protection from strong winds. The female forms bear seeds with a fleshy red aril. Usually dioecious.

> GROWTH RATE:　fast
> LIGHT:　　　　full sun, versatile
> MOISTURE:　　roots moist, versatile

T. baccata English Yew   Zones 6–8.
Tall, to 60 feet, dramatic tree, with dark, lustrous needles. There is a form suitable for almost every landscape use; a good topiary and hedge subject. 'Fastigiata' is naturally columnar, with branches very erect and close together. 'Fastigiata Aurea' has golden or gold-variegated needles. Beautiful only well within its temperature range.

T. × *media*   Zones 5–8.
A hybrid with the beauty of the English yews and the hardiness of the Japanese form (*T. cuspidata*.) Size is variable, since these are hybrids. There are many useful, slow-growing, wide, shrubby cultivars (see

Shrubs 7). 'Hicksii', Hick's Yew, is naturally columnar, growing slowly to 20 feet in 10 years. 'Hatfieldii' grows to about 12 feet in 20 years.

THUJA *thew-juh* Arborvitae

Beautiful evergreens for specimens, windbreaks, tall hedges, foundation planting—with scalelike, lacy leaves in flat sprays. Formal, dense, and clippable, easy to grow. Fruits are small, dried capsules. Height can be 40 to 60 feet, but more often reaches 12 to 15 feet. Best growth is on fertile, moist, well-drained soil. Choose established cultivars known to maintain good color in winter. Good in full sun, though they adapt to some shade.

> GROWTH RATE:　medium/slow
> LIGHT:　　　　full sun, semi-sunny
> MOISTURE:　　roots moist

T. occidentalis American Arborvitae
　　　　　　　　　　　　　　Zones 2–7/8.
Superb for specimen planting, accents, hedges. In the North it can grow to 40 or 60 feet but is usually seen under 25. Needs lots of moisture and tolerates limestone soils. 'Nigra' is cold-hardy, though it can turn yellow or brown in too-cold weather. 'Emerald Green' holds its color in winter.

T. orientalis, Oriental Arborvitae, now listed as *Platycladus orientalis* (see above).

T. plicata Giant Arborvitae,
Western Red Cedar   Zones 5–7.
Beautiful, fast-growing specimen 30 to 50 feet tall, native from northern California to Alaska. Prefers moist, well-drained, fertile soil—succeeds in bogs and swamps. Needs moist atmosphere. Several cultivars have good yellow color—including 'Rogersii', 'Hillier', and 'Stoneham.'

TORREYA *torr-ee-uh*

Handsome needled evergreens rather like yews, with whorled branches. The plumlike fruits of one species are used for food. Grown in warm regions as a change of pace from other, overused, evergreens.

> GROWTH RATE:　medium
> LIGHT:　　　　full sun, semi-sunny
> MOISTURE:　　roots moist

T. californica California Nutmeg   Zones 7–8.
Grows to 60 or 70 feet and has drooping branches with shiny dark green leaves about 3 inches long. The inch-long oval fruits are green streaked with purple.

T. nucifera Kaya, Japanese Torreya
　　　　　　　　　　　　　　Zones 7–8.
Taller species with horizontal branches and pyramidal form. Hardier and can be grown with shelter in Zone 6. Leaves have a strong odor when bruised. In Japan, the fruits are used for food.

TSUGA *tsoo-guh* Hemlock

Graceful pyramidal evergreens with feathery drooping branches, short, long-lived aromatic needles with two white bands beneath. Pretty little cones are ½ to 1 inch long. Shearable, great hedge plants. A shallow root system makes transplanting easy at any age.

Need plenty of moisture, prefer well-drained, somewhat acid soil, and are not tolerant of pollution.

GROWTH RATE: fast/medium
LIGHT: full sun, semi-sunny
MOISTURE: roots moist, versatile

T. canadensis Canada Hemlock Zones 3–7.
Much used in the Northeast as a property divider or specimen, for screening and tall hedges. Birds like to nest in the branches. New growth is light yellow-green, changing to dark green. Holds its needles for several years, so it always seems dense. Height is 40 to 70 feet. Succeeds on rocky bluffs. 'Kingsville' is a good choice for row plantings. There are excellent cultivars in various shapes. 'Pendula', Weeping Canadian Hemlock, is a weeping form 10 to 20 feet high.

T. caroliniana Carolina Hemlock Zones 4–7.
For southern gardens. Needles are placed differently, the look is more feathery, and the cones slightly larger, but otherwise similar to the species above. Greater pollution tolerance.

SEE ALSO:
× *Cupressocyparis leylandii*, Leyland Cypress, Trees 18
Ilex latifolia, Luster-leaf Holly, Trees 19
Ilex opaca, American Holly, Trees 19
Juniperus spp., various lists
Laurus nobilis, Grecian Laurel, Sweet Bay, Herbs 1
Pittosporum undulatum, Victorian Box, Mock Orange, Trees 11
Taxus cuspidata, Japanese Yew, Shrubs 7

ALTERNATE:
Lagunaria patersonii

TREES 5
TREES WITH RED OR YELLOW FOLIAGE ALL SEASON

The new foliage of some deciduous trees is red, usually burgundy-red, or yellow; a few retain the color throughout the season. And there are several lovely yellow and yellow-green evergreens. They brighten the garden in seasons when everything else is green. The very best cultivars are breathtaking when the sun is shining through the leaves. Buy these plants late in the season to ascertain the summer color. See also Shrubs 8 and 9.

COMPANION PLANTINGS
For foliage contrast: *Ilex crenata*, Japanese Holly; *I. opaca*, American Holly; tall *Rhododendron* cvs.; *Viburnum* cvs.
Perennials: *Veronica latifolia* 'Crater Lake Blue', Speedwell; *V. spicata* 'Snow White', 'Sunny Borders', Speedwell.

ACER *ay-ser* Maple

Valuable trees ranging from small ornamentals to majestic shade and street trees, famous for spring and fall color. The red buds herald spring, and the brilliant foliage is a symbol of autumn all over the Northeast. Most maple species are slow-growing, adapta-

Closeup of *Acer palmatum* 'Bloodgood', Japanese Maple.

Acer palmatum 'Bloodgood', Japanese Maple.

ble, and flourish in well-drained, moist, somewhat acid soil. In dry spells, water even mature maples deeply.

GROWTH RATE: medium/slow
LIGHT: full sun, semi-sunny
MOISTURE: roots moist

A. negundo Box Elder Zones 2–7.
Bright color for difficult sites. Useful windbreak and screen in areas where winter cold and summer drought are destructive of more ornamental maples. 'Auratum' is a good gold-leaved tree where the climate is right. 'Aurea-variegatum' leaves are gold-edged. Height is to 50 feet. 'Variegatum' is a small tree whose leaves are beautifully edged with white; probably not hardy north of Zone 5.

A. palmatum Japanese Maple Zones 5/6–8.
Exquisite small trees treasured for foliage and form. The new leaves are usually red; some fade to green in the heat and regain color in the fall. In warm regions, leaves may burn in full sun; afford some protection. 'Bloodgood' is brilliant red in spring, and holds its color through the season, deepening to dark red;

insist on grafted cultivars—grown from seed, the color may be unreliable. The new leaves of 'Atropurpureum' are reddish purple, fading toward green in summer. 'Burgundy Lace' is a beautiful, open-branched, smaller plant, with lacy, brilliant burgundy-red leaves. Height is 15 to 25 feet in cultivation, though this species can reach 40 to 50 feet in the wild. See also Shrubs 8.

A. platanoides 'Crimson King' Norway Maple Zones 4–7.
One of the few large trees with rich crimson purple leaves throughout summer and fall. A big, vigorous tree for streets and parks, 40 to 50 feet tall. 'Crimson Sentry' is a colorful 25-foot columnar form; foliage in fall is maroon-bronze.

A. pseudoplatanus Sycamore Maple, Planetree Maple Zones 4–7.
The species form is relatively colorless, but flourishes in salt conditions and winds that other maples do not tolerate. Height is 40 to 60 feet. Choose colorful cultivars such as 'Brilliantissimum', which unfolds shrimp pink and changes from yellow to green; requires shade from noon sun. 'Worleei' starts a soft yellow-green; turns yellow, then green with red petioles.

A. saccharinum Silver Maple, River Maple Zones 3–8.
A pretty, silvery, fast-growing maple that spreads relentlessly in moist soil. Recommended only for fast cover, and naturalizing of large sites and wet places. 'Lutescens' is a warm yellow in spring and later turns green. Height is 50 to 70 feet in cultivation.

CHAMAECYPARIS *kam-ee-sip-ar-iss*
False Cypress

Tall, pyramidal conifers with flat, scalelike foliage that is white on the undersides. A number of cultivars are gold or gold-edged. Grow best where humidity is high, in well-drained sandy loam; need shelter from strong winds and severe cold.

GROWTH RATE: slow
LIGHT: full sun
MOISTURE: roots moist

Chamaecyparis obtusa 'Crippsii', Cripp's Golden Hinoki Cypress.

a grassy slope. Leaves emerge late and turn russet and golden brown in fall. Must have well-drained, loose soil in the acid range. There are many colorful, interesting cultivars, including fascinating weeping forms 'Pendula' and 'Purpurea Pendula'. 'Albo-variegata' has leaves variegated white. 'Cuprea', Copper Beech, is paler than 'Atropunicea' (syn. 'Purpurea'), Purple Beech, whose spring foliage is a deep, rich red changing to copper-green and then to green. 'Riversii' is a deep purple cultivar that holds the color in summer—the new leaves are almost black. 'Dawyck Purple' is columnar. 'Roseo-marginata' (syn. 'Tricolor' 'Purpurea Tricolor') has purple leaves with rose and pink-white edges. 'Rohan Gold' has yellowish foliage.

MATURE HEIGHT: 80'
GROWTH RATE: medium/slow
LIGHT: full sun
MOISTURE: roots moist

MALUS *may-lus* Apple

The flowering crab apples belong to this genus, small-trees—8 to 30 feet tall—covered in spring with masses of exquisite apple blossoms and in fall with small yellow and/or red fruits birds love. The foliage of some is purple-red in spring, an elegant foil for the blossoms. Though they have problems, beauty has made the crab apple the most important small landscape tree through the northern U.S. and southern Canada. Of the 700 to 800 cultivars, many are susceptible to disease; buy from an established local nursery and insist on disease-resistant cultivars. Those named here are among the most resistant, but there are many others. Plant in well-drained soil.

GROWTH RATE: medium
LIGHT: full sun, semi-sunny
MOISTURE: roots moist

M. 'Prairifire' Crab Apple Zones 4–8.
One of the best red-leaved crabs and very disease-resistant. It reaches about 20 feet with an equal spread, has purplish foliage becoming green in summer, bright pink-red flowers, and dark red fruit.

M. 'Strawberry Parfait' Crab Apple
Zones 4–8.
A very beautiful tree. The foliage is reddish purple fading to green, and the fragrant pink blossoms are exquisitely edged with red. Height is to 15 or 20 feet. The fruit is yellow with a red blush. Resistant to most problems. Definitely worth trying, but fire blight resistance is unknown; ask your local nurseryman for advice before buying.

PRUNUS *proon-us*

Small—rarely over 30 feet—hardy, flowering trees that bloom early and are among the most beautiful. All thrive in well-drained, sandy loam. They are subject to the problems that affect roses. Buy from responsible nurserymen, and insist on resistant cultivars.

GROWTH RATE: fast/medium
LIGHT: full sun
MOISTURE: roots moist

P. × *blireana* Flowering Plum Zones 5–8.
Very early and hardy, with pretty double flowers. The foliage is reddish purple in spring, greenish bronze in

C. obtusa 'Crippsii'
Cripp's Golden Hinoki Cypress Zones 4–8.
Cripp's Golden Hinoki Cypress is a valuable medium-fast-growing dense and pyramidal tree with rich, golden yellow foliage. It reaches 8 to 10 feet, 30 in time. Prefers moist, loamy, well-drained soil, a humid climate, and open conditions. Another cultivar, 'Tetragona Aurea', is not easily found, but worth looking for; it reaches to 30 feet and has bright yellow, ferny foliage.

C. pisifera Sawara Cypress Zones 4–8.
The species is handsome when young, but loses lower limbs with age and needs bottom screening. 'Filifera Aurea' is a slow-growing, striking plant with

droopy, stringy branches and golden foliage. It prefers some acid in the soil. 'Plumosa Aurea' is eventually tall, with soft, feathery, golden yellow foliage that retains its color through summer. 'Squarrosa Aurea' is also tall, with fine, needlelike, fluffy yellow-green foliage.

FAGUS *fay-gus*
sylvatica European Beech Zones 4–7.

The beech is one of the most beautiful of the big deciduous trees, stately, 80 or more feet tall at maturity, with branches that sweep the ground. Demands staging with space all around; it is stunning alone on summer, and reddish bronze in fall. Requires more pruning than others, and has purplish red fruits rather lost in the foliage. To 15 or 20 feet tall and as wide. 'Moseri' retains its intensely red color well.

P. cerasifera 'Diversifolia'   Cherry Plum
Zones 5–8.

Small purple-leaved tree; brilliant red new leaves glow in the sun. The color is lasting. Masses of small pink flowers appear just before the leaves. 'Atropurpurea' foliage is cherry-red when new. 'Thundercloud' leaves remain purple through the growing season. 'Newport' leaves are popular dark purple, the flowers white. Height is about 25 feet; hardy to Zone 3. 'Mount St. Helens'™ PP 4987 Plum has light pink flowers and is especially hardy to Zone 3. 'Krauter Vesuvius' Plum has light pink flowers, is hardy to Zone 5, and is the plum most often grown in California.

P. × cistena   Purple-leaf Sand Cherry
Zones 2–7.

Reddish purple foliage color effective throughout summer. Height is about 14 feet. Light pink, fragrant flowers, small blackish purple fruits. 'Big Cis'™, Purple-leaf Plum, reaches 14 feet, and has light pink and very fragrant flowers; hardy to Zone 2. It is a good choice for pot culture.

P. virginiana   Chokecherry   Zones 2–7.

Wild tree with small, edible fruits loved by the birds. Small white flowers in dense racemes in early spring. Fast spreader and weedy, but a few cultivars are planted for the foliage, which is green in spring and turns red in summer. Among them are 'Canada Red', to 25 feet, and 'Shubert'. Very cold-hardy, not good in wet soil.

SEE ALSO:
Cupressus macrocarpa 'Golden Pillar', Monterey Cypress, Trees 4
Liquidambar styraciflua 'Aurea', 'Matthew's Gold', American Sweet Gum, Trees 7
Malus 'Candied Apple', Weeping Candied Crab Apple, Trees 2

Ilex aquifolium, 'Aureo-marginata', Golden-edge English Holly.

ALTERNATES:
Fagus sylvatica 'Zlatia', European Beech
Fraxinus excelsior 'Aurea', Golden European Ash
Gleditsia triacanthos var. *inermis* 'Sunburst', Thornless Locust
Robinia pseudoacacia 'Aurea', Golden Black Locust
Robinia pseudoacacia 'Frisia', Black Locust
Thuja plicata 'Hiller', 'Rogersii', 'Stoneham', Giant Arborvitae, Western Red Cedar

TREES 6
TREES WITH SILVER OR VARIEGATED FOLIAGE

Here are trees whose leaves are silvery, white-backed, or splotched or margined with white or cream. They are striking. Few gardens benefit from more than one of these attention-getters. However, some are used to create striking allees and tall screens. From a distance, the effect is often rather grayish.

COMPANION PLANTINGS
Background: *Juniperus chinensis* cvs. 'Keteleeri', 'Mas', 'Spartan', Chinese Juniper; *Pinus nigra,* Austrian Pine, Austrian Black Pine; *Rhododendron* cvs. Ground covers: *Vinca minor*, Periwinkle; *V. minor* 'Variegata', Variegated Periwinkle. Perennials: *Tulipa* Kaufmanniana Hybrids, Water-lily Tulips.

ACER *ay-ser*   Maple

Valuable trees ranging from small ornamentals to majestic shade and street trees, famous for spring and fall color. The red buds herald spring and the brilliant foliage is a symbol of autumn all over the Northeast. Most maple species are slow-growing, adaptable, and flourish in well-drained, moist soil. In dry spells, water even mature maples biweekly. Require well-drained, somewhat acid, soil.

GROWTH RATE: medium/slow
LIGHT: full sun, semi-sunny
MOISTURE: roots moist

A. palmatum   Japanese Maple
Zones 5/6–8.

Exquisite small trees treasured for foliage and form; they reach 15 to 25 feet in cultivation. The new leaves are usually red; some fade to green in the heat and regain color in the fall. In warm regions, leaves may burn in full sun; afford some protection. 'Butterfly' (syn. 'Kocho nishiki') has leaves edged in pink in spring. Height, to 15 feet. Good to Zone 4, but leaves need protection from sun-scorch. There are many specialized forms. See also Shrubs 8.

A. platanoides 'Drummondii'   Norway Maple
Zones 4–7.

Smaller than the species, with light green leaves edged with white. Reverts to green and must be pruned, but very bright and bold if the reversions are checked. 'Waldersei' leaves are mottled yellow; to about 30 feet.

CORNUS *korn-us*
kousa 'Snowboy'
Snowboy Chinese Dogwood   Zones 5–8

'Snowboy' has bright, attractively margined foliage, and white flowers. Dr. Frank Santamour recommends planting this species and its cultivars in place of *C. florida*, Flowering Dogwood. In tests for disease-resistant dogwoods from 20 geographic sources this species performed best. The bracts come a few weeks later than those of *C. florida* and face upward on the branch tops—most beautiful viewed from above. It has interesting mottled bark and reddish leaves in autumn. Some drought resistance. Height to 25 feet.

MATURE HEIGHT: 25'
GROWTH RATE: medium
LIGHT: full sun, semi-sunny
MOISTURE: roots moist

GINKGO *gink-go*
biloba 'Variegata'
Variegated Maidenhair Tree   Zones 4–9.

Small deciduous tree with characteristic fan-shaped leaves that turn a beautiful yellow in fall; especially tolerant of city conditions. Avoid female trees, whose fruit is messy and has an unpleasant odor. This collector's item has very showy foliage, mottled with white, and is rare. Prefers sandy, well-drained soil.

MATURE HEIGHT: 30'
GROWTH RATE: medium/slow
LIGHT;   full sun
MOISTURE: roots moist

ILEX *eye-lex*
aquifolium 'Argenteo-marginata'
White-edged English Holly   Zones 6–9.

Beautiful little broadleaved evergreen valued for brilliant fall and winter display of fruit attractive to robins and other birds. The species has white fragrant flowers in spring, followed by red berries and is usually seen in this country as a shrubby cultivar. The spiny-margined leaves of this cultivar have cheerful white edges; it is a female. 'Aureo-marginata' leaves are edged with bright yellow. Hollies are dioecious and most females require a male pollinator to fruit well. Need well-drained soil and are best in semi-sun. See also Shrubs 7.

MATURE HEIGHT: 35'
GROWTH RATE: medium
LIGHT: full sun, semi-sunny
MOISTURE: roots moist

LIRIODENDRON *lihr-ee-oh-den-dron*
tulipifera 'Aurea-marginatum'
Gold-edged Tulip Tree   Zones 5–9.

The species is a magnificent tree for the larger landscape. Reaching to 150 feet in the wild, it bears tuliplike, greenish yellow flowers flowers high in its branches in early summer or late spring. Bright green leaves turn golden yellow in fall. This cultivar is a smaller tree, and its leaves are prominently edged with yellow. Prefers rich, deep, moist loam, and slightly acid soil.

MATURE HEIGHT: 50'
GROWTH RATE: medium
LIGHT: full sun
MOISTURE: roots moist

TILIA *till-ee-uh*
tomentosa   Silver Linden   Zones 4–7.

Excellent, handsome, residential shade and street tree, pollution-tolerant and withstands heat and drought. It has smooth, light gray bark when young; the leaves are dark green above, white and tomentose beneath. Prefers moist, well-drained, fertile soil.

MATURE HEIGHT: 40'–60'
GROWTH RATE: medium/slow
LIGHT: full sun
MOISTURE: roots moist

SEE ALSO:
Acer negundo 'Aurea-variegatum', 'Variegatum', Variegated Box Elder, Trees 5
Juniperus chinensis 'Kaizuka Variegated', Variegated Chinese Juniper, Trees 4

ALTERNATES:
Liquidambar styraciflua 'Aurea', 'Matthew's Gold', American Sweet Gum
Liquidambar styraciflua 'Variegata', Variegated American Sweet Gum
Populus alba var. *nivea*, White Poplar, Silver-leaved Poplar
Salix alba, White Willow
Salix alba var. *seriacea*, White Willow

TREES 7
TREES WITH RED FOLIAGE IN FALL

In the fall, changing light, temperature, and moisture levels inhibit the production of chlorophyll in leaves. In some trees this creates a dramatic show of red and yellow. The maples are star performers.

Acer rubrum 'October Glory', Red Maple, Swamp Maple. (Neumann)

There are other favorites, but not all are as successfully cultivated as the maples—for instance sassafras and scarlet oak, which are suggested alternates on the list below.

Described here are trees whose autumn reds are brilliant, lasting, and usually reliable.

COMPANION PLANTINGS
Tree: *Picea pungens* 'Glauca', Colorado Blue Spruce.
Shrub: *Euonymus alata* 'Compacta', Dwarf Winged Spindle Tree.
Ground covers: *Pachysandra terminalis* 'Green Carpet', Japanese Pachysandra; *Vinca minor*, Periwinkle.
Flowers: *Anemone vitifolia* 'Robustissima', Grape-leaved Anemone; *Chrysanthemum* cvs., yellow and white.

ACER *ay-ser*   Maple

Long-lived, valuable trees ranging from small ornamentals to majestic shade and street trees, famous for spring and fall color. Their carmine-red buds herald spring and the brilliant foliage is a symbol of autumn all over the Northeast. Most maple species are slow-growing, adaptable, and flourish in well-drained, moist soil. In dry spells, water even mature maples biweekly. Prefer well-drained, somewhat acid soil. The maple leaf is the national emblem of Canada.

GROWTH RATE: slow/medium
LIGHT: full sun
MOISTURE: roots moist

A. circinatum   Vine Maple   Zones 5–7.
Brilliant fall color for coastal gardens from British Columbia through northern California. Mature height is 15 to 20 feet. Attractive bark. Summer fruits are a showy red.

A. ginnala   Amur Maple   Zones 2–8.
Yellowish white, fragrant flowers are followed by red-brown fruit in late summer. Reaches 8 to 10 feet at maturity. Color is from yellow to orange and red. Cultivars like 'Flame' have best color.

A. rubrum   Red Maple, Swamp Maple
Zones 3–10.
From Minnesota to the Florida Keys, local nursery varieties of the cultivars 'October Glory' and 'Red Sunset' are outstanding. In colder regions, plant extra-hardy cultivars, such as 'Autumn Flame' and 'Northwood'. Moderately fast-growing for a maple. Reaches 40 to 60 feet in cultivation, but well over 100 in the wild. Succeeds in wet places but will be smaller.

A. saccharum   Sugar Maple, Rock Maple, Hard Maple   Zones 3–8.
This species has great strength and character when mature, and has dazzling yellow-orange-red fall foliage. Reaches 60 to 75 in cultivation, over 100 feet in the wild. Cultivars such as 'Bonfire' may grow faster than the species and will have more reliable fall color. Don't confuse *A. saccharum* with the fast-growing but inferior *A. saccharinum*.

A. tataricum   Tatarian Maple   Zones 3–8.
As beautiful as *A. ginnala*, and similar, though not well known; 15 to 20 feet at maturity. Leaf color in fall is variable—red, yellow-red, and reddish brown. 'Rubrum' leaves are bloodred in fall.

COTINUS *kot-tye-nus*
obovatus   American Smoke Tree, Chittamwood   Zones 3–8

In June, chittamwood is enveloped in fluffy, pink-gray fruiting panicles 6 to 10 inches long. Bark at maturity is corky and beautiful. Fall foliage is brilliant orange-red. It succeeds in the Midwest, East, and South.

MATURE HEIGHT: 20'–30'
GROWTH RATE: medium/slow
LIGHT: full sun
MOISTURE: versatile

LIQUIDAMBAR *lik-wid-am-ber*
styraciflua American Sweet Gum
Zones 5–9.

A superb lawn, park, or street tree, the fall display is true red to dark crimson and yellow. Outstanding in southern California. In below-zero regions look for hardy cultivars like 'Moraine', which grows faster than the species and turns a rich red. A problem is prickly fruit which must be removed from the lawn before mowing. Prefers rich, moist, acid-range soil. Several small, colorful cultivars are known but none is easy to find in this country; 'Aurea' has gaudy yellow markings and 'Matthew's Gold' is gold. 'Variegata' leaves have creamy white margins that become rose blush in late summer.

MATURE HEIGHT: 60'–75'
GROWTH RATE: fast/medium
LIGHT: full sun
MOISTURE: roots moist

OXYDENDRUM *ox-ee-den-drum*
arboreum Sourwood, Sorrel Tree
Zones 4–9.

Among the most beautiful flowering trees and one of the best for crimson fall color. Very showy drooping racemes of fragrant white flowers cover the tree in summer. Attractive seedpods persist, heightening the fall display of red and red-purple. Attracts bees and is a source of superb honey. Good on dry soils, but not in polluted areas. Deeply grooved, interesting bark. Can take shade but does much better in full sun. Prefers well-drained, somewhat acid soil.

MATURE HEIGHT: 20'–25'
GROWTH RATE: medium/slow
LIGHT: full sun, semi-sunny
MOISTURE: roots moist

PISTACIA *pis-tay-shee-uh*
chinensis Pistachio
Zones 6–9.

Spectacular fall color in climates like that of southern California, but also thrives in the East. Good for lawn, park, and street use. Very adaptable species and free of problems.

MATURE HEIGHT: 30'–35'
GROWTH RATE: medium
LIGHT: full sun
MOISTURE: roots moist

TERMINALIA *ter-min-nay-lee-uh*
catappa Tropical Almond, Indian Almond
Zone 10.

A tropical tree whose leaves turn vibrant shades of red, yellow, and purple twice each year before falling in the dry seasons. Excellent shade tree for streets, it requires well-drained soil, and also survives sandy soils and salt spray.

MATURE HEIGHT: 20'–30'
GROWTH RATE: medium
LIGHT: full sun
MOISTURE: roots moist, versatile

ZELKOVA *zel-koh-vuh*
serrata Japanese Zelkova
Zones 5–8.

Choice for shade as well as for fall color in streets, parks, and larger landscapes. Popular bonsai subject. The Princeton Nurseries selection called 'Village Green' turns wine-red in fall and grows more rapidly than the species.

MATURE HEIGHT: 40'–50'
GROWTH RATE: medium
LIGHT: full sun
MOISTURE: roots moist

Nyssa sylvatica, Pepperidge, Sour Gum.

SEE ALSO:
Cornus kousa var. *chinensis* 'Summer Stars', Chinese Dogwood, Trees 2
Crataegus phaenopyrum, Washington Thorn, Trees 17
Pyrus calleryana 'Whitehouse', 'Capitol', Bradford Pear, Callery Pear, Trees 2
Stewartia spp., Trees 3

ALTERNATES:
Metasequoia glyptostroboides, Dawn Redwood
Nyssa sylvatica cvs., Pepperidge, Sour Gum
Quercus coccinea 'Superba', Scarlet Oak
Sapium sebiferum, Chinese Tallow Tree
Sassafras albidum
Sorbus alnifolia, Mountain Ash, Korean Mountain Ash

TREES 8
TREES WITH YELLOW FOLIAGE IN FALL

In cold weather, the leaves of these trees turn bright yellow. The color is lasting, and when the leaves do begin to fall, they carpet the ground with sunny gold.

COMPANION PLANTINGS
Background: *Acer palmatum* 'Bloodgood', Japanese Maple; *Nyssa sylvatica*, Pepperidge, Sour Gum. **Flowers:** *Antirrhinum majus* Giant, Giant Snapdragon; *Aster* cvs., Michaelmas Daisy; *Dahlia* × *hybrida* Unwin Hybrids, red; *Impatiens wallerana*, Zanzibar Balsam, Busy Lizzy, red.

Liquidambar styraciflua, American Sweet Gum.

Liriodendron tulipifera, Tulip Tree.

ACER *ay-ser* Maple

Most valuable trees ranging from small ornamentals to majestic shade and street trees, famous for spring and fall color. Their carmine-red buds herald spring and the brilliant foliage is a symbol of autumn. Most maple species are slow-growing, adaptable, and flourish in well-drained, moist soil. In dry spells, water even mature maples deeply. Prefer well-drained, somewhat acid, soil. The maple leaf is the national emblem of Canada.

GROWTH RATE:	slow/medium
LIGHT:	full sun
MOISTURE:	roots moist

A. macrophyllum Oregon Maple,
Big-leaf Maple   Zones 6–8.

Big Western trees for large parks and landscapes, with huge leaves—8 to 10 inches across, or more—which turn yellow-orange in fall. Fragrant yellow flowers in spring. Fast-growing for a maple and adaptable to soil pH. Colors best on the West Coast.

A. palmatum 'Okushimo' Japanese Maple
                                                             Zones 6–8.

Small upright tree, about 6 feet tall, whose foliage turns bright yellow in fall. Good choice for container growing and bonsai. There are other cultivars that also turn yellow in fall.

A. platanoides 'Summershade'
Norway Maple   Zones 4–7.

Big tree, 40 to 50 feet tall, one of the best maples,

with good bloom in spring and leathery dark green foliage. Like the species, foliage turns yellow in fall. Resists windburn and insect injury, and tolerates city conditions. Relatively fast-growing for a maple. 'Cleveland', superior choice for urban situations, is a columnar form with beautiful yellow fall foliage.

A. saccharum Sugar Maple, Rock Maple, Hard Maple   Zones 3–8.

The species has great presence when mature, reaching 60 to 75 feet high in cultivation, over 100 feet in the wild. Dazzling yellow-orange-red fall foliage. 'Globosum' is a rare 10-foot roundheaded form that turns a good yellow in fall. 'Green Mountain' turns yellow-red in the Pacific Northwest. 'Monumentale' is a broad columnar form that turns yellow-orange in fall.

GINKGO *gink-go*
biloba Maidenhair Tree   Zones 4–9.

Wonderful city and street tree with characteristic fan-shaped leaves that turn a beautiful yellow in fall. Lower length of the trunk usually is bare. 'Autumn Gold' is a broad-spreading male cultivar; 'Mayfield' is a narrow, columnar type. Prefers sandy, well-drained soil and has good salt tolerance. Avoid female trees; they produce malodorous, messy fruit. A long-lived tree, it is one of the oldest on the planet.

MATURE HEIGHT:	30'
GROWTH RATE:	medium/slow
LIGHT:	full sun
MOISTURE:	roots moist

GLEDITSIA *gled-dit-see-uh*
triacanthos var. *inermis*
'Shademaster' Thornless Honey Locust
                                                             Zones 4–9.

Fast-growing, thornless, feathery tree with a short trunk, open crown, and delicate leaves that turn clear yellow to yellow-green in autumn, and fall fairly early. Good for dappled shade. Prefers a high pH, thrives on rich, moist soils, but is tolerant of drought and very accepting of salt. The new leaves of 'Sunburst' are yellow, turning to bright green; grows relatively slowly to 30 or 35 feet.

MATURE HEIGHT:	30'–60'
GROWTH RATE:	fast
LIGHT:	full sun
MOISTURE:	roots moist

LIRIODENDRON *lihr-ee-oh-den-dron*
tulipifera Tulip Tree   Zones 5–9.

Magnificent tree for the larger landscape; it reaches to 150 feet in the wild. In late spring or early summer it bears lovely tuliplike flowers, greenish yellow outside and orange inside, but high in the branches so they are seen well only from above. Bright green leaves turn yellow and golden yellow in fall. Requires rich, deep, moist loam, and slightly acid soil, though it will adapt. 'Compactum' is a dwarf.

MATURE HEIGHT:	50'
GROWTH RATE:	medium
LIGHT:	full sun
MOISTURE:	roots moist

PARROTIA *par-roh-tee-uh*
persica Persian Parrotia   Zones 4–8.

Very desirable but hard to find small tree for home gardens, attractive in all seasons. Notable for foliage that is reddish purple when new, turns lustrous medium green in summer, and colors bright gold, yellow, orange, and crimson in fall. The crown is round. Mature bark exfoliates, peeling in plates to reveal a darker, mottled, inner bark. Flowers with ribbonlike petals and red stamens appear before the leaves. Requires well-drained, somewhat acid soil. 'Pendula' is described by Dr. Dirr as highly desirable but is not in widely circulated catalogs.

MATURE HEIGHT: 20'–40'
GROWTH RATE: medium
LIGHT: full sun, semi-sunny
MOISTURE: roots moist

PSEUDOLARIX *soo-doh-lar-ix*
amabilis Golden Larch   Zones 4–7.

Tall, spreading, graceful, needled conifer loved by those who know it. One of few deciduous conifers, the feathery needles wrap the tree in a green haze in spring, and turn lovely yellow-gold-orange before dropping in fall. Handsome, rugged, reddish brown bark. Attractive cones about 3 inches long. Requires well-drained, somewhat acid soil.

MATURE HEIGHT: 30'–50'
GROWTH RATE: slow
LIGHT: full sun
MOISTURE: roots moist

SEE ALSO:
Carpinus betulus, European Hornbeam, Trees 15
Fraxinus excelsior 'Aurea', Golden European Ash, Trees 13

ALTERNATES:
Acer pensylvanicum, Striped Maple, Moosewood
Aesculus flava (formerly octandra), Yellow Buckeye
Amelanchier canadensis, Shadblow, Serviceberry
Ulmus 'Sapporo Autumn Gold', Smooth-leaf Elm

TREES 9
TREES WITH COLUMNAR FORM

Narrow trees, both deciduous and evergreen, that make a dramatic statement in the landscape. Elegant as tall screening, they are used in Europe to line approaches to mansions and *châteaux*. Especially valuable with stark modern architecture and in large, formal gardens. Small specimens grown in containers are delightful design elements for patios, roof gardens, and condominium decks. "Fastigiate" describes a plant whose branches are erect and close together, as those of Lombardy poplars, which, although attractive when young, have proven unsatisfactory.

COMPANION PLANTINGS
Background: *Ilex crenata* 'Helleri', Heller's Japanese Holly; *Zelkova serrata* 'Village Green', Japanese Zelkova.

Perennials: *Achillea millefolium* 'Fire King', Yarrow; *Ceratotigma plumbaginoides,* Blue Cerastostigma, Plumbago; *Hemerocallis* 'Fragrant Light', Fragrant Lily Daylily; *H.* 'Ed Murray', Daylily.

ACER *ay-ser* Maple

Most valuable trees ranging from small ornamentals to majestic shade and street trees, famous for spring and fall color. Their carmine red buds herald spring and the brilliant foliage is a symbol of autumn. Most maple species are slow-growing, adaptable, and flourish in well-drained, moist soil. In dry spells, water even mature maples biweekly. Prefer well-drained, somewhat acid, soil. The maple leaf is the national emblem of Canada.

GROWTH RATE: slow/medium
LIGHT: full sun
MOISTURE: roots moist

A. platanoides Norway Maple   Zones 4–7.
A big tree, 40 to 50 feet tall or more in cultivation, whose yellow fall foliage can be spectacular. Resists windburn and insect injury, and tolerates city conditions. Relatively fast-growing for a maple. 'Cleveland', like 'Columnare', is a narrow form with yellow fall foliage, and one of the best for urban situations. 'Erectum' is a narrower, elegant tree, described as the Lombardy poplar of Norway maples. 'Crimson Sentry' is a columnar form of 'Crimson King', whose foliage turns red in fall.

A. rubrum Red Maple, Swamp Maple
                        Zones 3–10.
Moderately fast-growing for a maple, has rather small leaves, and is one of the best for brilliant red color in fall. Reaches 40 to 60 feet in cultivation, but well over 100 in the wild. Succeeds in wet places but will be smaller. 'Columnare' is a narrow, columnar form whose fall color is orange to deep red; height to 80 feet. Must have acid soil.

CARPINUS *kar-pye-nus*
betulus 'Columnaris'
Columnar European Hornbeam   Zones 5–7.

Excellent, dense, small landscape tree that grows slowly, used as a specimen, for screens, and tall hedges (it is shearable). The oval leaves turn yellow-green in fall, and there are decorative drooping clusters of fruit in summer and fall. This cultivar is a densely branched, slender, pyramidal tree to about 45 feet.

MATURE HEIGHT: 45'
GROWTH RATE: medium/slow
LIGHT: versatile
MOISTURE: versatile

FAGUS *fay-gus*
sylvatica 'Dawyck' (sym. 'Fastigiata')
European Beech   Zones 4–7.

The beech is one of the most beautiful of the big deciduous trees. Leaves emerge late and turn russet and golden brown in fall. This is a narrow form: to 90 feet tall, it remains about 10 feet wide. 'Dawyck Gold' and 'Dawyck Purple' are colorful and equally columnar. Beeches require well-drained, loose soil in the acid range.

MATURE HEIGHT: 90'
GROWTH RATE: medium/slow
LIGHT: full sun
MOISTURE: roots moist

GINKGO *gink-go*
biloba 'Princeton Sentry' Maidenhair Tree
                        Zones 4–9.

Wonderful form for this versatile city and street tree. Characteristic fan-shaped leaves turn a beautiful yellow in fall. Lower length of the trunk usually is bare. 'Princeton Sentry' PP 2726 is a grafted male, uniquely columnar, beautiful in its fall foliage. 'Mayfield' is another narrow, columnar type. Prefers sandy, well-drained soil and has good salt tolerance. A long-lived tree, it is one of the oldest on the planet.

MATURE HEIGHT: 60'–70'
GROWTH RATE: medium/slow
LIGHT: full sun
MOISTURE: roots moist

JUNIPERUS *joo-nip-er-us* Juniper

Mostly small conifers, with needlelike or scalelike leaves and very aromatic wood. The male cones are yellow, like catkins, and the female fruits are berry-like cones. A spreading root system makes junipers easy to transplant. Some blight exists: choose blight-resistant cultivars recommended by local nurseries. Set out container plants in spring or fall.

GROWTH RATE: medium
LIGHT: full sun
MOISTURE: versatile

Juniperus scopulorum 'Gray Gleam', Rocky Mountain Juniper.

J. chinensis Chinese Juniper Zones 4–9.
Species is mostly erect, and typically narrow, but sometimes very bushy. It includes tall forms 20 to 30 feet at maturity. 'Mas' is a narrow male tree. 'Mountbatten' is a very dense, narrow, upright tree that has soft gray green foliage.

J. scopulorum Rocky Mountain Juniper
Zones 3–7.
A narrow, pyramidal tree, 30 to 40 feet tall, successful from British Columbia to California. 'Blue Heaven' and 'Gray Gleam' are small trees known for their color. 'Skyrocket' is a very narrow form, 8 to 12 inches wide, and between 20 and 35 feet tall, with silvery blue foliage and dense branches; it was formerly listed as *J. virginiana.*

J. virginiana Red Cedar Zones 2–9.
Scalelike leaves and a form often columnar. It is a good specimen tree and is massed for windbreaks and screens, and used for hedges, specimen plantings, and topiary. The fragrant red wood is used for chests and cabinets. 'Glauca' is columnar, to 25 feet tall, with silver-blue foliage in spring. 'Hillii', slow-growing and columnar, to 16 feet tall, turns purple in winter.

PINUS *pye-nus* Pine

Big, important group of conifers known for long, pointed, but usually rather soft needles sheathed in bundles and lasting 2 or more years. Pyramidal in youth, but most eventually are flat-topped. The cones are large. Pines succeed in dry, sandy soils where little else grows, but they are sensitive to air pollution. Most require well-drained, somewhat acid soil, pH 5.0 to 6.0. Transplant with care in early spring. There are dwarf forms of many.

GROWTH RATE: medium/slow
LIGHT: full sun
MOISTURE: roots moist, versatile

P. cembra 'Columnaris'
Columnar Swiss Stone Pine,
Columnar Russian Cedar Zones 4–8.
The species is relatively narrow with blue-green needles, 35 to 40 feet tall, very handsome and slow-growing. The cultivar is narrower yet. One of the best.

P. strobus 'Fastigiata' Fastigiate White Pine
Zones 2–8.
Beautiful, rapid-grower, 50 to 80 feet tall, that is narrower than the species. The variety *glauca* has bluer needles. Excellent property divider, screen, specimen, and windbreak. One of the best for the East.

QUERCUS *kwurk-us*
robur 'Fastigiata' Fastigiate English Oak
Zones 4–8.

Lovely, tall, narrow oak with small, dark green leaves, densely branched. Superb windbreak, specimen, tall screen, or property divider. Prefers somewhat acid, well-drained sandy loam. See also Trees 13.

MATURE HEIGHT: 60'–70'
GROWTH RATE: medium
LIGHT: full sun
MOISTURE: roots moist

TAXUS *tax-us* Yew

Stately trees and vigorous shrubs with short, stiff, narrow, needlelike leaves, used since Roman times as lawn specimens, for hedges, and massing. May be sheared and pruned repeatedly to maintain size or to shape topiaries and espaliers. Prefer alkaline soil and are not good with azaleas and rhododendrons. Succeed in sun or shade, in moist soil with excellent drainage, but need protection from strong winds. The female forms bear seeds with a fleshy red aril. Usually dioecious.

GROWTH RATE: fast
LIGHT: full sun, versatile
MOISTURE: roots moist

T. baccata 'Fastigiata' English Yew
Zones 6–8.
Narrowly columnar with branches very erect and close together. Tall, to 60 or 75 feet, dramatic, with dark, lustrous needles. 'Fastigiata Aurea' has golden or gold-variegated needles. Beautiful only well within its hardiness range.

T. × *media* 'Hicksii' Hick Yew Zones 5–8.
'Hicksii' is naturally columnar with upright branches, growing slowly to 20 feet in 10 years. 'Hatfieldii' is similar, but more compact. 'Sentinalis' is a very narrow, slow-growing form. 'Stoveken' is a columnar male clone, to about 20 feet tall.

SEE ALSO:
Calocedrus decurrens, California Incense Cedar, Trees 4
Cedrus atlantica 'Fastigiata', Fastigiate Atlas Cedar, Trees 4
Chamaecyparis obtusa, Hinoki Cypress, Trees 4
Cupressus sempervirens, Italian Cypress, Trees 4
Laurus nobilis, Grecian Laurel, Sweet Bay, Herbs 1
Prunus sargentii 'Columnaris', Sargent Cherry, Trees 2

ALTERNATES:
Betula pendula 'Fastigiata', Fastigiate European Birch
Tilia americana var. *fastigiata*, Fastigiate American Linden

---

TREES 10
TREES WITH WEEPING FORM

Weeping trees are graceful, romantic, so popular that many species with pendulous features have been bred or grafted to the form. Some are grown as topiaries. We have weeping dogwoods, cherries, and evergreens, as well as the naturally weeping willows and birches. A healthy sweep of grass is perhaps the best way to set off a weeping tree. It needs little or nothing underneath. One weeping tree is all a small garden can handle visually. *Pendula* means hanging, pendant.

COMPANION PLANTINGS
Background: Columnar evergreens, see Trees 9.
Ground cover: Lawn.
Perennials: *Aurinia saxatilis* 'Compacta', Basket-of-gold, Goldentuft; *Dianthus caryophyllus*, Carnation, Clove Pink.

BETULA *bet-yew-la*
pendula 'Gracilis'
Cutleaf European White Birch Zones 2–6.

Small, slender tree valued for its graceful weeping habit and silky white bark striped dark gray or black. The deeply cut leaves turn yellow in autumn. Requires well-drained, moist, humusy soil in the somewhat acid range, but is rather tolerant. Birch borers are a real problem here and at present resistant cultivars are not established. The tree continues to be used because of its unique beauty, but the National Arboretum strongly recommends a regular spray program. 'Dalecarlica' is another elegant weeping cultivar. *B. p.* 'Fastigiata', Fastigiate European Birch, is a columnar form rather like a Lombardy Poplar.

GROWTH RATE: medium
LIGHT: tolerant
MOISTURE: versatile

CALLISTEMON *kal-liss-stee-mon*
viminalis 'Red Cascade'
Weeping Bottlebrush Zones 8–10.

Showy small tree from Australia, whose pendulous branches are covered in spring and fall with large rosy red flowers that look like reddish bottle brushes. There may be some summer bloom. This cultivar is an introduction of the Los Angeles State and County Arboretum. Tolerant of drought. Florida reports susceptibility to nematodes for the species.

MATURE HEIGHT: 10'–25'
GROWTH RATE: fast
LIGHT: full sun
MOISTURE: roots moist

CEDRUS *seed-rus* Cedar

Large, handsome conifers with small whorled, clustered needles, and large cones, graceful when young, impressive when mature, and demanding a large landscape. Long-lived and slow-growing. Prefer an open situation, but out of the wind, with well-drained and preferably somewhat acid soil.

GROWTH RATE: slow/medium
LIGHT: full sun, semi-sunny
MOISTURE: roots moist

C. atlantica 'Glauca Pendula'
Weeping Blue Atlas Cedar Zones 7–8.
Beautiful form with blue foliage and drooping branchlets, fast-growing when young. A leader must be staked to obtain a good weeping form. Height is 40 to 60 feet.

C. deodara 'Pendula'
Weeping Deodar Cedar Zones 7–8.
A beautiful weeping form of this most graceful of the cedars. The height is 40 to 70 feet in 30 or 40 years. Color is light green, grayish green, or silver. Can be damaged by severe winters at the northern edge of its range.

CHAMAECYPARIS *kam-ee-sip-ar-iss*
nootkatensis Nootka Cypress, Alaska Cedar
Zones 5–8.

Small to medium conifer with flat, scalelike, gray green foliage and spreading branches that droop,

Picea omorika 'Pendula', Weeping Serbian Spruce.

then sweep upward. The species is native to the Northwest coast, very cold-tolerant. Grows best where humidity is high, in well-drained, sandy soil. Adapts to pollution if other conditions are right.

MATURE HEIGHT: 30'–45'
GROWTH RATE: slow
LIGHT: full sun
MOISTURE: roots moist

GEIJERA *gay-gee-ruh*
parviflora Australian Willow   Zones 8–10.

Shapely, small evergreen tree whose main branches sweep up and smaller branches droop down, display-

Pinus strobus 'Pendula', Weeping White Pine.

ing willowlike green leaves. In spring and fall, there are sprays of insignificant white flowers. Requires well-drained soil.

MATURE HEIGHT: 20'–30'
GROWTH RATE: fast
LIGHT: full sun
MOISTURE: roots moist

SALIX *say-lix*

Delicate trees and shrubs with long narrow leaves; they are fast-growing and flourish by the water. *S. caprea* is the "pussy willow," but the males of some other species also display the velvety buds in early spring. The ornamentals are medium-size shrubs and trees usually naturalized by water. The two plants below are among the best of the weeping sorts, but far from the only ones. Ask local nurserymen for recommendations. Research by the National Ar-

Prunus subhirtella, 'Pendula', Higan Cherry. (Neumann)

boretum's Dr. Frank S. Santamour has shown that nematode damage is responsible for the inadequate root system that often causes willows to topple in storms. Look for long-lived introductions in coming years.

MATURE HEIGHT: 30'
GROWTH RATE: fast
LIGHT: full sun
MOISTURE: soil surface damp

S. alba 'Vitellina'   Golden Weeping Willow
Zones 2–8.
Delicate, graceful, fast-growing, weeping tree that is a golden haze in early spring. Like all the willows it thrives in wet places, but can succeed in drier soil. Not a good street tree as it litters through the season. Best naturalized, or by water's edge, and away from water pipes, which it invades. Dioecious. The males present catkins like those of the "pussy willow."

S. babylonica   Weeping Willow   Zones 6–8.
Where it is hardy, most beautiful of the weeping willows. Height is 30 to 40 feet.

SEE ALSO:
Cercidiphyllum japonicum 'Pendula', Weeping Katsura Tree, Trees 13
Cornus kousa var. *chinensis* 'Elizabeth Lustgarten', Weeping Chinese Dogwood, Trees 2
Fagus sylvatica 'Pendula', 'Purpurea Pendula', Weeping European Beech, Trees 5
Malus 'Candied Apple' Weeping, Weeping Candied Crab Apple, Trees 2
Malus 'Louisa', 'Red Jade', 'White Cascade', Crab Apple, Trees 2
Murraya paniculata, Orange Jasmine, Trees 11
Picea omorika 'Pendula', Weeping Serbian Spruce, Trees 4
Pinus strobus 'Pendula', Weeping White Pine, Trees 4
Podocarpus gracilior, Weeping Fern Pine, Shrubs 21
Prunus subhirtella 'Pendula Plena Rosea', Double Weeping Cherry (syn. 'Yae-Shidare-Higan'), Trees 2

Tsuga canadensis 'Pendula', Weeping Canada Hemlock.

Prunus yedoensis 'Ivensii', Yoshino Cherry, Trees 2
Prunus yedoensis 'Shidare', Weeping Yoshino Cherry, Trees 2
Styrax japonicus, Japanese Snowbell, Trees 3
Tsuga canadensis 'Pendula', Weeping Canada Hemlock, Trees 4

ALTERNATES:
Acacia subporosa 'Emerald Cascade', River Wattle
Cedrus libani 'Pendula', Weeping Cedar-of-Lebanon
Ulmus parvifolia 'Sempervirens', Chinese Evergreen Elm

TREES 11
TREES WITH FRAGRANT FLOWERS

There are only a few trees whose fragrance scents the air. They are treasured and planted near porches, patios, and entrances. Some conifers are aromatic—balsam fir, the cedars, and some of the pines have fragrant needles, wood, or gum (sap), but they don't really perfume a small garden. The flowering fruit trees have some scent, but only a few qualify as really fragrant.

COMPANION PLANTINGS (FRAGRANT)
Perennials: *Dianthus* × *allwoodii*, Allwood Pink; *Galium odoratum*, Woodruff, Sweet Woodruff; *Hosta plantaginea* 'Grandiflora', Fragrant Hosta; *Lobularia maritima*, Sweet Alyssum; *Valeriana officinalis*, Valerian, Garden Heliotrope.

CANANGA *kan-ang-guh*
odorata Ilang-ilang   Zone 10.

An open, evergreen tropical tree whose name means "flower of flowers." Also known as Ylang-ylang. Blooms are yellow, showy, appear year-round, and so fragrant they are used in the making of perfume. Planted in warm Florida parks and home gardens.

MATURE HEIGHT:	30'–40'
GROWTH RATE:	slow
LIGHT:	full sun
MOISTURE:	roots moist

CHIONANTHUS *kye-oh-nanth-us*

Small trees or large deciduous bushes that bear fragrant fringelike panicles of small white or greenish white flowers in late spring on the current year's growth. Males are more effective as the petals are larger, but they do not bear the bloomy purple fruit seen on the females in late summer, a nice contrast with the yellow fall foliage, and it attracts birds. Bark is a lovely gray. Good specimen plants, or in groups and near buildings. Tolerant of air pollution. Prefer well-drained, acid-range soil, pH 6.0 to 6.5. Dioecious or poly-dioecious, and may need companion to fruit well.

GROWTH RATE:	slow
LIGHT:	full sun, semi-sunny
MOISTURE:	soil surface damp

C. retusus Fringe Tree   Zones 5–9.
Rare and prized, with leaves and flowers smaller than the species below, very fine texture, and a profusion of white flower clusters. Height is 15 feet or more.

C. virginicus Old-man's-beard   Zones 5–9.
Also called American Fringe Tree. Fall color is often a good yellow. In the wild it is usually found near water. Mature height 12 to 20 feet.

CLADRASTIS *klad-rast-iss*
lutea American Yellowwood   Zones 4–9.

Slow-growing, medium-size tree with silver bark, and brilliant orange-yellow autumn foliage. In late spring or early summer it produces foot-long pendulous clusters of fragrant white flowers resembling wisteria. Attracts bees. Drought-resistant and trouble-free. Nice as a shade tree. The cultivar 'Rosea' has pink flowers.

MATURE HEIGHT:	30'–50'
GROWTH RATE:	slow
LIGHT:	full sun, semi-sunny
MOISTURE:	versatile

CLETHRA *kleth-ruh*
barbinervis Japanese Clethra   Zones 5–8.

Small, lovely tree that may be hard to find but is praised for beautiful bark and very large clusters of fragrant white flowers in midsummer. Grows in soils ranging from gravelly banks to wet spots, but does

Chionanthus retusus, Fringe Tree.

Cladrastis lutea, American Yellowwood. (Neumann)

best in moist, mildly acid soils with high organic matter content. Tolerates seashore conditions.

MATURE HEIGHT: 15'–25'
GROWTH RATE: medium/slow
LIGHT: versatile
MOISTURE: versatile

MAGNOLIA *mag-nohl-ee-uh*

The genus includes tall deciduous shrubs that bloom in early to mid-spring before the foliage appears, as well as majestic evergreen trees that bloom later. Those described here are truly fragrant. Provide well-drained, humusy, acid soil, pH 5.0 to 6.0, and an acid mulch 4 inches deep up to the trunk to maintain essential moisture. Well-drained soil is needed, especially in cooler regions. Transplant with care before new growth begins in early spring.

GROWTH RATE: medium/slow
LIGHT: full sun, semi-sunny
MOISTURE: roots moist

M. grandiflora Bull Bay, Southern Magnolia
Zones 7–9.

Broadleaved evergreen flowering tree 60 to 80 feet and more, with handsome, stiff, glossy leaves to 8 inches long. Huge, wonderfully fragrant, creamy, waxy flowers are borne in spring and summer. Fruit cones to 4 inches long open to expose red seeds. Good choice for landscaping large buildings and for espalier. Prefers cool and shade, loose soil that is deep and fertile. Requires protection north of Washington, D.C. See also Trees 3. 'Majestic Beauty' is a magnificent pyramidal tree with cup-shaped white flowers to 12 inches across in summer, and large lustrous green leaves.

M. virginiana Sweet Bay Zones 5–9.
Superb, graceful smallish tree for patio or garden, evergreen in warmer regions, deciduous farther north. Very fragrant, lemon-scented, creamy white rounded flowers appear with the leaves in late spring

Magnolia grandiflora, Bull Bay.

and early summer, and sporadically to early fall. The fruit is dark red, to 2 inches long, and the leaves silver-backed. Adjusts to considerable shade and to wet or swampy soils. Height can be 25 to 60 feet. Growth rate is medium to fast.

MURRAYA *mur-ay-uh*
paniculata Orange Jasmine Zones 9–10.

A tall evergreen shrub trained as a small tree, with graceful, pendulous branches and showy, fragrant white flowers that bloom spring, summer, and sometimes sporadically, followed by and often accompanying vivid red oval berries. Used in warm Florida and California for residences, hedges, medians, parks, and even topiary. Requires well-drained soil. Attracts bees.

MATURE HEIGHT: 10'–20'
GROWTH RATE: slow
LIGHT: full sun
MOISTURE: versatile

PITTOSPORUM *pit-os-por-um*
undulatum Victorian Box, Mock Orange
Zones 9–10.

Small broadleaved flowering evergreen with a lovely dome shape and wavy margined, rich green, pointed leaves. In mid- to late spring, bears very fragrant, creamy white flowers followed by orange berries (which can be messy). Another form is described in Shrubs 21.

MATURE HEIGHT: 15'–30'
GROWTH RATE: fast
LIGHT: full sun
MOISTURE: roots moist

SEE ALSO:
Citrus limon 'Improved Meyer', Lemon, Trees 16
Eucalyptus spp., Australian Gum, Ironbark, Trees 4
Fortunella margarita, Nagami Kumquat, Trees 16
Franklinia alatamaha, Franklin Tree, Trees 3
Ilex aquifolium 'Argenteo-marginata', White-edged English Holly, Trees 6
Malus, Apple, Trees 2
Malus 'Strawberry Parfait', Crab Apple, Trees 5
Oxydendrum arboreum, Sourwood, Sorrel Tree, Trees 7
Prunus × cistena, Purple-leaf Sand Cherry, Trees 5
Prunus serrulata 'Shirotae' (syn. 'Mount Fuji'), Japanese Flowering Cherry, Trees 2
Prunus yedoensis, Yoshino Cherry, Trees 2
Syringa vulgaris, Lilac, Shrubs 4

ALTERNATES:
Albizia julibrissin, Silk Tree, Mimosa
Hamamelis × intermedia 'Arnold Promise', Witch Hazel
Lindera benzoin, Spicebush
Robinia pseudoacacia, Black Locust

TREES 12
TREES ATTRACTIVE TO BIRDS

There's increasing interest in working with the lovely native plants described here because they're healthy and easy to care for. They are excellent choices for naturalizing. Any of the flowering fruit trees—crab apple, cherry—attract birds, especially cultivars with persistent fruit. Birds need trees for perching and nesting, and plants that supply nesting materials as well as food. Check the See also list below and Shrubs 16 for additional suggestions. The National Bird Garden at the U.S. National Arboretum has many ideas for the gardener interested in this subject.

COMPANION PLANTINGS
Background: *Carpinus betulus,* European Hornbeam.
Shrubs: *Ilex* 'Sparkleberry', Holly; *Pyracantha coccinea* 'Mohave', Fire Thorn.

Amelanchier laevis, Serviceberry. (Neumann)

Ground covers: *Asarum europaeum*, European Wild Ginger; *Athyrium goeringianum*, Japanese Painted Fern; *Thymus praecox* subsp. *arcticus*, Creeping Thyme.

AMELANCHIER *am-el-lank-ee-uhr*
Serviceberry

Airy little trees or shrubs of the open woodland that bear clusters of delicate white flowers in early spring. Fall color may be yellow to orange or dark red. Persistent berrylike fruits are usually black, edible, and rather sweet, which the birds love. Grow in almost any soil, but thrive in moist, well-drained acid soil at the edge of woodlands or by streams or ponds.

GROWTH RATE:	medium
LIGHT:	full sun, semi-sunny
MOISTURE:	roots moist

A. alnifolia Saskatoon Serviceberry
Zones 4–8.
Erect small tree or large shrub that covers itself with white flower clusters in spring. A good choice for the Northwest.

A. arborea Downy Serviceberry, Juneberry
Zones 4–9.
Lovely little upright tree that is one of the first to bloom in New England woods. Fall color is excellent. Attractive gray bark streaked with red. Height 15 to 25 feet.

A. canadensis Shadblow Zones 4–8.
Erect multi-stemmed little tree 20 to 30 feet tall, found in bogs and swamps along the East Coast to the Carolinas. The berries are red-purple, edible, loved by birds. 'Robin Hill Pink' is a colorful selection, but is most successful in the cooler reaches of its zones.

A. laevis Zones 4–8.
Taller tree whose new leaves are bronzy. 'Prince Charles' PP 6039 is 25 feet tall and has good orange to red fall color.

CELTIS *sell-tiss*

Medium-tall trees widely used in street plantings because of their tolerance of urban pollution and because the roots don't tear up the streets. The leaves are elmlike, and orange-red fruits attract birds.

GROWTH RATE:	fast/medium
LIGHT:	versatile
MOISTURE:	versatile

C. laevigata Sugarberry Zones 5–9.
A broadheaded tree, somewhat taller, with sweeter fruits than *C. occidentalis*. Good choice for the South. Resistant to witches'-broom disease in warm regions where this is a problem.

C. occidentalis Hackberry Zones 2–9.
Reaches 40 to 60 feet or more in cultivation, and has a rounded head and big leaves that turn yellow in fall. Interesting corky ridges on the bark. Prefers rich, moist soils, but adapts to almost anything. Susceptible in warm regions to witches'-broom.

CRATAEGUS *krat-teeg-us*
phaenopyrum Washington Thorn
Zones 3–9.

A beautiful little tree with glossy foliage and a pretty habit, white flowers in clusters in late spring, and persistent bright red fruits in early fall. A thorny tree tolerant of urban conditions but best in gardens, median dividers, or parks where birds can enjoy the fruits. The leaves turn scarlet to orange in autumn. There are many cultivars successful in colder regions. Prefers moist but well-drained soil.

MATURE HEIGHT:	25'–30'
GROWTH RATE:	medium/slow
LIGHT:	full sun
MOISTURE:	roots moist

MORUS *moh-rus*
rubra Red Mulberry Zones 4–8.

Rather tall, broadheaded tree cultivated for its red-purple, juicy edible fruits—if only one tree is to be planted for the birds, this probably is the one. Messy, best planted in a place reserved for birds. Withstands drought, salt, urban and seashore conditions.

MATURE HEIGHT:	40'–70'
GROWTH RATE:	fast
LIGHT:	full sun
MOISTURE:	roots moist, versatile

PRUNUS *proon-us*

Small—rarely over 40 feet—hardy, flowering trees that include the flowering fruit trees as well as the wildlings described below. The flowers and fruits of the wild species are smaller, but birds love the sour-sweet edible fruits. Leaves color nicely in fall. For naturalizing only. Thrive in well-drained, sandy loam.

GROWTH RATE:	fast
LIGHT:	full sun
MOISTURE:	roots moist

P. pensylvanica Wild Red Cherry, Pin Cherry
Zones 2–8.
A small tree, 30 to 40 feet, fast-growing and short-lived, good in woodlands and for its fruit crop which attracts birds. White flowers in clusters in spring. Leaves are bright yellow and red in fall. 'Stockton' is a double-flowered form.

P. serotina Black Cherry Zones 3–9.
Taller, to 50 or 60 feet, quickly spread by birds who love the red-to-black bittersweet fruits that ripen in late summer and early fall. White flowers in mid-spring.

Cornus mas, Cornelian Cherry. (Neumann)

Ilex 'Sparkleberry', superb companion plant for winter color.

P. virginiana Chokecherry   Zones 2–8.
A small shrubby tree, to 30 feet, that bears racemes of white flowers in mid-spring. Red, acid fruit that later turns purple appears in late summer and early fall. It is used to make wine and jelly. Birds love it.

SEE ALSO:
Cornus kousa var. *chinensis*, Chinese Dogwood, Trees 2
Cornus mas, Cornelian Cherry, Trees 2
Ilex opaca, American Holly, Trees 19
Juniperus virginiana, Red Cedar, Trees 4
Malus, Apple, Trees 2
Pinus strobus, White Pine, Trees 4
Prunus, Trees 2
Tsuga canadensis, Canada Hemlock, Trees 4

ALTERNATES:
Melia azedarach, Chinaberry
Pinus rigida, Pitch Pine

TREES 13
LARGE SHADE TREES

Majestic spreading trees for big landscapes, considerably larger in the wild than the heights averaged in cultivation. When height allows light to slant in under the crowns, understory trees and shrubs that prefer semi-sun thrive there. Some adapt to urban situations. Smaller shade trees—generally not over 35 feet in cultivation—are described in the next list.

COMPANION PLANTINGS
Understory trees: *Cercis canadensis*, Redbud, Eastern Redbud; *Cornus kousa* var. *chinensis* 'Snowboy', 'Summer Stars', 'Milky Way', Chinese Dogwood cvs.
Shrub: *Calycanthus floridus*, Carolina Allspice.
Ferns: *Adiantum pedatum*, Maidenhair Fern; *Athyrium goeringianum* 'Pictum', Japanese Silver Painted Fern; *Osmunda cinnamomea*, Cinnamon Fern.
Flowers: *Astilbe* × *arendsii* 'Fanal', Spiraea; *Epimedium grandiflorum*, Long-spur Epimedium.

ACER *ay-ser*   Maple

Long-lived, valuable shade trees; very little grows in their dense shadow. Bright spring flowers and glorious fall color are two important assets. The big maples are relatively slow-growing, adaptable, and flourish in well-drained, moist soil. In dry spells, water even mature maples biweekly. Prefer well-drained somewhat acid soil.

GROWTH RATE: slow/medium
LIGHT: full sun
MOISTURE: roots moist

A. macrophyllum   Oregon Maple,
Big-leaf Maple   Zones 6–9.
Native of the West Coast, 40 to 50 feet tall or more, with leaves 6 or 8 to 15 inches across. Dense shade tree for parks and streets. Spring flowers are yellow and fragrant; fall foliage is orange; pH adaptable.

A. platanoides 'Crimson King'   Norway Maple
Zones 4–7.
Rich crimson-purple leaves throughout summer and fall. A big, vigorous tree for streets and parks, 40 to 50 feet tall. 'Crimson Sentry' is a colorful, 25-foot, columnar form; foliage in fall is maroon-bronze. 'Summershade' is heat resistant, with leathery dark green foliage that tolerates city conditions. Best flowers of all the maples, and good yellow foliage in fall.

A. rubrum   Red Maple, Swamp Maple
Zones 3–10.
The most brilliant for fall color. Moderately fast-growing; 40 to 60 feet in cultivation, but well over 100 in the wild. Succeeds in wet places but will be smaller. Excellent street tree and good for shade as well. From Minnesota to the Florida Keys, local nursery varieties of the cultivars 'October Glory' and 'Red Sunset' are outstanding. In colder regions plant extra-hardy cultivars, such as 'Autumn Flame' and 'Northwood'.

A. saccharum   Sugar Maple, Rock Maple,
Hard Maple   Zones 3–8.
Big, magnificent shade tree for parks and big landscapes, with dazzling yellow-orange-red fall foliage. Reaches 60 to 75 feet in cultivation, over 100 feet in the wild. Cultivars such as 'Bonfire' may grow faster than the species and will have more reliable fall color. Don't confuse *A. saccharum* with the fast-growing but inferior *A. saccharinum*.

Acer rubrum, Red Maple, turns a magnificent red in fall. (Neumann)

Fraxinus excelsior 'Aurea', Golden European Ash.

CERCIDIPHYLLUM *ser-sid-if-fill-um japonicum* Katsura Tree — Zones 4–8.

Very beautiful, dainty, deciduous shade tree whose new leaves are a reddish purple, changing to blue-green in summer. In fall the foliage turns apricot-orange, more yellow in the Midwest, and has a faintly spicy scent. The bark is brown and shaggy. Choice for the medium-size landscape, useful for street planting, parks. Grows best in rich, well-drained, moist, somewhat acid soil though it is versatile as to pH. Transplant in early spring. 'Pendula', a lovely weeping form, reaches 15 to 25 feet in cultivation.

MATURE HEIGHT:	40'–60'
GROWTH RATE:	fast/medium
LIGHT:	full sun
MOISTURE:	roots moist

FAGUS *fay-gus* Beech

Magnificent, stately deciduous trees, 80 to 100 feet and more in the wild, with branches that sweep the ground. Demand staging with space all around; stunning alone on a grassy slope. The low, sweeping branches of mature specimens tent the ground, making a shady hiding place—and nothing grows under them. Leaves emerge late and turn russet and golden brown in fall. Must have well-drained, loose soil in the acid range.

GROWTH RATE:	medium/slow
LIGHT:	full sun
MOISTURE:	roots moist

F. grandifolia American Beech — Zones 3–9.
Strikingly beautiful specimen and shade tree for large spaces. Handsome light gray bark. Birds and squirrels relish the nuts. Height in cultivation is 50 to 70 feet. Not successful in urban situations; the heavy surface roots are hard to cover, pH 5.0 to 6.5. Transplant with care in early spring.

F. sylvatica European Beech — Zones 4–7.
Similar, big, very beautiful shade tree. The bark is a darker gray. There are many colorful cultivars, including fascinating weeping forms 'Pendula' and 'Purpurea Pendula'. 'Albo-variegata' has leaves variegated with white. 'Cuprea', Copper Beech, is paler than 'Atropunicea' (syn. 'Purpurea'), Purple Beech, whose spring foliage is a deep, rich red changing to copper-green and then to green. 'Riversii' is a deep purple cultivar that holds the color in summer—the new leaves are almost black. 'Dawyck Purple' is columnar. 'Roseo-marginata' (syn. 'Tricolor' 'Purpurea Tricolor') has purple leaves with rose and pink-white edges. 'Rohan Gold' has yellowish foliage.

Height in cultivation is 50 to 60 feet. Somewhat easier to transplant than the American Beech.

FRAXINUS *frax-in-us* Ash

Fast-growing handsome shade trees for large parks and landscapes. Withstand smoky, dusty, dry conditions. Leaves are good green and color well in fall—yellow, purple, and maroon. There are problems; choose cultivars advertised as seedless, disease-resistant, with colorful fall foliage. Provide deep, moist loamy soil. Adaptable to pH.

GROWTH RATE:	fast
LIGHT:	full sun
MOISTURE:	roots moist

F. americana White Ash — Zones 3–9.
Large, vigorous shade tree for parks, 50 to 80 feet tall. Conspicuous black buds in winter and bark of mature trees is interestingly patterned. 'Autumn Purple' is a pyramidal tree with glossy leaves that color deep purple-mahogany in fall. 'Rosehill' PP 2678, is a large, fast-growing pyramidal form with fiery bronze-red fall color.

F. excelsior European Ash — Zones 4–9.
Large, vigorous tree, 70 to 80 feet in cultivation, that thrives on limestone soil. Among many popular cultivars are 'Aurea', Golden European Ash, a slow-growing tree whose young shoots and bark turn yellow when older. Fall foliage is a brilliant yellow. Highly rated in Ohio shade tree evaluations is 'Hessei', which reaches to 60 feet, has a straight sturdy trunk, and less fall color but is very disease-resistant.

F. ornus Flowering Ash, Manna Ash — Zones 6–9.
Reaches 40 feet in cultivation and bears fragrant, showy white flowers in dense clusters as the leaves appear. Long cultivated in Europe, it is one of the ashes for the home garden. May be hard to find.

Gingko biloba, Maidenhair Tree. (Golden)

*F. pennsylvanica** Red Ash, Green Ash
Zones 3–9.
A little smaller than White Ash, 50 to 60 feet tall, and a good shade tree in the Plains States. Fall color can be spectacular but is inconsistent. Succeeds in wet soil; in the wild it grows along stream banks and in moist bottomlands.

F. udhei Shamel Ash, Evergreen Ash
Zones 9–10.
Semi- or evergreen, well under 50 feet in cultivation, popular in California as a shade and street tree. Fast-grower that needs pruning to retain its shape.

GINKGO *gink-*go
biloba Maidenhair Tree Zones 4–9.

Pretty city and street tree with characteristic fan-shaped leaves that turn a beautiful yellow in fall. Lower length of the trunk usually is bare. Prefers sandy, well-drained soil and has good salt tolerance. Avoid female trees; they produce malodorous, messy fruit. A long-lived tree, it is one of the oldest on the planet. 'Autumn Gold' is a broad-spreading male cultivar. 'Princeton Sentry' PP 2726, a grafted male, is uniquely columnar, beautiful in its fall foliage. 'Mayfield' is another narrow, columnar type.

MATURE HEIGHT: 30'
GROWTH RATE: medium/slow
LIGHT: full sun
MOISTURE: roots moist

LIRIODENDRON *lihr-ee-oh-***den***-dron*
tulipifera Tulip Tree Zones 4–9.

Potentially a very tall shade tree for larger landscapes, reaching to 150 feet in the wild. It bears tuliplike greenish yellow flowers high in its branches in late

*(Green Ash was formerly listed as *F. pennsylvanica* var. *lanceolata*, and Red Ash was *F. pennsylvanica*. Both are now listed as here.)

spring or early summer, best seen from above. Blue-green leaves turn yellow in fall. Prefers rich, deep, moist loam, slightly acid soil. Successful in urban situations, but needs generous space. Not suitable for most streets. There are variegated, fastigiate, and contorted forms.

MATURE HEIGHT: 70'–90'
GROWTH RATE: fast
LIGHT: full sun
MOISTURE: roots moist

PLATANUS *plat-an-us* Sycamore

Very tall, long-lived trees known for beautiful bark, which sheds in plates, creating a mottled effect. When growing in moist, rich soil with ample space they develop into massive specimens suitable for large parks.

GROWTH RATE: medium
LIGHT: full sun, semi-sun
MOISTURE: roots moist

P. × *acerifolia* London Plane Zones 5–8.
Big, long-lived, large-trunked, beautiful tree with characteristic sycamore bark. The species, an excellent street and park tree, is under attack by sycamore anthracnose. Look for Dr. Frank S. Santamour's two highly resistant hybrids 'Columbia' and 'Liberty': they are erect, single-trunked trees with bark that is gray orange when the trees are young, shedding to reveal yellow-green bark. Prefer rich, deep, moist soil, but are pH adaptable. May be heavily pruned in winter. Height, 70 to 100 feet.

P. occidentalis Eastern Sycamore,
American Plane Zones 4–9.
Tall tree with a massive trunk and wide-spreading branches. Especially impressive in winter, when older when the truly beautiful mottled white bark stands out. Too untidy for street use. It has many disease problems but is an outstanding native tree that should be preserved where it is found growing.

QUERCUS *kwurk-us* Oak

Big, spreading, deciduous or evergreen hardwood trees commercially important the world over and perhaps the most magnificent of all shade trees. South of the Mason-Dixon line native species tend to be evergreen. Fall foliage in the North can be quite brilliant, and the acorn is food for wildlife. Suitable for large parks and estates. Taprooted, so transplant young, and in early spring. Guide and prune young trees to develop a strong leader. Most species prefer somewhat acid, well-drained soil, but are versatile and there are exceptions.

GROWTH RATE: medium
LIGHT: full sun
MOISTURE: roots moist

Q. acutissima Sawtooth Oak Zones 6–9.
Height is 35 to 45 feet. Foliage opens a clear yellow in spring and colors yellow to golden brown in late fall. Good choice and fast-growing in its southern range, and a superior shade tree. U.S.D.A. introduction.

Q. alba White Oak Zones 5–9.
Majestic tree to 70 feet in cultivation, the finest native oak, and the state tree of Illinois. Foliage tends toward blue-green in summer, and in fall ranges from brown to wine-red and persists. Production difficulties and slow growth make it rare in commerce.

Q. bicolor Swamp White Oak Zones 3–8.
A tall timber tree that grows wild in swampy places and bottomlands. One of the best for naturalizing in wet areas. To 50 or 60 feet tall. Requires acid soil.

Q. macrocarpa Bur Oak, Mossycup Oak
Zones 2–8.
Big, impressive, inspiring tree, 70 to 80 feet tall. Corky branches give it a picturesque appearance. Difficult to transplant but is very adaptable—thriving in alkaline soil, dry or wet. Tolerates urban conditions better than most oaks and is used in parks and large landscapes.

Q. palustris Pin Oak Zones 4–8.
Most widely used native oak. A handsome tree that reaches 60 to 75 feet high and usually colors bronze-red in fall—the leaves are very persistent. Used in big parks, golf courses, commercial landscapes. Must have acid soil. The cultivars are more adaptable as to soil.

Q. phellos Willow Oak Zones 5–8.
Good shade tree and a fine oak for the South. Variable height, from 30 to 90 feet, fast-growing, and relatively easy to transplant. Good for parks, boulevards, large lawns, and can be pruned for tall hedges. Leaves persist into winter. Prefers acid soil and full sun.

Q. robur English Oak Zones 4–8.
Lovely, usually tall tree, 40 to 60 feet or more in cultivation with small, dark green leaves, densely branched. Superb windbreak, tall screen, property divider, or specimen. Cultivars tend to have better foliage color. 'Fastigiata', Fastigiate English Oak, is a very narrow, columnar tree to 50 feet tall, one of the best columnar trees for appearance. 'Pendula' is handsome when trained—to 35 feet tall.

Q. rubra (syn. *borealis*) Red Oak
Zones 4–8.
Quick-growing, clean tree 60 to 95 feet tall. The new leaves are red in spring and turn russet to wine-red in fall. Withstands urban pollution and is a good tree for

Quercus alba, White Oak. (Golden)

lawns, parks, golf courses. Prefers moist, fertile soil. Needs somewhat acid, well-drained, sandy loam. 'Aurea' has bright yellow leaves in spring—to 30 feet tall.

Q. virginiana   Live Oak   Zones 7–10.
Massive, long-lived tree 50 to 80 feet high, used extensively in the South for street planting, parks, golf courses, campuses. A spreading evergreen, it is a superb shade tree. Old leaves tend to drop all together in spring. Wind-resistant.

SEE ALSO:
Ginkgo biloba, Maidenhair Tree, Trees 8
Ginkgo biloba, 'Princeton Sentry' PP 2726, Maidenhair Tree, Trees 9
Liquidambar styraciflua 'Aurea', Golden American Sweet Gum, Trees 7
Magnolia acuminata, Cucumber Tree, Trees 4
Magnolia grandiflora, Bull Bay, Southern Magnolia, Trees 3
Malus 'Dolgo', Crab Apple, Trees 2
Metasequoia glyptostroboides, Dawn Redwood, Trees 20
Picea, Spruce, Trees 4
Pinus strobus, White Pine, Trees 4
Sophora japonica 'Regent', Japanese Pagoda Tree, Trees 15
Tilia cordata 'Greenspire', Small-leaved European Linden, Trees 15
Tilia tomentosa, Silver Linden, Trees 6
Ulmus parvifolia 'Dynasty', Chinese Elm, Trees 15
Zelkova serrata 'Village Green', Japanese Zelkova, Trees 7

ALTERNATES:
Catalpa speciosa, Western Catawba
Celtis laevigata, Sugarberry
Celtis occidentalis, Hackberry
Cladrastis lutea, American Yellowwood
Eucommia ulmoides, Hardy Rubber Tree
Gleditsia triacanthos var. *inermis* 'Shademaster', 'Sunburst', Thornless Honey Locust
Nyssa sylvatica, Pepperidge, Sour Gum
Prunus sargentii, Sargent Cherry
Taxodium distichum, Bald Cypress

TREES 14
SMALL OR DWARF SHADE TREES

Smaller trees good for shade, from tiny dwarf flowering crab apples to larger foliage trees, usually under 35 to 40 feet tall in cultivation. Many of the weeping trees are small shade trees. See Trees 10. For large shade trees, see Trees 13.

COMPANION PLANTINGS
Shrubs: Azalea (*Rhododendron*) cvs.; *Hydrangea* cvs.; *Nandina domestica*, Heavenly Bamboo; *Rhododendron* cvs.
Perennials: Ferns (Ground Covers 4); *Heuchera sanguinea*, Coralbells; *Hosta undulata*, Wavy-leaved Hosta.
Ground covers: *Pachysandra procumbens*, Alleghany Pachysandra; *P. terminalis* 'Green Carpet', Japanese Pachysandra.

CARPINUS *kar-pye-nus*

Among the finest medium to small landscape trees for urban use in home gardens, malls, commercial developments, and streets. Interesting fruit. Fairly slow growers that give good shade when mature. Require well-drained soil. Difficult, so transplant when young, in early spring.

GROWTH RATE: medium/slow
LIGHT: full sun, semi-sunny
MOISTURE: roots moist

C. betulus   European Hornbeam
                               Zones 4–7.
Lovely dense, bushy tree with dark green foliage, 35 feet or taller in cultivation. Fall foliage is yellow-green, and there are decorative drooping fruit clusters summer and fall. Good hedge and screening plant, shearable. Withstands smoke, dust, and drought. 'Columnaris' and 'Fastigiata' are narrower forms. There are variegated and pendulous types.

C. caroliniana (syn. *americana*)
American Hornbeam   Zones 2–9.
Small, understory tree 20 to 30 feet tall in cultivation, with a rounded crown. Tolerates wet soil and shade, and usually has colorful fall foliage—yellow, orange, scarlet. Not easy to transplant, and requires moist, somewhat acid soil, but is a suitable street tree. 'Fastigiata' is pyramidal, to 35 feet tall, hardy to Zone 5, heat- and drought-resistant.

CORNUS *korn-us*
controversa   Giant Dogwood   Zones 5–7.

Lovely understory tree with layered branches covered in mid-spring with large star-shaped white flowers (pointed bracts). In late summer and early fall, red berries progress to purple and blue-black. Dogwoods require well-drained, humusy, somewhat acid soil.

MATURE HEIGHT: 30'–40'
GROWTH RATE: medium
LIGHT: full sun, versatile
MOISTURE: roots moist

MALUS *may-lus*   Apple

Flowering crab apples are small, with spreading branches covered in spring with masses of exquisite blossoms and in fall with small red fruits birds love. Though susceptible to serious problems, beauty has made them the most important small landscape trees through the northern U.S. and southern Canada. Of the 700 to 800 cultivars, many are susceptible to disease; buy from an established local nursery and insist on resistant cultivars. Plant in well-drained soil. Several are suitable as small shade trees in the home garden—see Trees 2. The two described here are particularly spreading—one tall, one dwarf.

GROWTH RATE: medium
LIGHT: full sun, semi-sunny
MOISTURE: roots moist

M. floribunda   Japanese Flowering
Crab Apple   Zones 4–7.
Height to 18 feet with a spread to 25 feet, and a fine winter silhouette of spreading branches. The flowers are particularly attractive, deep pink to red in bud,

pink fading to white as they open. Fruit is yellow-red, effective in early fall.

M. 'Parrsi'   Pink Princess™ Crab Apple
                               Zones 5–8.
Very low, 8 feet tall, spreading to 12 feet, crab with purple foliage turning bronze, rose pink flowers, and deep red fruit. This is a naturally dwarf tree with excellent resistance.

OXYDENDRUM *ox-ee-den-drum*
arboreum   Sourwood, Sorrel Tree
                               Zones 4–9.

Among the most beautiful flowering trees and one of the best for crimson fall color. Very showy drooping racemes of fragrant white flowers cover the tree in summer. Attractive seedpods persist, heightening the fall display of red and red-purple. Attracts bees and is a source of superb honey. Good on dry soils, but not in polluted areas. Deeply grooved, interesting bark. Can take shade but much better in full sun. Prefers well-drained, somewhat acid soil.

MATURE HEIGHT: 20'–25'
GROWTH RATE: medium/slow
LIGHT: full sun
MOISTURE: roots moist

PHELLODENDRON *fel-lo-den-dron*
amurense   Cork Tree   Zones 3–7.

Wide-spreading tree with glossy foliage that turns yellow or bronzy yellow in fall and persists briefly. Valued for bark that becomes very attractive with age. Good for city parks and large landscapes and very adaptable. Black fruits can be messy; choose a male tree.

MATURE HEIGHT: 25'–30'
GROWTH RATE: fast
LIGHT: full sun
MOISTURE: roots moist

TSUGA *tsoo-guh*   Hemlock

Graceful pyramidal evergreens with feathery drooping branches, short, long-lived aromatic needles with two white bands beneath. Pretty little cones are ½ to 1 inch long. Shearable, great hedge plants. A shallow root system makes transplanting easy at any age. Need plenty of moisture, prefer well-drained, somewhat acid soil, and are not tolerant of pollution.

GROWTH RATE: fast/medium
LIGHT: full sun, semi-sunny
MOISTURE: roots moist, versatile

T. canadensis   Canada Hemlock
                               Zones 3–7.
Much used in the Northeast as a property divider, specimen, for screening, and tall hedges. Birds like to nest in the branches. New growth is light yellow-green, changing to dark green. Holds its needles for several years, so it always seems dense. Height 40 to 70 feet. Succeeds on rocky bluffs. 'Kingsville' is a good choice for row plantings. There are excellent cultivars in various shapes. 'Pendula', Weeping Canadian Hemlock, is a weeping form 10 to 20 feet high.

T. caroliniana   Carolina Hemlock
                                        Zones 4–7.
For southern gardens. Needles are placed differently, the look is more feathery, and the cones slightly larger, but otherwise similar to the species above. Greater pollution tolerance.

SEE ALSO:

Acer buergeranum, Trident Maple, Trees 1
Acer palmatum cvs., Japanese Maple, Trees 5
Aesculus × *carnea*, Red Horse Chestnut, Trees 2
Cercidiphyllum japonicum 'Pendula', Weeping Katsura Tree, Trees 13
Cornus kousa var. *chinensis*, Chinese Dogwood, Trees 2
Ilex aquifolium, English Holly, Trees 6
Malus, spreading forms, Apple, Trees 2
Oxydendrum arboreum, Sourwood, Sorrel Tree, Trees 7
Pinus strobus, White Pine, Trees 4
Pistacia chinensis, Pistachio, Trees 7
Prunus 'Okame', Flowering Cherry, Trees 2
Prunus sargentii, Sargent Cherry, Trees 2
Prunus serrulata 'Kwanzan' (syn. 'Sekiyama'), Japanese Flowering Cherry, Trees 2
Prunus yedoensis 'Akebono', Yoshino Cherry, Trees 2
Styrax japonicus, Japanese Snowbell, Trees 3
Styrax obassia, Fragrant Snowbell, Trees 3

ALTERNATES:

Acer campestre, Hedge Maple
Acer davidii, David Maple
Acer ginnala 'Flame', Amur Maple
Albizia julibrissin, Silk Tree, Mimosa
Cercis canadensis, Redbud, Eastern Redbud
Cercis occidentalis, Western Redbud
Crataegus laevigata (syn. *oxyacantha*), English Hawthorn
Crataegus phaenopyrum, Washington Thorn
Halesia carolina, Wild Olive
Koelreuteria paniculata, Varnish Tree, Golden-rain Tree

Malus floribunda, Japanese Flowering Crab Apple
Prunus subhirtella 'Autumnalis Rosea', Autumn Flowering Cherry
Sophora japonica, Japanese Pagoda Tree
Syringa reticulata (syn. *amurensis* var. *japonica*), Japanese Tree Lilac
Viburnum prunifolium, Black Haw
Viburnum rufidulum, Southern Black Haw

TREES 15
TREES FOR CITY CONDITIONS AND DRY PLACES

These trees withstand urban pollution and neglect with varying but considerable success. Some are beautiful, well-loved trees. Two National Arboretum introductions of the London Plane Tree, *Platanus* × *acerifolia* (See also list below), are among the best. But some are recommended because they flourish despite grime, heat, drought, lack of space, soil compaction. In the worst environments, even the best trees live only an average of 10 years, according to Princeton Nurseries statistics.

COMPANION PLANTINGS

Low background: *Artemisia ludoviciana* var. *albula,* Silver-king Artemisia; *Ligustrum* × *vicaryi*, Vicary Golden Privet; *Pinus mugo* var. *mugo*, Mugho Pine; *Potentilla fruticosa*, Shrubby Cinquefoil. Many others. See Shrubs 20.

ACER *ay-ser*   Maple

Many maples withstand pollution but not prolonged drought. Most are better park than street trees unless watered in droughts. Maples are long-lived, valuable trees, ranging from small ornamentals to majestic shade trees, loved for spring and fall color. Most maple species are slow-growing, adaptable, and flourish in well-drained, somewhat acid, moist soil. In dry spells, water even mature maples deeply. Look for new highly resistant National Arboretum introductions by Dr. D. Townsend.

GROWTH RATE: slow/medium
LIGHT: full sun
MOISTURE: roots moist

A. buergeranum   Trident Maple
                                        Zones 4–8/9.
Small tree good for streets and small urban gardens, with lovely bark. Withstands smoky, dusty, dry conditions. Height, 25 to 35 feet in cultivation.

A. maximowiczianum (formerly *nikoense*)
Nikko Maple   Zones 4–8.
Excellent small tree for urban gardens with glorious red, yellow, purple foliage in fall. Slow-growing. Height: 25 to 35 feet.

A. platanoides   Norway Maple   Zones 3–7.
Among the most popular street trees. Tall, formal, heavy-shade tree with good yellow fall color. Among established cultivars are 'Columnare', to 60 feet; 'Emerald Queen', 25 to 30 feet, one of the best for urban plantings; 'Deborah', 'Crimson King', and 'Crimson Sentry' are other fine selections for city use.

A. rubrum   Red Maple, Swamp Maple
                                        Zones 3–10.
Tall, formal, heavy-shade tree with brilliant red fall color. Among the best-established cultivars for street planting are 'October Glory' and 'Red Sunset', 40 to 60 feet in cultivation. Narrower forms are *A. r.* var. *columnare* cultivars 'Armstrong', which is well adapted to narrow streets, and 'Scarlet Sentinel.'

A. saccharum   Sugar Maple, Rock Maple, Hard Maple   Zones 3–8.
Big, formal, heavy-shade tree with beautiful fall color, for large landscapes. Too big for most streets. Among suggested cultivars are 'Green Mountain' and 'Bonfire'. Height: 60 to 75 feet in cultivation.

Tsuga canadensis 'Aurea', Canada Hemlock.

Acer buergeranum, Trident Maple.

Quercus phellos, Willow Oak. (Neumann)

BROUSSONETIA *broo-soh-**nee**-she-uh*
papyrifera   Paper Mulberry   Zones 6–10.

Fast-growing, large-leaved tree with colorful catkins in late summer. Not a great tree, and it suckers readily, but it is one of the most widely planted in cities because it withstands dirt, heat, drought, alkaline soils, and full sun.

MATURE HEIGHT: 40′–50′
GROWTH RATE: fast
LIGHT: full sun
MOISTURE: versatile

CARPINUS *kar-**pye**-nus*

Among the finest medium to small landscape trees for urban use in home gardens, malls, commercial developments, and streets. Interesting fruit. Fairly slow growers that give good shade when mature. Require well-drained soil. Difficult, so transplant when young, in early spring.

GROWTH RATE: medium/slow
LIGHT: full sun, semi-sunny
MOISTURE: roots moist

C. betulus   European Hornbeam
                          Zones 4–7.
Lovely dense, bushy tree with dark green foliage, 35 feet or taller in cultivation. Fall foliage is yellow-green, and there are decorative drooping fruit clusters summer and fall. Good hedge and screening plant, shearable. Withstands smoke, dust, and

drought. 'Columnaris' and 'Fastigiata' are narrower forms. There are variegated and pendulous types.

C. caroliniana (syn. *americana*)
American Hornbeam   Zones 2–9.
Small, understory tree 20 to 30 feet tall in cultivation, with a rounded crown. Tolerates wet soil and shade, and usually has colorful fall foliage—yellow, orange, scarlet. Not easy to transplant, and requires moist, somewhat acid soil, but is a suitable street tree. 'Fastigiata' is pyramidal, to 35 feet tall, hardy to Zone 5, heat- and drought-resistant.

CHAMAECYPARIS *kam-ee-**sip**-ar-iss*
nootkatensis   Nootka Cypress, Alaska Cedar
                          Zones 5–8.

Small to medium conifer with flat scalelike gray green foliage and spreading branches that droop, then sweep upward. The species is native to the Northwest coast, very cold-tolerant. Grows best where humidity is high, in well-drained, sandy soil.

MATURE HEIGHT: 30′–45′
GROWTH RATE: slow
LIGHT: full sun
MOISTURE: roots moist

CORYLUS *kor-il-us*
colurna   Turkish Filbert   Zones 4–7.

Formal, pyramidal, almost columnar tree, with very dark green summer foliage and corky branches. Good for street planting, parks, large properties. Suc-

ceeds even in climates that swing between scorching hot, dry summers and cold winters. Suitable for urban and street planting. Transplant in early spring and maintain moisture until established.

MATURE HEIGHT: 40′–50′
GROWTH RATE: medium
LIGHT: full sun
MOISTURE: roots moist, versatile

CUPANIOPSIS *coo-pan-ee-**op**-siss*
anacardioides   Carrotwood Tree
                          Zones 9–10.

Fine evergreen tree with rounded form and beautiful, dark green, leathery leaflets. Good city and street tree for warm California and Florida. A canopy of spreading branches gives dense shade. Mature tree may produce yellow-orange fruit. It has high tolerance to heat, drought, high coastal winds. Prefers well-drained soil.

MATURE HEIGHT: 30′–40′
GROWTH RATE: slow
LIGHT: full sun
MOISTURE: versatile

EUCOMMIA *yew-**kom**-ee-uh*
ulmoides   Hardy Rubber Tree   Zones 4–7.

Good shade tree with very dark green glossy leaves 4 to 6 inches long, tolerant of drought and poor soils. The outstanding summer foliage is free of problems. Though most often recommended for the Midwest,

It is now available from at least one major wholesaler in the East: Princeton Nurseries, Princeton, N.J. Not well known but worth looking for.

MATURE HEIGHT: 40'–60'
GROWTH RATE: medium
LIGHT: full sun
MOISTURE: versatile

GINKGO *gink-go*
biloba   Maidenhair Tree   Zones 4–9.

Outstanding city and street tree with characteristic fan-shaped leaves that turn a beautiful yellow in fall. Adapts to smoke, dust, drought. Lower length of the trunk usually is bare. Prefers sandy, well-drained soil and has good salt tolerance. Avoid female trees: they produce malodorous, messy fruit. A long-lived tree, it is one of the oldest on the planet. 'Autumn Gold' is a broad-spreading male cultivar. 'Princeton Sentry' PP 2726 is a tall grafted male, uniquely columnar, beautiful in its fall foliage. 'Mayfield' is another narrow, columnar type. 'Magyar', 50 to 60 feet tall, can withstand very severe urban conditions. There are many fine, colorful cultivars.

MATURE HEIGHT: 30'–40'
GROWTH RATE: medium/slow
LIGHT: full sun
MOISTURE: roots moist

GLEDITSIA *gled-dit-see-uh*
triacanthos var. *inermis* 'Shademaster'
Thornless Honey Locust   Zones 4–9.

Fast-growing, thornless, feathery tree with a short trunk, open crown, and delicate leaves that turn clear yellow to yellow-green in autumn. They fall fairly early. Good for dappled shade. Prefers a high pH, thrives on rich, moist soils, but is tolerant of drought and salinity—a consideration where roads are salted. The new leaves of 'Sunburst' are yellow, turning to bright green—this cultivar grows relatively slowly to 30 or 35 feet.

MATURE HEIGHT: 30'–60'
GROWTH RATE: fast
LIGHT: full sun
MOISTURE: roots moist

GYMNOCLADUS *jim-nok-lad-us*
dioicus   Kentucky Coffee Tree   Zones 4–8.

Tall, with bold, picturesque branching, handsome bark and light blue-green foliage. Specimen for larger parks and golf courses. Withstands limestone soils, drought, and city conditions. Prefers deep, rich, moist soil.

MATURE HEIGHT: 50'–60'
GROWTH RATE: medium/slow
LIGHT: full sun
MOISTURE: roots moist, versatile

QUERCUS *kwurk-us*   Oak

Big, spreading, deciduous or evergreen hardwood trees commercially important the world over and the most magnificent shade tree. South of the Mason-Dixon line native species tend to be evergreen. Fall foliage in the North can be quite brilliant. Acorns are food for wildlife. Suitable for large parks and estates.

Taprooted, so transplant young, and in early spring. Guide and prune young trees to develop a strong leader. Most species prefer somewhat acid, well-drained soil but are versatile, and there are exceptions.

GROWTH RATE: medium
LIGHT: full sun
MOISTURE: roots moist

Q. macrocarpa   Bur Oak, Mossycup Oak
                                     Zones 2–8.
Big, impressive, inspiring tree 70 to 80 feet tall. Corky branches are picturesque. Difficult to transplant but very adaptable—thriving in alkaline soil, dry or wet. Tolerates poor urban conditions better than most oaks and is used in parks and large landscapes.

Q. palustris   Pin Oak   Zones 4–8.
Handsome, widely used native oak, 60 to 75 feet high. Very persistent foliage usually colors bronze red in fall. Used in big parks, golf courses, commercial landscapes. Must have acid soil. The cultivars are more soil-adaptable.

Q. phellos   Willow Oak   Zones 5–8.
Good shade tree and a fine oak for the South. Variable height, from 30 to 90 feet, fast-growing and fairly easy to transplant. Good for parks, boulevards, large lawns, and accepts pruning for tall screening. Leaves persist into winter. Prefers acid soil and full sun.

Q. rubra (syn. *borealis*)   Red Oak
                                     Zones 4–8.
Quick-growing, clean tree 60 to 95 feet tall. New leaves are red and in fall turn russet to wine-red. Withstands pollution and is a good tree for lawns, parks, golf courses. Prefers moist, fertile soil somewhat acid and well drained. 'Aurea' has bright yellow leaves in spring—to 30 feet tall. Widely used for city planting.

ROBINIA *roh-bin-ee-uh*

Medium to small thorny trees with light, airy leaves and white, fragrant flowers borne in drooping clusters, followed by persistent pods. Attractive to bees. Rugged, surviving poor soils, salt, drought, and other difficult conditions—but not permanently wet soils. Most successful in rich, loamy soils that are alkaline.

GROWTH RATE: fast
LIGHT: versatile
MOISTURE: versatile

R. × ambigua 'Idahoensis'   Pink Idaho Locust
                                     Zones 4–8.
Rugged, tolerates hot summers and icy winters. The form is upright, and the late spring flowers are rose-pink and fragrant. Fall foliage is yellow. Height 35 to 40 feet.

R. pseudoacacia   Black Locust   Zones 3–8.
Very fast-growing, 30 to 50 feet tall, with extremely fragrant flowers and a dense, compact, round habit, good for shade. Not a beauty, but a successful stabilizer of highway slopes, strip-mined areas, and very difficult conditions. 'Inermis' is thornless, about 20 feet high. 'Semperflorens' is a large tree that blooms in late spring and intermittently thereafter or again in early fall. 'Frisia' has leaves a more or less stable golden color. The new leaves of 'Aurea' are a beautiful yellow when young, but fade to green in some climates.

SOPHORA *sof-foh-ruh*
japonica   Japanese Pagoda Tree
                                     Zones 4–8.

Handsome tree and shrub with airy foliage, attractive bark; showy clusters of pealike flowers in summer are followed by winged pods. Thrives in heat, drought, and difficult city conditions. Prefers well-

Robinia pseudoacacia, Black Locust. (Neumann)

drained sandy loam and sun. 'Regent' PP 2338 has a large oval crown of glossy dark green leaves, and comes into bloom at an early age. 'Princeton Upright' is suitable for narrow streets and small parks. There are weeping forms.

MATURE HEIGHT: 40'–50'
GROWTH RATE: fast
LIGHT: full sun
MOISTURE: versatile

TILIA *till-ee-uh* Linden

Excellent big shade and street trees that tolerate pollution. Smooth, light gray bark when young, small yellowish white flowers in drooping clusters. In some species the flowers are rather fragrant. Prefer rich, moist, well-drained soil.

GROWTH RATE: slow
LIGHT: full sun
MOISTURE: roots moist

T. americana var. *fastigiata*
Fastigiate American Linden   Zones 4–8.
Tightly pyramidal tree 65 to 75 feet tall, with large glossy leaves. Hardy and rugged.

T. cordata 'Greenspire' PP 2086
Small-leaved European Linden   Zones 3–8.
Rapid-growing, somewhat smaller tree, with a very straight trunk suited to planting along avenues. The flowers are fragrant. Height is 60 to 70 feet.

T. × euchlora Crimean Linden   Zones 4–8.
Somewhat smaller, beautiful linden with smooth glossy leaves, well suited to avenue planting. Height is 40 to 60 feet.

T. tomentosa Silver Linden   Zones 4–7.
Beautiful residential shade and street tree, pollution tolerant and withstands heat and drought. Grows medium fast, suitable as windbreak or screen. The leaves are dark green above and white and tomentose beneath. Mature height 40 to 60 feet.

ULMUS *ul-mus* Elm

Tall, stately shade trees for cool regions, widely used in streets, parks, and for landscaping large properties. The magnificent American elm, *U. americana*, that once shaded village squares in New England, is the victim of several problems and no longer is planted. The National Arboretum is one of many introducing superior, resistant cultivars. Prefer rich, moist soils.

GROWTH RATE: fast/medium
LIGHT: full sun, versatile
MOISTURE: roots moist

U. 'Sapporo Autumn Gold' Smooth-leaf Elm
Zones 4–8.
Medium-small tree, 40 to 50 feet in cultivation, released by the University of Wisconsin, resistant to the Dutch elm disease. Compact growth with small, very dense, dark foliage. Young foliage is a golden yellow in fall.

U. parvifolia 'Dynasty' Chinese Elm
Zones 5–8.
Released by Dr. Frank S. Santamour of the National Arboretum, this is a moderately fast-growing tree, with the spreading form of the American elm. Has

produced attractive red autumn leaves in D.C. and usually colors well in colder climates. It is highly resistant to elm problems. Tolerates stressful conditions and is a good small street and park tree.

SEE ALSO:
Acer pseudoplatanus, Sycamore Maple, Planetree Maple, Trees 5
Aesculus × carnea, Red Horse Chestnut, Trees 2
Albizia julibrissin, Silk Tree, Mimosa, Trees 17
Amelanchier, Serviceberry, Trees 12
Betula, Birch, Trees 1
Chionanthus virginicus, Old-man's-beard, Trees 11
Cornus kousa, 'Snowboy', Chinese Dogwood, Trees 6
Cornus kousa var. *chinensis* 'Milky Way', 'Summer Stars', Chinese Dogwood, Trees 2
Crataegus phaenopyrum, Washington Thorn, Trees 12
Ficus retusa var. *nitida*, Indian Laurel, Trees 4
Fraxinus americana, White Ash, Trees 13
Juniperus spp., Trees 4
Koelreuteria paniculata, Varnish Tree, Golden-rain Tree, Trees 3
Liriodendron tulipifera, Tulip Tree, Trees 13
Magnolia, most, Trees 2
Malus, resistant cultivars, Trees 2
Malus baccata, Siberian Crab Apple, Trees 2
Metasequoia glyptostroboides, Dawn Redwood, Trees 20
Platanus × acerifolia 'Columbia', 'Liberty', London Plane, Trees 13
Prunus, resistant cultivars, Trees 2
Pyrus calleryana, Bradford Pear, Callery Pear, Trees 2
Zelkova serrata 'Village Green', Japanese Zelkova, Trees 7

ALTERNATES:
Acer campestre, Hedge Maple
Acer ginnala, Amur Maple
Acer griseum, Paperbark Maple
Acer negundo, Box Elder
Acer negundo 'Aurea-variegatum', Golden Variegated Box Elder
Acer tataricum, Tatarian Maple
Callistemon viminalis 'Red Cascade', Weeping Bottlebrush
Catalpa speciosa, Western Catawba
Celtis laevigata, Sugarberry
Celtis occidentalis, Hackberry
Cladrastis lutea, American Yellowwood
Phellodendron amurense, Cork Tree
Pinus nigra, Austrian Pine, Austrian Black Pine
Pistacia chinensis, Pistachio
Platanus occidentalis, Eastern Sycamore, American Plane

TREES 16
TREES FOR CONTAINER PLANTING

Many trees thrive in containers. The best subjects are dwarf, semi-dwarf, small, columnar, weeping, and slow-growing forms. Plants with variegated leaves are lovely up close. Plants that are especially slow-growing are the best choices for bonsai, since

Arbutus unedo, Strawberry Tree. (Monrovia Nursery Co.)

root pruning and the limitations imposed by container size create the miniaturization.

Plant container-grown young trees in wooden tubs at least 16 inches square. Expect to water almost daily in windy, dry summer months. Choose trees well within your cold hardiness range; plants freeze much sooner in pots than in the ground. Be aware that containers on rooftops generally receive more bottom heat than those on wooden decks or cement patios. Use lightweight soil mixes to keep down the weight of pots that will require seasonal moving. Move containers before watering.

COMPANION PLANTINGS
Background: *Ampelopsis arborea*, Pepper Vine; *Pyracantha coccinea* 'Mohave', Fire Thorn.
Shrubs: Low-growing Azaleas (*Rhododendron*) spp. and cvs.; *Chamaecyparis obtusa* 'Nana Gracilis', Dwarf Hinoki Cypress.
Flowers: *Campanula poscharskyana*, Serbian Bellflower; *Lobelia erinus*, Edging Lobelia.

ACACIA *ak-kay-se-uh*

Fast-growing short-lived evergreen trees or shrubs with clusters or spikes of showy yellow flowers in spring. Often grown in containers in warm regions of California and Florida, where they are free-flowering and get quite large.

GROWTH RATE: fast
LIGHT: full sun
MOISTURE: roots moist

A. baileyana Cootamundra Wattle,
Golden Mimosa   Zones 9–10.
Small tree with feathery blue-green foliage and, in early spring, fragrant, bright yellow flower clusters. Sometimes used as a street tree in southern California.

A. subporosa 'Emerald Cascade'
River Wattle   Zone 10.
Graceful little tree with weeping branches covered with drooping, delicate, very narrow bright green leaves and tiny yellow flower puffs.

ACER *ay-ser*
palmatum Japanese Maple Zones 5/6–8.

Exquisite small tree treasured for foliage and form. The new leaves are usually red; some cultivars fade to green in the heat and regain their color in the fall. In warm regions, leaves may burn in full sun; afford some noon protection. 'Butterfly' (syn. 'Kocho nishiki') has leaves edged in pink in spring, turning yellow in fall. Height: to 15 feet. Good to Zone 4. There are many beautiful cultivars. 'Okushimo' is upright, about 6 feet tall, with foliage that turns bright yellow in fall. Needs sustained moisture and slightly acid soil. 'Dissectum', cutleaf Japanese maple, is especially elegant.

MATURE HEIGHT: 15'–25'
GROWTH RATE: medium/slow
LIGHT: full sun, semi-sunny
MOISTURE: roots moist

ARBUTUS *arb-yew-tus*
unedo Strawberry Tree Zones 8–10.

Lovely little evergreen for the warm West Coast. Foliage is tinted amber. Bears masses of white flowers in fall, followed by long-lasting fruits, orange red like strawberries. Requires acid soil and a dry climate to succeed. 'Compacta' is a 5-foot shrub grown in containers in cooler regions and moved to shelter during cold weather.

MATURE HEIGHT: 30'
GROWTH RATE: medium/slow
LIGHT: full sun, semi-sunny
MOISTURE: roots moist

CITRUS *sit-rus*

Lemons, grapefruits, and limes are garden-grown in the South—in cooler regions they make fruitful pot plants to summer outdoors in the sun, and winter indoors. Lovely, fragrant white flowers in spring. Prefer somewhat acid soil.

GROWTH RATE: slow
LIGHT: full sun
MOISTURE: roots moist

C. limon Lemon Zone 10.
In southern gardens lemon trees reach 20 feet. The tree is spiny, and has lemon-tasting winged leaves. 'Improved Meyer' reaches about 6 feet, has fragrant flowers, fruits all year in the right climate, and is a virus-free strain.

C. reticulata Mandarin Orange, Tangerine Zone 10.
Small spiny evergreen tree, erect branching, with small, fragrant white flowers followed by flavorful red-orange fruits that ripen in winter. Good espalier choice. 'Clementine', the Algerian Tangerine, is larger, hardier, and fruits only if there is another variety nearby.

C. sinensis Sweet Orange Zone 10.
To 40 feet in cultivation; container plants are half that size. Dwarfs are for pot culture. Extremely fragrant flowers in late fall, followed by sweet oranges. 'Valencia' is a dwarf that bears thin-skinned fruits in summer and is virus-free. There are many cultivars.

CLETHRA *kleth-ruh*
barbinervis Japanese Clethra Zones 5–8.

Small, lovely tree, hard to find but praised for its beautiful bark and very large clusters of fragrant white flowers in midsummer. Grows in soils ranging from gravelly banks to wet spots, but does best in moist, mildly acid soils with much organic content. Tolerates seashore conditions. Suitable for pot culture.

MATURE HEIGHT: 15'–25'
GROWTH RATE: medium/slow
LIGHT: versatile
MOISTURE: versatile

DELONIX *del-lon-ix*
regia Royal Poinciana, Flame Tree Zone 10.

Deciduous summer-flowering tree that makes a fantastic show; the growing range is limited to southern Florida, California, and Hawaii. Fernlike foliage, and clusters of bright scarlet and yellow flowers to 4 inches wide that are followed by flat pods to 2 feet long and 2 inches wide. Greenhouse or pot subject in cooler regions. Tolerates some salt and considerable drought.

MATURE HEIGHT: 25'–40'
GROWTH RATE: fast
LIGHT: full sun
MOISTURE: roots moist

FORTUNELLA *for-tew-nell-uh*
margarita Nagami Kumquat Zones 9–10.

Small, usually thornless evergreen tree or shrub related to citrus and grown in California and southern Florida, often as an espalier. It produces small, fragrant white flowers followed in October by aromatic, acid, little orangelike oval fruits used in Oriental

Fortunella margarita 'Variegata', Nagami Kumquat. (Monrovia Nursery Co.)

meals and marmalades. Very good pot plant, sometimes used in hedges.

MATURE HEIGHT: 10'–15'
GROWTH RATE: medium
LIGHT: full sun
MOISTURE: roots moist

LABURNUM *lab-burn-um*
× *watereri* 'Vossii' Golden-chain Tree Zones 5–7.

Airy, pretty, tall shrub or small tree with rich yellow, wisterialike flower panicles 18 to 24 inches long in late spring or early summer. Easily grown in a protected spot in well-drained soil with high organic content. May be rather short-lived.

MATURE HEIGHT: 15'–25'
GROWTH RATE: medium
LIGHT: full sun, semi-sunny
MOISTURE: roots moist

MALUS *may-lus* Apple

Apples and the beautiful crab apples and flowering crab apples belong to this genus. The flowering crab apples are small—8 to 30 feet tall—trees with spreading branches covered in spring with masses of exquisite apple blossoms and in fall with small red fruits birds love. Though susceptible to serious problems, beauty has made them the most important small landscape trees through the northern U.S. and southern Canada. Of the 700 to 800 cultivars, many are susceptible to disease; buy from an established local nursery and insist on resistant cultivars. Plant in well-drained soil. Those named here are highly resistant and typical of small cultivars suited to pot culture.

GROWTH RATE: medium
LIGHT: full sun, semi-sunny
MOISTURE: roots moist

'Coralburst', to 15 feet, coral pink buds, double rose flowers, bronze fruit ½ inch in diameter. Hardy to Zone 4.
'Doubloons', to 18 feet, spreading branches, double white flowers, persistent yellow fruits ⅜ inch in diameter. Hardy to −25° F.
'Jewelberry', to 8 feet, flowers are white, edged in pink, fruits bright red and ½ inch in diameter. Hardy to Zone 4.
'Louisa', to 15 feet, weeping form, flowers true pink, fruits ⅜ inch in diameter. Hardy to Zone 4.
'Mary Potter', to 10 feet, spreading branches, single, pink buds open white, fruits ⅜ inch in diameter, relished by birds, persistent. Hardy to Zone 4.
'Parrsi' Pink Princess™, to 8 feet, spreading branches, foliage purple becoming bronze-green, flowers rose-pink, red fruits ¼ inch in diameter. Hardy to Zone 5.
M. sargentii, 6 to 10 feet, usually twice as broad as it is high; profuse flowers are single, fragrant, usually white, fruits red, ¼ inch in diameter, and persistent. Hardy to Zone 5.

SEE ALSO:
Cercidiphyllum japonicum 'Pendula', Weeping Katsura Tree, Trees 13
Cercis canadensis 'Forest Pansy', Redbud, Eastern Redbud, Trees 2

Chamaecyparis nootkatensis, Nootka Cypress, Alaska Cedar, Trees 15

Lagerstroemia indica, Crape Myrtle, Trees 3

Laurus nobilis, Grecian Laurel, Sweet Bay, Herbs 1

Pinus thunbergiana, Japanese Black Pine, Trees 4

Prunus × *cistena* 'Big Cis'™, Purple-leaf Plum, Trees 5

Prunus sargentii 'Columnaris', Sargent Cherry, Trees 2

Prunus serrulata cvs., Japanese Flowering Cherry, Trees 2

Prunus subhirtella 'Pendula Plena Rosea', (syn. 'Yae-Shidare-Higan'), Double Weeping Cherry, Trees 2

Taxus, Yew, Trees 4

ALTERNATES:

Cedrus atlantica 'Glauca', 'Glauca Pendula', Blue Atlas Cedar

Cornus kousa var. *chinensis,* Chinese Dogwood

Crataegus phaenopyrum, Washington Thorn

Eucalyptus globulus 'Compacta', Compact Blue Gum

Stewartia koreana

TREES 17
TREES FOR SCREENING

Here are the trees most often used for screening and windbreaks. Rapid growers described on other lists are included in the See also list. Be aware that some of the fastest growers are less appealing. Interplant fast growers with slow ones and remove the fast when the slow specimens reach screening height. Many of the columnar plants in Trees 9 make good tall screens and windbreaks.

ACER *ay-ser* Maple

Long-lived, valuable trees ranging from small ornamentals to majestic shade trees, famous for spring and fall color. Most maple species are slow-growing, adaptable, and flourish in well-drained, somewhat acid, moist soil. In dry spells, water even mature maples deeply.

GROWTH RATE:	slow/medium
LIGHT:	full sun
MOISTURE:	roots moist

A. campestre Hedge Maple Zones 4–8.
Low maple with yellow fall color that adapts to dry, alkaline soils. Useful as an underwire street tree and for screening in hot, dry areas. Shearable for tall hedges. Slow grower to 25 or 35 feet.

A. ginnala Amur Maple Zones 2–8.
Yellowish white, fragrant flowers; cultivars like 'Flame' have good fall color. Reaches 8 to 10 feet at maturity. Used for grouping, massing, hedges, screening.

A. platanoides Norway Maple Zones 3–7.
Second most popular street tree, and superb for screening when mature. Tall, formal, heavy-shade tree, with good yellow fall color. Among established cultivars are 'Columnare', to 60 feet; and 'Emerald Queen', 25 to 30 feet, one of the best for urban plantings. 'Deborah', 'Crimson King', and 'Crimson Sentry' are other fine selections for city use.

ALBIZIA *al-bizz-ee-uh*
julibrissin Silk Tree, Mimosa Zones 7–9.

Lovely small, wide-spreading tree with fragrant, feathery, white to rosy pink flowers in spring to summer, followed by long, pendulous seedpods. Good naturalizer, since it self-sows abundantly (can be weedy), and withstands drought, salinity, high pH, and winds. Included here for use as a self-sowing, self-maintaining, naturalized barrier for wild lands. It is not recommended at this time as a landscaping specimen because it is susceptible to wilt and webworms. Resistant selections are not available at this writing, but are being developed; look for improved plants in the future.

MATURE HEIGHT:	20'–35'
GROWTH RATE:	medium
LIGHT:	full sun
MOISTURE:	roots moist, versatile

CARPINUS *kar-pye-nus*
betulus European Hornbeam Zones 4–7.

Among the finest medium to small trees. Dense, with dark green foliage that turns yellow-green in fall. Decorative drooping fruit clusters summer and fall. Good hedge and screening plant, shearable. Withstands smoke, dust, and drought. 'Columnaris' and 'Fastigiata' are narrower forms. There are variegated and pendulous types. Requires well-drained soil. Difficult, so transplant when young, in early spring.

MATURE HEIGHT:	35'–40'
GROWTH RATE:	medium/slow
LIGHT:	full sun, semi-sunny
MOISTURE:	roots moist

CRATAEGUS *krat-teeg-us*
phaenopyrum Washington Thorn
Zones 3–9.

Thorny little tree with glossy foliage, pretty form, white flowers in clusters in late spring, and persistent bright red fruits in early fall. Tolerant of urban conditions but best in gardens, as windbreaks and hedges, median dividers, or parks where birds can enjoy the fruits. Foliage scarlet to orange in autumn. There are many cultivars successful in colder regions. Prefers moist but well-drained soil.

MATURE HEIGHT:	25'–30'
GROWTH RATE:	medium/slow
LIGHT:	full sun
MOISTURE:	roots moist

FAGUS *fay-gus*
sylvatica European Beech Zones 4–7.

Magnificent, stately shade tree that screens with branches that sweep the ground. Elegant dark gray bark. Leaves emerge late and turn russet and golden brown in fall. Must have well-drained, loose soil in the acid range. There are many colorful cultivars, including weeping forms 'Pendula' and 'Purpurea Pendula'. Somewhat easier to transplant than the American Beech.

MATURE HEIGHT:	50'–60'
GROWTH RATE:	medium/slow
LIGHT:	full sun
MOISTURE:	roots moist

GLEDITSIA *gled-dit-see-uh*
triacanthos var. *inermis* 'Shademaster'
Thornless Honey Locust Zones 4–9.

Fast-growing, thornless, feathery tree with a short trunk, open crown, and delicate leaves that turn clear yellow to yellow-green in early autumn. Good for dappled shade. Prefers a high pH, thrives on rich, moist soils, but is tolerant of drought and very accepting of salt. The new leaves of 'Sunburst' are yellow, turning to bright green; grows relatively slowly to 30 or 35 feet.

MATURE HEIGHT:	30'–60'
GROWTH RATE:	fast
LIGHT:	full sun
MOISTURE:	surface soil dry, roots moist

Acer ginnala, Amur Maple. (Neumann)

Acer campestre, Hedge Maple.

JUNIPERUS *joo-nip-er-us*
virginiana Red Cedar Zones 2–9.

Small conifer with scalelike leaves and handsome red bark that shreds. Can be massed for windbreaks or naturalized, and is used in hedges and for topiary. The cultivar 'Burkii', about 30 feet tall, is a good blue that colors purple in winter. Some blight exists; choose blight-resistant cultivars recommended by local nurseries. Set out container plants in spring or fall.

MATURE HEIGHT: 40′–50′
GROWTH RATE: medium
LIGHT: full sun
MOISTURE: versatile

MALUS *may-lus*
baccata Siberian Crab Apple Zones 2–7.

One of the tallest and hardiest flowering crab apples, in mid-spring it produces fragrant white flowers, followed by long-lasting orange and yellow fruits. Good windbreak. The cultivar 'Jackii' is to 20 feet tall and as wide, with exceptionally bright red fruit and excellent disease resistance. One of the earliest.

MATURE HEIGHT: 20′–50′
GROWTH RATE: medium
LIGHT: full sun, semi-sunny
MOISTURE: roots moist

PICEA *pye-see-uh* Spruce

Big conifers with the rigid aromatic needles, large cones, and pyramidal form associated with Christmas trees. Spruces thrive in cool regions, open situations, and well-drained, humusy soil in the acid range, pH 5.0 to 6.0.

GROWTH RATE: medium/slow
LIGHT: full sun
MOISTURE: roots moist

P. abies Norway Spruce Zones 2–7.
Fast-growing, dense, 40 to 60 feet tall, useful as a windbreak or tall screen. Less attractive when older. There are beautiful cultivars with trailing branches.

P. pungens 'Glauca' Colorado Blue Spruce
Zones 3–8.
Stiff, formal pyramidal spruce with soft, silvery blue-gray foliage when young—later, silver-gray to blue-green. Height after 30 years is about 30 feet. 'Moerheimii' is very blue and the color is retained in winter. 'Hoopsii' is very silvery, one of the best cultivars for consistent color. More adaptable to urban situations than most other spruces.

PINUS *pye-nus*
strobus White Pine Zones 2–8.

Rapid grower for a pine, excellent property divider, screen, specimen, and windbreak. Recognized by its long, pointed but usually rather soft needles sheathed in bundles and lasting two or more years. Pyramidal in youth, but eventually flat-topped. The cones are large. Succeeds in dry, sandy soils where little else grows, but is sensitive to air pollution. Requires well-drained, somewhat acid soil, pH 5.0 to 6.0. Transplant with care in early spring.

Crataegus phaenopyrum, Washington Thorn.

MATURE HEIGHT: 50'–80'
GROWTH RATE: medium/slow
LIGHT: full sun
MOISTURE: roots moist, versatile

PLATANUS *plat-an-us*
× *acerifolia* London Plane   Zones 5–8.

Big, long-lived, large-trunked, beautiful tree with characteristic sycamore bark, to naturalize as an estate divider. The species is under attack by sycamore anthracnose. Look for Dr. Frank S. Santamour's two highly resistant hybrids 'Columbia' and 'Liberty'; they are erect, single-trunked trees with bark that is gray orange when the trees are young, shedding to reveal yellow-green bark. Prefers rich, deep, moist soil, but is versatile as to pH. May be heavily pruned in winter.

MATURE HEIGHT: 70'–100'
GROWTH RATE: medium
LIGHT: full sun, semi-sun
MOISTURE: roots moist

POPULUS *pop-yew-lus*
alba var. *nivea* White Poplar,
Silver-leaved Poplar   Zones 2–8.

Tall tree suitable for naturalizing in wild places. Leaves very white beneath. Easy to grow, and thrives in moist, deep loam. Tolerates pollution and salt spray. Poplars are fast-growing, weak-wooded, relatively short-lived trees not recommended for garden use. The tall, elegant Lombardy Poplars have too many problems to deal with. This variety is recommended for use only as a naturalized barrier.

MATURE HEIGHT: 40'–70'
GROWTH RATE: fast
LIGHT: versatile
MOISTURE: roots moist

SALIX *say-lix*
alba White Willow   Zones 2–8.

Fast-growing, easily rooted, upright, graceful tree of modest height, an airy barrier to naturalize, preferably over water. Plant where litter is not a problem. Succeeds in drier soil, but is best away from water pipes, which it invades. Dioecious. The males present the catkins whose buds are called "pussy willows." Foliage of the species *sericea* is silvery on the undersides. 'Vitellina', Golden Weeping Willow, is a beautiful weeping form.

MATURE HEIGHT: 30'
GROWTH RATE: fast
LIGHT: full sun
MOISTURE: soil surface damp

THUJA *thew-juh*
occidentalis 'Nigra' American Arborvitae
                                Zones 3–7.

Symmetrical, dark green, beautiful conifer with scalelike, lacy leaves in flat sprays. Sustains shearing and is used as a specimen, windbreak, tall hedge, or foundation planting. Formal, dense, and easy to grow. Fruits are small dried capsules. Needs lots of moisture and tolerates limestone soil as long as it is fertile and well-drained. Best in full sun, though it adapts to some shade. 'Emerald Green' holds its color in winter.

MATURE HEIGHT: 25'–40'
GROWTH RATE: medium/slow
LIGHT: full sun, semi-sunny
MOISTURE: roots moist

TILIA *till-ee-uh*
cordata 'Greenspire' PP 2086
Small-leaved European Linden   Zones 3–8.

More rapid-growing than the species, a shade and street tree that tolerates pollution, has a very straight trunk suited to planting along avenues, allees, and as a big windbreak. The flowers are fragrant and the bark of the young tree is smooth and light gray. Prefers rich, moist, well-drained soil.

MATURE HEIGHT: 60'–70'
GROWTH RATE: medium
LIGHT: full sun
MOISTURE: roots moist

SEE ALSO THESE FAST-GROWING TREES:
Acacia baileyana, Cootamundra Wattle, Golden Mimosa, Trees 16
Acacia subporosa 'Emerald Cascade', River Wattle, Trees 16

× *Cupressocyparis leilandii*, Leyland Cypress.

Acer saccharinum, Silver Maple, River Maple, Trees 5

Broussonetia papyrifera, Paper Mulberry, Trees 15

Callistemon viminalis 'Red Cascade', Weeping Bottlebrush, Trees 10

Cedrus atlantica 'Glauca', Blue Atlas Cedar, Trees 4

Celtis laevigata, Sugarberry, Trees 12

Celtis occidentalis, Hackberry, Trees 12

Cercidiphyllum japonicum, Katsura Tree, Trees 13

× *Cupressocyparis leylandii*, Leyland Cypress, Trees 18

Cupressus arizonica, Arizona Cypress, Trees 4

Delonix regia, Royal Poinciana, Flame Tree, Trees 3

Eucalyptus, Australian Gum, Ironbark, Trees 4

Fraxinus, Ash, Trees 13

Geijera parviflora, Australian Willow, Trees 10

Gleditsia triacanthos var. *inermis* 'Shademaster', Thornless Honey Locust, Trees 8

Lagerstroemia indica cvs., Crape Myrtle, Trees 3

Liquidambar styraciflua 'Moraine', American Sweet Gum, Trees 7

Liriodendron tulipifera, Tulip Tree, Trees 8

Metasequoia glyptostroboides, Dawn Redwood, Trees 20

Morus rubra, Red Mulberry, Trees 12

Phellodendron amurense, Cork Tree, Trees 14

Picea abies, Norway Spruce, Trees 4

Pinus ponderosa, Ponderosa Pine, Trees 18

Pittosporum undulatum, Victorian Box, Mock Orange, Trees 11

Prunus pensylvanica, Wild Red Cherry, Pin Cherry, Trees 12

Prunus virginiana, Chokecherry, Trees 5

Quercus acutissima, Sawtooth Oak, Trees 13

Quercus phellos, Willow Oak, Trees 13

Robinia pseudoacacia 'Frisia', 'Inermis', 'Semperflorens', Black Locust, Trees 15

Salix cvs., Willow, Trees 10

Sophora japonica, Japanese Pagoda Tree, Trees 15

Liriodendron tulipifera, Tulip Tree.

Tabebuia impetiginosa, Pink Trumpet Tree, Trees 2

Taxus, Yew, Trees 4

Tsuga canadensis, Canada Hemlock, Trees 14

ALTERNATES:

Amelanchier canadensis, Shadblow, Serviceberry

Chamaecyparis pisifera, Sawara Cypress

Cornus mas, Cornelian Cherry

Pseudotsuga menziesii, Douglas Fir

Thuja plicata, Giant Arborvitae, Western Red Cedar

TREES 18
TREES FOR SEASHORE GARDENS

Here are trees that stand up to the saline air and strong winds of the seashore.

COMPANION PLANTINGS

Shrubs: *Hydrangea arborescens* 'Annabelle', Hills-of-snow; *Juniperus conferta*, Shore Juniper.

Ground covers: *Leiophyllum buxifolium*, Sand Myrtle; *Myoporum* × 'Pacifica'; *Rosa virginiana*, Virginia Rose.

Flowers: *Aurinia saxatilis*, Basket-of-gold, Goldentuft; *Pelargonium* × *hortorum*, House Geranium; *Rudbeckia fulgida* var. *sullivanti* 'Goldsturm', Coneflower.

ACER *ay-ser*
pseudoplatanus cvs.   Sycamore Maple, Planetree Maple   Zones 4–7.

Medium-tall tree that succeeds in saline environments and high winds other maples cannot accept. Choose cultivars for color, for instance 'Brillliantissimum', which unfolds shrimp pink and changes from yellow to green; requires shade from noon sun. 'Worleei' starts a soft yellow-green, turns yellow, then green with red petioles. Versatile in well-drained, moist soil. In dry spells, water even mature maples deeply.

MATURE HEIGHT:	40'–60'
GROWTH RATE:	medium
LIGHT:	full sun, semi-sunny
MOISTURE:	roots moist

AMELANCHIER *am-el-lank-ee-uhr*
canadensis   Shadblow, Serviceberry
Zones 4–8.

Erect, multi-stemmed little tree found in open woodlands and bogs and swamps along the East Coast to the Carolinas. Clusters of delicate white flowers in early spring. The berries are red-purple, edible, loved by birds. Fall color may be yellow to orange or dark red. Grows in almost any soil, but thrives in moist, well-drained, acid soil at the edge of woodlands or by streams or ponds. 'Robin Hill Pink' is a colorful selection, but is most successful in the cooler reaches of its zones.

MATURE HEIGHT:	20'–30'
GROWTH RATE:	medium
LIGHT:	full sun, semi-sunny
MOISTURE:	roots moist

Acer pseudoplatanus, Sycamore Maple.

CELTIS *sell-tiss*
occidentalis 'Magnifica'   Hackberry
Zones 2–9.

Medium-tall tree widely used in street plantings because of its tolerance of urban pollution and because the roots don't tear up the streets. The cultivar resists drought and salt, and the roots withstand compacted soil low in oxygen. The elmlike leaves turn yellow in fall and the orange-red fruits attract birds. Interesting corky ridges on the bark. Prefers rich, moist soils, but adapts to almost anything. Susceptible in warm regions to witches'-broom disease.

MATURE HEIGHT:	50'–60'
GROWTH RATE:	fast/medium
LIGHT:	versatile
MOISTURE:	versatile

CLETHRA *kleth-ruh*
barbinervis   Japanese Clethra   Zones 5–8.

Small, lovely tree that may be hard to find, but is praised for its beautiful bark and very large clusters of fragrant white flowers in midsummer. Grows in soils ranging from gravelly banks to wet spots, but does best in moist, mildly acid soil with high organic matter content. Tolerates seashore conditions.

MATURE HEIGHT:	15'–25'
GROWTH RATE:	medium/slow
LIGHT:	versatile
MOISTURE:	versatile

CRATAEGUS *krat-teeg-us*
× *lavallei*   Lavalle Hawthorn   Zones 4–8.

Vigorous, upright little tree, with glossy foliage that colors bronze or copper-red in fall. White flowers bloom in clusters in late spring, followed by persistent bright orange-red berries in early fall. Used extensively as a street tree for it is tolerant of urban conditions. Should be set where birds can enjoy the fruits. Prefers moist but well-drained soil. Succeeds at the seashore.

Nyssa sylvatica, Sour Gum.

MATURE HEIGHT: 25'–30'
GROWTH RATE: medium
LIGHT: full sun
MOISTURE: roots moist

× **CUPRESSOCYPARIS** *kew-press-oh-sip-ar-iss leylandii*
Leyland Cypress   Zones 6–10.

Magnificent needled evergreen with bluish green, graceful, feathery foliage and scaly reddish brown bark. Excellent seashore plant, for formal situations and screening. Withstands heavy pruning and makes a good hedge. Once established, can grow 3 feet a year to over 100 feet, though it generally is smaller in cultivation. Often used as quick screening while slower-growing, more desirable shrubs mature. Needs no trimming and is easy to maintain. After about 5 years it outgrows hedge status. 'Naylor's Blue' is hardy to Zone 5, and has soft grayish blue foliage accents. 'Castlewellan' is equally hardy; its new growth is yellow.

MATURE HEIGHT: 60'–70'
GROWTH RATE: fast
LIGHT: full sun, semi-sunny
MOISTURE: roots moist

ILEX *eye-lex*
opaca American Holly   Zones 5–8.

Beautiful, pyramidal, broadleaf evergreen with smooth, shiny, toothed, leathery dark green leaves and a heavy crop of bright red berries in fall and winter. Hollies are long-lived and dioecious; one male tree pollinates up to 10 female trees, depending on species. Needs well-drained soil, partially shaded

location, and moisture. Succeeds at the seashore. Needs somewhat acid soil. 'Stewart's Silver Crown' has leaves edged in cream. There are yellow-fruiting forms.

MATURE HEIGHT: 45'–50'
GROWTH RATE: medium
LIGHT: shade
MOISTURE: roots moist

MORUS *moh-rus*
rubra Red Mulberry   Zones 4–8.

Rather tall, broadheaded tree cultivated for its red-purple, juicy, edible fruits—if only one tree is to be planted for the birds, this probably is the one. Messy, best planted in a place reserved for birds. Withstands drought, salt, urban and seashore conditions.

MATURE HEIGHT: 40'–70'
GROWTH RATE: fast
LIGHT: full sun
MOISTURE: roots moist, versatile

NYSSA *niss-uh*
sylvatica Pepperidge, Sour Gum
                              Zones 4–9.

Attractive, deciduous, pyramidal tree with somewhat pendulous branches, usually found near water, and known for its fine scarlet foliage in fall. Blue fruits are somewhat hidden under the foliage. Nice tree to naturalize. Must have well-drained acid soil, pH 5.5

Ilex opaca, American Holly.

to 6.5. Transplant in early spring, and afford some protection from drying winds. An exceptional honey is made by bees grazing on other trees of this genus, whose common name is Tupelo.

MATURE HEIGHT: 30'–50'
GROWTH RATE: medium/slow
LIGHT: full sun, semi-sunny
MOISTURE: soil surface damp

PINUS *pye-nus* Pine

Big, important group of conifers known for long, pointed but usually rather soft needles sheathed in bundles and lasting 2 or more years. Pyramidal in youth, but most eventually are flat-topped. The cones are large. Pines succeed in dry, sandy soils where little else grows, but they are sensitive to air pollution. Most require well-drained, somewhat acid soil, pH 5.0 to 6.0. Transplant with care in early spring. There are dwarf forms of many.

GROWTH RATE: medium/slow
LIGHT: full sun
MOISTURE: roots moist, versatile

P. halepensis Aleppo Pine, Jerusalem Pine
Zones 8–9.
Rugged pine with irregular, upward-reaching branches at maturity, good at the seashore, and thrives in hot, dry, windy places. Somewhat smaller tree, under 50 feet.

P. nigra Austrian Pine, Austrian Black Pine
Zones 4–7.
Rich, dark green, vigorous, dense, with stiffer needles than the commonly grown white pine, more interesting structure with age. Can live in the city and at the seashore, and can stand wind and adverse conditions as long as the soil is well drained and moist. Resists heat and drought. Succeeds in containers. Height 60 to 70 feet. May become diseased in the Midwest.

Pinus thunbergiana, Japanese Black Pine.

Sophora japonica, Japanese Pagoda Tree.

P. ponderosa Ponderosa Pine Zones 5–9.
Fast-growing, enormous conifer—to 230 feet in the wild—with yellowish green needles and 6-inch cones. In cultivation it reaches 60 to 100 feet. Useful only in the Northwest for mass plantings and shelter belts. Resists drought and tolerates alkaline soils, but must have full sun and protection from late frosts.

P. thunbergiana Japanese Black Pine
Zones 4–8.
Picturesque, to 30 or more feet tall, choice for bonsai, container-growing, informal accents. Prunable and adapts to semi-sunny situations. Outstanding salt tolerance and a great seashore plant. Requires fertile soil and more moisture than most other pines. 'Majestic Beauty', PP 5078, is offered as resistant to smog damage.

PLATANUS *plat-an-us*
× acerifolia London Plane Zones 5–8.

Big, long-lived, large-trunked, beautiful tree with characteristic sycamore bark, to naturalize as estate divider. It is not resistant to soil salt. The species is under attack by sycamore anthracnose. Look for Dr. Frank S. Santamour's two highly resistant hybrids 'Columbia' and 'Liberty'; they are erect, single-trunked trees with bark that is gray orange when the trees are young, shedding to reveal yellow-green bark. Prefers rich, deep, moist soil, but is pH versatile. May be heavily pruned in winter.

MATURE HEIGHT: 70'–100'
GROWTH RATE: medium
LIGHT: full sun, semi-sun
MOISTURE: roots moist

SOPHORA *sof-foh-ruh*
japonica Japanese Pagoda Tree
Zones 4–8.

Handsome tree or shrub with airy foliage, attractive bark; showy clusters of pealike flowers in summer are followed by winged pods. Thrives in heat, drought, and difficult city conditions. Prefers well-drained, sandy loam, and sun. 'Regent' PP 2338 has

Pinus nigra, Austrian Black Pine.

a large oval crown of glossy dark green leaves, and comes into bloom at an early age. 'Princeton Upright'PP 5524, is suitable for narrow streets and small parks. There are weeping forms.

MATURE HEIGHT: 40'–50'
GROWTH RATE: fast
LIGHT: full sun
MOISTURE: versatile

SEE ALSO:
Eucalyptus, Australian Gum, Ironbark, Trees 4
Juniperus virginiana, Red Cedar, Trees 4
Sequoia sempervirens 'Santa Cruz', 'Soquel', Redwood, Trees 4
Terminalia catappa, Tropical Almond, Indian Almond, Trees 7

ALTERNATES:
Acer rubrum, Red Maple, Swamp Maple
Cupaniopsis anacardioides, Carrotwood Tree
Cupressus macrocarpa, Monterey Cypress
Metrosideros excelsus (syn. *tomentosus*), Christmas Tree
Quercus ilex, Holly Oak

TREES 19
SHADE-TOLERANT TREES

Partial shade, or semi-sun, is defined as 2 hours of full sun or all-day dappled sun. Many small flowering trees are "understory" trees that thrive in this subdued light under tall trees.

COMPANION PLANTINGS
Shrubs: *Clethra alnifolia*, Sweet Pepperbush; *Sarcococca hookeriana* var. *humilis*, Sweet Box.

Cornus kousa var. *chinensis*, Chinese Dogwood.

Perennials: *Helleborus orientalis*, Lenten Rose; *Hosta* spp. and cvs.; *Pulmonaria saccharata* 'Mrs. Moon', Bethlehem Sage.
Ferns: See Ground Covers 4.

AMELANCHIER *am-el-lank-ee-uhr*
canadensis Shadblow, Serviceberry
Zones 4–8.

Erect, multi-stemmed little tree of open woodlands, bogs, and swamps along the East Coast to the Carolinas. Clusters of delicate white flowers in early spring followed by red-purple, edible berries that birds relish. Fall color may be yellow to orange or dark red. Grows in almost any soil, but thrives in moist, well-drained, acid soil at the edge of woodlands or by streams or ponds. 'Robin Hill Pink' is a colorful selection most successful in cooler regions.

MATURE HEIGHT: 20'–30'
GROWTH RATE: medium
LIGHT: full sun, semi-sunny
MOISTURE: roots moist

CHIONANTHUS *kye-oh-nanth-us*
virginicus Old-man's-beard   Zones 5–9.

Also called American Fringe Tree. Small, deciduous with panicles of greenish white, fragrant, fringelike flowers in mid-spring. Males are more effective as the petals are larger, but they do not bear the bloomy purple fruit of the females. Fall color is often a good yellow. Good specimen plant, or in groups and near buildings. Tolerant of air pollution. Prefers well-drained, acid-range soil, pH 6.0 to 6.5. In the wild it is usually found near water.

MATURE HEIGHT: 12'–20'
GROWTH RATE: slow
LIGHT: full sun, semi-sunny
MOISTURE: soil surface damp

CORNUS *korn-us*
kousa var. *chinensis*   Chinese Dogwood
Zones 5–8.

Beautiful understory flowering tree recommended by the U.S. National Arboretum as healthier than *C. florida*, Flowering Dogwood. The bracts are larger, come a few weeks later, and face up on branch tops—most beautiful viewed from above. Research seeking to produce the species with flowers more visible from the ground should net better cultivars in the next few years. Interesting mottled bark, reddish leaves, and persistent red fruits in autumn. Some drought resistance and prefers well-drained soil in the acid range. 'Milky Way' has large, pure white flowers, and raspberrylike fruits that attract birds. 'Summer Stars', an introduction by William Flemmer of Princeton Nurseries, blooms into August in the Washington, D.C., area and has very long-lasting flowers. *Kousa* is a good espalier plant.

MATURE HEIGHT: 25'
GROWTH RATE: medium
LIGHT: full sun, semi-sunny
MOISTURE: roots moist

FICUS *fye-kus*
retusa var. *nitida*   Indian Laurel   Zones 9–10.

Small, broad-headed evergreen with weeping branches when mature, used widely in southern and central California as a shade and street tree. The leaves are leathery and a good green. 'Green Gem'™ PP 5900 is resistant to ficus problems and a dense grower. Popular container plants in the North, summered outside and wintered indoors. Must be well drained.

MATURE HEIGHT: 25'–40'
GROWTH RATE: medium
LIGHT: full sun, semi-sunny
MOISTURE: roots moist

HALESIA *hay-lee-zee-uh*
carolina Wild Olive   Zones 4–8.

Lovely little deciduous understory tree known as Carolina Silverbell—for its early-spring clusters of bell-shaped white (or, rarely, pale rose) flowers that bloom on year-old wood. Thrives in rich, well-drained soil, along stream banks and hillsides in light shade. Excellent for naturalizing. Needs acid soil with a pH of 5.0 to 6.0.

MATURE HEIGHT: 30'–40'
GROWTH RATE: medium
LIGHT: full sun, semi-sunny
MOISTURE: soil surface damp

HAMAMELIS *ham-am-ee-liss*
Witch Hazel

Small deciduous trees or tall shrubs (witch hazel is also in the Shrubs section of this book) whose branches are covered with yellow, ribbonlike, often fragrant flowers in fall, late winter, or earliest spring. Usually the first trees to bloom. Grow well in light shade of deciduous woods. Good in the East and Midwest for screens, hedges, and excellent container plants. Brilliant fall color in leaves and bark. Provide soil in the acid range, well drained.

GROWTH RATE: medium/slow
LIGHT: semi-sunny
MOISTURE: roots moist

H. × intermedia   Zones 5–8.
'Arnold Promise' has large flowers, deep yellow and fragrant. Height to 20 feet. Autumn color of 'Diane' is exceptionally rich orange-red.

H. mollis   Chinese Witch Hazel
                                  Zones 5/6–8.
To 30 feet; it has the largest flowers and they are very fragrant. The fall color is orange-yellow.

ILEX *eye-lex*   Holly

Beautiful evergreen or deciduous shrubs and trees valued for brilliant fall and winter display of red fruit attractive to robins and other birds. Most are hardy only in Zones 4 to 7 and south. Leaf form varies from small, smooth, and shiny to large and very spiny—like the hollies that are a symbol of Christmas. Leaf color is green, except in some clones of English holly that have silver or yellow edges or are beautifully variegated ('Argenteo-marginata', 'Aureo-marginata'). Some have red berries, some have yellow or black. Hollies are long-lived and dioecious. Most require a pollinator: use one male tree for up to 10 female trees, depending on species. Need well-

Oxydendrum arboreum, Sourwood.

Styrax japonicus, Japanese Snowbell.

drained soil and are best in semi-sun. See also Shrubs 7.

GROWTH RATE: medium
LIGHT: full sun, semi-sunny
MOISTURE: roots moist

I. latifolia   Luster-leaf Holly   Zones 7–8.
Elegant pyramidal broadleaved evergreen tree to 50 feet tall in cultivation, with very large leaves, valued for brilliant fall and winter display of clusters of red fruit attractive to robins and other birds. Blends well with camellias and rhododendrons. 'Wirt L. Winn' is a much-praised cultivar.

I. opaca   American Holly   Zones 5–9.
Favorite in the East and South, a pyramidal tree reaching 40 to 50 feet, with single red berries that mature in October and persist through winter. Regional cultivars are best: ask local nurserymen for recommendations. Requires a pollinator, well-drained but moist, loose, acid soil, and protection from extreme drought and wind. Pollution tolerant.

MAGNOLIA *mag-nohl-ee-uh*
virginiana   Sweet Bay   Zones 5–9.

Graceful pyramidal flowering tree for patio or garden, evergreen in warmer regions, deciduous farther north. Very fragrant (lemon-scented), creamy white, rounded flowers appear with the leaves in late spring and early summer, then sporadically to early fall. The fruit is dark red, to 2 inches long, and the leaves are silver-backed. Adjusts to considerable shade and to wet or swampy soils. Provide humusy, acid soil, pH 5.0 to 6.0, and an acid mulch about 4 inches deep up to the trunk to maintain essential moisture. Well-drained soil is needed, especially in cooler regions. Transplant with care before new growth begins in early spring. It is also called Laurel, or Swamp Magnolia.

MATURE HEIGHT: 25'–60'
GROWTH RATE: fast/medium
LIGHT: full sun, semi-sunny
MOISTURE: roots moist

OXYDENDRUM *ox-ee-den-drum*
arboreum   Sourwood, Sorrel Tree
                                  Zones 4–9.

Among the most beautiful flowering trees and one of the best for crimson fall color. Very showy drooping racemes of fragrant white flowers cover the tree in summer. Attractive seedpods persist, heightening the fall display of red and red-purple. Attracts bees and is a source of superb honey. Good in dry soils, but not in polluted areas. Deeply grooved, interesting bark. Can take shade but does better in full sun. Prefers well-drained, somewhat acid soil.

MATURE HEIGHT: 20'–25'
GROWTH RATE: medium/slow
LIGHT: full sun, semi-sun
MOISTURE: roots moist

STYRAX *stye-rax*
japonicus   Japanese Snowbell   Zones 5–9.

Dainty little deciduous tree with a profusion of white, bell-shaped, pendant flowers in late spring and early summer, somewhat hidden by leaves. Most effective seen from below. Easiest to transplant when young. Prefers well drained, moist, somewhat acid soil rich in organic matter. Good companion to azaleas, kalmias, and rhododendrons. Notably trouble-free. Lovely in partial shade as a patio or shrub border specimen. Site for protection in cold climates.

MATURE HEIGHT: 15'–20'
GROWTH RATE: medium
LIGHT: full sun, semi-sunny
MOISTURE: roots moist

TSUGA *tsoo-guh*
canadensis   Canada Hemlock   Zones 3–7.

Graceful pyramidal evergreen with feathery drooping branches, short, long-lived aromatic needles with two white bands beneath. Pretty little cones are ½ to 1 inch long. Shearable, great hedge plant. A shallow root system makes transplanting easy at any age. Popular in the Northeast as a property divider, specimen, screen, or tall hedge. Birds like to nest in the branches. New growth is light yellow-green, changing to dark green. Holds its needles for several years, so it always seems dense. Needs plenty of moisture, prefers well drained, somewhat acid soil, and is not tolerant of pollution. 'Kingsville' is a good choice for row plantings. 'Pendula', Weeping Canadian Hemlock, is a weeping form 10 to 20 feet high.

MATURE HEIGHT: 40'–70'
GROWTH RATE: fast/medium
LIGHT: full sun, semi-sunny
MOISTURE: roots moist, versatile

SEE ALSO:
Acer palmatum, Japanese Maple, Trees 5
Cercis, Redbud, Trees 2
Lindera benzoin, Spicebush, Shrubs 25
Magnolia grandiflora, Bull Bay, Southern Magnolia, Trees 3
Taxus, Yew, Trees 4
Thuja, Arborvitae, Trees 4

ALTERNATES:
Acer circinatum, Vine Maple
Acer ginnala, Amur Maple
Acer pensylvanicum, Striped Maple, Moosewood
Acer pseudoplatanus cvs., Sycamore Maple, Planetree Maple
Carpinus carolinana (syn. *americana*), American Hornbeam

TREES 20
TREES FOR WET CONDITIONS

These trees are best able to stand wet soils and periodic flooding. Most of them are good ornamentals—a few are here simply because they thrive in wet places where more valuable trees do not. Development work is ongoing in the search for flowering trees that will flourish in wet soils.

COMPANION PLANTINGS
Shrubs: *Itea virginica*, Sweetspire; *Lindera benzoin*, Spicebush; *Myrica pensylvanica*, Bayberry; *Viburnum cassinoides*, Withe-rod, Appalachian Tea; *V. nudum*, Smooth Withe-rod, Swamp Haw.
Flowers: *Acorus calamus* 'Variegatus', Variegated Sweet Flag; *Lobelia cardinalis*, Cardinal Flower; *L. siphilitica*, Blue Cardinal Flower.

ALNUS *al-nus* Alder

Alders thrive in moist or wet soils where more beautiful trees do not. They are medium to tall, with coarse leaves, and flowers in the form of catkins in early spring before the leaves. Most alders fix nitrogen in the soil and are tolerant of almost every condition.

GROWTH RATE: fast/medium
LIGHT: full sun, semi-sunny
MOISTURE: soil surface damp, versatile

A. cordata Italian Alder   Zones 5–8.
Little known, but described as the best of the alders, a roundheaded tree 30 to 50 feet in cultivation, with handsome, glossy green, oval leaves. Succeeds in drier, high pH soils also. Grows fast in youth, slows later. Thrives in the Midwest.

A. glutinosa Black Alder   Zones 3–7.
Grows well in cool, wet places, even in water. Succeeds in drier land, but can spread widely in wet. Good for large parks, highway strips. 'Aurea' has golden yellow leaves early and is less vigorous than the species. 'Pyramidalis' is upright to 50 feet, a good form.

A. incana White Alder   Zones 2–7.
Reaches 40 to 60 feet, the choice for cold climates and wet land. 'Pendula' is considered a finer form.

AMELANCHIER *am-el-lank-ee-uhr*
Serviceberry

Airy little trees or shrubs of the open woodland that bear clusters of delicate white flowers in early spring. Fall color may be yellow to orange or dark red. Persistent berrylike fruits usually black, edible, and rather sweet, which the birds love. Grow in almost any soil, but thrive in moist, well-drained, acid soil at the edge of woodlands or by streams or ponds. Good for naturalizing.

GROWTH RATE: medium
LIGHT: full sun, semi-sunny
MOISTURE: roots moist

A. arborea Downy Serviceberry, Juneberry   Zones 4–9.
Lovely little upright tree that is one of the first to bloom in New England woods. Fall color is excellent. Attractive gray bark streaked with red. Height, 15 to 25 feet.

A. canadensis Shadblow, Serviceberry   Zones 4–8.
Erect, multi-stemmed shrub, 6 to 20 feet tall, found in bogs and swamps along the East Coast to the Carolinas. The berries are red-purple, edible, loved by birds. 'Robin Hill Pink' is a colorful selection, but is most successful in the cooler reaches of its zones.

A. laevis Serviceberry   Zones 4–8.
Taller tree whose new leaves are bronzy. 'Prince Charles' PP 6039 is 25 feet tall and has good orange to red fall color.

BETULA *bet-yew-la*
nigra 'Heritage'   River Birch   Zones 4–9.

Small tree whose handsome white outer bark exfoliates, exposing inner bark that may be salmon pink to grayish, cinnamon, or reddish brown. Grows medium fast, must have moist roots, and can stand periodic flooding. Nice in winter. Best in soil with a pH below 6.5. At the National Arboretum a good planting of this specimen separates the herb garden from the meadow. It is resistant to birch bark borer.

MATURE HEIGHT: 30'
GROWTH RATE: medium
LIGHT: versatile
MOISTURE: versatile

CARPINUS *kar-pye-nus*
caroliniana (syn. *americana*)
American Hornbeam   Zones 2–9.

Fine, small, understory tree with a rounded crown. Tolerates wet soil and shade, and usually has colorful fall foliage—yellow, orange, scarlet. Suitable for home gardens and commercial developments. Not easy to transplant and requires well-drained, moist, somewhat acid soil. 'Fastigiata' is pyramidal, to 35 feet tall, hardy to Zone 5, heat- and drought-resistant.

MATURE HEIGHT: 20'–30'
GROWTH RATE: medium/slow
LIGHT: full sun, semi-sunny
MOISTURE: roots moist

Halesia species, Wild Olive. (Neumann)

CHIONANTHUS *kye-oh-nanth-us*
virginicus Old-man's-beard Zones 5–9.

Also called American Fringe Tree. Small, deciduous, with panicles of greenish white, fragrant, fringelike flowers in mid-spring. Males are more effective, as the flower petals are larger, but they do not bear the bloomy purple fruit of the females. Fall color is often a good yellow. Fine as a specimen plant, or in groups and near buildings. Tolerant of air pollution. Prefers well-drained soil in the acid range, pH 6.0 to 6.5. In the wild it is usually found near water.

MATURE HEIGHT: 12'–20'
GROWTH RATE: slow
LIGHT: full sun, semi-sunny
MOISTURE: soil surface damp

CLETHRA *kleth-ruh*
barbinervis Japanese Clethra Zones 5–8.

A small, lovely tree that may be hard to find, but is praised for its beautiful bark and very large clusters of fragrant white flowers in midsummer. Grows in soils ranging from gravelly banks to wet spots, but does best in moist, mildly acid soils with much organic content. Tolerates seashore conditions.

MATURE HEIGHT: 15'–25'
GROWTH RATE: medium/slow
LIGHT: tolerant
MOISTURE: versatile

FRAXINUS *frax-in-us*
pennsylvanica* Red Ash, Green Ash Zones 3–9.

A little smaller than the better-known white ash, a good shade tree for large parks and landscapes in the Plains States. Fall color can be spectacular but is inconsistent. Succeeds in wet soil; in the wild, it grows along stream banks and in moist bottomlands. Withstands smoky, dusty, dry conditions. Leaves are

a good green and color well in fall—yellow, purple, and maroon. There are problems; choose cultivars advertised as seedless, disease-resistant, with colorful fall foliage. Provide deep, moist, loamy soil. Adaptable to pH.

MATURE HEIGHT: 50'–60'
GROWTH RATE: fast
LIGHT: full sun
MOISTURE: roots moist

HALESIA *hay-lee-zee-uh*
carolina Wild Olive Zones 4–8.

Lovely little deciduous understory tree known as Carolina Silverbell for the early-spring hanging clusters of bell-shaped white (or, rarely, pale rose) flowers that bloom on year-old wood. Thrives in rich, well-drained, moist, acid soil (pH 5.0 to 6.0), along stream banks and hillsides in light shade. Excellent for naturalizing. *H. monticola*, Silver-bell, a taller tree that succeeds at altitudes above 3,000 feet, is now grouped under *carolina*. Very disease-resistant. 'Rosea' is a beautiful pink form.

MATURE HEIGHT: 30'–40'
GROWTH RATE: medium
LIGHT: full sun, semi-sunny
MOISTURE: soil surface damp

LIQUIDAMBAR *lik-wid-am-ber*
styraciflua American Sweet Gum Zones 5–9.

A superb lawn, park, and street tree, the fall display is true red to dark crimson and yellow. Outstanding in southern California. In below-zero regions look for hardy cultivars like 'Moraine', which grows faster than the species and turns a rich red. A problem is the prickly fruit which must be removed from the lawn

*(Green Ash was formerly listed as *F. pennsylvanica* var. *lanceolata*, and Red Ash was *F. pennsylvanica*. Both are now listed as here.)

before mowing. Prefers rich, moist, acid-range soil. Several small, colorful cultivars are known, but none are easy to find in this country; 'Aurea' has gaudy yellow markings and 'Matthew's Gold' is gold. 'Variegata' leaves have creamy white margins that become rose-blush in late summer.

MATURE HEIGHT: 60'–75'
GROWTH RATE: fast/medium
LIGHT: full sun
MOISTURE: roots moist

MAGNOLIA *mag-nohl-ee-uh*
virginiana Sweet Bay Zones 5–9.

Graceful pyramidal flowering tree for patio or garden, evergreen in warmer regions, deciduous farther north. Very fragrant (lemon-scented), creamy white, rounded flowers appear with the leaves in late spring and early summer, and sporadically to early fall. The fruit is dark red, to 2 inches long, and the leaves silver-backed. Adjusts to considerable shade and wet or swampy soils. Provide well-drained, humusy, acid soil, pH 5.0 to 6.0, and an acid mulch about 4 inches deep up to the trunk to maintain essential moisture. Well-drained soil is needed, especially in cooler regions. Transplant with care before new growth begins in early spring. It is also called Laurel or Swamp Magnolia.

MATURE HEIGHT: 25'–60'
GROWTH RATE: fast/medium
LIGHT: full sun, semi-sunny
MOISTURE: roots moist

METASEQUOIA *met-uh-sek-woy-uh*
glyptostroboides Dawn Redwood Zones 6–8.

Big, stately, conical, deciduous conifer, which covered North America in prehistoric times and has been known until recently only as a fossil. Bright green, soft fernlike foliage, horizontal branches, and fall foliage that ranges from golden apricot to bronzy pink. It looks like an evergreen, but actually is deciduous. An interesting specimen for large parks and golf courses, and useful for fast screening. Does best in well-drained soil but succeeds in wet places and somewhat acid soil.

MATURE HEIGHT: 70'–100'
GROWTH RATE: fast
LIGHT: full sun
MOISTURE: versatile

PINUS *pye-nus*
nigra Austrian Pine, Austrian Black Pine Zones 4–7.

Rich, dark green, vigorous, dense, with stiffer needles than white pine, more interesting structure with age. Can live in the city and at the seashore, and withstands wind and adverse conditions as long as the soil is well drained and moist. Resists heat and drought. Succeeds in containers. May become diseased in the Midwest.

MATURE HEIGHT: 50'–60'
GROWTH RATE: medium/slow
LIGHT: full sun
MOISTURE: roots moist, versatile

Young planting of *Metasequoia glyptostroboides*, Dawn Redwood.

PLATANUS *plat-an-us* Sycamore

Very tall, long-lived trees known for beautiful bark, which sheds in plates, creating a beautiful mottled effect. When grown in moist, rich soil with ample space, they develop into massive specimens suitable for large parks.

GROWTH RATE: medium
LIGHT: full sun, semi-sunny
MOISTURE: roots moist

P. × acerifolia London Plane — Zones 5–8.
Big, large-trunked, beautiful trees with characteristic sycamore bark. The species, an excellent street and park tree, is under attack by sycamore anthracnose. Look for Frank S. Santamour's two highly resistant hybrids 'Columbia' and 'Liberty'; they are erect, single-trunked trees with bark that is gray orange when the trees are young, shedding to reveal yellow-green bark. Prefer rich, deep, moist soil, but are adaptable as to pH. May be heavily pruned in winter. Height, 70 to 100 feet.

P. occidentalis Eastern Sycamore, American Plane — Zones 4–9.
Tall tree with a massive trunk and wide-spreading branches. Impressive especially when older. In winter the beautiful mottled white bark stands out. Too untidy for street use. Many disease problems but is an outstanding native tree that should be preserved where it is found growing.

SALIX *say-lix* Willow

Fast-growing delicate trees and shrubs with long, narrow leaves; flourish by the water but can succeed in drier soil. Not good street trees as they litter through the season. Best kept away from water pipes, which they invade. Research by the National Arboretum's Dr. Frank S. Santamour has shown that nematode damage is responsible for the inadequate root system that often causes willows to topple in storms. Look for long-lived introductions in coming years. *S. caprea* is the "pussy willow," but the males of some other species also display the velvety, early-spring buds. The ornamentals are medium-size shrubs and trees usually used to naturalize by the water.

MATURE HEIGHT: 30'
GROWTH RATE: fast
LIGHT: full sun
MOISTURE: soil surface damp

S. alba White Willow — Zones 2–8.
Fast-growing, upright, and graceful tree of modest height, lovely when naturalized on the banks of a stream or pond. The leaves of the variety *sericea* are silvery on the undersides and very attractive. Dioecious. The males present catkins like those of "pussy willows." 'Vitellina', Golden Weeping Willow, is a beautiful weeping form.

S. babylonica Weeping Willow — Zones 6–8.
Most beautiful of the weeping willows where it is hardy. Height is 30 to 40 feet. May be hard to find.

TAXODIUM *tax-oh-dee-um*
distichum Bald Cypress — Zones 4–8.

Majestic deciduous conifer with beautiful, scaly bark and flat, needlelike, feathery foliage, yellow-green in

Taxodium distichum, Bald Cypress. (Neumann)

Quercus palustris, Pin Oak.

spring, sage-green in summer, russet in fall. Pyramidal to columnar, with a spreading head. Thrives in swamps, but is also successful as a specimen for large parks and estates (but it will be smaller). Needs fairly good drainage and acid soil; withstands very high winds even if it loses its head—therefore it is called "bald cypress." There are cultivars, including 'Pendens', a weeping form.

MATURE HEIGHT: 50′–70′
GROWTH RATE: medium
LIGHT: full sun
MOISTURE: soil surface damp

SEE ALSO:
Chamaecyparis obtusa, Hinoki Cypress, Trees 4
Eucalyptus globulus, Blue Gum, Trees 4
Eucalyptus leucoxylon, White Ironbark, Trees 4
Magnolia grandiflora, Bull Bay, Southern Magnolia, Trees 3

ALTERNATES:
Acer saccharinum, Silver Maple, River Maple
Nyssa sylvatica, Pepperidge, Sour Gum
Quercus bicolor, Swamp White Oak
Quercus palustris, Pin Oak

Salix species, Willow.

GARDENING VIEWS AT THE U.S. NATIONAL ARBORETUM

U.S. National Arboretum scientists conduct no specific research into cultural practices. However, they are in constant touch with scientists who do. And information flows in from their counterparts at the U.S.D.A. experimental stations and Extension Services at fifty-two state universities (see Appendix).

While there is no consensus on culture among these individuals and groups, here are some current research positions articulated by Dr. H. Marc Cathey, Director:

POLLUTION: Plants always have lived with the very real pollution of "natural" disasters, from the explosions of Krakatoa and Mount Etna to the more recent Mount St. Helens blow. Experiments on growing trees in "scrubbed air" produced highly variable results, from no measurable difference to strange shapes in the trees tested—this suggests that a certain amount of pollution is "natural" and even necessary. If we maintain the ambient levels we have, most familiar plants will continue to thrive.

GREENHOUSE EFFECT, ACID RAIN, OZONE LOSSES: It appears damage is being done. Much more research is needed before we will know how much damage and the long-term unchangeable impact. A recent failure of maples blamed on acid rain turned out to be the effect of drought. Damage in the Black Forest attributed to the interaction of acid rain and ozone loss apparently was enhanced by the European custom of scrubbing clean the forest floor, which destroys nature's cycle of renewal. The decomposition of fallen leaves and organic debris is an essential part of the ecosystem. A long-term study of decline in a stand of spruce at high altitudes concluded that acid rain was not the major factor: 90 percent of the difficulty was traced to an insect outbreak 10 years before. These questions have long been a concern of mankind and will continue to be so.

The understanding that we can damage our environment should make us protective of it. If poor management of a forest floor can accelerate acid-rain and lost-ozone damage, then good management can retard damage.

It is a fact that the deforestation of the tropics, specifically the rain forest in the Amazon basin—a major source of oxygen for the planet—is raising CO_2 levels, the "greenhouse effect." This problem must be addressed on a global level. The home gardener can give effective help: every single new tree or plant planted decreases the CO_2 content of the atmosphere and diminishes the greenhouse effect.

Gardeners also can help the environment by buying and planting only hardy, disease-free materials that can thrive in their gardens: this is the new gardening ethic that is the essential priority for all gardeners and environmental leaders.

STRENGTH FROM STRESS: The current research position is that trees and other woody plants take hold more successfully and grow stronger and more resistant if subject to natural stress. This is part of the reason the National Arboretum research staff is united behind the "new naturalism." Staking may not be helpful. At most, a tree may benefit from staking its first year after transplanting. A windbreak is better protection from weather than a stake.

Heavily amended soil is not now recommended for big plants. As noted elsewhere, adding masses of organic material to planting holes for large woody plants can have no lasting benefit. The sooner a plant begins to tie into the naturally occurring soil, the better.

Research suggests that annual fertilization and frequent watering of woody plants may stimulate rapid growth but result in weaker structures—more vulnerable to windstorms, frosts, droughts, extremes of temperature, pests, and diseases. Use fertilizers high in organic content; they are least likely to acidify the soil to killing intensities. Fertilize lightly: frequent light applications are likely to be more beneficial.

BUYING WOODY PLANTS: Scientists combine trees, shrubs, woody vines, and ground covers in one category—woody plants. For this book, the forestry definition of a tree is used: a plant having a single main trunk and reaching not less than 10 to 20 feet at maturity. Many genera include species that may be trees, shrubs, ground covers, or vines. Junipers, for instance, and roses come in almost every form: tree, shrub, vine, ground cover.

A woody plant is long-lived, costly to bring to market: to offset the loss of a big established plant is expensive and challenging. Insist on buying only top-quality, pest- and disease-resistant plants. Ask for resistant plants recommended here by their cultivar names, and include the American Association of Nurserymen Nursery Crops Code, which appears in the Index of this book. The code indicates the parentage of a plant and ensures the qualities needed for long-term success. A plant with a lovely new name may be a just-developed and untried introduction with no guarantee of good performance in the years to come. Even if your nursery is not yet using the AAN Nursery Crops Code, the fact that you identify a plant by its code name will hasten the establishment of performance standards in the industry and all over the world.

Monoculture may encourage problems. The most popular plants exhibit the most problems—beautiful flowering crab apples and cherries are examples. When buying plants flagged as having problems, accept only selections recommended as problem-free or resistant in your area by established and reliable local nurserymen and the local U.S.D.A. Cooperative State Extension Service.

Deliberately choose diversity in your garden and neighborhood. Avoid duplicating neighbors' plantings. Healthy new cultivars of wild species should be looked into. Choose only plants sure to thrive in your soil and climate. These best withstand insect attacks and diseases to which the species may be susceptible, and are better able to survive droughts.

When there is a choice, consider grafted or own-root trees and shrubs from cuttings: they are more consistent than plants grown from seed. Nursery specialists can graft a stem or bud from one superior species onto a root system from another, selected for strength and disease resistance, gaining more highly desirable characteristics where only one or two were present before. Grafted or own-root plants are surer to reproduce desired characteristics.

Select flowering plants, especially trees and big shrubs, well within their cold hardiness range: late frosts can devastate flower buds season after season even if the plant's foliage thrives. Smaller plants may succeed in the microclimate of a sheltered corner warmed by reflected light and protected from prevailing winds. Foliage plants will perform more reliably on the outer fringes of their hardiness zones than flowering plants.

The root system of a large plant, and especially a tree, eventually extends far beyond the improved soil of its planting hole. If it requires acid soil and the native soil is alkaline, it will have trouble. The roots of a small shrub are limited, and in many cases, native soil can be modified (see below) to suit the plant's requirements.

Choose plants according to mature height, especially trees and large shrubs. Authoritative gardening literature generally gives the height of very mature trees growing in the wild—and this may be 30 to 50 percent taller than trees growing in cultivation. In the warm South, plants generally grow taller and reach maturity sooner than those growing in the North's shorter season. The heights given here usually are the average seen in cultivation.

Set out young, rather than mature, trees and tall shrubs, and always choose young material of hard-to-transplant species. In most species, a young plant grows faster and adapts better to the new environment than an older one. In just two to three seasons, a transplanted young tree may reach and even surpass the height of a more mature tree transplanted at the same time. Or you can hire a landscape service which with mechanized equipment can move even 12-inch-caliper trees to your site safely any time of year the ground is workable.

Buy container-grown or balled-and-burlapped plants, rather than bare-root plants, when possible. They tie in to the new environment with less shock. Bare-root plants can be put into the garden successfully only in late winter/early spring. Container-grown plants can be planted any time the soil is not frozen.

The nearest responsible, established nursery is the best source of plants that will perform reliably in your garden. The National Arboretum can state that *Acer rubrum*, the Red or Swamp Maple, flourishes in Zone 3, but which varieties and cultivars will color best in your backyard, only experienced local plantsmen and gardeners know for sure. The maple species that has great color in northeast Vermont is not necessarily the one that colors best in southern Georgia, and toward the Rockies the soil/rainfall/day length changes. Plant performance depends on many, many variables. Investigate local plant societies: they are helpful, informed, and a place to meet folks who share your interests.

DIOECIOUS: When a fruiting plant is described as dioecious, be aware that a male plant may be needed within bee-flying/wind distance to ensure fruit production in a female. One male will cross-pollinate up to ten females, depending on species: check with your supplier on the pollinating needs of fruiting plants you plan to buy. *Malus* and *Prunus* and many other popular fruiting plants often are within range of a neighborhood pollinator. If a fruiting plants fails to produce, discuss with an informed gardener its sex and pollination needs. Some plants include both male and female flowers and do not require pollinators, just a little shaking by the wind.

In general, female plants produce the showiest fruit and litter most; males have the showiest flowers, but the show does not persist over the growing season.

LIGHT AND HEAT: When a flowering species fails to flower, check the hours of direct sun it receives: unless noted as flowering in shade, plants require 6 hours of direct sun to bloom well. In the hottest parts of the country, some noon shelter—a light trellis, for instance, or the dappled shade of tall trees—may be beneficial. Plants receiving full sunlight are often the most cold-hardy.

Plants can usually stand more drought and heat when growing in soil kept moist by a supply of humus and when the roots are kept cool by a mulch. (But don't over-mulch—see below.)

PLANTING TIME: The most vigorous growth occurs in spring. Late winter and early spring are the preferred planting times at the National Arboretum—particularly recommended for woody plants that transplant with difficulty.

Container-grown specimens for fall planting are offered in late summer and early autumn. Fall planting is usually successful if undertaken before Indian summer. The earth remains warm even after the air cools

and leaves fall, so roots continue to develop. That's why watering is recommended when it becomes dry in fall.

SOIL IMPROVEMENT: Fertility, structure, and pH are three separate qualities of soil. Fertility (see below) refers to the soil's content of the nutrients needed for sturdy plant growth. The pH reaction, a term that refers to relative acidity or alkalinity, determines whether or not those nutrients will be available to the plants. Structure or composition of soil governs its ability to admit and retain moisture, as well as the ease with which tender rootlets grow and seek out moisture and the nutrients dissolved in moisture.

The pH (potential of hydrogen) of soils determines whether they are acid, alkaline, or neutral. The neutral point is pH 7.0. Below pH 7.0 is classified as acid, and soil above that as alkaline. As a generalization, the elements required for growth are available in pH range 5.0 to 7.0, and most plants grow well toward the middle of this range. In the acid ranges, iron becomes more available. But as acidity increases many elements become less available, and some, such as aluminum, become available in quantities toxic to plant growth. Conifers and many evergreens do well in acid soils. Few woody plants succeed in soils near pH 8.0; lilacs are one exception and there are a few others. Flowers (herbaceous annuals and perennials) are generally versatile, but tend to prefer soils near neutral.

Home soil testing kits are sold by garden centers. Test your soil before amending it—do not guess what needs adding. If a soil test determines that the acidity in your soil needs to be increased to meet the needs of plants you have selected, you can add aluminum sulfate. Most soils in the Midwest tend to be alkaline and may need to be acidified. Better yet, have the soil tested by your Agricultural Extension Service. The fee is minimal. Do this some months ahead to have your recommendations in time for your gardening schedule.

To determine the structure or composition of the soil, use the snowball test. As a generalization, it can be said that good garden loam is composed of ⅓ each sand, clay, and humus. Pack a handful of moist — not wet and not dry—garden soil the way a snowball is packed. Soil with good structure will easily compact into a "snowball" and will also crumble under a little pressure. Soil that is too sandy or has too much humus (soil from the forest floor soil, for instance) won't pack; clay soil packs hard and won't easily crumble. To heavier clay soils add liberal quantities of "sharp," or builder's, coarse sand. Do not use sand from salt shores. Gypsum added at the rate of 50 pounds for every 1,000 square feet of soil improves the drainage and structure of clay soils in the East and the Far West. To improve lighter textured soils, add clay.

Humus, or organic matter, loosens soil and improves its water-holding capacities and drainage. It decomposes, releasing nitrogen and other elements to the soil, and the decomposition organisms release certain acids that made soil minerals available to the plants. However, the primary function of humus is not to improve soil fertility but rather structure, making it easier for tender rootlets to survive.

Soil literally shrinks as the humus dissipates. New supplies are required to keep the soil in good condition and plants growing strongly. Add only composted organic material to soil. When fresh humus, such as chopped weeds or leaves, is added to soil the decomposition organisms temporarily rob the soil of some nutrients, particularly the key element, nitrogen. If you do add fresh rather than composted humus, always also add a little fertilizer. Not a lot, because as the decay continues, the soil nutrients are released back into the soil.

FERTILIZING: The major elements generally added to soil to increase fertility are nitrogen (N), phosphates (P), and potash, (K). Nitrogen encourages rich green leaves. Phosphates help a good root system to develop and promote luxuriant flowering. Potash helps promote bloom, gives strength to stems, and is vital in plant resistance to diseases. All told, about 14 major and minor elements, in varying amounts, may be required for plant growth. Most fertilizers contain trace amounts of the desired elements.

All-purpose plant foods contain these elements in various ratios, expressed on the package as, for instance, 18(N)–6(P)–12(K). Ratios are according to the purpose of the plant food. To bring foliage plants and woody ornamentals to market, many nurserymen use a complete fertilizer with percentages like 18–6–12; 5–10–5 might be better for young plants whose goal must be root growth. A 7–6–19 composition would be meant for established plants, to encourage good health.

Acid fertilizer must be used for acid-loving plants, such as rhododendrons and gardenias, but with caution. Acid supplements can be overdone. Tests on failing rhododendrons showed that constant applications of acid fertilizers had pushed soil acidity beyond the effective range.

Newly planted materials generally cannot respond favorably to fertilizing the first season or two. They usually already have been heavily fertilized to encourage rapid growth for marketing.

When the decision is made that a large established woody plant or a tree needs fertilizing, spread the fertilizer on the soil surface. At least 90 percent of the feeder roots are located in the upper 8 to 18 inches of soil. Apply fertilizer from the tree drip line to the outer reaches of its root spread. If the tree is 80 feet tall, the roots will reach 80 to 120 feet out from the trunk. Deep root feeding close to the main stem pollutes the water table and often misses the feeder roots.

COMPOST: Compost is organic material that has decomposed into crumbly black soil-like particles. It is produced commercially from animal manures—rotted horse, cow, or sheep manure—often mixed with soil.

Composting of organic garden waste, such as leaves, weeds, or grass clippings, or kitchen refuse is made easier and tidier by the use of compost bins, barrels, or boxes offered at garden centers and in catalogs. You can also compost on the ground or in a shallow rectangle in the ground. Layer a pile of leaves 4 feet deep, preferably shredded (decomposition is faster), and other organic debris with soil, fertilizer, gypsum, and lime—make a depression in the center, moisten the pile, and turn it every six weeks until it has disintegrated. The pile should naturally heat and accelerate decomposition. Complex combinations of chemicals and fertilizers may be added—it's a whole study and there are books on the subject.

A simple way to get a continuing supply of humus to return to the soil is to use a shredder to break up fall leaves, together with green weeds if available, then mix with a compost starter and fertilizer. Lime may be added to sweeten compost meant for flower beds, herbs, and vegetables, which generally prefer a neutral or alkaline soil. Do not add lime to compost intended for acid-loving plants. Bag the fluffy mass and pour over it 2 gallons of hot water (per large garbage bag) to get decomposition started. Leave the top of the bag open so rain can keep it moist. Turn it upside down as often as you think of it. Depending on the warmth of the weather, it will all become crumbly black compost in four months to a year.

Use compost to enrich soil. It may be spread over the soil to a depth of 2 or 3 inches and dug or rototilled in, or it may be scratched into the soil around growing plants.

"SOIL" FOR CONTAINER PLANTS: The U.S. National Arboretum recommends commercially prepared soilless mixes for container plants.

Follow directions on the bag.

If you wish to prepare your own mix:

Soilless Mix:	Per bushel, add:
1 part coarse peat moss	1 cup 5–10–5
1 part horticultural perlite	1 cup limestone
	1 cup gypsum

Fertilize plants growing in this mix every few weeks: for slow-growing plants, water with ¼ teaspoon of 20–10–20 dissolved in 1 gallon of lukewarm water; for rapidly growing plants, water with 1 teaspoon of 20–10–20 per gallon of water.

PLANTING INSTRUCTIONS: Good drainage is needed by all but a few woody plants. To check drainage, dig a 24-inch-deep hole on the site selected and fill it with water: if the water has not drained away in 24 hours, correct the drainage. Dig the hole a foot deeper than the plant rootball and fill it with a drain of 8 to 10 inches of gravel to help move the water out of the area. Cover with 2 to 4 inches of soil, and plant the woody plant. To direct water flow out of a whole area, install a French drain, a trench filled with large stones wrapped in wire mesh.

Dig a wide, shallow planting hole twice or three times the width of the rootball. The primary roots grow in the top 8 to 18 inches of soil. Plant high. Newly planted trees lost in the first five years usually fail because they are planted too deep or sink after planting.

To improve the soil from the hole, work into it 25 to 50 percent of humus. Use peat moss for acid-loving plants; for others, use neutral leaf compost, well-rotted manure, or other organic soil amendment. Return a layer of improved soil to the bottom of the hole and tamp it down. In 6 weeks, the humus will be gone and the plant will begin to tie into the native soil.

Always lift a woody plant by the rootball, not by the stem. If the plant is wrapped in burlap (balled-and-burlapped), slit the ropes, then the burlap from top to bottom on either side. Peel away as much burlap as possible without endangering the rootball.

For balled-and-burlapped and container-grown plants, it is essential to get the roots developing out and tied into the soil. Cut away damaged roots. If roots are wound around the rootball, slash it from top to bottom on all four sides, making the gash about 1 inch deep. If this isn't done, over the years the roots likely will continue to grow around the rootball, and eventually will strangle the plant. Even if there are no roots winding around the rootball, score the rootball or rough it up. Then plant high, making sure the stem is straight. Expect the soil ball to settle in the first weeks.

Half fill the hole with water. When the water has drained, fill the hole with a layer of improved soil. Tamp it down firmly to eliminate air pockets. Water again. Slope the soil away from the plant. Mulch the entire area with 3 inches of an organic covering. In time, the plant will settle into the area. Water again deeply every two weeks of the first season, and less often the second, unless rainfall is regular.

MULCH: Research gathered by Dr. Francis R. Gouin, of the University of Maryland Horticulture Department, suggests that mulch is misunderstood and dangerously overdone. Mulch over 3 inches deep frequently results in root rot, stem rot, and suffocation, particularly in shallow-rooted plants such as azaleas.

Apply mulch after planting, but keep it under 3 inches. Apply more only as required to maintain that depth. The current research position recommends mulch as effective in only two areas: to keep the soil temperature even (avoiding heaving in winter and overheating in summer) and to add to the beauty of the garden. Shredded pine bark is considered the best mulch by Dr. Gouin. It is acid, the choice for acid-loving plants.

Mulch does not stop weeds from rooting, nor maintain soil moisture, and has been shown to act as a wick. To maintain soil moisture, black plastic and other forms of Pliofilm are recommended. The plastic must be perforated to allow rain to get through. It can be hidden under shredded pine bark or soil.

WATERING: Occasional watering of established woody plants in droughts is necessary: the watering must be deep to be beneficial. But constant watering in droughts is to be avoided. Plants have fail-safe systems that throw them into semi-dormancy in high heat and drought. Respecting a plant's inherent strengths and reinforcing its process allows it to develop into a vigorous, problem-resistant specimen.

PRUNING: Flowering plants that bloom on current year's growth, such as crape myrtle, are pruned in winter. Flowering plants that bloom in spring on 1-year-old wood, such as dogwoods and the flowering fruit trees, are pruned when the flowers fade.

Winter-prune deciduous plants during dormancy, just after the coldest part of the season. If a tree bleeds when sap start to flow, do not be concerned. It will cease when the tree leafs out.

Summer-prune when seasonal growth is complete if the intention is to slow or dwarf the development. Reducing the leaf surface reduces the "food" manufactured for the roots and limits next year's growth.

Avoid fall pruning: wounds heal more slowly.

It is not necessary to paint, tar, or otherwise cover a pruning cut or wound. Find the ring or collar from which each branch grows. Cut back just to it, but do not damage it. From that point the plant will develop an attractive, healthy covering for the wounded area.

Plants growing in hanging baskets should be pinched back regularly. This involves cutting the tip—1 to 3 inches— off each stem. Make the cut just above a node, the point where a leaf is attached to the stem. Regular pruning results in bushier specimens.

PESTS AND DISEASES: The National Arboretum scientists have found in sixty years of maintaining extensive gardens of every sort, from vegetable to herbs and roses, that plants stressed by their environment are stronger and more successful than coddled plants.

Their whole purpose is to select those plants that have innate resistance, and to breed for improved resistances the desirable ornamentals that have problems. They discourage the planting of disease-prone materials that survive only with constant interference from the gardener.

This book therefore deals only with plants the research staff believes will succeed without time-consuming, costly chemical and physical interventions.

AGRICULTURAL EXTENSION SERVICES

A gardener's best recourse can be the U.S.D.A. Agriculture Extension Service, located in the state university. The Service will test your soil in most states for a nominal charge and give sound advice on cultivars and species most likely to succeed in your area. The service is not, as sometimes supposed, interested in helping only the professional grower or farmer; it is also intended to serve you, the tax-paying home gardener. Look for the U.S.D.A. Extension Service at:

ALABAMA
Agricultural Experiment Station
Auburn University
Auburn, AL 36830

ALASKA
Institute of Agricultural Sciences
University of Alaska
Fairbanks, AK 99701

ARIZONA
Agricultural Experiment Station
University of Arizona,
Tucson, AZ 85721

ARKANSAS
Agricultural Experiment Station
University of Arkansas
Fayetteville, AR 72701

CALIFORNIA
Universitywide Admin.
Agricultural Experiment Station
University of California,
Berkeley, CA 94720

COLORADO
Agricultural Experiment Station
Colorado State University
Fort Collins, CO 80521

CONNECTICUT
Agricultural Experiment Station
P. O. Box 1106
New Haven, CT 06504

Agricultural Experiment Station
University of Connecticut
Storrs, CT 06268

DELAWARE
Agricultural Experiment Station
University of Delaware
Newark, DE 19711

FLORIDA
University of Florida
Institute of Food and Agricultural Sciences
Gainesville, FL 32601

GEORGIA
Agricultural Experiment Station
University of Georgia
Athens, GA 30602

HAWAII
Agricultural Experiment Station
University of Hawaii
Honolulu, HI 96822

IDAHO
Agricultural Experiment Station
University of Idaho
Moscow, ID 83843

ILLINOIS
Agricultural Experiment Station
109 Mumford Hall
College of Agriculture
University of Illinois,
Urbana, IL 61801

INDIANA
Agricultural Experiment Station
Purdue University
West Lafayette, IN 47907

IOWA
Agricultural & Home Economics
Experiment Station
Iowa State University
Ames, IO 50010

KANSAS
Agricultural Experiment Station
113 Waters Hall
Kansas State University
Manhattan, KS 66506

KENTUCKY
Agricultural Experiment Station
University of Kentucky
Lexington, KN 40506

LOUISIANA
Agricultural Experiment Station
Louisiana State University
and A&M College
Drawer E, University Station
Baton Route, LA 70803

MAINE
Agricultural Experiment Station
105 Winslow Hall
University of Maine
Orono, ME 04473

MARYLAND
Agricultural Experiment Station
University of Maryland
College Park, MD 20742

MASSACHUSETTS
Agricultural Experiment Station
University of Massachusetts
Amherst, MA 01002

MICHIGAN
Agricultural Experiment Station
Michigan State University
East Lansing, MI 48823

MINNESOTA
Agricultural Experiment Station
University of Minnesota
St. Paul Campus
St. Paul, MN 55101

MISSISSIPPI
Agricultural and Forestry Experiment Station
Mississippi State University
PO Drawer ES
Mississippi State, MS 39762

MISSOURI
Agricultural Experiment Station
University of Missouri
Columbia, MO 65201

MONTANA
Agricultural Experiment Station
Montana State University
Bozeman, MT 59615

NEBRASKA
Agricultural Experiment Station
University of Nebraska
Lincoln, NB 68503

NEVADA
Agricultural Experiment Station
University of Nevada
Reno, NV 89507

NEW HAMPSHIRE
Agricultural Experiment Station
University of New Hampshire
Durham, NH 03824

NEW JERSEY
Agricultural Experiment Station
Rutgers University
P. O. Box 231
New Brunswick, NJ 08903

NEW MEXICO
Agricultural Experiment Station
New Mexico State University
P. O. Box 3BF
Las Cruces, NM 88003

NEW YORK
Agricultural Experiment Station
Cornell University
Cornell Station, NY 14850

Agricultural Experiment Station
State Station
Geneva, NY 14456

NORTH CAROLINA
Agricultural Experiment Station
North Carolina State University
Box 5847
Raleigh, NC 27607

NORTH DAKOTA
Agricultural Experiment Station
North Dakota State University
State University Station
Fargo, ND 58102

OHIO
Ohio Agricultural Research
and Development Center
Ohio State University
Columbus, OH 43210

OKLAHOMA
Agricultural Experiment Station
Oklahoma State University
Stillwater, OK 74074

OREGON
Agricultural Experiment Station
Oregon State University
Corvallis, OR 97331

PENNSYLVANIA
Agricultural Experiment Station
229 Agricultural Admin. Bldg.
Pennsylvania State University
University Park, PA 16802

PUERTO RICO
Agricultural Experiment Station
University of Puerto Rico
P. O. Box 8
Rio Piedras, PR 00928

RHODE ISLAND
Agricultural Experiment Station
University of Rhode Island
Kingston, RI 02881

SOUTH CAROLINA
Agricultural Experiment Station
Clemson University
Clemson, SC 29631

SOUTH DAKOTA
Agricultural Experiment Station
South Dakota State University
Brookings, SD 57006

TENNESSEE
Agricultural Experiment Station
University of Tennessee
P. O. Box 1071
Knoxville, TN 37901

TEXAS
Agricultural Experiment Station
Texas A&M University
College Station, TX 77843

UTAH
Agricultural Experiment Station
Utah State University
Logan, UT 84322

VERMONT
Agricultural Experiment Station
University of Vermont
Burlington, VT 05401

VIRGIN ISLANDS
Agricultural Experiment Station
P. O. Box 166
College of the Virgin Islands
Kingshill, St. Croix, VI 00850

VIRGINIA
Agricultural Experiment Station
Virginia Polytechnic Institute
and State University
Blacksburg, VA 24061

WASHINGTON
Agricultural Experiment Station
Washington State University
Pullman, WA 99163

WEST VIRGINIA
Agricultural Experiment Station
West Virginia University
Morgantown, WV 26506

WISCONSIN
Agricultural Experiment Station
University of Wisconsin
Madison, WI 53706

WYOMING
Agricultural Experiment Station
University of Wyoming
University Station, Box 3354
Laramie, WY 82070

GUIDE

PLANT SMALL SEEDS by broadcasting over damp, prepared soil surface, then tamp firmly with hands.

PLANT LARGE SEEDS at three times the depth of the seed's largest measurement.

PLANT PERFORMANCE CODES are listed with botanical names in the Index. Include the code when identifying plants to nurserymen. Some will not yet be using the codes. The sooner we exact quality control, the sooner we'll have it.

TIME OF BLOOM for any given plant differs from region to region. It is expressed here as early spring, mid-spring, late spring, and so on. Plants whose performance spans seasonal boundaries may appear on several lists.

MATURE HEIGHT given for woody plants is usually that attained in cultivation, which is 30 to 50 percent less than the mature height of plants growing in the wild. Cultivated trees are long-lived, and our judgment of how they perform in North America is sometimes relatively new.

LIGHT:
full sun: means a minimum 6 hours full sun daily
semi-sunny: means 2 to 6 hours sun daily
shade: means 2 hours full sun, or dappled sun all day
versatile: means the plant tolerates a range of light.

MOISTURE:
surface moist: means a moist atmosphere is best
roots moist: means sustained moisture at root level, but the surface can be dry
versatile: adapts to drought and to some wetness

FERTILIZE new installations of woody plants only in the second or third season. They have just been through a period of heavy fertilization to maximize growth. Avoid fertilizing flowers in bloom: it stimulates growth at the expense of the flowers.

INDEX

This index includes the coding system developed by the American Association of Nurserymen. If readers use these codes when purchasing plants at suppliers using them, they can then be certain of getting the plant and the variety they want. Codes appear in capital letters between parentheses.

A

Aaron's Beard, 119
ABELIA X *grandiflora* 'Edward Goucher' (ABLGREG), 157–158, 182
ABIES (ABS), 212
ABIES concolor (ABSCN), 212
   'Conica' (ABSCNCC), 212
   'Violacea' (ABSCNVV), 212
ABIES firma (ABSFM), 212
Abyssinian, 8
ACACIA (ACC), 236
ACACIA baileyana (ACCBL), 236
ACACIA subporosa 'Emerald Cascade' (ACCSBEC), 236
ACER (ACR), 172, 189–190, 204, 217, 219, 220, 222, 223, 229, 233, 238
ACER buergeranum (ACRBG), 204, 233
ACER campestre (ACRCM), 238
ACER circinatum (ACRCR), 220
ACER davidii (ACRDV), 204
ACER ginnala (ACRGN), 220, 238
   'Flame' (ACRGNFL), 220, 238
ACER griseum (ACRGS), 204
ACER macrophyllum (ACRMC), 222, 229
ACER maximowiczianum (ACRMX), 233
ACER negundo (ACRNG), 217
   'Auratum' (ACRNGAT), 217
   'Aurea-variegatum' (ACRNGAR), 217
   'Variegatum' (ACRNGVR), 217
ACER palmatum (ACRPL), 167, 189, 217, 219, 222, 237
   'Atropurpureum' (ACRPLAT), 217
   'Bloodgood' (ACRPLBL), 217
   'Burgundy Lace' (ACRPLBA), 217
   'Butterfly' (syn. 'Kocho nishiki') (ACRPLBT), 219, 237
   'Crimson Queen' (ACRPLCQ), 167, 189
   'Dissectum' (ACRPLDS), 237
   'Dissectum Atropurpureum' (ACRPLDT), 167, 189
   'Dissectum Variegatum' (ACRPLDU), 167
   'Okushimo' (ACRPLOH), 222, 237
   'Osakazuki' (ACRPLOK), 167, 172, 189
   'Sangokaku' (ACRPLSN), 172, 189–190, 204
ACER pensylvanicum (ACRPN), 204
ACER platanoides (ACRPT), 217, 219, 222, 223, 229, 233, 238
   'Cleveland' (ACRPTCL), 222, 223
   'Columnare' (ACRPTCM), 223, 233, 238
   'Crimson King' (ACRPTCK), 217, 223, 229, 233, 238
   'Crimson Sentry' (ACRPTCS), 217, 223, 229, 233, 238
   'Deborah' (ACRPTDB), 233, 238
   'Drummondii' (ACRPTDR), 49
   'Emerald Queen' (ACRPTEQ), 233, 238
   'Erectum' (ACRPTER), 223
   'Summershade' (ACRPTSM), 222, 229
   'Waldersei' (ACRPTWW), 49
ACER pseudoplatanus cvs. (ACRPS), 217, 241
   'Brilliantissimum' (ACRPSBB), 217, 241
   'Worleei' (ACRPSWW), 217, 241
ACER rubrum (ACRRB), 220, 223, 229, 233

'Autumn Flame' (ACRRBAF), 220, 229
'Columnare' (ACRRBCL), 223
'Northwood' (ACRRBNR), 220, 229
'October Glory' (ACRRBOG), 220, 229, 233
'Red Sunset' (ACRRBRS), 220, 229, 233
ACER rubrum var. columnare 'Armstrong' (ACRRRAR), 233
'Scarlet Sentinel' (ACRRRSS), 233
ACER saccharinum (ACRSC), 217, 220
'Lutescens' (ACRSCLL), 217
ACER saccharum (ACRSH), 220, 222, 229, 233
'Bonfire' (ACRSHBB), 220, 229, 233
'Globosum' (ACRSHGG), 222
'Green Mountain' (ACRSHGM), 222, 233
'Monumentale' (ACRSHMN), 222
ACER tataricum (ACRTT), 220
'Rubrum' (ACRTTRR), 220
ACHILLEA (ACH), 26
ACHILLEA filipendulina 'Coronation Gold' (ACHFLCG), 26
ACHILLEA millefolium 'Fire King' (ACHMLFK), 26
ACHILLEA taygetea 'Moonshine' (ACHTGMM), 26
ACHILLEA tomentosa (ACHTM), 81–82
ACHIMENES (ACE), 42
ACIDANTHERA bicolor var. murieliae (ACDBL), 8
ACORUS calamus 'Variegatus' (ACSCLW), 57
ACORUS gramineus 'Ogon' (ACSGROG), 98
ACTINIDIA (ACA), 131
ACTINIDIA arguta (ACAAG), 131
ACTINIDIA chinensis. See ACTINIDIA deliciosa
ACTINIDIA deliciosa (syn. chinensis) (ACADL), 131
ACTINIDIA kolomikta (ACAKL), 131
ACTINIDIA polygama (ACAPL), 131
Adam's-needle, 28–29, 194
ADIANTUM pedatum (ADNPD), 109–110
ADLUMIA fungosa (ADLFN), 136
AEGOPODIUM podagraria 'Variegatum' (AGPPDVR), 106
AESCULUS X *carnea* (ASCCR), 205
'Briotii' (ASCCRBR), 205
African Marigold, 39–40
AGAPANTHUS orientalis (AGNOR), 41
'Peter Pan' (AGNORPP), 41
AGERATUM houstonianum (AGRHS), 37
'Blue Bedder' (AGRHSBB), 37
AJUGA genevensis (AJGGN), 106
AJUGA reptans (AJGRP), 106
'Atropurpurea' (AJGRPAT), 106
'Burgundy Glow' (AJGRPBG), 106
'Rubra' (AJGRPRR), 106
'Variegata' (AJGRPVV), 106
AKEBIA quinata (AKBQN), 138
Alaska Cedar, 224–225, 234
ALBIZIA julibrissin (ALBJL), 238
Alchemilla vulgaris (ALHVL), 76
Alder, 246
Aleppo Pine, 215, 243
Algerian Ivy, 108, 132, 139
Algerian Tangerine, 237
ALLAMANDA cathartica (ALMCT), 126
Alleghany Pachysandra, 117

ALLIUM (ALL), 47, 68
ALLIUM christophii (ALLCH), 47
ALLIUM fistulosum (ALLFS), 68
ALLIUM giganteum (ALLGG), 30, 47, 117
ALLIUM moly (ALLML), 47
ALLIUM neapolitanum (ALLNP), 41, 47
ALLIUM rosenbachianum (ALLRS), 30, 47, 117
ALLIUM schoenoprasum (ALLSC), 68
ALLIUM sphaerocephalum (ALLSP), 8, 47
ALLIUM tuberosum (ALLTB), 47, 68
Allwood Pink, 48
ALNUS (ALN), 246
ALNUS cordata (ALNCR), 246
ALNUS glutinosa (ALNGL), 246
'Aurea' (ALNGLAR), 246
'Pyramidalis' (ALNGLPR), 246
ALNUS incana (ALNIN), 246
'Pendula' (ALNINPP), 246
ALOYSIA triphylla (ALITR), 72
AMELANCHIER (AML), 228, 246
AMELANCHIER alnifolia (AMLAL), 228
AMELANCHIER arborea (AMLAR), 228, 246
AMELANCHIER canadensis (AMLCN), 228, 241, 244, 246
'Robin Hill Pink' (AMLCNRL), 228, 241, 244, 246
AMELANCHIER laevis (AMLLV), 228, 246
'Prince Charles' PP 6039 (AMLLVPC), 228, 246
Americana. See CARPINUS caroliniana
American Arborvitae, 166, 213, 215, 216, 240
American Beachgrass, 93
American Beauty Rose, 76
American Beech, 230, 238
American Bittersweet, 135
American Elder, 181, 199
American Fringe Tree, 226, 244, 247
American Holly, 242, 245
American Hornbeam, 232, 234, 246
American Native Azaleas, 153
'Galle's Choice' (RHDHBGI), 153
'Marydel' (RHDHBME), 153
American Plane, 231, 248
American Smoke Tree, 220
American Sweet Gum, 221, 247
American Wall Fern, 111
American Wisteria, 129
American Yellowwood, 210, 226
AMMOPHILA (AMM), 93
AMMOPHILA arenaria (AMMAR), 93
AMMOPHILA breviligulata (AMMBR), 93
AMPELOPSIS (AMS), 131, 140
AMPELOPSIS arborea (AMSAR), 131, 140
AMPELOPSIS brevipedunculata (AMSBR), 131, 140
'Elegans' (AMSBREL), 131, 140
Amur Cherry, 204
Amurensis var. *japonica. See SYRINGA reticulata*
Amur Maple, 220, 238
Amur Privet, 185
ANCHUSA capensis (ANC), 37
ANEMONE (ANM), 6, 31

ANEMONE blanda 'White Splendor' (ANMBL), 6
Anemone Clematis, 127
ANEMONE coronaria (ANMCR), 6
   'DeCaen' (ANMCRDD), 6
ANEMONE hupehensis var. *japonica* (ANMJP), 31
ANEMONE pulsatilla 'Rubra' (ANMPLRC), 6
   'Red Cloak' (ANMPLRR), 6
ANEMONE vitifolia 'Robustissima' (ANMVTRR), 31
ANETHUM graveolens (ANUGR), 68
ANGELICA archangelica (ANLAR), 44
Annual Marjoram, 70
Anthemis nobilis, 82
ANTHRISCUS cerefolium (ANSCR), 70
ANTIGONON leptopus (ANGLP), 126
ANTIRRHINUM majus (ANHMJ), 37
   Giant (ANHMJ), 37
   Intermediate (ANHMJ), 37
   Tom Thumb (ANHMJ), 37
Apothecary Rose, 76
Appalachian Tea, 199
Apple, 207, 218, 232, 237
Apple Geranium, 75
Apple Mint, 69
Aquatics, 54–59. *See also* specific aquatics
AQUILEGIA (AQL), 24, 25
   Spring Song Strain (AQLHRSS), 4
AQUILEGIA flabellata 'Nana' (AQLFLNN), 24
   'Alba' (AQLFLAL), 24
ARABIS alpina (AABAL), 113
ARABIS caucasia (AABCC), 113
Arborvitae, 166, 216
ARBUTUS (ARB), 204, 212–213
ARBUTUS menziesii (ARBMN), 204, 212
ARBUTUS unedo (ARBUN), 204, 212, 237
   'Compacta' (ARBUNCM), 204, 212, 237
ARCTOSTAPHYLOS uva-ursi (ARTUV), 107
   'Massachusetts' (ARTUVMS), 107
Argentine Trumpet Vine, 132
ARGYREIA splendens (ARGSP), 138
ARISAEMA triphyllum (ARMTR), 24
ARISTOLOCHIA durior (ARADR), 138, 140
Arizona Cypress, 213
Armand Clematis, 126
Arnold Arboretum, 150
ARONIA arbutifolia 'Brilliantissima' (ARNARBB), 172
Arrow Broom, 119
Arrowhead, 58
Arrowwood, 181–182
ARTEMISIA (ARI), 114–115
ARTEMISIA abrotanum (ARIAR), 115
ARTEMISIA annua (ARIAN), 115
ARTEMISIA dracunculus var. *sativa* (ARIDRST), 68–69
ARTEMISIA ludoviciana var. *albula* (ARILDAL), 106, 115, 169, 188
ARTEMISIA stellerana (ARISL), 115
Artichoke, 45
Artillery Plant, 106–107
ARUNCUS dioicus (AUNDC), 29
   'Kneiffii' (AUNDCKK), 29

ARUNDO (ARO), 91–92
ARUNDO donax 'Versicolor' (ARODN), 92
ASARINA (ASA), 136
ASARINA barclaiana (ASABR), 136
ASARINA erubescens (ASAER), 136
ASARINA procumbens (ASAPR), 136
ASARINA scandens (ASASC), 136
ASARUM (ASR), 78
ASARUM caudatum (ASRCD), 78
ASARUM europaeum (ASRER), 78
ASCLEPIAS (ASL), 44
ASCLEPIAS currasavica (ASLCR), 44
ASCLEPIAS tuberosa (ASLTR), 44
Ash, 230
   European, 230
   Evergreen, 231
   Flowering, 230
   Green, 230
   Manna, 230
   Red, 231, 247
   Shamel, 231
   White, 230
Asparagus asparagoides (ASPAS), 136
ASTER (AST), 31
ASTER X *frikartii* 'Wonder of Staffa' (ASTFRWF), 31
ASTER novae-angliae (ASTNN), 31
   'Harrington's Pink' (ASTNNHP), 31
ASTER novi-belgii (ASTNV), 31
   'Professor Kippenburg' (ASTNVPK), 31
ASTILBE (ASB), 24
ASTILBE X *arendsii* (ASBAR), 24
   'Fanal' (ASBARFN), 24
   'Feuer' (ASBARFF), 24
   'Professor van der Wielen' (ASBARPV), 24
ASTILBE chinensis 'Pumila' (ASBCHPM), 24
ATHYRIUM (ATH), 110
ATHYRIUM felix-femina (ATHFX), 110
ATHYRIUM goeringianum 'Pictum' (ATHGRPP), 110
ATHYRIUM thelypteroides (ATHTH), 110
Atlantic Pea, 136
AUBRIETA (ABR), 113
AUCUBA japonica (ACBJP), 162, 170, 190
   'Crotonifolia' (ACBJPCR), 162, 170, 190
   'Maculata' (ACBJPMM), 162, 170, 190
   'Picturata' (ACBJPPC), 162, 170, 190
   'Variegata' (ACBJPVR), 162, 170, 190
Aurelian Lily, 8, 47
AURINIA saxatilis (AURSX), 113
   'Compacta' (AURSXCC), 113
Australian Gum, 213
Australian Water Clover, 58
Australian Willow, 224–225
Austrian Black Pine, 215, 243, 247
Austrian Pine, 215, 243, 247
Autumn Crocus, 10, 11, 66
Autumn Moor Grass, 98
Autumn Olive, 181
Autumn Zephyr Lily, 11, 112

Azaleas, 149–153, 212, 216
   evergreen, 149–152
   deciduous, 152–153
   see also RHODODENDRON; specific types, e.g., Belgian Indian
   Azaleas; Pennington Azaleas
X *Azaleodendron* (AZL), 154
Aztec Lily, 9

B

Baby Rose, 187
Baby's-breath, 67
BACCHARIS (BCC), 192
BACCHARIS halimifolia (BCCHL), 192
BACCHARIS pilularis (BCCPL), 118, 192
   'Twin Peaks' (BCCPLTP), 118, 192
Back Acres Azaleas, 150
   'Margaret Douglas' (RHDHBMU), 150
   'Marian Lee' (RHDHBAE), 150
Bald Cypress, 248
Balloon Flower, 28
Balloon Vine, 136
Balsam Apple, 137
Balsam Pear, 137
Bamboo, 96
BAPTISIA australis (BPTAS), 26–27
Barberry, 162, 167, 172–173, 182, 184–185
Barnhaven Strains, 25
Basil, 69
Basket Flower, 8–9
Basket-of-gold, 113
Bayberry, 64, 193
Beachgrass, 93
Beach Morning-glory, 115
Beach Plum, 193–194
Bearberry, 107
Bearberry Cotoneaster, 104
Beautybush, 183
Bedding Begonia, 9
Bee Balm, 72–73
Beech, 230
   American, 230, 238
   European, 218, 223, 230, 238
Beech Fern, 111
BEGONIA (BGN), 9
BEGONIA grandis (BGNGR), 9
BEGONIA X *semperflorens-cultorum* (BGNSR), 9
BEGONIA X *tuberhybrida* (BGNTB), 9
BEGONIA X *tuberhybrida* Pendula (BGNTBPP), 9
BELAMCANDA chinensis (BLMCII), 66
Belgian-Glenn Dale Azaleas, 150
   'Green Mist' (RHDHBGT), 150
   'Pink Ice' (RHDHBPI), 150
Belgian Indian Azaleas, 149–150
   'Albert-Elizabeth' (RHDHBAR), 149

'Vervaeneana' (RHDHBVA), 149
Bellflower, 22, 29, 132, 139
Bengal Clock Vine, 138
BERBERIS (BRB), 172–173, 182, 184–185
BERBERIS buxifolia 'Nana' (BRBBXNA), 184
BERBERIS X *gladwynensis* 'William Penn' (BRBGLWP), 172
BERBERIS julianae (BRBJL), 184
   'Nana' (BRBJLNN), 184
BERBERIS koreana (BRBKR), 173, 182
BERBERIS X *mentorensis* (BRBMN), 184
BERBERIS thunbergii 'Aurea' (BRBTHAR), 167, 168
   'Crimson Pygmy' (BRBTHCP), 167, 182
BERBERIS verruculosa (BRBVR), 162, 184–185
Bergamot Mint, 69
Bethlehem Sage, 25–26
Betony, 107
BETULA (BTL), 204
BETULA nigra 'Heritage' (BTLNGHR), 174, 204, 246
BETULA papyrifera (BTLPP), 165, 204
BETULA pendula (BTLPN), 224
   'Dalecarlica' (BTLPNDL), 224
   'Fastigiata', Fastigiate European Birch (BTLPNFF), 224
   'Gracilis' (BTLPNGG), 224
BETULA platyphylla var. *japonica* 'Whitespire' (BTLPTWW), 204
Bigflower Tickseed, 27
Bigleaf Ligularia, 33
Big-leaf Maple, 222, 229
BIGNONIA capreolata (BGACP), 138
Birch, 204
   Canoe, 165, 204
   Japanese White, 204
   Paper, 204
   River, 174, 204, 246
   White, 204
Bird's Nest Spruce, 165
Bishop's Weed, 106
Bitter Cucumber, 137
Bittersweet, 135
Black Alder, 246
Blackberry Lily, 66
Black Cherry, 228
Black-eyed Susan, 28
Black-eyed Susan Vine, 138
Black Haw, 148
Black Locust, 235
Blackthorn, 167
Blanket Flower, 45
Bleeding-heart, 19, 22
Bloodflower, 44
Blood-red Cranesbill, 23
Bloodroot, 26
Blood-trumpet, 128
Blue Atlas Cedar, 213, 224
Bluebeard, 66
Bluebell, 25
   Mexican, 119
   Spanish, 6
   Virginia, 25

Blueberry, 65
Blue Cardinal Flower, 30
Blue Ceratostigma, 104
Blue Clump Bamboo, 96
Blue-devil, 197
Blue Fescue, 97
Blue Gum, 214
Blue Oat Grass, 89
Blue Passionflower, 128
Blue Pfitzer Juniper, 108, 164
Blue Ridge St.-John's-wort, 119
Blue Rug Creeping Juniper, 108, 164
Blue Salvia, 32
Blue Sargent's Juniper, 169
Blue Sedge, 90
Blue Selaginella, 121
Blue Sheep's Fescue, 89
Blue Trumpet Vine, 138
Blue Verbena, 76
Blueweed, 197
Bog Lily, 59
Bog Plants, 57–59
BOLTONIA asteroides 'Snowbank' (BLNASSS), 31
Borealis. See QUERCUS rubra
Boston Ivy, 132, 141
Botanical Tulips, 21
BOUGAINVILLEA (BGV), 126
  'Crimson Jewel' (BGVHBCJ), 126
  'Oo-la-la' (BGVHBOL), 126
Bourbon Rose, 76, 130
BOUTELOUA gracilis (BTUGR), 88
Bower Actinidia, 131
Box, 162, 176, 185
Box Elder, 217
Box Holly, 79
Boxwood, 162, 176, 185
Bradford Pear, 209
Braun's Holly Fern, 111
Brazil Cherry, 185
Brazilian Morning-glory, 137
BRIZA subaristata (BRZSB), 88
Broad Beech Fern, 111
Broom, 115, 119, 192
Broombrush, 158–159, 175
BROUSSONETIA papyrifera (BRTPP), 234
BROWALLIA speciosa (BRWSP), 42
  'Major' (BRWSPMJ), 42
Brown's Honeysuckle, 134
Brown's Yew, 166, 178
BUDDLEIA davidii (BDLDV), 158
Bugloss, 37
Bulbs, 6–11, 41–42. *See also* specific bulbs
Bull Bay, 211, 214, 227
Burford Horned Holly, 163
Burford's Chinese Holly, 163
Burnet, 71
Bur Oak, 231, 235
Busy Lizzy, 38

Butcher's Broom, 79
Butterfly Daffodils, 15
Butterfly Weed, 44
Buttonbush, 78
BUXUS (BXS), 162, 176, 185
BUXUS microphylla (BXSMC), 162, 176, 185
  'Compacta' (BXSMCCC), 162, 176, 185
  'Green Beauty' (BXSMCGB), 176
  'Morris Midget' (BXSMCMM), 162, 176, 185
  'Tide Hill' (BXSMCTH), 162, 176, 185
BUXUS sempervirens 'Myrtifolia' (BXSSMMM), 176
  'Suffruticosa' (BXSSMSF), 162, 176, 185

C

Cabbage Rose, 76
CALADIUM X *hortulanum* (CLDHR), 9
CALAMAGROSTIS (CLG), 92
CALAMAGROSTIS acutiflora 'Stricta' (CLGACSS), 92
  'Karl Foerster' (CLGACKF), 92
  'Stricta', 92
Calamondin, 80
Calamondin Orange, 190
California Bay, 64
California Incense Cedar, 213
California Nutmeg, 216
California Privet, 185
Callery Pear, 209
CALLISTEMON viminalis 'Red Cascade' (CLSVMRC), 224
CALLUNA vulgaris (CLNVL), 174
  'Alba' (CLNVLAL), 174
  'Foxii Nana' (CLNVLFN), 174
  'Gold Haze' (CLNVLGH), 174
CALOCEDRUS decurrens (CLCDC), 213
Calonyction aculeatum, 137
CALYCANTHUS floridus (CLTFL), 178
CAMELLIA (CML), 176–177, 194–195
CAMELLIA japonica (CMLJP), 176–177, 194–195
CAMELLIA sasanqua (CLMSS), 176–177, 194, 195
  'Cinnamon Cindy' (CMLSSCN), 176, 194
  'Flower Girl' (CMLSSFG), 177, 195
  'Frost Queen' (CMLSSFQ), 176, 194
  'Jean May' (CMLSSJM), 177, 195
  'Showa-no-Sakac' (CMLSSSN), 177, 195
CAMPANULA carpatica (CMNCR), 22, 29
CAMPANULA poscharskyana (CMNPS), 29
Campernelle Jonquil, 74–75
CAMPSIS (CMP), 135
CAMPSIS grandiflora (CMPGR), 135
CAMPSIS radicans (CMPRD), 135, 140
CAMPSIS X *tagliabuana* 'Madame Galen' (CMPTGMG), 135
Canada Hemlock, 186, 217, 232, 245–246
Canada Lily, 18
Canadian Burnet, 33–34
CANANGA odorata (CAGOD), 226
Canary-bird Flower, 71

Canary Creeper, 71
Candle Larkspur, 44
CANNA X *hybrida* (CNNHB), 59
  'Endeavour' (CNNHBEN), 59
  'Erebus' (CNNHBER), 59
  'Ra' (CNNHBRR), 59
  'Taney' (CNNHBTT), 59
Canoe Birch, 165, 204
Cape Honeysuckle, 128
Cape Jasmine, 80, 191, 195
Capparis spinosa (CPISP), 71
Caraway Thyme, 83
Cardinal Flower, 30
CARDIOSPERMUM halicacabum (CADHL), 136
CAREX (CRX), 90, 95
CAREX buchananii (CRXBC), 95
CAREX flacca (CRXFLBS), 90
CAREX glauca (CRXGLBS), 90
CAREX humilis (CRXHM), 90
CAREX morrowii 'Variegata' (CRXMRVV), 95
CAREX muskingumensis (CRXMS), 95
CAREX pendula (CRXPN), 98–99
Carnation, 48, 67
Carolina Allspice, 178
Carolina Hemlock, 186, 217, 233
Carolina Moonseed, 135
Carolina Silverbell, 244, 247
Carolina Yellow Jasmine, 132
Carosella, 70
Carpathian Bellflower, 22, 29
Carpet Bugle, 106
CARPINUS (CRP), 232, 234
CARPINUS americana. See CARPINUS caroliniana
CARPINUS betulus (CRPBT), 223, 232, 234, 238
  'Columnaris' (CRPBTCC), 223, 232, 234, 238
  'Fastigiata' (CRPBTFS), 232, 234, 238
CARPINUS caroliniana (syn. *americana*) (CRPCR), 232, 234, 246
  'Fastigiata' (CRPBTFS), 232, 234
Carrotwood Tree, 213, 234
CARYOPTERIS X *clandonensis* (CRTCL), 66
CATALPA speciosa (CTLSP), 210
Cat's-claw, 133
Cattail, 58
CEANOTHUS (CNT), 196
CEANOTHUS americanus (CNTAM), 162, 177, 196
CEANOTHUS X *delilianus* (CNTDL), 162, 177, 196
  'Gloire de Plantieres' (CNTDLGD), 162, 177, 196
  'Gloire de Versailles' (CNTDLGV), 162, 177, 196
CEANOTHUS ovatus (CNTOV), 196
Cedar, 213, 224
  Alaska, 224–225, 235
  Blue Atlas, 213, 224
  California Incense, 213
  Columnar Russian, 224
  Deodar, 213
  Japanese, 213
  Red, 214, 224, 239
  Russian, 215

  Weeping Deodar, 224
  Western Red, 216
Cedar-of-Lebanon, 213
CEDRUS (CDR), 213, 224
CEDRUS atlantica 'Glauca' (CDRATGL), 213
  'Fastigiata' (CDRATFF), 213
  'Glauca Pendula' (CDRATGP), 213, 224
CEDRUS deodara (CDRDD), 213, 224
  'Pendula' (CDRDDPN), 213 224
CEDRUS libani (CDRLB), 213
  'Pendula' (CDRLBPN), 213
CELASTRUS (CLR), 135
CELASTRUS orbiculatus (CLROR), 135
CELASTRUS scandens (CLRSC), 135
CELOSIA argentea (CELAR), 37–38
CELTIS (CLI), 228
CELTIS laevigata (CLILV), 228
CELTIS occidentalis (CLIOC), 228, 241
  'Magnifica' (CLIOCMM), 241
CEPHALANTHUS occidentalis (CPLOC), 78
CERATOSTIGMA plumbaginoides (CRM), 104
CERCIDIPHYLLUM japonicum (CRCJP), 230
  'Pendula' (CRCJPPPP), 230
CERCIS (CRI), 205
CERCIS canadensis (CRICN), 205
  'Flame' (CRICNFL), 205
  'Forest Pansy' (CRICNFP), 205
  'Royal' (CRICNRR), 205
  'Silver Cloud' (CRICNSC), 205
  'Wither's Pink Charm' (CRICNWP), 205
CERCIS occidentalis (CRIOC), 205
CERCIS reniformis (CRIRN), 205
Ceriman, 133
CHAENOMELES speciosa (CHNSP), 146
  'Apple Blossom' (CHNSPAB), 146
  'Cardinalis' (CHNSPCC), 146
  'Nivalis' (CHNSPNN), 146
  'Phyllis Moore' (CHNSPPM), 146
  'Rubra Grandiflora' (CHNSPRG), 146
Chalice Vine, 133–134
CHAMAECYPARIS (CHM), 168, 213, 217–218
CHAMAECYPARIS nootkatensis (CHMNT), 224–225, 234
CHAMAECYPARIS obtusa (CHMOB), 162, 168, 213
  'Crippsii', Cripp's Golden Hinoki Cypress (CHMOBCR), 168, 213
  'Filicoides' (CHMOBFL), 213
  'Nana Aurea' (CHMOBNR), 162, 168
  'Nana Gracilis' (CHMOBNC), 162, 168
  'Pygmaea' (CHMOBPP), 162
  'Tetragona Aurea' (CHMOBTA), 218
CHAMAECYPARIS pisifera (CHMPS), 168, 169, 218
  'Boulevard' (syn. 'Cyanoviridis') (CHMPSBL), 169, 213
  'Filifera Aurea' (CHMPSFA), 168, 218
  'Plumosa Aurea' (CHMPSPR), 218
  'Squarrosa Aurea' (CHMPSSR), 218
CHAMAEMELUM nobile (CAMNB), 82
Chamomile, 82
Chaparral Broom, 118, 192
Chapeau de Napoleon, 76

CHASMANTHIUM latifolium (CAULT), 95
Chaste Tree, 65
Checkerberry, 78
CHEIRANTHUS cheiri (CENCH), 47
CHELONE obliqua (CEEOB), 120
Cherry, 204, 209, 228
Cherry Laurel, 196
Cherry Pie, 74
Cherry Plum, 219
Chervil, 70
Chilean Bellflower, 132, 139
CHIMONANTHUS praecox (CIMPR), 179
China Fleece Vine, 138, 141
China Rose, 75, 76, 77, 187
Chinese Chives, 47, 68
Chinese Date, 65
Chinese Dogwood, 206, 244
Chinese Elm, 236
Chinese Gooseberry, 131
Chinese Hibiscus, 158, 177, 183
Chinese Holly, 171, 181
Chinese Juniper, 168, 214, 224
Chinese Magnolia, 207
Chinese Olive, 180
Chinese Parsley, 70
Chinese Podocarpus, 191
Chinese Trumpet Creeper, 135
Chinese Wisteria, 129, 141
Chinese Witch Hazel, 146, 183, 191, 245
CHIONANTHUS (CHT), 226
CHIONANTHUS retusus (CHTRT), 156, 226
CHIONANTHUS virginicus (CHTVR), 226, 244, 247
CHIONODOXA (CHX), 41
CHIONODOXA luciliae (CHXLC), 41
CHIONODOXA sardensis (CHXSR), 41
Chittamwood, 220
Chives, 68
Chokeberry, 172
Chokecherry, 219, 229
CHONDROPETALUM tectorum (CHETC), 97
Christmas Fern, 111
Christmas Trees, 212
CHRYSANTHEMUM (CHH), 15, 31–32
CHRYSANTHEMUM X morifolium (CHHMRCC), 31–32
  'Cloud 9' (CHHMRGG), 32
CHRYSANTHEMUM X superbum 'Polaris' (CHHSPPP), 32
CHRYSOGONUM virginianum (CHGVR), 120
Ciboule, 68
Cigar Flower, 42
Cilantro, 70
Cinnamon Fern, 111
X *Citrofortunella mitis* (CTRMT), 80, 190
CITRUS (CTS), 80, 237
CITRUS aurantium (CTSAN), 80
CITRUS limon (CTSLM), 80, 237
  'Improved Meyer' (CTSLMIM), 237
  'Ponderosa' (CTSLMPP), 80
CITRUS X limonia otaitensis (CTSLN), 80

CITRUS mitis. See Citrofortunella var. mitis
CITRUS reticulata (CTSRT), 237
  'Clementine' (CTSRTCC), 237
CITRUS sinensis (CTSSN), 237
  'Valencia' (CTSSNVL), 237
CLADRASTIS lutea (CLALT), 210, 226
  'Rosea' (CLALTRR), 226
CLEMATIS (CLM), 126–127
CLEMATIS armandii (CLMAR), 126
CLEMATIS balearica (CLMBL), 126
CLEMATIS cirrhosa (CLMCR), 126
CLEMATIS dioscoreifolia (CLMDS), 126
CLEMATIS flammula (CLMFL), 126
CLEMATIS X jackmanii (CLMJC), 126
CLEMATIS maximowicziana (syn. *paniculata*) (CLMMX), 126, 140
CLEMATIS montana (CLMMN), 127
CLEMATIS montana var. rubens (CLMMNRS), 127
CLEMATIS paniculata. See CLEMATIS maximowicziana
CLEMATIS recta (CLMRC), 126
CLEMATIS rehderana (CLMRH), 126
CLEMATIS tangutica (CLMTN), 127
CLEMATIS texensis (CLMTX), 127
  'Duchess of Albany' (CLMTXDF), 127
CLEMATIS viticella 'Betty Corning' (CLMVTBC), 127
  'Huldine' (CLMVTHH), 127
CLEOME hassleriana (CEMHL), 38
CLETHRA alnifolia (CLHAL), 195, 198
  'Paniculata' (CLHALPP), 195
  'Pink Spires' (CLHALPS), 195, 198
  'Rosea' (CLHALRR), 195, 198
CLETHRA barbinervis (CLHBR), 226–227, 237, 241, 247
Cliff Green, 106
Climbing Bittersweet, 135
Climbing Fumatory, 136
Climbing Hydrangea, 128, 139, 140–141, 192
CLITORIA ternatea (CITTR), 136
CLIVIA X cyrtanthiflora (CLVCR), 41
CLIVIA miniata (CLVMN), 41
Cloak Pasque-flower, 6
Clove Pink, 48, 67
Cloves, 185
CLYTOSTOMA callistegioides (CLYCL), 132
COBAEA scandens (CBASC), 136
COCCULUS carolinus (CCLCR), 135
CODIAEUM variegatum (CDMVR), 170, 190
COLCHICUM autumnale (CLUAT), 10, 11, 66
  'Albo-plenum' (CLUATAB), 66
  'Album' (CLUATAL), 10
  'The Giant' (CLUATTG), 10
  'Pleniflorum' (CLUATPP), 66
  'Waterlily' (CLUATWW), 10
COLEUS blumei (COUBL), 42
COLEUS pumilus (COUPM), 42
COLOCASIA esculenta (COLES), 59
Colorado Blue Spruce, 165, 169, 215, 239
Columbine, 24, 25
Columnar European Hornbeam, 223
Columnar Russian Cedar, 224

Columnar Swiss Stone Pine, 224
Compact Pampas Grass, 88
COMPTONIA peregrina, (CMTPR), 118, 196
Coneflower, 28
Confederate Jasmine, 139–140
CONSOLIDA ambigua (CNSAM), 38, 44
CONVALLARIA majalis (CNVMJ), 116–117
Cootamundra Wattle, 236
COPROSMA X kirkii (CPMKR), 197
Coral Bark Maple, 172, 189–190, 204
Coralbells, 23
Coralberry, 197
Coral Greenbrier, 136
Coral Honeysuckle, 135
Coral Vine, 126
COREOPSIS (CRO), 27, 66
COREOPSIS grandiflora 'Sunray' (CROGRSS), 27, 66
COREOPSIS lanceolata 'Goldfink' (CROLNGG), 27, 46, 66
COREOPSIS tinctoria (CROTN), 66
COREOPSIS verticillata (CROVR), 27, 66
    'Golden Showers' (CROVRGS), 27, 66
    'Moonbeam' (CROVRMN), 27, 66
Coriander, 70
CORIANDRUM sativum (COMST), 70
Cork Tree, 232
Cornelian Cherry, 206
Corn Flag, 8
Cornish Heath, 158
CORNUS (COR), 173, 190, 198, 205–207
CORNUS alba (CORAL), 170
    'Argenteo-marginata' (CORALAG), 170
    'Sibirica' (CORALSB), 173, 190, 198
    'Spaethii' (CORALSS), 170
CORNUS amomum (CORAM), 198
CORNUS capitata (CORCP), 206
CORNUS controversa (CORCT), 232
CORNUS florida (CORFL), 205, 206, 207, 219, 244
CORNUS kousa var. chinensis (CORKSCN), 206, 219, 244
    'Elizabeth Lustgarten' (CORKCEL), 206
    'Milky Way' (CORKCMW), 206, 244
    'Snowboy' (CORKCSS), 219
    'Summer Stars' (CORKCST), 206, 244
CORNUS mas (CORMS), 206
CORNUS nuttallii (CORNT), 207
    'Corigo Giant' (CORNTCN), 207
CORNUS sericea (syn. stolonifera (CORSR), 173, 190, 198
    'Flaviramea', Golden-twig Dogwood (CORSRFL), 173, 190, 198
CORNUS stolonifera. See CORNUS sericea
CORONILLA varia (CRLVR), 118
    'Penngift' (CRLVRPP), 118
CORTADERIA selloana 'Pumila' (COTSLPP), 88
CORYLUS colurna (COSCL), 234
CORYLUS maxima 'Purpurea' (COSMXPR), 167
COSMOS (CSO), 38
COSMOS bipinnatus (CSOBP), 38
COSMOS sulphureus (CSOSL), 38
COTINUS coggygria (CTNCG), 167
    'Notcutt's Variety' (syn. Rubrifolium) (CTNCGNV), 167

    'Royal Purple' (CTNCGRP), 167
COTINUS obovatus (CTNOB), 220
COTONEASTER (CTT), 104–105
COTONEASTER adpressus (CTTAD), 104
COTONEASTER adpressus var. praecox (CTTADPC), 104
COTONEASTER dammeri (CTTDM), 104
COTONEASTER horizontalis (CTTHR), 104
    'Variegata' (CTTHRVV), 104
COTONEASTER microphyllus (CTTMC), 105
COTONEASTER salicifolius (CTTSL), 105, 173, 190–191, 195
    'Autumn Fire' (CTTSLAF), 173, 190–191, 195
COTONEASTER salicifolius var. repens (CTTSLRN), 105
    'Scarlet Leader' (CTTSFSL), 105
Cottage Pink, 48
Cottage Tulips, 19, 20
Coyote Brush, 118, 192
Crab Apple, 207, 208, 218
Cranesbill, 23, 39, 43, 75
Crape Myrtle, 159, 211
CRATAEGUS X lavallei (CATLL), 241–242
CRATAEGUS phaenopyrum (CATPH), 228, 238
Cream Honeysuckle, 134
Creech, John, 159, 204
Creeping Charlie, 112
Creeping Cotoneaster, 104
Creeping Fig, 132
Creeping Gloxinia, 136
Creeping Gypsophila, 67
Creeping Jennie, 112
Creeping Lilyturf, 112
Creeping Mint, 69
Creeping Oregon Grape, 165
Creeping St.-John's-wort, 119
Creeping Thyme, 83
Crested Iris, 16
Crested Rose, 76
Crimean Linden, 236
Crimson Glory Vine, 136
CRINUM americanum (CINAM), 59
Crinum Lily, 8
CRINUM X powelli (CINPW), 8
    'Cecil Houdyshel' (CINPWCH), 8
Cripp's Golden Hinoki Cypress, 168, 218
Crispa, 20
CROCUS (COC), 11–12
    early hybrids, 12
    early species, 11
    fall species, 12
    'Lady Killer' (COCHBLK), 12
    'Peter Pan' (COCHBPN), 12
    'Pickwick' (COCHBPP), 12
    'Purpureus Grandiflorus' (COCHBPG), 12
    'Vernus Vanguard' (COCHBVV), 12
    'Yellow Mammoth' (COCHBYM), 12
CROCUS chrysanthus (COCCR), 11
    'Blue Pearl' (COCHBBP), 11
    'E.A. Bowles' (COCHBEB), 11
CROCUS sativus (COCST), 12, 66–67

CROCUS sieberi (COCSB), 11
   'Firefly' (COCHBFF), 11
CROCUS speciosus (COCSP), 12
CROCUS tomasinianus (COCTM), 11
   'Whitewell Purple' (COCHBWP), 11
CROCUS vernus (COCVR), 11
   'Remembrance' (COCHBRR), 11
Cross Vine, 138
Croton, 170, 190
Crown Vetch, 118
CRYPTOMERIA japonica (CYPJP), 213
   'Compacta' (CYPJPCC), 213
   'Elegans' (CYPJPEL), 213
   'Lobbii' (CYPJPLB), 213
   'Yoshino' (CYPJPYS), 213
CRYPTOSTEGIA madagascariensis (CYTMD), 128
Cuban Zephyr Lily, 11, 112
Cucumber Tree, 214
Cup-and-saucer Vine, 136
CUPANIOPSIS anacardioides (CPNAC), 213, 234
CUPHEA ignea (CPHIN), 42
X *CUPRESSOCYPARIS leylandii* (CPRLL), 242
   'Castlewellan' (CPRLLCS), 242
   'Naylor's Blue' (CPRLLNB), 242
CUPRESSUS (CPS), 213
CUPRESSUS arizonica (CPSAR), 213
CUPRESSUS macrocarpa (CPSMC), 213
   'Golden Pillar' (CPSMCGP), 213
CUPRESSUS sempervirens (CPSSM), 213
Cutleaf European White Birch, 224
CYMBOPOGON citratus (CMGCT), 70
CYPERUS (CPU), 59
CYPERUS alternifolius (CPUAT), 59
CYPERUS haspans (CPUHS), 59
Cypress, 213
   Arizona, 213
   Bald, 248
   Dwarf Golden Hinoki, 162, 168
   Hinoki, 213
   Italian, 213
   Leyland, 242
   Monterey, 213
   Nootka, 224–225, 234
   Sawara, 169, 213, 218
CYRTOMIUM falcatum (CYRFL), 110
CYTISUS (CTU), 115, 192
CYTISUS albus (CTUAL), 115, 192
CYTISUS X *kewensis* (CTUKW), 115, 192
CYTISUS scoparius (CTUSC), 192

D

Daffodil, 12–15, 25, 74–75
   Butterfly, 15
   Peruvian, 8–9
   Polyanthus, 14

   Winter, 10–11
Daffodil Garlic, 41, 47
DAHLIA X *hybrida* (DHLHB), 38
Daisy, 31–32
Damask Rose, 76
Dame's Rocket, 46
DAPHNE (DPH), 179
DAPHNE X *burkwoodii* (DPHBR), 179
   'Carol Mackie' (DPHBRCM), 179
   'Somerset' (DPHBRSM), 179
DAPHNE cneorum (DPHCN), 179
   'Pygmaea' (DPHCNPP), 179
   'Variegata' (DPHCNVV), 179
DAPHNE odora 'Aureo-marginata' (DPHODAR), 179
Darwins, 19, 20
Dasheen, 59
DAUCUS carota (DCSCR), 44
DAVIDIA involucrata (DVDIN), 210
DAVIDIA involucrata var. *vilmoriniana* (DVDINVL), 210
David Maple, 204
Dawn Redwood, 247
Daylily, 34–35, 15, 16, 22, 24
Deciduous Azaleas, 152–153
DELONIX regina (DLNRG), 210, 237
Delphinium ajacis, 38, 44
DELPHINIUM elatum (DLPEL), 44
DENNSTAEDTIA punctilobula (DNNPN), 110
Deodar Cedar, 213
DESCHAMPSIA (DSH), 95–96
DESCHAMPSIA caespitosa (DSHCS), 96
DESCHAMPSIA caespitosa var. *vivipara* (DSHCSVV), 96
   'Fairy's Joke' (DSHCPFJ), 96
DEUTZIA gracilis 'Nikko' (DTZGRNN), 105, 182–183
Devil-weed, 179–180
DIANTHUS 'Tiny Rubies' (DNT), 47–48, 113
DIANTHUS X *allwoodii* (DNTAL), 48
DIANTHUS barbatus (DNTBR), 48
DIANTHUS caryophyllus (DNTCR), 48, 67
   'Golden Sun' (DNTCRGS), 48, 67
DIANTHUS chinensis (DNTCH), 48
   'Heddewigii' (DNTCHHH), 48
DIANTHUS plumarius (DNTPL), 48
DICENTRA spectabilis (DCNSP), 19, 22
   'Adrian Bloom' (DCNSPAB), 22
DICHONDRA micrantha (DCDMC), 120–121
DICTAMNUS albus (DCTAL), 22
Digitalis purpurea (DGTPR), 76
Dill, 68
DISTICTIS (DST), 128
DISTICTIS buccinatoria (DSTBC), 128
DISTICTIS 'Rivers', 'Royal Trumpet Vine' (DSTHBRR), 128
Dittany, 22
Dogwood, 173, 190, 198, 205–207
   Chinese, 206, 244
   Evergreen, 206
   Flowering, 205, 206, 207, 244
   Giant, 232
   Golden-twig, 173, 190

Mountain, 207
Pacific, 207
Red-osier, 173, 190, 198
Red Twig, 173
Siberian, 173, 190, 198
Silky, 198
Variegated Tartarian, 170
DOLICHOS lablab (DLCLB), 137
Double File Viburnum, 157
Double Oldworld Arrowhead, 58
Douglas Fir, 216
Dove Tree, 210
Downy Jasmine, 134
Downy Serviceberry, 228, 246
Drooping Leucothoe, 195
Drooping Sedge Grass, 98–99
Drumsticks, 8, 47
DRYOPTERIS (DRP), 110
DRYOPTERIS erythrospora (DRPET), 110
DRYOPTERIS marginalis (DRPMR), 110
Dusty-miller, 115
Dutch Hyacinth, 6–7
Dutch Iris, 7
Dutchman's–Pipe, 138, 140
Dwarf Baccharis, 118, 192
Dwarf Balloon Flower, 28
Dwarf Box, 162, 176, 185
Dwarf Brush Cherry, 185
Dwarf English Yew, 166, 178
Dwarf Fan Columbine, 24
Dwarf Golden Hinoki Cypress, 162, 168
Dwarf Japanese Garden Juniper, 108
Dwarf Japanese Yew, 166, 178
Dwarf Lantana, 105
Dwarf Papyrus, 59
Dwarf Pfitzer Juniper, 108, 164
Dwarf Sumac, 197
Dwarf Winged Spindle Tree, 173, 183
Dwarf Witch Alder, 173
Dwarf Yaupon Holly, 115
Dwarf Yellow Daylily, 72

E

Eastern Ninebark, 168
Eastern Redbud, 205
Eastern Sycamore, 231, 248
East Indian Lotus, 57
ECHINACEA purpurea (ECCPR), 78
  'Bright Star' (ECCPRBS), 78
Echinops ritro (ECNRTTB), 23
ECHIUM (ECU), 197
ECHIUM fastuosum (ECUFS), 197
ECHIUM vulgare (ECUVL), 197
Edging Box, 162, 176, 185
Edging Lobelia, 30

Eglantine, 76
Egolf, Donald, 159
ELAEAGNUS (ELG), 169, 197
ELAEAGNUS angustifolia (ELGAN), 169, 197
ELAEAGNUS philippinensis (ELGPH), 169, 197
ELAEAGNUS pungens 'Maculata' (ELGPNMC), 162–163, 170
ELAEAGNUS umbellata (ELGUM), 181
Elder, 181, 199, 217
Elm, 236
ELYMUS arenarius (ELMAR), 93
ELYMUS glaucus (ELMGL), 93–94
ENDYMION hispanicus (ENDHS), 6
English Holly, 163, 181
English Ivy, 108, 111, 132, 139, 140
English Lavender, 74
English Oak, 231
English Primrose, 25
English Thyme, 42
English Yew, 216, 224
EPIMEDIUM grandiflorum (EPMGR), 113
  'Rose Queen' (EPDRBRQ), 113
EPIMEDIUM X rubrum (EPMRB), 113
EPIPREMNUM aureum (EPPAR), 138–139
  'Marble Queen' (EPPARMQ), 138
EQUISETUM hyemale (EQSHM), 58, 97
Eranthis hyemalis (ERNHM), 6, 11
Erect Selaginella, 121
ERIANTHUS ravennae (ERURV), 88
ERICA vagans (ERCVG), 158
  'Alba' (ERCVGAL), 158
  'Lyonesse' (ERCVGLL), 158
  'Mrs. D.F. Maxwell' (ERCVGMM), 158
  'St. Keverne' (ERCVGSK), 158
ERYNGIUM giganteum (ERGGG), 27
ERYNGIUM maritimum (ERGMR), 27
Eryngo, 27
EUCALYPTUS (ECL), 119, 213–214
EUCALYPTUS cinerea (ECLCN), 213
EUCALYPTUS citriodora (ECLCT), 74, 213
EUCALYPTUS globulus (ECLGL), 214
EUCALYPTUS leucoxylon (ECLLC), 214
  'Rosea' (ECLLCRR), 214
EUCOMMIA ulmoides (ECAUL), 234–235
EUGENIA (EGN), 185
EUGENIA aromatica (syn. *Syzygium aromaticum*) (EGNAR), 185
EUGENIA brasiliensis (EGNBR), 185
EUGENIA myrtifolia (syn. *Syzygium paniculatum*) 'Globulus' (EGNMRGL), 185
EUGENIA uniflora (EGNUN), 185
EUONYMUS (ENM), 170
EUONYMUS alata 'Compacta' (ENMALCM), 173, 183
EUONYMUS fortunei (ENMFR), 139
  'Emerald Beauty' (ENMFREB), 139
  'Emerald Leader' (ENMFREL), 139
  'Emerald 'n Gold' (ENMFRED), 171
  'Erecta' (ENMFRET), 139
  'Golden Prince' (ENMFRGG), 171
EUONYMUS japonica 'Aurea-variegata' (ENMJNAG), 171

EUPHORBIA epithymoides var. *griffithii* 'Fire Glow' (EPHETFG), 23
European Ash, 230
European Beachgrass, 93
European Beech, 218, 223, 230, 238
European Dune Grass, 93–94
European Hornbeam, 232, 234, 238
European Wild Ginger, 78
Evening Primrose, 23
Everblooming Honeysuckle, 135
Evergreen Ash, 231
Evergreen Azaleas, 149–152
Evergreen Candytuft, 76, 113–114
Evergreen Dogwood, 206
Ewers White Stonecrop, 33
Exbury Azaleas. *See* Knap Hill and Exbury Azaleas

F

FAGUS (FGS), 230
FAGUS grandifolia (FGSGR), 230
FAGUS sylvatica (FGSSL), 218, 223, 230, 238
   'Albo-variegata' (FGSSLAL), 218, 230
   'Atropunicea' (syn. 'Purpurea'), Purple Beech (FGSSLAT), 218, 230
   'Cuprea', Copper Beech (FGSSLCC), 218, 230
   'Dawyck' (syn. 'Fastigiata') (FGSSLDD), 223
   'Dawyck Gold' (FGSSLDG), 223
   'Dawyck Purple' (FGSSLDP), 218, 223, 230
   'Pendula' (FGSSLPN), 218, 230, 238
   'Purpurea Pendula' (FGSSLPP), 218, 230, 238
   'Riversii' (FGSSLRV), 218, 230
   'Rohan Gold' (FGSSLRG), 218, 230
   'Roseo-marginata' (syn. 'Tricolor', 'Purpurea Tricolor') (FGSSLRR), 218, 230
Fairy Lily, 11, 112
Fairy Primrose, 25
Fairy Rose, 186
False Cypress, 213, 217–218
False Indigo, 26–27
Fancy-leaved Caladium, 9
Fastigiate American Linden, 236
Fastigiate English Oak, 224
Fastigiate White Pine, 224
Feather Reed Grass, 92
FEIJOA sellowiana (FJISL), 169
   'Beachwood' (FJISLBB), 169
   'Coolidge' (FJISLCC), 169
   'Pineapple Gem' (FJISLPG), 169
Fennel, 70
Fern, 109–111
   American Wall, 111
   Beech, 111
   Braun's Holly, 111
   Broad Beech, 111
   Christmas, 111

Cinnamon, 111
   Hartford, 132–133
   Hay-scented, 110
   Holly, 110
   Japanese Holly, 110
   Japanese Shield, 110
   Japanese Silver Painted, 110
   Lady, 110
   Leatherleaf, 111
   Leather Wood, 110
   Maidenhair, 109–110
   New York, 111
   Ostrich, 78–79
   Rainbow, 121
   Shield, 111
   Sweet, 118, 196
   Sword, 111
Fern-leaf Tansy, 73
Fern-leaved Peony, 36
Fern-leaved Yarrow, 26
Fescue, 88–89, 97
FESTUCA (FST), 88–89
FESTUCA amethystina var. *superba* (FSTAMSP), 89
   'Rainbow Fescue' (FSTAMRF), 89
FESTUCA cinerea (FSTCN), 89, 97
   'April Grun' (FSTCNAG), 89
FESTUCA mairei (FSTMR), 89
Fetterbush, 148, 165
FICUS pumila (FCSPM), 132
   'Variegatus' (FCSPMVV), 132
FICUS retusa var. *nitida* (FCSRTNT), 214, 244
   'Green Gem' PP5900 (FCSRTGG), 214, 244
FILIPENDULA purpurea (FLPPR), 67
FILIPENDULA ulmaria (FLPUL), 67
Finger Bowl Pelargonium, 75
Finocchio, 70
Fir, 212
Fire Thorn, 178, 181
Fish Geranium, 39
Five-leaf Akebia, 138
Flag, 15
Flame Tree, 210, 237
Flame Vine, 128
Flannel Plant, 46
Flemmer, William, 244
Floating-heart, 58
Floribunda Roses, 129, 160, 161, 186, 187–188
   'Betty Prior' (RSAHBBP), 187–188
   'Europeana' (RSAHBER), 129
   'Redgold' (RSAHBRR), 161
   'Showbiz' (RSAHBSH), 161
   'Simplicity' (RSAHBSY), 188
   'Sunsprite' (RSAHBUP), 161
   'Trumpeter' (RSAHBTM), 161
Florida Flame Azalea, 153
Florist's Chrysanthemum, 31–32
Flossflower, 37
Flowering Ash, 230

Flowering Dogwood, 205, 206, 207, 244
Flowering Onion, 41, 47
Flowering Plum, 209, 218–219
Flowering Quince, 146
Flowering Tobacco, 38–39
Flowers, 6–49
    annuals, biennials, and tender perennials, 36–41
    for baskets and windowboxes, 42–43
    for bees, birds, and butterflies, 43–46
    fall and winter bulbs, corms, and rhizomes, 10–11
    fall perennials, 31–34
    fragrant, 47–49
    small spring bulbs, corms, and rhizomes, 6–8
    spring perennials, 22–26
    summer bulbs, corms, and rhizomes, 8–10
    summer perennials, 27–31
    See also specific flowers
FOENICULUM var. *piperitum* (FNCVLPP), 70
FOENICULUM vulgare (FNCVL), 70
FOENICULUM vulgare var. *dulce* (FNCVLDL), 70
Forget-me-not, 46
FORSYTHIA X *intermedia* (FRTIN), 118–119, 146, 177
    'Arnold Dwarf' (FRTINAD), 118–119, 197
    'Arnold Giant' (FRTINAG), 146, 177
    'Lynwood' (FRTINLN), 146, 177
    'Nana' (FRTINNN), 146, 177
FORTUNELLA margarita (FRLMR), 237
Fortune's Rhododendron, 154, 155
FOTHERGILLA (FTH), 173
FOTHERGILLA gardenii (FTHGR), 173, 212
FOTHERGILLA major (syn. *monticola*) (FTHMJ), 173, 212
FOTHERGILLA monticola. See FOTHERGILLA major
Fountain Grass, 90–91
Foxglove, 76
Fox Grape, 136
Fox Red Curly Sedge, 95
Fragrant Gladiolus, 8
Fragrant Hosta, 29–30, 117
Fragrant Snowbell, 212
Fragrant Sumac, 197
FRANKLINIA alatamaha (FRNAL), 210
Franklin Tree, 210
Fraser's Photinia, 186
FRAXINUS (FRX), 230–231
FRAXINUS americana (FRXAM), 230
    'Autumn Purple' (FRXAMAP), 230
    'Rosehill' (FRXAMRS), 230
FRAXINUS excelsior (FRXEX), 230
    'Aurea' Golden European Ash (FRXEXAR), 230
    'Hessei' (FRXEXHS), 230
FRAXINUS ornus (FRXOR), 230
FRAXINUS pennsylvanica (FRXPS), 231, 247
FRAXINUS udhei (FRXUD), 231
FREESIA X *hybrida* (FRIHB), 41
French Hydrangea, 171
French Lavender, 74
French Marigold, 40
French Thyme, 83

Fringed Hibiscus, 158, 177
Fringe Tree, 156, 226
FUCHSIA X *hybrida* (FCHHB), 42
FUCHSIA magellanica (FCHMG), 195
Fujiyama Rhododendron, 155

G

Gable Azaleas, 151
    'Louise Gable' (RHDHBLL), 151
    'Purple Splendor' (RHDHBPD), 151
GAILLARDIA (GLL), 45
GAILLARDIA aristata 'Goblin' (GLLARGG), 45
GAILLARDIA pulchella (GLLPL), 45
GALANTHUS elwesii (GLNEL), 6
GALANTHUS nivalis (GLNNV), 11
GALAX urceolata (GLXUR), 121
GALIUM odoratum (GLMOD), 82
Gallberry, 193
Garden Balsam, 38
Garden Forget-me-not, 46
Garden Heliotrope, 49, 74
Gardenia, 80
GARDENIA jasminoides (GRDJS), 80, 191, 195
    'Fortuniana' (GRDJSFR), 80, 191, 195
Garden Phlox, 28
Garden Verbena, 40
Garland Flower, 179
Garlic, 8, 47, 105–106
Garlic Chives, 47, 68
Gas Plant, 22
GAULTHERIA procumbens (GLTPR), 78
GAULTHERIA veitchiana (GLTVT), 198
Gay-feather, 32
GEIJERA parviflora (GJRPR), 225
GELSEMIUM sempervirens (GLSSM), 132
    'Pride of Augusta' (GLSSMPF), 132
Geneva Bugle, 106
GENISTA (GNS), 119
GENISTA pilosa 'Vancouver Gold' (GNSPLVG), 119
GENISTA sagittalis (GNSSGBR), 119
Gentian, 45
GENTIANA asclepiadea (GNTAS), 45
Geranium, 75
    Apple, 75
    Fish, 39
    Hardy, 23, 39, 43
    House, 39
    Ivy, 43
    Lemon, 75
    Peppermint, 75
    Rose, 75
    Zonal, 39
GERANIUM (GRM), 39, 43, 75
GERANIUM sanguineum var. *prostratum* (GRMSNPR), 23
German chamomile, 72

Germander, 186
Ghent Azaleas, 152
  'Coccinea Speciosa' (RHDHBOA), 152
  'Daviesi' (RHDHBDD), 152
Giant Arborvitae, 216
Giant Dogwood, 232
Giant Feather Grass, 89
Giant Onion, 47
Giant Reed, 92
Giant Sequoia, 216
Giant Silver Grass, 92
Giant Snowdrop, 6
Giant Snowflake, 7
Giant Stripe, 92
GINKGO biloba (GNKBL), 219, 222, 223, 231, 235
  'Autumn Gold' (GNKBLAG), 222, 231, 235
  'Magyar' (GNKBLMG), 235
  'Mayfield' (GNKBLMM), 222, 223, 231, 235
  'Princeton Sentry' (GNKBLPS), 223, 231, 235
  'Variegata' (GNKBLVV), 219
Girard Azaleas, 151
  'Girard's Hot Shot' (RHDHBIH), 151
  'Girard's Scarlet' (RHDHBIS), 151
GLADIOLUS (GLD), 8
GLEDITSIA triacanthos var. *inermis* 'Shademaster' (GLATCSS), 222, 235, 238
  'Sunburst' (GLATCSN), 222, 235, 238
Glenn Dale Azaleas, 150
  'Glacier' (RHDHBGC), 150
  'Martha Hitchcock' (RHDHBAH), 150
Globeflower, 31
Glory-of-the-snow, 41
Glossy Privet, 185
Goatsbeard, 29
Gold-band Lily, 18
Goldcup, 133–134
Gold-dust Tree, 162, 170, 190
Gold-edged Tulip Tree, 220
Golden-bells, 146
Golden-carpet, 114
Golden-chain Tree, 211, 237
Golden Clematis, 127
Golden-club, 58
Golden Larch, 223
Golden Mimosa, 236
Golden Pfitzer Juniper, 108, 164
Golden Pothos, 138–139
Golden-rain Tree, 210–211
Goldenrod, 79
Golden Star, 120
Golden Thread Sawara Cypress, 168
Golden-trumpet, 126
Goldentuft, 113
Golden-twig Dogwood, 173, 190
Golden Variegated Japanese Spindle Tree, 171
Golden Variegated Spindle Tree, 171
Golden Weeping Willow, 225
Gold Flower, 119, 175
Gold Moss, 114

Grape Hyacinth, 7
Grape-leaved Anemone, 31
Grape Vine, 136
Grasses. *See* Ornamental Grasses; specific grasses
Grass Pink, 48
Great Blue Lobelia, 30
Greater Periwinkle, 109
Great Stonecrop, 33
Grecian Laurel, 64
Grecian Silk Vine, 141
Greek Windflower, 6
Green Ash, 231, 247
Greenbrier, 135–136
Green Santolina, 73, 175, 192
Greenwood Azaleas, 151
  'Greenwood Orange' (RHDHBGG), 151
  'Pink Cloud' (RHDHBPU), 151
Ground Covers, 104–121
  with deciduous foliage, 106–107
  with evergreen foliage, 107–109
  flowering, 104–106
  lawn alternatives, 111–113
  for nooks and crannies, 113–114
  for seashore gardens, 114–116
  for shade, 116–118
  for slopes and erosion control, 118–119
  for wet conditions, 120–121
  See also specific ground covers
Groundsel-bush, 192
Gulftide Yaupon Holly, 177
GYMNOCLADUS dioicus (GMNDS), 235
GYPSOPHILA paniculata (GPSPN), 67
  'Bristol Fairy' (GPSPNBF), 67
  'Pink Fairy' (GPSPNPF), 67
GYPSOPHILA repens (GPSRP), 67

H

Hackberry, 228, 241
HAKONECHLOA macra 'Aureola', Golden Variegated Hakonechloa (HKNMCAR), 96
HALESIA carolina (HLSCR), 244–245, 247
HALESIA monticola (HLSMN), 247
  'Rosea' (HLSMNRR), 247
Hall's Honeysuckle, 134
HAMAMELIS (HMM), 146, 183, 191, 245
HAMAMELIS X *intermedia* (HMMIN), 146, 183, 191, 245
  'Arnold Promise' (HMMINAP), 146, 183, 191, 245
  'Diane' (HMMINDN), 146, 183, 191, 245
HAMAMELIS mollis (HMMML), 146, 183, 191, 245
HAMAMELIS virginiana (HMMVG), 146, 191
Handkerchief Tree, 210
Hanging Basket Begonia Group, 9
Hanson Lily, 19
Hard Maple, 220, 222, 229, 233
Hardy Begonia, 9
Hardy Fuchsia, 195

Hardy Geranium, 23, 39, 43
Hardy Rubber Tree, 234
Harison's Yellow, 76
Harris Azaleas, 151–152
  'Fascination' (RHDHBFS), 152
  'Parfait' (RHDHBPF), 152
Hartford Fern, 132–133
Hay-scented Fern, 110
Heart Vine, 136
Heather, 174
Heavenly Bamboo, 165, 174, 191
HEDERA (HDR), 107–108, 132, 139
HEDERA canariensis (HDRCN), 108, 132, 139
  'Variegata' (HDRCNVR), 108, 132, 139
HEDERA helix (HDRHL), 108, 111, 132, 139, 140
  'Argenteo-variegata' (HDRHLAG), 108, 132, 139
  'Aureo-variegata' (HDRHLAV), 108, 132, 139
  'Baltic' (HDRHLBL), 108, 132, 139
  'Bulgaria' (HDRHLBG), 108, 132, 139
  'Wilson' (HDRHLWL), 108, 132, 139
Hedge Maple, 238
HELENIUM autumnale (HLMAT), 32
  'Butterpat' (HLMATBB), 32
HELIANTHUS (HLH), 45
HELIANTHUS annuus (HLHAN), 45
HELIANTHUS salicifolius (HLHSL), 45
HELIANTHUS tuberosus (HLHTB), 45
HELICTOTRICHON sempervirens (HLRSM), 89
Heliotrope, 74
HELIOTROPIUM arborescens (HLTAR), 74
HELLEBORUS orientalis (HLLOR), 24–25
HEMEROCALLIS (HMR), 34–35
  'Bertie Ferris' (HMRHBBF), 34
  'Bountiful Valley' (HMRHBBV), 35
  'Double Decker' (HMRHBDD), 34
  early, 34
  early midseason, 34
  'Ed Murray' (HMRHBEM), 35
  'Fragrant Light' (HMRHBFL), 35
  'Mary Todd' (HMRHBMD), 34
  midseason, 35
  midseason late, 35
  'Netsuki' (HMRHBNN), 34
  'Ollalie Red' (HMRHBOR), 35
  'Pardon Me' (HMRHBPM), 35
  'Prairie Moonlight' (HMRHBPN), 35
  'Ruffled Apricot' (HMRHBRP), 34
  'Sombrero Way' (HMRHBSW), 35
  'Stella de Oro' (HMRHBSD), 34
HEMEROCALLIS fulva (HMRFL), 72
HEMEROCALLIS minor (HMRMN), 72
Hemlock, 186, 216–217, 232
  Canada, 186, 217, 232, 245–246
  Carolina, 186, 217, 233
  Mountain, 186
  Western, 186
Hen-and-chickens, 114
Henry Lilac, 212
Herbs, 64–83

  for baskets and pots, 80–81
  culinary, 68–71
  flowering, 66–68
  fragrant for drying, 71–74
  fragrant for garden, 74–75
  historic, 78–79
  for nooks and crannies, 81–83
  trees and shrubs for gardens, 64–65
  See also specific herbs
HESPERIS matronalis (HSRMT), 46
HEUCHERA sanguinea (HCHSN), 23
HIBISCUS (HBS), 158, 177, 183
HIBISCUS moscheutos (HBSMS), 27
HIBISCUS rosa-sinensis (HBSRS), 158, 177, 183
HIBISCUS schizopetalus (HBSSH), 158, 177
HIBISCUS syriacus (HBSSR), 158, 183
  'Diane' (HBSSRDD), 158, 183
  'Helene' (HBSSRHH), 158, 183
  'Minerva' (HBSSRMM), 158
Hick Yew, 224
Higan Cherry, 209
Highbush Blueberry, 65
Hills-of-snow, 192–193
Hinoki Cypress, 213
HOLBOELLIA grandiflora (HLBGR), 134
Holly, 163, 177, 181, 193, 245
  American, 242, 245
  Box, 79
  Burford Horned, 163
  Burford's Chinese, 163
  Chinese, 171, 181
  Dwarf Yaupon, 115
  English, 163, 181
  Gulftide Yaupon, 177
  Horned, 171, 181
  Japanese, 163
  Luster-leaf, 163, 177, 181, 245
  Sea, 27
  Spreading Japanese, 177
  White-edged English, 219–220
  Yaupon, 163, 177
Holly Barberry, 78
Holly Fern, 110
Holly Olive, 180
Honeysuckle, 134–135, 179
  Brown's, 134
  Cape, 128
  Coral, 135
  Cream, 134
  Everblooming, 135
  Hall's, 134
  Privet, 134, 135
  Trumpet, 135
  Winter, 179
Horned Holly, 171, 181
Horsemint, 72
Horsetail, 58
HOSTA (HST), 29–30
  'Honeybells' (HSTHBHN), 29, 117

HOSTA lancifolia var. *Albomarginata* (HSTLNAL), 29, 117
HOSTA montana 'Aureo-marginata' (HSTMNAR), 29, 117
HOSTA X *moseranum* (HSTMS), 119
HOSTA plantaginea 'Grandiflora' (HSTPLGR), 29–30, 117
HOSTA sieboldiana 'Frances Williams', 'Gold Circle', 'Gold Edge' (HSTSBFW), 30, 117
HOSTA tardiflora (HSTTR), 30, 117
HOSTA undulata (HSTUN), 30, 117
House Geranium, 39
Hyacinth, 6–7
Hyacinth Bean, 137
HYACINTHUS orientalis (HCNOR), 6–7
   'Blue Magic' (HCNORBM), 6
   'Carnegie' (HCNORCC), 6
Hybrid Perpetual Roses, 76–77
Hybrid Tea Roses, 159, 160
   'Double Delight' (RSAHBDD), 160
   'Fragrant Cloud' (RSAHBFC), 160
   'Miss All-American Beauty' (RSAHBML), 160
   'Olympiad' (RSAHBOP), 160
   'Pascali' (RSAHBAP), 160
   'Touch of Class' (RSAHBTC), 160
Hybrid Tuberous Begonia, 9
HYDRANGEA (HDN), 192–193
HYDRANGEA anomala subsp. *petiolaris* (HDNANPL), 139, 140–141, 192
HYDRANGEA arborescens (HDNAR), 192–193
   'Annabelle' (HDNARAN), 193
   'Grandiflora' (HDNARGR), 193
HYDRANGEA macrophylla (HDNMC), 171
   'Variegata' (HDNMCVV), 171
HYDRANGEA paniculata 'Grandiflora' (HDNPNGR), 193
HYDRANGEA quercifolia (HDNQR), 193
HYDROCLEYS nymphoides (HDCNM), 59
HYMENOCALLIS liriosme (HMNLR), 59
HYMENOCALLIS narcissiflora (HMNNR), 8–9
   'Sulphur Queen' (HMNNRSQ), 9
HYPERICUM (HPR), 119, 174–175
HYPERICUM buckleyi (HPRBC), 119
HYPERICUM calycinum (HPRCL), 119
HYPERICUM X *moseranum* (HPRMS), 175
HYPERICUM prolificum (HPRPR), 158–159, 175
   'Hidcote' (HPRPRHH), 159, 175

I

IBERIS sempervirens (IBRSM), 76, 113–114
   'Autumn Snow' (IBRSMAS), 114
   'Snowflake' (IBRSMSS), 114
Iceland Poppy, 27–28
Ilang–ilang, 226
ILEX (ILX), 163, 177, 181, 245
   'Apollo' (ILXHBAP), 181
   'Argenteo-marginata' (ILXAQAR), 245
   'Aureo-marginata' (ILXAQAM), 245
   'Edward J. Stevens' (ILXHBEJ), 163

   'John Morris' (ILXHBJM), 181
   'Lydia Morris' (ILXHBLM), 181
   'Nellie R. Stevens' (ILXHBNR), 163
   'Sparkleberry' (ILXHBSS), 181
ILEX aquifolium (ILXAQ), 163, 181, 219–220
   'Argenteo-marginata' (ILXAQAR), 163, 181, 219–220, 245
   'Aureo-marginata' (ILXAQAM), 163, 181, 245
ILEX cornuta (ILXCR), 163, 181
   'Burfordii' (ILXCRBF), 163, 181
   'China Boy' (ILXCRCB), 163, 181
   'China Girl' (ILXCRCG), 163, 181
   'O'Spring' (ILXCROS), 171
ILEX cornuta var. *rotunda* (ILXCRRN), 163
ILEX crenata (ILXCN), 163, 177
   'Convexa' (ILXCNCN), 163, 177
   'Glory' (ILXCNGL), 163, 177
   'Golden Heller' (ILXCNGH), 163, 177
   'Helleri' (ILXCNHL), 163, 177
   'Repandens' (ILXCNRR), 177
   'Tiny Tim' (ILXCNTT), 163, 177
ILEX glabra (ILXGL), 193
   'Compacta' (ILXGLCM), 193
   'Leucocarpa' (ILXGLLL), 193
   'Viridis' (ILXGLVV), 193
ILEX latifolia (ILXLT), 163, 177, 181, 245
   'Wirt L. Winn' (ILXLTWL), 245
ILEX opaca (ILXOP), 242, 245
   'Stewart's Silver Crown' (ILXOPSS), 242
ILEX verticillata (ILXVR), 198–199
   'Chrysocarpa' (ILXVRCC), 199
   'Nana' (ILXVRNN), 199
   'Winter Red' (ILXVRWR), 198–199
ILEX vomitoria (ILXVM), 163, 177
   'Emily Brunner' (ILXVMEB), 163, 177
   'Gulftide' (ILXVMGL), 163, 177
   'James Swann' (ILXVMJS), 163, 177
   'Schellings Dwarf' (ILXVMSD), 115
IMPATIENS (IMP), 38
IMPATIENS balsamina (IMPBL), 38
IMPATIENS wallerana (IMPWL), 38
IMPERATA cylindrica (IMRCL), 88, 89, 96
   'Red Baron' (IMRCLRB), 88, 89, 96
Imperial Japanese Morning-glory, 137
Indian Almond, 221
Indian Currant, 197
Indian Laurel, 214, 244
Inkberry, 193
IPOMOEA (IPM), 137
IPOMOEA alba (IPMAL), 137
IPOMOEA coccinea (IPMCC), 137
IPOMOEA hederacea (IPMHD), 137
   'Grandiflora' (IPMHDGG), 137
   'Superba' (IPMHDSS), 137
IPOMOEA nil (IPMNL), 137
IPOMOEA pes-caprae (IPMPS), 115
IPOMOEA purpurea (IPMPR), 137
IPOMOEA setosa (IPMST), 137
IPOMOEA tricolor (IPMTR), 137

IRIS (IRS), 15–17, 22
   'Baby Blessed' (IRSHBBB), 15
   Bearded, 15–16, 17
   Beardless, 16–17
   'Beverly Sills' (IRSHBBH), 15
   'Butter Pecan' (IRSHBBP), 15
   'Canary Prince' (IRSHBCP), 15
   'Corn Harvest' (IRSHBCH), 16
   'Denver Mint' (IRSHBDM), 16
   dwarf, 15
   'Immortality' (IRSHBIM), 15, 16
   intermediate, 15
   Japanese, 16, 58
   'Orange Parade' (IRSHBOP), 16
   'Pink Sleigh' (IRSHBPS), 16
   Siberian, 16, 17, 58
   Species, 16–17
   Tall, 15, 17
   'Wedgewood' (IRSHBWW), 7
   'White Swirl' (IRSHBWS), 16
IRIS cristata (IRSCR), 16
IRIS Dutch Hybrids, 7
IRIS X *germanica* (IRSGR), 15
IRIS kaempferi (IRSKM), 16
   'Grape Fizz' (IRSHBGF), 16
   'Marhigo' (IRSHBMM), 16
IRIS pseudacorus (IRSPS), 17, 58
IRIS sibirica (IRSSB), 16
   'Blue Burgee' (IRSHBBB), 16
   'Blue Pennant' (IRSHBBP), 16
   'Early Bluebird' (IRSHBEB), 16
   'Harpswell Haze' (IRSHBHH), 16
   'Outset' (IRSHBOT), 16
IRIS tectorum (IRSTC), 17
   'Alba' (IRSHBAL), 17
   'Rainbow Gold' (IRSHBRG), 17
   'Snow Cloud' (IRSHBSC), 17
   'Ultrapoise' (IRSHBUL), 17
Ironbark, 213
Italian Alder, 246
Italian Cypress, 213
Italian Jasmine, 134
Italian Woodbine, 134
ITEA virginica (ITAVR), 199
Ivy, 107–108, 132, 139
   Algerian, 108, 132, 139
   Boston, 132, 141
   English, 108, 111, 132, 139, 140,
   Mexican, 136
Ivy Geranium, 43
Ivy-leaved Morning-glory, 137

J

Jack-in-the-pulpit, 24
Jackman Clematis, 126

Jacobean Lily, 9
Japanese Anemone, 31
Japanese Apricot, 64
Japanese Barberry, 167, 182
Japanese Black Pine, 215, 243
Japanese Blood Grass, 88, 89, 96
Japanese Box, 162
Japanese Bunching Onion, 68
Japanese Cedar, 213
Japanese Clematis, 126
Japanese Clethra, 226–227, 237, 241, 247
Japanese Fir, 212
Japanese Flowering Cherry, 209
Japanese Flowering Crab Apple, 207, 232
Japanese Hibiscus, 158, 177
Japanese Holly, 163
Japanese Holly Fern, 110
Japanese Hydrangea Vine, 128
Japanese Iris, 16, 58
Japanese Maple, 172, 189, 217, 219, 222, 237
Japanese Mint, 69
Japanese Pachysandra, 117
Japanese Pagoda Tree, 235–236, 243
Japanese Photinia, 186
Japanese Pittosporum, 191
Japanese Primrose, 134
Japanese Privet, 171, 185
Japanese Quince, 146
Japanese Rose, 77, 114, 187, 188
Japanese Sedge, 95
Japanese Shield Fern, 110
Japanese Silver Grass, 93, 99
Japanese Silver Painted Fern, 110
Japanese Snowbell, 212, 245
Japanese Spirea, 105
Japanese Staunton Vine, 134
Japanese Stewartia, 212
Japanese Torreya, 216
Japanese Tree Lilac, 212
Japanese Umbrella Pine, 216
Japanese White Birch, 204
Japanese Wisteria, 129
Japanese Yellow Bells, 33
Japanese Zelkova, 221
Jasmine, 134
JASMINUM (JSM), 134
JASMINUM humile var. *glabrum* 'Revolutum' (JSMHMRR), 134
JASMINUM mesnyi (JSMMS), 134
JASMINUM officinale (JSMOF), 134
   'Grandiflorum' (JASOFGG), 134
JASMINUM polyanthum (JSMPL), 134
JASMINUM X *stephanense* (JSMST), 134
Jefferson, Roland, 209
Jerusalem Artichoke, 45
Jerusalem Pine, 215, 243
Jerusalem Sage, 25
Johnny-jump-up, 40
Jonquil, 12–13

Campernelle, 74–75
Judd Viburnum, 148
Jujube, 65
Juneberry, 228, 246
Juniper, 108, 163–164, 165, 169, 174, 193, 214, 223–224
  Blue Pfitzer, 108, 164
  Blue Rug Creeping, 108, 164
  Blue Sargent's, 169
  Chinese, 168, 214, 224
  Dwarf Japanese Garden, 108
  Dwarf Pfitzer, 108, 164
  Golden Pfitzer, 108, 164
  Pfitzer, 193
  Rocky Mountain, 214, 224
  Sargent's, 108, 163
  Savin, 108, 164
  Shore, 108, 163, 193
  Singleseed, 108, 164
  Waukegan, 108, 164
Juniper Hybrid, 108, 164
JUNIPERUS (JNP), 108, 163–164, 165, 169, 174, 193, 214, 223–224
JUNIPERUS chinensis (JNPCH), 168, 214, 224
  'Gold Coast' (JNPCHGC), 168
  'Kaizuka' (syn. 'Torulosa') (JNPCHKT), 214
  'Kaizuka variegated' (JNPCHKV), 214
  'Keteleeri' (JNPCHKT), 214
  'Mas' (JNPCHMM), 214, 224
  'Mountbatten' (JNPCHMT), 224
  'Old Gold' (JNPCHOG), 168
  'Spartan' (JNPCHSP), 214
JUNIPERUS chinensis var. *sargentii* (JNPCHST), 108, 163
  'Glauca' (JNPCSGL), 108, 163, 169
JUNIPERUS conferta (JNPCN), 108, 163, 193
  'Emerald Sea' (JNPCNES), 108, 163, 193
JUNIPERUS horizontalis 'Bar Harbor' (JNPHRBH), 108, 164, 169
  'Douglasii' (JNPHRDG), 108, 164
  'Wiltonii' (JNPHRWL), 108, 164
JUNIPERUS X *media* (JNPMD), 108, 164, 193
  'Pfitzerana Aurea' (JNPMDPR), 108, 164, 193
  'Pfitzerana Compacta' (JNPMDPC), 108, 164, 193
  'Pfitzerana Glauca' (JNPMDPG), 108, 164, 193
  'Sea Spray' (JNPMDSS), 108, 164, 193
JUNIPERUS procumbens 'Nana' (JNPPRNN), 108
JUNIPERUS sabina (JNPSB), 108, 164
  'Broadmoor' (JNPSBBR), 108, 164
  'Moor-Dense' (JNPSBMM), 108, 164
  'Skandia' (JNPSBSK), 108, 164
  'Tamariscifolia No Blight' (JNPSBTN), 108, 164
JUNIPERUS scopulorum (JNPSC), 214, 224
  'Blue Heaven' (JNPSCBH), 214, 224
  'Gray Gleam' (JNPSCGG), 214, 224
  'Skyrocket' (JNPSCSS), 214, 224
JUNIPERUS squamata (JNPSQ), 108, 164
  'Blue Star' (JNPSQBS), 108, 164
  'Variegata' (JNPSQVV), 108, 164
JUNIPERUS virginiana (JNPVR), 214, 224, 239
  'Burkii' (JNPVRBR), 214, 239

'Canaertii' (JNPVRCN), 214
'Glauca' (JNPVRGL), 224
'Hillii' (JNPVRHL), 224

K

KADSURA japonica (KDSJP), 135
Kaempferi Azaleas, 151
  'Louise' (RHDHBLL), 151
  'Willy' (RHDHBWW), 151
Kaffir Lily, 41
KALMIA (KLM), 164, 212
KALMIA angustifolia (KLMAN), 164
KALMIA latifolia (KLMLT), 156, 164
  'Elf' (KLMLTEL), 164
  'Ostbo Red' (KLMLTOD), 156
Kalo, 59
Katsura Tree, 230
Kaya, 216
Kehr Azaleas, 150
  'Anna Kehr' (RHDHBAK), 150
  'Kehr's White Rosebud' (RHDHBKH), 150
Kentucky Coffee Tree, 235
Kentucky Wisteria, 129
KERRIA japonica 'Pleniflora' (KRRJPPL), 188
Kew Broom, 115, 192
KIRINGESHOMA palmata (KRNPL), 33
Kiwi, 131
Klondyke Dwarfs, 38
Knap Hill and Exbury Azaleas, 152–153
  'George Reynolds' (RHDHBGY), 153
  'Gibraltar' (RHDHBGB), 153
KNIPHOFIA tucki (KNPTC), 46
KNIPHOFIA uvaria (KNPUV), 46
KOELREUTERIA paniculata (KLRPN), 210–211
KOLKWITZIA amabilis (KLKAM), 183
Korean Barberry, 173, 182
Kurume Azaleas, 150
  'Coral Bells' (RHDHBOB), 150
  'Pink Pearl' (RHDHBIP), 150
  'Snow' (RHDHBSO), 150

L

LABURNUM X *watereri* 'Vossil' (LBRWTVV), 211, 237
Lace-bark Pine, 204, 215
Lady Fern, 110
Lady Palm, 191
Lady's Mantle, 76
Lady Tulip, 21–22
LAGERSTROEMIA indica (LGRIN), 159, 211
  'Acoma' (LGRINAC), 159
  'Apalachee' (LGRHBAP), 159, 211
  'Biloxi' (LGRHBBB), 211

'Catawba' (LGRINCC), 159
'Comanche' (LGRHBCC), 211
'Hopi' (LGRINHH), 159
'Lipan' (LGRHBLL), 211
'Miami' (LGRHBMI), 211
'Muskogee' (LGRHBMS), 211
'Natchez' (LGRHBNT), 211
'Osage' (LGRHBOS), 211
'Pecos' (LGRINPC), 159
'Potomac' (LGRINPP), 159
'Powhatan' (LGRINPW), 159
'Scarlett O'Hara' (LGRINSH), 159
'Seminole' (LGRINSS), 159
'Sioux' (LGRHBSS), 211
'Tuscarora' (LGRINTT), 159
'Tuskegee' (LGRHBTT), 211
'Wichita' (LGRHBWW), 211
'Yuma' (LGRHBYM), 211
'Zuni' (LGRINZZ), 159
Lamb's-ears, 16, 107
LAMIUM maculatum (LMMMC), 121
    'Beacon Silver' (LMMMCBS), 121
    'Variegatum' (LMMMCVR), 121
LANTANA (LTN), 42, 105
LANTANA camara (LTNCA), 43
LANTANA montevidensis (LTNMN), 43, 105
LANTANA ovatifolia var. *reclinata* (LNTOVRC), 105
LAPAGERIA rosea (LPGRS), 132, 139
    'Albiflora' (LPGRSAL), 132
LARDIZSABALA biternata (LRZBT), 134
Large Climbing Roses, 129, 130–131
    'America' (RSAHBAR), 130
    'Blaze' (RSAHBBZ), 130–131
    'Climbing Peace' (RSAHBIE), 129
    'Dortmund' (RSAHBDM), 131
    'Golden Showers' (RSAHBGH), 131
    'New Dawn' (RSAHBND), 131
    'Viking Queen' (RSAHBVQ), 131
Larkspur, 44
LATHYRUS odoratus (LTSOD), 137
Laurel, 245, 247
LAURUS nobilis (LRSNB), 64
Lavalle Hawthorn, 241–242
LAVANDULA (LVN), 74
LAVANDULA angustifolia (LVNAN), 74
    'Hidcote' (LVNANHH), 74
LAVANDULA dentata (LVNDN), 74
LAVANDULA stoechas subsp. *pedunculata* (LVNST), 74
Lavender, 74
Lavender Cotton, 73, 175, 192
Leatherleaf Fern, 111
Leatherleaf Mahonia, 165
Leatherleaf Rhododendron, 155
Leather Wood Fern, 110
LEIOPHYLLUM buxifolium (LPHBX), 115–116
Lemon, 80, 237
Lemon Balm, 72
Lemon Geranium, 75

Lemongrass, 70
Lemon Mint, 69
Lemon-scented Gum, 74, 213
Lemon Thyme, 83
Lemon Verbena, 72
Lenten Rose, 24–25
Leopard Plant, 33
LEUCOJUM aestivum (LCJAS), 7
    'Gravetye Giant' (LCJAEGG), 7
LEUCOTHOE fontanesiana (LCTFN), 195
LEUCOTHOE fontanesiana var. *nana* (LCTFNNN), 195
LEVISTICUM officinale (LVTOF), 71
Leyland Cypress, 242
Liang-ilang, 226
LIATRIS (LTR), 32
LIATRIS scariosa (LTRSC), 32
    'September Glory' (LTRSCSG), 32
LIATRIS spicata 'Kobold' (LTRSPKK), 32
LIGULARIA (LGL), 33
LIGULARIA dentata 'Desdemona' (LGLDNDD), 33
LIGULARIA stenocephala (LGLST), 33
    'The Rocket' (LGLSTTR), 33
LIGULARIA tussilaginea 'Auero-maculata' (LGHLTSAR), 33
LIGUSTRUM (LGS), 183–184, 185
LIGUSTRUM amurense (LGSAM), 185
LIGUSTRUM X *ibolium* (LGSIB), 184
    'Variegatum' (LGSIBVR), 184
LIGUSTRUM japonicum 'Silver Star' (LGSJPSS), 171, 185
LIGUSTRUM lucidum (LGSLC), 185
LIGUSTRUM obtusifolium (LGSOB), 184
LIGUSTRUM obtusifolium var. *regelianum* (LGSOBRL), 184
LIGUSTRUM ovalifolium (LGSOV), 185
LIGUSTRUM X *vicaryi* (LGSVC), 168, 185, 188
    'Storzinger Strain' (LGSVCSS), 168, 185, 188
Lilac, 156–157, 212
LILIUM (LLM), 17–19
    Asiatic Hybrids, 17–18
    Aurelian Hybrids, 18
    'Black Beauty' (LLMHBBB), 18
    'Black Dragon' (LLMHBBD), 18
    'Burgundy Strain' (LLMHBBS), 18
    'Gold Eagle' (LLMHBGG), 18
    'Gold Lode' (LLMHBGL), 18
    'Imperial Silver' (LLMHBIS), 18
    'Jamboree' (LLMHBJJ), 18
    Oriental Hybrids, 18
    'Showtime' (LLMHBST), 18
    Species, 18–19
    'Stargazer' (LLMHBST), 18
    'Tiger Babies' (LLMHBTB), 18
    Trumpet Hybrids, 18
    'White Henryi' (LLMHBWH), 18
LILIUM auratum var. *platyphyllum* (LLMARPL), 18
LILIUM canadense 'Coccineum' (LLMCDCC), 18
LILIUM candidum (LLMCD), 18, 72
    'Cascade' (LLMCDCS), 18
LILIUM hansonii (LLMHN), 19
LILIUM lancifolium (LLMLN), 19

LILIUM regale (LLMRG), 19
Lily, 17–19, 22, 41
  Aurelian, 8, 47
  Autumn Zephyr, 11, 112
  Aztec, 9
  Blackberry, 66
  Bog, 59
  Canada, 18
  Crinum, 8
  Cuban Zephyr, 11, 112
  Fairy, 11, 112
  Gold-band, 18
  Hanson, 19
  Jacobean, 9
  Kaffir, 41
  Madonna, 18, 72
  Magic, 9–10
  Rain, 11, 112
  Regal, 19
  Resurrection, 9–10, 117
  Scarlet Kaffir, 41
  Spider, 8, 59
  Sword, 8
  Tiger, 19
  Water, 54–56
  Wild Yellow, 18
  Zephyr, 11, 112
Lily Leek, 47
Lily Magnolia, 156
Lily-of-the-field, 10–11
Lily-of-the-Nile, 41
Lily-of-the-valley, 116–117
Lily-of-the-valley Bush, 148, 165
Lilyturf, 109, 111–112
Linden, 236
LINDERA benzoin (LNDBN), 199
Lingaro, 169, 197
Linwood Azaleas, 151
  'Garden State Garnet' (RHDHBAN), 151
  'Hardy Gardenia' (RHDHBHG), 151
Lippia citriodora (LPPCT), 72
Lippia graveolens (LPPGR), 70
Lipstick Tulip, 21–22
LIQUIDAMBAR styraciflua (LQDST), 221, 247
  'Aurea' (LQDSTAR), 221, 247
  'Matthew's Gold' (LQDSTMG), 221, 247
  'Moraine' (LQDSTMM), 221, 247
  'Variegata' (LQDSTVV), 221, 247
LIRIODENDRON tulipifera (LRDTL), 220, 222, 231
  'Aurea-marginatum' (LRDTLAM), 220
  'Compactum' (LRDTLCC), 222
LIRIOPE (LRP), 111–112
LIRIOPE platyphylla (LRPPL), 109, 111–112
  'Christmas Tree' (LRPPLCT), 112
  'Variegata' (LRPPLVV), 111
LIRIOPE spicata (LRPSP), 112
Live Oak, 232
LOBELIA (LBL), 30
LOBELIA cardinalis (LBLCR), 30

LOBELIA erinus (LBLER), 30
LOBELIA siphilitica (LBLSP), 30
LOBULARIA maritima (LBAMR), 48, 113
Lombardy Poplar, 240
London Plane, 231, 240, 243, 248
Long-spur Epimedium, 113
LONICERA (LNC), 134–135, 179
LONICERA X brownii (LNCBR), 134
  'Dropmore Scarlet' (LNCBRDS), 134
LONICERA caprifolium (LNCCP), 134
LONICERA etrusca 'Superba' (LNCETSS), 134
LONICERA fragrantissima (LNCFR), 179
LONICERA X heckrottii (LNCHC), 135
Lonicera japonica 'Halliana', (LNCJPHL), 134
LONICERA periclymenum (LNCPR), 135
  'Graham Thomas' (LNCPRGT), 135
LONICERA pileata (LNCPL), 134, 135
LONICERA sempervirens (LNCSM), 135
  'Magnifica' (LNCSMMG), 135
  'Sulfurea' (LNCSMSS), 135
  'Superba' (LNCSMSP), 135
LONICERA tatarica (LNCTT), 179
  'Arnold Red' (LNCTTAR), 179
  'Grandiflora' (LNCTTGG), 179
  'Morden Orange' (LNCTTMR), 179
  'Virginalis' (LNCTTVV), 179
Lotus, 57
Lovage, 71
Lowbush Blueberry, 65
Luster-leaf Holly, 163, 177, 181, 245
LUZULA nivea (LZLNV), 96
LYCORIS (LYC), 117
LYCORIS squamigera (LYCSQ), 9–10, 30
LYGODIUM palmatum (LGDPL), 132–133
LYGODIUM scandens (LGDSC), 132
LYSIMACHIA (LSM), 112
LYSIMACHIA nummularia (LSMNM), 112
  'Aurea' (LSMNMAR), 112
LYSIMACHIA punctata (LSMPN), 112

M

MACFADYENA unguis-cati (MCFUG), 133
Macranthum Azalea, 152
Madagascar Rubber Vine, 128
Madonna Lily, 18, 72
Madrone, 204, 212
Magic Lily, 9–10, 117
MAGNOLIA (MGNHB), 146–148, 207, 211–212, 214, 227
  'Galaxy' (MGNHBGL), 207
  'Spectrum' (MGNHBSP), 207
  'Timeless Beauty' (MGNHBTM), 211
MAGNOLIA acuminata (MGNAC), 214
MAGNOLIA grandiflora (MGNGR), 211, 214, 227
  'Little Gem' (MGNGRLC), 211, 214
  'Majestic Beauty' (MGNGRMT), 211, 214, 227
  'St. Mary's' (MGNGRSY), 211, 214

'Victoria' (MGNGRVC), 211, 214
MAGNOLIA kobus (MGNKB), 147
MAGNOLIA liliiflora (MGNLL), 156
   'Ann' (MGNLLAN), 156
   'Betty' (MGNLLBB), 156
   'Jane' (MGNLLJJ), 156
   'Jody' (MGNLLJD), 156
MAGNOLIA X *loebneri* 'Merrill' (MGNLBMR), 147
MAGNOLIA X *soulangeana* (MGNSL), 207
   'Lennei' (MGNSLLN), 207
   'Lennei Alba' (MGNSLLL), 207
MAGNOLIA stellata (MGNST), 146, 147
   'Betty' (MGNSTBB), 148
   'Centennial' (MGNSTCC), 147
   'Dandy' (MGNSTDD), 148
   'June' (MGNSTJJ), 148
   'Rosea' (MGNSTRA), 147
   'Royal Star' (MGNSTRS), 147
   'Susan' (MGNSTSS), 148
MAGNOLIA virginiana (MGNVR), 64, 211–212, 214, 227, 245, 247
MAHONIA (MHN), 164–165
MAHONIA aquifolium (MHNAQ), 78, 165
   'Atropurpureum' (MHNAQAT), 78
   'Charity' (MHNAQCC), 78
MAHONIA bealei (MHNBL), 165
MAHONIA repens (MHNRP), 78, 165
Maiden Grass, 93
Maidenhair Fern, 109–110
Maidenhair Tree, 222, 223, 231, 235
Maire's Fescue, 89
MALUS (MLS), 207, 218, 232, 237
   'Candied Apple' (MLSHBCP), 207
   'Coralburst' (MLSHBCL), 237
   'Dolgo' (MLSHBDD), 207
   'Doubloons' (MLSHBDB), 237
   'Jewelberry' (MLSHBJJ), 237
   'Louisa' (MLSHBLL), 207, 237
   'Mary Potter' (MLSHBMP), 237
   'Narragansett' (MLSHBNN), 207
   'Parrsi', Pink Princess (MLSHBPP), 207–208, 232, 237
   'Prairifire' (MLSHBPR), 218
   'Red Jade' (MLSHBRJ), 208
   'Strawberry Parfait' (MLSHBSP), 218
   'White Cascade' (MLSHBWC), 208
MALUS baccata (MLSBC), 207, 239
   'Jackii' (MLSBCJC), 207, 239
MALUS floribunda (MLSFL), 207, 232
MALUS hupehensis (MLSHP), 207
MALUS sargentii (MLSSR), 148, 237
MALUS sieboldi 'Fuji' (MLSSDFF), 208
Manchurian Lilac, 157
Mandarin Orange, 237
MANDEVILLA splendens (MNDSP), 133
Manna Ash, 230
Maple, 172, 189–190, 204, 217, 219, 220, 222, 223, 229, 233, 238
   Amur, 220, 238
   Big-leaf, 222, 229

Coral Bark, 172, 189–190, 204
David, 204
Hard, 220, 222, 229, 233
Hedge, 238
Japanese, 172, 189, 217, 219, 222, 237
Norway, 217, 219, 222, 229, 233, 238
Oregon, 222, 229
Paperbark, 204
Planetree, 217, 241
Red, 220, 223, 229, 233
River, 217
Rock, 220, 222, 229, 233
Silver, 217
Striped, 204
Sugar, 220, 222, 229, 233
Swamp, 220, 223, 229, 233
Sycamore, 217, 241
Tatarian, 220
Threadleaf Japanese, 167, 189
Trident, 204, 233
Vine, 220
Marginal Shield Fern, 110
Marigold, 15, 39–40
   African, 39–40
   French, 40
   Signet, 40
Marjoram, 70
MARSILEA mutica (MRLMT), 58
MATRICARIA recutita (MTCRC), 72, 82
MATTEUCCIA pensylvanica (MTAPN), 78–79
MATTEUCCIA struthiopteris (MTAST), 79
Maurandya, 136
Meadow Saffron, 10, 66
Mealycup Sage, 32
Medlar, 64
MELISSA officinalis (MLEOF), 72
Memorial Rose, 119
MENISPERMUM canadense (MNPCN), 139
MENTHA arvensis var. *piperescens* (MNTARPP), 69
MENTHA X *piperita* (MNTPP), 69
MENTHA X *piperita* var. *citrata* (MNTPPCT), 69
MENTHA requienii (MNTRQ), 69
MENTHA spicata (MNTSP), 69
MENTHA suaveolens 'Variegata' (MNTSVVV), 69
MERTENSIA virginica (MRTVR), 25
MESPILUS germanica (MSPGR), 64
METASEQUOIA glyptostroboides (MTSGL), 247
Mexican Bluebell, 119
Mexican Ivy, 136
Mexican Oregano, 70
Michaelmas Daisy, 31
MICHELIA figo (syn. *fuscata*) (MCHFG), 179
MICHELIA fuscata. See *MICHELIA figo*
MICROBIOTA decussata (MCRDC), 108–109
Mignonette, 49
Milfoil, 26
Milkweed, 44
Mimosa, 238
Miniature Climbing Roses, 129, 130

'Hi-Ho' (RSAHBHI), 130
'Little Girl' (RSAHBLG), 130
Miniature Roses, 186, 187
  'Centerpiece' (RSAHBEE), 187
  'Cupcake' (RSAHBCK), 187
  'Lavender Jewel' (RSAHBLW), 187
  'Rise 'N Shine' (RSAHBRI), 187
  'Snow Bride' (RSAHBOB), 187
  'Starina' (RSAHBAA), 187
Mint, 69
  Apple, 69
  Bergamot, 69
  Creeping, 69
  Japanese, 69
  Lemon, 69
MISCANTHUS (MSC), 92–93, 99
MISCANTHUS floridulus (MSCFL), 92
MISCANTHUS sacchariflorus (MSCSC), 90
MISCANTHUS sinensis (MSCSN), 93
  'Gracillimus' (MSCSNGR), 93
  'Purpurascens' (MSCSNPP), 93
  'Variegatus' (MSCSNVR), 99
  'Yaku Jima' (MSCSNYJ), 93
  'Zebrinus' (MSCSNZZ), 99
Mock Orange, 180, 227
MOLINIA caerulea subsp. *arundinacea* (MLNCRAR), 97
  'Karl Foerster' (MLNCLKF), 97
  'Transparent' (MLNCLTT), 97
Mollis Azaleas, 152
  'Koeningin Emma' (RHDHBKA), 152
  'Koster's Yellow' (RHDHBKO), 152
Momi Fir, 212
MOMORDICA (MMR), 137
MOMORDICA balsamina (MMRBL), 137
MOMORDICA charantia (MMRCH), 137
MONARDA didyma (MNRDD), 72–73
  'Croftway Pink' (MNRDDCP), 72
MONARDA punctata (MNRPN), 72
Mondo Grass, 109
Monkey Plant, 121
MONSTERA deliciosa (MNSDL), 133
Monterey Cypress, 213
Moonflower, 137
Moonseed, 139
Moosewood, 204
Morning-glory, 137
  Beach, 115
  Brazilian, 137
  Imperial Japanese, 137
  Ivy-leaved, 137
  Red, 137
  Silver, 138
  White Edge, 137
Morrison, B.Y., 91
MORUS rubra (MRSRB), 228, 242
Moses-on-a-raft, 119
Mosquito Grass, 88
Moss Phlox, 105

Moss Pink, 28, 105, 113
Moss Rose, 76
Mossycup Oak, 231, 235
Mountain Andromeda, 148, 165
Mountain Camellia, 212
Mountain Dogwood, 207
Mountain Hemlock, 186
Mountain Laurel, 156, 164
Mountain Lover, 106
Mountain Rock Cress, 113
MUEHLENBECKIA complexa (MHLCM), 141
Mugho Pine, 165–166, 188
Mugwort, 114–115
Mullein, 46
Mum, 31–32
MURRAYA paniculata (MRRPN), 227
MUSCARI azureum (MSRAZ), 7
  'Album' (MSRAZAL), 7
  'Heavenly Blue' (MSRAZHB), 7
MYOPORUM X 'Pacifica' (MPRHBPC), 116
MYOSOTIS (MST), 46
MYOSOTIS alpestris (MSTAL), 46
  'Victoria' (MSTALVV), 46
MYOSOTIS scorpioides var. *semperflorens* (MSTSCSM), 46
MYRICA asplenifolia, 118, 196
MYRICA pensylvanica (MRCPN), 64, 193
Myrtle, 80, 178
MYRTUS communis (MRUCM), 80, 178

N

Nagami Kumquat, 237
NANDINA domestica (NNDDM), 165, 174, 191
  'Fire Power' (NNDHBFP), 165, 174, 191
  'Harbor Dwarf' (NNDHBHD), 165, 174, 191
  'Woods Dwarf' (NNDHBWD), 165, 174, 191
Narcissus, 12–13
NARCISSUS (NRC), 12–15, 74–75
  'Actaea' (NRCHBAC), 14
  'Amor' (NRCHBAM), 13
  'April Tears' (NRCHBAT), 14
  'Baby Moon' (NRCHBBM), 14
  'Baccarat' (NRCHBBB), 15
  'Binkie' (NRCHBBN), 13
  'Cantabile' (NRCHBCC), 15
  'Ceylon' (NRCHBCL), 13
  'Cragford' (NRCHBCR), 14
  Cyclamineus Hybrids, 14
  Doubles, 13
  'February Gold' (NRCHBFG), 14
  'Foresight' (NRCHBFF), 13
  'Geranium' (NRCHBGG), 14
  'Hawera' (NRCHBHH), 14
  'Ice Follies' (NRCHBIF), 13
  'Jack Snipe' (NRCHBJS), 14
  Jonquilla hybrids, 14

'Kinglet' (NRCHBKK), 14
Large Cups, 13
'Mount Hood' (NRCHBMH), 13
'Orangery' (NRCHBOR), 15
'Peeping Tom' (NRCHBPT), 14
Poeticus Hybrids, 14–15
'Salome' (NRCHBSS), 13
'Silver Salver' (NRCHBSL), 13
'Sir Winston Churchill' (NRCHBSW), 13
Small Cups, 13
Species, 15
'Spellbinder' (NRCHBSP), 13
Split Coronas, 15
'Sunapee' (NRCHBSN), 13
'Tahiti' (NRCHBTT), 13
Tazettas, 14
'Tete-a-tete' (NRCHBTE), 14
'Thalia' (NRCHBTH), 14
'Trevithian' (NRCHBTR), 14
Triandrus hybrids, 13–14
Trumpets, 13
'Unsurpassable' (NRCHBUN), 13
'White Lion' (NRCHBWL), 13
NARCISSUS asturiensis (NRCAS), 12, 15
NARCISSUS X *odorus* (NRCOD), 74–75
NARCISSUS poeticus (NRCPT), 74
NARCISSUS poeticus var. *recurvus* (NRCPTRC), 15
Narrow-leaved Cattail, 58
Narrow-leaved Hosta, 29, 117
Nasturtium, 71
NELUMBO nucifera 'Alba Grandiflora' (NLMNCAG), 57
   'Momo Botan Minima' (NLMNCMB), 57
   'Mrs. Perry D. Slocum' (NLMHBMP), 57
NEPHROLEPIS (NPH), 111
NERIUM oleander (NRMOL), 81, 185, 191
New England Aster, 31
New York Aster, 31
New York Fern, 111
New Zealand Flax, 167
NICOTIANA alata (NCTAL), 38–39
   'Nikki White' (NCTALNW), 39
Nikko Maple, 233
Noisette Rose, 77
Nootka Cypress, 224–225, 234
Northern Oats, 95
North Tisbury Azaleas, 150–151
   'Alexander' (RHDHBAX), 150–151
   'Marilee' (RHDHBMA), 151
Norway Maple, 217, 219, 222, 229, 233, 238
Norway Spruce, 214, 239
Nutmeg Pelargonium, 75
NYMPHAEA (NMH), 54–56
   'Attraction' (NMHHBAT), 54
   'Blue Beauty' (NMHHBBB), 56
   'Chromatella' (NMHHBCC), 55
   'Comanche' (NMHHBCM), 55
   Day Bloomers, 56
   'Emily Grant Hutchings' (NMHHBEG), 56

   'Escarboucle' (NMHHBES), 54
   'Fabiola' (NMHHBFF), 54
   'General Pershing' (NMHHBGP), 56
   'Gladstone' (NMHHBGG), 55
   'Hollandia' (NMHHBHH), 55
   'James Brydon' (NMHHBJB), 54
   'Marian Strawn' (NMHHBMS), 56
   Night Bloomers, 56
   'Panama Pacific' (NMHHBPP), 56
   'Pink Sensation' (NMHHBPS), 54
   Pink Water Lilies, 54–55
   'Red Flare' (NMHHBRF), 56
   Red Water Lilies, 54
   'Sioux' (NMHHBSS), 55
   'Sunrise' (NMHHBSN), 55
   'Texas Shell Pink' (NMHHBTS), 56
   'Virginalis' (NMHHBVV), 55
   White Water Lilies, 55
   'Yellow Dazzler' (NMHHBYD), 56
   Yellow Water Lilies, 55
NYMPHOIDES (NMP), 58
NYMPHOIDES cristatum (NMPCR), 58
NYMPHOIDES geminata (NMPGM), 58
NYMPHOIDES peltata (NMPPL), 58
NYSSA sylvatica (NSSSL), 242–243

O

Oak, 231–232, 235
   English, 231
   Fastigiate English, 224
   Live, 232
   Mossycup, 231, 235
   Pin, 231, 235
   Red, 231–232, 235
   Sawtooth, 231
   Swamp White, 231
   White, 231
   Willow, 231
Oak-leaved Hydrangea, 193
Occidentale Azaleas, 152
   'Foggy Dew' (RHDHBFE), 152
   'Irene Koster' (RHDHBIK), 152
OCIMUM basilicum 'Spicy Globe' (OCMBS), 69
October Daphne, 33, 82
OENOTHERA tetragona 'Fireworks' (ONTTTFF), 23
   'Illuminations' (ONTTTIL), 23
Old Garden Roses, 75–77, 130
Old-man's-beard, 226, 244, 247
Oleander, 81, 185, 191
Olive-green Sheep's Fescue, 89
Onion, 41, 47, 68
OPHIOPOGON japonicus (OPHJP), 109
Orange Jasmine, 227
Orchid-flowering Tulip, 20
Oregano, 70

Oregon Grape, 78, 164–165
Oregon Maple, 222, 229
Oregon Myrtle, 64
Oriental Arborvitae, 166, 215, 216
Oriental Bittersweet, 135
Oriental Fountain Grass, 98
Oriental Poppy, 28
Oriental Spruce, 215
ORIGANUM (ORG), 69–70
ORIGANUM majorana (ORGMJ), 70
ORIGANUM vulgare (ORGVL), 70
Ornamental Grasses, 88–89
  for color and texture, 88–90
  for naturalizing and slopes, 90–91
  for rapid growth and summer screening, 91–93
  for seashore gardens, 93–94
  for shade, 94–97
  for sunny, dry, urban areas, 97–98
  for wet conditions, 98–99
  See also specific grasses
Ornamental Onion, 47
ORONTIUM aquaticum (ORTAQ), 58
OSMANTHUS (OSM), 179–180
OSMANTHUS X fortunei (OSMFT), 180
OSMANTHUS fragrans (OSMFR), 180
OSMANTHUS heterophyllus (OSMHT), 180
  'Aureo-marginatus' (OSMHTAR), 180
  'Aureus' (OSMHTAS), 180
  'Gulftide' (OSMHTGL), 180
  'Variegatus' (OSMHTVG), 180
OSMUNDA cinnamomea (OSNCN), 111
Ostrich Fern, 78–79
Otaheite Orange, 80
OXYDENDRUM arboreum (OXDAR), 221, 232, 245
Oyster Plant, 119

P

PACHYSANDRA (PCH), 117
PACHYSANDRA procumbens (PCHPR), 117
PACHYSANDRA terminalis (PCHTR), 117
  'Green Carpet' (PCHTRGC), 117
  'Variegata' (PCHTRVR), 117
Pacific Dogwood, 207
Pacific Madrone, 204, 212
PAEONIA (PNA), 35–36
  'Age of Gold' (PNAHBAF), 36
  'Alice Harding' (PNAHBAH), 35
  'Bowl of Cream' (PNAHBBF), 35
  Chinese, 36
  'Dinner Plate' (PNAHBDP), 36
  Double, 35–36
  European, 36
  'Felix Supreme' (PNAHBFS), 36
  'Flame' (PNAHBFF), 36
  'Godaishu' (PNAHBGG), 36
  'Hatsi Garashu' (PNAHBHG), 36
  Herbaceous, 35–36
  Japanese, 36
  'Karl Rosenfield' (PNAHBKR), 36
  'Krinkled White' (PNAHBKW), 36
  'Midnight Sun' (PNAHBMS), 36
  'Rare China' (PNAHBRC), 36
  'Renkaku' (PNAHBRR), 36
  'Rimpon' (PNAHBRM), 36
  Saunders Hybrids, 36
  Single, 36
  'Thunderbolt' (PNAHBTT), 36
  tree, 36
PAEONIA tenuifolia (PNATN), 36
Painted Gaillardia, 44
Painted Nettle, 42
Palm Sedge Grass, 95
Panama Orange, 80
Paniculata. See CLEMATIS maximowicziana
PANICUM virgatum (PNMVR), 97, 99
  'Haense Herms' (PNMVRHH), 97
Pansy, 40
PAPAVER (PPV), 27–28
PAPAVER nudicaule (PPVND), 27–28
PAPAVER orientale (PPVOR), 28
  'Maya' (PPVORMM), 28
  'Minicap' (PPVORMN), 28
  'Tara' (PPVORTT), 28
Paperbark Maple, 204
Paper Birch, 204
Paper Mulberry, 234
PARROTIA persica (PRRPR), 223
  'Pendula' (PRRPRPP), 223
Parsley, 70
PARTHENOCISSUS (PRT), 131–132, 141
PARTHENOCISSUS henryana (PRTHN), 132
PARTHENOCISSUS quinquefolia (PRTQN), 132, 141
PARTHENOCISSUS tricuspidata (PRTTR), 132, 141
  'Lowii' (PRTTRLW), 132, 141
  'Veitchii' (PRTRVT), 132, 141
PASSIFLORA (PSS), 128
PASSIFLORA caerula (PSSCR), 128
PASSIFLORA coccinea (PSSCC), 128
PASSIFLORA edulis (PSSED), 128
Passionflower, 128
Passion Fruit, 128
PAXISTIMA canbyi (PXSCN), 106
Peacock Moss, 121
Peacock Orchid, 8
Peegee Hydrangea, 193
PELARGONIUM (PLI), 23, 75
PELARGONIUM crispum (PLICR), 75
PELARGONIUM graveolens (PLIGR), 75
PELARGONIUM X hortorum (PLIHR), 23, 39
PELARGONIUM odoratissimum (PLIOD), 75
PELARGONIUM peltatum (PLIPL), 43
PELARGONIUM tomentosum (PLITM), 75
Pennington Azaleas, 150

'Beth Bullard' (RHDHBEU), 150
'Pennington White' (RHDHBEW), 150
PENNISETUM alopecuroides (PNNAL), 89
PENNISETUM incomptum (PNNIN), 90–91
PENNISETUM orientale (PNNOR), 98
PENNISETUM setaceum (PNNST), 89
Peony, 15, 16, 22, 35–36
Pepperidge, 242–243
Peppermint Geranium, 75
Pepper Vine, 131
Perennial Phlox, 28
PERIPLOCA graeca (PROGR), 141
Periwinkle, 80, 109
PERNETTYA mucronata (PRAMC), 199
PEROVSKIA atriplicifolia (PRVAT), 67, 89
Persian Onion, 47
Persian Parrotia, 223
Peruvian Daffodil, 8–9
PETROSELINUM crispum (PTSCR), 70
PETUNIA X *hybrida* (PTAHB), 39
Pfitzer Juniper, 193
PHASEOLUS coccineus (PHUCC), 137
Pheasant's eye, 15, 74
PHELLODENDRON amurense (PHLAM), 232
PHILADELPHUS (PHD), 180
  'Miniature Snowflake' (PHDHBMS), 180
  'Minnesota Snowflake' (PHDHBMN), 180
PHILADELPHUS X *limonei* (PHDLM), 180
  'Avalanche' (PHDHBAV), 180
  'Frosty Morn' (PHDHBFM), 180
  'Innocence' (PHDHBIN), 180
PHILADELPHUS X *virginalis* (PHDVR), 180
  'Bouquet Blanc' (PHDVRBB), 180
  'Glacier' (PHDVRGG), 180
Philodendron pertusum, 133
Phlox, 28
  Garden, 28
  Moss, 105
  Perennial, 28
PHLOX paniculata 'Mount Fujiyama' (PHXPNMF), 28
PHLOX subulata (PHXSB), 23, 28, 105, 113
  'Chattahoochee' (PHXHBCC), 105
  'Millstream Coraleye' (PHXSBMC), 23
PHORMIUM tenax (PHRTN), 167
PHOTINIA (PHT), 185–186
PHOTINIA X *fraseri* (PHTFR), 186
  'Indian Princess' (PHTFRIP), 186
PHOTINIA glabra (PHTGL), 186
PHRAGMITES australis (PHGAS), 94
PHYSOCARPUS opulifolius 'Dart's Gold' (PHSOPDL), 168
PICEA (PCA), 165, 214, 239
PICEA abies (PCAAB), 165, 214, 239
  'Nidiformis' (PCAABND), 165, 214
PICEA glauca (PCAGL), 165, 214
  'Conica' (PCAGLCN), 165, 214
PICEA omorika (PCAOM), 214
  'Pendula' (PCAOMPN), 214
PICEA orientalis (PCAOR), 215

'Gracilis' (PCAORGG), 215
PICEA pungens (PCAPN), 165, 169, 215, 239
  'Fat Albert' (PCAPNFL), 165, 169
  'Glauca' (PCAPNGL), 215, 239
  'Hoopsii' (PCAPNHP), 215, 239
  'Moerheimii' (PCAPNMR), 215, 239
  'R.H. Montgomery' (PCAPNRH), 165, 169
Pickerel Rush, 58
Pickerel Weed, 58
PIERIS (PRS), 148, 165
PIERIS floribunda (PRSFL), 148, 165
PIERIS japonica (PRSJP), 148, 165
  'Red Mill' (PRSJPRM), 148, 165
  'Variegata' (PRSJPVG), 165, 171
PILEA microphylla (PLAMC), 106–107
PILEOSTEGIA viburnoides (PLEVB), 133
Pin Cherry, 228
Pincushion Flower, 46
Pine, 215, 224, 243
  Aleppo, 215, 243
  Austrian, 215, 243, 247
  Fastigiate White, 224
  Japanese Black, 215, 243
  Japanese Umbrella, 216
  Jerusalem, 215, 243
  Lace-bark, 204, 215
  Mugho, 165–166, 188
  Ponderosa, 243
  Swiss Stone, 215
  Umbrella, 216
  Weeping Fern, 191
Pineapple Guava, 169
Pineapple Sage, 32
Pink Allamanda, 133
Pink Idaho Locust, 235
Pink Jasmine, 134
Pink Princess, 207–208
Pink Princess Crab Apple, 232
Pink-shell Azalea, 153
Pink Trumpet Tree, 209, 212
Pin Oak, 231, 235
PINUS (PNS), 215, 224, 243
PINUS bungeana (PNSBG), 204, 215
PINUS cembra (PNSCM), 215, 224
  'Columnaris' (PNSCMCC), 224
PINUS halepensis (PNSHL), 215, 243
PINUS mugo var. *mugo* (PNSMGMO), 165–166, 188
PINUS nigra (PNSNG), 215, 243, 247
PINUS ponderosa (PNSPD), 243
PINUS strobus (PNSST), 215, 224, 239–240
  'Fastigiata' (PNSSTFS), 215, 224
  'Pendula' (PNSSTPN), 215
PINUS thunbergiana (PNSTH), 215, 243
  'Majestic Beauty' PP 5078 (PNSTHMB), 215, 243
Pistachio, 221
PISTACIA chinensis (PSTCH), 221
PITTOSPORUM tobira (PTTTB), 191
  'Variegata' (PTTTBVR), 191

PITTOSPORUM undulatum (PTTUN), 227
Planetree Maple, 217, 241
Plantain Lily, 29–30
PLATANUS (PLT), 231, 248
PLATANUS X *acerifolia* (PLTAC), 231, 240, 243, 248
   'Columbia' (PLTACCC), 231, 240, 243, 248
   'Liberty' (PLTACLL), 231, 240, 243, 248
PLATANUS occidentalis, (PLTOC), 231, 248
PLATYCLADUS orientalis (syn. *Thuja orientalis)* (PLLOR), 166, 215
PLATYCODON grandiflorus var. *mariesii* (PLDGRMR), 28
   'Apoyama' (PLDGRAP), 28
   'Autumnalis' (PLDGRAT), 28
Plum, 209, 218–219
Plumbago, 104
Poetaz Daffodils, 14
PODOCARPUS (PDC), 191
PODOCARPUS gracilior (PDCGR), 191
PODOCARPUS macrophyllus (PDCMC), 191
PODOCARPUS macrophyllus var. *maki* (PDCMCMI), 191
Poet's Jasmine, 134
Poet's Narcissus, 74
POLIANTHES geminiflora (PLNGM), 49
POLIANTHES tuberosa (PLNTB), 49
Polyantha Primrose, 25
Polyantha Roses, 186, 187
   'China Doll' (RSAHBCD), 187
   'The Fairy' (RSAHBTF), 187
Polyanthus, 25
Polyanthus Daffodils, 14
POLYGONUM aubertii, (PLUAB), 138, 141
POLYPODIUM virginianum (PLPVR), 111
POLYSTICHUM (PLH), 111
POLYSTICHUM acrostichoides (PLHAC), 111
POLYSTICHUM braunii (PLHBR), 111
Ponderosa Pine, 243
PONTEDERIA cordata (PNICR), 58
Poplar, 240
Poppy, 27–28
Poppy Anemone, 6
POPULUS alba var. *nivea* (PPLALNV), 240
Porcelain Ampelopsis, 131, 140
Portuguese Broom, 115, 192
PORTULACA grandiflora (PRLGR), 39
POTENTILLA fruticosa (PTNFR), 159, 188–189
   'Coronation Triumph' (PTNFRCT), 159, 188
   'Katherine Dykes' (PTNFRKD), 159, 188
   'Knaphill' (PTNFRKK), 159, 188
POTENTILLA tridentata (PTNTR), 114
POTERIUM sanguisorba (PTMSN), 71
Pothos, 138–139
Pot Marjoram, 70
Prairie Cord Grass, 99
Princeton Nurseries, 244
Pride of Madeira, 197
Primrose, 25
PRIMULA (PRM), 25
PRIMULA X *hybrida* (PRMHB), 25
PRIMULA malacoides (PRMML), 25

PRIMULA X *polyantha* (PRMPL), 25
   'Pacific Giants' (PRMPLPG), 25
PRIMULA vulgaris (PRMVL), 25
Privet, 183–184, 185
Privet Honeysuckle, 134, 135
PRUNUS (PRN), 208–209, 218–219, 228
   'Okame', Flowering Cherry (PRNHBOK), 209
   'Tai Haku' (PRNHBTH), 209
PRUNUS X *blireiana* (PRNBL), 209, 218–219
   'Moseri' (PRNBNMM), 219
PRUNUS cerasifera (PRNCS), 209, 219
   'Atropurpurea' (PRNCSAT), 219
   'Diversifolia' (PRNCSDD), 219
   'Krauter Vesuvius' (PRNCSKV), 209, 219
   'Mount St. Helens' PP 4987 (PRNCSMS), 219
   'Newport' (PRNCSNN), 219
   'Thundercloud' (PRNCSTH), 219
PRUNUS X *cistena* (PRNCT), 219
   'Big Cis', Purple-leaf Plum (PRNCTBC), 219
PRUNUS laurocerasus (PRNLR), 196
   'Rotundifolia' (PRNLRRR), 196
PRUNUS laurocerasus var. *schipkaensis* (PRNLRSP), 196
PRUNUS maackii (PRNMC), 204
PRUNUS maritima (PRNMR), 193–194
PRUNUS mume (PRNMM), 64
PRUNUS pensylvanica (PRNPN), 228
   'Stockton' (PRNPNSS), 228
PRUNUS sargentii (PRNSR), 209
   'Columnaris' (PRNSRCL), 209
PRUNUS serotina (PRNST), 228
PRUNUS serrulata (PRNSL), 209
   'Kwanzan' (syn. 'Sekiyama') (PRNSLKW), 209
   'Shiro-fugan' (PRNSLSS), 209
   'Shirotae' (syn. 'Mount Fuji') (PRNSLSR), 209
PRUNUS spinosa var. *purpurea* (PRNSPPR), 167
   'Plena' (PRNSNPP), 167
PRUNUS subhirtella 'Autumnalis Roseae', Autumn Flowering
   Cherry (PRNSBAR), 209
   'Pendula' (PRNSBPN), 209
   'Pendula Plena Rosea' (syn. 'Yae-Shidare-Higan') (PRNSBPP), 209
PRUNUS virginiana (PRNVR), 219, 229
   'Canada Red' (PRNVRCR), 219
   'Shubert' (PRNVRSS), 219
PRUNUS yedoensis (PRNYD), 209
   'Akebono' (PRNYDAK), 209
   'Ivensii' (PRNYDIV), 209
   'Shidare Yoshino', Weeping Yoshino Cherry (PRNYDSS), 209
PSEUDOLARIX amabilis (PSLAM), 223
PSEUDOTSUGA menziesii (PSDMN), 216
PSEUDOTSUGA menziesii var. *glauca* (PSDMNGC), 216
Puccoon, 26
PULMONARIA officinalis (PLOOF), 25
PULMONARIA saccharata 'Mrs. Moon' (PLOSCMM), 25–26
Purple Coneflower, 78
Purple Giant Filbert, 167
Purple-leaf Sand Cherry, 219
Purple Tabebuia, 209
Purslane, 116

Pussy-willow, 199
PYRACANTHA coccinea (PRCCC), 178, 181
   'Mohave' (PRCCCMM), 178, 181
   'Navaho' (PRCCCNN), 178, 181
   'Shawnee' (PRCCCSS), 178, 181
   'Teton' (PRCCCTT), 178, 181
PYROSTEGIA ignea. See PYROSTEGIA venusta
PYROSTEGIA venusta (syn. *ignea*) (PRGVN), 128
PYRUS calleryana 'Bradford' (PRUCLBR), 209
   'Capitol' (PRUCLCP), 209
   'Whitehouse' (PRUCLWS), 209

Q

Quaking Grass, 88
Queen-Anne's-lace, 44, 106
Queen-of-the-meadow, 67
QUERCUS (QRC), 231–232, 235
QUERCUS acutissima (QRCAC), 231
QUERCUS alba (QRCAL), 231
QUERCUS bicolor (QRCBC), 231
QUERCUS borealis. See QUERCUS rubra
QUERCUS macrocarpa (QRCMC), 231, 235
QUERCUS palustris (QRCPL), 231, 235
QUERCUS phellos (QRCPH), 231, 235
QUERCUS robur (QRCRB), 224, 231
   'Fastigiata' Fastigiate English Oak (QRCRBFS), 224, 231
   'Pendula' (QRCRBPP), 231
QUERCUS rubra (syn. *borealis*) (QRCRR), 231–232, 235
   'Aurea' (QRCRRAR), 232, 235
QUERCUS virginiana (QRCVR), 232
Quince, 146

R

Radish Tulip, 21–22
Railroad Vine, 115
Rainbow Fern, 121
Rainbow Pink, 48
Rain Lily, 11, 112
Ravenna Grass, 88
Red Alpine Epimedium, 113
Red Ash, 231, 247
Red-berried Bamboo, 136
Redbud, 205
Red Cedar, 214, 224, 239
Red Horse Chestnut, 205
Red-hot poker, 46
Red Maple, 220, 223, 229, 233
Red Morning-glory, 137
Red Mulberry, 228, 242
Red Oak, 231–232, 235
Red-osier Dogwood, 173, 190, 198
Red Passionflower, 128

Red Puccoon, 26
Redroot, 196
Red Silver Grass, 93
Red-stemmed Thalia, 59
Red Switch Grass, 97
Red Twig Dogwood, 173
Red Willow, 198
Redwood, 216
Reed, 91–92, 94
Regal Lily, 19
Regel's Privet, 184
RESEDA odorata (RSDOD), 49
Resurrection Lily, 9–10, 117
RHAMNUS frangula 'Columnaris' (RHMFRCL), 189
RHAPIS excelsa (RHSEX), 191
RHODODENDRON (RHD), 149–155, 212, 216
   'Anna Rose Whitney' (RHDHBAW), 155
   'Apple Blossom' (RHDHBAB), 155
   'Ben Moseley' (RHDHBEM), 154, 155
   'Besse Howells' (RHDHBEO), 155
   'Brown Eyes' (RHDHBOE), 155
   'Cadis' (RHDHBCI), 154, 155
   'Carolina Rose' (RHDHBAS), 154
   'Caroline' (RHDHBCO), 154
   'Catawbiense Album', (RHDHBCL), 155
   'Elizabeth' (RHDHBEL), 155
   'English Roseum' (RHDHBIR), 155
   'Gomer Waterer' (RHDHBGW), 155
   Great Lakes Region, 155
   'Hallelujah' (RHDHBHU), 155
   'Harold Amateis' (RHDHBAT), 155
   'Holden' (RHDHBHD), 154
   'The Honorable Jean Marie de Montague' (RHDHBTB), 155
   'Janet Blair' (RHDHBJL), 154, 155
   'Lenape' (RHDHBLP), 154
   'Llenroc' (RHDHBEN), 155
   'Loder's White' (RHDHBLW), 155
   'Lodestar' (RHDHBLT), 155
   'Mary Fleming' (RHDHBMF), 154, 155
   Mid-Atlantic Region, 154
   'Mrs. Furnival' (RHDHBMV), 155
   New England Region, 155
   'Nova Zembla' (RHDHBNZ), 154, 155
   'Olga Mezitt' (RHDHBOM), 155
   'Olin O. Dobbs' (RHDHBOD), 154
   Pacific Northwest, 155
   'Parker's Pink' (RHDHBPK), 154
   'P.J.M.' (RHDHBMJ), 154
   'Ramapo' (RHDHBRR), 155
   'Rochelle' (RHDHBRE), 154, 155
   'Roseum Elegans' (RHDHBRG), 154
   'Scintillation' (RHDHBSN), 154, 155
   Southern United States, 154
   'Tom Everitt' (RHDHBTV), 154
   'Tom Koenig' (RHDHBTK), 154
   'Trude Webster' (RHDHBTW), 155
   'Unique' (RHDHBUN), 155
   'Van Ness Sensation' (RHDHBVT), 155

'Vernus' (RHDHBVS), 155
'Vulcan's Flame' (RHDHBVF), 155
'Westbury' (RHDHBWB), 155
'Weston's Pink Diamond' (RHDHBWP), 155
'Wheatley' (RHDHBWY), 154, 155
'Windbeam' (RHDHBWA), 154, 155
RHODODENDRON arborescens (RHDAR), 153
RHODODENDRON augustini (RHDAG), 155
RHODODENDRON austrinum (RHDAS), 153
  'My Mary' (RHDASMM), 153
RHODODENDRON brachycarpum (RHDBR), 155
RHODODENDRON dauricum (RHDDR), 154
RHODODENDRON dauricum var. *sempervirens* (RHDDRSM), 154
RHODODENDRON fortunei (RHDFR), 154, 155
RHODODENDRON indicum (RHDIN), 152
RHODODENDRON X *laetevirens* (RHDLT), 155
RHODODENDRON makinoi (RHDMK), 154
RHODODENDRON metternichii (RHDMT), 155
RHODODENDRON mucronulatum (RHDMC), 154, 155
  'Cornell Pink' (RHDMCCP), 154, 155
RHODODENDRON occidentale (RHDOC), 152, 153
RHODODENDRON schlippenbachii (RHDSC), 153
RHODODENDRON smirnowii (RHDSM), 155
RHODODENDRON tamurae (RHDTM), 152
RHODODENDRON vaseyi (RHDVS), 153
  'Pinkerbell' (RHDVSPP), 153
RHODODENDRON yakusimanum (RHDYK), 154, 155
  'Yaku Princess' (RHDYKYP), 154, 155
RHOEO spathacea (RHOST), 119
  'Vittata' (RHOSTVV), 119
RHUS (RUS), 197
RHUS aromatica (syn. *canadensis*) (RUSAR), 197
RHUS canadensis. See RHUS aromatica
RHUS copalina (RUSCP), 197
RHUS typhina (RUSTP), 197
  'Laciniata' (RUSTPLC), 197
River Birch, 174, 204, 246
River Maple, 217
River Wattle, 236
Robin Hill Azaleas, 151
  'Betty Anne Voss' (RHDHBBV), 151
  'Nancy of Robinhill' (RHDHBNF), 151
ROBINIA (RBN), 235
ROBINIA X *ambigua* 'Idahoensis' (RBNAMID), 235
ROBINIA pseudoacacia (RBNPS), 235
  'Aurea' (RBNPSAR), 235
  'Frisia' (RBNPSFF), 235
  'Inermis' (RBNPSIN), 235
  'Semperflorens' (RBNPSSS), 235
Rocket Larkspur, 38, 44
Rock Maple, 220, 222, 229, 233
Rock Polypody, 111
Rocky Mountain Douglas Fir, 216
Rocky Mountain Juniper, 214, 224
Roof Iris, 17
ROSA (RSA), 76–77, 129–131, 159–161, 186–188
  Floribundas, 129, 160, 161, 186, 187–188
  Hybrid Perpetual Roses, 76

Hybrid Tea Roses, 159, 160
Large Climbing Roses, 129, 130–131
Miniature Climbing Roses, 129, 130
Miniatures, 186, 187
Old Garden Roses, 130
Polyanthas, 186, 187
Shrub Roses, 186–188
ROSA X *alba* (RSAAL), 76–77
  'Celestial' (RSAALCC), 76
ROSA X *borboniana* (RSABR), 76
  'La Reine Victoria' (RSABRLR), 76
ROSA centifolia (RSACT), 76
  'Cristata' (RSACTCC), 76
  'Fantin Latour' (RSACT), 76
  'Gloire des Mousseuses' (RSACTGD), 76
  'Muscosa' (RSACTMM), 76
  'William Lobb' (RSACTWL), 76
ROSA chinensis (RSACH), 75, 76, 77, 186
  'Minima' (RSACHMM), 186
  'Mutabilis' (RSACHMT), 76
  'Old Blush' (RSACHOB), 76
  'Rouletti' (RSACHRR), 186
ROSA damascena (RSADM), 76
  'Autumn Damask' (RSADMAD), 76
  'Madame Hardy' (RSADM), 76
ROSA eglanteria (RSAEG), 76
ROSA gallica 'Officinalis' (RSAGCOF), 76
ROSA gallica var. *versicolor* (RSAGCVR), 76
ROSA glauca (RSAGL), 76
ROSA X *harisonii* (RSAHR), 76
ROSA multiflora (RSAML), 187
Rosa Mundi, 76
ROSA X *noisettiana* (RSANS), 77
  'Champney's Pink Cluster' (RSANSCP), 77
ROSA X *odorata* (RSAOD), 75, 77
  'Mrs. Dudley Cross' (RSAODMD), 77
  'Niphetos' (RSAODNN), 77
ROSA rugosa (RSARG), 77, 114, 187, 188
  'Blanc Double de Coubert' (RSARGBD), 77
  'Frau Dagmar Hartopp' (RSARGFD), 77
  'Sir Thomas Lipton' (RSARGST), 188
ROSA virginiana (RSAVR), 77, 197
  'Plena' (RSAVRPP), 197
ROSA wichuraiana (RSAWC), 119
Rose, 76–77, 129–131, 159–161, 186–188
  See also specific types, e.g., Floribunda Roses; Large
  Climbing Roses; Miniature Roses; Shrub Roses
Rose-bay, 81, 185, 191
Rosebud Cherry, 209
Rose Fountain Grass, 89
Rose Geranium, 75
Rose Mallow, 27
Rosemary, 81, 178
Rose Moss, 39
Rosenbach Onion, 47
Rose-of-Sharon, 158, 183
Rose Verbena, 112
ROSMARINUS officinalis (RSMOF), 81, 178

'Arp' (RSMOFAR), 81, 178
'Prostratus' (RSMOFPP), 81, 178
ROSMARINUS officinalis var. *humilis* (RSMOFHM), 81, 178
Round-headed Garlic, 8, 47
Royal Azalea, 153
Royal Poinciana, 210, 237
Rubra Flora Piena, 36
Rubrifolium. See COTINUS coggygria, 'Notcutt's Variety'
RUDBECKIA fulgida var. *sullivanti* 'Goldsturm' (RDBFDGG), 28
RUDBECKIA hirta (RDBHR), 28
RUELLIA brittoniana (RLLBR), 119
RUELLIA makoyana (RLLMK), 121
RUMOHRA adiantiformis (RMHAD), 111
Running Myrtle, 80
RUSCUS aculeatus (RSCAC), 79
Russian Cedar, 215
Russian Chamomile, 82
Russian Olive, 169, 197
Russian Sage, 67, 89

S

Sacred Lotus, 57
Saffron Crocus, 12, 66–67
Sage, 32, 81
    Bethlehem, 25–26
    Jerusalem, 25
    Mealycup, 32
    Russian, 67, 89
    Scarlet, 32
Sagebrush, 114–115
SAGITTARIA (SGT), 58
SAGITTARIA lancifolia (SGTLN), 58
SAGITTARIA sagittifolia 'Flore Pleno' (SGTSGFP), 58
St.-John's-wort, 119, 174–175
SALIX (SLX), 225, 248
SALIX alba (SLXAL), 225, 240, 248
    'Vitellina', Golden Weeping Willow (SLXALVV), 225, 240, 248
SALIX babylonica (SLXBB), 225, 248
SALIX caprea (SLXCP), 225
Salt Cedar, 194, 199
SALVIA (SLV), 32
SALVIA azurea X *grandiflora* (SLVAZGR), 32
SALVIA elegans (SLVEL), 32
SALVIA farinacea (SLVFR), 32
    'Blue Bedder' (SLVFRBB), 32
SALVIA officinalis (SLVOF), 81
    'Ictarina' (SLVOFIC), 81
SALVIA splendens (SLVSP), 32
SALVIA X superba 'East Friesland' (SLVSREF), 32
SAMBUCUS canadensis (SMBCN), 181, 199
    'Aurea' (SMBCNAR), 181, 199
Sand Myrtle, 115–116
SANGUINARIA canadensis (SNRCN), 26
SANGUISORBA canadensis (SNBCN), 33–34
Santamour, Frank S., 206, 207, 231, 246

SANTOLINA (SNT), 175, 191–192
SANTOLINA chamaecyparissus (SNTCH), 73, 175, 192
SANTOLINA virens (SNTVR), 73, 175, 192
Sapphire Flower, 42
SARCOCOCCA hookerana var. *humilis* (SRCHKHL), 117–118
Sargent Cherry, 209
Sargent Crab Apple, 148
Sargent's Juniper, 108, 163
Saskatoon Serviceberry, 228
Sassafras, 65
SASSAFRAS albidum (SSSAL), 65
SATUREJA hortensis (STJHR), 82
SATUREJA montana (STJMN), 82
Satzuki Azaleas, 152
    'Macrantha Purple' (RHDHBAP), 152
    'Shinnyo-no-tsuki' (RHDHBSS), 152
Saucer Magnolia, 207
Savin Juniper, 108, 164
Sawara Cypress, 169, 213, 218
Sawtooth Oak, 231
SCABIOSA caucasica (SCBCC), 46
    'Alba' (SCBCCAL), 46
    'Blue Perfection' (SCBCCBP), 46
Scarlet Clematis, 127
Scarlet Fire Thorn, 181
Scarlet Kadsura, 135
Scarlet Kaffir Lily, 41
Scarlet Runner Bean, 137
Scarlet Sage, 32
SCHIZOPHRAGMA hydrangeoides (SCPHD), 128
Schroeder Azaleas, 151
    'Carrie Amanda' (RHDHBAM), 151
    'Hoosier Sunrise' (RHDHBOS), 151
SCIADOPYTIS verticillata (SCTVR), 216
Scilla hispanica, 6
SCILLA siberica (SCLSB), 7
    'Spring Beauty' (SCLSBSB), 7
Scindapsus aureus, 138
SCIRPUS albescens (SCRAL), 58
Scotch Broom, 192
Scouring Rush, 58
Sea Holly, 27
Sea Oats, 94
Sea Purslane, 116
Sedge, 90, 95
SEDUM (SDM), 32–33
SEDUM acre (SDMAC), 114
SEDUM ewersii 'Album' (SDMEWAL), 33
SEDUM maximum 'Atropurpureum' (SDMMXAT), 33
SEDUM sieboldii (SDMSB), 33, 82
    'Ruby Glow' (SDMSBRG), 33
SEDUM spectabile (SDMSC), 33
    'Autumn Joy' (SDMSCAJ), 33
SELAGINELLA (SLG), 121
SELAGINELLA involvens (SLGIN), 121
SELAGINELLA uncinata (SLGUN), 121
SEMPERVIVUM tectorum (SMPTC), 114
Senecio, 33

Sequoiadendron giganteum (SQDGG), 216
SEQUOIA sempervirens 'Santa Cruz' (SQASMSC), 216
   'Soquel' (SQASMSQ), 216
Serbian Bellflower, 29
Serbian Spruce, 214
Serviceberry, 228, 241, 244, 246
SESLERIA autumnalis (SSLAT), 98
SESUVIUM portulacastrum (SSVPR), 116
Shadblow, 228, 241, 244
Shamel Ash, 231
Shammarello Azaleas, 151
   'Elsie Lee' (RHDHBIL), 151
   'Helen Curtis' (RHDHBHC), 151
Shasta Daisy, 32
Sheep Laurel, 164
Shield Fern, 111
Shining Sumac, 197
Shore Juniper, 108, 163, 193
Shrub Althaea, 158, 183
Shrubby Cinquefoil, 159, 188
Shrubby St.-John's-wort, 158–159, 175
Shrub Roses, 159–161, 186–188
   'Meidomonac' (RSAHBMM), 188
Shrubs, 146–199
   attractive to birds, 180–182
   with blue, gray, and silver foliage, 168–169
   for container planting, 189–192
   deciduous, 182–183
   dwarf and slow-growing, 174–175
   evergreen, 161–166, 184–186
   flowering, 146–148, 156–159
   with fragrant flowers, 178–179
   with red foliage all season, 166–167
   with red, orange, and yellow foliage in fall, 172–174
   seashore gardens, 192–194
   for shade, 194–195
   for slopes and erosion control, 196
   for topiary and espalier, 176–178
   with variegated foliage, 170–171
   for wet conditions, 198–199
   with yellow foliage all season, 167–168
   See also specific shrubs
Siberian Carpet Cypress, 108–109
Siberian Crab Apple, 207, 239
Siberian Dogwood, 173, 190, 198
Siberian Iris, 16, 17, 58
Siberian Squill, 7
Sieber Crocus, 11
Signet Marigold, 40
Silk Tree, 238
Silky Dogwood, 198
Silver Banner Grass, 90
Silverbell, 244, 247
Silver-dollar Tree, 213
Silver Edge Pachysandra, 117
Silver Grass, 92–93
Silver-king Artemisia, 106, 115, 169, 188
Silver Lace Vine, 138, 141
Silver-leaved Poplar, 240

Silver Linden, 220, 236
Silver Maple, 217
Silver Morning-glory, 138
Silver Spike, 91
Silver Vine, 131
Silvery Spleenwort, 110
SINARUNDINARIA nitida (SNDNT), 96
Singleseed Juniper, 108, 164
SKIMMIA (SKM), 25, 166, 175, 189, 192
SKIMMIA japonica (SKMJP), 166, 175, 189, 192
SKIMMIA reevesiana (SKMRV), 166, 175, 189, 192
Slender Deutzia, 105, 182–183
Sloe, 167
Small Globe Thistle, 23
Small-leaved Cotoneaster, 105
Small-leaved European Linden, 236, 240
Small's Brier, 136
SMILAX (SMX), 135–136
SMILAX lanceolata. See SMILAX smallii
SMILAX megalantha (SMXMG), 136
SMILAX rotundifolia (SMXRT), 136
SMILAX smallii (syn. *lanceolata*) (SMXSM), 136
SMILAX walteri (SMXWL), 136
Smirnow Rhododendron, 155
Smokebush, 167
Smoke Tree, 167
Smooth-leaf Elm, 236
Smooth Withe-rod, 199
Snakehead, 120
Snapdragon, 37
Sneezeweed, 32
Snowbell, 212
Snowboy Chinese Dogwood, 219
Snowdrop, 7, 11
Snowy Wood Rush, 96
Soapweed, 29, 194
Society Garlic, 105–106
SOLANDRA guttata (SLNGT), 133–134
SOLIDAGO odora (SLDOD), 79
SOLIDAGO virgaurea 'Cloth of Gold' (SLDVRCF), 79
   'Golden Shower' (SLDVRGS), 79
SOPHORA japonica (SPHJP), 235–236, 243
   'Princeton Upright' PP 5524 (SPHJPPP), 236, 243
   'Regent' PP 2338 (SPHJPRG), 236, 243
Sorbet, 206
Sorrel Tree, 221, 232, 245
Sour Gum, 242–243
Sour Orange, 80
Sourwood, 221, 232, 245
Southern Arrowwood, 181–182
Southern Black Haw, 148
Southern Indian Azaleas, 150
   'Formosa' (RHDHBFM), 150
   'George L. Tabor' (RHDHBGL), 150
   'Mrs. G.G. Gerbing' (RHDHBIG), 150
Southern Magnolia, 211, 214, 227
Southern Swamp Crinum, 59
Southernwood, 115
Southern Yew, 191

Spanish Bluebell, 6
Spanish Lavender, 74
SPARTINA pectinata (SPIPC), 99
   'Aureo-marginata' (SPIPCAG), 99
Spearmint, 69
Speedwell, 23–24
Spicebush, 199
Spider Flower, 38
Spider Lily, 8, 59
Spiderwort, 23
Spike Gay-feather, 32
Spindle Tree, 171
Spiraea, 24
SPIRAEA X *bumalda* 'Limemound' (SPRBMAW), 168
SPIRAEA japonica (SPRJP), 105
   'Alpina' (SPRJPAL), 105
SPIRAEA nipponica (SPRNP), 105
SPIRAEA X *vanhouttei* (SPRVH), 184
SPODIOPOGON sibiricus (SPDSB), 91
Spotted Dead Nettle, 121
Spreading Japanese Holly, 177
SPREKELIA formosissima (SPKFR), 9
Spruce, 165, 214, 239
   Bird's Nest, 165
   Colorado Blue, 165, 169, 215, 239
   Norway, 214, 239
   Oriental, 215
   Serbian, 214
   White, 165, 214
Spurge, 23
STACHYS (STC), 107
STACHYS byzantina (STCBN), 16, 107
STACHYS officinalis (STCOF), 107
Staghorn Sumac, 197
Standish English Yew, 166, 168, 178
Star Jasmine, 139–140
Star Magnolia, 147–148
STAUNTONIA hexaphylla (STIHX), 134
Stephan Jasmine, 134
STERNBERGIA lutea (STBLT), 10–11
STEWARTIA (STW), 212
STEWARTIA koreana (STWKR), 212
STEWARTIA ovata var. *grandiflora* (STWOVGR), 212
STEWARTIA pseudocamellia (STWPS), 212
STIPA gigantea (STAGG), 89
Stolonifera. See CORNUS sericea
Stonecrop, 32–33
Strawberry Tree, 204, 212, 237
Striped Giant Reed, 92
Striped Maple, 204
STYRAX (STX), 212
STYRAX japonicus (STXJN), 212, 245
STYRAX obassia (STXOB), 212
Sugarberry, 228
Sugar Maple, 220, 222, 229, 233
Sumac, 197
Summer Grape, 136
Summer Lilac, 158
Summer Savory, 82

Summer Snowflake, 7
Summersweet, 198
Sunflower, 45
Surinam Cherry, 185
Swamp Haw, 199
Swamp Magnolia, 245, 247
Swamp Maple, 220, 223, 229, 233
Swamp White Oak, 231
Sweet Alder, 198
Sweet Alyssum, 48, 113
Sweet Autumn Clematis, 126, 140
Sweet Azalea, 153
Sweet Bay, 64, 211–212, 214, 227, 245, 247
Sweet Box, 117–118
Sweet Briar, 76
Sweet Clock Vine, 138
Sweet Elder, 181, 199
Sweet False Chamomile, 72
Sweet Fern, 118, 196
Sweet Goldenrod, 79
Sweet Gum, 221, 247
Sweet Marjoram, 70
Sweet Olive, 180
Sweet Orange, 237
Sweet Pea, 137
Sweet Pepper bush, 195, 198
Sweetspire, 199
Sweet Viburnum, 157
Sweet Violet, 36, 40, 71
Sweet William, 48
Sweet Woodruff, 82
Sweet Wormwood, 115
Swiss Stone Pine, 215
Switch Grass, 99
Sword Fern, 111
Sword Lily, 8
Sycamore, 231, 248
Sycamore Maple, 217, 241
SYMPHORICARPOS orbiculatus (SMHOR), 197
SYRINGA (SRN), 156–157, 212
SYRINGA amurensis var. *japonica. See SYRINGA reticulata*
SYRINGA X *henryi* (SRNHN), 212
   'Lutece' (SRNHNLL), 212
SYRINGA meyeri (SRNMR), 157
   'Palabin' (SRNMRPP), 157
SYRINGA patula 'Miss Kim' (SRNPTMK), 157
SYRINGA reticulata (syn. *amurensis* var. *japonica*), 212
SYRINGA vulgaris (SRNVL), 157, 212
   'Sensation' (SRNVLSS), 157
Syzygium aromaticum. See EUGENIA aromatica
Syzygium paniculatum. See EUGENIA aromatica

T

TABEBUIA chrysotricha (TBBCH), 209
TABEBUIA impetiginosa (TBBIM), 209, 212
TAGETES (TGT), 39–40

TAGETES erecta (TGTER), 39–40
TAGETES patula (TGTPT), 40
TAGETES tenuifolia (TGTTN), 40
Tall Gay-feather, 32
Tallhedge Alder Buckthorn, 189
Tall Purple Moor Grass, 97
Tamarisk, 194, 199
TAMARIX pentandra. See TAMARIX ramosissima
TAMARIX ramosissima (syn. *pentandra*) (TMRRM), 194, 199
TANACETUM vulgare var. *crispum* (TNCVLCR), 73
Tangerine, 237
Tanglehead, 133
Tara Vine, 131
Taro, 59
Tarragon, 68–69
Tatarian Maple, 220
TAXODIUM distichum (TXDDS), 248–249
  'Pendens' (TXDDSPP), 249
TAXUS (TXS), 166, 178, 216, 224
TAXUS baccata (TXSBC), 166, 168, 178, 216, 224
  'Fastigiata' (TXSBCFS), 216, 224
  'Fastigiata Aurea' (TXSBCFR), 216, 224
  'Nana' (TXSBCNN), 166, 178
  'Pygmaea' (TXSBCPP), 166, 178
  'Repandens' (TXSBCRP), 166, 178
  'Standishii' (TXSBCSS), 166, 168, 178
  'Washingtonii' (TXSBCSS), 166, 168, 178
TAXUS cuspidata (TXSCS), 166, 178, 216
  'Densa' (TXSCSDD), 166, 178
  'Nana' (TXSCSNN), 166, 178
TAXUS X *media* (TXSMD), 166, 178, 216, 224
  'Brownii' (TXSMDBW), 166, 178
  'Densiformis' (TXSMDDN), 166, 178
  'Hatfieldii' (TXSMDHT), 166, 178, 216, 224
  'Hicksii', Hick's Yew (TXSMDHC), 166, 178, 216, 224
  'Kelseyi' (TXSMDKK), 166, 178
  'Sentinalis' (TXSMDSS), 224
  'Stoveken' (TXSMDST), 224
  'Wardii' (TXSMDWR), 166, 178
Tea Crab, 207
Tea Olive, 180
Tea Rose, 75, 77
TECOMARIA capensis (TCMCP), 128
TERMINALIA catappa (TRICT), 221
TEUCRIUM chamaedrys (TCRCH), 186
TEUCRIUM chamaedrys var. *prostratum* (TCRCHPR), 186
Texanum, 171, 185
THALIA geniculata (THLGN), 59
THELYPTERIS (THT), 111
THELYPTERIS hexagonoptera (THTHX), 111
THELYPTERIS novboracensis (THTNV), 111
Thornless Honey Locust, 222, 235, 238
Thorny Elaeagnus, 162–163, 170
Threadleaf Japanese Maple, 167, 189
Threadleaf Tickseed, 27, 66
Three-toothed Cinquefoil, 114
THUJA (THJ), 166, 215, 216
THUJA occidentalis (THJOC), 166, 213, 215, 216, 240

'Emerald Green' (THJOCEG), 166, 216, 240
'Hetz Junior' (THJOCHJ), 166
'Hetz Midget' (THJOCHD), 166
'Nigra' (THJOCNG), 166, 216, 240
'Rheingold' (THJOCRH), 166
'Wareana' (THJOCWR), 166
THUJA orientalis. See Platycladus orientalis
THUJA plicata (THJPL), 216
  'Hillier' (THJPLHH), 216
  'Rogersii' (THJPLRR), 216
  'Stoneham' (THJPLSS), 216
Thumbelinas, 40
THUNBERGIA (THN), 137–138
THUNBERGIA alata (THNAL), 138
THUNBERGIA fragrans (THNFR), 138
THUNBERGIA grandiflora (THNGN), 138
THUNBERGIA gregorii (THNGR), 138
Thyme, 83
THYMUS (THM), 83
  'Doone Valley' (THMHBDV), 83
THYMUS X *citriodorus* (THMCT), 83
  'Aureus' (THMCTAR), 83
THYMUS herba-barona (THMHR), 83
THYMUS praecox subsp. *arcticus* (THMPRAR), 83
  'Albus' (THMPCAL), 83
  'Coccineus' (THMPCCC), 83
  'Splendens' (THMPCSS), 83
THYMUS vulgaris (THMVL), 83
  'Argenteus', Silver Thyme (THMVLAR), 83
  'English' (THMVLEN), 83
  French (THMVL), 83
Tickseed, 27, 66
Tiger Lily, 19
TILIA (TLA), 236
TILIA americana var. *fastigiata* (TLAAMFT), 236
TILIA cordata 'Greenspire' PP 2086 (TLACRGR), 236, 240
TILIA X *euchlora* (TLAEC), 236
TILIA tomentosa (TLATM), 220, 236
TORREYA (TRR), 216
TORREYA californica (TRRCL), 216
TORREYA nucifera (TRRNC), 216
Tosa Spirea, 105
TRACHELOSPERMUM jasminoides (TRCJS), 139–140
Tradescantia virginiana (TRDVR), 23
Trailing Lantana, 43, 105
Trees, 204–248
  attractive to birds, 227–229
  for city conditions and dry places, 233–236
  with columnar form, 223–224
  for container planting, 236–237
  with distinctive bark, 204
  with evergreen foliage, 212–217
  with flowers, 205–212, 226–227
  large shade, 229–232
  red foliage, 217–219, 220–221
  for screening, 238–240
  for seashore gardens, 241–243
  shade-tolerant, 243–246

silver or variegated foliage, 219–220
small or dwarf shade, 232
with weeping form, 224–225
for wet conditions, 246–249
yellow foliage, 217–219, 220–221
See also specific trees
Trident Maple, 204, 233
TRILLIUM grandiflorum (TRUGR), 26
TROLLIUS ledebourii 'Golden Queen' (TROLDGQ), 31
TROPAEOLUM (TRM), 71
TROPAEOLUM majus (TRMMJ), 71
TROPAEOLUM peregrinum (TRMPR), 71
TROPAEOLUM polyphyllum (TRMPL), 71
Tropical Almond, 221
Trumpet Creeper, 135, 140
Trumpet Honeysuckle, 135
Trumpet Tree, 209, 212
Trumpet Vine, 132, 135, 140
TSUGA (TSG), 186, 216–217, 232–233
TSUGA canadensis (TSGCN), 166, 186, 217, 232, 245–246
   'Kingsville' (TSGCNKK), 217, 232, 246
   'Pendula', Weeping Canadian Hemlock (TSGCNPN), 166, 186, 217, 232, 246
TSUGA caroliniana (TSGCR), 186, 217, 233
TSUGA heterophylla (TSGHT), 186
TSUGA mertensiana (TSGMR), 186
Tuberose, 49
Tufted Hair Grass, 96
TULBAGHIA violacea (TLBVL), 105–106
Tulip, 19–22, 25
   Cottage, 19, 20
   Lady, 21–22
   Radish, 21–22
   Waterlily, 21
TULIPA (TLP), 19–22
   'Ace of Spades' (TLPHBAF), 20
   'Bellona' (TLPHBBL), 19
   Bunch-flowered, 19
   'Burgundy Lace' (TLPHBBC), 20
   Darwin Hybrids, 19
   double early, 19
   Double Late, 20–21
   'Estella Rynveld' (TLPHBER), 20
   Fosterana hybrids, 21
   Fringed, 20
   'Garden Party' (TLPHBGP), 19
   'Georgette' (TLPHBGG), 19
   'Golden Parade' (TLPHBGR), 19
   Greigii Hybrids, 21
   'Jewel of Spring' (TLPHBJF), 19
   Kaufmanniana Hybrids, 21
   lace, 20
   Lily-flowered, 19
   'Mariette' (TLPHBMM), 19
   'Mickey Mouse' (TLPHBMS), 19
   'Mount Tacoma' (TLPHBMT), 21
   'Parade' (TLPHBPP), 19
   Parrot, 20
   'Peach Blossom' (TLPHBPB), 19
   'Purissima' (TLPHBPR), 21
   'Queen of Sheba' (TLPHBQF), 20
   'Red Emperor' (TLPHBRM), 21
   'Red Riding Hood' (TLPHBRR), 21
   'Shakespeare' (TLPHBSS), 21
   Single Early, 19
   Single Late, 20
   'Sorbet' (TLPHBSR), 20
   Species, 21–22
   Triumph, 19
TULIPA clusiana (TLPCL), 21–22
TULIPA marjolettii (TLPMR), 22
TULIPA pulchella 'Violacea' (TLPPLVV), 22
Tulip Tree, 222, 231
Tupelo, 243
Turkish Filbert, 234
Turtlehead, 120
Tussock Bellflower, 22
Twin Flower, 49
Two-men-in-a-boat, 119
TYPHA (TPH), 58
TYPHA angustifolia (TPHAN), 58
TYPHA latifolia var. *variegata* (TPHLTVR), 59

U

ULMUS (ULM), 236
   'Sapporo Autumn Gold' (ULMHBST), 236
ULMUS americana (ULMAM), 236
ULMUS parvifolia 'Dynasty' (ULMPRDD), 236
Umbellularia californica (UMLCL), 64
Umbrella Palm, 59
Umbrella Pine, 216
Umbrella Plant, 59
UNIOLA paniculata (UNLPN), 94
Unwin hybrids, 38

V

VACCINIUM (VCC), 65
VACCINIUM angustifolium (VCCAN), 65
VACCINIUM corymbosum (VCCRM), 65
Valerian, 49, 74
VALERIANA officinalis (VLROF), 49, 74
Variegated Andromeda, 171
Variegated Bigleaf Hydrangea, 171
Variegated Cattail, 59
Variegated Dwarf Weigela, 171
Variegated Grassy-leaved Sweet Flag, 98
Variegated Japanese Silver Grass, 99
Variegated Maidenhair Tree, 219
Variegated Sweet Flag, 57
Variegated Tartarian Dogwood, 170

Variegated Weigela, 171
Varnish Tree, 210–211
VERBASCUM chaixii 'Album' (VRCCHAL), 46
VERBASCUM thapsus (VRCTH), 46
VERBENA (VRB), 112
VERBENA canadensis (VRBCN), 112
Verbena hastata (VRBHS), 76
VERBENA X *hybrida* (VRBHB), 40
VERBENA platensis (VRBPL), 112
VERBENA rigida (VRBRG), 112
  'Flame' (VRBRGFF), 112
VERONICA (VRN), 23–24
VERONICA latifolia 'Crater Lake Blue' (VRNLTCL), 23–24, 28, 47
VERONICA spicata 'Blue Fox' (VRNLTCL), 24
  'Blue Peter' (VRNSPBP), 24
  'Snow White' (VRNSPSW), 24
  'Sunny Borders' (VRNSPSB), 24
Vervain, 112
VIBURNUM (VBR), 148, 157, 199
  'Chesapeake' (VBRHBCC), 148
VIBURNUM X *burkwoodii* 'Mohawk' (VBRBRMM), 148
VIBURNUM X *carlecephalum* 'Cayuga' (VBRCCCC), 148
VIBURNUM carlesii (VBRCR), 148
VIBURNUM cassinoides (VBRCS), 199
VIBURNUM dentatum (VBRDN), 181–182
VIBURNUM dilatatum 'Catskill' (VBRDLCC), 157
VIBURNUM X *juddii* (VBRJI), 148
VIBURNUM nudum (VBRND), 199
VIBURNUM odoratissimum (VBROD), 157
VIBURNUM 'Oneida' (VBRHBON), 157
VIBURNUM plicatum var. *tomentosum* (VBRPLTN), 157
  'Mariesii' (VBRPCMM), 157
  'Shasta' (VBRPCSS), 157
VIBURNUM prunifolium (VBRPN), 148
  'Gladwyne' (VBRPNGG), 148
  'Holden' (VBRPNHH), 148
VIBURNUM rufidulum (VBRRF), 148
VIBURNUM sargentii 'Susquehanna' (VBRSRSS), 157
Vicary Golden Privet, 168, 185, 188
Victorian Box, 227
VINCA (VNC), 109
VINCA major (VNCMJ), 109
  'Variegata' (VNCMJVR), 109
VINCA minor (VNCMN), 42, 80, 109
  'Alba' (VNCMNAL), 109
  'Variegata' (VNCMNVR), 109
Vine Maple, 220
Vines, 126–141
  attractive to birds, 135–136
  flowering, 126–131
  for foliage, 131–134
  with fragrant flowers, 134–135
  for rapid growth or screening, 136–138
  for shade, 138–140
  slopes and erosion control, 138
  for urban conditions, 140–141
  See also specific vines
VIOLA (VLA), 6, 40

VIOLA odorata (VLAOD), 40, 71
  'Royal Robe' (VLAODRR), 40, 71
  'White Czar' (VLAODWT), 40, 71
VIOLA tricolor (VLATR), 40
VIOLA X *wittrockiana* (VLAWT), 40
Viper's Bugloss, 197
Virginia Bluebells, 25
Virginia Creeper, 132, 141
Virginia Rose, 77, 197
Virgin's Bower, 126
VITEX agnus-castus (VTXAG), 65
VITIS (VTS), 136
VITIS aestivalis (VTSAS), 136
VITIS cognetiae (VTSCG), 136
VITIS labrusca (VTSLB), 136
Viviparous Hair Grass, 96

W

Wallflower, 47
Wall Rock Cress, 113
Wandering Jew, 118
Washington Thorn, 228, 238
Water Canna, 59
Water Iris, 17, 58
Water Lily, 54–56
Water-lily Tulips, 21
Water Poppy, 59
Water Snowflake, 58
Waukegan Juniper, 108, 164
Wax Begonia, 9
Wax-leaf Privet, 171, 185
WEDELIA triloba (WDLTL), 116
Weeping Bottlebrush, 224
Weeping Canadian Hemlock, 166
Weeping Candied Crab Apple, 207
Weeping Deodar Cedar, 224
Weeping Fern Pine, 191
Weeping Lantana, 43, 105
Weeping Willow, 225, 248
WEIGELA (WGL), 171
WEIGELA florida 'Variegata Nana' (WGLFLVN), 171
WEIGELA praecox 'Variegata' (WGLPRVV), 171
Welwyn Hybrids, 32
Western Azalea, 152, 153
Western Catawba, 210
Western Hemlock, 186
Western Red Cedar, 216
Western Redbud, 205
White Alder, 246
White Ash, 230
White Birch, 204
White Bullrush, 58
White-edged English Holly, 219–220
White Edge Morning-glory, 137
White Fir, 212

White Flowering Cherry, 209
White Ironbark, 214
White Oak, 231
White Pine, 215, 239–240
White Poplar, 240
White Rose of York, 76
White Snow–flake, 58
White Spruce, 165, 214
White Wake-robin, 26
White Willow, 240, 248
Wild Carrot, 44
Wild Ginger, 78
Wild Oats, 95
Wild Olive, 244–245, 247
Wild Red Cherry, 228
Wild Yellow Lily, 18
Willow, 224–225, 240, 248
Willowleaf Cotoneaster, 105, 173, 190–191, 195
Willow leaved Sunflower, 45
Willow Oak, 231
Wilson Rhododendron, 155
Windflower, 6, 31
Windowleaf, 133
Winter Aconite, 6, 11
Winterberry, 198–199
Wintercreeper, 171
Winter Daffodil, 10–11
Winter Daphne, 179
Wintergreen, 78
Wintergreen Barberry, 184
Winter Honeysuckle, 179
Winter Savory, 82
Wintersweet, 179
Wire Vine, 141
WISTERIA (WST), 128–129
  'Alba' (WSTAL), 128
  'Purpurea' (WSTPP), 128
WISTERIA floribunda (WSTFL), 129
WISTERIA frutescens (WSTFR), 129
WISTERIA macrostachya (WSTMC), 129
WISTERIA sinensis (WSTSN), 129, 141
  'Alba' (WSTSNAL), 141
  'Purpurea' (WSTSNPP), 141
Witch Hazel, 146, 183, 191
Withe-rod, 199
Woodbine, 131–132, 134, 135, 141
Woolflower, 37–38
Woodruff, 82
Woolly Betony, 16, 107
Woolly Pelargonium, 75
Woolly Yarrow, 81–82
Wreath Nasturtium, 71

Y

Yarrow, 26
Yaupon Holly, 163, 177
Yellow Cosmos, 38
Yellow Floating-heart, 58
Yellow Iris, 17, 58
Yellow Japanese Barberry, 168
Yellow Jasmine, 132, 134
Yellow Loosestrife, 112
Yellow Parilla, 139
Yellowroot, 121
Yellow Snowflake, 58
Yew, 166, 168, 178, 216, 224
  Brown's, 166, 178
  Dwarf English, 166, 178
  Dwarf Japanese, 166, 178
  English, 216, 224
  Hick, 224
  Southern, 191
  Standish English, 166, 168, 178
Ylang-ylang, 226
Yoshino Cherry, 209
YUCCA (YCC), 28–29, 194
YUCCA filamentosa 'Bright Edge' (YCCFLBE), 28–29, 194
  'Gold Sword' (YCCFLGW), 194
YUCCA glauca (YCCGL), 29, 194

Z

Zanzibar Balsam, 38
Zebra Grass, 99
ZEBRINA pendula (ZBRPN), 118
ZELKOVA serrata (ZLKSR), 221
  'Village Green' (ZLKSRVG), 221
ZEPHYRANTHES (ZPH), 10, 11, 112
ZEPHYRANTHES candida (ZPHCN), 11, 112
ZEPHYRANTHES rosea (ZPHRS), 11, 112
Zephyr Lily, 11, 112
Zinnia, 40
ZINNIA elegans (ZNNEL), 40
  'Fantastic Light Pink' (ZNNELFL), 40
  'Liliput' (ZNNELLL), 40
  'Peter Pan' (ZNNELPN), 40
  'Pumila' (ZNNELPP), 40
  'Small World' (ZNNELSW), 40
  'Tom Thumb' (ZNNELTT), 40
ZIZYPHUS jujuba (ZZPJJ), 65
Zonal Geranium, 39
Zoysia Grass, 112–113
ZOYSIA tenuifolia (ZSATF), 112–113

X

XANTHORHIZA simplicissima (XNTSM), 121

The key locations and zones given below are based on the new hardiness research for Canada and Mexico. The zone numbers correspond to the information given on the end papers. Maps for Canada and Mexico were not available for this edition.

CANADA

Province or Territory	Location	USDA Plant Hardiness Zone
Alberta	Calgary	3
	Edmondton	3
	Fort McMurray	2
	Jasper	3
British Columbia	Fort Nelson	2
	Hazelton	4
	Vancouver	8
Manitoba	Churchill	·2
	Lynn Lake	2
	Winnipeg	3
New Brunswick	Bathurst	4
	Fredericton	4
	Grand Falls	4
Newfoundland	Corner Brook	6
	Springdale	4
	St. Anthony	5
	St. John's	6
Northwest Territories	Inuvik	1
	Yellowknife	2
Nova Scotia	Halifax	6
	Sydney	6
Ontario	Big Trout Lake	2
	Dryden	3
	Toronto	5
Prince Edward Island	Alberton	5
	Charlottetown	5
Quebec	Drummondville	4
	Inukjuak	3
	Montreal	5
Saskatchewan	La Ronge	2
	Regina	3
	Saskatoon	3
Yukon Territory	Dawson	1
	Mayo	1
	Watson Lake	1
	Whitehorse	2

MEXICO
(Partial List of States)

State	Location	USDA Plant Hardiness Zone
Baja North	El Rosario	10
	Ensenada	10
	Mexicali	9
Baja South	San Ignacio	10
	San Jose Del Cabo	11
	Santiago	10
Campeche	Campeche	11
Chiapas	Tuxtla Gutierrez	11
Chihuahua	Chihuahua	9
Coahuila	Saltillo	9
Durango	Durango	9
Guerrero	Acapulco	11
Hidalgo	Tulancingo	8
Mexico	Toluca	9
Nuevo Leon	Monterrey	9
Oaxaca	Oaxaca	10
Queretaro	Queretaro	10
Quintana Roo	Cozumel	11
San Luis Potosi	San Luis Potosi	9
Sinaloa	Culiacan	10
Tamaulipas	Ciudad Victoria	10
Veracruz	Veracruz	11
Yucatan	Merida	11

THE FRIENDS OF
THE NATIONAL ARBORETUM

Since the U.S. National Arboretum is a government entity, it can't be subsidized. But it can be supported with volunteers and with funds.

The Friends of the National Arboretum was formed to help this incredible garden and educational facility, rightly known as "the World's Greatest Garden." With private funds this organization helps propagate new plant species, carry on research projects, organize worldwide plant exploration and acquisition programs, develop educational programs and create collections at the Arboretum.

If you would like more information about supporting the Friends of the National Arboretum, please write or call the FONA national office at 3299 K Street, Northwest—7th Fl., Washington, DC 20007, (202) 965-7510.

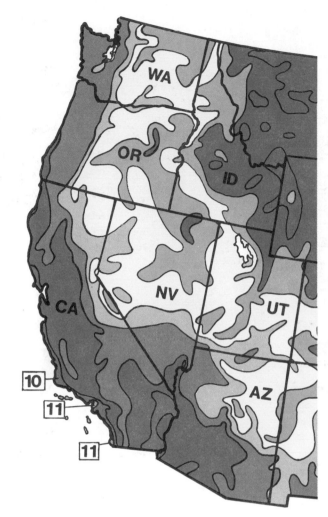

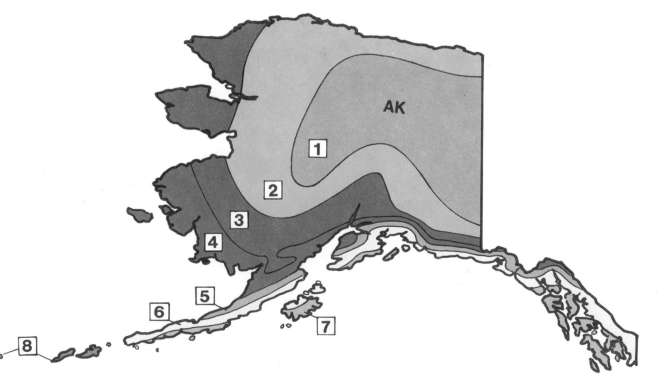